The Producers

The Producers

◆

Profiles in Frustration

Luke Ford

iUniverse, Inc.
New York Lincoln Shanghai

The Producers
Profiles in Frustration

iUniverse, Inc.

For information address:
iUniverse, Inc.
2021 Pine Lake Road, Suite 100
Lincoln, NE 68512
www.iuniverse.com

ISBN: 0-595-32016-3 (pbk)
ISBN: 0-595-66463-6 (cloth)

Printed in the United States of America

For Amy Alkon, Donna Burstyn, Lisa Herman, Debbie Kollin, Emmanuelle Richard, Cathy Seipp

What Producers Said To Luke Ford

"I don't think there's anything terrible about masturbating a horse if you're doing it for a good reason." **Larry Brezner, *Good Morning, Vietnam, Throw Momma from the Train***

"Tonight they want you to fuck Lassie." **Jeff Wald, *Roseanne***

"I can make you not fucking breathe." **Jeff Wald**

"I am going to finance everybody's lawsuit against you." **Jeff Wald**

"I still can't figure out what the point of your book will be." **Al Burton, *Diff'rent Strokes, Facts of Life, Square Pegs, Silver Spoons***

"You need a job. You need something grown up to do." **Brian Reilly, *Don't Tell Mom the Babysitter's Dead, The Santa Clause, Joe Somebody***

"I'm not sure that this book will be read, if it is ever published. Or if you will actually write the book." **Brian Reilly**

"I don't know what I'd thank you for. I don't know why you're writing this book." **Stuart Benjamin, *La Bamba, White Nights, Against All Odds***

"If you publish this, I'm sunk." **Susan Cartsonis, *What Women Want***

"I don't know why any of this has to do with how to get movies made," **Phyllis Carlyle, *Se7en, The Accidental Tourist***

"I don't think your book is going to be too interesting based on these questions you're asking." **Edgar J. Scherick, *Wide World of Sports***

Contents

Preface

After six years confined to bed by Chronic Fatigue Syndrome, I moved to Los Angeles in March 1994 to start a new life. Looking for a job, I browsed the help wanted sections of the *Daily Bruin* and the *LA Weekly*. Ads for "actors, models" caught my attention.

On a whim, I decided to go in the opposite direction of my life prior to illness (studying economics), and pursue acting.

In addition to getting an agent, taking classes and going on auditions, I devoted myself over the next two years to reading on the industry, attending seminars and talking to anyone with wisdom to share. From this, I concluded that producers were the most under-rated players in Hollywood.

I vowed that one day I would write a book about them.

In the summer of 1996, I interviewed a dozen producers. Then in 2001-2002, I talked to another hundred. The stuff I could not fit in this book is on my website www.lukeford.net, including interviews with such producers as Evgeny Afineevsky, Mary Aloe, Mark Amin, Suzanne Bauman, Frank Beddor, Richard Berman, Alain Bernheim, Robert Boden, John Bunzel, Roy Campanella Jr, Rob Carliner, Chris Castallo, Stanley Chase, Rob Cowan, Carl Craig, H.M. Coakley, Ellis Cohen, Lorena David, Pierre David, Deborah Del Prete, Moshe Diamant, Dennis Doty, Neal Edelstein, Steven Feder, Bruce Ferber, Roger Gimbel, Don Glut, Michael Z. Gordon, Phil Gurin, James Hirsch, Richard Hull, Diane Sillan Isaacs, Stanley Isaacs, Charles Johnson, Steven A. Jones, Fred Kuehnert, David Korda, Jim Kouf, David Lancaster, Franklin Lett, Si Litvinoff, Doug Mankoff, John Manulis, Paul Maslak, Mitchel Matovich, Lori McCreary, Eric Mittleman, John Moffitt, Robert Newmyer, Michael Phillips, Ilene Kahn Power, Hadeel Reda, Mathew Rhodes, Mark Roberts, Rick Rosenthal, Morris Ruskin, Aaron J. Shuster, Sheri Singer, Lloyd Silverman, Pierre Spengler, John Quinn, Ladd Vance, Steven J. Wolfe, Frank von Zerneck, and Shelley Zimmerman.

1

Harry Bernsen

June, 1996

Harry Bernsen (father of actors Corbin and Collin) was born in 1925. In 1943, he joined the Marine Corp and served in World War II. "I was the first one to land in Nagasaki after the atomic bomb."

In 1953, Bernsen met and married actress Jeanne Cooper, who starred in the CBS soap opera *The Young and the Restless* for more than two decades. They divorced in 1977.

"I created this thing for television called *Two Women Abroad*. A big name American woman spends two weeks with a major foreign woman like Raisa Gorbachev in Russia or [the widow of Sadat] in Egypt or Benazir Bhutto in Pakistan. I adore women."

Harry pauses to adore several beautiful women in the our cafe. "It's everything about women. We would give Susan Sarandon a list of 50 women around the world and ask her who would you like to spend two weeks with and talk about politics, birth, sexuality, food, clothes, everything. Not just talk, they go. Sophia Loren wants to start hers out with Italian cooking and then go through everything. [A French actress] wants to talk about the sexuality of the French man. Raisa Gorbachev wants to talk about the loneliness of politics in Russia. [Sadat's widow] wants to talk about the psyche of the Egyptian male. Princess Diana wants to do England.

"I love to have women involved. I'm working with a woman director in Sausalito right now. She makes erotic films for women.

"I fell in love with an actress [Dolores Hart born October 20, 1938] while I was married. She was my client. She was going to be the next Grace Kelly. She was in Rome while I was living there (in the early 1960s). She was a converted Catholic. We spent a lot of time in Rome together. No sexuality just the relationship was great. My wife always resented it.

"Dolores left Rome and came back here. She got engaged. She was under contract to Hal Wallis, one of the major producers in the world. Hal threw a party for her [in 1963] and gave her a beautiful mink coat for her engagement. She threw up all over the mink coat and backed out of the engagement. She called Maria Cooper, Gary Cooper's daughter, and joined the Abbey of Regina Laudes in Bethlehem, Connecticut, as a cloistered nun.

"I got angry with her. I told her, 'You've got the ability to reach millions of people, why are you going in this abbey with 45 nuns?' She's been there for 33 years.

"I used to go up there two or three times a year. We'd have dinner under a thing because she was cloistered. I ended up with a ridge under my nose because I kissed her through the latticework.

"I'm a very religious person. I go to church every Sunday. I go to a lot of churches. I read the Bible every day.

"I don't believe in evil. I don't believe in death. I don't believe in sickness. It's nothing to me. Say a friend of yours died. A lot of people say that's the end of it. His ashes are in Forest Lawn. But if you go to the ocean, and you see somebody sailing until he goes over the horizon and you don't see him anymore, he's still sailing.

"If you see an ambulance going down the street, what do you think?"

"That somebody's hurt."

"I always think that somebody's giving birth.

"I'm 71 years old. I work out three days a week with a trainer. I lost 30 pounds in the last four months and I want to live another 30 years. I want to have babies with this woman. To be fair to her, I want to live another 30 years.

"I spent time with the Dalai Llama last week. I believe in everything. I love the entertainment business because of what it has the ability to do to people—[to change] how they talk, make love, think.

"I can say anything to anybody. How do you think I could talk to this girl [in our cafe] like that? Could you have done that? Give her your card."

"I could but I almost never would."

"I do it because I just want to love her."

"I want to take her to bed."

"I'm strange that way. I'm very much in love. I'm finally with a woman that I don't want to screw around on. I just think you can influence people and show them how to love. Isn't that true?"

Harry speaks to an attractive girl sitting next to us.

He turns back to me. "See, she agrees.

"There are a few things that I'm doing that I have a hard time justifying why I'm doing them. But there's a lot of money involved. I try to find a reason. As a producer, you get the shit kicked out of you every day. You're rejected.

"I loved *Independence Day* (1996). The idea of a Jew and a black guy saving the world, I loved it. A person who was a wimp became a hero. The world got together to fight a common enemy. I want the world to get together to find a common good—angels. That's a script I'm working on.

"I'm working on a picture with this director in Sausalito about Edna St. Vincent Millay, the American poet laureate and Pulitzer Prize winner. Have you heard of the expression 'burning a candle at both ends'? That's one of her poems. She was a forerunner of [open] sexuality, bisexuality, drugs, dope.

"There was a terrorist conference in Egypt four months ago. There were 29 world leaders there and only one was a woman—Mary Robinson of Ireland. If there had been 29 women there, it would've been a better place."

"Do you think women are ethically superior to men?"

"That's a good question. I don't think they're jaded. I think they're compassionate and nurturing.

"I saw this mother of a Muslim terrorist on TV talking about now her son is dead, he can have all the beautiful things in the world. Seventy virgins. I don't believe in that. This is where the beauty is. Like that woman there. I don't believe in death."

In a 1970s interview, Harry praised Idi Amin, the former Ugandan dictator who killed about 500,000 of his own people.

"I'm a DeGaullist. I believe that France is for France and the world is for the world. I agreed with a lot of the things that Idi Amin was saying at the time. He wanted the teachers to be Ugandans. I believed in that. I was proved wrong."

Five years later, I find on sexvigor.com this quote from Harry Bernsen for the video *Secrets of History's Greatest Lovers*: "What women have wanted us to know, but we were afraid to ask."

2

Jon Brown

A manager-producer, Jon has the affable manner, ready smile and fast delivery of the Hollywood agent.

Born May 21, 1956, he grew up in the entertainment industry. His mother, Myra Berry Brown, wrote children's books. His father, Ned Brown, ran MCA's [Music Corporation of America] literary division until it was divested by government order in 1963. Then Ned started his own agency.

"My dad represented Frank Herbert, Carlos Castaneda, William Bradford Huie, John Barth, Jackie Collins, Paul Gallico, John Michael Hayes, and Leigh Brackett. I was pretty friendly with Carlos. I was a senior in college and he was a best-selling author of a series of books that dealt with hallucinogenics. The guy was eating peyote and getting loaded. I hung with him. We talked about our similar experiences. I believe everything that he wrote."

A phone rings.

"Is that my ex-wife? Oh fuck. I'll call her back."

Jon turns to me. "I just got through an ugly divorce."

I was born on the same day (May 28) as Jon's ex-wife.

"I should introduce you two," he laughs.

"When I graduated from college [U.C. Santa Barbara], I spent the next two years sitting on a couch in front of my dad's desk, listening to him talk on the phone and make deals. Then he gave me contracts to read and learn. Then turned me loose to run the office while he returned to his beach house and relaxed.

"There isn't a lot of work to do [with] authors. People would just call and if the book was available, he'd send it out.

"I used my dad's license and worked out of my garage for years.

"Now I represent (for film rights) screenwriters, directors, estates of famous authors (Paul Gallico, Cornell Woolridge, Daman Runyon and Shirley Jackson,

Leigh Brackett, Ed Hamilton), and a couple of living authors (South African novelist Wilbur Smith, Irish author Julie Parsons). I represent hundreds of short stories and novels."

"The IMDB.com credits you with the 1999 film *Solo*?"

"We were getting ready to start a rewrite on it and the writer of it, Gary DeVore, disappeared and was tragically killed. He was found dead a year later."

Gary disappeared June 28, 1997. His body was found July 9, 1998, in the Mojave Desert Canal. His car apparently slid off Highway 14 into the California Aqueduct.

"They claim he had an accident. It's still very suspicious. I think he was killed. After he disappeared, the project died.

"There are few movies with sole producers anymore. Everyone brings a little something. What do I bring? I have a good eye for material and I help get it to the next step in the studios. I've got a dozen projects around town in development. I'm not a nuts and bolts guy. I'm a creative guy.

"It's so hard to get a movie made. It's a crap shoot. I have big talent attached to all of my movies and none of them have been made. Thankfully it's not my only job. The life of an independent producer is a lonely one. There are just a handful of guys that have lots of movies being made. Today 65 percent of my job is managing and 35 percent is producing.

"The reason this manager-producer thing has gotten so ugly is that certain managers attach themselves to the material or actors and demand that the studio take on the manager as a producer. In return, the manager says to the client, you don't have to pay me my commission because we're getting a fee from the studio. I think that's unethical.

"I did it once early in my career. A screenwriter client of mine, probably my hottest client, wrote a movie. He asked me to produce it. I sold it to Showtime. I kept him on for three drafts. Showtime wanted to fire him after the second draft because they didn't think it was funny enough. I thought it was hilarious but they didn't have a sense of humor. Then I had to fire him and the client said, 'But you promised to keep me on this movie until we got it made together. That's why I brought it to you.' I said, 'I know, but I'm not paying the bills and ultimately all I can do is recommend. I can not say yes.'

"I realized that I shouldn't do this because I can't put on a producer hat if I'm trying to produce a movie that my client wrote. Because I might say something that he doesn't want to hear. And I'd rather have the client as a client, making money from their services, than me taking a shot of becoming a producer and attaching myself to a project of their's and hoping it gets made and getting my fee that way."

"Did you keep him as a client?"

"Yes."

"What's your typical day look like?"

"I get up, read the paper, work out and roll into work around 9 a.m.. I do my European calls. Then I'm in the office, emailing. A lot of the time it's easy for me to email executives. They can give me yes or no answers and I don't have to go through a phone conversation to do it. I read in the office. I get a lot of submissions. I have my assistant do coverage for me as well. I'm not so interested in his opinion of the material as his synopsis of what it is about. If it looks interesting, I'll read it.

"I usually have one to three lunch meetings a day. I purposefully double and triple book my lunches because this is a business of cancellations. At one time, I'd only have one lunch a day and I was getting cancelled constantly. So now I double book all my lunch so I always have a lunch. I'm invariably cancelled by one person a day. If I'm not cancelled, then I do the cancelling. My lunches are usually booked up two months in advance. I rarely have breakfast and dinner meetings. I do a lot of business in my out of office meetings."

"And this is your life."

"Yeah. I wouldn't know what else to do. It's the most exciting business in the world. It certainly is the last business to feel the hit of a recession. When everything else has turned to crap, people will always find a way to come up with $7:50 to escape to see a movie.

"I'm affected by the terrorist thing. Development has slowed way down. Movies are being put in turnaround that had anything to do with terrorism, buildings bombed, bio-chemical warfare. I had two movies that clients wrote that were in pre-production at a network and both went into turnaround. One was the JFK Jr story and he died in a plane crash. So they said, 'Well, we can't do that.'"

"Why can't you do a movie that has some of those elements?"

"Because people think it is in poor taste. Perhaps the advertisers are skittish because they don't want to advertise in a movie that promotes terrorism or even glorifies it. I think you will see PG family films make a big comeback. I've got a couple in development. I'm going to be right there to take advantage of that."

"What do you read every day?"

"The trades (*Daily Variety* and *Hollywood Reporter*). The newspaper (*LA Times*) is the only thing I read religiously. I don't have time to read books, except when I'm on vacation. I read 5-10 scripts a week."

"What do you do in your spare time?"

"I play golf every Thursday morning and whenever I have a lunch cancellation, I play tennis. I have a kid at home. I go out with my girlfriend. I'm not an all-nighter guy anymore. I used to be. I like to go home and relax and tinker with my cars. I think I'm the only Jew in Hollywood who gets dirt under his fingernails."

3

John Badham

I chat by phone with John, a director-producer whose credits include *Saturday Night Fever* (1977), *War Games* (1983) and *Blue Thunder* (1983)

"I had to give a speech today before 500 people to The Taskforce on Violence in the Media. I was the first guy out of the barrel. Then I was followed by director Peter Hyams who talked about how he was going to change his approach since September 11. He'd probably make fewer movies with the government as the bad guy. Yet he had made his career with the government as the bad guy. Then Laurence Andries, who produces HBO's *Six Feet Under* (2001) talked about the way they will try to handle violence. The network guys talked about how they promoted series."

"Did you hear about director Robert Altman's remarks that Hollywood served as an inspiration for September 11th's terror?"

"To quote Peter Hyams, 'That guy's a putz.' I think it's silly to place the blame on that. We're going to blame the IRA and the Arab-Israeli conflict on the movies? Here we're talking about a country (Afghanistan) where they're not allowed to go to the movies and they're not allowed to watch TV or listen to the radio.

"In *Saturday Night Fever*, about 90 percent of the way through the picture, there's a gang rape of one of the girls. I did not want to shoot the scene. I thought it was distasteful and unpleasant and unnecessary. We were not going to miss the point of the movie by not having this scene.

"And the producer, Robert Stigwood, the 600-pound gorilla, who had the final cut and was a terror, said, 'You're shooting it. I don't care what.' So now the question became how to do it. Here I now had to go as delicately as I could, if you can say good taste in a rape scene without being ridiculous. How can you do it without being grotesque? I had to put a lot of effort into that so that the point got made but we didn't do it the way some people wanted.

"It was one of those few scripts that I loved the second I saw it and I couldn't wait to do it. Even though it had to be done on an extremely low budget ($3 million) and quickly (52 days), with few resources, it was still a terrific experience. Doing musicals is about the most fun a human being can have. I think it's better than sex. Shooting dance numbers is so exciting when you get the music going loud and the cameras going and the dancers going."

"When you put your body of work together, what are the common themes?"

"Pictures that I like telling the story. That's my guiding principle. If I like the story. If the characters appeal to me. That's what I am going to make. And I don't think about guiding principles and themes. I don't want to get stuck doing the same picture time after time. Sometimes I've gotten roped into doing three techno movies in a row—*Blue Thunder*, *War Games* and *Short Circuit* (1986). Just what I was trying to avoid. Your creativity goes down the tubes as you do the same thing over and over. You might as well be on the Chevrolet assembly line sticking wheels on the cars. You start to think automatically instead of creatively.

"The approach to America of a foreign director is going to be different from somebody who sees America all the time.

"*Saturday Night Fever* for example. I've never been to Brooklyn in my life. Thank God my mother sent me to dance classes when I was in high school. Thank God I spent the previous six months preparing a movie that I left—*The Whiz* (1978). I left it the day they insisted Diana Ross was going to be the star. When you have a story built on a six-year old child's point of view of the world, and in the original *The Wizard of Oz* (1939) film, they'd already stretched it by putting Judy Garland in there. You're looking at a child's vision of scarecrow, a cowardly lion, a tin man.

"Now you propose putting a 30-year old woman into that same part with her worldliness and knowledge of the world. As good an actress, dancer and singer as Diana Ross is, she's in the wrong place. It was not going to work. I told the people at Universal, 'I have no idea what I would say to her on the stage. It makes no sense to me. I'm the wrong person to be there. I'm sure there's somebody who will have something to say.'"

"How many films have you walked off?"

"I think that might be it. I try to not get involved if I don't like it. When I got involved in that, it was a more open playing field. But the assorted partners got together and decided they needed this giant star. Sydney Lumet directed it."

On his third marriage, John has one child. "If you can't get it right the first time, try, try again."

"You started picking up credits as an executive producer with *Stakeout* (1987). Why?"

"I realized that I wanted more control over filmmaking. I was into a film with producers I didn't know and I thought this was a wise thing to do. Until this point, I had the fortune to work with experienced skill producers and I had no need to encroach on their territory. But starting with a couple of movies before *Stakeout*, I could sense a sea change, and I decided to get in there where I had more clout."

"Do you like working with actors?"

"I'm writing a book on how directors work with actors, how to understand the psychology of the actor. It is easy to get yourself into a contemptuous mode with actors. Their artistic temperaments and weird behaviors and make fun of them without understanding where the behavior comes from. Why are actors not like well-behaved electricians and grips who do exactly who you tell them to? Why do they have to always fuss about, 'I don't understand this line and why do I have to do this?'

"I believe that 99 percent of young directors are terrified of actors. They understand cameras and lenses and everything technical but that weird animal called the actor scares them. They don't know what to do and many of them are intimidated and they run away from them. I thought, let's talk to a lot of directors and see how they deal with actors.

"Actors are a great asset. You cannot create them. The greatest director in the world can not make a good actor out of a mediocre actor. All you can do is try to cover up the mediocrity. You can inspire an actor and bring the best out of them. But you have to like them and earn their trust and be on their side. They're not going to do their best work if they're in an atmosphere of fear."

4

Alan Sacks

Alan Sacks won an Emmy for his movie *The Color Of Friendship* (2000).

"In 1990," he remembers, "I read this story about California congressman Ron Dellums."

"The most left-wing congressman," I note.

"I don't know about that. He's most definitely a man of the people. When he and his wife went back to Washington D.C. in 1977, they decided to bring over an African exchange student. Because he was dealing with apartheid, he wanted his family to experience a real African student. And by mistake, they got a white South African racist girl, the daughter of a South African policeman whose job included enforcing apartheid.

"I contacted Dellums, wanting to develop a movie based on this story. And I pitched it to Michael Healy, a director of movies for TV at CBS. Michael said he loved the movie but it wasn't the kind of movie they were doing at CBS then. They were doing women in jeopardy stories.

"Then, Michael became an executive at the Disney Channel. He called me up in 2000, asking about the Ron Dellums idea. He said that if I could get the rights to it, he'd put it into development. So, within an hour, I had the rights back to the story and was on the phone with Ron."

"What happened with the white racist South African girl?"

"In the movie, she learned something. Her character arc was that she went back a changed person. In reality, she did go back a changed person but the Dellums family has lost contact with her.

"Every time I work on a project, it's my favorite one. I'm almost like a method producer, like a method actor. I totally live the project and they all become a part of me.

"I made a punk movie, *Du-beat-e-o* (1984). I was a hardcore punk while I was doing it and I had an arm full of tattoos that have since been laser removed. I made a skateboarding movie *Thrashin* (1986) and I was really a skateboarder. I produced and directed a documentary for PBS on cowboy poetry. I became totally immersed in the cowboy world. Some of my closest friends are true cowboys.

"I love getting into different cultures with my projects. I'm working on a TV series now, *Dance Dance Revolution*, on a new dance phase that's big in Korea and Japan. It's a game that kids play in the arcades and a whole culture has developed around it. The kids have their own language, dress code, clubs. I'm totally into it. I'm down there with the kids, in the arcade, and it's really a trip. This is about to explode in this country, with my help.

"I was born December 9, 1942. Growing up in Brooklyn, I was too young to be part of the Beat generation. But I liked to go into the Village and emulate the generations before me, like Allen Ginsberg and Kerouac. Then I got into the hippie thing. The punk thing happened in the late 1970s and it all seemed the same to me."

"What did the punk scene create that's lasting?"

"Fashion. The music is still there today. Limp Bizkit. The style and attitude."

"How would you sum up the punk attitude? Nihilistic? Anarchic?"

"A combination of both. Nihilistic and anarchic. I'm going to do my art my way, and fuck you. I can't live that way today."

"Anarchy and nihilism is a frightening combination to most of us bourgeois types."

"My values are bourgeois too. I'm not the guy to talk about politics. I'm just rolling along trying to educate my students and create some television programs."

October 31, 2001

I'm in Beverly Hills when the strawberry lemonade banana smoothie takes effect. I dash into the public library for a pit-stop and check out Hunter S. Thompson's book, *Fear and Loathing in Las Vegas*. I want to jazz up my writing.

Wearing my *yarmulke*, I drive to Los Angeles Valley Community College where I find Sacks in the "smartest classroom on campus." He's a short Jewish guy wearing glasses and Buddhist regalia.

Alan waves a copy of last week's *Los Angeles Daily News* with the banner headline "Valley Tops In Film Jobs."

He snickers, "They also said the porn industry is part of these film jobs. I was thinking, how many students are we training that are going to work in that industry?"

Film people look down on TV people who look down on commercials people. Everybody looks down on porn people.

Alan wears a small idol on a silver chain around his neck. "It's my own *mezzuzah*," he smiles. "It's a symbol. I've been interested in Tibetan Buddhism since 1975. I joke with my wife and kids that I am a Jew for Buddha."

"Do you practice it?"

"I went into a meditation center at lunch time today. Not to practice but to get a brochure. I like to sit and meditate every day, even if it is just for ten minutes.

"I try to remember to look at colors. I'm looking at the color of this tape recorder, seeing that pretty red color. Just to remember that that's out there. So that's a form of meditation for me. I like to think there is more compassion and peace in the world than exists right now."

Alan's just bought a copy of the classic *The Elements of Style*. A matronly looking woman beside him complains, "It is gender biased."

Sacks teleconference's with Derrick deKerckhove's class at the University of Toronto. Mentored by media theorist Marshall McLuhan, Dr. deKerckhove directs the McLuhan Program in Culture and Technology. The quality of the students in his class, many of them pursuing graduate degrees, is light years ahead of the dim bulbs in Alan's community college class. What the Los Angeles class lacks in intelligence, however, it makes up for in racial diversity. The Toronto class is white with the exception of two Japanese students.

Today's guest is 16-year old animation whiz kid Donovan Keith who participates via teleconferencing from Chabot Community College.

Alan read about Keith on Wired.com. "I want to help him get some jobs in the industry. I want to make a movie about him."

"If you wanted to develop a movie about him, what steps would you take?"

"First, I'd meet with him and figure out what the story would be. The story would probably be—this kid comes up with a program. And then big business comes in to corrupt him and somebody wants to buy him out. Is he going to sell out or is he going to remain a true artist? And he's going through this at 15 years old. Or, a kid like this could probably command a job for $200,000 a year. How would that change you?"

It's 4 p.m. and only a couple of people have come to the class. Alan gets on the phone and asks people to come by. At 4:15, we watch the Canadians come into their conference room and take off their jackets.

My attention is not on the program but on a woman. When I walked in the door, I noticed this pale Russian secretary. She wore a tight black miniskirt and a tight top.

I am overloaded by sexual stimuli. In my neighborhood, most of the people I know dress modestly. Here the girls wear tight jeans and revealing tops.

I want to address them in the style of Prime Minister Gladstone wandering the streets of 19th Century London, trying to rescue fallen women: "Hi, I'm your moral leader. I want to talk to you about modesty. Please get into my van."

Donovan Keith drones on about a recent animation feature. "The movie has some good aspects. Some Eastern philosophy and a female lead. That's always good. More diversity."

A black woman dressed as the devil walks in. She's the college president. She wants to buy souls.

A student asks Donovan about military uses for 3-D animation.

"There are far too many military applications for 3-D animation," he replies. "The military doesn't seem to have much artistic vision."

"They have the budget but not the story."

"They have a very old story," says Dr. Derrick.

Donovan talks about "simplicity of line and form." I stare at the secretary.

Another student asks where Donovan finds his stories?

"You have to go inside. You have to think about what message you want to get across. In Hollywood, far too much emphasis is put on focus groups instead of what we're trying to say to people. It really depends on if you're in it for money or if you're in it to tell people what you want them to hear."

Student: "Not the generic you, where do you get your stories?"

"I look at my life. And whatever is important to me in my life, I want to share with others. If I'm feeling really happy one day, I want to spread the love."

"If Disney offer you a lot of money to work with them, would you go with them or stay independent?"

"I'd go with them [Disney] long enough to get the money to afford to be independent."

The discussion turns to pirated software. Donovan, who is about to release his own animation software program, says, "I do not pirate software anymore. Now that I've become a developer and realize how much work goes into it. It all comes down to karma. If you want to have good karma, you don't pirate software."

The students deride this. They say stealing software is fine because they're poor and the corporations are rich.

March 25, 2002

Alan's disturbed by my write-up of my visit to his class (which I posted to Luke-ford.net). "I have some concerns about your point of view. It's fine as a journalist to interpret whatever you see, and that's cool. But you describe one person I'm talking to as matronly. You describe my students as dim bulbs. You describe someone else as black. You describe me as short and Jewish. Those are not positive images that you're laying out there. You walk in there with a *yarmulke* on and I was surprised to see that."

"Ethnicities and religion are of interest to me."

"What's so interesting about short and Jewish? Or matronly or black? If there was a reason for it, that's one thing. That almost seems anti-Semitic in a way?"

"Black and Jewish identify someone's ethnicity or religion. Matronly describes how someone looks."

"I understand but there are other ways to describe how somebody looks. Those are all negative. I'm proud to be short and Jewish. But the way it read. For somebody on the outside, that's just not a cool thing. That was completely stereotypical. It's like saying I'm cheap."

"I don't think of short and Jewish and black and matronly as negative."

"Nor do I, but the tone of it was. A reader would pick that up."

"I will go back and take a second look. The main thing is, I quoted you accurately?"

"Yes, pretty much. If you want to include it, just bring up this conversation. I'm cool with that."

5

Alain Silver

I interview Alain at his home in Santa Monica. We're surrounded by hundreds of 33rpm records, a reel-to-reel tape recorder and a TV that looks to date from the 1970s.

Born December 7, 1947, in LA's Chinatown, Alain grew up in the San Fernando Valley. After receiving his doctorate in Motion Picture History from UCLA, he published 14 books, produced 30 movies and approximately 120 CDs of music.

"I worked on this feature *Beat* (2000). There were many problems. The other producers suddenly found themselves with a picture that was not as easy to sell as they had thought.

"They wanted to re-cut it. I was caught in the middle [between the other producers and the director]. I said to one, 'I understand your situation but it's unfair to blame the director since he delivered the script.' The producer agreed. 'Yes, and I liked the script, but now that it is a movie, I can't sell it.'

"There's a shift in how you market independent pictures. It goes back to the '80s and what kind of budget you can expect to raise on an independent project. In the late '80s, you could shoot anything. You got by by attaching marginal names as actors to raise funds. Then the foreign buyers [realized] that the American independent product they were buying was substandard. Plus the video shelves in all those little stores filled up.

"I produced a couple of pictures in 1989 for Australian executive producer Tom Broadbridge. He'd been successful with a company that distributed Australian pictures including an early hit called *BMX Bandits* (1983), starring a teenage Nicole Kidman.

"Tom wanted to make some American movies for a price with some minor names with certain formula elements. He once told me about a trailer for *Prime*

16

Suspect (1989) for Cannes—'Make sure you put all the gun shots and all the tits in it.'

"Tom hired my partner Patrick Regan and me to produce the picture. It was written by Thomas Cost, who lived with actress Susan Strassberg, the daughter of [famed acting teacher] Lee Strassberg. She attached some other actors, such as Billy Drago and Frank Stallone.

"Thomas Cost, who mainly worked as a production designer, came in and told me that he thought he'd written a brilliant film noir and he wanted to shoot it in an impressionist manner. The first thing I said was, I don't think we want to talk to Tom about film noir and expressionism. It's not what he's relating to.

"We had a budget of $500,000, financed by a New Zealand bank. It was going to have a completion bond, which was surprising given the low budget. A completion bond means that a company comes in and for a percentage, 1.5-3 percent, and insures there's completion of the picture. The company gets take-over privileges if they see there's a problem. If there are overruns, they have to come in and spend money. Needless to say, they're not in the business of taking over and spending money. They want to make sure that doesn't happen. They make sure by significantly checking the budget and the schedule and feeling secure there's a good picture.

"The picture was doable but the problem was that the script made no sense, which I shared with Tom Broadbridge before he went back to Australia. He called me at a weird hour from Australia saying he'd read the script on the flight and it made no sense.

"We got it rewritten by Bruce Kimmel. The story is about a high school guy who goes on a weekend camping trip with his girlfriend. She's brutally murdered. He's so traumatized that he loses his voice and is put into an institution where his psychologist is Susan Strassberg. He escapes to clear his name and find the real murderers. Susan helps him. It was a hopelessly convoluted plot.

"Thomas Cost had written it so that after his first sexual experience with this girl, this kid's showering in this waterfall and her severed head comes over the waterfall. I read that and said that is impossible. I can't even get you a decent severed head with our budget.

"So on the spur of the moment, I said, instead of a waterfall, it's a small lake. And he's gone swimming and she's by the shore. And while he's 100 yards off shore, this dark figure comes out of the bushes with a knife. He sees her being killed. He swims as fast as he can but he cannot get there. He gets there just in time to have her die in his arms. That's what we shot. Thomas didn't like it.

"We were limited by the capabilities of the actors in the cast. As pre-production continued, we had far more problems. Our DP (Director of Photography) and Production Designer couldn't understand what Thomas wanted. It's the first movie he's ever directed.

"I remember a scene at the production meeting a week before shooting. There are two killers in the woods and there are cutaways to their hands holding knives. One actor is white and one actor is black but these cutaways are supposed to look the same.

"Both executive producers wanted to fire Thomas but I fought to keep him on. We'd made a deal with the guy who'd written the script and brought in the package [of actors].

"We started shooting and we saw the dailies and they were impossibly confused. We saw by day two or three that this was not working. I talked to the bond company and they agreed, but we didn't have a pretext. Thomas's deal was that he couldn't be arbitrarily fired. While the production attorney wrestled with those issues, we kept shooting. On day five, I was in the office. My partner was on the set. I just got off the phone with the attorney, still trying to find a pretext to find Thomas. My partner called to say, 'Thomas just attacked me. He tried to choke me. The first AD and the DP had to pull him off of me.' And my first reaction is great, we can fire him.' We did the next day.

"We brought in Bruce Kimmel, who did the rewrites under a pseudonym (Alex Josephs). He came in for a small fee and made the movie work on the remaining days, including re-shooting. We were rewriting the script before each scene. Bruce would be shooting a scene and I'd be rewriting the next scene.

"Susan Strassberg had to work the first day after Thomas, the man she lived with, was fired. She burst into tears the first four times she came out of make-up. She had to go back in. It was a long day. My producing partner was banned from the set because Susan held him responsible for Thomas's problems. I was the only producer allowed to speak to her.

"We finished on schedule and under budget. The problem was, we had a lot of Thomas Cost's material. As we cut the picture together, we got rid of many of Thomas's scenes. It came out 84 minutes long. Tom Broadbridge had a deal with an early incarnation of Sony Pictures. They were picking up pictures for distribution. He owed them a picture. One of the Australian pictures he gave them, they didn't want. So he gave them this one. They said, great, but it has to be at least 96 minutes long.

"That was impossible. We shot a really long title sequence in the cemetery and got it up to 88 minutes. My producing partner Patrick Regan quit. We thought about this character you never see, this aggressive district attorney. How about we make him like the Peter Coyote character in *Jagged Edge* (1985)? So we wrote and shot two full scenes and four transitional pieces, shot them in two days, for $8000. We got to 96 minutes. At the screening, Tom Broadbridge turned to me and said, 'You shot all these minutes for $8000. Why couldn't you have shot the whole picture at that ratio?'

"We delivered the picture to Sony. A couple of weeks later, there was an article in *The LA Times* with the president of Sony SBS. The president talked about our film, though he didn't mention it by name. He said we have to be more careful with these pickups. He didn't have a problem with the quality of the picture but in the shooting of the post-production inserts, we'd used a Panasonic TV. And when the people back in Japan at Sony first saw this movie, they focused on this instant of a Panasonic TV.

"*Prime Suspects* was made for $520,000. Tom sold it to Sony for $420,000 and then he made a deal for foreign distribution for $750,000. He was happy with his instantaneous profit. The company that bought the foreign rights, bought them off the original script. They realized when they took delivery of the picture that the budget was not as high as Tom had said. He told people the budget was $2 million bucks. They might've bought it if you said it cost one million but not two million. So when they got the picture, they realized they'd overpaid and they reneged on the deal.

"The case went to arbitration and the arbitrator nullified the contract because the picture was too different from the original script. I testified that all the changes we'd made were to improve the picture. Tom resold *Prime Suspects* for half the original amount, long after I did a second picture (*Night Visitor*, 1989) with Tom that was distributed by MGM-UA. It was the same formula—gratuitously violent and a tasteless script.

"Both of these instances, *Prime Suspects* and *Night Visitor*, reveals what it was like in the late '80s trying to fulfill audience requirements and trying to make a decent picture. At that point in my career as a producer, if I had a project offered, I couldn't just say no. That's different today. If somebody offers me a project I think is dreck, it is easy for me to say no. I don't need the money and I don't need another credit.

"You can never tell how a picture will turn out. I thought *Beat* would be well received. It's been finished for almost two years and it might eventually get a domestic release.

"Rupert Hitzig directed *Night Visitor*. It was the first movie he directed. He produced a lot of studio pictures. He was aware of the limitations. The only thing

I had to teach him was that he couldn't bring all of his friends from these big budget pictures to this million dollar picture. Because they just wouldn't understand this level. The problem with any picture of this level, the way they are put together dictates the range of aesthetic results.

"Sometimes directors can't stand back from what they're doing, they get so involved, that they can't tell when a scene works. Because of the short schedules and other constraints of independent pictures, it is easy for directors to lose focus of the whole picture and get lost in the details. The best thing a producer can do is try to pull the directors back and let them see what by definition they're supposed to see. If there's anything a director needs to do at any given moment, it is try to help situate an actor. Where is this scene in the movie? Where is your character? Directors are prone to getting sucked in to the details that blind them to the bigger picture.

"I had that experience with someone as sophisticated as Rupert on *Night Visitor*. We looked all over Los Angeles for a basement. And I said, Rupert, just build it on a stage. You can't find many basements in Los Angeles large enough to shoot in.

"It's hard enough doing these pictures. And when you have directors locked into certain concepts and don't understand that you've brought them a location better than what they wrote, it becomes a problem to do an independent picture for a budget.

"I did *Runaway Dreams* (1989) in Fort Lauderdale with first time director Michelle Noble. I gave her her first job in the business as a Production Assistant (PA) and she brought me onto this project to mollify the bond company and make them feel secure. And after I spent a few days in Fort Lauderdale, I said to Michelle, 'I'm sorry. I know the camera's facing east. But we could've shot this in LA.' And she agreed. It was a beach with palm trees. There was nothing about where we shot that said Fort Lauderdale.

"The movie was based on some *60 Minutes* reports about teenage runaways to Fort Lauderdale who became underage prostitutes. The producer on the movie had produced the *60 Minutes* reports. The movie played in a couple of film festivals but was never released in the United States. It was right there on the bubble of independent film sales that finished in 1990.

"I've shot some digital features on Sony DV (Digital Video) cameras with director Christopher Coppola. We shot *Palmer's Pickup* (1999) in Super 16mm for a million dollars. We shot while we drove across country with as small a crew as possible. When we cut the picture, we found that a minimum of 1,000 frames were ruined. The bond company freaked. They didn't want to extend the delivery date (because the financing for the film was based on it being delivered at a certain time). So we took the picture digital. We transferred the whole movie to high definition video and clean it up there. It cost about $200,000 to do that but the results were great. We went from 16mm to high definition video to 35mm.

"We premiered it at a film festival in Berlin at a huge 1000-seat theater with a monster screen. And the film looked great, though a little grainy.

"The major studios are not interested in taking risks to make a little money. They're interested in taking a big risk to make a lot of money. They're not interested in a guaranteed $5 million to $10 million unless there's no risk. If you want them to back a picture theatrically, they have to imagine a huge upside or it's not worth their effort. And that studio mentality makes it so difficult for independent pictures to compete for distribution slots.

"This has destroyed the mid-level market. The studios have bought out the largest independents like Miramax, October Films, and New Line and forced you to go to a much lower-level alternative where it is difficult to compete. What's the last independent picture to show on 2000 screens? *The Blair Witch Project* (1999)? It doesn't happen often. A lot of people out there making independent pictures think they're going to be the next *Blair Witch Project*. It's not realistic."

6

Chris Hanley

In 1991, Harvey Weinstein came to the home of Chris and Robert Hanley in London and offered them 50 percent of Miramax for $6 million. The Hanleys called a friend who warned them it was a dangerous investment because Miramax had so much debt. They said no.

Instead they formed Muse Productions, and during the 1990s, Chris produced the directorial debuts of Sofia Coppola (*Virgin Suicides*, 1999), Vincent Gallo (*Buffalo '66*, 1998) and Steve Buscemi (*Trees Lounge*, 1996).

"You have a tendency to like sex and to explore death," says Chris. "I'm not trying to lighten my day by reading things. People forget that most of the best stories ever told are tragic. What's *Tender is the Night* by F. Scott Fitzgerald? Was *Catcher in the Rye* light? *American Pie* was light but would that ever be a book that either of us would want to read?

"I have this background in the philosophy of science and the philosophy of mathematics, cybernetics, physics, neuroscience, neuro-physiology. I like things that play with time. I'm interested in mind-brain theory. What defines the self? A pile of neurons? The writers of novels seem to be more into science than people who turn in screenplays.

"When I watch a horror thing, I just get scared. It pumps up my hormone level into fight or flight. I watch horror movies with my hands over my eyes. The first *Alien* (1979) movie made me feel more alive, not because it was scary, but because the imagery was tapping into something essential, like a cancer cell, as a primitive essential form.

"I liked the movie *The Others* (2001) because it was gothic and it reifies a whole world of dreams that people walk around with. It makes it feel that dreams could be truer reality. I like it when the house is used as a metaphor for the mind, the creepy house with all the little rooms in it and unknown horrors that you stumble into. Or medieval thinking, with castles, like Bergman films like the *The*

Seventh Seal (1957) which was about the Black Death. Ending up in the castle and having to face death and the knight does it one way. The strongest person is actually the weakest.

"Jim Thompson's novel which I bought, *The Killer Inside Me*, isn't so much about murder and fear and death but it has a sadomasochistic thing with the sexuality that made it interesting."

"When were you born?"

"No. I don't want that published anywhere. A long time ago. I saw the Beatles on Ed Sullivan. I'm doing a movie called *The Family* about Charles Manson's rock n'roll career (based on the book by Ed Saunders, *Charles Manson And The Dune Buggie Attack Battalion*). Dennis Wilson financed his rock career [before Manson turned into a mass murderer]. Doris Day's son Terry Melcher owned the house Roman Polanski rented where Sharon Tate was killed. Manson did NOT go to the site of any of the murders—he is a mass murderer on the basis of conspiracy, due to his cultish mind control of his 'Family.'

"These murders were not something I read about. I remember when it was taking place. I think that by 1970-71, the cat was out of the bag that there was a death poet, murderer, cultist out there that's attractive and destructive to society at the same time.

"I feel that I was a part of the time. The directors of *The Family*, Don Murphy and Susan Montcord, just inherited the spirit of the sexual revolution."

"Was there still free love in the '70s?"

"I was a virgin at the time but that was the deal, yes. Half the movie is free love."

"What was your breakout film?"

"*Freeway* (1996), starring Reese Witherspoon. It was controversial. It went out on HBO and teenagers across the nation embraced it. It shipped tons of videos. People 15-25 felt it had a voice they hadn't seen. In the end, *Pulp Fiction* appeals to the college intelligentsia, not a trashy teenager. *Freeway* appealed to an audience closer to the street.

"Roger Ebert said *Freeway* was one of his favorites. *Trees Lounge* was a poignant look at a real person in a real place with a nothing ending. It's about a guy who drank too much and never got out. The movie never sold anything. And people thought, oh, that really is the way life is. We called it 'bleak chic.' It got a cool hip reception in the media even though it didn't knock off a lot of tickets.

"They were shot two weeks apart and I had two of them pumping out in the fiercely competitive independent world. I experienced the same thing with *Virgin*

Suicides and *American Psycho* (1999). Their premieres in New York were one day apart. *American Psycho* was on 15 magazine covers.

"*Buffalo 66* ($2.3 million directed by Vincent Gallo, starring Mickey Rourke, Christina Ricci) and *Two Girls and a Guy* ($1.26 million directed by James Toback and starring Robert Downey and Heather Graham) came out at the same time and got a high ranking reception in the media, from *Entertainment Weekly* to *Premiere* to *The Wall Street Journal* to *The New York Times*.

"I've produced a few films with Ed Pressman. After a while, with the low budget films of less than seven million, I've probably got the hotter reputation because I just kept churning them out. I was always on the set, getting to know the actors, staying in touch with them. Finding out who they wanted to work with and which directors. Christina Ricci's directing something with Adam, who has office space here. I've been trying to get her to direct for years.

"*American Psycho* was our biggest budgeted film at $7 million."

"How did you get *Buffalo 66*?"

"I've known Vincent Gallo since late 1983, when he recorded in my studio in New York. He was into art and I'd become an art dealer. He went into acting and I got into producing. He moved out here first. We hung out. His screenplay circulated around town. He reluctantly sent me over a copy, because everything he does is reluctant. I read it and said, 'Are you kidding? No one else could direct this but you. It's your life.' And so he did.

"Lions Gate Entertainment (distributor) thought they were going to have a light comedy. It wasn't what they expected at first. Over the years it panned out as being more significant for the way we did it. We shot the movie on Kodak Ektachrome Reversal film 35mm (and it had not ever been used before as a replacement for negative film—it is basically a positive transparency film). Kodak had to make a special batch for us just for *Buffalo 66*. In 16mm format it had been used for war photography (dating back to late World War II and Vietnam etc, and also for football cinematography up until a period in the early 1980's when it was switched over to negative film).

"Vincent had grown up with the Buffalo Bills. His mother really was a Buffalo Bills freak who only had one photo of him and hundreds of them. He really spent time in jail for stealing a car. The whole painfulness of existence was drawn from his relationship with his father.

"Ben singing that song in that one scene is actually Vincent's father's real voice from a cassette recording he'd done years earlier. Vincent's father had a great voice and never did anything with it, just sung in bars. Some of the scenes were shot in the house he lived in while growing up. Most of the people he grew up with are still there. It's that kind of town where people never get out. It's a strange jail sentence. They're all sports freaks walking around with Buffalo Bills regalia.

"I was the only producer on that and work 23-hour days with him threatening me at 4 a.m. that he was going to stab me in the face if I didn't do this or that. I spent more concentrated effort on that, getting the financing, getting the crew members and keeping them in line, dealing with the unions, than I have on any other film."

"How did you get Sofia Coppola, Francis Ford Coppola's daughter, to make her directorial debut?"

"I knew Jackie, her sister-in-law. Jackie was married to the son that died in the boat accident. Jackie is deeply involved with the Coppola family. Sofia and Jackie and my wife and I would go to dinner from time to time. Sofia stumbled on the book *The Virgin Suicides* and wrote a script for the hell of it. She looked up who owned it and lo and behold it's the friend she eats dinner with. My wife Roberta lobbied to get Sofia the directing job.

"I originally wanted Nick Gomez to direct. He wrote a script that didn't quite work. I don't like to jump from director to director. But Sofia's passion for the project became apparent to me.

"It was hard to finance the picture. The title alone was difficult. Using the words 'Virgin' and 'Suicides' in the same title. They wouldn't even let me register it in the state of New York. I had to call it the Virgin S. corporation. We form shell corporations every time we make a movie, to limit the liability of the movie to that property. So I tried to register Virgin Suicides Inc Productions and the state said it was pornographic. Even though at one point Disney owned the film rights to the book."

7

David Permut

David is developing a feature film called *Promoter*. "My mentor Bill Sargent was a promoter.

"I've always wanted to be in the movie business. My family moved out here from New York when I was 13 years of age. My first job in the business was selling maps on Sunset Blvd to the stars' homes. I was 15. The prices for the maps were negotiable, from $1-3 depending on the appetite of the customer. Joe Hyams, who was married to Elke Summer, wrote a novel, *The Pool*, about a kid on the corner who sells maps to the stars homes. He spent hours on the corner talking to me and I was one of the people he dedicated the book to.

"Fred Astaire used to come by and sign the map. Katherine Hepburn and Elvis Presley lived near me. I met a lot of people. And as I got their autograph, the price of the map went up. In the early '70s, I was known as the kid on the corner of Sunset Boulevard and Holmby Hills. There was a lawyer across the street named Sam Zagong. He used to come over and encourage me. He used to sell newspapers in Chicago. He handled Stanley Kramer and every major director of that era.

"My business was Beverly Hills Map Company. I made my own maps and updated them every few months. I can't tell you how I got my own addresses. I had a license to sell the maps. I wanted to get cars to stop so I body painted my brother's girlfriend. 'Movie Maps Here. Stop.' And she was dancing in a bikini. The police didn't like that.

"A number of the neighbors in Bel Air, Beverly Hills and Holmby Hills wanted to get rid of me and two old ladies who sold maps. Francis's corner was Mapleton and Holmby Hills and the other woman Vivian sold in front of Gary Cooper's old house. They didn't want us around.

"We lived in the area. I came home from work one day and my mother showed me a letter that went out to all the people in the area explaining why they wanted to get rid of the maps. They're unsightly and they cause accidents.

"I found a personal injury lawyer willing to take our case because he saw publicity. I spoke at City Hall. I said I just wanted to make some money. These women could be on welfare, instead they're earning a living. Star Maps are a tradition in Hollywood. People come here by the millions. The Beverly Hills City Council made it illegal to sell the maps.

"The case went to the California State Supreme Court which ruled in our favor. The only reason you see any kids on Hollywood Blvd with signs is because of this court case.

"It was a different era. There was an innocence. Now with surveillance and stalking and the problems of the world today. Those issues didn't exist in 1971.

"My dad comes home one night and he says he met a guy who's going to reunite the Beatles. I said, 'Give me a break. You met a guy in the bar and he said he was getting the Beatles together? And you believed him?' I was cynical. Then I turned on the TV that night to see a news flash that the Beatles were meeting in Hollywood for a proposed reunion. My eyes lit up like saucers and I ran to my dad. 'Where did you meet this guy? Who is this guy?' Dad gives me his business card with a Beverly Hills address. I thought, 'Wow, he's in Beverly Hills. He must be legitimate.'

"I tracked him down and this guy had an office on Little Santa Monica Blvd across from what is now the Peninsula Hotel. He was above a tailor shop working out of a utility room. There were no windows. He worked out of a closet with a card table and two folding chairs. He drove a Corvair that never started and he lived in Howard Weekly Apartments in the San Fernando Valley right next to the Ventura Freeway. He obviously had no money. And this fiery red-haired Irishman from Cato, Oklahoma, by the name of Horace William Sargent III was the guy who was going to get the Beatles together?

"He told me that he did *Hamlet* and made millions during the Burton/Taylor era of the '60s with a new video process called Electronovision. And he made one version of Harlow with Carole Lindley and he made millions. And he told me he made the first rock show with the Rolling Stones, James Brown, Jan Dean, Leslie Gore and every major rock star of the '60s. And he filmed it, the first filmed rock show. I go to the library and check him out and he did it all. Sargent was a promoter who was consistently erratic. He was either flying high or he was on the canvas and everybody said it was his last stand. That's when he had the resilience to pull rabbits out of the hat.

"I told Sargent about a play about the Harding Teapot Dome Scandal written by prominent writers Robert E. Lee and Jerry Lawrence who wrote *Inherit the Wind*. He optioned the play for one dollar. He and I joined forces to produce it. I'm 15-16 years old. I became his gopher. He's got no money. I'm loaning him money from my movie maps business. Meanwhile I'm telling my dad that I'm getting into the business. And he said, 'I don't know about this guy Sargent.' I said, 'This is how it works. You put the deal together and then you find the money. Don't worry about it. This guy knows what he's doing.'

"We got an all-star cast for the play—Lloyd Bridges, Beau Bridges, Lee Grant, Robert Culp, William Wyndham, Tom Bosley. It was going to be a limited-run stage show filmed on stage in San Francisco. This is one that Sargent couldn't pull off. He was screwing around trying to get the money. Ultimately, he disappears four weeks before the curtain was set to go up and the play never went on.

"About three years later, in 1974, I went to college. Sargent called me at my job as a junior agent. They said, 'There's somebody on the phone who says you'll know him by his initials.' What are his initials? 'BS.' I pick up the phone and he says, 'Goddamn, where are you, you little Jew?' He used to call me 'LJ.' I say, 'Where are you? You let me down.' He said, 'I'm sending my limo to pick you up.'

"He sends an angel-white phantom Rolls Royce to drive me three blocks to the Beverly Wilshire Hotel. He's in the penthouse suite. Warren Beatty had the other penthouse suite. This elderly guy in Sargent's apartment turns out to be John Tanent, the largest shareholder in Georgia Pacific and in the lumber business. Sargent bought a Mormon church in Salt Lake City with Tanent's money and converted it into a 32-track state-of-the-art soundstage studio.

"We go see a play, *Give 'Em Hell, Harry*. Sargent buys the one-man play and four weeks later, we videotape the film (1975). It cost $230,000 including a lavish party we threw in Seattle. We transferred the tape to film. The quality was horrific. It looked grainy and terrible. But it didn't matter because the actor, James Whitmore, was brilliant. No studio wanted to distribute the film. Sargent said, 'We will distribute it ourselves.' How do we do that? He picked up the phone and called Sumner Redstone and Sal Halassee, Chairman of United Artists, and he booked the theaters. You couldn't do that today but in 1975, there weren't several major releases every week. There were openings in schedules.

"The picture opened on 300 screens that Sargent booked. Whitmore gets an Academy Award nomination for Best Actor. The picture does about $11.5 million. As Bill Sargent used to say, 'We're shitting in high cotton.'

"Sargent takes over 1888 Century Park East, in Century City, the entire sev- enth floor of the high-rise. I'm president of the company and he's chairman of the board. We're on the map in a big way. The floor is decorated like a gothic castle. When the elevator doors open, the voice activated recording booms, 'Welcome to Bill Sargent's Theater Television Operation.' Flickering lights. My office is the size of a football field. I have a sunken wet bar and I don't drink. I had a library with vintage books. At the time, I wasn't an avid reader.

"His big dream was to reunite the Beatles. I wanted to capitalize on *Give 'Em Hell, Harry* and do other shows along that line. Other shows we could videotape and film.

"In 1975, Bill Sargent convinced the world that the Beatle were getting back together when he made them a $50 million offer. And Bill Sargent wound up on the cover of *People* magazine convincing the world that the Beatles were getting together. Lorne Michaels does a takeoff of Bill Sargent on *Saturday Night Live*, offering him $7 to get together again.

"We had $3 million in the bank. Where were we going to get the other $47 million? Sargent said, 'Don't worry about that. It's a technicality.' I'd set up a meeting with George Harrison's attorney David Braun. Sargent started by offering him $30 million then upped it to $50 million. It was a seven-and-a-half minute meeting then David threw us out. I'm depressed because the meeting went whacky. And Sargent says, 'We've got 'em.' And in five minutes, he went back to our offices, picked up the phone, called Western Union and sent four telegrams to the Beatles offering them $50 million.

"Then our offices are barricaded. You can't get near our offices. Security is called in. He convinced the world that the Beatles were getting together. The phone lines lit up like Christmas trees. I had friends of mine from high school who I didn't care for particularly, who said, 'Hey Permut, are you part of the Beatles now?'

"Sargent said, 'You're young. You talk to the media.' I'm doing interviews with the media. I'm living at home at the time. I'd come home for dinner and my dad would say, 'You were on the news tonight talking about the Beatles.'

"What made Sargent such a great promoter is that he believed that the Beatles were getting together. And the irony is, if they would've answered the telegram, he would've gotten the $50 million and we would've enjoyed a Beatles reunion.

"His next promotion was a fight between a man and an 18-foot Great White killer shark. 'Death Match.' Either the man or the shark would die, live under water. It was on the heels of the success of *Jaws*.

"Sargent used to be a boxing promoter. He promoted Cassius Clay a.k.a. Mohammed Ali.

"An 80-foot diameter ring was constructed with nine cameras under water. Universal threatens to sue us. The letter comes to the office and Sargent loves that. 'Oh God, we're being sued.' As though it is the greatest thing that's ever happened.

"David Binder, who directed *Give 'Em Hell, Harry* is now scouting locations for the shark fight. Our offices are now barricaded again. The International Humane Association holds a special session at the U.N. to ban the fight in United States waters. But our attorneys say that we come under the same provisions as bull fights. As long as we hold it outside of the U.S., we can promote it. Jimmy the Greek places odds on the shark in Las Vegas.

"Meanwhile, we're having problems because we can't catch a shark. So the project went south. And Sargent disappears again.

"I got started in the business at that time cultivating stories. I wanted to make movies not promote fights between a man and a shark. I realized that the power is in the material. I didn't have access to stars and directors but I did have access to writers. And I started working with a number of young writers. I started my own production company. Most of the writers were bartenders and stereo salesmen. I make my first development deal with Columbia Pictures.

"Then a phone call comes. 'Goddamn you little Jew. Where are you?' It's Sargent and it is 1979. He's infectious and seductive and I love him for that. He's got a glint in his eye. He's like the Pied Piper. You get a magic carpet ride with him. We made history again when we shot *Richard Pryor Live in Concert* over two nights at the Long Beach Terrace Theater. Every studio turned the film down. And again we released it ourselves, about four weeks after it was shot. It grossed $32.5 million on a budget of less than one million.

"It was the most successful concert film ever and was turning point in the career of Richard Pryor.

"One night I was having dinner with a television executive who asked me how I got started in the business. So I regaled him with stories about Sargent. And he said, 'This is a series. We've got to talk to the network.'

"I always knew it would be a book or a movie. I tape-recorded, with Sargent's approval, hours of telephone conversations with him about the shark fight and the Beatles.

"When I went around to the networks, I was very prepared with a colorful show. Pictures and videos. All three networks wanted to do the show. We developed it at NBC before we realized that it is more of a movie. Eventually perhaps we can spin it off as a series.

"Sargent's living in Cato, Oklahoma. He's not wealthy, but when he's on the canvas and counted out, that's when he has the resilience to bounce back. The last time I spoke to him, he told me, 'I'm building an indoor city. I have an 822-room hotel. You know what's the biggest waste in hotel space? Halls. I've got no halls. I'm talking to the Japanese.'

"I don't know what the hell he's talking about but you could read about him on the front page of the *Wall Street Journal* tomorrow. He's the same guy who offered to buy the Super Bowl and take it off free television and put in on pay cable."

8

Dale Pollock

November 21, 2001

I call Dale in North Carolina. "How did George Lucas like your biography, *Skywalking: The Life and Films of George Lucas?*"

Dale laughs. "He didn't like my book after the fact. He liked it when he first read it but the reality of seeing his life on a page disturbed him. Mostly because he wants to control every aspect of his creative and personal life and he didn't control my book. He is not a fan of it and he has made that clear in his public statements."

"How many of your peers, when you were an entertainment journalist, wanted to work in the business they covered?"

"Fewer when I came but more now. Unfortunately, that may have been a trail I helped blaze. And I feel bad about it sometimes. Before Charles Schrager and I and a couple of other people left, the trades weren't considered a way in to the business. And we showed that they were. And we've seen a lot of people now make that transition."

"What was it like working for David Geffen?"

"That was my film school. I learned more in one year than I had learned up to that point covering the entertainment industry for eight years. Watching him in action. Watching him work the phones. Watching him deal with creative people in the story meetings. I couldn't have worked for him much longer. He was difficult."

"Did he scream at you?"

"He screamed at everybody. You didn't take it personally."

"What did you think of Tom King's bio of Geffen?"

"I wasn't too impressed by it. I thought he soft-pedaled some things and bore in too hard on others. Geffen is a complex guy and has achieved amazing things in multiple fields. He's had major success in three areas—music, film and legitimate stage."

"What was Tom too soft on?"

"I thought he was too soft on the issue of how much Geffen's sexuality influenced the decisions he made. Tom King never made any attempt to contact me or any of the people I knew.

"Geffen's films had a sexual quality to them that a lot of films during that era didn't. And I thought that made them interesting. *Risky Business* (1983) is a very sexual movie. Geffen was able to embrace subject matter that a lot of other people weren't able to. He was willing to take chances. I found the script for *Beetlejuice* (1988). I don't know if any other company would've been willing to make that film other than Geffen."

"Is there a Hollywood Gay Mafia?"

"It's like saying, is there a Jewish Mafia? Yes, there are a lot of Jews but do they act in concert to advance their Jewishness? There are a lot of people who are gay. Do they act in concert to advance a gay agenda? I don't think so. I've never regarded that as a Gay Mafia and I've never felt that it hurt me in my career that I wasn't gay."

"Are you Jewish?"

"Yes, and I never felt like that helped me."

"When did you find you wanted to produce movies?"

"That was at Geffen when I found two scripts, *Beetlejuice* and *The 'burbs* (1989). And I wanted to work on both of those films. And Geffen said to me, no, no, no. I produce the films, you go find more material. And I said, I want to work on these movies which I found. And he said no, that's not your job. That's when I said, I want to be a producer. And he said, that's not going to happen here."

"Why did you move to North Carolina in 1999?"

"Because the kind of films I was interested in producing were becoming more and more difficult to make. My last film was *Meet The Deedles* (1998). I walked off a picture called *I'll Be Home For Christmas* (1998) because those weren't the kind of movies I was interested in making and I was doing it for a paycheck. I was head of the producing program at the American Film Institute and teaching in the USC professional writing program. I was getting more out of my teaching than out of the frustrating business of trying to produce good movies."

"Most journalists advise aspiring journalists to not major in journalism at college. Would that apply to film schools?"

"If I really believed that, I wouldn't be doing what I was doing."

"How did you go in 1985 from the *LA Times* to Geffen?"

"I had written my book on Lucas. I was burned out. The *LA Times* wouldn't give me a leave of absence to finish my book so I was pissed off at them. I left the

Times and then got hired by Geffen. I never wrote a piece on Geffen in my whole career.

"I was fortunate to produce twelve movies in ten years. I had a knack for getting movies made. Now, how good they were, how commercial they were?

My budgets ranged from $4-32 million (*Mrs Winterbourne*, 1996). Columbia made us cast Rikki Lake for *Winterbourne* because they owned her TV show which was really hot when we cast the film. By the time the film came out, the TV show was not so hot. The audience didn't embrace her as a leading woman. I enjoyed working with her but she's not a leading lady. That's the bad side of synergy—when the studio owns two things and decides to combine them.

"Three films have had the most meaning to me—*The Beast* (1988), *A Midnight Clear* (1991), and *Set It Off* (1996).

"*A Midnight Clear* was the best film I produced. I went to everybody in town to raise the money and nobody wanted to make a little anti-war film. At that time, World War II was not a fashionable subject. Finally, we pre-sold the foreign and video rights and raised the money. That film fell apart five times before we got it made. At one point I was scouting locations in Yugoslavia when there was still a Yugoslavia. We ended up making it in Park City, Utah. On every movie, I had to raise the money. Either sell it to a studio or do a split-rights deal or raise it independently.

"I would get calls, like with *Set It Off* [four black women rob banks], saying, 'This is material I can't sell anywhere. Are you interested?' I had a reputation for getting tough movies made."

9

Dorothea Petrie

November 29, 2001

Married to director Daniel Petrie, Dorothea Petrie has four children who work in Hollywood—Daniel Petrie Jr, Donald Petrie, June Petrie and Mary Petrie.

Dorothea began her career as an actress. Then she became a casting director and agent. She began her producing career in 1979 with *Orphan Train* for CBS.

"In my next life, I'm going to have a business degree and a law degree. When our girls were in high school and our boys were in college, I realized that I would soon have some time and I felt that producing was the thing that I could do best. I know material. I've worked with good writers like Carl Sandberg. Dan had a fine reputation but I didn't want to go on that reputation. I didn't want people to hire me because of Dan and expect Dan to direct the picture.

"I found this historical story about trains in the 1850s that took 100,000 orphan kids around different cities to find homes for them. I researched it and sold it first to United Artists as a feature film with Steve McQueen (as the gambler on the trains) and Ali McGraw (as the woman shepherding the orphans). Steve and Ali broke up and the project died. I bought it back and sold it to CBS as a TV movie. This was 1979 and the Sam Peckinpah period.

"I felt more comfortable in the world of television. I took the project to EMI, to Roger Gimbel and Marian Rees. It was the kind of picture that had something to say aside from being an important story. I want the audience to say, 'Oh, that's interesting,' without knowing they're getting a message.

"I'm occasionally asked to do a picture that's not like that and I say that another producer can do that better. I don't do rape or the latest headlines.

"It's harder to sell my type of movies right now because the networks aren't buying as many films. They now need the marketing and the star names as much or more than the story. That's why we have a lot of films being done that perhaps shouldn't be.

"I've been in the fortunate position over the years to have people ask me to bring them projects. I'm known for my niche. I can do any subject, but I like to have something positive."

"Would you judge any of your projects as failures or are all of them successes?"

"In degrees, I think they're all good to terrific. The last one I did, for Masterpiece Theater, called *Song of the Lark* (2000), is a lovely picture. We were using Willa Cather's 400-plus page novel. I hesitated to do it because each of her characters could've been a film in itself. We used the most autobiographical part of her novel—about a girl who felt like a fish out of water in her home town. She's a talented writer and nobody understands her goal to be someone. Willa Cather was most interested in the struggle to become an artist. I think our movie was good but it was not good enough. And I don't think we could've made it good enough unless we had done it as a mini-series.

"It sounds pollyanish, but I try not to do anything that I know I'm not going to be pleased with ahead of time. Directors often think they can do anything.

"When you're asked to do something in a real hurry, that's when you're found out. I had problems with shows but the biggest problems I had was with *Crash Landing: The Rescue of Flight 232* (1992). I told the sponsor AT&T that I don't do crash pictures but they told me that this was different. And it was. It was about a young guy, Gary Brown, in the Sioux City, sheriff's department. He said we should have a rescue unit in case we have a tornado or something. The hospitals aren't ready. And he bugged everybody so much they gave him some space and let him do his thing. He ran practice rescue operations and people would smile.

"So when that plane lost its transmission, they asked, 'Where can we land? Keep us away from the city.' And Sioux City said, come to us, we're ready. And they were. And they saved almost everybody on board.

"AT&T had to downsize, so we lost them as a sponsor. When I went to the Sioux City community and said that I had to shoot the movie in Canada because of the exchange rate, they said no. We can help you. And they did. We had someone donate a plastic silo. As a producer, you have to find ways to get things done.

"All the rescue operations around the country that had their budgets slashed, the monies were restored because of our picture.

"The second film I did was *License to Kill* (1984), about drunk driving. My father was killed by a drunk driver when I was a youngster. I didn't want to do that story but MADD (Mothers Against Drunk Driving) came to me to do their story. I wanted people to sit in the audience of *License to Kill* and say, 'That could've been me. I had an extra martini at lunch.' The story is about an upright citizen, with a wife and kids, who had a couple of drinks at lunch and was driving with his drink. And it is a high school girl, the Valedictorian, who's driving along and is killed."

"Isn't there a level of ruthlessness required in getting films made? Have you ever felt that you had to sell your soul to do a project?"

"No. And I wouldn't. I've never had to be ruthless. I have had to fire people. I'm not afraid to be tough. Actress Jean Stapleton said about me, 'She's so nice but she has a spine of steel.'"

"Your background as a casting director has helped you working with actors?"

"Oh yes. I used to think I knew every actor in New York. Many people that are well known today, we gave their first job."

"Many producers fear actors."

"Oh that would be terrible. I've only had a couple of prima donnas who thought they knew everything. That's unfortunate because it shows up on the face of the actor. They're not the best they can be. Those kind of people I don't understand. I think they're hurting themselves. I wish that we could do pictures now that didn't depend on a name. Many times you have to cast someone who is not as good as can be for a role, and as a result, the movie is not as good as it could be.

"When I was doing *Orphan Train* at CBS, the casting head was Jeanne Guess. She said to me, 'Dorothea, I love this project but they're going to drop it because there isn't a prominent enough star.' Remember we had 24 children and a man and a woman. A big star wouldn't do it because of the 24 kids. Jeanne said to me, 'Tell me who you want for the picture and that's who we'll get.'

"I had the cover on *New York* magazine. There were four actresses—including Jill Eikenberry. Jill had only done theater and wore her hair in a Victorian style. I wanted her to play Emma Symms. Kevin Dobson played Frank Carlin the gambler. We couldn't cast such unknowns today."

"Can movies only do good or can they also do harm?"

"Movies can do terrible things. You only have to see children going around shooting with their fingers. I think the people that do features with violence for violence sake are just awful. I truly think that kids on the border [of sanity and morality] see themselves being heroes. I think commercials can be a great danger. Every time we sit down and see a car commercial which shows someone going from 0 to 60 mph in three seconds. If I was a kid looking at that, I'd say, 'I have to get into a car and go like that.' I think that's very destructive.

"I wouldn't make anything that I wouldn't want my children or grandchildren to see.

"If I found the right story, I'd deal with suicide or mental illness. But it can't be about those subjects, it has to be a wonderful story."

"How did you balance your career with being a wife and mother?"

"Fortunately, I never had a problem balancing work and being a wife and mother to four children. As casting director for the U.S. Steel Hour at the Theatre Guild, and later an associate with Lucy Kroll, a prominent New York agent, my work schedule ended at 3 p.m.—deliberately timed to match the children's coming home from school. Because my schedule was timed to my husband and children, there never seemed to be any resentment."

"Is Hollywood a nice place to raise a family?"

"Yes and no. Our permanent move to Los Angeles came when our oldest son was entering college, our second son entering high school, and our twin daughters in elementary school. One of the first questions our daughters asked after attending school was, 'Who do we know who's famous?' In the East they had been around celebrities, and they were just the same as all our friends. Los Angeles is a star-struck community and the need for status in Hollywood does affect children and families more than in other communities."

"How do you measure success?"

"Any person who is fortunate enough to work at something they truly love is successful. It is hard for me to imagine spending hours at a job I disliked. I am pleased to be respected by my peers. Good reviews are always gratifying. Earnings are important in Hollywood. I was told, 'Do you know that you are the most expensive television movie producer in Hollywood?' That fact is important and impressive to some folks in our business. What they don't know is that if I truly love a project, I'd do it no matter what it paid."

10

Daniel H. Blatt

Born in 1937, Dan Blatt attended Philips Andover Academy from 1951-55. In 1959, he graduated from Duke and in 1962 from Northwestern University School of Law.

He served on the civil rights group Lawyers' Constitutional Defense Committee in Jackson, Mississippi in 1964.

After working a thousand legal cases, Blatt moved into entertainment. From 1970-75, he was Vice President of Palomar Pictures, overseeing *Sleuth* (1972), *The Heartbreak Kid* (1972), *The Taking of Pelham 123* (1974), and *The Stepford Wives* (1974).

Moving to Los Angeles in 1976, Blatt produced seven feature films and almost 30 TV movies.

Dan stands 5'8" and walks with a severe limp due to nerve damage in his right leg. He plays golf regularly (handicap 11).

"Which projects have had the most meaning for you?" I ask.

Daniel pauses for 30 seconds and looks through his resume. He speaks in a soft voice. "The first one I really produced, *The Raid On Entebbe* (1977). My parents (Kurt and Trudy) fled the Nazis in Germany in 1934. I grew up in a household where persecution of the Jews was drilled into my soul.

"My father was a doctor working at a Jewish hospital. Shortly after the Nazis took over, he noticed regulations for Jewish doctors. He took my mother to Paris for their honeymoon for two weeks and then met his brother Max in Barcelona. Then they came to America.

"After my parents arrived, they brought my mother's side of the family over to Buenos Aires, Argentina. My mother didn't see her family for 17 years.

"My father brought his side of the family to America. They didn't have any money. Travel wasn't easy. There was a depression.

"*The Raid On Entebbe* represented the Jews reacting to victimhood in a positive way. I grew up in a very Jewish house. Then after I was *bar mitzvah*ed, I said 'enough of this' and I moved away from it. And then suddenly to be brought back into this thing was almost like a gift, a circle that I'd completed. Also, *Sadat* (1983) was part of that cycle."

"Did working on that *Entebbe* movie affect your Jewish identity afterwards?"

"Yes, that's what I was trying to say."

"How?"

"It was coming back to my roots."

"So did you start keeping *Shabbos*?"

Daniel laughs. "Let's not go that far.

"The raid on Entebbe happened July 14, 1976. We started shooting in October. And it aired on January 14th, 1977."

"Did you have to buy the rights?"

"No, it was a big thing. Everybody wanted this story. Every studio. There were three Entebbe movies made.

"The *Sadat* miniseries was difficult to make. We shot it over 42 days in Mexico. The Egyptians didn't like it for three reasons. One, it was obviously pro-Israel. Two, they felt it didn't portray them accurately. Three, Sadat was a hero to the world but not to them."

"Have you been to Egypt?"

"No. I could never go now.

"I thought my miniseries *Common Ground* (1989) was good. It was adapted from Anthony J. Lukas's Pulitzer Prize winning book. It's a story of America trying to deal with its racism and failing."

"How would you feel if a bunch of blacks suddenly moved into your neighborhood?" I ask.

Dan chuckles. "It would reduce the property values."

"Did you come to any personal conclusions on bussing because of this project?"

"Yes, that it doesn't quite work.

"I did a lot of these stories about real people who believed in something and tried to effect change."

Blatt's proud of several movies he made with Christian themes such as *Tecumseh: The Last Warrior* (1995), *Miracle On The 17th Green* (1999), *A Town Without Christmas* (2001).

"How do you measure whether a picture was a success? By an internal or external barometer?"

"If you consider yourself an artist, you do it for yourself. But in today's world, you have to measure your audience. We don't operate in our own world, we operate in a commercial world.

"If my family and friends like my movie, they call. If they don't like it, they don't call."

"What are your favorite and least favorite parts of your job?"

"I like working on scripts and on post-production. Shooting is not my favorite."

"Working on scripts and post is where you have the most control. Is that why it is your favorite? Because there are fewer variables?"

"Yes. When you're shooting, you're dealing with limited time. You've got to be careful. You're limited in how many times you can ask to do it differently. Egos, tension, time and money."

"Why can you tweak a script and make it better than the professional screenwriter can?"

"First, I've made all these pictures. I've got a track record. For a good screenplay you need a good plot, a story that keeps moving. Scenes have to have conflict. And in each scene, you should learn more about your characters. In the end, it's about your characters. When you think about all the great movies, it's about the characters. When you think about all the great movies, you don't think of the plot. You think of the characters. You need characters that are interesting, unpredictable, faulty."

"What do you think are your strengths as a producer? Finding good material?"

"Yes, and that I am a leader. And I'm not afraid to work. And I have a lot of enthusiasm."

"What makes a good leader in producing a movie?"

"It's like playing sports. If you grew up playing sports, you saw what it was like to have a good coach or a bad coach. First thing, you have to be honest and knowledgeable. You have to see the entire picture and be able to get the best out of every person. Every person who works on a picture is an artist in his own way whether it is a costume designer, prop guy, writer, DP. Each person has to be treated to be differently. Some people you have to be tougher on and some people you have to encourage. And if they're not doing a good job, you have to get rid of them."

"What's it like raising kids in Hollywood?"

"It's tough on a marriage because you're not around much."

"Your sister [Dr. Ruth Blatt Merkatz who was the first Director of the FDA's Office of Women's Health] was such a driven woman."

"We were all driven. That's what we were taught. 'You've got to work hard.'"

"Aren't German Jews regarded as the elite of American Jews?"

"They'd like to think that. I grew up thinking that German Jews were the smartest. Then they sent me to Andover. And there I was told we were the cream of the crop."

"What do you remember about *The Stepford Wives*?"

"It's had an interesting afterlife. It's had a greater afterlife than it had an initial run. It's a famous film now."

"What did you think of the content of the film. It was an angry feminist film."

"Maybe it was in front of its time. I went to visit a friend in Woodland Hills. She says, 'Come up here and visit us. We're in Stepfordville.' I thought it was an interesting concept."

"Could you make a film you passionately disagreed with?"

"I couldn't."

"So your films are a reflection of your sensibilities?"

"Unless you're independently wealthy, you have to make a living. There are some things that you do to get by. But if someone has done more than five films, you can look at the body of work and see the humanity of the person behind it."

"Some people then really scare me. Like Martin Scorsese and his bloody violent vision."

"He's got a dark violent view. If a person has had the opportunity to have a say in what he's making, and then you look at the pictures in totality, eventually you will see a common thread. I'd like to think that my pictures reflect my belief that one person can make a difference. If people are passionate about some issue, they can effect change. *Tecumseh* was about one man who wanted to unite all the Indian tribes and drive the white man out of North America. Tecumseh was a Christ-like figure. He was born under a sign."

"In your *Kissinger and Nixon* (1995) movie," I ask, "did you deal with Kissinger?"

"Only when he was trying to sue me," Dan says.

"Why did he threaten to sue you?"

"Because he said that what we were saying about him wasn't true."

"Wasn't it based on the book by Walter Isaacson?"

"Yes."

"Why didn't he sue Isaacson?"

"A book is read by a few thousand people. A TV movie is seen by millions of people.

"Our movie had two terrific performances by Ron Silver and Beau Bridges. Kissinger grew up in Washington Heights which is where my Aunt Gretchen lived. When I watched Ron Silver portray him with the little belly and the ferocious temper. He couldn't suffer fools gladly. It was like watching my father.

"When you're telling stories about people, I've realized that the cradle to grave approach doesn't work. When I did *Tecumseh*, it was cradle to grave. They made a mistake in *Ali* in trying to cover the whole story. And you wind up with no story. You don't get a sense of the character. *Kissinger and Nixon* was them negotiating the peace treaty in 1972. And if you do it properly, you will learn everything there is to know about the characters."

"What did Kissinger deny?"

"In the original script, there was a lot of stuff about wiretapping between him and the president. Kissinger said he'd never behave like that. He wanted to be portrayed as a man who only wore white clothes and a white hat."

"Because of his legal threats, you changed the script?"

"We made some changes because of fear of a lawsuit."

"If Isaacson had documented it, how could you get sued?"

"It came down to how far the corporation wanted to go taking a legal risk."

"How did Kissinger like the final product?"

"I don't know. He certainly didn't call me."

"I thought the movie was sympathetic to Kissinger. He came across far more admirably than did Nixon."

"Yeah. Kissinger engineered that great peace treaty. But he was questioning our portrayal of his methods. 'I never told a lie. I never wiretapped. I never misled the president. I never told a lie to the North Vietnamese. I didn't leave the South Vietnamese hanging in the wind. I totally trusted Haig.'"

"Were you disappointed with any of your movies?"

"They were all disappointing. Initially I see all the things that could've been better. Then I look at them later and I realize they weren't bad. You get too close to a picture."

11

Paul Colichman

<u>**January 11, 2002**</u>

Paul, 39, has produced 100 movies.

Growing up in Brentwood, he began working as an usher in a movie theater at age 12. By 16, he was booking movies. By 24, he had an MBA from UCLA.

I visit him at Regent Entertainment's headquarters on Ocean Blvd in Santa Monica. We walk out of his office to the deck overlooking the Pacific Ocean and sit down at a table. Within a few minutes, we have our feet up.

"Which of your projects had the most meaning for you?"

Paul names off his most critically acclaimed features: *Gods and Monsters* (1998), *Twilight of the Golds* (1997), *Tom and Viv* (1994), and *One False Move* (1992).

"None of them are on the list of our most financially successful films. At least ten of the smaller more commercial films have made more money. We try to balance it out. If we just made the purely artistic projects, we'd go broke. For every one that hits, three miss. With the more commercial projects, even if you don't creatively hit it right on the nose, you can still be profitable. With artistic projects, there's no room for error.

"We try to make these movies that are very commercial that have an art edge, like *One False Move*."

"Where do you make the cash?"

"The films you don't know about are the ones that make us the most money. *Circuitry Man*, a sci-fi series. *The Brotherhoods*, a little video series. These cost under a million dollars each to make."

"What pulls your trigger to decide to make a movie?"

"A script that is a cut above. Once I have the material, I can get the actors, directors and packaging.

"A good film is like love—you know it when you feel it. There's chemistry with the crew, the director is creatively on and the actors are crackling."

"How have you grown as a filmmaker over the past 14 years?" I ask.

"I've gained more respect for the basic rules of a good screenplay. When I was younger, I believed that you could do a deconstructionist work and it would be good. I now don't. It has never worked for me. I need the good solid three-act American screenplay. Anything other than that, doesn't work. You'd be amazed at how few screenplays are even structured well enough to consider. People submit us things that are more artistic. People think that artistry gives one the right to ignore the rules. Quite the contrary. Artistry is using the rules in a creative and unique way. So it has gotten easier for me to decide what to make. I can throw out the poorly structured stuff right away unless I feel I can fix the structure easily. Then I take the ones that are well structured and work with that smaller set, about one in four. I get a lot of movies that have no third act. I get movies that have no second act.

"The television movie structure is the three-act structure cut in half into seven sections. All the movies I've made that didn't turn out well are the ones that weren't structured right."

"Can you make a good movie where the lead characters are not sympathetic?"

"They can be seriously flawed but they should be sympathetic. They have to have a redeeming quality. If they don't, it's hard to emotionally look into the film. The audience must identify with someone."

"Would you rather marry a Jew or a non-Jew?"

"I don't think I care."

"Many of my Jewish male friends long for *shiksas*."

"Oh. I'm gay, so maybe it makes a difference. My boyfriend is half-Jewish even though he does not look it or act it."

"Why are there a disproportionate number of gays in Hollywood? Gays seem to have a better visual sense."

"I think there is an artistic bent that goes with the orientation. This business needs people on the cutting edge who are visually astute. You've got to integrate a lot of things on the production side—not just smart with the written word, but visual, and a good businessman."

"And gays tend to be the most empathic people I know."

"The ability to empathize is essential for producing. Because most of the time the people you are talking to can't tell you what they want to say. They can't get it out. Or they have a feeling and they can't even express it. If we can translate those feelings, we can get a group of people to work together and succeed. Every time you start a movie, you're starting a new company with 120 people who've rarely worked together before. And everybody brings all of their issues to the table."

"We've seen more films dealing with gay themes in the last five years than in the previous 100 years."

"True."

"Is that reflecting or driving a societal change?"

"Reflecting. Film rarely drives anything. It reflects. Gay liberation started in 1969 in New York with the Stonewall riots. There came a point in history where we said enough is enough. We're going to start to fight. It's been a 30-year fight. It is the civil rights movement of our generation."

"Are there still distributors loathe to deal with gay-themed films?"

"Yes. There's homophobia everywhere. It's rampant."

"I'm a liberal Hollywood Jew. But as a straight, seeing two men on screen kissing is very jarring and disturbing."

"You'll get over it."

"Do you remember any particularly biting comments from distributors?"

"I remember a thousand of them. I've made a lot of movies. I know when I've made a really good one because it doesn't happen all that often. No producer makes a really brilliant film all that often. I was pitching a distributor who should've bought *Gods and Monsters*. And he said, 'We already have one of those kind of movies.' And their other one of those kind of movies turned out to be a dismal failure while *Gods and Monsters* got three Oscar nominations. They thought they were allowed one per customer. Could you imagine saying that to a black producer? 'Oh, we already have a black movie.'"

"I can imagine people thinking it."

"But they wouldn't have the guts to say it. These are people who are supposedly my colleagues and have known me for years and without hesitation will make a statement like that to me. It doesn't even make an impression on their cerebellum that that might be a problem. Homophobia is so accepted. That too will change."

"When I grew up, when you were mad at someone, you called them a fag."

"You are one of the few straight Australian men I've met. I remember one thing about Sydney—the huge gay population and very open."

"Was that epithet used where you grew up?"

"Yes. All kinds of awful things were used. Abuse of gay people is still accepted. Stuff that no other group would have to put up with, we have to put up with."

"When did you come out?"

"When I was 24."

"How did your parents react?"

"It didn't bother them."

"Do any of your movies reflect themes from your childhood?"

"No. Growing up as a gay youth, you're managing your way through childhood. You're not embracing it."

"One producer told me that his movies were his psychotherapy."

"Not mine. I find that a poor use of film. I don't make these things for me. They're not self-serving. They're designed to entertain the world."

"Many movies are self-serving."

"I have no patience for such things. We have responsibility as producers to entertain and inform. If we're going to be self-indulgent, we should do it on our own time."

"Is there a thread through your work?"

"On the contrary, they are eclectic. I'm looking for that quality piece that can come in any form. It could be a science fiction movie or a romance."

"Could you make a film where you disliked the moral?"

"Disliked the moral? I don't know if I look at the morals that much when I make them. I look at the quality of the work. With a good third act, you bring the action to an end but it keeps you thinking as you walk out the door. The best movies aren't so simple that they give you a moral. The really good movies don't give you a moral message. They're not that manipulative. They're able to tell an exquisitely structured story without manipulating you or leading you to a firm conclusion."

"Could you make a film where the main character is a homophobe?"

"Yes, just like I could make *American History X* (1998) where the main character is a racist."

"It seems there is still a PC attitude in Hollywood where the characters can have any flaw except be racist or homophobic?"

"I could give you a list of movies that are homophobic in their approach. Most mainstream comedies treat gay people as a joke and marginalize them. You could go through a history of film and be shocked at how homophobic so many movies are."

"They've been instinctively used as a gag."

"Yes. What could be more homophobic than taking someone's lifestyle and making it the butt of a joke? A lot of the teen comedies, from *Porky's* (1982) forward, did you ever see any gay characters in those movies? Did you see any of them referred to in a nice way?"

"No. They're usually the butt of jokes."

"Talk about homophobia. It's everywhere. It's omnipresent. People are naturally homophobic. You have to be educated out of it. People are naturally anti-Semitic. Even though you are not gay, you are Jewish and you know what that is like. Now take that and multiply it by ten."

"*As Good As It Gets* (1997). Jack Nicholson."

"Plays a homophobe. And the movie starts with a gay bashing scene. But would I make that movie? You bet your ass. Because of what surrounded it and the understanding that was gained throughout it."

"Can a film be a great film and yet be too immoral to make? Do you ever feel that tension? Such as *Lolita* (1962, 1997)."

Paul looks mystified. "I didn't find that particularly immoral."

"You never read a script and say, Jesus, this is a great script and would be a great movie but it is immoral."

"Out of all the scripts I've read, I don't think that has ever come up for me. I'm not terribly judgmental when it comes to morality. If I can find a brilliant screenplay, I will make it. Some people would've thought *Gods and Monsters* was immoral."

"What about gratuitous violence?"

"If the violence is an important part of the story, it should be there. What defines gratuitous is purely subjective. I would say it is gratuitous if it doesn't move the story along. If it is not moving the story along, it needs to be removed, not because it is violent but because it doesn't move the story along. Anything gratuitous shouldn't be there. Movies are supposed to be pithy."

"How would you feel about making a movie that promotes the war on terrorism?"

"I can't imagine a movie that would do that other than a propaganda film. I suppose if one could find a sympathetic terrorist, good luck."

"Isn't the Bush administration meeting with Hollywood types to get them involved in the war on terrorism?"

"That's utter nonsense, of course."

"We did that in WWII."

"They were all lousy movies. The best film from WWII was *Casablanca* (1942), probably the best war film ever made, but not much in the propaganda area. The lead character was a soldier of fortune."

12

Judith James

Richard Dreyfuss's feature producing partner Judith James is tall, silver-haired and, despite her fifty plus years, full of energy.

We discuss Wayne Wang's movie *Center of the World*, which James liked. "It's only got one pornographic moment with the lollipop scene," says James. "It was an honest examination of the American psyche with regards to its sexual life. For Europeans, sex is a simple function of life. For Americans, it is veiled and secret and hidden and more exciting because it is not permitted."

"What are your moral obligations as a movie producer?" I ask.

"Whatever your own moral obligations are. I wouldn't set down any standards for the industry but I am appalled by some things that happen. I do think there are people who should look themselves in the mirror. Censorship is way too complicated but I do get surprised at people's ability to forget what their mothers taught them when they were growing up. It's like once they walk in the door in Hollywood, all bets are off and they can do anything they want."

"Is it more profitable to make immoral films rather than moral films?"

"I don't think so. I do worry that there is a fear that if you aren't outlandish, you won't make money. I think distributors sometimes say this is soft and it probably won't do as well so we won't push it as hard."

"I wonder how much transgressiveness is done to grab the attention of one's peers?" I muse.

"Read the trades six month late. Whew! Unbelievable, the fuss and announcements done for the attention of one's peers."

"Most of the projects announced in the trades are never made."

"If you hear of a new source of money, get to them because they are not going to be there long. A movie will go through five or six castings before it is finally cast. But they'll announce every damn one. I'll read the trades for three months and then not read them for three months. I try not to read them at all but then you lose touch with what's going on with people you know."

"Is there a common thread through your movies?"

"The common thread is what interests the producer or what he thinks he can make money on. What interests Richard and me is what is the project saying. It's hard to make money doing that. There's so much stuff you want to open a window on. 'Did you see THAT?' It sounds like I'm being educative but it can also be commercial."

"Many of your films have a moral."

"Yes. It's hard to withstand the criticism. 'Oh wow, then, it must not be entertaining.' You have to not think about that."

"How did you come to partner up with Richard Dreyfuss?"

"I was the co-head of the Film and Television Department experiment at the Mark Taper Forum, Los Angeles's regional theater company. It wasn't a good marriage. You take the nonprofit regional theater with the for-profit film and television industry and I had to spend money before we got paid and that scared them.

"Richard was working at the Taper a lot because he'd suffered a setback with a drug arrest. He's a smart man and he knew he needed to sit down and rethink who he was and what he was doing. And he was doing a lot of workshops. We liked the same authors, we had the same politics [left-wing]. We bought [film rights to] a book together. The bicentennial of the U.S. Constitution was coming around and we had said to each other that it was possible to do something commercial about the Constitution. Why does it always have to be relegated to PBS which Richard and I and 17 other people would watch?

"We put together a one-hour special for ABC TV called *Funny, You Don't Look 200* (1987) and went on from there."

"Tell me about *Mr. Holland's Opus* (1995)."

"Bob Court, who was head of the production company Interscope, which was distributed by Disney, sent over the script in 1993. I read it and I called him to say it was a Richard project. It's just what an audience wants from Richard. Audiences want something from their stars. They expect comedy from Richard or if not comedy, they want him to be a doctor, lawyer or teacher. He's got an inherent intelligence in his face. I always kid him about the number of people I do business with who all want to have lunch with Richard Dreyfuss. They just imagine themselves to be a friend of Richard's. The warts on the character were interesting. He wasn't a namby pamby character.

"To play the part, Richard had to learn music, how to conduct, and how to do sign language. So I worked on the script, casting and everything leading up to the shoot.

"In the final product, we had to cut 25 minutes. It was a difficult film for the studio to market because they perceived it as too soft while test audiences were giving it phenomenal reviews. But newspaper editors and those assigning reviewers said it was sentimental drivel. Not until we pushed until we were blue in the face did the film begin to pick up steam. It got dropped out of the Thanksgiving, 1995 release and not put out until March 1996 [aside from a brief one week run at two theaters in late 1995 to qualify for Oscar nominations].

"There are greed aspects to the studio system that approach evil but the everyday business of what studios do is just a bunch of human beings just trying to get a film out. Who says that something wonderful can't also be commercial? Who patented this word soft?"

"After seeing the trailer to *Mr. Holland's Opus*, you have no desire to see the film, because you've already seen the highlights of the film."

"You could say that about any trailer over the past five years. They suck the life out of a movie. Try to get that changed? We had another trailer cut. But their evidence is that people come to the movie. *Shine* had a bad trailer and it overcame that."

"Tell me about *Quiz Show* (1994)."

"Dick Goodwin [the Jewish House investigator who uncovers the scandal] gave us his book. He was unrehearsed in the ways to move in Hollywood. It wasn't a book that appeared to be a movie. It was years of his life in politics. The quiz show scandal was one chapter. At one time, Dick thought Richard could play the part [of Goodwin]. Richard and I said the book was great and could become a movie but Richard can't play the part. The character is fifteen years younger than Richard, just starting out.

"It took director Barry Levinson 11 months to read the book because he was doing another film. Dick Goodwin kept wondering why he couldn't read the book more quickly. When Barry finally read it, he said absolutely this is a movie and I want to write it. Then Barry decided he couldn't write it. He and his partner Mark Johnson produced it. And finally Paul Attanasio wrote it. And Robert Redford came on board to direct it. The script had a problem—the TV audience today is more cynical and less likely to be shocked by the fixing of quiz shows.

"*Quiz Show* got a lot of attention in the circles in which we travel—New York intelligentsia and the media. People who read *The New York Times* and care deeply about our country. But it wasn't a major commercial success.

"It's become an old story that when people accept their Academy Award, they say, 'It took us ten years to get this movie done.' The fastest movie [*Trigger Happy*, 2001] I ever did was seven months from the time we decided to do it to production. And we had to raise over five million from 27 different territories. But if you talked to the writer-director of that, it did take him seven years to get it done."

"*Quiz Show* took a hammering over historical accuracy," I say.

"No, it did not take a hammering over historical accuracy. The *Quiz Show*'s facts and conventional wisdom coincide. There are people who say that is not how it happened, Herbie Stemple being one. There are people who were annoyed by the central position of Richard Goodwin but it was his story. It was from his perspective."

"There ended up being 13 producers on the Quiz Show. Producing also got split up on *Kissinger and Nixon*. Walter Isaacson's book was sent to me and I thought it could be a movie. I was asked if Richard was interested in playing Kissinger. I knew it would interest him way more than playing the Richard Goodwin part in *Quiz Show*.

"We got the money to make the movie. Then I thought, if Richard and I do a movie on Kissinger, and we're left of left politically, we can be vulnerable to criticism that we're going after Kissinger. Richard and I have a strong friendship with Lionel Chetwynd, known as one of the few vocal Republicans in the entertainment community. There are a lot of Republicans in Hollywood despite what people say. If you include studio executives, I'd say the breakdown was 70 percent/30 percent Democrat/Republican but the discussion would have you believe that it is 95 percent/5 percent. What is rare is for someone in the ranks of people who write and direct admitting that they are Republican. Lionel is able to speak intelligently on why the Republican position is a valid choice. He is a joy and a worthy debater.

"So I went to Lionel and asked him to join us. We discussed just a couple of chapters from the book (just before and after Nixon got elected the second time) because you have to select, you can't float around. Right now I'm looking at Edmund Morris's book *Theodore Rex*. And I'm beginning to get a handle on what the film might be based on. Richard has always wanted to do Teddy Roosevelt. We've had several different projects with different takes on his life.

"Richard finally decided he wouldn't play Kissinger. People said, 'Thank you Judy for developing a good script but if you can't deliver Richard, goodbye.' This was a project that almost broke my heart. I felt that I understood that movie better than [eventual producer] Daniel Blatt. I have nothing against Dan Blatt except that he was there and not me. He's a good line producer [production manager].

"I liked how the movie turned out except for the use of prosthetics. They stood in the way of the audience and broke the audience's acceptance of the piece. They were always looking at the wrinkles and the nose. I think they should've just had us accept the two actors."

Judith says Walter Isaacson was able to substantiate allegations in his book about Kissinger that Henry threatened to sue over. And that the script wasn't changed to avoid a suit from Kissinger.

"There were a couple of scenes that determined how you looked at the next scene that were cut. But there's no scandal here. Lionel tweaked the book. He removed some language from the book."

"Didn't you lose a scene of Kissinger secretly taping?"

"My recollection is that it was removed because it wasn't needed."

"Did you ever make a movie about Winnie Mandela?"

"No, I owned, for ten years, the rights to her life story. Camille Cosby [Bill's wife] and I bought them from her. She's a difficult person. We bought the rights from her four years before Nelson Mandela got out of prison. She was an entirely different person then. I'm a much greater supporter of hers than 92 percent of the people in the United States. I defy any person in this world to stand up to what she stood up to and not go crazy. She went nuts and she has not come back from the other side completely but she's a great woman. Her story is a Shakespearian tragedy.

"We got money from NBC to do a mini-series. We sent writer Emily Mann to South Africa two years before Nelson got out. Then HBO did a movie on Nelson. But we were doing it from Winnie's point of view. It ended with her, a little drunk, refused entry to her home in Soweto. She punched a white cop and scared the shit out of all the cops. And she said, 'I'm going home and you're not going to stop me.' And she did walk into Soweto. And that was six months before Nelson got out. Then she became so blind and so badly thought of, before the football episodes.

"It wasn't two months after Nelson got out of jail, that they were closing Winnie Mandela out of every single meeting of the ANC (African National Congress). She had run it for years and kept the idea of Nelson alive. She had an inherent sense of what to do to call attention to herself. She got noisy and difficult and he divorced her. When she was down, there may have been drugs, there was a lot of drinking, and they say there were a lot of young men, particularly around the 'football' episodes.

"Did we have trouble with her? Yes. Did we find that she tried to sell the rights to her life two and three times? Yes. But she has a great story and people should hear about it. There's a little imp in me that says, 'You don't want to hear it? Fuck you, I'm going to tell it to you anyway.'

"The writer of our play and TV movie, *Having Our Say* (1999), Emily Mann, was the writer we hired to do the Winnie Mandella story. Emily is a close friend. I was at her house, driving up to see my mother who had Alzheimer's. Emily's sister is a book agent and had sent Emily the book. I picked it up, read the back cover, and asked to borrow it. I read it at a truck stop between New Jersey and Massachusetts and got on the phone calling agents. In between the lines of these two old ladies talking to each was the history of the last 100 years of this country. It was so colloquially done and so important.

"Sadie was dignified and quiet and believed you could find a way without confronting. And Bessie was a confronter. And the two of them were not the black urban bullshit myth about black people. Their father was a slave until he was seven years old. They were two of ten kids. Nine of the ten graduated from college through determination and saving their pennies. They were lawyers, doctors, teachers and dentists.

"The book was being bid upon as a mini-series: they lived and they didn't die."

"What's wrong with a mini-series?"

"American mini-series tend to be bio-pics."

"So?"

"Why do you want to tell their stories? The book was about what these 101 and 103-year old women thought about the world. It was not about what they had gone through. What the project needed was the personality of Bessie and Sadie.

"I called my close friend Camille Cosby and she'd read the book the week before. So we decided to do it together.

"I come from a theater background. You think about movies as magical. To me, commercials are magical. Movies are linear. Plays are magical. You can go into people's minds in a way you don't do as a movie. So Camille, Emily and I thought about doing it first as a play."

"You can do more interior monologue in a play."

"Of course. You can do a one-man play. You could never do that as a movie or you'd end up with *My Dinner With Andre* (1981) and how many of those can you do? You are in the internal with a play, which is a lot closer to a book. The problems of going from a book to a film are difficult. Have you seen *A Beautiful Mind* (2001)? Why did Nash do what he did is better approached in books.

"In our play, we had two women chatting with each other and a third person. Emily made the audience the third person and welcomed them in for tea. We never flash-backed on stage. When we did it as a movie for CBS, we had to flash back. We had two offers to do it as a low budget film. We talked to many people and looked at statistics. Movies on a black theme had become more common and were relegated to a certain audience and a certain distribution pattern. We weren't going to reach as many people on film as by television."

13

Stan Rogow

"I have an eight year old boy, Jackson, who is the principle reason I got involved with children's television," says Stan. "There wasn't much of my work that he could see. I started watching the stuff he was watching and I thought that I could do better.

"I saw that there was stuff people were putting into these shows that I got that he didn't get. There was an episode of *Rugrats* (2001) where a character drops his head into his hands and goes, 'the horror, the horror.' My son has not yet seen *Apocalypse Now* (1979) [nor read the Joseph Conrad novel that inspired it, *Heart Of Darkness*]. And we in *Lizzie McGuire* (2001-???) do stuff like that on a regular basis. We did an homage scene from the *Great Escape* (1963) where Steve McQueen is in the cooler throwing a ball against the wall.

"I found an opportunity in children's television to do more adventurous material. Mainstream television was afraid of fast cuts, jump cuts, throwing an animated character in, having digital stills and doing adventurous storytelling. Part of the visual inspiration for *Lizzie McGuire* was the movie *Run Lola Run* (1998) which had cartoons and jump cuts. Nobody could do that in primetime television though now they've started to copy *Lizzie*'s style in primetime. We were aggressive in our filmic style and every week tried to invent some new way to be aggressive while still telling fundamentally human relatable stories that kids respond to.

"Great television is about connecting to the audience at some emotional level that they want to experience on a weekly basis. Kids today have grown up with MTV, Instant Messaging while listening to their MP3 players while talking on the phone. The information bombardment is easier for kids to accept that it is for grownups."

"How did you come up with *Lizzie McGuire*?" I ask.

"I've known its creator Terri Minsky for years. He'd written a script seven years ago which I'd thought charming and appropriate for the Disney Channel. It started out as a soft low-concept show about a girl and her family. Originally it was just a voice-over where she'd talk her inner thoughts. The network asked for a higher-concept. I said we could visualize the voice-over with pop-up videos where words come up, or we could do an animated character. They said let's do the animated character. Then when we went into the production, we amped up the approach.

"That was something that children's television never seemed to care about. My point of view is that kids do not only watch kid shows. They watch $100 million features, primetime television, great special effects. They're used to seeing good stuff. I come from that world and I didn't want to diminish my level of production."

"What's the story behind *State of Grace* (2001-2002)?"

"It was created by Brenda Lilly and Hollis Rich, loosely derived from their own experiences. I was good match for the project because I too grew up during that period from the 1960s. It's a story about a Jewish family that moves to the South during the 1960s. My family didn't move to the South but my father always traveled there. The show was intended for teenagers but we've broadened its appeal to women 18-54. We've discovered that we've made a show that kids can tell their parents to come watch with them and parents can tell their kids to come watch with them. This is a show that brings people together. It's true family programming.

"The show has an original tone. It's a comedy that makes you cry. It's a show that probably would not have been bought by a network. It started in the niche market of the Fox Family Channel now owned by Disney.

"I was born in New York in 1950 and grew up in Brooklyn. I went to college and law school in Boston. I never wanted to be a part of this business except when I was five years old and someone wanted to put me under contract at Paramount because I could sing and dance. But I would've had to move to LA and my parents weren't interested. The president of Paramount at the time told me, 'Son, if show business is in your blood, don't worry about it. It will always be there.'

"I was a radical lawyer in the '70s working in the ghetto in Boston doing poor-people law. I thought that would be my life. Bill Kunstler was an inspiration to me. But I discovered that I wasn't changing the world. I became frustrated because poverty was so institutionalized. Nobody really wanted out of the institution, they just wanted the institution to work better for them. I would say, 'Wait, you can take control of your lives.' They'd say, 'We don't want to take control of our lives. We've got you. You can straighten it out and get us more money.' There was no perception of a legitimate way out. There wasn't a way out. By the time you've frittered away most of your elementary and high school education, it's done. Unless you want to go back and do a lot of pick and shovel work and get your high school diploma. That's why there are more colored people in jail than there are in college.

"While living in Wellesley, Boston, there was a 15-room mansion with a ballroom to rent. The people moving out were video freaks who were using computer graphics and doing documentaries and taping rock n' roll groups. I hooked up with them. I did three movies with them including *Playing For Time* (1980) about the Oxford Auschwitz starring Vanessa Redgrave.

"That was incredibly controversial because of her anti-Zionist statements at the Academy Awards."

"Did you know about her anti-Zionist statements?"

"Absolutely and we also knew she was a great actor. The day I closed the deal, I called my parents. I said, 'Guess what? Today we closed the deal with Vanessa.' They said, 'Which movie?' I said, '*Playing For Time*.' They said, 'Are you crazy?' I said, 'What do you mean? She's fabulous. She's the best actress on the planet.'

"They said, 'Apparently you don't understand. Nobody is going to like this.' It hadn't dawned on us. She's an actor, who cares about her politics. At the end of the day, she certainly isn't anti-Semitic. Why would she take this role if she was anti-Semitic? She has issues with how Zionism is playing itself out but that is not the whole of Judaism. So the movie became infamous and we had our offices attacked by the JDL. They came up to our offices and threw paint all over our offices. I was standing there saying, 'Now wait a second. I understand. I used to be the guy who broke into offices in college and do all this but I've never been on this side of the thrown paint.'

"The final answer to that one was that Vanessa won an Emmy, Jane Alexander won for Best Supporting Actress and Arthur Miller won for Best Screenplay. Then I moved out to Los Angeles and produced the pilot of the TV show *Fame*. I wasn't interested in doing series television. I wanted to do movies. I was a snob and I didn't watch much television. During a good hunk of the 1970s, I didn't even own a television."

"Though you've worked through the network system, you don't seem terribly cynical?"

"I'm realistic. It is what it is. It doesn't necessarily bring the best out in anything. Do I have a collection of unbelievably stupid notes I've been given over the years [by network executives]? Yes, and they're all the same because they are all based on not knowing how to make anything. As Brandon Tartikoff taught me, all you can ask of a network is at bats. Maybe I'll strike out. Maybe I'll hit a single or a double or even get lucky and hit a home run. Most stuff fails. If we only knew how to make hits, we'd only have hits. Please, just let me take my best swing and if I fail, I fail. But at least you will have the benefit of my vision, and that might just be the thing that works. But I don't know if a collective group of people ever made great anything, certainly not great art, if we pretend we are doing art. I keep some illusion that that is what we're doing. There are moments when I want out of the business and go back to New England and teach."

"How long have you been married?"

"Nine years."

"First marriage?"

"I was kinda married in law school."

"A lawyer says kinda married?"

"Back then, it was so uncool to be married. We were just living together, in the '70s in Boston. Our parents started getting on us. So we said, 'For their sake, let's get married. But let's not tell anybody' because it will be a colossal embarrassment to tell anyone we're married. So we got married and didn't tell anybody. Then people started hearing we were married. And we said, 'No, no, no. We only did it for our parents and we got divorced.' And quickly we did get divorced."

"Is it tough staying married and raising a kid in Hollywood?"

"I think it is tough staying married and raising a kid, period. I'm fortunate that at this stage of my career, I get to be home for dinner. I don't partake in the Hollywoodness of it all. I like my job. I get to live a mundane life with soccer games, basketball games. I've also made it a point to shoot in Los Angeles. Everything else comes second to my being a husband and a father.

"A couple of weeks ago, I was channel-surfing. And *The Man In The Grey Flannel Suit* (1956) was on, which is all about can you have both family and career. It is difficult. It's why I was a selfish bachelor for all those years. For *Clan Of The Cave Bear*, I was mostly away for three years. We were scouting locations around the world. I couldn't do that today. I couldn't attempt to be this good of a husband or a father 15 years ago."

"Did you have a *bar mitzvah* as a kid?"

"Yes."

"Is your wife Jewish?"

"Madeleine has an interesting background. She was born Jewish and ended up going to Catholic school, which is exactly what happens in *State of Grace*, a Jewish girl ends up having to go to Catholic school. What is she? She doesn't know, but Jackson's Jewish. He knows he's Jewish. We certainly celebrate *Chanukah*. We celebrate Christmas and Easter. We celebrate everything.

"My *bar mitzvah* was such a mixed thing. I learned more about Judaism in college when I took a class in the Old Testament than going to Hebrew School learning for my *bar mitzvah*. If it is something that he wants, he can be *bar mitzvah*ed. If he doesn't want, he doesn't have to. I struggle to find a way because we've never belonged to a temple. The rabbi that married us (Don Singer in Malibu) practices Judaism meets Buddhism. I called him right before 9/11 to say that I've got to find a way to get Jackson some information about his heritage.

"My mother kept a kosher home. My father was much more secular like me. We went to an Orthodox synagogue for the high holidays. I went to Hebrew School four days a week from age eight to thirteen, and was thrown out almost on a daily basis for being a wiseass. It was fine with me so I could get out and play stickball. My parents would always get called in and the rabbi would complain, 'He's trying to kill me.'"

14

Donald Zuckerman

January 21, 2002

I sit down with Donald Zuckerman at Lulu's restaurant on Beverly Blvd.

"There are a few major film markets each year," he says. "The AFM in Santa Monica, the Cannes Film Festival, MIFED in Milan and now the London festival. Apparently [the distributor of Zuckerman's $8 million film *The Man From Elysian Fields*, 2001] didn't show up for the first two days of the London screening. We missed a big opportunity. The people at Gold Circle Films [financiers] were livid.

"We shot the movie during the last three months of 2000 and finished the editing in July of 2001. Toronto was our big festival for selling it. I was in New York a couple of days before. I ended up waiting in line for three hours on September 12, and rented a car and drove to Toronto. When the planes hit the World Trade Center September 11th, I was on 86th St and Madison Ave in upper Manhattan.

"Roger Ebert called *The Man From Elysian Fields* the best film he'd seen at the Sundance Festival. Mick Jagger plays the owner of an escort service."

Born and raised in New Jersey, Zuckerman attended the small private school Mount Claire Academy. He majored in Political Science at the University of Pennsylvania, "because it was an easy major. I wasn't a motivated student. There weren't many black people there either. Only one in my prep school, the son of a chauffeur. The blacks at college were Africans. Their fathers were royalty and presidents, or athletes. I didn't get to know black people until I was a public defender for four years in the Bronx.

"I was a young liberal idealist who got mugged by reality. I got tired of getting guilty people off. And I was good at it. Then I went into private practice, but I didn't want to do anymore criminal defense. In 1980, I opened The Ritz, which became a famous night club. Almost every major band in the world played there—the Police, Genesis, Sting, Tina Turner."

"Tell me about *Beat*."

"While we were shooting *Dog Town* (1997), I met this guy Gary Walkow, a writer-director. He had a script that I read and liked. He'd done a couple of low budget movies that played Sundance.

"My partner and I made a deal with Avi Lerner from New Image. He took the foreign distribution rights and we agreed to put up the money for domestic distribution. The movie premiered at Sundance. We had a lot of trouble selling it. Ultimately we sold it to Lions Gate and it will come out on video this year.

"We shot in Mexico. It was a blast. My ex-girlfriend Wendy Pier Cassileth came down with me and co-produced the movie. We all had a good time with the exception of the fact that Courtney Love was there. She was really really hard to deal with. She's an extremely angry person who takes delight in having people not like her. She takes delight in being cruel and mean to people. She made me fire the make-up people. And as far as I could tell, their only crime was that they were attractive. Not good to have other attractive women around."

"How did the other actors react to Courtney?"

"I don't think they liked her much. She was disrespectful to their time. They would be ready and on the set and she would take forever in hair and makeup to come out. And then as soon as she got there, she'd be like, 'I don't like this light.' And, 'Where do I put my chin?' That was her favorite question.

"It was hard to get a good performance out of her. Instead of having five takes where there were a couple of good ones, there was a line here and a line there. And whatever actor was acting against her, you frequently had to use his worst performance to get one acceptable performance from her.

"Norman Reedus and Ron Livingston went to her when she wanted to fire their make-up people. 'Look, Donald says you're insisting that he fire our people, and they don't even have anything to do with you. It's not fair. How would you like it if we didn't like your crew?' And she said, 'Hey, too bad.'"

"Do you regret casting her?"

"No, not really. What can you do?"

"I heard she got into a fist fight with Kirk Honeycutt, the lead critic of the *Hollywood Reporter*, at Sundance?"

"She did. She was unbelievable. We had a little dinner party the day before our screening. Kirk and his wife Mira were there. Kirk's wife asked if she could take some photos. So I asked Courtney's PR person from PMK and she said fine. A couple of hours later, I turn around and Courtney has yanked the camera out of Mira's hand because Mira took a picture of her. Kirk goes for the camera and they're in a tug of war over it. And Courtney starts yelling, 'You hit me. You hit me.' Courtney's boyfriend/record producer Jim Barbour goes after Kirk. I got in between both of them."

"I heard a distributor made an offer on the picture if Courtney would help promote it, and she told him in an expletive laden manner that she wouldn't."

"The chairman of the board of Trimark Pictures, Mark Amin, made an offer the night of our premiere. I said, 'I appreciate that but we have more money in the picture than you're offering.' So he said, 'Why don't you and I sit down tomorrow and see what we can do?' So I was feeling good about that.

"Half an hour later, we're talking to Avi Lerner and we see Mark talking to Courtney. Then he storms over to us and says, 'Fuck her. There's no way I'm buying this movie.' So we don't know what she said to him. We just know that there was an extreme reaction to what was said."

Mark Amin says, "I was dragged to this party by the producer. Then he dragged me over to Courtney. Then she was extremely rude and dismissive. I had an emotional reaction."

"There were some bad reviews," I say.

"It's not a great movie," Donald admits. "We had a director who was unwilling to take any notes. My partner and I thought there were a lot of things that could've been done to improve the movie. He refused to discuss it with us. He said, 'I got us into Sundance and I know what's best.' We didn't have any time before Sundance to get any work done. So we screened it the way he wanted it at Sundance and got a mediocre response. Then we took the picture, re-cut it, and got accepted to the LA Independent Film Festival. The director objected to our cuts. The people at the festival who had seen both versions said our version was much better. We played at the LA Independent Film Festival and all the actors, Kiefer Sutherland, Ron Livingston, Norman Reedus, and their people, all saw the second version and all said it was superior to the first version.

"The director, of course, because he's so talented, didn't need to see the second version to know that his version was better. Because he already knew it wasn't any good, he wouldn't watch it. And one got one review from F.X. Feeny who said it was good but the movie was already damaged goods from not having sold at Sundance. That's why it's sat around for a long time. The version being released is Gary's version because we don't feel like spending the money."

"I wonder if some of the bad reviews come from the uncomfortable presentation of William Burroughs and the Beats?"

"There were scenes in the movie of William Burroughs chasing after a young man. It was very unflattering. The young man would only have sex with him every other day. It was almost like he was paying for it. It wasn't like, 'I'm gay and I'm enjoying myself.' It was portrayed in an unattractive way.

"Gary tried to be true to the subject matter. He went out of his way to shoot in the actual locations. We went to Lake Patzcurao in Mexico because they went to Lake Patzcurao. We went to the volcano they went to. We shot across the street from Burroughs apartment. Gary did a lot of research. Burroughs was probably the way Gary portrayed him."

"I think people have a more romantic view of Burroughs and the Beats and this film was a downer for them."

"That's probably true.

"When I saw Gary's rough cut of the movie, I was happy, because I worried if he would be able to get a performance out of Courtney, which was essential. He did. He pieced together the bits and pieces."

"I heard the Mexican producers tried to extort you and held parts of the negative and sound track?"

"They did. We're in court. They claim that Courtney slandered them. The line producer says she had to have back surgery because Courtney called her names. Courtney did call her names. Courtney called everybody names."

I talk to Alain Silver, who also worked on *Beat*. "The producers suddenly found themselves with a picture that was not as easy to sell as they had thought.

"The nexus of producing is creatively helping to get the best picture done but fiscally trying to stay within budget and make sure that what you finally have is something that can be sold and return the cost. The two challenges are intricately woven together. Most directors are fiscally responsible. I don't encourage them to worry about how much something will cost. I encourage them to try to get the most possible and it is my job to tell them whether it can or cannot be done.

"*Beat* was in casting for 16 months. It couldn't get made without particular actors agreeing to do it for particular prices. It was my first time working with Gary Walkow. We met at the Directors Guild. We were on a couple of committees together. He told me he had a number of projects and asked me to read them. I took a look and passed on a number of strategies to get them made.

"Originally *Beat*, written by Gary, was planned for a $400,000 budget. After a year, Gary spoke again with producers Andrew Pfeffer and Donald Zuckerman.

"The movie is about two events in the early history of the Beat literary movement. One in 1944 and the other, which is most of the picture, culminating in Mexico in 1951.

"Lucien Carr is under pseudonym in a lot of Kerouac novels. Lucien introduced Burroughs to Ginsberg. They hung out at a salon in an apartment shared by a woman who was to become Kerouac's first wife and the future Joan Burroughs.

"That Lucien's still living added a whole new level of complication once we finally got the go-ahead on the picture and had to get Errors and Omissions insurance [for libel].

"Eventually Zuckerman and Pfeffer got financial backing from German Willi Bar, who's backed a lot of pictures. I'm using this as an example of how independent pictures work. You've got a script. You want to make a movie. You don't have a studio to give you money. You either find equity money, private investors who will permit you to make a picture without any requirements, or you attach some actors and off the actors you sell territories, either in chunks or in small pieces. And off the sales of the territories, you borrow the money under the understanding from a motion picture lender that all these sales are in place. And you can also borrow against 'air,' or what is called 'the gap.' If you've sold X number of territories for this amount of money, it's simple to predict what the remaining territories are worth. That's how *Beat* was put together.

"A deal was made for foreign distribution with Millennium for two-thirds of the budget. He didn't put up cash. He just put up a contract. Since Millennium's been in business for over ten years, it is possible to borrow against the full value of that contract. Enough of them have been honored that lenders feel secure to lend against those contracts.

"The other producers then had to scramble around to come up with the other third of the budget.

"Over six months, various offers were made to various women (like Winona Ryder) for the part of Joan and to various men (such as John Malkovich and Ethan Hawke) for the part of Burroughs. And the offers varied from $250-750,000 with a total budget between $4.2–$4.8 million. None of the offers were accepted. So Gary and I started doing another picture with these other two producers (Andrew and Donald), a digital project for a $150,000 total budget.

"We were a few weeks from shooting after spending $30-40,000, when there was an offer accepted on *Beat* by an actor named Norman Reedus. The problem with signing an actor like Reedus is that he doesn't get you financing. A former male model, Norman's done a lot of independent pictures. I'd only seen him in a brief scene in *8mm* when we cast him. He was a good choice. A lot of studio casting directors thought he was going to break out.

"In Hollywood, when you make an actor an offer, and it is accepted, you're obligated to pay. It's known as 'pay or play.' So now there's an obligation to pay Norman and there's a start date. Gary, the director, wanted a woman named Allison Elliot (*Wings of the Dove*, 1997, *Spitfire Grill*, 1996) to play Joan. The problem was, with Norman and Allison as the leads, there was still no way to get the movie funded. So the search continued and finally there was an acceptance from Courtney Love. And based on that, it was possible to get the Millennium deal.

"Later, Kiefer Sutherland signed on to play Burroughs and Ron Livingston to play Lucien Carr. Gary, the director, was upset that he was forced to accept these actors. He now agrees that Kiefer and Ron are the best things in the movie. Nobody saw Kiefer as Burroughs but he did his homework on Burroughs before coming down to Mexico. He only worked two weeks of the five week shooting schedule. That's all we could afford to pay him for.

"We compressed his part. He was originally in less than a third of the script. He was only in the Mexico City portion of the shoot, not in the western location. One of the things we did on the fly in Mexico was to add him to some scenes. Once we saw that his performance was what we really needed to anchor the second two acts of the movie with, he disappeared for the second act, we added three short scenes that kept him from disappearing for 18 pages of script. And focused towards the third act, which was Burroughs and Joan. Lucien and Ginsberg leave by the beginning of the third act.

"We ended up cutting many of Joan's scenes. As valiantly as Courtney tried, she was just not giving the kind of performance that had been owed. We shot her in a lot of scenes that we couldn't use. That cost Ron Livingston two big scenes. He understood. Despite many physical problems, we actually came in under schedule.

"We had some other issues. The Mexican producers wanted more money. They held parts of the negative and half the soundtrack to try to extort it. Ultimately they did not succeed in doing that, but it caused some big problems with the post-production schedule. For six weeks, there was nothing we could do.

"The idea was to try to get it into Sundance. Even though we got it into Sundance (the print only a day-and-a-half old), I don't think Gary and the two other editors really had the time to get the picture into the best possible shape. But we didn't have a choice.

"The Mexican producers are suing over a bunch of different issues. They're mostly suing Courtney Love for inflicting emotional distress. They presume Courtney has the deepest pockets."

"A producer suing an actor for emotional distress?" I smile. "That's so funny."

"Not if you know Courtney. I have to say in Courtney's defense, she's dedicated to becoming a better actress. She understands this. It's a difficult situation for her to come from being a star in one medium to an ordinary player in another. Many of the complaints about Courtney were not made by the producers. They were made by the other actors.

"Courtney's name came up two years before the shooting of the film. She was always on the list for Joan.

"Performance is a delicate thing and the whole idea there was to get actors to give quality performances. This is an art movie. It's not terribly commercial. It needed those kind of performances.

"*Beat* got into Sundance but it came out of Sundance very badly. First, we lost six weeks of post production. Then it didn't help that Courtney almost got into a fist fight with the lead reviewer for the *Hollywood Reporter*, Kirk Honeycutt. They settled their squabble but the next day she yelled at some kid on the street. The biggest problem was that after the main screening, one of the offers on the picture [to distribute it], when that gentleman made an offer on it and went up to Courtney and asked if she'd help promote it, she told him in an expletive-laden manner that no, she wouldn't. And in fact, there's no reason why she should. It's not something that she's required to do.

"After all that time in casting, we had to deal with hail storms [on location], difficult terrain in these lava fields. The actors had to ride horses into the location, then the squabble with the Mexican producers, and to end up with a marketing strategy that deteriorated to the point that we went from good offers before Sundance to fractions of that after. It's part of independent production. It's not over when the picture's through shooting. If you've still got territories to sell, there's still an ongoing fight.

"*Beat* got a decent reception at the Sundance screening. We couldn't go to the Salt Lake screening because we had this dinner in Park City for trade and other newspaper folk to meet the actors. It was the only day that Kiefer could be there. *Beat* got bad reviews in the *Hollywood Reporter* and *Variety*.

"There was resentment by many members of the audience about the liberties taken with the historical story. I would say the pictures is 90-95 percent accurate. Most of the presumption is about a romantic involvement between Lucien Carr and Joan Vollmer which is supported in a lot of books on the Beats. A lot of people did not like the way that Ginsberg and Burroughs were portrayed. They were portrayed as gay men in the 1950s. I don't think Burroughs would've had a problem with the portrayal. He's written extensively about the events. The shock of killing Joan is what finally propelled him into finishing his two novels *Junkie* and *Queers*. *Queers* is about events parallel to Joan driving around Mexico with Lucien Carr and Ginsberg. They'd come down to visit Burroughs and he wasn't there. He'd gone away on an excursion into Central America with a quasi-hired male lover."

"Was Burroughs primarily a homosexual?"

"Yes."

"Ginsberg?"

"Yes."

"Lucien Carr?"

"No. His son is a best selling novelist named Caleb Carr."

"Why did people object to the '50s portrayal of Ginsberg and Burroughs homosexuality?"

"There's an implication in the picture that in the '50s, that if these guys could choose not to be gay, it would make their lives easier. Ginsberg and Burroughs were wrestling with their sexual identities."

"While the thinking today is, if you think you're gay, you should just run with it."

"Yes. Gary wanted to portray Burroughs' genuine intellectual love for Joan. There's a scene early on with Joan and Burroughs in the kitchen. And the toast is, 'Oh Joan, if only you were a man.' And her reply is, 'Well, Bill, nobody's perfect.'

"I think this '50s attitude towards relationships didn't sit well with a lot of people who have very protective attitudes towards Ginsberg, Burroughs and the Beats. They look at their sexual identities from a 21st Century perspective.

"I remember that within a week, Gary went from a high after finishing the picture to a low after two very bad reviews.

"A guy who's part of the Burroughs estate, who to the best of my knowledge, has never seen the picture, nevertheless posted a negative diatribe about it on a website.

"Gary started working on the script when Ginsberg and Burroughs were still alive. From the point of view of the Errors and Omissions insurance, it became much simpler once they were dead. In the United States, you can't libel the dead. And they were both public figures [who are harder to libel]. Joan was also dead. Lucien Carr was the biggest issue because he's still alive. And a few changes were made to the script to satisfy the insurance carrier. That we weren't speculating in a way that was beyond the bounds of permissible speculation."

"Did you ever get any reaction from Lucien Carr?"

"No. Courtney tried to contact him. Our attorneys advised us not to contact him. For a while, it looked like the whole project might fall apart because we couldn't get that Errors and Omissions (E&O) coverage. If we couldn't get that

E&O coverage, we couldn't get a bank loan to fund the picture. You can't borrow money or get a completion bond without all the insurance in place.

"We didn't close the loan on the picture, which gave us the bulk of the funding, until the fourth week of shooting. This is not the ideal way to proceed. It was difficult keeping the budget going with limited cash flow. Fortunately Millennium advanced against the loan or we couldn't have continued."

Courtney Love responded to these criticisms on her website Hole.com, and then deleted the thread for legal reasons. She says she never had a problem with Donald Zuckerman and that she hates the rich kid Mexican producers of Background Productions, Antonio Zavala Kugler, Victor Zavala Kugler, and Alexandra Cardenas.

Courtney writes that she wanted the make-up artists fired because they were trying to give drugs to Norman Reedus and Kiefer Sutherland, and that she can't work with actors who are on drugs. And she says the make-up artists were not attractive.

In Mexico, says Courtney, even PAs are rich kids who require bodyguards out of fear of kidnapping.

According to Courtney, Zuckerman tried to get her to persuade the crew to stay on even though they had not been paid in three weeks. Zuckerman approached her in the middle of the night, and asked her to stand on a platform and speak to the crew through a megaphone. She refused.

Despite not being paid, the workers were allowed only one water [bottle?] a day, one coffee with no milk or sugar, and one meal. Although she had been promised fresh fruit and clean water, Courtney says she ate what the crew ate—a slop of refried beans, buttered spaghetti, reconstituted potatoes, and local water. Zuckerman got hepatitis and others got dysentery.

One of the female producers became obsessed with Kiefer Sutherland and slept in his hallway.

Still, the worst problem with the film was that the script sucked.

15

Joel Rice

"I started as an actor in the film industry. I became a social worker because I wanted to do things like helping people and raising awareness. I missed the entertainment industry and the larger scale impact you could have. So I developed some ideas for movies that were social work in their orientation.

"I had this idea for a movie. I got the *LA Times* to write an article about this true story that I had the rights to. That brought the industry to me and that's how I got started. The movie was eventually released in 1998, *About Sarah*, a drama about role reversal. A woman must cope with her mentally retarded mother. It's similar to *I Am Sam* (2001) starring Sean Penn and Michelle Pfeifer.

"*About Sarah* is the most meaningful movie I've done. I grew up with a mother who was chronically ill. As a child, I was a parent in my own family. When I was a psycho-therapist, I worked with many mothers and sons for Big Brothers. My mission is to help kids be kids and parents be adults.

"The first movie I produced was *Bonds of Love* (1993). And I continued to try to do movies that raised awareness, that raised consciousness, that brought up subject matter that hadn't been explored. That's always been my goal as a social worker-producer. I did a *Dare to Love* (1995) that dealt with the impact of schizophrenia on a family. My consultant was John Nash's psychiatrist."

Joel speaks in a soft reassuring therapeutic voice.

"I've done this movie [*Cries from the Heart*, 1994] on autism and this technique called 'facilitated communication' which helps some autistic kids communicate when they are not able to communicate in a normal way.

"I did *One Kill* (2000) that dealt with women in the military, and how women are treated in a man's world. And it also dealt with the issue of guns and that kind of thing. It was a military thriller but my reason for doing it was to explore the treatment of women in the military and the issue of guns and shooting and how that could affect your life. I'm smart enough to know that I just can't do a movie about gun control. You have to find a compelling entertaining story to tell these things in.

"I haven't gotten to do every single movie about something meaningful but 85 percent of the 15 films I've done have dealt with some kind of psychological or social issue.

"I became an actor when I left college and I was cast as the lead in the film *Final Exam* (1981) when horror films were popular. I continued to do a lot of theater and television but my career never took off. So I would always work in psychiatric hospitals. I taught acting to people with mental retardation. As an actor, I didn't have enough opportunity to express what I wanted to express. So then I got my masters in Social Work at UCLA and eventually found my way back into the industry in a way that felt like I could have a greater impact.

"I now have my own company that deficit-finances movies, pays the difference between what the network pays you to do movies and what the movie really costs.

"When I didn't have kids, the driving force in my life was making movies. Now I have kids, I want to be with them. I'm more discriminating how I use my time. When I was an actor, I remember inviting a casting director to my show-case. She said, 'I never go out during the week. I'm with my children.' She said it as a hard and fast rule. When I am making a movie, it usually takes me completely away.

"These days there aren't that many [movie] slots to fill for the networks. In the past two years, I've moved from just doing network movies to doing movies for the Disney Channel, Lifetime, Showtime, TV series work and reality work."

"Isn't it hard to sell movies centering on mental illness?"

"Yes and it has gotten progressively harder. I don't think I could sell one now as I did these other ones. Mental retardation is not mental illness. Mental illness is more specifically something they're afraid of because it is harder for the audience to experience. Mental retardation has always been a subject, a la *Rain Man* (1988).

"I did a movie about a deaf kid also. All those disabilities are hard. The networks are afraid it feels like some 1980s disease of the week movie. You have to find a compelling story, and if within that compelling story there's mental illness or disability, then it is O.K.

"I did a movie about schizophrenia [*Dare to Love*]. It was one of my best movies. We were careful to only have one act of seven in an institution. The protagonist got on a drug that was able to help. It was a love story. The opening was provocative. We did everything we could to get people to the table and we still didn't do that well, even though it was critically acclaimed. People are afraid.

They want to escape in a movie though hour-dramas can explore great issues. It's a bigger commitment to take that on for two hours than to do it for an episode of something where you already know the characters."

"How do you know when you've made a movie that's made a difference?"

"I often have 1-800 numbers on after my movies so people can find more information about whatever is at the center of the story. There's an organization NARC, which used to stand for the National Association of Retarded Citizens but they don't use those words anymore. I've gotten many awards from those organizations. But it's hard to know. I used to be in-house at CBS and NBC and people would call the network after a show.

"I try to hire people with disabilities in all my films."

"Working with them must be a real challenge?"

"It isn't really. I think people are afraid, that it is hard enough to make a movie. But it isn't anymore of a challenge than any other challenge. It's just accommodating whatever the needs are, whether you're working with a person with a disability. In one film, we used seven deaf actors and 30 deaf extras.

"I've done two movies about mental retardation and I didn't cast a person with mental retardation in the starring role. But I made sure that the star's best friend was a person who was really mentally retarded. In *I Am Sam*, you could tell that Sean Penn's four friends really did have mental retardation. It's important for authenticity and for giving people opportunities."

"How do your peers react to your niche?"

"As far as the people I sell stuff to, it's good to have a niche. It shows that I can be trusted. They know the project won't be criticized for inaccuracy. They don't need a consultant. *One Kill* was a compelling military thriller. Even though I have my own agenda, it isn't really what the movies are when you see them. I'm more typecast by my peers as someone who feels he needs to be on the set every second of every day. Some producers just sell it and move on.

"*One Kill* still meets my agenda for my movies, and that is to say something. *One Kill* speaks to how women are treated in a man's world and also to the use of guns and how that can impact your life. I always have something like that as my personal mission. The genre doesn't matter to me. *One Kill* had a lot of male appeal, and that was who I was trying to reach about the way women are treated. You don't need to reach women with the way women are treated. So that [thriller] genre was a good way to get that message across."

"We have a lot of movies about the terrible way men treat women, but not so many movies about the terrible way women treat men?"

"Primarily because the audience they're trying to reach is female. Men don't come to the table for movies on television unless it is something geared towards them. Today they're trying to get audiences of men and women so they're doing fewer movies about how badly men treat women.

"One of the biggest rated movies for CBS, *Men Don't Tell*, was about a man who was physically abused by his wife. It did extremely well because we'd already seen enough movies on spousal abuse where the woman was a victim. Recently on Lifetime, they did a movie about an adolescent boy who was physically abusing his mom."

"As a heterosexual male, particularly in Los Angeles, you just go through this bombardment of sexual temptation. You go to the office and often women are dressed provocatively. Why doesn't anyone tell this story?"

"I think they've explored that on one-hour dramas. I remember an *Ally McBeal* (1997-2002). It's not a big enough issue to be a movie."

"Do you ever get criticized for being too preachy with your films?"

"No, because I don't think I am. I have my own agenda, but I don't think anyone would say I'm preachy. If a movie feels preachy, you haven't done a good job. Nobody would come away from *One Kill* thinking that it had preached that men should treat women better. It's a thriller."

"What is your stance on gun ownership?"

"I'm not into guns. I think guns are too easily accessed. Too many people have guns. Too much happens as the result of guns in the home. Kids can access guns way too easily. I don't believe in hunting."

"Jay Bernstein, producer of the *Mike Hammer* series, laments the decline of manly men on television."

"I think they've broadened the definition of a man but there are definitely shows with manly men at the center. Maybe they're manly men with more going on now? David James Elliot, who was in my last film, is a manly man and his show *JAG* is popular. He's more complex than the one-dimensional manly man. So I don't agree. But I'm not a manly man myself. I would not be interested if it was a one-dimensional manly man. I'm not interested in action and shoot-ups."

"Has manhood changed since 9/11?"

"No. Because if you saw the [New York] firemen, you also saw them crying at the memorial service. The level of emotional access that these guys have about the pain of what they saw and losing their peers. We want to celebrate heroism but these men have more dimensions. Everyone was touched by September 11. We love heroes and firemen are especially seen as a heroic group. And always have been.

"In terms of Bush and the government stance, there's a certain kind of manly manness going on. I do think there is a resurgence of machoism going on in the government."

"How do TV executives react when you bring them films about mental illness?"

"They're completely negative because they worry that people don't want to turn on the TV to watch something like that. It's hard to sell."

"How frustrating is the seven act TV movie structure?"

"Not at all. It's smart to have a certain number of dramatic high points in a piece. You can't meander in a TV movie with something that is just character oriented. You need to think that you're going to be within an act and on to the next act, and people are going to leave and come back. I find it easy. I've sold scripts that were not developed for television and I could just look through it and put the acts in without changing anything.

"The end of the first act is the same [on TV] as the [feature] three act structure. The only big difference is that you need a turning point in the middle of the piece. Features don't require a high point in the middle."

"In the early '90s, we had all these women-in-peril TV movies."

"In the '80s, we had disease of the week movies. Then women-in-jeopardy and then true crime. For several years, NBC did all these young adolescent issues. The market gets saturated. Everyone's right to try to brand the movie, so that people know what they're getting, but if you do the same movie every week, people will stop watching."

"Which of your movies have most surprised you?"

"I'm aware of every single step [in production] so it is not easy to be surprised. I can tell through the dailies whether we have something or not. I thought *One Kill* was going to be good, then it got so complicated that I feared it would not be as good as I hoped, but ultimately it was better than I had ever dreamed. In *Cries from the Heart* (1994), this phenomenal young actor Bradley Pierce surprised me with how well he captured this autistic kid.

"I did this movie, *The Secret She Carried* (1996), it was almost embarrassing that I was doing it because it was more of an assignment than my own idea. It was about a woman who was trying to get pregnant with her husband and then got raped and she didn't know who the father was. It was originally conceived she was being tracked by the rapist while eight months pregnant and held captive. My wife was pregnant at the time and I couldn't do a movie where the victim was going to be a pregnant woman running around. So I made it about what it's like for a couple dealing with rape and what it's like for the husband to feel powerless and not know whether he was the father of the child. The movie was directed so well [by Dan Lerner] that it became more powerful than I expected."

"Are there any topics you want to tackle that execs tell you are taboo?"

"I want to do a movie about guns, and kids and violence [such as Columbine] but it is almost getting too late. Many of the series have explored it. *Boston Public*'s (2000-2004) doing it tonight.

"I have these books that are fantastic and explore issues but they're hard to sell."

"How are you going to handle your own children's access to TV and movies?"

"So far we don't allow our three-and-a-half year old to watch anything with commercials or adult content. She either watches videos or PBS or Nicklelodeon or the Disney Channel. I think TV is fantastic for young people in the way that these shows explore things that are hard for kids. Bill Cosby has this show, *Little Bill*, who has to go get an X-ray because he broke his arm. And my daughter had to go for an appointment, so I said she'd be like *Little Bill*. So all of a sudden she knows that it is not scary and that she'll be O.K.

"We were watching the Super Bowl yesterday and she loved it. Then the commercials come on and you have to stand in front of her. But we've never taken her to a theater. It seems like too much stimulation."

"Would you rather your kid was addicted to television or to cigarettes?"

"Television. I'm a big television person. It helped me through my adolescence."

16

J. Todd Harris

Born March 30, 1959, Jonathan has made 18 films in the past seven years.

Harris made a splashy debut with the critically acclaimed $600,000 film *Denise Calls Up* (1994).

"You've made three films with gay themes—*Urbania* (2000), *Sordid Lives* (2000), *Rites of Passage* (1999). Has their homosexuality hurt their distribution?"

"I think that gives them a niche. I'm not damning gay films as much as I am damning getting distribution and getting paid. Gay films are hard to sell overseas."

"Many of my friends and I can't watch two men kiss."

"*Urbania* is not a sex film. There's a gay bashing in it and a chance for a guy who's lover was bashed to come back for retribution. Only 90 seconds of this movie will you have to cover your eyes."

"It's hard for independent films to make any money from the domestic theatrical release."

"Right. All the money that *In the Bedroom* (2001) makes in theatrical will get sucked into P&A (prints and advertising), but they'll have an Academy Award nominated film."

"Have any of your films made money from domestic theatrical release?"

"Ones that have sold outright to TV and video. I haven't had my *Boys Don't Cry* (1999). I haven't had my *Pi* (1998), my *Go* (1999), my *Requiem for a Dream* (2000), my *In the Company of Men* (1997). I haven't had my little movie that's popped out but goddamn it, I'm going to make one. Producing a film is so much work to make $50-100,000. I have to make three of those a year to survive. I have three people working fulltime for me.

"I'm struggling to put the money together for my latest film [*Burial Society*, 2002]. It's just getting harder. I still believe in independent film but I'm a married man with two kids. I'm not a bachelor living in a pad in Venice. I have house payments. I'm going to keep living this fantasy life of not having a boss. I work harder being my own boss. I'm online at 7 a.m. and 11 p.m."

"Which films have you made primarily just to make money?"

"*Tick Tock* (2000). Though I do love the script of *Partners in Crime* (2000). I couldn't make them at the level I wanted to. I settled for making them and knowing I could get paid for doing it. I can't say that I loved making [the $43 million Universal picture] *Dudley Do-Right* (1999). I thought the script was hogwash, but I made almost half a million dollars from that film and bought a house. I made that film for the money. I hoped it would be *George of the Jungle* (1997) [created by the same man who came up with *Dudley*, the late Jay Ward], a film that I could be proud of it, take the kids to see it, make a damn sequel and get a beach house and put the kids through school. I hope that I can make more studio films that I can be proud of and make money. I've got this independent film habit. It's like heroin."

Todd smacks two fingers against the underside of his arm and imitates shooting up. His eyes grow wide. "No, no, no!"

He sits back tranquilized. "A man came to the office. He wants to make a movie of his play about four people having dinner. He wants to shoot it for $250,000 on digital video. I love the play. I'm thinking about it. I believe there are still discoveries to be made. If I can mix in one or two charity cases a year with more commercial fare. Ideally, I'd like to make one studio movie a year, one medium-sized thriller like *Sexy Beast* (2000), *Deep End* (2001), and one Sundance special. I've been to Sundance three times and I'd go again if I had a film there.

"Everybody's so risk averse that you become responsible for everything. It's all these corporations saying, 'You make the film and take all the responsibility. You get a smidgin' of the upside and have all of this freakin' risk.

"Last year I made a film, *29 Palms* (2002). Bless the company for giving us the resources to make it, but I ran up $300,000 in uncovered pre-production costs and the bank loan closed 72 hours before principle photography. Production was a cluster fuck. I had to draw lines with the production crew. I had to bully people. I had to convince everyone that everything would be all right and I barely believed it myself. I lost 16 pounds during the month of February.

"In the second week of production, I thought I was having a heart attack. I was driven to the hospital and they said I was having an anxiety attack. I went on seratonin uptake inhibitors for a few months. Even when I got the whole film financed and my $300,000 back, I didn't want to throw up my fists in joy and triumph. I wanted to go into my little corner and weep. I borrowed the last $100,000 from my own portfolio without telling my wife. I was like a gambler rolling the dice. 'I'm going to get it all back on this roll.' I was risking three times as much as I stood to make. I cornered myself so if I didn't make it happen, I was going to explode.

"We were due to start principle photography on Monday. The Thursday night before that, [lead actor] Chris O'Donnell's deal fell apart over a ridiculous insurance question. And my line producer calls from the desert and says that we're $250,000 over what the minimum guarantee is from the bank. In 12 hours, I had to solve these issues. My wife is on vacation with the kids. I'm losing weight like the stock market is plunging. I woke up at 5 a.m. with the shakes. I called Toronto to work out the Chris O'Donnell thing. I had to tell the bond company, 'It will be O.K. It will be O.K. Just sign here. It's fine. Just sign here.' I had to get a $270,000 check to SAG by 5 p.m. or the actor weren't coming. We got there at 4:15. It wasn't even a triumph. It was just horrible.

"*29 Palms* was a nightmare shoot. We had a first-time commercial director [Leonardo Ricagni]. He wouldn't take the script as gospel. The script turned out to be a more complex than I realized with a series of flashbacks that if you didn't follow right, if one thread fell through, none of it made sense. I had a low-budget production staff that the director couldn't get along with. He was Latin American and had his own ego thing working. I had a production manager who couldn't talk to the director. I had an AD (assistant director) who spoke Spanish. I thought that was good. But he was a horrible AD and I ended up firing him. We were through the contingency funding the day I signed the papers. My production manager kept that from the bond company [which guarantees completion of the film in exchange for 2-3 percent of the total budget] for two weeks. And two weeks in, all hell broke loose. Every day of that movie was dreadful. Actor and Native American activist Russell Meads held me up and accused me of putting him in a hotel room I wouldn't put a white man in.

"We're now six months late delivering the film to distributors. I've lost at least $50,000 due me. We couldn't get it into Sundance or Berlin.

"The film is going to suffer from being finished by committee. I would work with the director again. Everybody says I'm crazy. He's brilliant. The film looks stunning. People might say he's crazy to work with me again, but if we had the right circumstances, it would work out. He wasn't ready to make an independent film. I don't think he caught on to what the distributor wanted until they'd run out of patience with him. We brought in a friend of his to help him finish the film. And we were so panicked about how late we were and problematic things were, that we clung to his friend's vision of the film. I think the director's instincts were more Jim Jarmusch than Coen Brothers. For four million dollars, we wanted a Coen Brothers film. We don't need an artsy black-and-white film. We need something that will play at the AMC if it gets lucky, or at least at the Sunset Five. Right down to doing the music, everything was hard about the film.

"*Happy Hour* (2001) is a simpler film. It was made for $1.5 million. We shot in New York. Again we had a first time filmmaker [Mike Bencivenga] who did not finish the film because the financiers ran out of patience. The financiers felt he was not delivering anything close to what was on the page. They brought in another guy to re-shoot some stuff and rewrite some stuff. We re-shot 15 percent of the film.

"Mike's a wonderful guy. A theater guy. ABC News guy out of New York. Smart, engaging. But at the end of the day, it just didn't go smoothly. We didn't get enough coverage. Some of the secondary casting was weak and we had to cut around it. I don't know yet. The jury is out on if we're taking this film from an 83 to an 87 [out of 100]. Or, as the people who wrote the checks fear, we're taking a 55 to an 87. We have no distribution on this film and there's a million-and-a-half dollars at stake. I haven't shown it to anybody yet because it is not done. It's a personal film with sparkling dialogue and three great performances. The question is will the guy [Mark Malone] who's taking over bring out the gist of what was in this film or is he going to fuzz out the original voice. Fortunately this is a book and won't be in print for a year or two. If you were a print journalist, I couldn't let this appear in the next few months. Too scary.

"*Liberty, Maine* (2001) was a film I godfathered. A friend of mine [Josiah Emery] came to me and said, 'I've raised all the cash. I need your credibility.' He didn't take all my advice and now he's got a sweet family drama that will be really really hard to sell. We got lucky and got a star interested in one of the parts and it fell apart over $5-10,000. I don't think he was convinced the actor was perfect for the part but at least on the video box we would've had some safety net. He's teetering on a high wire and he could lose $400,000.

"*Burial Society* is a really smart fun script, a thriller about a Jewish guy who joins a Jewish burial society, a *chevra kadisha*. We need to cast a Canadian in the lead [to get Canadian government grants]."

"How many movies did you do with Francis Ford Coppola's Zoetrope?"

"Just *Jeepers Creepers* and I really didn't do anything. Did I meet Francis Ford Coppola? Only on email. We had a very spirited email exchange at one point as I was losing my grip on the film. I didn't feel I was being treated fairly. Once I made my appeal to Francis (which really upset director Victor Salva) and Francis said no, I didn't grapple with him.

"I made movies with [actor and producer] Timothy Daly for three years. I had offices in Century City and Paramount. He had a producing deal at Paramount. Today he's in town doing voiceovers for the video game of Superman. He did *The Fugitive* (1993). He gave me a chunk of money and I was able to have a staff and make deals. I made seven films. I never let go of my Century City office with Davis Entertainment because I knew that Tim's deal with Paramount wasn't forever.

"I made a six million dollar film for TV, the bio-pic *Little Richard* (2000). Richard was coming in on a daily basis with his posse. He's the ageless architect of rock 'n' roll. He has hair down his back, extensions, make-up. He's wild-eyed."

"How much influence did you have over your studio pic *Dudley Do-Right*?"

"Very little. The only influence I could have over it was negative. I could've said, hey, this script is ridiculous and killed my $500,000 payday."

"It must've been cool working with $43 million?"

"It was. My biggest concern was, 'When's lunch? And where are the dailies?' We shot two pages a day. All the responsibilities that are normally mine were the studio's. I'm dying to do it again. I'm dying to do it again better and where I have some say. Universal changed regimes in the middle of it and they buried the release in the end of August, the graveyard for films. It only did three million its first weekend."

"Your most blessed film of all was your first one, *Denise Calls Up*."

"It was the most profitable, the most fun, we knew the least about what was going on."

"Which films have had the most meaning for you?"

"*Denise Calls Up* because it gave me my start. *Urbania* because it was a provocative film. It's the reason independent films exist. Stunning, controversial, engaging. I'm proud of *Bad Manners* (1997) because it is smart, engaging, with good actors. David Straithairn is classy. Bonnie Bedelia was not used to such a low budget film. With David, you could say, 'Here is your hammock and this portapotty is your dressing room,' and he'd go O.K. So mellow. I have high hopes for *Happy Hour*. It's about a drinker with a writing problem. The protagonist is a talented writer who's been blocked for ten years. And he finds love and meaning and a reason to live when it is too late. He's played by Anthony LaPaglia, the lead in *Lantana* (2001)."

"What have you learned from your 15 years in the independent movie biz?"

"You have to shut up and do it. I'll never know if I should've just taken that $250,000 I brought with me to Hollywood and just made a movie. Too many people just want to make a movie without thinking what will happen to it when it's done and who it is for. When I walk into a studio pitching a movie, I say, 'this is the poster. It will be this guy riding a horse.' Something they can see. They want to know the logline. They want to know who will star and who will see it. And the tighter your script is before you start, the better. It's nerve-racking to fix a script during the shoot.

"I've never worked with the same director twice."

"Is there a common thread through your films?"

"I like films about the human condition. I liked *Lantana*. My nickname for it is *Australian Beauty*. I like Woody Allen's better films. I still think *Crimes and Misdemeanors* (1989) is like a Swiss watch. It's my favorite film of all time. It's so heart breaking and funny. *Sex, Lies and Videotape* (1989) is a favorite. It still gives me goose bumps. *In The Company Of Men*. I like being in the hands of an assured filmmaker. It's hard for a director to cut scenes that he loves. *Denise Calls Up* at 83 minutes was dragging. At 79 minutes, it was rocking. *Monster's Ball* (2001) is a high concept film (can be summed up in one line)—a racist falls in love with a black woman.

"We're trying to do a sequel to *Denise Calls Up*. The theme is all the technology which is supposed to bring us together is really keeping us apart. Why get together if I can send you an email? Why call you? I'm online six hours a day."

"Is your [lyricist] wife Amy Powers Jewish?"

"Mercifully. She's the first Jewish woman I've been out with in a long time. We married four years ago and we have two children. I had a long fun robust bachelorhood. I got all my yayas out and a few yayas that weren't even mine. We have a lot of common values. I didn't want to marry somebody who'd just roll over and do whatever I wanted to. She challenges me to become a better person. I find her sexy. It's the first six years of my life that I've been monogamous. I have friends who say, 'Come on, you've horsed around.' And I haven't. I consider myself lucky to have emerged from the sexual revolution without any permanent damage. As much as I see women every day that I'd like to grab, the consequences are too severe. I have too good of a thing going."

"Your wife wouldn't be understanding?"

"I think she'd be furious. And I'd be devastated if she fucked around on me. And I think that I would be devastated if I fucked around on her as much as fun as it might be for a few minutes. She's talented and she's funny and we have kids together. And once you have kids, you're not just cheating on your wife, you're cheating on your kids. I'd go home and look at my children and start to ball. 'What have I done?' I'd be cheating on my in-laws who are terrific to me. It hasn't always been easy. I just wish that we were making more money. We're both in our early 40s with professional degrees and our lives have been financial roller coasters. She's an MBA from Columbia with a law degree from Harvard and an undergraduate degree from Vassar. I've got my Stanford degrees and by L.A. standards we're barely getting by. She wrote the lyrics for [Andrew Lloyd Webber's play] *Sunset Blvd.*"

"What are some of the common values that bind you together?"

"It helps to be Jewish. It was never that important to me but [now] there are no issues about how to raise the children. She wishes that I was more spiritual. She thinks about the after-life. We belong to a Reform temple. It's where our kids go to school. We come from upper-middle class white families who had enough resources but not too much. We both want a certain standard of living but we're not slaves to it.

"We had our youngest kid go to the emergency room two weeks ago. He fell and smacked his nose. It was like *Kramer vs Kramer* (1979) as I ran him to the hospital thinking, 'Oh no, our baby's getting stitches in his nose and is going to have a scar.' It was six hours in the emergency room.

"She's great at reading scripts. She reads lightning fast. And I can help her with her business. I can get her work. We're not using our contacts enough. We're just exhausted. We have a nanny 50 hours a week."

"How many of your films would you count as a success?"

"About half. It's exhausting. I've got to search for a new sales company for *Urbania*. How much money am I going to get for that? It's almost a pride thing. I feel that I have to get people to see it in other countries. I'm trying to think bigger and more commercial. More studio films."

17

Marc Frydman

"If *West Wing* is about a bunch of good guys doing the right thing," says Marc about a political drama (*Capital City*) he's producing for TV, "we're a bunch of bad guys doing the wrong thing. We have one good character, who is pure. The rest is horse trading and blackmail and shakedowns. It's funny. It's a drama with a lot of comedic twists. It's not a lecture."

"Is it slanted liberal?"

"I would be dishonest to say it is right in the middle. I think there will always will a liberal slant to it because that is what we are.

"I've known [right-wing] actor Gary Oldman for ten years. We've been friends. I made a movie in which he starred [*Murder in the First*, 1995]. I produced his directorial debut, *Nil by Mouth* (1997). We went to Cannes together when *Nil* was an official selection. And with *The Contender* (2000), it unraveled [Oldman and his manager Douglas Urbanski alleged it was edited to make points for the Democrats].

"Little did anyone on the set know that this raw nerve was an early sign of what would become a postproduction battle, with distributor DreamWorks and [director Rod] Lurie on one side, and Oldman and Urbanski on the other. What had once been an amusing irony—that *The Contender*, a rare politically charged drama with obvious Oscar potential, was being made by the conservative-leaning Oldman and Urbanski in partnership with the self-proclaimed "die-hard liberal" Lurie—became the seed of a struggle that involved allegations of breach of contract and the charge that the film's true spirit had been sold out by its director."

"Does he hate you for what happened?"

"I don't think he hates me. I'm not happy with the way he behaved. I think much of it came from his entourage. I don't think he's totally his own man. He once was divorced. The relationship became heated. It was not that way on the set. When we sold the movie to DreamWorks, that's when things got really bad.

Gary wanted his character to be more like the good guy. We liked the movie the way it was. DreamWorks [strong supporter of the Democratic Party] asked us to trim the movie. We had two meetings with Steven Spielberg in the cutting room that were benign.

"From the moment Urbanski saw the movie, they were not happy with the cut. When you have such a deep disagreement, you are not going to resolve it. I was happy with how the movie turned out. The writing was good. The movie delivered. The reviews were good. The domestic box office was fine and it did even better overseas. We had great actors [Joan Allen, Jeff Bridges, Christian Slater, Oldman] but no movie stars. Jeff Bridges and Gary Oldman are bigger stars overseas than in America. It was difficult subject matter. Like *The Big Lebowski* (1998), the movie has grown in stature since its theatrical release. In some countries, it made more money than *Titanic*. It's a cult movie. If we did *Contender 2*, we'd probably make more money.

"Rod Lurie's first movie, *Deterrence* (1999), was low-budget. It was more like a calling card for Rod so that he could convince big investors that he could direct. He wrote the script. He also wrote and directed a 22-minute short movie before that called *Four Second Delay* (1998). It's about a radio talk show host who invites *Washington Post* reporter Bob Woodward (played by Rigg Kennedy) to come on his show. And the host tries to get Woodward to reveal the identity of his Deep Throat Watergate source. One of the callers says he's holding hostages that he will kill one by one unless Woodward identifies his source.

"Rod was a movie critic for *Los Angeles* magazine and he hosted a radio show on KABC. I met him in 1994, when he had a class and was showing *Murder in the First*. He loved the movie. He gave us a screenplay called *Pork Chop*, which I thought was brilliant but extremely violent. We couldn't put it together. I told him to write something small and contained. That was *Deterrence*. It's about a president of the United States stuck in a diner during a snowstorm while campaigning. And while he's stuck, he must deal with a nuclear threat made by Iraq without his normal staff and means of operation.

"It's difficult to do a one-location movie because you have no way to tell time passage. We sold the movie to Paramount and then Rod wrote *The Contender*. I went to my normal sources for independent financing. I didn't want to depend on studios.

"The original budget for *Star Gate* was $30 million and we ended up at $55 million. It wasn't budgeted properly. I knew something was wrong when we built a set in Yuma, Arizona that was bigger than the production company's building on Sunset Blvd. We'd been misled by production designers. I was green. I knew that I liked the screenplay and I knew I had the financing. We cast it well. But nobody trusted the movie. It had a smell of disaster. MGM, which distributed it, told us that our $55 million movie was going to make $5 million opening weekend. So go and hide because it's going to be a disaster.

"Roland Emmerich, the director, and Dean Devlin, the writer, and I went to hide as instructed. They called us Friday night to say we're at $8 million already. So we came back to town. We did $17 million that weekend and ended up at $70 domestic box office with huge ancillary sales and a TV show after that."

"Were you guys involved in the TV show?"

"No, because we hated MGM's take. Our relationship with MGM was so damaged. They were not supportive of the movie and then they became big credit grabbers when the movie performed. Roland and Dean were hurt by how they had been treated by the studio. They hated MGM. The head of marketing at MGM then was Albert Nimzicki and he became the villain in *Independence Day* (1996). They hated him. MGM called Roland and Dean hacks. So they felt totally abandoned. And when their movie performed, MGM came to them and said, 'Let's do our next movie.' And they laughed. 'Are you kidding? Do you think we have such a short memory?' And they made a killer deal for *Independence Day* which became one of the top grossers of all time. MGM could've had this movie if they had behaved properly. Even if you don't trust a movie, don't openly despise it."

"Have all your films made money?"

"Yes, because of my low budget approach."

Frydman worked in French television from 1982-1992 before moving to Los Angeles to make movies.

"*Nil by Mouth* was a strange movie based on Gary's personal life as a poor boy in a lowlife district of London. It's about his childhood memories.

"Gary didn't want to compromise on anything in that movie. He did it the way he wanted. It was primarily by Luc Besson because he wanted Gary to be in *The Fifth Element* (1997). Gary said, O.K, but instead of paying me, pay for my [four million dollar] movie."

"Did it make any money?"

"No. It's a tough movie. It's a well crafted movie but it is not aimed at any kind of audience. Gary did the movie more for himself than anything else. We all knew that."

"It was a tough film to watch."

"I don't know why anyone would want to. I didn't want to watch it."

"Is there a common thread through your movies?"

"They're mainly true-story or issue-oriented. I find contemporary American history fascinating, from Watergate on.

"Rod Lurie is the first movie critic turned director in America. The closest example, Peter Bogdanovich, was not a critic but an essayist about movies. In France, all the big directors used to be critics. A lot of people told me I was crazy producing a movie for a critic turned director. Critic—director roles have nothing to do with each other. I was not so antagonistic because I came from a different background."

"European filmmakers don't seem to make films that people want to see as much as American films?"

"Yes."

"What's your critique of the European film industry, particularly the French one?"

"I wouldn't know where to start. I think it is a disaster. The movie industry in Europe has been decimated. The French system is under subsidy, on IV, and artificially protected."

"They're making films for themselves."

"I think the problem with French film goes back to the auteur idea, that the director is like the author. He creates the movie and is all powerful. But movies are different from books. They are much more expensive. You can't afford to have authorship status and be in your own world without regard for what the audience wants to see. That's why they need subsidies. If Americans knew about the system, they'd laugh at it. It's as if the U.S. government would pay for 50 percent of every movie made regardless of how it performs. Now that Canal Plus became Vivendi and has bought Universal and the chairman of the company has acquired clout. He's saying, enough of the French system as we knew it. I think things will change.

"Most of the money to make French movies comes from TV. And all those guys who called themselves auteurs, they are basically now in the paw of TV. TV executives now decide on cast and story. The French directors who think differently, like Luc Besson, come to America. He would never accept the French system. He rolled up his sleeves and came here."

18

Bryce Zabel

January 28, 2002

"When you're a television journalist," says Bryce, "you fall into the rules of television. That means shows get cancelled and [employment] terms are limited. At CNN, there was a staff turnover [in 1981] and suddenly I found myself in Los Angeles looking for another television job. I managed to find one doing a *60 Minutes* kind of job for PBS. And that was great. Then that show got cancelled. I'm on the horns of the television beast. I was more involved in television than in journalism.

"So I asked myself, what's my desire? Do I stay in Los Angeles? I had met the woman who is now my wife [writer-producer Jackie Zabel]. I didn't want to move. So I decided to modify what I was doing. I came to the conclusion that if I took another job as an anchor or reporter, I'd end up anchoring the news in Buffalo, and then anchoring the news in Indianapolis. So I changed what I wanted and I sought work in Hollywood. So instead of just going vertically from one place to another, I moved horizontally to what was available on the horizon in Los Angeles.

"Ultimately, the woman I married [in 1984] said, 'Have you ever written a screenplay?' I had never done it. I didn't even know what one looked like. We got one and I read it. And I said, 'This looks pretty easy. There aren't a lot of adjectives and adverbs in it. I can do this.' The first two things I wrote [in 1984] became TV series—*E.N.G.* [Electronic News Gathering, a 60-minute series about television news which ran in Canada from 1989-94] and *Kay O'Brien* (1986)."

"Is it difficult to stay married in Hollywood?"

"I haven't had any problem. We've always been in the television/entertainment/news business and we've always complemented each other in our interests. It's probably hard to stay married as an actor in Hollywood."

"I was just reading the latest issues of *Scientific American*, which has a devastating cover story about TV addiction. How do you feel about the medium?"

"I'd love to read the article and respond. Anything in life can be abused. It's a wonderful thing to enjoy a glass of wine with a fine meal on a Saturday night. It's a different thing to wake up in the morning and slam down your first hit of vodka. There's good television and there's bad television. There's quality television and mindless diversion. There's no problem with watching mindless diversion once in a while. It allows you to relax. If you become addicted to only mindless diversion, it's going to affect your life in a negative way.

"I look around at television now. And I'm also a member of the board of directors of the Writers Guild. The writing in television is stronger today than the writing in movies. The best most thoughtful work is being done in TV. The amount of great hour dramas on television has never been better. As chairman of the TV academy, I can't join an outcry against TV. I've found TV a great way to express almost every thought that has come to me over the past 15 years."

"Journalism for many journalists is a religious calling. Do you ever wake up at 2 a.m. and think that you've sold out?"

"No. I haven't had anyone attack me for it. I miss journalism. On the other hand, what I do now for a living allows me to use all the skills of journalism. When you create a pilot, it's necessary for you to understand that world. And the best way to understand it is to go back to journalism. To do your research and call people up and interview them. I'm one of the best interviewers I know. I get things out of people I need information from that make my scripts better and more realistic. I've never quit being a journalist. I'm just practicing a different form of expression.

"The TV Academy job expresses another aspect of my journalistic life. When the Emmys were in controversy this year and we had to postpone them twice, and I became the spokesperson for the TV Academy, that called on every skill I'd ever learned in journalism. It's a state of mind that follows you all your life."

"Have you learned anything about the news business from your past four months in the spotlight?"

"Absolutely. Like all journalists, I know what the deadline can do to you. It means that you've got to be on at a certain time. And I've been burned a couple of times by people who had a story they were bound and determined to report whether or not it fit with the facts. And I've been personally attacked in what I see as an unfair way.

"I realized during the Emmy situation that someone who is smart about journalism can have a significant impact on the stories written about their organization by understanding the mind of the journalist interviewing them and what their needs are. I probably give a good sound bite when called upon because I have listened to sound bites for thousands of hours, picking out 15-20 second sound bites.

"Have I become disenchanted by virtue of the experience? No. Ninety eight percent of the journalists I encounter are good at what they do and I feel like I am in good hands. One thing I've had to learn. I'm having a casual conversation with you now. I'm just rambling on and trying to be responsive. When you're talking to a journalist on the record, there's no such thing as a casual comment. You need to think carefully about what your message is. I don't mean in a spin doctor kind of way but in a communication kind of way. What message do you want out?

"If your message is that the Emmys are a secure venue and you can feel secure coming to them, then don't talk about where the toilet facilities are going to be located. Talk about security. Better still, come up with a descriptive way of saying it. For example, at the Emmys, the phrase I used was that 'we would have presidential level security.' That turned out to not only be a good sound bite but a descriptive way for people to understand the truth."

"I couldn't find any of your bad press," I say.

"During the Emmys, it was all positive. We just went through a period where our executive committee chose not to renew the contract of our chief executive staff person. The Emmys was a positive situation because I was attempting to be resolved and resolute about the fact that they would go on, and that there was a reason for them to go on."

"What have you learned from presiding over the Television Academy, particularly as it applies to producing television?"

"I'd put it the other way. What have I learned from producing television that applies to running the Television Academy. As a show runner, you learn a lot of skills. You learn how to run a good meeting and be productive. You learn how to delegate authority and trust people. Those are all important skills for running a large organization because you need to inspire people to see a common vision. You need to give them the adequate time and tools to achieve that vision. Then let them do their work. That's what I'm trying to do with the Television Academy. It's a volunteer position and I still have to work for a living. I can't afford to make it a fulltime obsession.

"I'm always enterprising new things. I have a pilot at DreamWorks Television. I just optioned a script to Fireworks, a major TV producer. I'm finishing up the first draft of a feature film. And my wife and I have the *Atlantis* credit this year for story. It's tough to juggle all these things but I've always juggled many projects at a time. That goes back to CNN days when I was reporting four stories a day when the big network guys reported one story every three days. I've always been good at compartmentalizing and juggling multiple projects and that's what I must do now."

"What does your typical day look like?"

"I haven't had the chance to evolve a typical day. During the Emmys, for instance, this was a story that people had an incredible amount of interest in because this was the first cultural touchstone to be affected by 9/11. I got to the Emmys and realized that I hadn't talked to anybody about who was nominated. I'd talked about security. During the Emmys, my typical day was to wake up and put on a suit and tie, which is something a writer-producer in this town almost never does. I would drive to CNN or MSNBC or talk to the AP or stop at the Academy for a security meeting. I had to say, 'greater good here. I've been called upon at this particular moment in history through no reason than the election to step in and do the best I can.' That was a fulltime gig for a couple of months.

"Now I'm trying to do less of that. I'm trying to set specific hours that I work at the Academy and to continue my regular creative life. Most days involve Academy maintenance, idea generation and pitches and lunches. I hope in the next twelve months to end up on a series."

"Can you leverage your position with the Academy to further your career?"

"It's the other way around. You have to spend your time assuring people that you're still working because they so saw me so actively involved with the Academy on the Emmys, that many people simply assumed that that was my new job. I don't think I am going to get any work out of any new relationship that only exists because of the Academy. Everything that I'm involved with right now that could lead to work is with people I've worked with before. For the past 15 years, I've done four to eight scripts a year and pitched 20 times. I know most people. People who know me probably say, 'He's a maniac. He can run the Academy and run a show at the same time.'"

"Where does your fascination with government conspiracies and UFOs come from?"

"My first show was about a TV news room and my next show was *Kay O'Brien*, about a female surgeon in New York City. You are defined by your successes and I've been in a string where, as my career crested as a show runner, I also did a string of sci-fi shows, *Lois and Clark* (1993), *Dark Skies* (1996), *M.A.N.T.I.S.* (1994), and *Crow: Stairway to Heaven* (1998). I think it would be harder to sell a conspiracy themed show now because people realize that implying

that government is up to no good is a tough sell during a time when the only people who can potentially protect you from a terrorist is your government.

"I do believe there is a reality to UFOs. Therefore, if you believe that, you
must also believe that there are people who have information about that reality
that has not been shared on an official level. I've gone through periods when I
was really into that because it was the show that I was doing, such as *Dark Skies*.
You play a role. My role was as television producer of *Dark Skies* who was willing
to speak up about the conspiracy. Now I don't have that role anymore. It doesn't
mean that I don't believe. I just don't play it as much.

"It is not surprising to me that the government doesn't call a news conference
and say, 'Here's what we know.' Because they'd have to admit that they don't
know much. They'd create panic by saying there is a reality to UFOs but we
don't know where they come from, whether from the rest of universe or another
dimension or they are time travelers. We have some excellent photos of some
UFOs.

"I think that some time in the next 20 years, there will be a UFO incident that .
is captured on multiple cameras at different locations and multiple videotapes
and authoritative witnesses numbering in the hundreds and at that point it will
wind up on the cover of *Time* and *Newsweek* and every network will have to cover
it. And at that point, the big global discussion will have to kick in. I also don't
think it will change things. When we learn that there are UFOs who visit us from
time to time, people will still get up in the morning and go to work."

"Do you believe that Lee Harvey Oswald was the lone gunman who killed
John F. Kennedy?"

"No, I do not. I believe that the greatest work of American fiction is the Warren Commission."

"Do you believe in any cover-ups analogous to that?"

"I'm not a raving paranoid. I'm really quite a patriot these days. I believe that
our government by and large is actively trying to protect the interests of the
American people and the rest of the world. I do think that as with any large organization, and our government is one of the largest ever created, there are things
that have happened that people aren't proud of institutionally. For example, I
don't think you're paranoid or a conspiracy theorist to point out things we now
know to be true. We now know there were LSD experiments that were con-
ducted by our own government."

"Bottom line, who do you think was truly behind the Kennedy assassination?"

"Some version of organized crime, Cuban exiles and our own government
played a shadowy coalition that allowed it to happen. I think we've reached that

point where unless some evidence is unearthed later, which I doubt, it will always have a big asterisk by it in the history books. I think it is clear that multiple groups were involved."

"I went through a phase where I went through two dozen books on the matter and they say what you just said."

"*Dark Skies* is an entire series that combined the two big conspiracy theories of all time—the Kennedy assassination and UFOs—into one. I don't personally believe the *Dark* Skies mythology but it made for a helluva good story."

"What are your latest thoughts on the Bush administrations overtures to Hollywood to join the war against terrorism?"

"I don't see any reason why we creative individuals who are also Americans observing the world can't have creative discussions amongst ourselves about some legitimate stories. If you told writers now to come up with an idea for a relevant idea to the war on terrorism, about 90 percent would come up with an idea of a Muslim American being discriminated against. I think what would really help America's case around the world is if there was a regular character on *ER* who was Muslim, but wasn't discriminated against and just did his job well. We're bending over backwards to be fair Americans when we should also ask ourselves if there are realistic programs to be developed about our ability to sustain a long term war against terrorism. While everyone's pitching ideas about Muslim-Americans who are discriminated against, we could also postulate a show that takes place in a small New Jersey town across from the World Trade Center where 15 of their men and women went to work one morning and never came back. And wouldn't that be an interesting one hour drama to see how that city was healing itself and moving on.

"I think there may be lots of interesting conversations we've missed out on by virtue of taking content off the table. When I went to those meetings, it seemed like they were more technical than creative. It was, 'Let's get a DVD of Harry Potter to the U.S.S. Carl Vincent.' That's not going to save the world or end the war on terrorism."

"I think there's a perception in the heartland that the Hollywood community is not as patriotic."

"I live in Agoura Hills. It's 35 miles north of Los Angeles. I live next to people who don't work in Hollywood. I'd like to believe that most of us in Hollywood are so shocked by the outrageousness of the attack of September 11, if the standard [of patriotism] is an appropriate response to September 11, I'd believe that we're patriotic. If the question is, in peace time, are Hollywood types as comfortable waving the flag as someone in Middle America on the Fourth of July, maybe they're not. But they're not that much different. I'd love to have dinner with Michael Medved and hear his view on that."

"One example Michael gives is that there was no movie made celebrating the Gulf War."

"I agree that didn't happen. I don't know if that supports his point. Historically it has always taken Hollywood a longer time to come to grips with war. Hollywood deals with wars of the past more successfully than war of the recent past. Hollywood is in the business of spectacle. Is *Black Hawk Down* (2001) patriotic or not? I'm not sure. It's honest. It's disturbing. In some respects, I see it as patriotic. It is young guys doing their best to do what their country needs them to do, to the point of laying down their lives."

"Which of your shows have had the most meaning to you?"

"The one that I wrote that has the most meaning to me, that was never made, was the *Lewis and Clark*, a feature I wrote for Warner Brothers. Kevin Costner was supposed to star. I'm an Oregonian and I grew up 50 miles away from where Louis and Clark spent the winter on the Pacific coast. That's a patriotic inspirational story about brave people who did the impossible. It's about the American spirit and the human spirit and I love that story. I love bringing something that was meaningful to me as a young kid to life in a screenplay.

"The thing I'm most proud of that was produced, *Dark Skies*, is a demonstration of free speech. Think about the ideas that were floated in that series. I was allowed to tell this outrageous story that had political overtones and fans have put more metaphorical spin on it than I ever thought I had on it when I did it. I got a full season to take $45 million to create this alternative universe over 20 hours of programming.

"We've been granted the publishing rights, so we can if we wish to continue to tell the story in book form, although that is a lot of energy.

"I came to love *The Crow*. *The Crow* character is my favorite character that wasn't mine that I've ever had to develop in a series. I made him over in my vision. By the time the series was over, he was not at all the character from the feature film but a different person. The TV series was more about redemption than revenge and the character reflected that.

"I loved being part of the team that reinvented Superman on *Lois and Clark*. *Kay O'Brien* was the first series I did that actually got made. I participated in it on a daily basis and everything about that experience was intense and unique and original."

"Does a TV show need to go five years and hit syndication to be a success?"

"It helps. You can do it with less. The expanding television universe has changed the playing field. *Dark Skies* and *The Crow*, even though they each only did a single season, have been airing nonstop on the scifi channel for years now. They have *Dark Skies* and *Crow* marathons where they will air all episodes in a single day. The biggest problem for most TV producers and writers over the years was that whatever they did was lost forever. The great thing about tape and the exploding TV universe, is that it is all available to people again."

"How much are you able to put your vision into reality?"

"It depends on the project, though clearly more in television than features. My vision, if you will, on [the 1997 feature] *Mortal Kombat: Annihilation*, was limited. We had to make sure if fit with the videogame people, the first movie, the producers. There were so many people it had to march to that drummer for that it wasn't a big creative highpoint. Television is different. *Dark Skies*, even though it was an incredible struggle to finish, is 95 percent the vision that Brett Freeman and I set out to do. Even though I had some of the lowest moments of my career during that show trying to hang on to certain things that I knew had to be part of the series, and yet I was being asked to give them up. It's situational. It's depends on whether you are the show-runner or not. Different projects require less 'vision' than others. *Dark Skies* was a big bold weird vision. Working on *Life Goes On* (1989-1993) in its third or fourth season doesn't require a big bold vision. It was, 'O.K, we've got the franchise. How do we keep making the burgers here?'

"One of the greatest things that a writer can be involved in is writing the pilot for a series because for at least those few moments while you're writing it, you're creating a template that you hope will go forward. There aren't a thousand voices in your head."

"What does your work say about you?"

"I believe that things are going to work out. I believe there's a profoundly optimistic streak in humanity that I choose to think about most of the time. It's clear that our human traits make the best drama. No matter how fantastic the story, whether it is the invasion of the planet or a character who comes back from the dead, it's really about being a human being and surviving. It's the struggle to do the right thing and to be a good person is what ennobles almost every story that people tell."

"Do you believe that human nature is basically good?"

"I don't know. If you look around the world, the good guys seem to be winning by a whisker. Maybe that means we're basically good. I don't know. I think there's a good streak in the majority of human beings and I choose to think about that most of the time."

"How did you and your philosophy of life handle September 11?"

"The first thing that I did was stay home with my children that day. I instantly knew that this was for them what the Kennedy assassination was for me and what Pearl Harbor was for my father. And that their generation was going to be defined by it. It's such a cataclysmic event that people could be so misguided that in the name of their God take so many lives in such a brutal and senseless way. That's why it gave me pause when you asked me about whether people are basically good. It causes you to question some of your bedrock values. It's changed how I feel about what I want to write and what I want to do with my life. You tend to make sure that you use your time as a valuable investment. You wake up every morning and ask, 'How can I be of service today.' And if that is the unintended consequence of 9/11, that we may look back on it and say that it had a positive upside because it made us stop taking things for granted."

"You say that America's diversity is its strength. Yet almost all of your peers, the folks who make TV and movies, are white males, two-thirds Jewish. So if diversity is so great, why don't you guys practice it too?"

"I'm not Jewish, by the way. My wife is. We're making progress with diversity. We're more sensitive to the notion that diversity is a strength. I believe you change the world one act at a time. You don't change it by issuing proclamations. You change it by doing the right thing from moment to moment. As more people have their consciousness raised on this issue, the world will become a more equal diverse and positive place. And that will happen in Hollywood as well. I don't think we want to condemn people for being white males. White males are a part of our population and they should be able to make a living as well. On the ground floor, I see it changing. I see inclusion happening. I certainly work for it. I see it reflected in many of the stories and movies that are told. Most of the tapes that I get for the Emmys that come from Showtime and HBO are incredibly diverse. Almost to the point where you go, if this were a story about a white male, it would never be made."

"What's it been like for you a non-Jew from Oregon moving into Jewish Hollywood?"

"I guess I should be happy that people assume that I am Jewish then. This is something that I did not grow up tuned in to. I didn't have Jewish friends growing up. I did when I went to college but it surprised me that they were Jewish. Maybe the majority of my friends now are Jewish but I don't think of them in that way. My wife was disowned by her mother for eight years for marrying me. My three kids have been raised in the Jewish religion."

19

Jay Bernstein

January 30, 2002

In a recent issue of *The National Enquirer* (TNE), Jay said we need tough guys like John Wayne to help defeat terrorism, "but Hollywood and the networks are not interested."

Hollywood is failing America in its time of crisis. We should be inspired to fight for our country. "There's a mindset since Vietnam that war is bad."

Bernstein says that studio chiefs and TV bosses won't listen to him. "They don't get it. Hollywood's hunkered down in a foxhole of fear."

The article takes up two-thirds of a page and features a big picture of John Wayne with a small inset photo of Jay.

"Would you take a look at my eyes and take a look at John Wayne's eyes?" asks Jay. "Take a look at my nose and take a look at John Wayne's nose."

"They're similar."

We talk about Jay's *Mike Hammer* series.

"When Barbara Corday, who was the co-creator of *Cagney and Lacey*, became the head of Columbia, she hated *Mike Hammer* because it was the antithesis of *Cagney and Lacey*. She wanted to get rid of the decollatage. We had terrible fights. She just wanted the show cancelled. She once said that the series set back the women's movement a decade.

"It was a genre piece. Mike Hammer was never rude to women and even when they would come on to him, he didn't do anything lascivious. He'd probably have an affair with somebody in every episode.

"Barbara Corday was the precursor of now. We don't have any male shows. We have *Alias* and *Jordan's Crossing* and *Dark Angel*. There's nothing going on for men. They were trying to get rid of us and *Mike Hammer* was a good place to start. And she finally did get the show cancelled. I then got it on again. It's the first time anyone's done a series more than once with the same actor [Stacy

Keach]. And I did it three times over 12 years. It's always been a cult hit, not a number one show."

"How did you get involved?"

"In 1979, I was flying first class on an airplane to New York. You should always fly first class. I've made two big deals that way. I was sitting next to Mickey Spillane, author of the Mike Hammer detective novel series. Mickey was a childhood hero of mine. I said to him, 'She walked towards me, her hips waving a happy hello.' He put down his paper and smiled and talked to me for a minute.

"He told me later, 'I thought I was going to be sitting next to a fan for the next five hours.' About 30 minutes later, I said, 'Women stuck to Mike Hammer like lint on a blue Serge suit.' And he laughed and we started talking again. He said he hadn't worked in Hollywood for 15 years. He didn't like the people there. By the time the plane landed, he gave me the rights to Mike Hammer for $1.

"We'd like to redo the whole Mike Hammer thing and make it contemporary. Make him a John Wayne type character who fights terrorists. In the original books, Hammer was fighting the communists. He'd go into the cell meetings and machine-gun communists."

"How are the Hollywood execs reacting to you?"

"I haven't gone out [pitching] since September 11. I'm letting this sink in. It will still be difficult. You notice that the flags are down. We have a feminine attitude here and a lot of the country. It seems that the men are doing the mergers and acquisitions while the creative is controlled by women. Women give life while men have been the warriors who take life and protect it. Women are saving the seals and the whales while we got bombed in New York City.

"So many people have said that I should do a book, but…in New York, whenever people have asked, it's clear that I am not their kind of person. I'm not politically correct.

"I found that the synonym for 'producer' was 'problem.' Nobody ever calls you with anything but problems. If you were shooting a two hour movie, it would take four months. I was doing the equivalent of four months work every six days. You had to be John Wayne tough to deal with these people. The minute you get a green light to go with your team, with Columbia (the producer) and CBS (the network), I become the enemy of both of them. Columbia's trying to save money. They kept trying to cut me down. Then CBS would have their point of view. When you make a TV show, you do it by committee. When you try to make a horse by committee, you end up with a camel. So I had to fight. I wasn't popular as a producer because I fired more producers than anyone had else fired.

"I had spent a decade as a publicist and a decade as a manager, so when I got into production, I didn't know who were the best people to work with. And the studio wanted to give you people who were cheaper and couldn't work anywhere else. You don't know that at the beginning. You're told that all these people are wonderful.

"Primarily I had to fire writers. I've never gotten along well with writers. When *Mike Hammer* (1984-87) was most popular, I made a deal with CBS that we would hire three writers to do three scripts for each episode. And I was lucky to get one script that was any good. The writer is the only person whoever gets paid [regardless of production]. The writers let you think that's the only thing they're doing but they're doing five other scripts at the same time. The agents, in many cases, won't let you meet the writer until you've made a firm offer. I found that the writers who had the best personalities were usually the worst writers. They knew how to sell. I ended up doing much of the writing myself, and I'm not a writer. But I'd structure it from stories I'd make up.

"Some of the writers they gave me were people who'd written for radio in the 1940s. I was getting all this corn stuff that had been done 40 times.

"Mickey Spillane's Mike Hammer books have always been closed-end mysteries. You didn't know who did it until the end. Columbia had no problem with that but CBS said we have to worry about our sponsors. We don't want closed-end shows because when someone gets up and goes to the bathroom and comes back to the TV set, they don't know what's going on. 'So we want you to show at the beginning, like *Columbo*, who the killer is.' That's not what *Mike Hammer* is. When it finally worked, the way CBS rewarded me was to steal my ideas and come up with a show called *Murder She Wrote* (1984-96).

"When I came up with the ad campaign, they didn't like, 'When the police won't help you, *Mike Hammer* will.' But I finally got it in. Then when Stacy Keen went to prison [for drugs], they stole it and came up with a show called *The Equalizer* (1985-89). 'When the police won't help you, *The Equalizer* will.'

"*Mike Hammer* was the first hard-guy P.I. The others were the Jimmy Carter soft detectives—*Barnaby Jones* (1973-80), *The Rockford Files*, (1974-80), *Magnum P.I.* (1980-88). Mike Hammer was a Charles '*Death Wish*' Bronson type who would kick the shit out of you. He'd be like a pit bull.

"We invented the voice over and then ABC stole that with *Spenser: For Hire* (1985-88). Anything that you do that works, somebody takes it from you.

"Girls are told that they shouldn't sleep with the producer, but I slept with the executive producer of Mike Hammer, Jay Bernstein, which is me. He hired me as a writer and I wrote several episodes and got in the Writers Guild. Then I slept with Jay Bernstein again, and he let me direct. So I got into the Directors Guild of America. Then I slept with him again and he let me act and I got into the Screen Actors Guild.

"Producing was fun but hard. You had to get yourself ready each day to stay in shape for a fight. No one ever calls you with a compliment. Every other business I've been in was the same way. In management, when I made someone into a star, I'd just get fired. Once I got them to where they wanted to be, the air would get rarified, they'd get deified and I'd get nullified. Because 15 percent of nothing is nothing while 15 percent of $10 million is $1.5 million. It is hard for them to write those checks. I've been fired hundreds of times."

"You've stayed on good terms with Farrah Fawcett and Suzanne Sommers."

"I'm not on bad terms. But when someone fires you, they're like ex-wives. It's not like any of them would throw a benefit for me. Because they would have to feel bad about firing me. It all gets tricky. They could owe you money and some smart lawyer will say, 'You don't have to pay him. Just sue him. Say he ruined your career.' Then you have to go get a lawyer and spend the same amount of money you would've gotten.

"I've been engaged three times but married only once. I only knew my wife (Cabrina Finn) two days when I proposed. We were in Cozumel, Mexico, scuba diving. I was shark hunting, down about 100 feet. I shot the shark and it was the first time I had ever missed. The shark was circling to kill me. I went to get the other spearhead and this girl I'd just met, was holding it. The current was against me and I couldn't get there. The shark was about to rip me apart and she just leans in, doesn't know what she's doing, and kills the shark. The next morning, I proposed.

"We ended up scuba diving halfway around the world. We had a million dollar wedding at St. Marten's island in the West Indies paid for by Robin Leach's *Lifestyles of the Rich and Famous.* Eddie Fisher was my best man.

"Cabrina and I got along well under water. We just had problems on land."

"The most devastating article I ever read in *TV Guide* was an expose on Suzanne Somers after she left *Three's Company.*"

"That was after she left me. Her husband Allen Hammel went in and asked for a huge raise for her. They had fights and she got blacklisted. She didn't work in film or television for eight years."

"Why would anyone else care that she'd stood up ABC?"

"Like when Farrah left *Charlie's Angels.* If you walk out on a hit show, even though you have a contract, you're not going to want to hire such a person. Just like you wouldn't want to hire a girl who's been divorced eight times.

"Suzanne's now on the Home Shopping Network three hours a week selling exercise equipment, candy, jewelry. She's written books on exercise and diet. They're close to billionaires."

"What effect has it had on you to spend most of your adult life around beautiful women?"

"The good news about beautiful women is that there seems to be a never-ending supply. Because I'm Jay Bernstein, I get 1200 pictures and resumes every month. Do they want me for my body? No. We're all a package. Everybody wants us for more than just what we would want them to want us for. I don't think I've ever dated a humpback.

"I've never been a cheater. When I've had a relationship, I've always been faithful to that relationship. But I was always so busy, I was working 25 hours a day. It was hard for anyone to put up with that. Many times I would take a woman somewhere and leave her at the table for four hours. Not meaning to, but by the time I came back, they were gone.

"If I were to say how many women I've slept with, it would be as tacky as Wilt Chamberlain. There's no upside to saying. When you're 18 years old, you and I thought we could fuck everybody there was. But then as you get more mature, and you realize that there's a new crop coming in every year, you realize that you can't do that. At this stage in my life, sex for sex sake is a bore.

"I would love to have someone in my life as a lover/companion/friend, but with the way the world is, I don't think it is going to happen. I think that the women have become men and the men are becoming women. And I'm certainly not attracted to men. The women that I've liked have been the most beautiful because all I've met are beautiful women.

"The birth control pill came in in the 1960s. Before that, divorce wasn't in. I remember Oklahoma City, where I grew up, we would drive by the Deaconess School where the unwed mothers would be. In Oklahoma City, I only knew one person who'd been divorced. Then came the pill and freedom. An abortion prior to the pill, you could serve the same prison time as being a heroin dealer now. There were no abortionists. You had to go Mexico and the rusty knife.

"Girls today in their 20s think that the birth control pill, if they think about it, has been around since the late 1800s. I am traditional in what I want. The reason that I haven't been married eight times is that it has changed too much for me to want to deal with the downside that you see with all your friends. You lose your house, your bank account, your mind. I've always been the caretaker. The women were always younger. It would sure be nice at this point to have someone who wanted to take care of me. But they're not out there unless you want to go for someone older, which I never did. For years, I haven't gone out with a woman at least 25 years younger than me."

"There are women out there who want to nurture and care for a man, but they're not actresses."

"I haven't met anyone who wasn't an actress and a model. A lot of these movie stars, beautiful actresses like Susan Hayward, can't meet a man. Where could she meet a man? Look at Farrah Fawcett. What's she going to do to meet a man? She's certainly not going to go to a bar. If she goes out with somebody who loves the publicity of being with her, that's dangerous. You don't want somebody with you just for that, and if you go out with somebody who hates the publicity and can't handle it, then that's a problem too. If someone fixes you up and you go to their house, you could be in a situation you don't want to deal with. If they come to your house, then you've got another problem. A lot of us are stuck in our own worlds. I don't meet people who aren't in the business.

"The problem with my marriage is that I had no experience with it. To me, it was like heavy going steady. My parents were married for 53 years before my dad died. People don't do that anymore. Ten years is about as long as anyone in this town lasts.

"Each of us is a package. Women like me for being Jay Bernstein and for what I can do for them and for my intelligence. With you, because you're handsome, you can get people outside the business, nurses, secretaries, whatever, based on your looks. That's why you get to meet more people outside the business than I did. Even though I would rather have looked more like you than like me, what happens is when you have someone really handsome and intelligent, like you are, and you go on television and talk about something, women just look at the handsome people and don't listen to them. I'm in the middle so people can look at me and listen to me at the same time.

"What I am supposed to do in my own life is help America. I gave them role models at a time when we didn't have any. In the 1970s, when Nixon was impeached and nobody wanted to be in politics because you go to prison, music was spiked hair and spike bracelets, sports, the most looked-up to person was Joe Namath, that's when I started working on the role models—Farrah Fawcett, Suzanne Somers, Mary Hart, Linda Evans.

"It used to be that 25 was the age where women, who weren't married, were considered old maids. But when Farrah was 30 on Charlie's Angels, I publicized that. And it took women from 25–30. They moved up those five years. Then with Linda Evans, I made women perfect at 40. My friend Dr. Joyce Brothers says that we were cutting down women's suicide rate 25 percent between the ages of 30–40. Say someone is 36, and instead of being depressed and suicidal that they were six years over the hill, they could say, 'Gee, I have four years to get it all together and be perfect, just like Linda Evans.' It gave them more to feel good about themselves."

"So when you look back on a career of over 30 years in Hollywood, which things have you done that have the most meaning to you?"

"I created role models for a country that didn't have any. Right now we don't have role models. This [TNE] article reminds guys about our responsibilities. Women will ignore it. They're not dropping *Charlie's Angels* into Afghanistan. That's what I've tried to do—keep myself where I can help. With *Mike Hammer*, the reason I fought so hard to keep that on was not for any of the reasons you would think. It was because I believe there is a difference between good and evil. Good should be rewarded and evil should be punished. And as much as I like to watch shows like *Law & Order* (1990-???), with its great acting, I hate what it's about. Because it shows that evil can get off with a good lawyer on a technicality. In every episode of *Mike Hammer*, the audience knew who was guilty. Mike Hammer knew. Then they pulled a gun on him first and he'd get rid of them. Nobody went to court."

"America had this great victory in the Persian Gulf ten years ago and there hasn't been one movie or TV series to celebrate it?"

"We're living in the world of Vietnam. People think war is bad because Vietnam was bad. I hate the fact that *Black Hawk Down* is doing so well. They make it sound like it is patriotic. It's an anti-war film. It's back to *Platoon* (1986). We look like the villains. We're machine-gunning children. It sure doesn't make you want to put your flag out. It makes you want to take it down."

"I think there's a great yearning in the American breast for patriotic entertainment."

"I don't think so. I think it should be put there. Movies are primarily for young people who don't want to see war. They want to be entertained. The average age for movie audiences is under 23. And on television, the audience you go for is women. So men are not an audience anywhere except for sports. As for the rest, 98 percent of the time, the bad person is a guy."

"When you were creating your role models, men and women still had more traditional roles on TV. When did it change?"

"With the growth of feminism. Men weren't watching this. It was happening all around them. Take the black situation. When I grew up in Oklahoma City and you got on the bus, it said 'rear seats for colored.' The only colored people you met were in your home working for you. They lived in a segregated part of town. Then in the 1960s you had Martin Luther King and negroes. Then we watched the rise of equality. And we could see it. But with the feminism, it just kept coming.

"Women are able to communicate. The typical American male does his job all day, has lunch with his friends, discusses business, goes home and he's tired. Women all day long are communicating. If a guy calls his friend and says, 'I want you to know that Cabrina and I are getting a divorce.' And he says, 'That's terrible. And any time you want to talk about it, 24/7, you call me.' And I'd get off the phone thinking that is really nice.

"The woman gets on the phone and calls her best friend to say, 'I'm going to be getting a divorce from Jay.' The friend will say, 'What did that sonofabitch do to you? Let me tell you a lawyer that you ought to get right now. And if I were you, I'd get right down to the bank and lock up the accounts.' And three hours later, you're screwed. We have 'Women in Film' organizations. Do you ever see 'Men in Film' groups? You'd go to jail if you started a white men's organization. They'd think you were the grand dragons of the Klu Klux Klan.

"Men are individuals. We don't work in groups. Even in the animal kingdom as with elephants. There's only one bull in the herd and all the rest are cows. When men are young, they talk about sex all the time. When you get older, it's not gallant to talk about the women you've been with. Women, when they're young, never talk about sex because it is not polite. But when they get older, that's all they talk about.

"I nearly gave in with *Mike Hammer* before September 11 because I couldn't sell it. And I still wanted to show the difference between good and evil without the lawyer getting you off like every one of these legal shows. I had a script written called *'Mickey Spillane's Ms. Hammer.'* I nearly had to turn Mike Hammer into a woman.

"The things that I produce are 90 percent about the things that I believe. I produce, not out of addiction, but out of obligation. I wouldn't produce something for any amount of money that had a message that was the opposite of what I believed. I am not a zealot. I just feel responsible since nobody else is doing it. I want to produce patriotic entertainment. Second. If England and Ireland can't get along because of Catholics vs Protestants, how are we going to get along here with Muslims, Christians, Buddhists?

"Have you been to Japan? Have you ever heard of an African-Japanese? Or a Mexican-Japanese? Or a Russian-Japanese? We haven't faced our problem. I'd like to take a Vietnamese-American old fashioned family who believe in Buddhism who have a 19-year old daughter who falls in love with a conservative

Catholic Hispanic. Both families discourage the relationship but the kids run away, get married and have a child. A year-and-a-half later, while they are both working in the World Trade Center, they're killed. Now you've got a child who's half Vietnamese-American and half Hispanic-American and these two families need to raise it together. We may be integrated but we're segregated and separated."

"Hollywood pushes projects that say that diversity is a wonderful thing. I'm not so sure."

"I'm not either but we're stuck with it."

"We get along by leading separate lives. Ninety five percent of my friends are Jewish."

"How do you feel about the Hasidic Jews?"

"They're my fellow Jews. I've had good and bad interactions with them."

"Did you know that they seem to be the most powerful group now in Israel? That's difficult for me to deal with just on a personal prejudice level. I'm not comfortable with that nor do I understand it. It's as foreign to me as Buddhism. I've never met a Hasidic Jew. The only people I knew who wore black hats were cowboys.

"If Pakistan and India go to war, one of them will land some missiles into Israel. We have a pact with Israel. I'm trying to raise some Jewish money to make patriotic entertainment. Because if that happens, I'm afraid there will be a lot of anti-Semitism in this country. I don't think Americans can identify with Hasidic Jews. If we have a WASPy Mike Hammer side-by-side with an Israeli who looks like you, there will be more of an identification. You don't think Jews are a different race, do you?"

"No. I think they are a people, like the American people, composed of many different races."

"Like a nationality but not a race. So many people, like Hitler and many people here, thought the Jews were a race. I went to an Episcopal private school for six years. I was the only Jew in the school. Many of the fathers of the girls wouldn't let me date their daughters after 16 years old because they didn't want their girls to get pregnant and have their baby with horns. Where did that one come from?"

"From *John* 8: 44 in the New Testament. Jesus calls the Jews children of the Devil. And the Devil has horns. So the Jews have horns too."

"The literalists think the baby will be born with horns. I remember being at the home of Lee Majors (*The Six Million Dollar Man*, 1974-78) in Kentucky, with his family. They were older. We went to the Holiday Inn, the nicest restaurant in town. This woman kept looking at me. She said, 'Are you a Jew?' I said yes. Then she asked, 'Where are your horns?' I said, 'I had those manicured off when I was very young.'

"Technology was supposed to make things better but it's just made things faster. You go to the shrink on Wednesdays and I go to the shrink on Wednesdays. Things have gone so fast with no real sense to it. I've had to make a purpose to what I was doing to stay around to do it. I don't get any applause for that but that's O.K. I get applause from the emails, but those are all blank faces."

"From the Hollywood community?"

"No. To them, I'm like a rogue. All those people I managed and help maximize their potential into superstardom, they all thought I was Prince Valiant and Sir Lancelot. The people that I got all that from thought I was Jesse James or John Dillinger. Then, when these people fired me, I didn't have anybody thinking I was the good guy anymore. That's why I took some time away from it · because it is hard to be the villain all the time when you know you're doing good things.

"Those Al Qaeda prisoners we have in Cuba should be shot. Now they're talking about giving us their life stories.

"The agent called today. I want him to send this TNE article to the executives making decisions, even though the story will piss them off. I've always thought that if you can't go over the fence, you go under the fence. If you can't go under the fence, then you better suggest that they move their fence, because if they don't, you might just blow it up. I'm ready to blow up fences again. They may not want to see me at NBC. But if I've got enough power to get this in print, I have enough power to get seen at some network. If NBC turns me down, I can go to ABC and if they make it and it is successful, then the person at NBC who turned me down will get fired. We're sending covers of Mickey Spillane's Mike Hammer books translated into 19 different languages."

"Is Mike Hammer a Jay Bernstein alter ego?"

"Yes. My hero growing up was WWII hero Audie Murphy. In WWI, Sergeant York killed 18 Germans. In WWII, Audie Murphy killed 240. And he was my hero growing up. Then my heroes became Alan Ladd, and Clark Gables, and those who wore the white hat, who were doing what I'm trying to do. *The Lone Ranger* (1949-57) didn't get any thanks for what he did. The last thing they always said in the show was, 'Who was that masked man? Why, didn't you know? That was the Lone Ranger. Ho, ho, ho Silver!' He didn't get praise either.

"*The Green Berets* (1968), starring John Wayne, is what I'm talking about. Make us heroes. Don't show us slaughtering the children and killing civilians.

"Did you see the movie *No Man's Land* (2001)? It's about Bosnia. It shows how bad war can be but in a different way. I think we need to have some heroes who have balls. They took everything we had. Tarzan is now Sheena. In every one of them, they switched what the man was into a woman. It's just wrong because the women aren't doing any of the real fighting. They're the ones who wanted equality, and they took ours away. We used to have the organization Big Brothers, which did a lot of good. Then they made it Big Brothers and Sisters."

20

Doug McHenry

Doug is a rare breed—a movie producer who is black.

"You're going to pay for this?" says McHenry when we meet at the Four Seasons in Beverly Hills.

I nod but my heart skips a beat.

"Otherwise we could go down the street to McDonalds. O.K., I've only got 40 minutes."

Doug speaks and gestures in an extravagant way. His words pour out and my mind races to catch up with his idiom.

McHenry graduated from Stanford with an Economics degree in 1973, and from Harvard with an MBA/JD in 1977. He then passed the California Bar and went to work for producer Peter Guber's Casablanca Records as head of business affairs. Doug's next boss was film head David Putnam (*Chariots of Fire*, 1981).

"You're the first black movie producer I've met."

"A lot of the [black] guys I know who went to Harvard are with the big corporations. They're either the affirmative action officer or in finance. Everyone who was smart did finance. I wanted to work for a Washington law firm but the people lie so much there."

"They lie just as much in Hollywood."

"It's different. Politicians say that I am going to make my life better with health care to create a more humane society. Hollywood says this is the fucking product, you either buy it or not. I don't promise to make you healthy. I don't promise you Social Security. I don't promise to defend the country or defend the schools."

"So the movie maker has no moral responsibilities?"

"Not true. We have a moral responsibility to not bore the client. I've made 13 movies. I've never lost money because I never bore the client. My movies have cost up to eight million dollars and all of them except one have done at least $20 million domestic box office. And we sell a shit load of records.

"Working for Peter Guber was exciting. I didn't want to be stuck away in some affirmative action office. Casablanca was a small lean company. They didn't give a shit what color you were. There were four owners, one of whom was black. The music business is probably the most integrated business next to the beer commercial."

I see white people giving us the eye when McHenry swears loudly.

The Vietnamese waitress comes over. I order the black bean soup for $7:50.

Doug: "I will take the soup as well and the Cobb salad. You've got something in it like avocado. Now, where is it on the menu? Could you find it for me."

The waitress points it out on the menu.

"Please, could I have some escarole in there in addition to the green romaine? No red romaine. Butter lettuce. No anchovies and put some chicken in it. And no papaya and no avocado. If you send me something that is a mistake, I will eat it anyway. Thank you."

McHenry was fired in 1984. "I'd never been fired in my life. And I don't like the feeling. I'm good at what I do. Fuck that. I will never work for anyone again. So I bit the bullet.

"Mom and dad want you to have some security. When you choose to do what you and I do, you've got to jump off and glide. It's scary. I was running out of money. I was three months behind on my rent. I'm rolling pennies for four days to get $180.

"My partner for 17 years, George Jackson, died last year of a stroke. We were trying to sell a picture of hip hop rap. We got in our raggedy car in 1984 and we go down to the Long Beach Arena. It is rowdy with radical white kids, Latino kids and all kinds of black people. There was electricity and excitement that something unbelievable would happen. It was the first rap fest. Run DMC, the Fat Boys, Houdini. We said, 'We're making a movie of this shit.' We met [promoter] Russell Simmons, Rick Reuben, Jive Records. We hang with them. And we write up a proposal and go around the studios.

"If you go to a movie executive's office, and you look around, there's no fucking stereo. There's no CD player. If you ask him what the number one song in the country is, he doesn't know. Mark Canton was the only guy with a fucking stereo in his office.

"If you ask a movie exec what is the number one TV show, they don't know. They don't understand that it is all the same thing. When a creative idea starts as a Broadway play, as a magazine article, as a book, as a screenplay or this, you want to run this creative idea through all the proper distribution channels. Mark Canton knows about rap. We were the first people to put rappers in a movie.

"I fly to New York to meet with Parkway Records and they take us to meet Morris Levy. I didn't know who he was but he's this notorious record underworld giant. Ultimately, all these record things are owned by this guy Morris Levy who started [the club] Birdland with his brother. Levy's brother was assassinated. Levy went to jail and shit. [He died in 1989 after being sentenced for federal racketeering and extortion.] I had no idea that my life was on the line with some mobster."

Doug, a Congregationalist Christian, says grace before eating.

"Tell me about *New Jack City* (1991)."

"We've always wanted to do a gangster movie. We loved *The Conformist* (1970), *Third Man* (1949), the Dutch angles and shit, the fucking monochromatic colors. *New Jack City* is about a dark gangster who is not dumb. The lead character Nino Brown (played by Wesley Snipes) is dark, handsome. A motherfucker on screen.

"This shit called crack was going around. Before that, it was heroin and cocaine. There was a guy from my home town of Oakland who was on the cover of California magazine. They called him the MBA gangster. He studied all the loopholes in the [drug] law. For example, you can't get busted for selling drugs unless there's a hand-to-hand transfer. So he took over these projects and you'd go up to one end of the project and place your order. Then you'd all the way round to pick it up. So there was no hand-to-hand transfer. So we thought of a [character in the movie]. Then the third guy came from a story in Washington D.C., where this 21-year old guy was busted and found with $10 million cash in show boxes.

"We had a hip-hop cop. There'd never been a hip-hip cop. The hip-hop sensibility is identified with the street and the bad guys but we made him a good guy. The bad guy was cool. He had the suits and shit, the bodyguards, the champagne. The man with the baggy pants and shit like that, the cop, is Ice T.

"A hip-hop cop sounds like a contradiction in terms but it sure did fucking work. You can be cool and be a good guy. You can be of the hip-hop generation with a hip-hop consciousness that focuses on the real bad guys and leaves the guy with two rocks [of cocaine] alone.

"When I produce a movie, I produce the music at the same time. The idea of rap being a bridge between R&B choruses was mine. I flew in Queen Latifa and in ten minutes she does a rap bridge for *Money, Money, Money*. And R&B has never been the same. The picture grossed over $50 million domestic and sold over four million records and a shit load of cassettes.

"It was time that Warner Brothers was having all kinds of failures. We were their first hit that year. We got a ring. It was Bob Daley and Terry Semel, who ran WB at the time, and the president of production. They bring us in and serve us champagne and say that we have a deal there for the next four years. And then we didn't make one other fucking picture for them."

"Have you used cocaine?"

"No comment. I've seen others do it. I've seen it on TV."

"How well do you know the hood?"

"I'm comfortable under the freeway underpass. That hood could be Nebraska. I love people. You could put me in the middle of Afghanistan and I'm going to get along. I love people. I'm sincere with them and I treat them with respect. When I'm in the hood, I don't speak [black urban lingo]. I speak the way I'm speaking to you. I don't talk down to people. People know that. Fuck that.

"I've made four movies this past year, about 40 percent of the [black] market-place.

"When you walk into a movie theater, you say, make me feel something. Make me laugh, make me cry. People have laughed and cried at stuff I've been involved in that wouldn't let me move next door and marry their daughters. For the average family that goes to my films, they've got to wait for the 15th and the 1st [for their welfare checks]. Many families can't afford a baby sitter for my movies. When I go to a theater, there are crazy characters in the aisles and screaming babies. And I don't play 'em cheap. My shit looks good.

"I shoot Wesley Snipes better than any director he's ever been with. They blotch him. They put blue light on him instead of amber. When you see Vanessa Williams in the thing I just did [*Keep the Faith, Baby*, 2002], she looks more incredible than in the Arnold Schwarzenegger movie. Because they don't give a fuck and they don't know how to shoot 'em [blacks]. Blue light looks good on you and shitty on him. He should be in amber and golds and lucentas. But he's too busy shooting Sean Connery to know what to do with Wesley.

"I always try to have a point and I always try to make them look real good. And I'm proud that every picture I've produced looks stunning compared to how much it costs. That's out of a desire to give that person who can't afford that baby sitter to give them their fucking money's worth. That's my job. Not to tell them how to think. Not to promulgate or be pedantic. But make them feel something."

"What do your movies say about you?"

"The movie that's closest to me is *Jason's Lyric* (1994). I decided that I was going to direct something. I read a script that had potential. I saw my background in it. I said, I have the power to do it. I don't give a shit. I'm directing this movie. I got the money and I did it. It was *Romeo and Juliet* in the ghetto. It had a lot of different themes in it. The message to me was two things. Sometimes to be a hero, you have to walk away. The hero doesn't always kick the bad guy's ass. Sometimes you have to destroy the person, and sometimes you walk away. If you truly love someone unconditionally, you have to let that person go, because that person's destiny may not be intertwined with yours."

Doug tears up. "I'm an emotional guy. I just got done speaking with my dead partner's [George Jackson] mother who's having a hard time. I'm going to see her in Harlem on Monday. I'm having a premiere for my new film, *Keep The Faith, Baby* [true story of politician Adam Clayton Powell Jr.]. It stars another new actor, Harry Lennix.

"George Jackson and I shot a scene from *New Jack City* at the Adam Clayton Powell government building, the tallest building in Harlem, on 125th Street. We turned each to other and said, we're going to make a movie about this man."

Doug cries. "George didn't have to die. He was 43 years old. He was in good health but he was president of Motown Records. He was in a bad domestic situation. His ex is suing George's mother for back taxes. George's mother has not seen his baby in two years because she won't let her."

"How did you handle the critical reaction to *Jason's Lyric*?"

"There are two communities. Reviewers don't understand black movies. They don't understand the vernacular and they don't understand the situation the actors are portraying. I don't know how anybody could not like the movie.

"Take *Kingdom Come* (2001) with Whoopi Goldberg and Loretta Divine. Do you think the Academy Awards people will pay any attention to these fine performances? If my name was Woody Allen, and I didn't have to raise a fucking dime, and could make anything I want because he's got a tribe of people that support his ass, I would get Academy award nominations.

"African-Americans are a minority in this industry. Being black has no biological significance at all. We're not a different species. Racism is in the interest of the majority or we wouldn't have it.

"If I want to sell cars to Britain, I better put the steering wheel on the right side of the car. If we want to tour these [black] films in Europe, we must have black film festivals. We should lead with the music. Give it four years, and you will see a sizeable increase in the foreign market for these films."

"What's it like being a non-Jew in a predominantly Jewish industry?"

"I don't knock them. They founded this business. They took off with Edison's invention. What I find shameless is that these agents, who represent 40 percent black talent—such as actors, singers, dancers, athletes—are so damn liberal, and are all white. There are no black agents.

"To be a producer, it helps to have grown up in the business. It's difficult to break in. If I was white and 6' tall and Methodist, it would be tough. It's tough for the Jewish guy who doesn't have Jewish relatives in the business. The industry is paternalistic and nepotistic.

"I don't believe that Jewish people are prejudiced against anybody else. A lot of people are jealous of Jewish people. Rather than hate people, I'd rather imitate success. If I wanted to be a great long distance runner, I'd imitate what the great runners do.

"When I was a partner in a management agency, people would say to my white partner, why are you involved with that black guy? To the client, the white guy's ice is colder. If we both have an ice machine, the white guy's ice must be colder. That's why this whole affirmative action thing is so fucking ridiculous. I went to Stanford and Harvard. Those schools make no compunction that there are a certain amount of spots made for legacies. If my daughter wants to go to Stanford, and has 100 points less on the SAT than your daughter, my daughter's ass is getting in. I give money and I went there. Nobody talks about them getting in. Why is it a better social policy to discriminate on the basis of private donations than to train some doctors who actually go to the black community and the fucking Indian reservations?

"That's bullshit. Because people who talk about open competition, don't really want to compete. They want to keep it for them.

"The test of morality is what a person will do to his worst enemy. To the exact same extent you promise freedom to your enemy, is the exact same extent I will trust your ass in a leadership position."

"Do you think it was truly racism that caused *Jason's Lyric* to get an initial NC17 from the ratings board?"

"I don't know. Bruce Willis get to take a shower and show a dick. There are two kinds of racism. Racism that we all suffer from. Just like men. We all suffer from chauvinism just like women. Were you born wanting to sleep with women naked with high heeled shoes on? Where does this come from? If you like women. I don't care whether you do or not. If you have a wet dream about making love to a woman with a pair of stilettos on, that's not necessarily natural. This is chauvinism because every centerfold has a naked woman with shoes. That men have trouble with intimacy is all chauvinism. Therefore, a white censorship board [can't win]. If they allow the poster, then the black churches say, 'If it was two white people they would never have allowed it. They think that blacks are animals. Racism, racism.' If they don't allow the poster, it's racism. Two naked white people, we'll leave it alone, but two naked black people, that's just too strong. It will cause people to riot."

Doug picks up the check.

21

Mark Lester

January 31, 2002

Mark Lester was born November 26, 1946. "I segued into the business by working for a documentary film company (American Documentary Films) in San Francisco in 1970 that was making political films. I had been a campaign manager and running the Young Democrats of California for four years. I had a degree in Political Science from Cal State Northridge.

"I did a little picture called *Cops of the World* about American involvement in Vietnam. The company was operated as a commune with everybody voting on which pictures to make. I was a more independent type person. I was in charge of raising the money. I thought, hey, if I can raise the money, that means I finance a movie. So why do I need to be voting with all these people when I'm raising the money?

"A professor of anthropology at U.C. Berkeley got me interested in the Mayan Indians in Mexico. So I went down there and lived with them for three months and made a documentary, *Twilight of the Mayans*, which won Best Documentary at the Venice Film Festival. Twenty five years later, these Indians got weapons and started fighting the Mexican government.

"Tricia Nixon was getting married in 1971. I met this troupe called The Cockettes, San Francisco drag queens. I decided to spoof the Nixon Whitehouse with a film called *Tricia's Wedding*. It was a sensation, the *Rocky Horror Picture Show* of its time. It ran across the street from the Whitehouse.

"John Dean told the story on Johnny Carson how a burglar was ordered to break into the lab so a print could be screened in the White House basement, that bunker where all the guys would hide, just like it was a stag film. I think it's amazing that a $3000 underground comedy could so distract the top level of our government. Nixon was outraged by these drag queens playing all these Nixon Whitehouse people. They ran a clip on the Johnny Carson Show.

"I four-walled the theaters and showed the movie and took in all the revenue and got enough money to make another movie. I met some investors in Oakland who wanted to know what I was doing next. I was with my girlfriend rafting on a river at Sacramento and I met some auto daredevils called 'The Circus of Death' led by Dusty Russell. They were Hells Angel types who traveled from town to town and put on these death defying shows. One guy blew himself up with dynamite and other guys crashed head on into each other. They don't even have these kind of shows anymore because cars aren't made to crash like that.

"So I wrote my first feature length movie called *Steel Arena* (1972). I raised the money and did everything. *Rolling Stone* called it the most original movie of the year. I put political layers underneath it all. I thought it was symbolic of the country at the time.

"*Truck Stop Women* (1974) was a comedy action movie with women hijacking trucks in the desert. It became a cult hit. *Rolling Stone* loved it.

"Two years later, Nixon was in the Watergate fiasco and I decided it was time to do a sequel. I decided to do a spoof of the Whitehouse called *Whitehouse Madness* (1975). That picture didn't do well because it came out the night he resigned. I shot the movie in ten days. I built the Whitehouse on a soundstage. Nixon gets exorcised by Billy Graham and he's walking naked through the Whitehouse, which turned out to be true. He was talking to pictures on the wall while walking nude through the Whitehouse. The picture failed because nobody wanted to hear about Nixon after he resigned. I thought there was going to be a big trial.

"Years later, when Phil Gramm was running for president, it turned out he was an investor in the movie. I was in Doonesbury [cartoon strip] for a week. Phil Gramm was directing me behind the scenes.

"George Caton was a friend of mine who was raising money for my different movies. The reality is Phil Gramm didn't know what we were really doing. Originally he was going to invest in *Beauty Queens*.

"The movie business at the time was wide-open. There were 5000 drive-ins around the country. We took it city by city. I distributed it myself. Today if you make a video like that, it's strictly a direct to video movie. In the '70s, they were theatrical pictures.

"I made a movie *Bobby Jo and the Outlaw* (1976) starring Lynda Carter, who became *Wonder Woman* (1976-79). That was released theatrically all over and the picture grossed $5 million. That's like $40 million today. It was the trilogy of sorts and my biggest success yet.

"*Stunts* (1977) was the first movie where someone hired me as a director. It was New Line Cinema's first movie. It turned out sensationally. When New Line Cinema went public, they used the movie as an example because they netted a $2 million profit on the sale to NBC.

"*Roller Boogie* (1979) was the last movie of the 1970s. It was released on the last day of 1979. Thank God for *Heaven's Gate*. It was pulled from the theaters by United Artists, and *Roller Boogie* was put in its place. Linda Blair was hot at the time.

"Linda was having some personal problems and she was not working at the studios. That's the good thing about independents. We don't have to worry about that stuff.

"*Gold of the Amazon Women* (1979) is the only movie I made directly for TV. I called it *Spaghetti Jungle*. Alfredo Leone, of Italian horror film fame, was the producer. He wanted to shoot it in Trinidad because he served in the Navy there during the war. We shot in the middle of a rain forest. It rained every day which made things difficult. Anita Enkberg made her semi-comeback.

"It was a strange experience. I'm sure it is the only film to be shot in Trinidad. We built big villages and sets on these abandoned bunkers where the planes used to be hidden from the Nazis. We had to bring everything in. Customs was a nightmare.

"Bo Svenson was a crazy actor. He ended up attacking some local girl. I saw it happened. He stands about 6'8" and he threw a chair at this tiny girl. He got arrested. He had to escape from the island. The police surrounded the set and allowed him to shoot, then on the last day, they took him away.

"It's funny to see how far censorship has come. Now you have *Baywatch* (1989-2001) where they're wearing bikinis on TV. The NBC censors came down to Trinidad and ruled that the girl's loincloths were an inch too high. They came just below their knees. They made us close down and sew another inch on every dress."

"I think your best film is *The Class of 1984* (1982)."

"I think it is. It's the one I love the most. I'm putting together now a DVD for its 25th anniversary release. I thought of the idea. I went back to my high school in the San Fernando Valley and researched it. At the time, there was little violence in high schools but it was coming. The warning at the beginning of the film says that if society doesn't do anything about this issue, this problem will spread all across the country. Now with Columbine, etc, it turns out to be true. At the time, people were laughing at me. How could they be checking all the kids for guns before they come into school?

"My idea was to update *Blackboard Jungle* (1955) which I liked as a teenager. I spent a year with the script and I did everything exactly right and it became a huge success. It was a classic film and also about a political issue. I used my original interest in politics and put it into a commercial context. The film became controversial. I was on the *CBS Morning News*. *Time* magazine reviewed it. *Newsweek* gave it two pages.

"Nobody wanted to distribute the movie. I screened the film at every studio. I had a deal at Columbia Pictures and at the last minute they said, 'Frank Price has vetoed it. It's too controversial.' It was a big hit at the Cannes Film Festival. Then I got to America and they said it was too vile and too controversial and not mainstream enough.

"Paramount's Frank Mancuso said he'd take it if I brought the film to his neighborhood in New Jersey and the people like it. I said O.K, if it plays with *Death Wish* (1974). So I flew with a print to the New Jersey. When I got to the theater, they screened it with *Porky's* (1982). They had a special advertisement that all 12-year old boys get in free to *Porky's*. So the theater was filled with 12-year old boys and when they saw *Class of 1984*, they were outraged. They came into the lobby and threw things at Frank Mancuso.

"Warner Brothers said they would take it if I could prove that a theater will take it. So I started calling theater chains. I got a hold of Sal Hasinine, who was president of United Artists theaters. I screened it for him at his home on Long Island. He said it was great, 'I will play it in all my theaters.' He said I didn't need Warner Brothers. 'I'll give you a half million dollar advance. I've got theaters all over the country.'

"I said, 'You've got to open it in the summer time.' He said, 'We're playing *Best Little Whorehouse in Texas* (1982).' I said, 'Isn't that a Warner Brothers film?' He said yes, and it's doing terrible. I said pull it and replace it with my film. My film became the number one picture in New York."

"What should society do to prevent school shootings?"

"Zero tolerance is a good idea. If a student does one thing, they're out. I always tell my kids to be aware of kids in the class who are left out of things. Be nice to them. It seems that the people who shoot are always these loners who are cast aside by the other kids and not integrated into the school."

John has an 18-year old girl, a 9-year old boy and a 6-year old boy. He's been married ten years.

"I can show my kids some of my films—*Roller Boogie*, and *Stunts*, and the ones they're not interested in. Kids want to see R-rated films. It's a great thing to my 9-year old to see R-rated films like *Black Hawk Down*. These pictures have the F-word through all these movies. I think, they hear these words all through school. So you're not going to take them to a good movie because they say fuck? It seems silly to object to showing kids a film based on language only."

"How do you decide what R-rated films to take your kids to?"

"If it is a good movie, I don't care what the rating is. I keep them away from sexual content. *Black Hawk Down* is a good movie, about an important subject…that happened. So if a 9-year old is able to comprehend, which he was, why not take him?

"I don't like censorship. I don't like ratings boards. I did this picture *Extreme Justice* (1993) and it got an X-rating. There's no sex in it. They rated it X because of the political content. It was about the L.A. Police Department's SIS secret squad. It was based on a true story, all these newspaper stories, a *60 Minutes* piece and there's a book on it now. The L.A. riots were happening as we were shooting. The producer claims that the police were following me.

"It was supposed to be an anti-police movie but I made it so people could take it either way. I like the SIS. I like what they did, following these criminals and shooting them down when they leave the bank. The only problem was, as portrayed in the movie, that they would watch the crime take place and arrest them after. They put innocent people in jeopardy while they waited to knock them off.

"After it was rated X, I said that's outrageous. I flew to New York and fought the ratings board. They changed the rating to an R without making any cuts. *The Night of the Running Man* (1994) was rated X. I had to trim sex scenes to get an R.

"People immediately think that X is hardcore. It was just a simulated lovemaking scene. The actors aren't even nude. They're wearing G-strings. It just looks like they're having sex. Now they're saying, oh, it's cumulative, when I ask what specific scenes they object to.

"It's all turned around now. The Democrats are now for censorship and the Republicans are against it.

"*Firestarter* [a 1984 movie based on the Stephen King novel] was the first book that I had adapted. I made it for Dino DeLaurentiis. I found this place (an old plantation) to shoot in Wilmington, North Carolina. Nobody had ever made a film there before.

"Dino was originally going to do it as a union film but he didn't have the budget. John Carpenter was originally going to direct but the budget got to $18 million. So Dino asked, can anybody make it for $10 million? I raised my hand.

"We followed the book exactly. Stephen King was on the set and loved the whole project. But he hates every movie when it's finished.

"*Commando* (1985) starring Arnold Schwarzenegger was my most commercial movie, made for $12 million for a big studio. It was wildly successful and set Schwarzenegger off on his routine of one-liners and comedy bits in different movies like *The Terminator* (1984).

"I've always tried to put something working class in my films. It comes from my political background. At the time, the CIA were accused of training contras to go down to Nicaragua. I put different news items in the film. I remember Roger Corman once saying that even in a movie like *Candy Striper Nurses* (1974), they're trying to form a union. I think the same way. You put these different elements in the film and they become stronger pictures because they have something to say."

"Where does your political bent come from?"

"My parents were very left-wing. I grew up in Ohio and moved to Los Angeles in my teens. My dad was a court reporter. We used to go around Los Angeles and if there was even a right-wing John Birch Society meeting, we'd go.

"Once you establish yourself as a producer-director, it's hard to get hired because producers tend not to be as interested if you are also a producer.

"I think of myself as more of a thriller director. I'm buying books now. I have a book agent. I buy books once they've been passed on by the studios. I'm buying suspense thrillers because with action movies, you're competing with major studios and all these incredible action sequences that can be done when you spend $50 million on a movie. With a suspense thriller, like *In The Bedroom* or *Memento* (2000), you can do something interesting on a low budget because it relies more on the characters and suspense you can build.

"*Sacrifice* (2000 TV movie) was based on a book by Mitchell Smith about the killer at an abortion clinic."

"Thrillers are about the most profitable genre for independent films."

"Yes but you can never have a big hit."

"What's your favorite part of your job?"

"I like everything. I like principle photography. I like staging scenes. Then it's exciting to see what you've done. It's like painting. I prefer shooting on location than in L.A. I remember spending three weeks traveling through the Mid-West to find the perfect 1930s town to use for a movie. I came across Guthrie, Oklahoma. It was exciting to tear down the old storefronts and replace them with 1930s storefronts. You have control of the whole town. You're creating the cars and the characters within this setting.

"I even like sales. People say, 'You must have a right brain and a left brain. How do you go from selling a movie, to raising the money, to directing?' There is a big separation because with selling, you're dealing with straight business. Even there, you're pitching a story to people and you're learning what they might be interested in buying.

"We have our own foreign sales company here. There are few directors (such as Menahem Golan, Steven Spielberg) who have their own foreign sales company. I ask, what does my sales company need to sell? Now I'm looking for art-ploitation—an art film with exploitation elements. It's really risky to make an art film. We see a hundred of these films every day that never get distributed. If one pops out, it's incredible."

"Which of your films has been the biggest risk?"

Mark sits and thinks. "None of them are a risk. None of them can lose their investment. We haven't taken risks here but I want to. The risk these days is in staying in business. I made three films last year and I financed them all myself. The budgets are over $2 million. The average is $5 million. Up to $10 million."

"Tell me about working with the late Brandon Lee in *Showdown in Little Tokyo* (1991)."

"This was his first [American] movie. He'd done a couple of pictures in Hong Kong. I wanted a little sidekick to Dolph Lundgren. Brandon was so good in the movie that when Warner Brothers saw him in the movie, they said we've got to cut this into a Brandon Lee movie."

"Other notable actors?"

"Meg Ryan had done one scene in *Top Gun* (1986). I read her for *Armed and Dangerous* (1986) and I hired her immediately. Everybody knew she was going to be a star. The casting people came in and said, 'You've got to use her.' [One of] Michael J. Fox's first movie[s] was *Class of 1984*. He came in for a reading and the minute I saw him, I said, 'This guy's a star.' Sometimes you can tell right away and other times I go over our casting list and say, 'Ohmigod, I saw Matt Damon? He came in for that?' He was 18. 'Ben Affleck? How come we couldn't catch him?' You can't always tell."

"What do you think your body of work says about you?"

Mark thinks for 30 seconds. "I've thought a lot about that. I look back through all these pictures and other people see them and go, 'The minute one of your movies comes on TV, I know it's you. Even if I've missed the credits. You have a certain style.' What is that? I've always tried to put some kind of statement in all these movies. They have political overtones. I'm a fast-paced person. My movies move quickly. I would hope that I have some humanity to them but there's also a dark side. I must have a dark side because my pictures have a dark side. There aren't too many comedies. I have many hard-edged thrillers. I mainly dress in black. People meet me and go, 'You seem so soft spoken and nice, then you see the movie.' I've had an angry side over the years that I've portrayed on the screen. Now I've mellowed.

"I'm no longer the young angry guy making *The Class of 1984*. Upset by some issue, and now I'm going to make a movie about a bad experience in high school. Or, a guy who didn't like authority growing up so now I'm going to make a movie like *Extreme Justice*, which attacks authority. It is true that you're kind of like your movies if you make them and you choose this kind of material. Obviously you're projecting out.

"Growing up, I was always an outsider. I was raised outside the system. Through the McCarthy era, my father was always afraid that he'd lose his security clearance. I had a lot of fears growing up. I was always an outsider at school. So the pictures all have an outsider. I'm giving you good information. I was going to write this in my own book. I suppose that's why I'm an independent film company and go outside the system. We're distributing ourselves. I've been an outlaw."

"What clique were you in in high school?"

"I was never in a clique because I was in drama class. Now my son loves drama and all the girls love drama. All the boys want to be in drama. When I was taking drama in high school, that was a gay thing to do. You were a nerdy gay kid in high school if you were in drama. Even the girls in drama didn't like you. The sports guys got all the girls. When I sat at lunch, they came in and stole my lunch."

22

Marian Brayton, Anne Carlucci

February 5, 2002

I chat with the two spirited TV movie producers in their 50s at Hearst Entertainment.

Anne speaks with a gravelly voice, the result of years of smoking. She's just quit cigarettes and sucks on lollipops. She's more talkative and flamboyant than Marian.

"I almost got the chance to shoot a movie in Australia last year," she begins. "It's a good thing I didn't do it because it will never air. It's about a serial killer in a 747—not a popular type of movie anymore."

"I'm writing a book on producers."

"Are you finding we're all interchangeable?" asks Marian.

"Maybe, but producers take very different approaches to their work. I've interviewed many male movie producers who take great pride in not putting messages or morals into their films while other producers, particularly TV movie producers, take great pride in putting messages into their movies."

"We love to send messages," says Marian. The first movie we did together [*The Littlest Victims*, 1989] was about a doctor who discovered AIDS in children."

"I can't tell you how unpopular the subject matter was in 1983," says Anne.

"The advertising community did not look on this favorably."

"AIDS wasn't even a word yet," says Anne. "It was called GRIDS—Gay Related Immune Deficiency Syndrome. It's the story of Dr. Jim Oleski from Newark, New Jersey, who was a pediatric immunologist. He went into pediatrics because he wanted to be in the life business, and the clean end of medicine, only to discover that his children were dying. He started keeping records and running tests and he soon discovered the kids were getting AIDS from their birth mothers. This little doctor had to take on the AMA and the US government. Nobody wanted to hear this story.

"Marian was a senior Vice-President of CBS Dramatic Specials. This was where we brought all the projects nobody would buy because they were about something. Marian wanted the project because it was a story of an ordinary person who finds himself in extraordinary circumstances. Marian fought like crazy to get the movie made.

"I got a call one day saying the movie is dead. I went into such a deep depression. I'd just had a wisdom tooth pulled. My dentist had said to me, 'Whatever you do, don't get yourself all worked up because you need the blood to clot. Don't get your adrenaline going.' So the minute she said the movie was dead, my mouth started to bleed. Then 15 minutes later she called to say we had a reprieve.

"The movie airs. In Paris is Countess Albina DuBoisrouvray from Belgium. Her 23-year old son had died that year. He was a search-and-rescue helicopter pilot. His helicopter went down on a mission and he was killed. She was looking for a children's charity to endow in his name.

"Countess DuBoisrouvray is so moved by the film that she sets up an appointment with Dr. Oleski. Now Jim Oleski is like Captain Kangaroo in a lab coat. He's not good with business. He practiced in Newark, New Jersey, in the ghetto. The Countess meets with him and says that she'd like to donate to his clinic. He's delighted but he has no idea to what extent. She says, 'Tell me what you need?' He says, 'There's a big AIDS conference and I can't afford to go. It would cost about $15,000.' She says, 'Well, that's not a problem. I'm talking about a wish list, if you could have anything you wanted for your work.' He was clueless. She ended up giving him $5 million to open his own clinic and help these children. She sold the family jewels because she decided that there was so much work to be done. Now there's a charity and building endowed in her son's name. And there are all these children whose lives have been saved."

"We did *Unforgivable* (1996)," says Marian, "about a batterer (played by John Ritter) who redeems himself, gets in touch with his behavior, and started a program to help batterers. And we got 5000 phone calls in 48 hours. We shut down the CBS switchboard with the number of calls."

"These calls are impulse calls," says Anne. "If you're beating your wife, and you see John Ritter, and you see yourself in John Ritter's behavior, and you want to change but you don't know how to do it, well, this guy did it. At the end of the movie, there's an 800 number, you might reach for the phone and dial. If you are not put in touch immediately with someone who's going to take control of you and give you the help you need. The first question they asked was what city did you live in. Then they patched you through immediately to a domestic violence program in your neighborhood. That's the power of television. A movie that hauls you emotionally and informs you and entertains you with John Ritter. That was casting against type."

"We developed *The Burning Bed*, the 1984 breakthrough movie starring Farrah Fawcett."

"I started developing that movie in 1978," says Anne. "I was working for Norman Lear. I bought the book. I sold it to CBS but when we submitted the script, there was no way CBS was going to do it. The white boys at the network at that time were horrified by it. It was not for the Tiffany network. Farrah Fawcett had just come out of *Charlie's Angels* (1976) and had a deal with NBC. So we put Farrah in the movie and took it to NBC. It was passed on because one of the executives said, 'I don't really believe that men do these kind of things.' Not an evolved period. The project languished. Farrah held on to it. And five years later it got made."

"I did a movie [*Rape and Marriage*, 1980] about the first case a woman sued her husband on trial for rape. Another time I developed a movie about a woman who tried desperately to get police protection because her husband was threatening her. The police were literally standing outside on the lawn while he beat her to a pulp and injured her permanently. The more we can bring attention to these things by trying to show ways to break these patterns, it helps.

"I remember when I was at CBS, I'd just read a book about a strange new illness, Alzheimer's. A script came across my desk on it and the movie *Do You Remember Love?* (1985) won numerous awards."

Marian and Anne agree that women have long been the majority of viewers of television movies. Male driven movies appear largely on USA, UPN, TNT, and TBS. "But if they changed that to female-driven material," says Anne, "they'd get a bigger audience because women are the movie watchers on television. Of all the businesses, television is most open to women."

"There's been an extraordinary growth of women in power positions in the industry," says Marian. "When I first went to CBS, I was one of the first women in the MOW [Movie of the Week] field. Guys would come in and they had never had to relate to women who had the perception of power. I was one of the first women Vice-Presidents at CBS. Now we have women heading up everything."

"How would TV movies be different if men were still in positions of power like 1975?"

"They wouldn't be," says Marian. "They would still have to be driven by the numbers and it is a fact that women watch more. I don't think it matters if women produce these movies or men."

"Women speak a special language and often it is not even necessary to finish the thought," says Anne. "Women get it. And men never get it the way a woman gets it unless it is Edward Albee (playwright who wrote *Who's Afraid of Virginia Wolf?*) who totally gets it.

"The film that I had the most fun making was *The Soul Collector* (1999) and *Out of Sync* (2000). It was so much fun to make a movie like *Out of Sync* that had no bearing on reality and didn't have a message in it except follow your dream. It had a lot of music. The cast jelled and liked each other. We enjoyed making it and we went into a major depression when it was over.

"You need enormous stamina to make a movie. For certain executive producers, it is more a question of deal-making rather than movie-making. That's why Marian and I are not rich. We're more about film-making than money-making. That means that I am on set from crew-call to crew-wrap.

"Marian and I spend months and years developing a movie. I will be fucked if I let a director throw me off my movie. TV movies are producer-driven, not director-driven. I lay it right out. When we're interested in a director, he comes in and we have a meeting. I say it, because I'm the one who's going to be on the street corner with him at 2 a.m.. I say, 'Look, I'm there. I won't get in your way but it's my vision. If you're not there to make the same movie that I'm going to make, we're going to have problems. Because at the end of the day, I'm going to win that war. It's my movie. I'm not going to let anyone cut me off from the process.'

"When we go into the editing room, I'm in the editing room with the director. I'm in the mix. I'm in the looping. I'm in everything. I have never worked with a director who resented me. They're not accustomed to being supported that way. It's a producer's job to support the director and protect their stars. If they see you're not just a role-player, that you're not just dropping in between shopping trips, or dropping by for lunch to schmooze your star, but that you work and you care. They respect you and they respond to you."

Marian writes scripts under a pseudonym she won't reveal. "Comedy, but nobody wants to make a comedy movie on television."

"The network executives don't believe that people are capable of laughing on their own, that they need a laugh track. I wouldn't do a slapstick comedy like *Space Balls* for television but I would do a romantic comedy like *Sleepless in Seattle*."

"Years ago when I was first at CBS, they said they didn't want to do any romantic comedies. I loved comedies. I found a script and convinced them to make a romantic comedy set in a bird watching camp. It was a big hit and for a while everybody wanted to make romantic comedies. I even made a black comedy about a [black] family who moved in to what they thought was a lovely rural area, and they were in the middle of a survivalist community."

"Putting ethics aside, how could you have made more money?" I ask.

"You could make backdoor deals with publishing companies and give them an undeclared cash bonus for every book they bring you that you get set up and made," says Anne. "Thievery always works."

"Like cooking the books?"

"Creative book-keeping, without exception, is the rule. The Hearst Corporation is a scrupulously honest company. There are certain things you can do to get a movie green lit. You've got a script close but you're out of steps. You don't want to go back to the writer who's doing a crappy job. But you have a friend who works for a series who will do you a favor if you slip him $10,000 in cash. We can't do that sort of thing here. If I were an independent producer, I could do that. Get in tight with network executives and give them expensive presents. 'Oh, let's shoot this movie in [exotic locale] and we'll all go there and you can bring your family.'"

"Have you been offered bribes?"

They say no.

"I got some awfully nice Christmas presents," says Marian. "When major feature players came in and tried to sell me something, and if I didn't like it, I didn't buy it. I should've bought everything, gotten to know them, and gone back into features. I was always too concerned with the story."

"Same thing with agents. You feather your nest. If you own your own movie, it's a cost of doing business. So you buy the hot agent who can help you a fabulous gift at Christmas. And he knows that if he gives you his star, there will be more of those little gifts coming down the road. It's only unethical if it is something the agent would be embarrassed to talk about it. That makes it unethical."

"Is there a movie that describes your job?"

"*The Player* (1992) and *Swimming with Sharks* (1994)," says Anne.

"*Network* (1976)," says Marian. "When I was invited to go to work for CBS, I had no idea what a woman wore. So I saw the movie a second time so I could look again at Faye Dunaway's outfit so that I could find something to wear."

"She was fashioned after a real network executive. The rumor has it, it was Lynn Bowlin, married to director Paul Wendkos. She was one of the pioneers and because she didn't just turn the other cheek and do what the man wanted her to, and behave the way women are supposed to behave, she was labeled a bitch, and a killer, and a barracuda and all those names that are applied to women who don't conform to the male world of doing business. Because men don't get emotional."

"Men usually say about attractive women who get ahead," I note, "that they slept their way to the top."

"It's the famous story of Sherry Lansing," says Anne. "How else could she do it? She was too pretty to have a functioning brain cell. It's absurd. Sherry Lansing started as a secretary, assistant, story editor. She happened to work for a bunch of guys over the years who were impressed by her. I met her socially a number of times. She was always a nice woman. Then I had a business meeting with her, and here is her specialness. When you have a meeting with Sherry Lansing, the door is closed and the phone is off and no one interrupts and you become the most important person in her life. That's an art."

"And she always returned phone calls," says Marian

"If there was a movie made about your life, what would the character arc be?"

"Oh God," says Anne. "My life story? Marian, dare I bore him to death?"

"Go ahead. I may have to go out."

"I'll just give you the character arc. Poor working class Italian Catholic girl [who] was the first to graduate high school in her family [and] is now a producer whose name is on national television through hard work."

"Your parents must be kvelling."

"My father died when I was six," says Anne. "My mother died this past November, still not understanding what it was that I did for a living. The moral of that story is never look to your family for approval."

"I grew up isolated on a farm in Nebraska. Went to New York to be a musical comedy star but ended up a book reviewer at *Kirkus Reviews*. I was happy but poor. I came to Los Angeles in 1972 to see if I could make some money."

"Is there anything in your movies that you can point to and say, 'Nobody else could've done that'?"

"I don't think so," says Marian. "Though we can usually do our movies better than anyone else."

"We each bring something different to it. I love every single movie that we've done. And I love every single actor we've worked with except one. And that actor doesn't know how I feel.

"When you get a green light on a movie, and you want Stockard Channing or Anjelica Houston or Susan Sarandon and you wind up with someone less stellar. You have a choice here. You can rant and rave, resent, get angry and spit. Or you can take that less stellar actress and embrace her because that is your actress. And if you don't love that actress, she's dead. You embrace what you've got. And you make the best movie you can.

"Actors bring the magic to the film. They breathe life into the character. Would you like to deal with rejection every day? And your product is yourself. That's hard to live with on a daily basis. So is it any wonder that actors can be on edge in new situations? It's new people they've never met before. Are they going to be safe? Are they going to be secure? They've been screwed over a thousand times on other movies they've done, why should this be any different? My experience is that you embrace that actor and that you create a safe and comfortable zone for that actor. And that actor will kill for you. You give the actor what the actor needs so that he can get out there every day and hang out on a limb for you."

"Where do you find your material?"

"Everywhere," says Anne. "Newspapers, magazines. The feature people get first crack at everything. They've got people in New York publishing. They've got their hands on the first 30 pages of a major writer's manuscript. You don't get near stuff like that with television because you can't spend that kind of money. There are so many wonderful books out there that if nobody ever wrote another book, you'd never run out of material.

"Today the emphasis [in TV movies] is on branding. Pre-sold titles. Events. Something immediately recognizable. You know what you're getting. You don't have to sell it."

"What makes you interested in a project?"

"Do I find it compelling?" says Anne. "*The Soul Collector* was a romance novel. I didn't show the novel to the network because they would not have bought it. Because they're not in the romance novel business. We sold them a story based on a synopsis. They loved it. Only after they bought it and they were making a deal, did I get a call from my network executive who says, 'My business affairs people are telling me we have to buy this book?' I say, 'Yeah, you have to buy this book. Didn't I tell you it is based on a book?' 'No.' 'Yeah, it's based on a book. But it's not necessary to read the book because we've changed so much in the book.'

"It was the second highest rated two-hour movie for CBS that year."

"What are the other blind spots you deal with?"

"First time writers," says Marian. "We had a perfect mini-series but the network wouldn't buy it because the writer wasn't well known enough. And now that writer is an enormous best selling author. The network has acquired several of the author's books, maybe the entire line. The quote from the network was,

'This is not the type of writer that we want to get into business with. It's not a Tiffany network kind of writer.' And this is not a porn writer."

"We can just tell it like it is," says Anne. "We're not political. That's what happens when you reach a certain age. You don't give a damn anymore. We work hard. We make terrific movies. Our movies have always done well. We've always pulled a good number. We're well respected.

"We had a deal come through our door 18 months ago. A script came in. Marian read it and gave it to me. I read it and said, 'That's a nice story. It's very soft. There's only one place for this. Let's option it.' These two baby producers, two young men who had never produced anything in their lives.. We put the paperwork through and business affairs start the deal-making process. And one afternoon I get a call from our business affairs people that so-and-so want $150,000 and executive producing credit. Well, Marian and I are executive producers. It takes a lot of years to work up to executive producers.

"I said no. Who are these guys? They can have the money but they can't have the executive producer title. I'll make them a co-executive producer. But if they need that executive producer title, then blow the deal. Those two writers would not take a co-executive producing credit and they wound up setting the script up on their own at the network where I knew they had a chance. I didn't care.

"Who are these people? What is that about? What are your credentials? Who are you to tell me that I can't have my credit because you're taking my credit? When you're not even going to be there to make the movie? I resent it and I didn't cave and I didn't make the deal and I lost a network movie. I still don't care. I would do that all over again. You have to draw a line somewhere.

"Nobody ever gave me anything for nothing. Today nobody wants to start their business life as anything less than a VP. I don't have to feed that. I have no patience for that."

"Everything is so segmented now," says Marian. "There's little innovation. If you come in with something fresh and never been done before, which they claim they want, then they get insecure. They don't want to make a decision. The project sits for weeks while all the enthusiasm which could carry it forward, dies. People don't make decisions quickly anymore. They don't rely on their gut instincts. Everyone's running so scared at the networks that it's slowed the process down and made it difficult to make interesting project."

"You'll lose a project because when they buy it, it's timely, and then it sits, and they'll pass on it. It was timely two years ago. You had it for two years, why didn't you just fucking order it? What gets both of us crazy is hearing, 'We're looking for different. We're looking for new.' Then they do the Bible again. We had an incredible pitch about this true spousal abuse story, *Exiled In Paradise* (2001), about a woman, a professional writer, who must run away with her kids from her insane abusive husband. She winds up on an island in some paradise, weaving together shells to make a living. For her ex-husband not to find her, she can't have a social security card, a driver's license, because all that stuff is on computer and you can be found.

"We came up with a different approach to tell the story. In the opening of the movie, the woman has a meeting with a bunch of security people. They have a file in front of them and they know why she's there. And they can't help her. They can't keep her safe from her crazy ex-husband."

"They gave her two choices: Either you disappear or you have him killed."

"At that moment, we go into *Sliding Doors* (1998). In one scenario, she's plotting his murder. In the other scenario, she's plotting her disappearance. At the end, it could be interactive. The network told me the material was too derivative. Then there's a shift at the network and people lose their jobs. So you bring the story back in. You hear that they now have several projects using the *Sliding Doors* approach. Now, I ask you, how many people are coming up with the *Sliding Doors* approach all of a sudden?

"So they don't buy your project, but they take your approach. That's the problem with a novel and innovative approach. I pitched that idea over lunch to another network executive. This was obviously the first time she'd heard of it. She loved it. So when it fell out at the first network, so I call and I hear they have a number of *Sliding Doors* projects. How could that be? They glommed on to the approach and applied it to a different story."

"Where do you do most of your pitches?"

"You don't do them over lunch," says Anne. "If you ever want to have lunch with a network executive, don't pitch them. You make an appointment, you go to their office, and you make a professional presentation. You do whatever you have to do to sell your project."

"I got a call from an agent at a prestigious agency. They wanted to come in and pitch this fabulous idea. It's unusual that these agents would do this. So they came in and the basic idea of the pitch was, *Adam and Eve—The True Story*. And they'd say things like, 'Don't be afraid of nudity, because we'll be careful how we shoot it. Through the leaves, the trees, etc.' Finally, I asked, 'How are you planning to deal with the notion of God in this picture?' They looked at each other and they didn't know how to answer the question. They said, 'Here's what we're not going to do. We're not going to have any arm come down and point a finger at them.' They finally left and my assistant and I were on the floor, cracking up.

"I had one pitch meeting where someone came and took off their leg. One morning, I had barely had my coffee, I had a guy, with gusto, tell me how he had murdered somebody. He was sitting there talking with the priest about how he'd been rehabilitated. From the gleam in his eye, I wasn't so sure."

"We had two guys come in to pitch a story," says Anne. "They came in with flow charts and color coordinated charts that covered the whole sofa. Each character was color coded. It was like an advertising meeting. We'd never had that before.

"Marian would get these pitches all the time at the network. They'd come in and pitch a book. 'You've got to move on it right away, Marian, because other people will lap it up. Marian, who diligently did her job, would go home on her weekend and plough through 1200 pages of this turgid book."

"I'd find some real problems in the book. I'd call up the producer and ask, 'How are you planning to address these problems?' They would go, 'We didn't read the book. We read the coverage.'"

"That's common," says Anne.

23

Stuart Benjamin

February 12, 2002

I walk down the corridor of Crusader Entertainment in Beverly Hills and poke my head in Stuart's doorway. A fierce man looks up at me from his computer.

"Stuart?"

"Yes, come in. Please give me a minute."

I sit on the white couch and read a book.

"How do you replace the same word multiple times?" asks Stuart.

I get up and walk over to his desk. "You go to Edit, then Replace, then write in the word as it appears in the original, and then write in the word as you want it spelled."

Five minutes later, we settle down to talk.

In his early 50s, Benjamin stands about 6'1 and weighs about 200 pounds. He wears jeans.

He's worked on such films as *An Officer and a Gentleman* (1982), *Against All Odds* (1984), *White Nights* (1985) and *La Bamba* (1987).

Stuart grew up in the San Fernando Valley. At North Hollywood High School, he played varsity basketball, served in student government and got A grades.

"I went to USC as an undergraduate with future director Taylor Hackford. He was my best friend. I went to law school [Harvard] while he went into the Peace Corp.

"The guy who wrote the book *The Paper Chase* was in my class at Harvard but nobody knew him because he was off writing the book. The John Houseman character was like my contracts professor Dr. Clark Byse. He was a tough crusty guy with a soft heart underneath. If you didn't come into class prepared, he kicked your ass.

"At a place like Harvard, you have to opt to do one of two things. You can lock yourself in your room for 20 hours a day for the next three years, do the

Harvard Law Review and graduate in the upper five percent of your class. Or you take the easy way out, which I did."

"Were you on the set of *Officer*? What do you remember?"

"Nothing that I can talk about. The stories are legion about Debra Winger and Richard Gere."

"But their conflicts don't come through on the screen."

"The chemistry was there on screen which was a testament to their acting skills, and to Taylor's skills as a director, and to the editing staff. Stuff happens on movies that is best left on the set. Debra Winger has been quoted heavily about Richard Gere."

"Your legal training has taught you discretion."

"I think that's part of it. I'm not a good interview because of that. Because I'm a private person, I tend to respect other people's privacy. Making movies is a funny business. It's great fun.

"We shot *Against All Odds* in Mexico, where there was a cave that we wanted to use for the steam bath thing. When we got down there, they wouldn't let us shoot the scene because of the nature of the scene. Too sexy to shoot near sacred ruins. So we came back here and built the cave.

"*La Bamba* is the highlight of my career. I grew up in the San Fernando Valley. Ritchie Valens was a local hero. Everybody who went to school with me remembered well the plane crash [which killed Valens, Buddy Holly and the Big Bopper]. I remember slow dancing in junior high school gyms to Ritchie Valens.

"In the 1970s, a friend of ours, Daniel Valdez, was the brother of Luis, who directed *La Bamba*. Danny traveled up and down the Central Valley [of California]. He always wanted to be Richie. In the 1970s, none of us had a clue how to get a movie made. Then in the early 1980s, Danny calls from Watsonville, in Northern California. He's become close to the Valens family. Would we be interested in the rights to do a movie? By then, Taylor and I had a deal at Columbia Pictures. We'd made *Against All Odds*.

"We started having meetings with the Valens family. A whole group of them, the mother, the brothers, the sisters, would drive down from Watsonville, near Santa Cruz, and meet with us. Ritchie was the light of their life. He was what he was in the movie—a sweet kid who grew up into this great America success story who died way before his time. So a legend grew up of Ritchie Valens. In the minds of the family, his legend grew over time. No matter how wonderful Ritchie really was, he was ten times more wonderful 20 years later. That memory of Ritchie Valens was precious to them and they were not easily going to give it up. They were concerned about creative control and how we were going to depict Richie.

"So one day I said to them, 'We know how important Ritchie is to you. And we wouldn't do anything to tarnish that image. Part of the process of making a movie is a bit of trust. You've got to trust us that we will do justice to Richie's image. So when you're comfortable that we will do that, call us.'

"Taylor and I wrote a check out of our pockets to the family to option the rights. This is one of those stories which I believe belongs in the book.

"We're about to go off to make *White Nights*. We're having lunch with the head of Columbia, Guy McElwaine. We asked for $50,000 to develop the story of Ritchie Valens. He said, 'Who?' 'Ritchie Valens. The guy who sang *La Bamba* who went down on the plane with Buddy Holly and the Big Bopper.' 'Oh? Who'd want to see a movie about that?'

"'Guy, we're going to off to make a really expensive movie. Give us $50,000 to develop a script.' He did. Luis Valdez writes the script. Many months later, we turn it into Columbia Pictures. At the screening room at Columbia, to show them a rough cut of *White Nights*, and in walk a couple of senior production executives. Taylor asked them what they thought of the Ritchie Valens script. One of them said, 'There's no fucking way this studio will ever make that movie.' It was clear that the reason they were never going to make the movie was not that they didn't like the script or the story. They just didn't think anyone would go see a movie about a Hispanic kid that nobody remembered.

"Coca Cola owned Columbia at the time. Guy said he'd go to Atlanta and fight for the Ritchie Valens story. We had budgeted the movie at $8.5 million. He comes back and says that Coca Cola doesn't want to make the movie for $8.5 million. We ask for a price and he comes back with $6.5. We agree to make the movie for that amount but you have to give us the money and let us go off and make the movie. We can't do a studio movie.

"They said, fine, we'll do that, but you have to put off your fees to guarantee completion. If the movie goes over budget, that cuts dollar for dollar into our fees. We said fine. I had $6.5 million deposited into our bank account in the name of R. Valensuela Productions, which I controlled, without a piece of paper between us and the studio. You couldn't get $2000 today without a blood oath. You can't even get a dinner reimbursed without going through expense reports.

"Probably the most amazing moment I've ever spent on a movie was a day in July at the airport in Pocoima. We shot the scene where the plane takes off in the snow with Richie, Buddy Holly, and the Big Bopper. It's the middle of the night. It's hot. We're blowing the Styrofoam snow everywhere. There's this little teeny

Cessna. Before we shoot, I decide to get in the plane. When you step on the wing of the plane, the plane tilts. The plane must weigh 150 pounds. You get in and it seems like the backseat of a VW.

"Richie's mom and a couple of his sisters break down in tears and plead with actor Lou Diamond Phillips, who plays Richie, to not get on that airplane. It's the end of the shoot and they've really bonded with Lou. He's become Richie's alter-ego. They don't want him to get on that airplane because they know what happened last time.

"The picture was finished shooting in July of 1986. We got a release date for August, 1987. We knew we had a [good] movie. We went to Kansas City to a whitebread audience and it tested well. Taylor and I controlled the music rights. Coca Cola held its marketing meeting that year in Monterey, California. We wanted Coke to help market *La Bamba* and we offered them the song La Bamba for free to use in their commercials. They said they weren't interested.

"Then the song by Los Lobos became the number one song in the country for several weeks in a row. The sountrack album became number one. The movie does serious business. Now the Coke marketing people knock on our door to use the song. We say, 'Sure, you can use our song for the commercial. How a big a check are you going to write?' They wrote a substantial check.

"*La Bamba* changed my life. Right afterwards I stopped practicing law to concentrate on movies. I bought a Porsche, which I still drive."

"Crusader Entertainment's mission statement says: 'We believe that gratuitous violence, use of drugs and smoking, sex and profanity will obscure the positive message we wish to impart and compromise the entertainment and commercial value of our projects.' You would not have been able to make most of your 1980s films with these guidelines."

"Crusader is a new company that's trying to find its identity. It's making one of my pet projects—*The Ray Charles Story.*"

Stuart reclines on the couch. I try to take advantage of him while he appears relaxed and vulnerable.

"If you were to put ethics aside, how could you have made more money as a producer?"

"Which of your films have had the most meaning to you?"

"Have any of your movies broken your heart?"

"What movie would best describe your producing work?"

Stuart "Quote Machine" Benjamin thinks through each question and says no, nothing, not really.

"If we were to make a movie of your life, what would the character arc be?"

Stuart thinks for five seconds before he stumbles into an answer. "Character arcs are artificial. We design arcs for characters to justify making the movie. So we pull and squeeze our characters. In real life, the growth process is not easy and not clear.

"I've never been willing to cross certain lines. I've always tried to keep balance in my life. I did not give up my life in law school. I know I'm smart. And being smart enables you often to accomplish what you want to accomplish by being smarter, as opposed to working harder. And sometimes it becomes an excuse for not working hard."

"You don't think the movie business is a particularly vicious business?"

"No more than anything else. Read the business section."

"What's it like for you dealing with actors, these incredibly needy people?"

"I'm not sure that they are anymore needy than any other group. I've been around athletes all my life. In the 1970s, I was invested in the Boston Celtics. In the late '70s, in the Clippers. You meet needy people all over the place."

Benjamin has two children who live in New York—a 24 year old daughter Jennifer who writes for Cosmopolitan, and a 23-year old actor-waiter son Mathew.

I give Stuart a release form. He becomes the first producer to decline to sign it until he sees how I use his quotes. "I'm very careful," he says.

I turn to leave. "Thank you for your time."

"You're welcome," says Stuart. "And thank you..."

He pauses and thinks hard. "I don't know what I'd thank you for. I don't know why you're writing this book."

24

Larry Brezner

February 12, 2002

"How are you?" asks Larry Brezner as he welcomes me into his spacious Beverly Hills office.

"Great," I reply.

"You're Australian," Larry picks up.

Brezner's a partner in Morra, Brezner, Steinberg & Tenenbaum Entertainment, a management company which shepherds the careers of such stars as Robin Williams, Woody Allen, Billy Crystal and David Letterman.

Larry looks at his secretary. "You didn't tell me he was Australian? How did we let an Australian in here?"

He turns to me with a smile. "What do you make of the Australian invasion? They've always had good directors. Now they have good actors [Russell Crowe, Nicole Kidman, etc]."

I smile and bask in the success of my countrymen.

Brezner's an amiable balding chap around 50 years of age, dressed casually in jeans. He stands about 5'10 and weighs about 180 pounds. He has two degrees in psychology including a masters from John Hopkins University.

"I was a school teacher during Vietnam because it was an automatic deferment from the draft. As I walked home every day, I passed by this nightclub that was never open. So I bought it for a dollar and opened a small club with organic food for hippies. Then I started bringing entertainers into the club. Big managers would come in. I met my wife Melissa Manchester there."

"How long were you married?"

"About 150-200 years. We never had kids. We're still on good terms. I became her manager. There was this big manager who came to my club all the time—Jack Rollins. Jack had discovered Woody Allen. I took Melissa to him and said that I wanted to manage her for him. Jack didn't have to pay me. So I did what I recommend to people who graduate from film school—get a job in entertainment, even if you have to work for free.

"I decided to become a movie producer as part of the management business, but not necessarily with my clients. I was more interested in producing movies than in managing talent. Although I continue to manage talent and I continue to produce movies, I recognize that we're a management company first and a production company second. If our clients said, 'We don't want you to produce movies anymore,' we wouldn't produce movies anymore. Many of our clients, like Robin and Billy, have been with us for over 25 years.

"Now we're in an age where all managers try to be producers by simply attaching themselves to their client's projects. We never do that. When we produce something, I'm on the set all the time. I devote myself to that movie. We don't put our names on a project for a fee. That's why we've had production deals at studios since I've come to LA.

"We generate our own material. I have a number of people who work for me just in generating material.

"I was deeply involved with the production of *Arthur* (1981) on a day-to-day basis. Steve Gordon, who wrote and directed *Arthur*, was such a great writer that we sold his series *Goodtime Harry* (1980) to the network just so that he could practice directing before making his film debut with *Arthur*. That was stupid because directing three-camera film [for television] is entirely different from directing a feature film. He had written a film [*The One and Only*, 1978] before that was so destroyed by the director [Rob Reiner], that he said he'd never let that happen again.

"We took Woody Allen's entire crew and put Steve on it to direct *Arthur*. And everybody on that film knew what they were doing except the director. He had no idea that he was surrounded by people, which is what you have to do with a new director. His assistant-director was Woody's line producer, Robert Greenhut, who clearly directed the film.

"Steve directing Sir John Gielgud was funny. Steve would say, 'Would you like me to call you Sir John? Or can I call you John?' Gielgud never quite got the movie. He didn't see what was particularly funny about it. He didn't see what was particularly funny [about such lines as], 'I'll alert the media.' Or, 'Would you like me to wash your dick for you, sir?' He found it ironic that after the great Shakespearean work he'd done over his lifetime, he won an Academy Award for *Arthur*."

Larry takes a call from his 18-year old daughter at university in Colorado. She's hurt her leg in a snowboarding accident and this distracts him throughout our interview.

"Steve died of a heart attack right after *Arthur*. I just thought he was a major hypochondriac. Every day we'd walk into his office, he'd be on the phone with Lew Wasserman complaining about the air conditioning. That's how crazy Steve was. He'd call Lew Wasserman to complain about a maintenance problem.

"I've produced several TV shows only because I said, 'I'm the producer,' and nobody said no. I had some run-ins with Barry Diller over the [1990 series] *Good Grief*, which took place in a funeral home. Barry Diller can be the most intimidating individual on the planet. Joe Roth was one of my closest friends. I produced the film *Coupe de Ville* (1990) that Joe directed. Joe was head of Fox at the time. Diller was above him. Joe would say, 'Diller can be a tough guy. Don't let him intimidate you. He'll say some really vicious things to you. If you allow it to happen, he'll just continue and you'll just be a lackey.'

"We'd got into this dispute about the television show *Good Grief*, which he wanted desperately. We had a hilarious pilot script. We wanted to do it as a movie and he said no, I'll give you 13 shows. Well, he never gave us the 13 shows, so I took the show away from him and he got furious.

"I get a message that Diller wants to see me immediately. I'm thinking about the warning from Joe. How do I protect myself? Peter Chernin is sitting in Diller's office. Diller starts in a soft spoken way. 'I hear you pulled the show from us?' I said, 'Yes, because you did not live up to some of the agreements we made.'

"Diller says, 'So you're an expert in television now? So you're an expert in comedy now?' Slowly he starts to build. He says, 'Let me tell you something about you.' Then he starts to insult me in a way you can't believe. 'You don't know anything about comedy. You know fuck-all about the television business. You don't know what you're doing. Who the fuck do you think you are?' He just went on and on. He started getting really out of hand.

"Even though in my stomach, I was getting tied up in knots, for some reason, I got up and walked up to one inch from his nose. I said to him, 'I've got to tell you something.' He said, 'What?' I said, 'In this light, your eyes are just fabulous.' He just looked at me. There was a long pause. He started smiling and he said, 'Get out of here.' He threw me out of his office. I could hear him laughing as I was leaving. It was just one of those situations where you had to protect yourself by going in another direction.

"*Throw Momma from the Train* (1987). Stu Silver came to me with the idea to a version of the Alfred Hitchcock film, *Strangers on a Train* (1951), as a comedy.

I didn't get it but I told him to write it on spec. So I worked with him on scenes. We decided to make it in Hawaii so that in case someone makes the film, we can go to Hawaii.

"I needed the rights from *Strangers*, owned by Warner Brothers. WB doesn't give up rights. We gave them the script and they said, 'Pass. We're not doing it and we're not giving up the rights. So forget it.' We were dead. We needed the rights and we needed a film clip from *Strangers*. He gets the whole idea of throwing momma from the train from watching *Strangers*.

"Something strange happened. *Arthur* was a tremendous hit. Warner Brothers developed a sequel. Even though we were the producers, they never mentioned this to us. Certain executives were dishonest. Dudley had come to them to do a sequel. I called up the head of the studio and asked him if they were doing this. He said yes. I said, 'You better check your contract. You can't do this without us. You have no sequel.' I got a call a day later from that executive. 'We want you to produce the movie.'

"They told me the idea and I said pass. I think that film will fail. I think that Arthur without his money is not funny. They said, what can we offer you because we want to do the movie? I said, give me my fee for the movie and give me the rights to *Strangers on a Train*. And they said, we can't give you the rights. I said, well, give me a letter saying you won't sue me if we do *Throw Momma from the Train*. They were willing to do that.

"*Good Morning Vietnam* (1987) was a two-page treatment, not a comedy, about the true story of Adrian Cronauer, a disc jockey in Vietnam who became known for two things: His morning call 'Goooooood Morning Vietnam.' He was the first guy to play rock n' roll on Armed Forces Radio. I saw it as a comedy. I went to New York to interview Adrian Cronauer. Stu Silver wrote the first half of the movie.

"We developed the script at Norman Lear's company. Alan Hall ran the company. He said, 'We're not going to do a film about Vietnam. No film has been done about Vietnam. It's too soon.' This is before *Platoon* had come out. So Lindsay Duran, an executive who was in that meeting, went to Paramount. She called up, 'We want it over here.' We took it to Dawn Steel, a good friend who ran Paramount at the time. She said, 'If we ever disagree about the concept, I'll let it go.' Ned Tannen, number two at Paramount, and I disagreed about the last act of the film. He thought it should continue as a comedy. I said no. I think this film is a metaphor for the war. The whole thing was a joke for a while until it wasn't a joke anymore. That's the way the film should be. Ned disagreed and Dawn Steel let the film go.

"I got a call the next day from Jeffrey Katzenberg. It was a Saturday morning and I was playing tennis. Jeffrey said he wanted to make the movie but he wouldn't get into a bidding war. I said, 'Jeffrey, you have my word I won't shop it to other people. I will talk to you on Monday. But I've got to finish this set. It's more important than the movie.' So we made a deal on Monday and we went to look for directors.

"We met with many directors, from Peter Bogdanovitch to Hal Ashby. Jeffrey mentioned Spike Lee. Robin Williams was not attached as we developed the film. He just read the script and liked it.

"We met with Barry Levinson, who'd just done *Tin Men*. We had a meeting. I did a little too much talking about the film because I was so passionate about the movie. Four years had gone by since I'd started developing the movie. I said, the character should do this. The character should do that. I got a phone call at midnight from Jeffrey. He said he had good news and bad news. Barry wants to direct the film but he doesn't want you involved. I was devastated. I asked why. Jeffrey said, 'He thinks you are so passionately involved with the thing. And there can only be one captain of the ship. The only way he can do the movie is if he's completely autonomous to do the film.'

"I said, I'll let you know tomorrow. That night was a restless night. I was giving up my baby, which I'd developed and I thought was an important movie. I cried because I was being rejected over something that I so loved. I knew that Barry Levinson was the right person to direct the film so I had to step away. Just before I called Jeffrey, I got a call from Orion Pictures. They wanted to green light *Throw Momma*. Both pictures were set on a start date for the same week. So as one thing was taken away from me, another thing was given to me.

"I hired Danny De Vito to direct *Throw Momma*. I worked on the film every day. I was in Thailand for three weeks before Barry started shooting *Good Morning Vietnam* but I then had to go back to *Throw Momma*. With two films shooting simultaneously, I became the hottest producer in the business.

"The entirety of *Good Morning Vietnam* with the exception of one shot was done in Thailand. They wouldn't let us blow up the restaurant in Thailand. They kept asking for more payment. So we rebuilt the restaurant here and blew it up.

"When Anne Ramsey came in to audition for *Throw Momma*, she'd just come out of a cancer operation where half of her tongue had been removed. So she didn't make much sense. One of her lines in the movie was momma hitting Billy Crystal and says, 'Get out of the way, you black bastard.' That's how nuts she is. She's calling him racial slurs but the wrong racial slurs.

"We could hardly figure out what she was saying in the audition. Danny and I were terrified of the woman. We looked at each other and said, 'That's momma.' Barry Sonnenfeld served as the cameraman on the picture.

"I was able to suggest ideas to Danny during the shoot. One of the basic rules of the producer—director relationship is to make any idea the director's idea."

"Is Danny DeVito a naturally funny guy?" I ask.

"No. He's not a million laughs.

"What I'm best known for on that film was cutting the trailer. I went in to Orion and cut it together from one scene. The guys at Orion said, are you out of your mind? You've got to show scenes from throughout the movie. I said, this scene is all you have to know. Then I took it to Danny. He said, 'I'm not using that trailer. It's our best fucking scene. I'm not doing that. You want to give away our best joke.' Danny's wife, Rhea Perlman, came over and said, 'Danny, are you crazy? That trailer is perfect.' He reluctantly agreed.

"Orion said no to the trailer. I begged them to test it. It tested high. So they agreed to go along with it. The exhibitors just played the shit out of the trailer. The movie ultimately did well. We never changed the trailer. We used it on TV.

"*Good Morning Vietnam* did about $130 million domestic box office. Jeffrey said this was a film they were going to platform. Meaning, they would start it at a couple of theaters and let the movie build word of mouth and critical acclaim. Jeffrey was concerned that Robin wasn't coming off a hit film.

"We shot *The 'burbs* (1989) on one street on the Universal lot. I had fundamental disagreements with the director [Joe Dante]. After I looked at the first day's dailies, I realized that this wasn't working. So I had a meeting with Joe Dante. I said, 'You can't have a guy who's military minded wearing camouflage. That's not funny.' He looked at me and said something I will never forget, because he was fundamentally right. 'I like The Three Stooges and you like Mel Brooks. We're never going to get along in comedy. I'm the director and you're going to have go along. Tom Hanks is in the movie and he agreed to do the movie with my vision.' I realized that I was powerless. He was exactly right. From the time he says action, he's the captain of the ship.

"It was a tiny script in the sense that it was a small story. Just a small scary comedy. But once Joe Dante and Tom Hanks came on board, this small movie had to be changed. At the end of the movie in the original script, the hero gets killed because he's been making a wrong judgment all along. You never see it coming. In the new version, we realized that we can't kill Tom Hanks. People will rush the screen. So we had to change the ending and we ruined the concept of the film. Everything got bigger and broader. Joe made the film he wanted to make but I don't find it funny, though I've never had a more enjoyable experience on a film.

"There are all kinds of producers on various levels. Jerry Bruckheimer doesn't hire Sydney Pollack to do his movies because the clash would be too great. Jerry hires a director like Michael Bay, who he created. Jerry will have a lot of say on his pictures. Nobody would tell Jerry Bruckheimer, 'I don't care what you think. This is the way I'm making the film.' Jerry's too powerful a producer. Most producers are not in that position.

"The producer is in charge during the buying stage, the development stage, the hiring stage, right up until 'Action!' Then you give over power to the director. This can change if you have a first-time director, but every director who's had a hit film sees himself as in charge. It almost has to be that way. If actors think that the producer is really in charge on set, there's chaos. You have to always create the illusion, even if you are running the set, that the director is in charge. The studio is the ultimate arbiter of any dispute. Usually if there's a difference of opinion between a producer and a director, the studio will go with the director, unless you are one of the few producers who has the power to tell the studio what you're going to do."

"Which producers have that kind of power?"

"Joel Silver, Brian Grazer, Scott Rudin. They're usually fanatic crazy people who will rip down a studio office brick by brick if they don't get what they want. Scott can be strong in his point of view."

"Has there been any other film where your vision has so diverged from the director?"

"There have been many. Every director has his own point of view."

Larry takes another call from his daughter, who's waiting for an X-ray to see what's wrong with her leg.

"Tell me about 1990's *Coupe de Ville* which Joe Roth directed."

"Joe was running Morgan Creek, a small production company. I sent the film over to him and he said, 'I love this. I want to direct.' It's a sweet film done for no money. Joe and I became close friends on the film, which can happen. Either you become gigantic enemies or close friends. I remained with Joe for a lot of years after that. When he was at Fox, I took a producing deal at Fox. When he went to Disney, I took a producing deal at Disney. Joe now runs his own little studio Revolution which produced *Black Hawk Down*.

"*Coupe de Ville* never got much of a release. Two days after he finished the movie, he announced he was taking over Fox. That made the people at Universal, which was distributing the movie, unhappy. They had our movie. At one point, they agreed to sell us the movie. Then they changed their mind. One of the wives of the executives had seen it and said it was a good movie. They decided to not give it back and angry at Joe, they didn't give it much of a release.

"Mike Binder wrote the film. He was a standup comic who I encouraged to write. *Coupe de Ville* was a story about his family. I know his family and the story hit close to home. It was a father with three sons who didn't get along, and his little trick to try to get them to like each other."

"Which of your other films have had the most meaning to you?"

"Gosh, I don't know. There are major disappointments and there are films I don't care about. We did *Passed Away* (1992) for Disney. I had a huge disagreement with Jeffrey over the casting of the lead character. Even though Bob Hoskins was a fine actor, it was supposed to be about a traditional Irish-American family at a wake. I wanted Brian Denney to play that role. Disney pushed Bob because he'd done *Who Framed Roger Rabbit* (1988) for them.

"I can't think of any film I've done where I don't ask, what could we have done better. The biggest embarrassment of my life was making *Freddie Got Fingered* (2001).

"I think Tom Green's a funny guy but has no experience in doing movies. When the director quit because Tom wouldn't go along with the new version of the script, Tom decided he wanted to direct. He looked at me and I said, 'Well, you'll have to talk to the studio about that.' I never thought in a million years would they allow him to direct. He'd never directed anything. They let Tom direct and Tom made the film he wanted to make but it was just not a good film. It was just shock for shock's sake. That's not what I do. Tom said to the studio, 'If 30 people get up and leave the first time they've seen the movie, then I'll know I've made the movie I wanted to make.' I'm thinking to myself, 'My God, if 30 people get up and leave, I'm going to kill myself.' Guess what? They left. He was pleased.

"Tom was directing his script and he was starring. What can you tell him? The studio was not going to support me. I went to the studio 25 times and said, 'You don't know what is going on here. We're making a film that you can't show.' There's a guy masturbating a horse in the opening scene for no reason. I'm not shocked by anything. I don't think there's anything terrible about masturbating a horse if you're doing it for a good reason. I can't think of a reason right now."

Freddie Got Fingered bombed at the box office but did well on home video.

"It was such a hard-R that kids couldn't get into see it. His audience was younger kids. I wouldn't want my kids to see it. It was embarrassing. There's nothing worse that I can imagine as a producer of premiering a film with all the people you love and respect in the business and at home are sitting in the audience and you're looking at something that's as bad as anything you've seen, and your name is on it. They're looking. They come up to you after the movie and say, 'Interesting. Really. That was interesting.' They have all those euphemisms for, I can't really talk about the film and tell you how bad I think it is. 'Gee, I thought Tom was interesting. Congratulations.'

"It's so personally embarrassing. I don't think anybody outside the industry realizes how hard it is to make a film. And to make a bad film. To put all that time and effort into making a bad film. It's just so terrible on so many levels. It's embarrassing personally. It's professionally embarrassing. It's a waste of such time and energy. It's almost impossible to imagine a worse feeling. I know there are people starving right now in Argentina who are saying, 'What's your problem, buddy?' But I'm just talking on a producer level."

"You read the script."

"Yeah, well, we didn't. We started with an idea. I sold the idea to Joe Roth. Then Tom Green wrote the script and showed it to Todd Garner at Disney. They said we're not making this movie. If Michael Eisner saw this movie with a Touchstone label he'd fire us all. Go with God. Take the script and sell it anywhere you can. So I sold it to New Regency. Yeah, I read the script. All I could hope was that we could bring in a director and another writer and turn it into a decent funny outrageous comedy. We didn't accomplish that particular goal.

"*Krippendorf's Tribe* (1998) was a film that also didn't succeed at the box office. It came from a book I'd read by Frank Parkin. I thought, what a funny idea. A college professor takes a grant to visit tribes in New Guinea and spends all the money on his kids and has nothing to present. So he decides that his kids are as primitive as any tribe one could imagine. He'd just write a paper on them. The idea was enhanced by a memory from college. One of the classes studied an unusual group of people known as the Nacirema [spells American backwards]. All the strange things they do like shave the hair off their face every morning. They wear things in their ear. When you look at it from a sociological way, the things we do are as odd as any tribe.

"I loved the idea of the film. We were accused of being racist because the kids put on makeup. I think the film direction-wise did not succeed. The director [Todd Holland] was a nice guy but again it was his first feature film [and last]. There was a clash with the stars."

25

Barnet Bain

February 14, 2002

Barnet grew up in Northern Quebec, an hour's drive north of Montreal, in the small town of Saint Agatha of the Mountains. The fulltime population was about 3000 people, largely Catholic. There were about ten Jewish families.

The town was located in a tourist district by a lake, surrounded by ski mountains, and on weekends the population swelled to 30,000. During summer, it would go to 60,000.

"There was a local synagogue that was affluent because it was supported by a membership that was non-resident," remembers Bain. "I, to my chagrin, was a beneficiary of all that largess because I lived up the street from the synagogue and next door to the rabbi. So from the day I turned 13, it was my misfortune to be conveniently accessed to make a *minyan* [prayer quorum]. So no matter how much earlier I arose from week to week, the rabbi was always standing at the door, ready to pull me from the pleasures of being young to go make a *minyan*. My skis, my skates had to wait. Everything waited for the *minyan*.

"At one point, I thought I was going to be a rabbi, but I think this period of my life when I was tyrannized by the constant quest for a *minyan* drove me from it.

"Being a film producer is exactly the same job. The food is better. You're always trying to get a *minyan* together. I thought about leading a religious life. Now is an opportunity to do it on a canvas that is worldwide [and] non-sectarian. I now make a distinction between a religious life and a spiritual life.

"Values and ethics are moving targets. There's no such thing as ultimate values. Values are a trail of bread crumbs. You follow them, you pick them up, you digest them and you move on. As a producer, it's only about story telling and ritual. Ritual being the performance side of story telling. I am interested in stories that will open me and others to greater intimacy with ourselves so that we have greater self-knowing and the ability to access a larger domain of personal choice.

"In 1979, I was asked to adopt the *Gospel of Luke* as a script for Warner Brothers."

"Why did they turn to you as an expert in Jesus?"

"Producer John Heyman hired me because I was around and available and cheap. John told Warners he already had a script. When they asked to see it, he said, 'It's not very good. He'll start over.' They said, 'We'd like to see the script anyway.' So he said, 'I'll go back to New York and I'll punch it up.'

"I get a call. John says, 'I'm going to hire you to do this and I'm going to pay you an obscenely small amount of money.' For me, it was a king's ransom. He said, 'I'm going to pay you this a week to adapt this movie. You will have exactly one week to do it.'

"I went off and wrote the script in three weeks. Warners called him up and said the script was fine. 'We'll shoot this.' He hired me just to produce a bunch of pages. He had no expectation that I would produce a script they would shoot.

"In the summer of 2001, I saw an article in *Forbes* magazine that that movie *Jesus* is the most widely seen film. It's been seen by a billion-and-a-half people. It's been translated into over 450 languages. It's been used as an evangelical tool. It was financed by the Hunt brothers of Texas silver fame.

"I made $8750 from the film. Agents get a bad rap. Where are they when you need them?

"Last summer, I was stuck overnight in Rome. There was a youth jubilee. There were kids wall-to-wall marching through the streets. They were all clutching these bags that had these little cassettes of this movie. The box had an endorsement from the Pope. My 12-year old daughter never had any idea that I had anything to do with this movie. 'My God, dad, there's the Pope and there's you.'

"I wrote a few more scripts and discovered development hell [the hell of trying to get a movie made]. I moved to LA in 1982. I met my future [Jewish] wife on Thanksgiving, 1982. We spent the next afternoon together and we've never parted. We married in August, 1983. We had a daughter in 1988.

"I wrote for years for everyone and never had another movie made. I sold a lot and I worked a lot and I never had another movie made. It became difficult, lonely and bitter."

The first film Barnet produced was the undistinguished 1996 TV movie *The Conspiracy of Fear*.

Bain met producer Stephen Simon, who shared his metaphysical interests. In 1995, they formed the company Metafilmics to make spiritual films. Their biggest production was the $70 million *What Dreams May Come* (1998) starring Robin Williams.

"We wanted to make mainstream popular entertainment that spoke to spiritual issues and looked for what was magnificent in people. It wasn't about making goody goody movies. They could be difficult, even violent, movies, but they should be movies where you came away feeling that you understood more about who you were, why you were.

"I wish one could make a movie about big metaphysical themes and market it as a movie about metaphysical themes without relying on big special effects. Stephen and I would've liked to have made the movie for half the money without the special effects. We would've had the same audience and it would've been more profitable.

"New Age has proved to be the most successful niche of publishing in many years. I hope a similar niche emerges in film. The film business looks to leverage everything so they can deliver to the widest possible audience.

"Somebody once said that being with Robin Williams is like traveling with a Shriners' convention. It's like being with all of the Shriners in one guy. Robin lives in his heart. His heart is not just on his sleeve, it is all over. That he had the courage to step into a performance like that…"

"What did you think of Ron Bass's script?"

"I loved it. The first time I read it, it brought me to tears. It was powerful, wise and insightful. It either moved people or made them feel uncomfortable. You don't make films that deal with spirituality and emotional literacy without raising the temperature.

"Ron is probably the most successful screenwriter alive today. He understands the power of diving into people's emotional states. As Ron taught me, movies are not about what is said from one person to another. They're about what's going on unsaid between people. Unless you can conjure up states of heightened emotion, there's no subtext for a camera to read in a scene. It just becomes the lines that people are throwing at each other. That does not create a state of heightened reality.

"Ron knows how to conjure a state of heightened reality. It is not in the words that he puts into the mouths of his characters. It is in the climate that exists between the characters around the words. Sometimes that climate spills over in ways that are uncomfortable for the audience. They react with either curiosity, exploration and humility and rewarded deeply, or they react with cynicism and denial."

"Tell me about *The Linda McCartney Story* (2000) TV movie."

"She was half of one of the great popular love stories of our time. It's well known that these lovers never spent more than two days apart in their entire marriage. There was a mythology to the story that appealed to me. Love stories are only as good as the challenges they meet. In the case of *What Dreams May Come*, we had the ultimate obstacle—they were dead. In the case of McCartneys, they struggled with the demands of fame. They put under the microscope the seductions we all have. We lead fast paced lives and are pulled away from what is really valuable."

"If we were to make a movie about your life, what would the character arc be?"

"It would be about a man who looked for meaning and connection. But he has meaning and connection and doesn't know it. He comes full circle to where he began—a connection with the divine and a sense of being in dominion with all the forces around and beyond us. A man of God. I acknowledge my talents as a father, a husband and as a lover. I mean that in the sense of giving and receiving safety and security and value and making people feel known and visible for who and what they are."

Barnet was last in synagogue a year ago—for a *bar mitzvah*. "I feel powerfully connected, most of the day, to the mystery. My daughter did not have a *bat mitzvah*. She identifies with being Jewish but I am not sure what she has hooked up to it. She didn't go to Hebrew school. We talked about some of the esoteric energies around Judaism. She's familiar with that in an experiential way. She's familiar with conjuring those energies of Shechina [the divine presence] even though she doesn't do it as a Friday night ritual. When she wants that kind of intimacy and connection, she knows exactly how to do that.

"We don't instruct her in that manner, but she has many connections to kabbalistic Judaism."

26

Peter Hyams

I sit down with Sol Hurok's grandson at his spacious office on Third Street in Santa Monica.

"I started as an arts student at a young age," says Peter. "I was trained in conservatories. I became consumed with photography. I began writing at a young age. Not well, just precociously. My politicized family worked in the theater. I knew that I wanted to combine imagery with writing and relevance. My stepfather Arthur Lief was blacklisted. I heard of his arrest on the radio."

"Was he a communist?"

"Probably."

"Were you a red diaper baby?"

"I don't know what that means. I was the son of intellectuals and artists. My father Darren Hyams (a theatrical producer and publicist on Broadway) and my stepfather were certainly. I think my father was a socialist and I think my stepfather was a member of the Communist Party though he'd never admit it to me. I'm the kid of people who were young intellectuals in the depression. The equivalent of civil rights marches and anti-war demonstrators in the '30s were socialists and communists. They were also the people who wanted America to fight fascism.

"In college, the craft that interested me in combining imagery and writing was documentary filmmaking. I graduated at age 21 and was hired by CBS News where I worked for more than six years (from 1964-70).

"I happened to be very bad [at journalism]. I was much more concerned with taking a photograph that was beautiful than a photograph that was accurate. I dedicated myself to being unencumbered by fact. I thought fact was an unfair restriction to put on writing. I wanted to write something that would elicit a response. Documentary directing is the ability to capture an event. Film directing is the ability to shape an event. They are two disparate talents. I'm scrambling to be good at one.

"I remember covering a fire and coming back and going to the assignment editor and saying, 'I really got some great stuff. I did this cop. It was his job to have his back to the fire and hold people back. He's a real Irish New York hard working *Archie Bunker* cop. My country right or wrong. Now his son is in Vietnam and he's questioning it all. Some of his friends' kids have come back in little wooden boxes. The underpinnings of everything he's almost robotically believed in have come into question.

"The assignment editor says, 'How many people were injured in the fire?' I said, 'Gee, I don't know. But this guy was so good.' 'Well, what happened to the building?' 'I don't know. This guy is really terrific.' That was my level as a reporter."

"Does anyone get discriminated against in Hollywood today for their political beliefs?"

"I don't think anyone's that political. Arnold Schwarzenegger is a real Republican. Tim Robbins is on the other side. I think the Hollywood community is probably more Democratic than Republican."

"Of course."

"It's not as liberal as you think it is."

"80/20."

"No. It's more 60/40."

"Has anyone not wanted to work with you because of your political beliefs?"

"No. I imagine if I were running around saying, 'Free John Walker. I support the Taliban,' people would be offended. It would offend me.

"If I have one gift that I was given by my parents, as dysfunctional as my home was, is that I was brought up with absolutely no sense of color or religion. Everybody is equal. Color and religion are not part of my visual or emotional vocabulary. I've liked to arbitrarily cast a woman in a man's role or somebody of a different ethnicity in a role. It just adds texture."

"What motivates you?"

"If I got out of bed in the morning and picked up *The Los Angeles Times* and saw a banner headline that Russia and China have launched their entire nuclear arsenal at America, my only thought would be, 'Do I have a cover set for that day's shooting?'

"I'm truly obsessed with getting to where I'm not. I want to get good so much that it hurts. More now than ever. I can see better now the gulf between where I am and where I want to go. I see good stuff that people do. That raises the bar.

"When you go to art school, you spend years training your hand to reproduce whatever it is that you see. If you want to play an instrument, you spend 10-15 years training your hands to reproduce the notes, if you are lucky enough to be able to do that. I remember where I was. I remember what the light was like coming through the studio window. I realized I could do it.

"That day was the biggest trauma of my life. It's a day from which I still have not recovered. That was the day that the heavens opened up and a shaft of light came down. God reached from the clouds with a celestial hammer in his hand and hit me on the forehead and said, 'Schmuck, being an artist has nothing to do with your hands and only to do with what you see.' It's like fluency in a language. At one point, you can speak. Now, what do you have to say?

"My definition of an artist is someone who has an FM receiver in an AM world. Do I see anything interesting or am I just an illustrator?"

"Are movies an art like painting?"

"Of course. It's like saying, is theater an art? It's writing, it's painting, it's music. It's everything. I think it is the most relevant art form. There's nothing in the world that I would rather do than make movies. I just want to do it well. I'm like Charlie Brown. I keep on thinking that one time Lucy won't drop the ball when I go to kick it.

"I carry with me a quote from Sir Carol Reed: 'When you're finally done with a film, and there's nothing left to do, it's like falling out of love. Making a film is all work and worry, fear and panic. Not making a film is worse.'"

"You left CBS News and you…"

"I didn't know anything. I had a wife and two little babies. I figured that all I had to do was write and somebody would make it. I had no concept of what the odds were. I wrote a screenplay and it was made [*T.R. Baskin*, 1971].

"The early '70s was a time of great retrenchment in the film industry and a very tough time for new directors, despite all the books [such as] *Easy Riders, Raging Bulls*. The studios had each given a young denim-shirt-wearing director his first film and got back something unreleasable. I was mildly sought after to write and produce films, as is anybody who is new and writes something. I didn't want to do that anymore.

"Barry Diller was head of ABC's movie of the week. ABC made two or three 90-minute films a week. They were shot in 12 days. I consider Diller to be the smartest executive ever in this business. He hired me, Michael Chricton and Steven Spielberg within weeks of each other.

"I met with him at a time when television was considered by [film people] as a vat of sulfuric acid. If you put your hand in, you'll come out with a stump. I didn't believe that.

"I told Diller I would write a television movie for him if he'd let me direct. I said I had two ideas. One was an attempt by the U.S. government to fake a space shot. He said, 'What else?' 'I'd like to do a homage to Raymond Chandler. A period detective piece.' He said, 'Do the detective thing.' I did it [*Goodnight My Love*, 1972] and it was praised. Over-praised. One of the trades called it the *Citizen Kane* (1941) of television movies, which, trust me, it wasn't.

"Nobody in this industry is properly rated. You're either overrated or under-rated. Having been both, overrated is better. It pays better and it makes you feel better. Unless you're Jim Cameron or Steven Spielberg, your temperature can fluctuate widely.

"My first feature, *Busting* (1974), was all about vice cops. Like a journalist, I went around to New York, Boston, Chicago and Los Angeles and spoke with hookers, pimps, strippers and cops and DAs. Every episode in the film was true."

"You were your own cinematographer?"

"I wasn't in the [cinematographer's] union then, so I had to hire a camera-man. The camera issue has always been a tough issue. It's an acrimonious dispute. They wouldn't let me in the union [until 1983]. It was grudging. In 1997, Conrad Hall was talking to me on the phone. He's one of my idols. And he asked me, 'How come you're not in the ASC (American Society of Cinematographers)?' I said, 'Well, they don't like me. It's not that I don't like them.'

"He said, 'That's nonsense. If I [and another cinematographer] sign your application, will you join?' I said yes. So I send in my application and I was summoned to this meeting for 90 minutes. And a couple of days later, this rejection letter came."

Peter points to a frame on the wall.

"I don't understand why they don't like you?"

"I don't think another director has ever been admitted to the cinematographer's union. There were people who were just opposed to it."

Steven Soderberg is the only other director who officially handles his own camera.

"I know some directors who do it without getting credit and they're not union cameramen—Stanley Kubrick did it. Somehow every movie that Ridley Scott makes is the most beautiful movie you've ever seen.

"Not only am I not in the ASC, there has never been a word written about any of my movies in the American Cinematographers magazine. It's not like *2010*

(1984) and *End of Days* (1999) are invisible little movies. Academy Award nominations are not going to come my way, and they may not be merited."

"Why do you like to use natural light so much?"

"I don't. I never have. I don't like it. The camera is not a recording device. The camera's a negative. I think photography should be heightened. I love shadow. I love the dark. I love changing the color of light. People write about cinematography and they don't know what they're talking about. Nobody knows what natural light is. When you build a set, how can it be natural light?"

"I guess there's that perception because you work so much with shadow."

"You make shadow. I love the dark. I love the source of light. I love the bent of light. I remember going to museums as a kid and studying painting. Look at Rembrandt. I think I've spent my life looking for the perfect terminator, for that miraculous moment when light seems to expire of old age around somebody's cheek.

"I think there's no excuse for photography not being adventurous. I think the biggest sin that anyone can commit is conservatism in any art form. I don't think there's an excuse for a photograph to be mundane."

"You try to approximate natural light?"

"No. I try to make something that I think is dramatic. Somebody sitting beside a window [as I am], I like to see the window. I like to see the light coming through that window. I like to see the key side of their face X amount of stops over and the shadow side of their face X amount of stops under. And whatever that X factor is is part of the skill of exposure."

"*Our Time* (1974)."

"A romantic comedy. I was trying to do the opposite of what I had done before. I had done a hard tough R-rated movie about vice cops. It was not a popular success. With *Peeper* (1975), I managed to combine critical and commercial failure. That made me colder than ice. Nobody wanted me. One studio signed me to write and direct something specifically so I would write. Then they brought in another director. I remember this one studio executive would not return my phone calls for two years. Then I went off, and under the radar, made *Capricorn One* (1978). Audiences just stood up and cheered at one point in the film. It wasn't because it was such a great movie, it's just that certain movies strike certain chords with people. In a successful movie, the audience, almost before they see it, know they're going to like it.

"I remember standing in the back of the theater and crying because I knew that something had changed in my life. Sitting on the film cans outside the screening room, I felt my cheeks were wet with tears. A bright man, [studio executive] David Picker, came over to me and said, 'You're going to have a lot of new best friends tomorrow. You better know how to handle it.' I was at home the next morning at eight o'clock when the phone rang. The guy was talking without saying who it was. It was the guy who hadn't returned my phone calls in two years.

"It was so vulgar and so obnoxious that I was saved from ever thinking that I am good. If it was anything less horrific than that, I might have believed it. I don't think this is an industry that cares about good or bad. It cares about commercial success. A director is hot on Saturday morning. You know Friday at 5 p.m. what the 8 p.m. movies are on the East Coast. Between 11 p.m.–midnight, you know what the weekend gross is going to be. You get a call from the head of the studio and the head of distribution and it's either a wonderful phone call or a terrible phone call. If it is a wonderful phone call, then Saturday morning you are hot. If it is 100 minutes of drivel and it is the number one picture that weekend, you are hot. If it is *Citizen Kane*, and nobody's gone to see it, your phone is not going to ring. If your film did well that weekend, then that Monday, that person is getting offered stuff.

"I think that giving directors credit for or blame for the financial success of their films is completely wrong. Directors should be given credit for or blame for the quality of the film. The financial outcome belongs with the studio who chose to make it. Steven Spielberg doesn't make a movie successful for any other reason than he's wonderful. He makes wonderful movies that we all want to see. When Jim Cameron makes a movie, I'm first in line. If nobody went to see *Traffic* (2000), it would be just as good a film. If I was running a movie studio and I saw *Traffic*, and it didn't make a dime, I'd say, 'Get me the guy who made that movie. He's talented. If we put the right material in his hands, it's going to be a monster.'

"Peter Weir makes *Witness* (1984) and *Mosquito Coast* (1986). One is wildly successful and one is not. Did he suddenly lose talent? Is he not a talented guy because people didn't go to *Mosquito Coast*?"

"What happens to me is that quickly into a film, I either buy it or I don't."

"When you talk about wonderful filmmakers, in the first two minutes of the movie, you feel a hand of talent. So you watch it differently. It's not necessarily buying a movie."

"Do you have fond memories of working with Sean Connery in 1981's *Outland*?"

"I'm not anecdotal. Someone once asked me if I have fun making a movie? I don't know if a heroin addict has fun taking heroin. I would die without it. It is by definition the process of failure. It is falling short of what I wanted to do. If you aim high enough, you have to fall short.

"I'm working on a film right now and I can't tell you how extraordinary that film is in my head. When the process [of shooting] starts, it's going to pass through me. What's going to be between it and perfection and is me. The only thing that stands between me and genius is genius. It's the only thing I lack. I've got all the neuroses of genius. I've got all the compulsions of a genius. I've got all the phobias of a genius. I'm as obnoxious as a genius."

"When did you start thinking about *2010*?"

"When I was asked to do it. The chairman of MGM asked me to do it. 'Here's this book [by Arthur Clark]. It's got to be in the theaters 17 months from now.' I was petrified and reluctant and intrigued. When I read the book, I said, 'It's a fascinating book but there are things about it that I really don't agree with. If you want me to do this film, two things have to happen. One, Stanley Kubrick has to say that it is O.K. with him. He's God and I will not displease God. Two, I want to change the film from the book. The book was written without politics. This was 1984 and Ronald Reagen. I'd like to make this a movie about Americans and Russians not getting along whereas in the book they got along. I want to add something about brinkmanship. He said fine. They asked Stanley Kubrick and Kubrick said O.K.

"We arranged the first phone call between us. I was in the office when the first phone call came through and I stood up. I picked up the phone and stood up. Kubrick didn't even say hello. He said, 'In *Outland*, you've got a shot that went through. How did you do that?' He talked about all the crap he'd gone through with the cinematographer's union and how they wouldn't let him in. He was asking me about shot after shot after shot. I was on the phone with him for almost three hours. I told him everything and he told me nothing.

"A couple of months later, I was sitting around at a club and talking to someone. I asked him what it was like when he first met Stanley Kubrick. He said, 'We sat on a park bench and we spoke for about three hours. And I told him everything and he told me nothing.'

"Stanley and I spoke a lot. He was so kind and unassuming. I was so scared that right before we started the movie, I got a panic attack. The chairman of MGM sent me a bound volume of the bad reviews of *2001*.

"The only thing to do with *2010* was to make a film so unlike *2001* that people could not compare it. I met Jim Cameron because I'd seen *Aliens* (1986). I got his number and I called him up. I said, 'You did exactly what I tried to do. You made a film so unlike the first movie that you can't compare them.'"

"*2010* is often called your most ambitious film."

"I hope not. I hope that I get more ambitious. I hope that the most ambitious thing I've done is the thing I'm doing.

"I can't look at a film I've made when I can no longer do anything to it. It's too frustrating. When I'm still working on it, I can look at it a thousand times."

"Does the size of the budget affect your enthusiasm for a project?"

"No. Enthusiasm? What I lack in talent, I try to make up for in passion. Nobody works harder than me."

"Have you been passionate about all of your movies?"

"Of course. How could you do it if you weren't? Isn't every director passionate about his movie? You can't work that hard on a project and not be passionate about it. I work 20 hours a day, seven days a week. I'm not cynical. I don't know anybody who makes films who isn't passionate. I've backed out of a couple of projects because I saw that I would lose enthusiasm for them."

"How did you come to direct *End of Days*?"

"Jim Cameron and I tried to work together on several projects. At one point, we flirted with doing *Godzilla*. At one point, he was going to write and produce *Planet of the Apes*. He asked if I would like to direct.

"Right after Cameron made *Titanic*, he had this idea for a film. He fleshed out a 200 page novella *Bright Angel Falling*. Then he wanted me to write a script. It was the best thing I've ever written. Unfortunately it was about a comet. Then Disney and Paramount both announced movies about comets—*Armageddon* and *Deep Impact* (1998). So we didn't make ours. We didn't want to get in that race. It was like a death.

"One day I walked into Jim's office and he said, "You're going to do this film *End of Days*. Read the script. You're going to start shooting in X number of weeks.'

"The budget was over $80 million. When you make a film with a big star, everything gets swollen. Suddenly when you want locations, and they hear it's a big Schwarzenegger movie, they charge more. I'm used to guerilla filmmaking. I'm used to not getting everything I want.

"I'm working on my fourth film with Moshe Diamant. I've never seen anybody manage to get more on the screen for less. He says to me, 'Don't talk to me about money. Tell me how many days you need and what you need, and you will have that.'

"Our last movie was *The Musketeer*. It opened on September 7th and was the number one picture in the country and was on its way. Then Tuesday was September 11th. Complaining about that is like going through a cancer ward complaining about a hang nail."

"Do you have a predilection for action movies?"

"I have a predilection for movies that are larger than life. I love movies that are exotic. I love going to a theater when the lights go down, and I never sit past the fourth row because I don't want to see the edges of the screen, and the movie takes you some place. I love movies that are thrilling.

"When I go to a movie like *As Good As It Gets*, I'm awestruck at that kind of talent. I couldn't begin to make a film with the kind of intellect that James Brooks has, but I love seeing it."

"Which of your films has the most meaning for you?"

"I hope the last one."

"Which do you think is your best film?"

"I hope the last one [*The Musketeer*]. If a film doesn't show lessons learned, then you're not getting better. I didn't start out making *Citizen Kane*, so I have to get better. Someone once described a career as a horse race without a finish line.

"My middle son John, 32, is a painter and a filmmaker and he has the talent that I wish I had. He made one independent film, *One Dog Day* (1997) and he's just finished a documentary, which is the best documentary I've ever seen in my life. I've my three kids talk about directors and if they made a list of their top ten, I would not be on it. I would not be on my own list of my top ten directors.

"Chris (into computers) is my oldest son and Nick (passionate about music) is my youngest.

"I have the kind of personality that makes each person think that they are what stands between me and megalomania. They have to cut me down a peg or two. Everybody I'm with seems to take on that responsibility and they kick the living shit out of me."

"What's it like staying married (37 years) and raising kids in Hollywood?"

"I would be pushing a shopping cart down the Third Street Promenade and talking to myself if I wasn't married. I married out of my league. I met George-Ann [Spota] when I was 17 and we've been together since. It was the only way I could've survived. I married somebody who is interested in the world around her, involved in the issues of the day, and tolerates what I do because it affords us a nice home. Other than that, if I could've been a congressman, she would've been much happier and more impressed with me. If she could've been elected to Congress, she would've been even happier. Frankly, she should be.

"When I was in that period when my phone calls were not being returned, I wrote two screenplays, one called *Hanover Street*. We were getting broke and a prominent producer wanted to buy the script for a shocking amount of money. I came home and told my wife, 'All of our money worries are over.' She said, 'Do they want you to direct?' I said no. She didn't say anything.

"I was sitting at my desk when she walked out and closed the door. I felt down. And she walked back in and stood in the doorway and said, 'I just want you to know that if you sell that script without directing it, I'm leaving you.'

"Her name is George, after the novelist George Elliot, and the priest said, 'I'm not baptizing any girl named George.'"

"Do you guys socialize much with the industry?"

"No. Our cadre of friends all came from the same school where we were parents. The only exception is my oldest friend in the world, Steven Bochco. Steven and I were born within five months of each other and our mothers were best friends. We grew up together. We were raised together. We bathed together. We learned how to piss together. We were clothed, fed, and scolded by each other's mother. Steven was a parent at the same school. Since then, I've made a couple of friends in this business—Billy Crystal and Candice Bergen."

"What does your wife think of this industry?"

"She thinks it is hard, quixotic, ephemeral, overrated and underrated. Underrated in that people in this business are much smarter than they are given credit for. Overrated in the sense that it is glamorous, fun. It's not."

"Your wife's views sound like your views."

"They are. They diverge in that she's not compulsive. She recognizes that she is married to a compulsive. Similarly if you were married to Michael Jordan, you would understand that his compulsion was practicing basketball. If I were a professor of history, or if I were involved with the government, she would be much more impressed."

27

Robert Kosberg

February 22, 2002

"How has the pitching environment changed in the past year?" I ask.

"Each year has gotten progressively tougher. I started pitching ideas a lot in the 1980s. You could go to any studio, pitch an idea, and get a development deal easily. Then through the 1990s, it became tougher as the studios became more consolidated. Everyone knows the business has shrunk. Development, along with other divisions, has shrunk, so there's not as much money to gamble on pitching. Studios run in cycles. Every year you will find different studios who don't want to hear, let alone buy pitches. There are alone four or five studios to begin with to pitch to, then when one or two don't want to hear pitches, you're going to just a few buyers.

"What I do to negate that problem, I try to find partners they can't say no to. There are always powerful people in Hollywood. I was just on a conference call to Julia Roberts' company, for instance. If I get her company interested on a pitch, and then we go to her favorite studio, which is Joe Roth's Revolution, my odds go up tremendously. Even in a world where pitching is difficult, there's always another way to skin the cat. Teaming up with powerful entities, be it a star, a producer, a director or a writer, works. You can pitch to production companies which have discretionary funds to buy ideas, hire a writer, develop a screenplay and then go to a studio."

"Contacts are even more valuable."

"The more people you know, the more ammunition you can load up to make your pitch even stronger and fight against the odds."

"Is this tougher pitching environment related to Hollywood becoming increasingly corporate?"

"Yes. When I started out pitching and it was a more freewheeling atmosphere, people weren't responsible to these corporate boards and the conservative nature of the boards which want studios to do sequels and brand name projects and not take chances on movies. You hear directors and writer and stars, want to make interesting films, complain about studios not wanting to take chances. The philosophy of studios not wanting to take chances filters down first from not wanting to make that kind of movie to we don't want to develop that kind of script to we don't want to buy that kind of idea. There's less development in general and . that affects everybody. It's a hard business to be in."

"I've been struck how every producer I've met is nice and professional and educated and hard working. I thought there would be more cowboys like Scott Rudin."

"The wild world where there were all types of people functioning in Hollywood and you could meet a million different types has gone away. In a more conservative, more corporate world, it squeezes everybody into the same box. It's harder to be original, outrageous and different because everything is squeezed into a corporate image. Everyone knows how tough it is to make a living so everyone is playing a similar game. If it is a difficult game, you better be good. You better be bright. You better be educated and have your stuff together. The people who are too speculative and superficial are probably going to fall by the wayside. Making a living in Hollywood is so tough that the people you talk to who are making a living will have similar characteristics. I find it in my travels also.

"How creative everyone is, is a different question to ask. The people who go to law school might be terrific in figuring out a good contract, but does that mean they are the right person for a position with creative power? I come from a creative background. I went to UCLA film school. I was strictly interested in stories and ideas and the creative side of movie-making. Not the physical, technical, editing, how to use a camera, how to be a line producer. I'm concerned that when I walk into a room to convince someone that I have a great story, and people listening on the other side of the desk, haven't come from that background. There is a contradiction that creative types have to face every day and that's why there's a lot of frustration."

"I think that in LA, many people in the production process don't know much about filmmaking."

"Square pegs in round holes. There are a lot of people who know a lot about filmmaking and they're not in the right place. A lot of people on the creative side find themselves in legal or agent positions. There are a lot of people scrambling for jobs and they're not always in the best place. Life isn't fair. The more independent maverick types really struggle because there is nobody out there who hears and understands and sympathizes with what they want to do. That's why the independent Sundance world is becoming as strong as it is. It's an outgrowth of how frustrating it is for most people, who used to be in the Hollywood system, to get their movies made. The two worlds overlap. Many of the movies that get nominated for Academy Awards, like *Memento*, feel like they are independent films."

"This past year, 2001, was not a good one for movies."

"If you knock down the amount of films that Hollywood makes, which had to happen because of budgets (average Hollywood picture costs $70 million), and you realize that the studios are conservative and want to make sequels, then you realize that the number of new and wonderful films is going to be smaller. That's why you have to look to the independent world to supplement."

"Few people will be able to survive and pay their bills working in the independent world."

"Few people will be able to survive and pay their bills working in the movie business period. On the level that I work on, development and creating ideas and stories, you can't make a living in the independent world. I have to work with the studios. With a good idea or pitch, I don't even go to the independent companies because they don't have the development budgets to finance ideas into scripts. They don't have development budgets. They only buy screenplays. The movies they make are based on scripts they've found that they love that they might option and package to do foreign sales and the things they do to push their movies into existence. But they can't risk spending money to hire a writer to develop just an idea. Because what happens most of the time when you do that is you go through months of development hell and many of the scripts don't get made. That expenditure would make most independent companies go broke. The only people who can afford to have development budgets are studios. I have to play the studio game."

"Did you see *The Player*?"

"I liked it. I didn't love it. I was entertained by it. They did a good job of poking fun at the silliness inherent in the world of pitching and selling ideas. It's true that most everyone who walks into a room [to pitch] sounds the same way and talks about Julia Roberts and Bruce Willis within 30 seconds."

"What movie would best describe what you do, particularly the pitching?"

"There hasn't been a movie aside from *The Player* that particularly looks at the world of pitching. Some of the smaller independent films such as *Swimming With Sharks*, and *State and Main*, are a good inside look at the making of a movie."

"What about books and novels?"

"The book that everyone looks at in a love/hate way that is the most legendary story of anyone who comes to Hollywood is *What Makes Sammy Run* by Budd

Schulberg. Even though it was written as an indictment of the type of person who will step on anyone to get to the top, as Budd Schulberg points out, the irony is that people today look at it as the Bible for how you should behave. They don't realize that he wrote it as something you're supposed to be ashamed of. That's a sad comment on Hollywood. I read it in high school and as despicable as the character might have been, it was an exciting look at inside Hollywood.

"Hollywood is stimulating and fast paced. You have to be very aggressive to make it. Maybe Sammy Glick is way over the top, but the people I work with in Hollywood all have a little bit of Sammy in them. On the positive side, I mean, the side that won't take no for an answer. That won't give up when they're rejected. That will just find a way to persevere no matter what. That part of it is what makes the book so popular. Everyone sees in it a little bit of what they know deep down they will have to be to survive, because every day, it's *The Myth of Sisyphus*. You feel like you are pushing a boulder up the hill and the boulder continues to fall back on you and crush you. It is hard to get up every morning and say, 'I am going to push the boulder again today and I may only get one or two feet up the hill, and I am inevitably going to get crushed, and tomorrow I will do it again.' There are few people with the personality to deal with that day in and day out.

"The movie business, from a pitch point of view, demands that you have a personality that is resilient. When I take a pitch out, I know that I am going to be rejected 40 times. Then on the 41st time, I'm a genius, if I'm lucky, but on a lot of projects, I'm never a genius. I'm just rejected 40 times."

"What keeps you grounded?"

"Having a family. If you have a separate life away from Hollywood, that also helps. I also love what I do. If you're doing something that you've wanted to do since high school, that allows you to be grounded because it reminds you that that's what you wanted in the first place. If you're just succeeding on that level, you can be happy. If you have all kinds of wild and crazy dreams, and they're not coming true every day, you are going to be disappointed and you're not going to be very grounded."

"What does your wife think of the business?"

"She's amused by it. She finds it difficult to hear me talk about the rejections on a daily basis because she shares my enthusiasm for a given project. She'll say, 'I can't wait to see that.' I'll have to remind her that she may never see it. The business frequently does not reward things that deserve to be seen. I'm not saying that every idea I have deserves to be seen, but lots of people I know, including myself, have had terrific projects that, for various reasons, never see the light of day.

"The film magazines over the years have frequently run articles about the top ten screenplays never made. You read them and they're brilliant, but for various economic reasons, they never happen and they become tarnished goods. Or they become too expensive to ever get out of turnaround from a studio. They languish. People wonder about this great script they heard about. How come with Julia Roberts and Tom Cruise attached, it never got made. *Shakespeare in Love* (1998) languished for years at Universal.

"My wife is a good support system and she has the same overall philosophy that I do—you have to laugh. You have to be amused by it or you cry."

"Do you guys go to Hollywood parties together?"

"No, that's not part of our lives. I almost regret that I don't do a lot of that because a lot of business is done on the golf course or at the party. I tend to keep the two worlds separate. I don't go to a lot of breakfast, lunch or dinner meetings or after hours parties. I like to go to screenings because I love movies. Sometimes I look at friends who are doing well because of relationships they make in that network and I wish that I could do more of it, but then it would be 24 hours a day, seven days a week with no sleep."

"Remember the Bob Levi character in *The Player* who went to AA meetings because that's where the deals were?"

"It's not a joke. The people I know who are looking for material find it everywhere from car washes to funerals to AA. There's no place so sacred that you won't hear someone talking about Hollywood. I was talking to someone yesterday who was followed into a restroom by someone who wanted to hand them a script. There are just those endless anecdotal stories about people who feel desperate and do desperate things.

"I just got off the phone from a nice call. Disney has bought one of the projects that I submitted. You're catching me in a good mood today. I think the reasons it sold are: (A) I identified a commercial idea, and, (B), I brought the project to the right company. I got the right partners who added the right strength to the pitch."

"How many people do you talk to on a given day?"

"Anywhere from 50 to 200."

"Do you have a secretary and say, 'Roll calls'?"

"That's a studio executive persona. I'm more casual."

"What does an average day look like for you?"

"I get up around 7 a.m. and read three or four newspapers (*LA Times, NY Times*, and the trades). I flip the dial and see what is going on in radio and television. I just enjoy learning. The old expression, 'Knowledge is power.' It's also entertainment.

"I come in to the office and keep a television on. I'll listen to the radio. I'll have meetings with writers and other producers who are pitching me. I'll talk on the phone. Then I'll usually get in the car and drive to a studio or production company and do two or three meetings where I will pitch some of my current material. I think that what I do best is pitch. I may pitch 15 different ideas in a day to five different buyers. Interspersed with that, I will meet with writers on projects I've already sold.

"Now, I could just concentrate on pitching one project. But that's not my personality. I'm hyper. The winds of Hollywood mean that if you spend all of your time on one project, it will cut your heart out when it doesn't get made. By having as many balls in the air as I do, I can watch them all rise and fall with a bemused eye, because ultimately I don't know which projects will get made. That's in the hands of the gods. I don't know if another studio is going make a similar movie which will ruin my project. I read articles in the trades almost daily about a story that negates something I'm currently pitching."

"Is the deal the thing for you?"

"I love stories and ideas. It's terrific high trying to develop those and convince other people in the business that you're right and they should buy your idea. It's fun prospecting for those nuggets like a gold miner. I don't disappear after the deal, even though I put such an emphasis on finding ideas that I get put into a niche in Hollywood. I'm known as an idea guy and a pitching producer, so people assume that once I've pitched an idea and sold it, that I'm gone. That's far from the truth. Once you've sold an idea begins the hard work of finding a writer, meeting a writer, working with the writer on the script. I'm involved all the creative meetings that a producer would go on. What I am not involved in is the physical day-to-day making of a movie because that's not where my skill lies. Once they're on the set, that's not where I want to be. I want to be back at my desk finding the next project. All the development process before going on set, I'm totally involved in because that's where I get to protect the original vision. I'm the one who gets to raise his hand in a meeting and remind everybody that we're starting to veer too far away from the original concept because I'm the one who either found it or thought of it. I'm usually the one fighting to keep the integrity of the idea alive so we don't end up on Mars making a Western when it is supposed to be a romantic comedy set in New York."

"Casting?"

"Once a director gets hired, you're at his mercy. As everyone talks about, the director is really the king of Hollywood. If you have a good relationship with the director, he wants you involved in all those meetings. If I have a more distant relationship, then I am not involved."

"What are your favorite projects?"

"The first one is always your favorite. *Commando* (1985) was the first big project I sold. The movie was a huge success and I still receive a check every year. *In The Mood* (1987) was a movie I sold around the same time. My writing partner David Simon and I read an article about Sonny Wisecarver. The one-line high concept is still good to this day—the 14-year old boy who was known as America's greatest lover.

"David and I flew to Las Vegas and bought the rights from Sonny Wisecarver. We came back to Los Angeles and sold the project. Then we wrote the script. I remember going to the movie theater in Orange County where it was being tested. The lights went down and the curtain went up and my name was on the screen. That's the biggest thrill of all. You've gone through this entire process and suddenly an actual physical movie is up there on the screen. And you're realizing that that thing on the screen might not have been there if it hadn't been for you. That's an amazing moment.

"More recently, the movie *Twelve Monkeys* (1995), starring Brad Pitt and Bruce Willis, directed by Terry Gilliam. I couldn't have been luckier to have brought something into the Hollywood system. I got it to the producer Chuck Roven who had a great relationship with a top screenwriter David Peoples. The script attracted Gilliam, Willis and Pitt. Then seeing a final film come out that's considered a classic science fiction film that was commercially successful. That's as much sheer happiness as you can get.

"I had an idea called *A Novel Life*, which has still not been made, but I got to spend a week with Tom Stoppard developing the story. Tom Stoppard may be the most famous living playwright. To have Tom Stoppard fly over from London and say to me that he was willing to work with me on my idea because he wished he'd thought of it himself. I couldn't be more flattered to have someone like that recognize that one of my ideas was worthy of his time. The fun of the process of working with bright stimulating interesting people keeps me excited every day. I just love stories. When someone tells me a good story, I want to see it get made."

"I've never done this with any producer, but may I pitch you an idea?"

"Sure. The last person who did this, I sold their project, with their permission, to Meg Ryan. Be careful what you wish for."

"Son of Christian evangelist converts to Orthodox Judaism writes a book on the pornography industry, exposes an HIV outbreak, saving lives, and as recompense gets thrown out of all the Orthodox shuls in his neighborhood."

"Number one it's smart. It's about issues and those are tougher to sell as issues because people are afraid that you'll never be able to get a script by most writers that will properly execute the level that that kind of subject matter inherently demands. Most studio executives don't want to go towards religion, philosophy, and certainly if you throw in something like AIDS, you're in a lot of red flags. Subject matter areas that are difficult. I tend to pitch things that are much simpler and probably more trivial. The opposite of that would be, a man meets a girl and she turns out to be a mermaid. Something as silly as a man meets a fish [*Splash*, 1984] not only ended up a huge success but made the careers of Brian Grazer, Ron Howard and Tom Hanks. A cultural phenomenon. Your kind of movie would never see the light of day unless it was written by Paddy Chayefsky. So I would never take on something like yours because it is too difficult. The niche market that would try to do your movie is so small and narrow.

"It is so difficult pitching commercial high concept ideas, but if I had to pitch your idea, I'd kill myself. I wouldn't even get up in the morning. The person who's going to sell that idea for you is someone who's as passionate about it as you are and decides that it is going to be a passion project. They know it is not traditionally commercial. They're going to beat down every door of people with similar interests to sell that project."

28

Kenneth Kaufman

"I made a film in my second year [of graduate work at the Annenberg School of Communications at Penn]," Kenneth says, "and it was looked at by producer/ director Otto Preminger. Mr. Preminger hired me to be his assistant [after Kaufman completed his masters degree in 1973]. It was a terrible film, a typical student film without much money spent. Looking back at it years later, it was about the worst thing I've seen in my life.

"Preminger was working on his second to last film at the time, *Rosebud* (1975). I stayed with him for three-and-a-half years. It was a remarkable experience. I traveled all over the world with him. His memory was starting to fail. He had the beginnings of Alzheimer's Disease. I became his memory. Otto tended to be larger than life. The kind of things that a young person could learn from him were not necessarily the technical things but that everybody was equal in his eyes. For example, whether it be the driver who drove him to the set or the head of the studio, they were all equal to him. They were all idiots to him. They were all subject to his wrath. I was never scared by anybody after that, or overly impressed by anybody because he managed to cut them all down to size."

"What is it with the rageaholics in this business?"

"Power does that. I've never found that the best way to the finish line. Otto was a guy who was used to getting his way. He had a huge power of personality. There wasn't a day on a movie or a play when everybody else didn't talk about him at dinner. Everybody talked about what he did that day and how he acted that day. That shows his power of personality. It had nothing to do with his talent."

"How would you rate him as a director?"

"If you look at his films now, he was an old fashioned director. He came out of the theater. In today's world of fast-cutting and moving cameras, he would not have fit in. He would set up a scene and photograph it. It was more of the actors moving than the cameras moving. He was however a remarkable producer. He produced almost all the films he directed in the latter half of his career. He went after controversial material. He understood that breaking barriers got publicity. He had a tremendous knack for publicity and promotion. He had excellent artistic taste. He had a good sense of casting and was able to attract the biggest stars.

"I wanted to make documentaries that changed the world. Preminger would say, 'Why would you want to make documentaries? In a fiction film, you can do anything you want. You can write it, hire the actors, and set them up the way you want. You don't have to go photograph what is actually happening.' It's ironic that I've become known for making docu-dramas.

"My first film appeared around Christmas 1983 on CBS—*The Gift of Love: A Christmas Story* starring Angela Lansbury, Lee Remick and Polly Holliday. We made ten TV movies over the next six years and received many Emmy nominations. *The Attic: The Hiding of Anne Frank* (1987) was nominated for six Emmys.

"It was possible to make that kind of material in those days. As time wore on, it became more difficult to make material we were proud of."

"It became more disease-of-the-week and women in peril fads."

"I made a dozen films in the NBC cop series *In the Line of Duty*. They were one of the few groups of films that appealed to men.

"We made the first one [in 1988]. It was called *The FBI Murders* and was about an infamous day in FBI history when a number of FBI agents were shot in Miami. Two were killed. The head of movies at NBC movies at the time, Tony Mesucci thought we should add a handle to the title. 'How about: *In the Line of Duty: The FBI Murders.*'

"It turned out to be a great idea he had. We were able to make another ten or so in the series. Luck plays a huge part in producing films. We had a good story. We took it to ABC and ABC passed on it. Then I called NBC about the story and they said, 'Don't even bother to bring it here. We're really not buying anything that is male oriented.' I said, 'I hear you, but it's really a great story. Let me come in to talk to you about it.' The executive said, O.K., but it's going to be a waste of time.'

"We made an appointment for three weeks hence. On the day of the appointment, he called me to say, 'Good thing you're coming in today. You're going to sell this to us. We just had a meeting and we need to buy some male oriented stuff.' So I walked in and they weren't even listening. They were ready to go. So we wrote a script and made it and its ratings were high.

"Then they called and said, 'Let's make some more.' We did, including one that was their highest rated film in four years—about Waco."

"When you have one sponsor behind a program, it tends to have a higher quality."

"Yes. They will want to make something where their brands will feel comfortable residing."

"We had more of this in 1950s television."

"That's when the advertising agencies really controlled it until things went another way. We might circle back to that because of the difficulties networks are having financially."

"If we returned to that model, I bet we wouldn't have as much crap on television."

Ken laughs. "It depends on who the advertiser is. An advertiser tends to spend more because they know they're going to be identified by the movie and they want it to be excellent. Some of the best movies of all time were made by advertisers."

"Tell me about your NBC movie *Howard Beach: Making the Case for Murder* (1989)."

"That was a fabulous thing to do. I'm a huge fan of Joe Hines, the special prosecutor brought in to the case, who is now the Brooklyn DA, but at that time was an ex-fire commissioner attorney for New York City, who was brought in to prove that this was not an accident but really a murder motivated by race. He did such a brilliant job that he became the main character of the movie. It was a complex and cerebral case and not easy to make a movie out of. We couldn't afford to shoot in New York so we recreated Brooklyn in Chicago."

In December, 1986, three black men ran into car trouble in Howard Beach, a middle-class white neighborhood in New York City. They sought refuge in a nearby restaurant. They were driven out into the street and one man was run over and killed by a car.

"I have always been a news junkie. The late '80s was a time before the explosion of news magazines. We had an opportunity in television movies to get behind the headlines and tell the human side of the story. The movies had the built-in promotion of nationally known stories."

In 1992, CBS televised Kaufman's *A Woman Scorned: The Betty Broderick Story*.

"Betty was a wealthy San Diego housewife. Her husband was a successful attorney. They had a rocky marriage and a bunch of kids. They got divorced. He ended up marrying his assistant after having an affair with her. Betty could not cope with it. She got up in the middle of the night, drove 20 minutes to his house, with keys stolen from one of their daughters, let herself in, went upstairs and shot both her husband and his new wife while they slept. She killed them.

"It became a huge event in San Diego. Oddly, much sympathy was on the side of Betty because he married his secretary. Even though this woman premeditated a murder, there were all these women's groups lining up behind her. We were fortunate enough to obtain an *LA Times* magazine piece by a brilliant journalist named Amy Wallace. We had the aid of a Pulitzer Prize winning researcher working with us, Sonny Rawls.

"We got Meredith Baxter to play the part. Meredith was at the age where she could relate to the issue of younger women in men's lives. We made a film that was not only widely watched, but it became a tremendous talking piece. So we made a sequel about her trial: *Her Final Fury: Betty Broderick, the Last Chapter* (1994). Her first trial was a mistrial, and then ultimately she was convicted of murder and sentenced to life in prison.

"It was a perfect example of a news story that was fascinating and an ability to get behind it and explore what it was like for a woman in her early 40s, with kids who were teenagers, whose husband falls for a younger woman. Betty was a bit loony. There was every reason in the world for her husband to turn away from her. Amy Wallace exchanged correspondence with Betty. We always try to tell both sides."

"How much creative license do you give yourself to fictionalize for dramatic effect?"

"We try as best we can [due to the limitations of the medium] to stick to the facts. You always have to do some reordering and compressing. You have to composite characters. If there were three investigators, we made them into one character. I had a couple of rules I always followed. One—never fictionalize the dead cops. Two—do not buy one side's rights so we were not forced into taking a position. Rather, we worked from public records, books, and articles that were even-handed."

"Is there a common denominator in the movies you've made that haven't worked?"

"You work as hard on the bad ones as the good ones. You think they're going to be fine and sometimes it just doesn't turn out that way. Often the ones that attract the biggest audiences are not the ones I like the best. They may be the most simplistic or the easiest to promote.

"The common denominator in bad movies is cast. You just made the wrong choice. Often times, those choices are made by committee. The network has a point of view and you give in because you want to get the film made.

"Our most controversial film was *In the Line of Duty: Ambush in Waco* (1993). February 28, 1993 was the day when the ATF and the FBI attacked David Koresh's compound. That began the siege which lasted until April 19, when the FBI went in there was a conflagration.

"On February 28, NBC called and asked if we wanted to make the movie. The siege had just begun. I said, 'I'm not really comfortable. Why don't we wait a year?' Then NBC said, 'We're not waiting. We want to make this right away. Either you're going to do it or someone else is going to do it.' I asked for 24 hours to think about it. I called a bunch of people, we had a team making these movies, and asked them if we could pull it off. NBC wanted it on the air in May. I called Sonny Rawls and asked him to come on board. He said yes.

"We began the project on March 1. We knew we had to start shooting within five weeks. We didn't have a script. We didn't know what the story was. We didn't know where to shoot it. The siege was still going on. So the ATF and FBI wouldn't give us any information. They wouldn't let us talk to anybody. Luckily, Sonny Rawls had the ability and the sources to get inside law enforcement. We got information that nobody else got because they knew we wouldn't be out until May. We got floor plans. We got interviews with the wounded law enforcement people. We decided that we weren't going to take any sides. If people had information, we were going to pay $500.

"Everybody was trying to sell us rights but we wouldn't buy any rights. We got a lot of information and we structured a script. The writer left blank the law enforcement scenes because we didn't know the exact facts of what went on.

"We decided to shoot in Tulsa, Oklahoma, because it has the same topography as Waco, Texas. I was friendly with actor Tim Daly, who was on *Wings* (1990-97). I described the David Koresh role to Tim and he took a flier [committed to the project], even though we didn't have a script. He was enormously instrumental in crafting his role. He studied Koresh and the Bible and the type of quotes that Koresh used. He ended up looking remarkably like Koresh.

"At the last minute, we were able to get a couple of key interviews with people involved in Waco. That enabled us to answer such key questions as, 'Why did the FBI go in when they did? And how did they know where Koresh was?'

"We were 14 days into shooting [on April 19th] when the FBI moved into [Koresh's compound] and there was the tragedy of all the people killed. We had to stop shooting that day because our actors were so freaked that the people they were playing were just killed. It was the most surreal experience.

"I was in somebody's trailer working on the script when the production manager ran over and turned on the TV. Here was this structure [going up in flames] that looked exactly like our structure 50 yards away. Our [movie] story ended February 28 [the day of the initial assault on the compound] so this was never going to be in the movie.

"The press descended on us. They went directly from Waco to Tulsa. At the same time, there were hearing in Washington about violence on television. Our trailer for Ambush in Waco got to the Congress subcommittee. Warren Little-field, head of NBC at the time, told us we had to take some specific shots out of the picture. It was the highest rated movie of the year for NBC.

"We dodged a bullet. I was on the hook financially. If I knew now what I didn't know then, I would never have made the project. We were playing with fire. We were making a movie without having enough information, not having the script done. It could've bankrupted our company. We could've made a really terrible movie. I think the movie holds. It's interesting and factually, it's about 98 percent correct. A couple of things we got wrong that nobody could've known until five years later.

"Our movie ended February 28 when the FBI agents were killed in Waco. Our movie was about how did Koresh get all this power and how did the FBI track him. What was the FBI doing that day.

"While we built our replica structure, we had to plant our explosions. That came before the words on the page. I was asked to do a bunch more quickie crime stories afterwards and I said no.

"I took a lot of heat for the violence issue. Congress was very excited. Every few years they get into the violence on television issue. We're the pornographers of our era. They used as an example the *In the Line of Duty* series because it was about violent issues. In fact, in our films, you always see the consequences of violence. That's the point of them. I'm against gratuitous violence.

"Our first *FBI Murders* movie did set precedents for explicit violence, but compared to what is on TV now, it is not even close.

"The other movie we did, which I would not have done if I knew then what I know now, was *In the Line of Duty: Smoke Jumpers* (1996). It was about the guys who jump into forest fires to put them out. A bunch of these terrific guys were killed horribly in Colorado.

"We had to recreate forest fires and I had no idea how difficult it was going to be. We had the cooperation of the fire protection people in Northern California. We found an area near Placerville where they were going to do a controlled burn anyway. We shot in the first week of the film all the fire we had to shoot.

"I didn't realize the danger until two weeks before we started shooting. I didn't realize that if it rained, we couldn't shoot. I didn't realize that if the humidity was too low, we couldn't have shot. Unlike feature films, where you can wait and shoot three months later, a TV movie has a small margin of financial success. You're only going to get X amount of dollars.

"We spent as much money on safety as we did on actors for that film. It was lucky that we got away without any problem. We ultimately had to do some of our aerial photography in Southern California and we ended up losing money on the movie. It could've been a true disaster.

"We shot on the week after Thanksgiving. They'd just had a heatwave and they didn't have any rain and they didn't have low humidity, and they were able to burn down a forest. We had prisoners working for us. We had the California Department of Forestry working for us. We were lucky.

"The television movie has changed dramatically. Four years ago, a producer would make a film and retain all ancillary rights. Now the networks demand domestic rights and there becomes little reason for me as an entrepreneur to make those pictures. I need to keep my [film] library fresh. If I don't get domestic rights, then I have to make other kinds of movies.

"Foreign rights, which used to finance the pictures, have dropped in value dramatically. The pictures are more expensive to make. So the independent producer has been in a position of tight margins.

"Lifetime movies are owned by Lifetime. So as a producer for Lifetime, you're making films for a fee. The company that I built was built on making films and owning rights."

"You've moved away from docu-dramas."

"They're not getting made anymore. The networks aren't interested. The television movie form may be a dinosaur. The only films that seem to be working are entertainment oriented films like showbiz biographies."

"How are you adjusting to the changing times?"

"I'm developing small feature films about subjects that I care about. Independent producing is getting tougher every year. I'm glad that I got into this business 20 years ago and not today, because independent producing of TV movies is barely alive."

"I don't understand why foreign rights to independent movies have declined so dramatically?"

"Number one—there was a tremendous oversupply. Number two–there's been a move outside the United States for independent national productions. They're not as reliant on American product. Number three, there's a worldwide recession. Advertising revenues are way down and people aren't spending as much money. When you have a fragmented marketplace, like you have here, there's not enough money generated by any one channel to pay for new television movies. Foreign rights were driven before by German rights, and the German rights market has gone down dramatically."

"Yes, the market is far more fragmented, but aren't there more places to sell your projects to?"

"Yes there are more channels but fewer owners. About six entities own almost everything. They have their production arms and they can afford to hire their own people to produce for them. It is not in any of the big six's interest to keep that outside producer alive. In fact, the outsiders are competitors who are easily squashed.

"I've seen the writing on the wall for many years. I had a project that ultimately got made by somebody else. It was a book called *Strange Justice* about Supreme Court Judge Clarence Thomas. I acquired the book to be made at TNT. We had a fantastic script and it was waiting to go and there were political reasons within the Turner organization that related to politics and court decisions."

"Clarence Thomas was to cast a vote on deregulation which affected the fortunes of TNT's parent company."

"Ahh, you're into it. You understand. TNT waited and waited to make the movie and ultimately they didn't make the movie. I don't know why but it appeared to be political reasons. I couldn't take the project to HBO because it was owned by the same people. Two years before, when TNT and HBO wasn't both owned by Time-Warner, HBO was very interested in the book. Now they weren't interested at all. TBS (Turner Broadcasting Service), I couldn't go there. There were all these places I couldn't go anymore with this project because they were all owned by the same people. That's the problem for the independent producer. If one guy doesn't like it, that's going to close off a lot of outlets. Or if somebody does like it, they will say, 'We'd love for you to make it, but we're going to own it.' What do you mean? 'If you want to play it on our air, we have to own it.'"

"From your economics background, you know that big business tends towards monopoly."

"You don't have to go to graduate school to know that."

"Adam Smith said that businessmen seldom gather to eat and drink without making deals that will defraud the public."

"We're certainly seeing it in today's headlines."

"Where do you think you and your peers will be in five years?"

"Television movies thrived when the networks played two or three TV movies a week. During the 1970s and '80s, despite the wide-ranging subject matters, the audience knew that if they turned into the NBC Sunday night movie, they'd get a certain quality. Then they became a series in another sense. The Monday Night Movie became 'movies that mothers and daughters could watch together.' That worked in a fragmented market. The TV movies became another kind of series. I think the next phase is that movies are going to be special events. As special events, I think they will continue to thrive. But special events don't create enough volume for a business. They are one-time events. I don't think the independent producer of TV movies will exist five years from now unless there's a dramatic change—government regulations, a breakup [of the leading oligopolies]."

29

Nicholas Loeb

February 26, 2002

I meet Nicholas Loeb (born August 2, 1975) at his mansion in the Hollywood Hills. He suffers from a head cold. We speak in his office, covered with pictures of Nick with famous people such as Presidents Clinton and Reagen and *Playboy* Playmate Sandy Bentley.

"Why did you become a movie producer?"

"Since I was six years old, I've acted in school plays. I went to boarding school Loomis Chaffee in Connecticut. It was a coed WASPy pretentious snobby upper class boarding school which I hated."

"You didn't make any contacts?"

"No. I don't even speak to anyone in my school. Every year the headmaster or someone from the school flies out to California to meet with me to try to raise money for the school.

"When I got to Tulane University in New Orleans, I thought I wanted to be the next Ronald Reagen. So I was a Theater/Political Science major. I soon realized that theater was more the history of theater and setting stage design than how to be an actor. When I realized that Political Science was more history of politics than how to be a politician, I dropped that too. When you go to college, you don't know what's what. So I jumped on the bandwagon and did what the rest of my friends were doing, and went to business school.

"I wasn't going to come out here because I did not know what I wanted to do. Growing up, everyone says, 'Don't be an actor. It's a terrible business to go into. You're never going to make it.' Nobody ever says you're going to make it.

"Then, sometime in my freshmen year, my cousin bought a studio. I saw a little ray of hope. I've got a relationship in Hollywood. I've got a door that might be open to me."

"Who was your cousin?"

"Edgar Bronfman Jr. So I started coming down here in the summers interning. I worked for Universal. I worked in corporate development for Brian Mulligan. I worked in motion picture finance for Chris McGurk, who's now president of MGM. I worked for two months as a PA for director Mike Nichols on *Primary Colors*. It was great."

"Why do you think that movie didn't work? [Made for $80 million, it grossed less than half of that in the United States.]"

"The marketing. That movie came out the same time as the Monica Lewinsky scandal. The studio wanted to downplay that because it didn't want to exploit Clinton. You know Clinton exploited Monica. The ad could've been perfect. You could've seen Travolta hitting on a girl on one half of the screen and Clinton and Monica on the other. And it would've been the biggest movie ever. They didn't do any advertising. While I was living in New Orleans, I saw one advertisement on television for it. For an $80 million movie, you should've been seeing it every day. No one knew the movie was coming out and that's why it flopped.

"It was probably too intellectual for the public and not enough sex and violence."

"Did you work with Mike Nichols?"

"Yeah, I got him coffee. I ran errands for him and for everyone else on set as well. All the PAs on the set had a relationship to be a PA. Everyone was Mike Nichols' cousin or John Travolta's wife's nephew. Everyone had some sort of hookup to get them the lowest job on the set. They had 12 PAs.

"It was a great experience to see how a set worked and what everybody's job was. To see how much the studio blew on a movie."

"Where did that $80 million go?"

"Catering was $1.2 million. I could've made a movie from the catering budget. We had Chateau Brian for lunch. They flew in lobster from Maine for dinner. They had sushi chefs on the set. Travolta wanted all that. Travolta had three trailers and four meals every meal. He had four different platters of food he could pick and choose from, and a $20 million salary.

"The only problem that I saw on the set was when they shot a scene in Santa Monica. Mike Nichols was on his cell phone. The First A.D. set up the shot and yelled, 'Action!' And Mike Nichols turned around and said, 'Who the fuck is the director?' Mike whigged out.

"All the actors were great. I spent half my time playing baseball with Billy Bob Thornton at night. That was one of my jobs—to play catch with him. Travolta never came out of his trailer. All the other actors were friendly with the crew. Travolta was aloof and private. He goes to the set and stays in his trailer. I don't think that's good. I think an actor should get more involved with the crew because the crew makes the film work. You want to love your talent because your talent are the stars.

"Even if you've been in this business for 20-30 years, hopefully you still get starstruck, because that's why we're here, tthe glitz and the glamor. If it gets old, why be here?

"The funny thing about this business is that people at the top, or even going to the top, never want to help anybody else. Nobody wants to help anyone in this town. Everyone's out for themselves. It sucks because a lot of people work hard and never make it. It would be nice if once in a while you saw a star reach out and give a helping hand. You know how lawyers have to do pro-bono work. I think every star should have to do one cameo in a low budget movie every year because it helps producers get their films made. If I had Travolta for two weeks to do a small supporting role in my film, I could raise all the money I needed to make my film.

"There's no union for producers. There is the Producers Guild of America, but it is not strong. If they set up a picket, the actors and directors would just be producers. Now the agencies are becoming producers. It's getting crazy.

"Every year the headmaster or someone from my prep school flies out to California to meet with me to try to raise money for the school. Last year the president of Tulane flew out to meet with me. I like Tulane. I won't give them any money yet."

"What do you tell your old headmaster?"

"I tell him all the stories that I have from the school, and why I hated it. Things they didn't do. Things they should do. If they make changes, I might donate. I spend 25 percent of my time doing charities.

"I came out here in September of 1998, soon after I graduated from Tulane. I wanted to be a producer. I had no idea what the fuck I was doing. I needed a script. I decided to write a script, with a girl I'd met over the previous summer. It was a fictional account of my life with a lot of truth thrown in. I thought I should write what I know. I fictionalized it to make it commercial.

"I had no idea how to write a script. Neither did this girl, Christina Peters, who'd never written or directed anything before. I submitted it to Universal and the comment that came back was: 'This sounds more like a psycho-analytical case study than a screenplay.' So that ended my screenwriting career.

"Do you mind if I smoke?"

"No."

Nicholas snorts and pulls out a cigarette. "I shouldn't even be smoking.

"I didn't know the difference between a good screenplay and bad screenplay.

"Christina had been trying to get her screenplay (*The Smokers*, 2000) made for ten years. I read it and I was not that interested in it. She kept telling me how all these people wanted to do it. I decided there might be something to it, so why not produce it? I borrowed $500,000.

"There's a funny story how I met Christina. I was a PA on *Primary Colors*. On my last night, I decided to take the cast out for drinks at the Sky Bar. Billy Bob Thornton, Emma Thompson, Adrian Lester, were there. I'm the only non-celebrity at the table. I go to the bathroom. I'm very naive. This guy approached me in the bathroom. He obviously thought I was a big shot. I told him that I wanted to do a movie when I graduated from college. He said he was a writer. I told him to send me material. I needed to meet writers.

"I read his material and I wasn't interested in any of it. I knew five people in LA. One night I called him up and I said, 'What goes on in LA?' I was from New York and New Orleans where things happened all hours of the night. Here everything closes at 2 a.m.. I thought there had to be a secret party scene that goes on after 2 a.m. that I had to find out about so I could go meet people.

"He said, 'There's not much that goes on here after 2 a.m., but there's a great girl I should set you up with.' I was confused why he would set up one of his girlfriends with a guy he met in the bathroom at Sky Bar. I thought that was amusing. The girl went out on a blind date with me. It was the most expensive blind date of my life. It cost me a movie.

"She had a producing partner already, Kenny Golde, who produced some TV. He'd helped her develop the script. He'd gotten her to register the script with his name attached as the co-writer. After I got the money, it took me nine months of contract negotiations to make the film because of him. He wanted sole producer credit. He wanted this and that. He wanted money. He wanted points. We couldn't afford him. I wasn't going to give this guy sole producing credit when all he did was give her some producer notes.

"Our three leads were Dominique Swain (*Lolita*), Busy Philips (*Dawsons Creek*), and Laura Birch (*American Beauty*) as well as Oliver Hudson, Kate's brother. We were set to shoot in Wisconsin.

"Remember, we had a director who had never directed. All the producers had never produced. None of us had done anything."

"Was Christina ever your girlfriend?"

"For a week, then we ended up just becoming friends."

"Why did you want to make this project? Just for her?"

"Yeah. I didn't know any better. Everyone seemed to like it. All these actresses wanted to do it. I thought they were going to be huge stars.

"I had a tough time dealing with agents. Nobody wanted to take me seriously. So I called the biggest producer I knew at the time, and the most famous person I knew at the time, Quincy Jones. I'd met him and he'd said, 'If you ever need help, give me a call.'

"I called him. 'I would like you to be a producer on this. You don't have to do anything. Let me just say that you're the executive producer on this movie.' He said, 'Send me the script.'

"I sent him the script. He said, 'Make me an offer.' I said, 'We'll give you three points [three percent of the gross revenues].' He said that's fine.

"He'd read the script. He said, 'This is some fucked up shit.' [That's a compliment.]

"The movie's about three girls at a boarding school who bring a gun back to school and decide to rape guys at gunpoint.

"In the summer of 1999, a week before we were to shoot the film, our lead actress Dominique Swain pulls out of the project. We're already in Wisconsin, ready to shoot. Her agent was named Tracy Brennan at ICM. And Thor Birch's agent was Jason Barrett at ICM. Their offices were next door. As soon as Dominique pulled out, Thor pulled out. Jason said that the only reason Thor was doing it was because Dominique was doing it.

"Dominique pulled out because she wanted Oliver [Hudson], who she was on a movie previously with, who she had a crush on, to play her boyfriend. There were three mediocre guy roles, supporting roles, and they were already cast. I was playing one of the roles. I could've moved around but we would've had to move another actor and I had already made my promises. And I wasn't going to break my word. I'd cast a friend of mine.

"Two of my leads had pulled out and I panicked. I barely even got the agents to return phone calls. I called Ron Meyer, president of Universal at the time. I knew him because of my cousin Edgar. I said, 'Ron, what should I do?' Ron said, 'Well, you could sue them. You would probably win, but you will win the battle and you will lose the war. It's not what you want, but let me think about it and I will see what I can do.

"I also talked to Jeff Korchek, head of legal affairs for Universal. He'd put me on *Primary Colors*. I said, 'Jeff, what should I do?' He said, 'We'll see. Let me make a call.'

"Five minutes after that phone call, Jason Barrett called me. He said that Thor Birch did not pull out. OK. So Thor was back. I said, 'What about Dominique?' He said, 'I know nothing about Dominique. It's not my business.'

"I don't know what calls went on. Jeff said, 'I don't know what they're doing but I advise you to get an attorney.' So I called an attorney and we sent a letter to Tracy Brennan and threatened to sue. She said, 'Ok, she'll do it. But we want this and that.'

"So I spent three or four hours a day panicking. She had all these demands. Her name can't be on the box. Then what's the whole point? Then she's not doing it. They strong-armed me into saying that at the end of the day, if we get a theatrical release, we had to pay her $150,000. At the time, I didn't care. If we sell the movie at a festival, the distributor will pay it. I had no choice. I was losing a lot of money.

"Dominique wanted a trailer. She wanted two first-class plane tickets. Finally, we came to an agreement. I had no choice. The day she's supposed to arrive, she misses her flight. The reason she missed her flight was that nobody sent her a car. The reason we did not send her a car was because we did not have her address because her agency would not give us her address. They said that wasn't their fault.

"We eventually got her to the airport by saying we'd reimburse them if they got her a car. We booked her on another flight. She misses her second flight. We had to buy her another First Class ticket to get her to Kenosha, Wisconsin. We got through to the gate agent. We're talking to the agent. 'Yes, she's here. She just checked in.' She missed her third flight. She went back to call a friend on the telephone.

"She finally arrived and she hated me. One day she asked for a second First Class plane ticket for her sister to come on the set. We said, 'Dominique, we already bought you three. You have to give us a week's notice. And the production is over in five days.'"

"Did she turn in a good performance?"

"She was O.K. I'm not going to comment on that.

"We finished the shoot in 18 days with a lot of fuck-ups. It was the first time for everybody on set. We made a lot of mistakes. It took us nine months to edit the film. I was the post-production supervisor and I didn't know the first thing about production. I thought it would save costs. It would've saved costs if I had hired a post-production supervisor. It was another mistake I'd made. I should've also gotten a director to help Christina on set.

"When it came time to do ADR (Audio Digital Recording), Dominique refused to do ADR. She was too busy.

"ADR is when the actors come in to do their lines so we have a clear track. When you have dialogue on a set, with a guy with a boom mike, a lot of it won't come across. So you have to go back and watch yourself on screen and redo it on a microphone on a clear track. On *Titanic*, 90 percent of the dialogue was done in ADR. In most films, it is done like that.

"Dominique's lines ended up sounding like crap. We didn't get the film into Sundance. We notified all the distributors and had a screening of the film in LA. We got a bunch of offers from foreign sales companies but no studios. I wasn't about to give my film away to a foreign sales rep. So six months went by and I said fine. I gave it to one foreign sales rep and I decided to keep my domestic. Another six months went by before I got a domestic distributor. After begging, I finally got MGM to buy the film. I would've expected help from Universal but they did send 11 people to my screening. MGM distributed it two weeks ago. It's in Blockbuster."

"Any reviews come back?"

"They're all terrible. The film ended up not being a success, but it was a great learning experience. I made a lot of relationships. I got a film done. I'll never do it again without having a distributor beforehand."

I talk to Christina Peters.

"I talked him into it?" she says incredulously. "Let me give you the real scoop. Yes, I was a blind date. I joked to him with that it was probably the most expensive blind date he ever had. We dated for about a month. Then we were just friends. He graduated college and wanted to produce a movie. And he asked me to produce it because I was going through ups and downs and all other shit."

"How did you feel about how the movie turned out?"

"It's a lot like life. I feel happy and not so happy. I was extremely happy that MGM picked it up and it went out to video stores and people can see it. That's the ultimate dream of an artist—that people see your work. I was disappointed in seeing how everything works. It's no longer your movie anymore. There are so many cooks in the kitchen and everyone changing something.

"I haven't seen the final product. I was so excited when I first made the movie but I did so much with it, it became like my firstborn child that I had to let go of. I know that they cut it from an NC17 to an R. I know that my favorite line in the movie is no longer in the movie. They changed the music. That was one of my biggest disappointments.

"I am so not complaining. I am so grateful to have made my movie. I glow whenever anyone says, 'I saw your movie at Blockbuster. My daughter loves it.' Of course I'm ecstatic. Somebody enjoys it and got something out of it. A lot of people really do get the message that I was trying to convey. That girls can't be boys. Women can't fuck like men and I don't think they have to. A lot of times, women in a men's world feel that they have to become a man. I'm saying there's an alternative in that route. There's power in being a woman and in being honest with what you want. Lisa realizes that she's not such a great person but that's who she is. Karen wishes that she had a boyfriend."

"How do you like making porn movies for LFP [Larry Flynt Publications, under the name Kat Slater]?"

Christina panics. "I don't want to talk about that."

Returning to my conversation with Nick: "[Veteran producer] Silvio Tabet gave me six scripts he was working on. He said to me, 'I've been around for a while. I like writing and developing. I don't like doing the hustling anymore. You do the hustling.'

"I read all six scripts and I liked one. It's a great action movie, like *Die Hard* (1988) on the tundra of Northern Canada. I've brought some writers in to do a polish. I rarely like anything. Since I've been here, I've optioned four things."

"It sounds like you are starting to establish yourself."

"I'm trying. It's really tough. Everybody wants to be in the business. I've gone further than most but I've had the benefit of my family who support me. It's hard to get anyone to listen to you.

"There are some producers who know development. There are some producers who just have relationships. There are some producers who just know physical production. I think a producer should know all those three.

"I was speaking to a 27-year old friend of mine at a production company with a deal at Warner Brothers. He says he wants to be a producer. I've sent him scripts for hopefully Morgan Creek to do. He says, 'We're looking for $30 million films, not $10 million.' I said, 'How do you know the difference? You've never produced a film.' He said, 'I just know.' I said, 'You've never worked on a set.' He said, 'I don't need to.'

"I said, 'What's a gaffer?' He said, 'I don't know.' I said, 'You want to be a producer and you don't know what a gaffer is? You are what's wrong with this industry. This is why producers end up overpaying and overspending. You could cut costs in half if top producers knew what everything costs and knew what everybody did. Then they'd know where they could cut corners.'

"Then you have producers who don't know development. They don't know how the story should work. Then there are those without the relationships, like me, which makes it harder to get anything done.

"I read an article in *The LA Times* about a month ago. It was a hysterical article about this agency in Japan that breaks people up for a living. They break up couples. They go on covert operations. It's a non-confrontational country. They hire this agency to help them break up with their girlfriends.

"So I emailed the writer in Japan. He emailed me back, saying he'd had a few offers. 'Let me get back to you.' He gets back to me and asks what I'm going to offer. In the meantime, I pitched my friend at Gold Miller who represents this director Keenan Ivory Wayans. My friend passed. He said he already had something like it.

"I didn't know what to do. I didn't have a writer to develop the story. So I blew it off.

"Last week, I'm sitting at dinner with an assistant at ICM. He said he had a funny story to tell me. At the end of every week, all the assistants have to come in and pitch story ideas to the story department to show what we've learned and how to pitch. I was reading this article in the *LA Times*. It was the same article. I pitched it. They loved it. They put a writer on it. The option was for $50,000. They pitched it and sold it to DreamWorks for $500,000.

"It's all about access. If I had that access, I could've pitched it and been a producer on it for DreamWorks."

"What type of access would you have needed to make that deal?"

"I would've needed access to a writer, who would read it without me having to call their agent and wait three months to get the writer to look at it. I would've needed someone to make a call to DreamWorks to get me a meeting. I don't know anyone at DreamWorks.

"I submitted a script to CAA four months ago. They said they really liked it and they were going to help me package it with a director and an actor so I could get it made. They haven't done anything. I'm a little producer.

"I had a script that a guy named Charlie Matthau who was attached to direct. Walter Matthau's son. Three years ago, he brought me in for a meeting. He showed me a bunch of scripts. He said that Aaron Abrams and Paul Sorvino were the co-writers of the script and he was attached to direct. I believed him.

"The script had been everywhere. It was a Mafia comedy.

"Three years later, I'm sitting at a table next to these guys from Fox. They start talking about Charlie Matthau. I said that I've got a script, would you be interested in this. This guy Eric Poticha was director of TV miniseries at Fox. We became close friends.

"He read it and said it was a cool project. It would be great for a TV movie. Everyone else had passed. Why not? I couldn't find Aaron Abrams manager but I found Paul Sorvino's manager. We had a meeting. The manager said Paul wanted to direct. He didn't know if he'd act. 'Make me an offer. He wants this amount of money.' He was being difficult.

"Eric at Fox says we don't really need Paul. Charlie says there's another draft written before, that Paul didn't write. I read it. It was the same thing except it wasn't Italianized. So we decided to run with this script. We didn't need Paul.

"My lawyer calls Aaron Abrams agent at ICM, Scott Seitel, who freaked out. 'Why is Nick Loeb running around town with this script? He doesn't have the rights to it.' Scott calls me up and screams at me. I said, 'Scott, I just got you a deal. Why are you screaming at me?' The reason he's screaming at me is that he didn't get his writer a deal.

"We all go into Fox for a meeting. Charlie and his manager, Michael Meltzer, who wants to produce. Charlie had read the script years ago and thought it was great. It was based on a true story. Charlie goes, 'I want to direct this. How do I get myself to direct this project? Hmm.' He decides to call the guys that the story is about, who are now in jail. He goes in and obtains their life rights so the script can't be made without Charlie Matthau. He backdoors the writer and the other producer.

"When I found out this, I knew this was all heading downhill. I decide to set up an LLC [Limited Liability Company] to produce it. I'm going to option the script. Fox will reimburse me for the option. Charlie will direct, I will produce.

"Michael Meltzer calls me. He wants to produce. I tell him I don't need a producer. If he wants to produce, he should call Fox. They tell him they don't need him, they have Nick to produce it.

"The next day, my lawyer tries to finish the deal with the agent Scott Seitel who tells me he won't option it to me anymore. He says he's working on a deal with Charlie Matthau and Michael Meltzer. I call Charlie and Michael and they say they're not optioning it.

"I get a call from Fox a couple of days later. My friend Eric [at Fox] says, 'Scott Seitel just pitched to me this script with Michael Meltzer and Charlie Matthau to produce. I said no because you bought it to me.' Michael and Charlie had lied to me.

"A day later, I got a call from Charlie Matthau. He denies he tried to backdoor me. He gets Michael on the phone and he says the same thing. I said, 'You just burned yourself a bridge. Not with me, but with Fox. They don't want to deal with this crap. If you want to pay my legal fees, option the material and then come to me to help produce, I might consider it. Then I'll go to Fox when I control it.'

"That's the last I heard from them, and it was two-three weeks ago. Unbelievable. The movie had sat around for three years. Charlie was finally going to get a chance to direct a movie. They fucked themselves by being greedy. This business gets more unbelievable every day."

"What type of movies do you want to make?"

"I want to do big concept movies. I want to make movies that are released on 2000 screens and that everybody in America wants to go see. Movies like *Armageddon, Independence Day, American Pie, There's Something About Mary* (1998).

"I'm working on a movie now about a married guy who loses three-quarters of his testicles in an industrial accident on the day he's going to make a baby with his wife. He goes on a journey to try to buy his sperm back that he had donated when he was young at sperm banks all over the country so he could buy his wife a ring. It's like *There's Something About Mary*. He's outside a sperm bank one day after they'd tossed away a lot of sperm. And he falls into the dumpster. It's really funny and grotesque. It's a cute story. It's all about his love for his wife. He wants to have this complete family because he was an orphan but he doesn't really understand what family values are all about. He could adopt a kid. It's a cute, fun, raunchy comedy.

"I'm working on a project about three guys who are cleaners. They clean up hits that have gone bad. And they get set up by the DA. When someone fucks up a hit, these guys come in and kill the hitman, clean up the area. They have specialty DNA where they can see all traces of DNA. A cool action comedy.

"I stay away from dramas and period pieces that aren't action based. They're hard to make."

"How would you compare New York society to Hollywood?"

"There is no society life here. The society consists of actors, directors and producers. There's no family society. There's no social register."

"Did you find those post 2 a.m. parties you looked for?"

"I started making them. I had a party for *American Pie 2*, which made the press. I invited Jenna and Barbara Bush and they showed up at 2 a.m. with the secret service.

"Yes, you can make contacts at parties. It's not difficult to make contacts. It is much more difficult to use those contacts. I had a friend who worked at AMG. He said, 'I'm leaving. There's a woman here you should meet with.' I met with her. She was really sweet. 'I'll help you out. I'll do this. I'll do that.' She didn't really do anything."

Nick shows me some T-shirts from his *Smokers* mover. For the guys, the shirts read "Rape me." For the girls, "Munch the Muffin."

A few days later, Charlie Mathau faxes Nick Loeb: "I was totally fine with your being a producer on *Picasso*, simply for your having the good sense to mention the project to Eric (and regardless of the fact that your only "rights" to the script was that you had read it—and regardless of the fact that I had shown the script to Eric a year ago). I did not and do not want to produce *Picasso*, only direct. I don't particularly care who produces it or how many producers there are. So, how am I greedy?

"I told you that we're not optioning the script. I don't have to option the script. I own the underlying rights. So what am I lying about?"

30

Mark Archer

March 1, 2002

Born October 6, 1973, Mark Archer is best known for producing *In the Company of Men* for $20,000.

"I've spent most of my life where I am now—Fort Wayne, Indiana. When I was 14, I was interested in broadcasting. I knew the church studio had a lot of cool gear. Part of my impetus for becoming part of the crew was that I didn't want to go to Sunday school. I discovered quickly that I enjoyed it and people started telling me that I had a knack for it. I did it all through high school. By age 17, I'd decided I wanted to do it as a career.

"In September of 1995, I shot a PSA against domestic violence. The group I'd been tossed into working with were on a no-budget film *In the Company of Men*. I took everything I'd learned from this $6500 PSA and applied it to a $20,000 film. We spent from January 1996 to June in sold pre-production. We had plans for every contingency. I'd learned that if you don't have any money, the best way to defend yourself is to have a plan for everything.

"So, for $20,000, we shot *In the Company of Men* on 35mm in eleven days in June.

"I remember doing a live call-in to an NPR station in Philadelphia. The question that was put to me was, 'What inspired you to take this film on? Did you believe in the story?'

"I said then, and I'll say it now: 'It had so little to do with believing in the script.' I thought it was an O.K. script. I'd never been into art films. My favorite films are *Terminator* and *Star Wars* (1977). It was the challenge of producing this film for $20,000. That's all I had into it. 'I'm going to prove that I can do this and hold the production together. If it gets seen, maybe I can get another film out of it.'

"We edited the film in July, August and September. We had no money to complete it so we did a video rough-cut and sent it off to Sundance. We didn't hear anything for five weeks. All of us had gone back to our day jobs. The week of Thanksgiving, I was completely broke from doing the film. I had incurred debt to finish the film. I was on the brink of bankruptcy. I was holding the debt load for the film.

"We had a little money left over. I called the director, Neil LaBlute. 'I have huge bills. I need to get some of this paid for.' He said, 'Well, O.K., we can take care of some of your bills, but I need to take some of the money and buy some snow boots.' I remember wanting to reach through the phone line and strangle him. I thought, 'Do you have any idea that I am dodging phone calls from creditors right now because I am about to go broke?' I said to him, 'Why is that?' He said, 'Because we're going to Sundance.' I will never forget that feeling because at that point, the universe turned upside down."

"Why haven't you worked with Neil since?"

"Neil and I were just going in different directions. I had read his script for what became *Your Friends and Neighbors* (1998), and I didn't want to do it. It was too much like *In the Company of Men*."

31

John D. Hancock

John D. Hancock directed *Bang the Drum Slowly* (1971). *Time* magazine critic Richard Schickel called it "possibly the best film made about sport in this country."

Hancock lived in Los Angeles from 1974 to 1993. "I was determined to like it and I succeeded for about six months. Our Malibu house was burned up in a big fire in 1993 and we moved to Indiana."

John married actress-screenwriter Dorothy Tristan in 1975. "I had several lucrative deals from Columbia following *Bang the Drum* that fell through.

"I was fired on *Jaws 2*. I was Dick Zanuck's choice for it. He and Sydney Sheinberg still had scores to settle on the overages [profit sharing] on the first *Jaws*. Sheinberg had my wife and I over to dinner. She was writing the screenplay. Sheinberg made a strong case that his wife Lorraine Gary, who played Roy Schneider's wife in the first *Jaws*, should go out on a boat in the second *Jaws* to rescue the kids. We went back and relayed this to Zanuck and he said, 'Over my dead body.'

"Not being used to dealing in a bureaucracy with powerful people, used to just running my own ship, I did not know that the thing to do at this point was to get the two of them in a room and say, 'Now you guys need to tell me which way we have to do this.' Instead, I thought that Zanuck is a person I've always liked. I've liked the pictures he's made. He's the son of a fabulous producer-director-studio head Daryl Zanuck. I thought Sid Sheinberg, he's just some lawyer. He'll come and go.

"So we turned in the next draft without Lorraine Gary going out on the boat to rescue the kids. Sheinberg never met my eyes in the commissary again. During rehearsals, I fired an actress for a small part. She turned out to be the girlfriend of another executive at Universal. That spelled my demise. Verna Fields [1918-1982, second unit director of 1975's *Jaws*, longtime editor] had a role in it. She felt she should have been offered the directorship based on her editing. It was politics and I made enough mistakes that I got in trouble. Directors are like baseball managers—they get fired sometimes.

"We were shooting *Jaws 2* on Martha's Vineyard in 1977. A Lear jet landed and the next day my wife and I were on our way to Rome to recover. I figured I should pull back. What was I doing doing *Jaws 2* anyway? That's not the kind of thing I went into business to do.

"I want to do an action picture. With *Bang the Drum Slowly*, I got typed as warm and human. I'm not."

"You're cold and inhuman?"

"Yes."

"Did it change you making *Bang the Drum Slowly?*"

"It changed my salability in the business enormously but no it didn't change me. I don't think it changed me inside."

"Do you prefer working on independent or studio films?"

"I just prefer working."

32

Stephen J. Cannell

Born May 2, 1941, Stephen J. Cannell has produced over $1 billion worth of television programs.

I meet him at his office building on Hollywood and La Brea Blvds. He wears gold jeans and an army jacket.

"I've spent hours reading about you," I begin. "Is there any one book or article that you think best captures you?"

"Most of them are condensed. One guy wrote his doctorate thesis on me but it was so wrong. I'm willing to cop to shortcomings but this guy had two theories. One theory was that everything I was writing was chronicling my personal life and career at the major studios. He was so fascinated by life at the studios that if I wrote *Baretta* (1975-78) as a wild man, it was because I was angry at Universal. I was never angry at Universal. Those guys were all my friends. I'm still friends with all of them. Then he had a theory of predominance—that the same themes reoccurred over and over again in my life and writing. There's some truth to that, but then he'd pick on episodes of some series, the scripts of which I didn't even write, that was similar to something I'd done in 1980. It was a doctorate thesis written by some kid. I interviewed with him because I wanted to help him but then I'd really disagreed with his conclusions.

"I know what my motor is. I know how I write. I know what intrigues me. I know how I get my ideas. I'm certainly not writing my own biography every time I sit down at the typewriter. There is one theme that reoccurs throughout my work—underdogs. I prefer underdogs. If that's recombinance, then I cop to that. As a dramatist, I'd rather write about David than Goliath.

"There have been some nice puff pieces, which have made me look much better than I am."

"I haven't seen anyone slam you."

"I don't get slammed often. I got slammed once in *Time* magazine around 1983. I was hot at the time. Both *Time* and *Newsweek* asked to do a story on me at the same time. I picked *Time* because it was a more prestigious magazine. This lady called me from *Time* and I brought her in like I'm talking to you. I talked to her. She shadowed me around. She writes her article. She calls me up for the fact-checking part of it. She says, 'It's a good article. You're going to enjoy it. It's really turned out good. I'm really happy with it. You'll be pleased.'

"So now the article comes out and it's titled, 'The Merchant of Mayhem.' It is a complete character assassination. It says that I am an egotist and that I do every-thing for money. There wasn't one nice thing about anything in there. So I called her up. 'I just saw the article in *Time* and I've got to tell you, I'm not real happy with it.' She starts to cry on the phone. I say, 'Don't cry. It's not the end of the world. I can take it.' She says, 'No, no. It's not the article I wrote. It's nothing like what I wrote.' So I said, 'Who wrote it?' She said, 'I can't tell you but it isn't my article. I apologize to you.'

"So I look at the bottom of the article and there's another name down there—Harry F. Waters, the entertainment editor of Time magazine. So I call the guy up. I've never met him. 'Harry, Stephen Cannell.' He goes, 'Oh yeah, hi.' 'Listen, I'm curious about this article in *Time* magazine. I hear that you rewrote it.' He said, 'I didn't get what I wanted from my writer in Los Angeles and so we did some changes.'

"I said, 'I may have a healthy ego but I don't know that I'm an egotist. People have to have healthy egos in this business because there's so much rejection. If you don't have a healthy ego, you get run out of the game, but I don't go around beating on my chest. As far as doing anything for money, I've never done any-thing for money. I was born wealthy.'

"He stops me right there. 'I've read your press package. Nobody's ever written anything bad about you. Maybe you just can't stand the heat.' I said, 'Well Harry, if you wrote the article, which I am now assuming you did, maybe you're just a complete asshole calling me an egotist when you've never met me. How can you make a personal evaluation of what kind of human being I am when you've never met me? It's perfectly O.K. by me if you hate my television, but to brand me an egotist and a money grubber never having spent a second in my presence.'

"Then he goes in to this whole thing about how he loved the *Rockford Files* and *Tenspeed and Brownshoe* and he hated *The A-Team*. His whole opinion of me as a sellout was that I'd done two shows he loved and now I'd turned on him. So he decided that he was going to smack me. The whole reason that he put her on the story was to get a negative article. When she didn't write it, because she came out and met me and she had some sense of who I was.

"A friend told me this once. 'The press is like a fuzzy cute furry little puppy and we all want to hold the puppy, but sometimes it bites you.' I was holding the puppy and I got bit. So you've just got to laugh about it and move on. Nobody remembers that article except me and Harry Waters and the woman he rewrote. Most of what has been written about me has been positive. I think that's because my motives for doing what I'm doing are simple. I really just want to make something that I like, whether it's *Rockford* or *Wiseguy* or *Tenspeed* or *The A-Team*, when I was making each of those shows well, I'd go home, watch them, and go, 'Yes!'"

Cannell makes a fist.

"One of the things that has surprised a lot of people, particularly my critics, is that such diverse product has come out of one head. You wouldn't think that the person who did *Wiseguy* would've also done *The A-Team*."

"Surely you are revealed in your body of work? What does your body of work say about you?"

"Some things but not every thing. There are certain things that intrigue me as a writer that wouldn't intrigue somebody else. I can't say what those things are. I tend to enjoy writing comedy more than heavy drama, but I'm good at writing dark things like *Wiseguy*. Several of my novels (*The Viking Funeral, Final Victim*) are dark.

"I'd imagine that my preference for underdogs and flawed characters comes from my own beginnings as a bad student, an underdog, dyslexic, branded the 'stupidest' kid in the class. I do respond emotionally to underdogs. I much prefer the flaws of my characters to the strengths. I don't find Superman to be an entertaining character. I enjoyed watching the Superman movies because of the special effects, but as a character, Superman doesn't appeal to me because he has too much going for him. One flaw—Kryptonite—and that only shows up occasionally. The guy's good looking, jumps buildings, bend steel bars. What's the problem?

"I much prefer a guy like Rockford who's put in prison for a crime he didn't commit. The cops think he's guilty all the time. His father thinks he's a jerk for being a private eye rather than a truck driver, which he views as a good solid manly job instead of running around trying to find divorced women's husbands. Rockford's flaws and his own sense of self-irony made him a fun character for me to write. I was always looking for the flaws in my characters. If you run down the list, *The A-Team* had the most flawed characters of any show I've created. Everybody on that show was dysfunctional.

"On *Wiseguy*, Vinnie Terranova was constantly in a moral struggle with himself. He had a set of values as a blue collar cop and all of a sudden he's undercover and accepted by a Mafia family in the first arc. He's driving some guy's Porsche and living in a high rise apartment with a view of the city. He's hanging out with a bunch of actresses from Broadway shows. All of a sudden he's being seduced by the very thing he's trying to bust.

"When I pitched that at NBC, and told them I was going to take five weeks to tell every story, they didn't want to do it. So I had to keep pitching it. I pitched it about ten times and I never sold it. But about four years later, I sold it to CBS and got it on the air. I never gave up on it. It was the flaw that attracted me, this guy struggling to stay on due north when all the input around him was driving him to want to veer south."

"Did you have to struggle to stay on due north?"

"No, I didn't because I love this work. It was what I wanted. My father was my greatest hero in life. My dad was a totally ethical guy, a tremendous role model for me, and my best friend. He taught me how to be and how to think and how not to take myself too seriously. He made me realize that you had to be a team player to get anywhere. All those things were ingrained in me.

"I was raised with money. My father [Joseph] was a self-made millionaire. My sister and I were raised great. I went to private schools even though I didn't get fuck all out of them. I was expected to learn. All I've ever wanted was to be a good writer. In my own mind, I'm an O.K. writer who's struggling always to get better. I have friends that I think are better than me. I read other novelists and think, 'Wow, this person is so great. Maybe one day I'll be like him.' That keeps me growing.

"My own fastball doesn't seem that good to me. I throw it real easy. Other writers tell me, 'Oh man, you're the best,' but since they're usually talking about my easy pitch, I tend not to believe them. And I'm looking at someone else's fastball and thinking, 'Wow, I could never do that.' I'm always calling writers that I admire to go to lunch with them.

"I was just reading Andrew Klavan's book, *Man and Wife*, and thinking, 'I could stretch in that direction.' So I'm now writing a book called *Love at First Sight*, which is a strange and different novel for me. It's nothing like his book at all but I'm using some of the technique that I saw in his book. I'm using the I-narrative. This guy displays his flaws more than his own strengths as he tells his narrative. I've never written a book in the I-narrative before."

"Who are your writer heroes?"

"David Chase (*Sopranos*) is one. We worked together on *Rockford*. I created the show and I was a boy wonder. I remember the first script of his that I ever read and I thought it was one of the best scripts I'd ever read. Better than anything I'd ever done on the show. I'm supposed to be the guru-writer of the show and I've got a guy working for me who's better than me. Instead of being frightened of his talent, I embraced it.

"Steve Bochco is another huge talent. We created a show together—*Ritchie Brockelman Private Eye* (1976). At the time we created the show, I was the hot guy at Universal. I had *Rockford, Baretta, Baa Baa Black Sheep*, all primetime network shows. Everything I was creating was going on the air. Bochco on the other hand was in purgatory at Universal. He'd been a writer-producer on a show called *Griff* (1973), which did not work. The executive producer, rather than taking the blame, which he should've because he was in charge, told the head of the studio that Bochco was doing the show. So Steve, at age 25, owned that whole network failure. He ended up hiding out as the story editor of *McMillan and Wife* (1971-76).

"Steven and I were friends on the lot. I was the David E. Kelley of that moment. We'd go to lunch together. One day, I had a meeting at the tower with Frank Price, head of the Universal studio. Frank asked me if I had any ideas for a new series. I could sell almost anything at that time. Without giving any thought to it at all, I said, 'Yeah, I've got this idea about a young guy who's a surfer and a private detective. He's got a surfboard on his car. He's up every morning busting through the curl at Malibu.' Frank says, 'I love it. I can sell it.' He took such a huge bite out of this thing. I'm going down in the elevator, and by the time I get to the bottom floor, I hated the idea.

"I was scheduled to have lunch that day with Bochco at this Mexican restaurant near Warner Brothers. We were sitting there having a margarita and looking at each other. He says, 'What's wrong? You're looking really down.' I said, 'I just pitched this idea to Frank Price and he took this huge bite out of it. And it's just about the worst idea I've ever had.'

"Steve said, 'Let's hear it.'

"I told him my idea and he thought it was a good idea. Steve said, 'But you've got the wrong take. It's not about surfing, it's about age. What if he looks so young nobody will take him seriously? What if clients walk into his office, see a guy who looks 16-years old sitting there and they do a U-turn and they're gone? So he has to get the guy down at the end of the hall who's an accountant to pretend to be him. So he tells the clients, 'No, no. I'm not Ritchie Brockelman. Let me go down the hall and get my dad.'

"So we sat there until 5 p.m. banging this thing out, putting the bones on it, coming up with the pilot idea [for *Ritchie Brockelman Private Eye*]. So when we were done, Boch said, 'This will be great. Go sell this to Frank.' I say, 'Boch, you've got to do it with me.' He says, 'I'm not going to do it. They think I suck.'

"I said, 'I would never have gone in this direction if it weren't for you. I just had a stupid idea. You've got it going in the right direction. I'm not going to write this without you.' He goes, 'If you put my name on it, there's no way it will ever go beyond the first meeting.'

"I said, O.K., why don't we just write it on spec? When we send it up to the Tower, I'll just put a cover page on it with no name. Once it's sold it, I'll say, 'By the way, this is a co-authored script with Bochco.'

"I called Frank Price up and said, 'I've got an idea for the script. I'm going to start work on it.' Frank said, 'I've already talked to NBC. They love it. They want to go forward.'

"Boch wrote half the script and I wrote half. We wrote a 90-minute pilot and sent it up to the studio with no cover page. NBC loved it. Then I said, 'Oh, by the way, Bochco is my co-author.' By that time, they didn't care because they had it sold.

"I always knew Steven Bochco would be huge. I was surprised that it took David Chase so long because David was as good when we did *Rockford* in 1976 as he is today.

"I love Dick Wolf, David Kelley, Don Bellisario. I gave him his first script assignment."

"Who are some of the other people who've worked for you?"

"Frank Lupo, Patrick Hasburg (*21 Jump Street*), Juanita Bartlett, Randall Wallace (*Braveheart, We Were Soldiers*), David Burke. Director Rob Bowman worked here as a gopher and then as a production assistant. I gave him his first directing jobs. He went on to do *The X-Files* feature. My job as a studio owner was to find people who were young and inexperienced but I thought had talent. I could buy them cheap and I would train them. Often they were diamonds in the rough and they didn't know how to plot a story or understand three act structure. I'd try to make them stars. If a writer did a good job on the script, and the picture turned out good, I would always take the writer to the network with me. We'd physically screen our pictures for the network. It was a great chance to expose young writers to the network. The network would tend to give me all the credit but I wasn't going to be able to grow my studio if everybody thought I was the only person with any ability over here.

"If it was a good movie and I brought the writer over and gave him credit, you could just see the writer begin to grow in their eyes. At some point, I would want that writer to have a pilot. If the network wouldn't go for it, often I'd have to say that I'd co-write. I hated doing that because I much preferred writing my own stuff, but to get the writer that first gig, I'd do it. If you'd ever see anything that was co-written by me and another writer, that writer's name is on top. I always took the second credit. My goal was to push those people up.

"Eventually, the network would offer these guys million dollar contracts. I'd be paying them half that. The writers would come in to me and say, 'What am I going to do? I want to stay here but Disney is offering me one million.' I'd tell them to go. You can't turn a million dollar deal down. I can't match it. So I'd be constantly looking for the new young person."

"Did you know that you had the producer in you?"

"My dad was my hero. He was an entrepreneur. He taught me that you need to support other people to be successful. My father used to say, 'Don't go around catching someone doing something wrong. Catch someone doing something right. It's much more effective.' As a kid, I used to watch him do it because I worked for him in the summers. He owned a bunch of furniture stores. Cannel & Chaffin. He'd walk the floor on these furniture stores and he'd see something he'd like. He'd stop and ask, 'Who did this?' 'Oh, Lowell did that.'

"My dad would hunt Lowell up and say, 'Lowell, come here. That is great. We need more like that.' He always had people just churning to do more.

"When I was at Universal, I believed in the value of a contract. It would never occur to me to threaten breach of contract to get a better deal. I signed a deal as a head writer to make $600 a week. I was the cheapest writer on the lot. It was the lowest deal you could do by Writers Guild standards, but I'd been working for my dad for $7000 a year. I was at Universal for eight years and I never renegotiated my deal but once. It was late in my arrangement with Universal. There was one thing in my deal that my agent had managed to get in there—I had good fees for my pilots. The reason they did it is that they never thought I was going to write a pilot. So they'd give me $70,000 to write a two-hour pilot and a $100,000 production bonus if it ever got made. Then I became the hottest pilot writer at Universal. I was writing two or three pilots a season. I was making $400,000 a year in pilot fees.

"Because people wanted me to write pilots, I eventually had four shows on for Universal. I was so under water, that I couldn't do any pilots. So in success, my gross income went down. So my agent said to Universal, 'Steve's been so success-ful that he can't do a pilot this year. He's got four shows on the air. This is good for Universal but bad for Steve.' They said, 'Yeah, we see the problem. We'll address it but we want two more years on his contract.'

"So I called up Sid Sheinberg, the head of the studio at the time. I told him the problem and added, 'You've got to know that if you don't give me a dollar, that's O.K. I signed this contract and I will live up to the terms of it. I'm not going to come in here and limp my way through the next two years. I'm going to come in here and swing from my heels like I always have. I just thought you guys wouldn't want to see me get punished because I did a good job for you. but I'm not going to give you two years.'

"Sid didn't know what to do. He wasn't used to hearing this kind of presenta-tion. I didn't threaten him. I just asked him to be paid. There was no anger and no recrimination. A month later, he changed my deal. My father would say, 'Live up to your agreements.' I used to call him up and ask what I should do. He'd say, 'Son, you're only as good as your word in life. If you give some guy your hand, they'll always remember that you didn't renege on it. Even if it wasn't in your best interests, that commitment will follow you through your entire career. That story will get told. And that's more valuable than the money.

"Another thing I learned was that many of my friends had a tendency to over-value themselves. I remember having lunch with a talented writer, producer and director. And he was trying to renegotiate to get his fees improved. So I was the wrong guy to be talking to.

"I sat listening to him yammer about how good he was. How Universal didn't know what they had. I'm thinking, this guy needs to cool down. He says, 'If I leave this goddamn show, nobody else can do it. Not a soul on this fucking lot can do it.' So when he took a breath, I leaned across the table and said, 'I can do it. I can do it good. If they call me up and ask me to do your show, I'll do it. You'll probably see the difference and I'll see the difference, but nobody watching television will see the difference. Calm down. You're going to make an enemy out of this studio. Don't do it. You're too angry and you're wrong. I can do your show and you can do mine.'

"I used to see so much of that. People saying, "We've been ripped off. We've been screwed. The studio is fucking us.' They're fucking you? You're making more money than heart surgeons, and many of you didn't even get out of college. They're fucking you? Maybe compared to other people in show business but this is never-never land. We should all be spanked for cashing our checks. This is lunacy.

"Everybody bought into that lunacy but I never did because my dad was so pragmatic. I'd say to myself, 'I'm lucky I'm here because these people don't know what a dollar's worth.' Since I was 13, I had to go to work in my father's factories. I was working with Mexican-Americans who had nothing. Who had no education and had no chance to see what was in life and the world. I'd work all summer with a guy and like the guy and I'd realize how limited his whole existence was because he didn't have opportunity. I'm being paid all this money to sit down and tell stories. That guy's working eight-hour shifts on a screenprinting machine in 100-degree heat for a little over minimum wage.

"Even though I was raised with in a lush environment, I was raised by a man determined that I wasn't going to become a bratty spoiled kid, and that I was going to know the value of a dollar. That I wasn't going to hang out at the tennis club all summer. When I got to Universal, it meant something to me to make my shows for the money. If Universal told me that I had to make a *Rockford Files* episode for X number of dollars, I'd make it. I really cared that I got it in the can for that price. They were paying my salary and I was their employee and I was being given an order. I understood on a business level that there is only so much profit studios can make on every hour of this stuff and if I spent twice the budget, I'd eat up the profit.

"I would work to stay on budget. Quickly the production department knew I was a good guy. The guys in the Universal production building knew that I gave a shit about that problem. So if I couldn't get a show on pattern budget, I'd tell them.

"Every series has a pattern budget—what the average show ought to cost. They're all custom shows, but we're not making Fords that all look the same. So each show would budget out differently though we'd have a pattern for what each show ought to cost. We'd shoot three days on the lot and four days off the lot. We'd use X number of actors as day players and guest stars. X number of stunts. Let's say that *Rockford* back then would cost $650,000 [per episode]. That was your pattern budget. Every show had to be on or below pattern before they would approve it.

"Sometimes you'd squeeze 'em down so they would be on pattern, but they weren't realistic boards. So when you went out and shot them, there'd be a lot of overtime and then you'd have a fucking budget disaster. The production department would yell at you and drag you into meetings. There was constant shit like that going on all the time. Producers on the lot wouldn't cut their scripts to bring them down to budget. So the production department wouldn't let the producers cast.

"The reality is that the better actors in the guest star acting pool work all the time. If you could get to the actor you wanted eight days before shooting, he might be available. But if it's two days before, he's probably already working.

"After I'd produced for a year or two, they realized that I took the pattern budget seriously. If I couldn't get a show on pattern, I'd call up Dick Berni, who was head of production at Universal. 'Dick, I've got a problem with this show. Let me tell you why it is going to go 10-15 percent over pattern. Here's the problem I can't solve. Maybe you can help me.' Eventually, he'd let me have the extra 15 percent if I promised to get it back to him in the next two shows. They trusted me. So I got some leeway that the other guys didn't get.

"When my eight-year contract with Universal expired in 1979, they offered me over a million dollars a year to re-sign. No writer had ever been offered a million dollar deal. I was flattered but I started thinking. I created all these shows and I make no money from them. I just get my fee and a tiny creator royalty. The programs are owned by Universal. If they make $300 million from *The Rockford Files*, I get none of that. Then my entrepreneurial spirit kicked in. Wanting to be my dad, my hero, I went to him and asked, 'What do you think? Do you think I should try to form my own independent studio?' If you look around, you'll see that David E. Kelly and Steve Bochco Productions are all underwritten by major studios. Those are Fox-owned shows.

"I decided that I didn't want to have a studio as a partner. I wanted to be myself and own my own shows. My dad asked, 'Can you do it?' I said, 'I think so. I think I understand how this animal works. I learned how to control budgets for Universal. I think I can do it for myself.'

"So I walked away from that Universal deal and I formed Cannell Studios. I made a deal with ABC. They guaranteed me three pilots. It was a complicated deal with trigger mechanisms in it for extra series and other things. I signed up. I went off and made *Tenspeed and Brownshoe*, for which I won a Writers Guild award for the Best Screenplay of 1981. It was a good script and I really needed a good script on my first privately produced deal."

"It was touch and go for you the first three years?"

"I made a lot of mistakes. It turned out that I didn't know what I was doing. I wasn't as smart as I thought I was.

"At the beginning of *Tenspeed*, I had a small company. I was trying to keep my overhead down, something I learned from my dad. You know what an alligator is? It's a business where the overhead eats the equity. I didn't want my company to be an alligator.

"The pilot sold. We were shooting the first episode of *Tenspeed.* I said to Alex Beaton, my line producer, 'I came in to my office this morning and I didn't see my daily production report.'

"At Universal, producers would get a daily production report on their desk every morning. The top of the report would have the budget of the show and then under that would be whatever additions or subtractions occurred when we shot last night. If we went over two hours, into union golden time, there's probably $15,000 in add-ons. If we went under an hour, maybe there'd be a $2000 savings. Underages never equal overages. If something went wrong, like our camera got hit by a car, that would be in there. Then at the end, it would have a new adjusted budget for the show. You could look at the new budget and drive the show economically. 'Geez, we're $100,00 over. Maybe we don't need 40 extras in this party scene. Maybe we can get away with 20.' But if you don't know what things cost you, you're flying blind.

"So Alex said to me, 'There isn't a daily production report.' I was personally at risk. I said, 'How can there not be a report?' Alex said, 'Steve, there's a whole building at Universal that generated these things for you every morning. A whole building that works all night long. And we've got one production accountant and he's working on next week's show.'

"I asked, 'How many people do we need?' Alex said that we needed at least four people to track this stuff and they won't be up to speed until the fourth episode. I couldn't afford four people. By the time of the fourth episode, I could be out a million dollars out of my own pocket. It had never occurred to me that I wouldn't be getting a daily production report every day because I'd never looked behind the curtain.

"I finally hired two people and they were slow getting these numbers to me. Well after the episode wrapped, I'd find out that I'd spent $250,000 of my own money. Then the next episode wrapped, and I'd find out that I'd spent another $250,000 of my own money. I was only 32 years old. I was thinking, 'I don't want to sell my house over this.' The network gives you a license fee for a show but it generally doesn't cover your entire cost of production. You sell your foreign rights, and if you're careful, you can get close to covering your costs. [The big TV payday comes in syndication.]

"I'm thinking that I'm going to be in debtor's prison by the end of this 13-episode production. I called Tony Themopolis, head of ABC. 'Tony, I have a major problem. I'm trying to manage a new studio. I've got the final figures on the first two shows and I'm out half a million dollars. You know that's out of my pocket.

If this keeps on, I will be out of business. I need you guys to underwrite some of this.'

"Tony says, 'I see you problem. The shows look really nice, but we have a contract.' I said, 'I know we have a contract. I'm begging you to give me some relief here.' I knew at the time that Aaron Spelling had a cost-plus deal at ABC [whereby ABC would shoulder his extra costs], so he could never go into his own pocket. Whatever his overages were, ABC would pay. Aaron would still own the negatives. Spelling had the best deal in town.

"I didn't want to say, 'Give me Aaron's deal.' They would laugh at me. We had several conversations until I said, 'Tony, I'm going to have to cut the value of the shows down.' He said, 'Don't do that.' I said, 'Put yourself in my place. I don't have any partners. It is me and my wife Marcia. I can't spend $250,000 dollars a week of my own money. I don't have that kind of cash. I only have one option. I have to cut down the value of the shows. I'm going to have to start making some pocket shows.' He says, 'Don't do that. If you do, you'll end your career with ABC.'

"I said, 'Tony, come on man.' He said, 'I'll call you back at 5 p.m..' He calls me back. 'You keep going the way you're going and we will make some accommodation at the end.' I asked, 'What kind of accommodation?' He said, 'I don't know.' I said, 'Will you put that in writing that you will make an accommodation?' He said no. I said, 'Tony, what if you get hit by a bus?' He said, 'Steve, that's the best I can do.'

"So I had to put my whole life on the line to make the last six episodes of *Tenspeed* and trust ABC not to let me swing when it's all over, to just look me in the eye and say, 'It didn't work and so we're not going to cover you.' I made a heroic choice to go forward with nothing more than Tony's word. When it was over, he took care of me. He didn't make me whole completely but he picked up 70 percent, enough to allow me to stay in business.

"I thought I knew what I was doing, but I plainly didn't. Even though I was a good advocate for Universal, they were still tougher than I was. There were times that they refused me things that I would've probably gone ahead and done if I was my own boss. They wouldn't have let me but I wanted the shows to be better. I didn't want it to look like shit so I'd spend the extra money. When you pile all those things up at the end of the year, it ends up being major dough.

"My overhead was too low and I had to start acquiring more people. Then along comes *The A-Team*, which we sold to NBC, and suddenly we have our first big hit. I couldn't afford it. It was costing me half a million dollars a week because of all the stunts. I knew if I took the stunts out, I didn't have a show.

NBC wasn't about to give me more money. So we had the whole board of my studio in this office and we did a cost analysis and we realized that we wouldn't be able to make our payroll in three months.

"My CFO said we were either going to have to get bank financing or we will have to sell the show to another studio. We'd be selling the number one show on television, which could be worth $100 million, but we've got to be able to stay in the game to collect.

"We hunted around and finally the Wells Fargo bank said they'd be interesting in financing our show. We worked the papers out and there was one thing that seemed odd to me. They wanted me to put my house up along with everything else. So I called my dad and he said not to do it. He asked me how many times had I met with the bank and for how long had we negotiated. I said we'd met four times and negotiated for six weeks. He said don't do it. They will make the deal without it. The only reason that they want your house in the deal is that they want you emotionally committed to this deal. They'll do the deal without making you commit your house. So I kept saying no and they kept saying they wouldn't make the deal. It went right to the eleventh hour on the deal and at the last minute they agreed to make the deal without forcing me to put my house on the line."

33

Eric Louzil

March 14, 2002

A hefty bearded man of over 200 pounds, Eric Louzil invites me into his cramped Sunset Blvd office.

"I almost became a ballet dancer. My mom was a dancer in Europe. I went to ballet classes for three years. I didn't tell anyone at school [in Sydney, Australia]. I was on the swim team too. As we were moving to the U.S. [around 1967, when Eric was 14], I was accepted into the Royal Australian ballet program. There was one guy there and about 200 girls."

Eric graduated UCLA film school in 1975. "*Sonic Boom* (1974) was my student short film. Most students do films about quadriplegics or handicapped people.

"Every weekend we took out the *LA Times* Calendar section and took out the list of what actors were in town. We'd then figure out how to go see them and put them in the film. Keith Moon was our biggest find. I still have the contract. It says that we had to give him a case of coke and one TV set. We drove to Palm Springs and spent $1400 for the cocaine to make him happy. It was a choice between him and Elton John, who at the time was playing at the Troubadour. Everybody thought Elton was too small. Keith was then considered one of the greatest drummers of all time. Keith was a party animal. He gave us a day for free.

"During my 13 years bouncing around the studios, I got 26,000 hours in. During the summer, when it was slow, we'd make a film. We'd shoot it on weekends. In 1986, I met Lloyd Kaufman from Troma Pictures and we hit it off. The first film I made for them was called *Georgia County Lockup*, a women-in-prison film changed to *Lust for Freedom* (1987). We used to say, 'You'll laugh. You'll cry. You'll kiss five bucks goodbye.'

"We made the film for $50,000 and then Troma gave me another $125,000 to improve the sound, add scenes and blow it up to 35mm for a theatrical release.

We made a ton of money on the film, more than $2 million, because those were the days when people were buying videos and paying high prices.

"Troma is still going strong, with a film library of over 2000 films. Lloyd never wanted to go public because he wanted to control the destiny of the company. They've been in business for about 30 years. Lloyd and his partner Michael Herz graduated from Yale. They were close friends with John Avildsen, who directed *Rocky* (1976). They used to work on pornos in New York. John Avildsen used to direct pornos. Sylvester Stallone was known as the Italian Stallion.

"Troma did all the post-production and location scouting for *Rocky*. Lloyd plays the bartender in all the *Rocky* movies. Lloyd worked as an associate producer on big films like *The Final Countdown* (1980).

"Lloyd's so energetic. He's into Chinese–Japanese culture. He speaks fluent Mandarin Chinese and Japanese. Troma has a cable TV show in Europe. Not here, because, as Lloyd puts it, 'The gatekeepers won't let me in.'

"They have a brand name. When you say, 'I'm going to watch a Troma film,' you know it's going to be mayhem and tits. Lloyd is not like that in person. I remember when we were going through the script for *Class of Nuke 'Em High* (1986) at Dennys on Sunset Blvd, Lloyd eliminated all the 'Fucks.' He crosses out everything that is derogatory.

"A lot of his reputation is misinterpretation. When *The Toxic Avenger* (1985) got screened in Canada for the censorship board, it was the first time in the history of the board that the censors walked out after about ten minutes. *The Toxic Avenger* is about a blind girl who lives in a junkyard. When she's feeling the guy's genitals out, she says, 'Oh my.' She's blind. Lloyd says they submitted the script to the Institute of the Blind in New York and they thought it was a funny scene. They approved it. Yet people criticized the film for making fun of blind people. But the blind people thought it was funny.

"I made about seven films for Troma. My second was *Fortress of Amerikkka* (1989). Lloyd put three 'Ks' in it. One of the presidents used that line years later. 'We will not return to a *Fortress of Amerikkka*.'

"I made *Sizzle Beach, USA* (1986) just as I was meeting Troma. It starred Kevin Costner as did *Shadows Run Black* (1986). I sold both films to Troma. Kevin was also a grip—stagehand at the time. He was very inquisitive. We worked together at Raleigh Studios.

"A lot of people were calling *Sizzle Beach, Silicone Summer*. More women then were getting breast implants than they are today. I don't think anyone in the film had natural breasts. Back then there was more nudity in films than there is today. Today you won't see full front female nudity but then it was common. On men it wasn't acceptable. You couldn't do a backshot of a male nude but now it is O.K. on TV.

"We shot *Sizzle* and *Shadows* on weekends and it took a year to finish them. Many films were shot on weekends then including a famous one, *You Light up my Life* (1977). People had jobs during the week. Today people just max out their credit cards and shoot.

"Kevin was just a stagehand. When you needed something then, you'd go to Kevin's boss and he'd tell Kevin to go get it. Kevin walked into my office one day and said he was thinking about getting into acting. He was a good looking guy so we gave him the part and made him one of the boyfriends of one of the girls in the film.

"My wife and I kidded at the time about signing him to a percentage deal of his future employment, in case he became a star.

"He was a terrible actor. I like him in some stuff today but I don't think he's a classic actor. He had a terrible habit of putting his hand in front of his mouth when he was talking. So we'd cut the camera and say, 'Kevin, you've got to take your hands away from your mouth.'

"Years later he did a film called *No Way Out* (1987). The critics said that the love scene he did in the backseat of the car with Sean Young was the steamiest love scene in a decade. We laughed because the first film we did with Kevin, we had to give him a bottle of wine. He was stiff. He didn't want to kiss the girl. He was shy. He had two kids at the time.

"The last interaction I had with Kevin was during *No Way Out*. He wanted to buy back the two films we did together but I'd already sold them to Troma. He was pissed. He didn't want anyone to know about his early films. He'd just gotten the lead role in *The Untouchables* (1987). Everybody knew that because he had the lead in a Paramount film, he was going to become a star. The producers and distributor of *No Way Out* held the film back a year because they knew they would have something valuable once the publicity machine for *Untouchables* came on board and made Kevin a star.

"You have to understand that when studios produce a film, they also own the media that promotes them. They own *Time* magazine, *Entertainment Weekly* and *People*. You think you're getting an independent source but you're not.

"If you read the *Time* magazine article on Kevin for *The Untouchables*, they had a front page picture of Kevin with the headline, 'The American Dream—struggling actor from Fullerton College makes it to the big time.' But they don't talk about his past in the article. The story of how he became a star was totally fabricated by the PR department at Paramount. They made him sound like a struggling student going through school studying, acting. It doesn't mention anything about him having a job at Raleigh Studios because that's not romantic.

"I've given about 300 interviews about Kevin. Once he became a star, everybody wanted to interview me because I'd made two of his early films. Once he became a star, he focused on eliminating his past.

"A German named Bill Harris had a live show on pay-per-view and Kevin was the guest. And all of a sudden, they showed clips from *Sizzle Beach, USA* and two other low budget films he'd done. After they'd shown the clips, Bill Harris turned to Kevin and asked, 'Is that you?' What could Kevin say? Of course it was him. That started the investigation into his real past. Paramount never mentioned that he did low budget films. He was known in those days as the kid on the cutting room floor. He'd gotten parts in three big features and was cut out of all three—*The Big Chill* (1983), *Frances* (1982), and *Night Shift*, (1982). The most famous once was Lawrence Kasdan's *The Big Chill.* They shot all his scenes and then the studio decided it was better to talk about his death than to actually show it.

"But that was instrumental in starting his career because Larry Kasdan felt sorry for him and decided to put him in *Silverado* (1985). If you look at early *Variety* listings on *Silverado* for casting, Kevin was about number ten. But Larry liked him and gradually his part increased. He ended up with third billing. Everyone was pissed. Linda Hunt, who just won an Academy Award, got low billing. It created a stir.

"Success does change people. Probably the only person it hasn't is Ron Howard, who's still down to earth.

"Many of the films I've made, even though shot for low budgets, keep turning up on TV and people know about them. I did a film called *Shock 'Em Dead* (1991). It was Traci Lords second straight film. Back then the AIDS thing was starting. She was a porno star and therefore she was 'dirty.' Nobody wanted to be near her. She had to have her own trailer and she wasn't allowed to drink out of the same water containers as other people. Traci was fun. She was a cute girl. She stuck with it. She was a smart business woman.

"She only made one porno movie after turning 18—*Traci, I Love You*, to which she owned the rights. People suspected that she turned herself in to the authorities so that all her previous porn movies would be banned. It was a great coup on her part.

"She had these puffy wide lips. She was always putting lipstick on.

"I'm pissed because back in those days, I had the Rob Lowe tape [of Rob having sex with an underage girl at the 1984 Democratic National Convention] and somebody stole the tape while I was making the Traci film. Boy, they did her [Lowe's underage girl] almost all night. They were taking turns. The tape ran for hours.

"We gave [porn star] Ron Jeremy bit parts in three films we did. Ron is a funny guy. He never sleeps. He takes cat naps. You've got to be careful getting in a car with him when drives. He'll fall asleep at a stop sign. He owed me a dinner once. He said, 'I've got to go to work for half an hour and then I'll take you to dinner. Follow me.' So we went to this porno setup in the San Fernando Valley. He wouldn't let me watch him. 'You've got to stay in the waiting room.' Which was O.K. because we were talking to a girl there. We asked her about getting tested for AIDS. He does his scene and then he drives like a maniac to the Rainbow [9015 Sunset Blvd]. We carry a film of his roommate Bob Gallagher. They've been roommates over 20 years and lead separate lives.

"Ron told me that his biggest problem is that he can't have a relationship with a woman. Once they find out what he does for a living, it's all over. I was directing a film in Miami. He had a small part. It was tough because everywhere we went, somebody recognized him. We almost lost one location when the family found out he was a porno star. People would act differently when they found out he was a porno star.

"There was a girl who wanted to go out with him, thinking he was a famous actor. He says it is typical for him to go out with a girl, and then a couple of days later, he'll call her up and all he'll hear on the other end of the line is screaming.

"Dana Plato appeared in a couple of my films. When I first met her, she was like a caged animal [from drugs]. We were shooting on Key Biscayne. We were all living in this Polynesian Village house. She didn't have any drugs. She'd make so-called 'Russian cocktails.' She'd go to the store and get Psuedofed, Nyquil, and just mix everything together. She was trying to straighten her life out.

"She had a miserable childhood. She was on [TV show] Diff'rent Strokes (1978-86). When she got pregnant on the show, she went in to the producer and said, 'I can either have an abortion or have the child on the show.' Within half an hour, she was fired [in the show's seventh, and next to last, season] because they didn't want to have anything to do with any of it. Her manager absconded with all her money, and the life savings of about 20 other clients. Because she was a minor on the show, all her checks went to him.

"When we met her, she was working as a hostess at a Mexican restaurant in Las Vegas. She was high all the time. That's where she held up the video store in Las Vegas.

"She met some guy who was a control freak. He would call her every ten minutes on the set to ask 'What are you doing?' He'd take all her money all the time. She was so afraid. She would tell stories about how she was electrocuted at her grandparents' house. How they would beat her. She had a troubled childhood and it never got any better. She appeared in three of my films—including *Bikini Beach Race* (1992) and *Silent Fury* (1994). Around the same time I did *Fatal Pursuit* (1998) with Malcom McDowell.

"We shot *Fatal Pursuit* in New Orleans so nobody was sober ever. Malcom is a fun guy. We had a shitty script. He just came up to me and said, 'Don't worry about it.' He could take something that was shitty on paper and make it work. He would take terrible material and make it look interesting. He had a 21-year old girlfriend or wife with him. She had a little dog. We had to rent a limo for her the whole time so she could go buy antiques. We also had Lydie Denier, a French actress, in the film. She refused to take her clothes off for the nude scene [though she does in numerous other films]. Her contract said nude scene. We used a body double.

"We shot the film in the same mansion where they shot *In the Heat of the Night* [TV series from 1988-94]. Malcom is in bed waiting for her and she announces, 'No, I am not going to take my clothes off.'"

"Was it fun auditioning all these women for nude parts?"

"It was a job. It's an interesting phenomena in this town. I met a lot of porno actresses in the early '90s. The porno actresses want to straighten out their lives and become legitimate actresses. I hired three porno actresses for *Nuke 'Em High*. On location, we went to Yuma, Arizona and Phoenix. It was funny. All the so-called straight girls on the film would party all night long and sleep with everybody. The porno chicks (including Kascha) went to bed early, read books, and were the only ones to have breakfast with me in the morning and were ready to go for work. Porno for them was just a business. The normal girls were all screwing around all night and wouldn't eat breakfast.

"Kascha was hot. If you're analyzing porno chicks, a lot of them come from the Midwest. They usually come from a religious background. Kascha had a master's degree in classical piano. She met her boyfriend-husband [Papillon] and she was going to change the porno industry by just sleeping with her husband, even though he didn't share that same philosophy. The first time I interviewed Kascha, we had a ground floor office with street parking. The first time she walked from the car to the front door, you'd hear nothing but cars screeching and coming to a halt. She was drop dead gorgeous. She had a body that was unbelievable. She was Tahitian looking, blonde hair. She was the most down to earth girl you've met. She was friendly. She offered to babysit my kids. She was really normal and most porno girls were like that. She just wanted to be a legit actress. She was a hot number then. She was in all the magazines and people wrote about her constantly.

"She was so cute. I remember all the porno chicks from *Nuke 'Em High* talked about Magic Johnson [Los Angeles Laker basketball star]. They said he would always rent a limo after a game and come into the [San Fernando] Valley and pick up all these porno chicks and party all night. Him and the other black talk-show host [would] party all night. The porno chicks would talk about Magic Johnson and how he was fucking every porno chick in the Valley. He was trying to take after Wilt Chamberlain.

"When I cast for Troma, they had me, when I was interviewing girls, have another guy and a woman in the room. And the door had to be open."

"Did the girls still try to sleep with you anyway?"

"I didn't get that. When you're working on a film as a producer-director, you're tired. You're wiped out. I thought that maybe one day I'd be able to direct a film, and that's it. I've always dreamed about being able to come on a set and just direct and then go home. But in the independent world, you're doing everything. Late at night on the Troma films, we spent an hour or two doing cash receipts for the day because they had to be Fed-Ex'd first thing in the morning to New York because they wouldn't wire anymore more until they had the receipts. Most films are like that. The completion bond companies today track everything you do every day.

"We just bought a film called *Hook, Gloves and Redemption*. It was made by the two world-famous French brothers [Jules and Gedeon Naudet] from that 9/11 documentary on CBS the other night. It's their only other documentary.

"It's tough to sell documentaries but I really liked these two brothers. I've been talking to them for a long time. Every time I went to New York, I'd see them. I wanted to help them out and sell their little documentary on boxing.

"We'd been talking about this fire thing they were doing. They are the only filmmakers to get permission to follow a unit ever. They got a one-year permit. They're now at the top of the list. Our phone is ringing off the hook from people wanting to talk to them. People are asking about their documentary. Everyone wants to get their hands on everything they've shot. The bids are going through the roof. We can't even deal with it. We figured we'd take a two week breather to figure out what to do.

"They're talented and into whatever they're doing. They're not in a rush. When they pick a subject, they want to get to know it. When you watch 9/11, you get a sense of how they want to be part of a thing. One brother cooked a dinner for all the firefighters."

"Have you gotten to see the raw tapes?"

"Not yet. I think that's going to be the real documentary that comes out. The version on TV was toned down. When you heard those loud noises on TV, those were bodies dropping. He panned the camera to film some of that. When they came upon the scene, there were arms and pieces and everything and they certainly didn't show that on TV. I'm sure another version will come out. That will take them to another level.

"The last film I did was *Dilemma* (1997). I had to change my name to Eric Larson. The buyers knew me from making low budget films and the distributor thought the buyers wouldn't buy the films for the higher price.

"The films I'm now working on will take about two years to go from script to screen. The discipline of that is unusual for me. Our budgets range from $8-15 million. I'm now concentrating on financing and distribution. I go to 14 film markets a year.

"The American Film Market this year was down 20 percent. Our *Wisegirls* (2002) film [starring Mariah Carey and Mira Sorvino, shown at Sundance] has given us recognition. We just closed a theatrical deal yesterday on *Long Ago and Far Away*. We've signed Joe Charbanic, who directed *The Watcher* (2000), to a movie called *Consent*. It deals with an actor raping someone during a rape scene. She presses charges. So we're doing quality projects. It will be tough to go back to making a low budget film.

"I've decided to get more into dealmaking. When you direct a film, you get so immersed that your quality of life declines. Now I can just make deals and enjoy life more. I go to Europe five times a year and life is good.

"It's tough when you start directing low budget things [to crossover]. It's even tough for an actor who's been on TV to cross over to features. It's tough to make the transition. It's easier to start out fresh."

Eric has two kids—aged 21 and 17. His third wife (married three years, lived together six), Rita, is a psychologist "who deals mostly with kids and people in the industry. Many of her clients are in the music industry. They're more screwed up than people in film. There's more backstabbing in music than in film. She can't stand the film business."

"What's her last name?"

"I can't say. One of her clients has been trying to find out for a long time what I do. He knows I'm in the film business and he is too. She told one patient what movies I'd done, figuring that nobody would ever have heard of me, and he turned out to be a big fan and I had to sign a *Nuke 'Em High* poster for him. She freaked out that anybody would know who I was."

"What do you think is your best film?"

"I should say what Lloyd says, 'They're all my best films.' As a straight movie, I like *Dilemma* (1997). As a Troma-type film, probably *Nuke 'Em High 2* (1991). Even today, it is such a classic. If my wife had seen *Nuke 'Em High 2*, prior to our getting married, I don't think she would've married me. I don't think I could ever do another film like that. It was so strange. It's totally different from anything out there. I still have people trying to track me down to find out things about *Nuke 'Em High 2*. I've got testimonials on video. My wife had a patient, 17-18 years of age, going on to college, and he begged her for a poster from me so that he could put it in his college dorm room.

"My first marriage was when I was 18. It lasted only one year though we were together for six years during high school and college. She was a primate paleontologist involved in the Leakey Foundation. She never got a 'B' [grade] in her life. She was the only non-medical student allowed [to study corpses at UCLA]. I used to pick her up after class and she'd smell of formaldehyde from bodies she'd been working on. The Leakey Foundation took an interest in her and she went to these mountains in Iran.

"After we were married a year, she wanted to go off to do her doctoral work [in Iran?]. She wanted me to come along to be a still photographer and catalogue the bones and stuff. She couldn't cook either. Next I married someone [Laurel Koernig] who could cook and just wanted to raise kids and have a family. We had two kids and we were married almost 20 years (1977-1995). She just wanted to find herself at one point."

"What did she think of your movies?"

"She worked on many of them. She thought they were nuts but she didn't care so long as I paid the bills and brought home the check."

34

Moustapha Akkad

"The media runs the world," says Moustapha. "No tanks or planes. The media and the public companies. This is what *The Protocols of [the Learned Elders of] Zion* [a notorious anti-Semitic forgery] is all about.

"The Zionists, last century, were persecuted in Europe. So they immigrated to the United States. They had a target. They were united. They did not permit [statements] critical of Zion. They went all the way to control the world and to control the minds of the people through the media. There's a lesson to learn from them.

"They have control of the media here. We know it. They did not do it through tanks or machine guns. They planned of course. They united. Did you see Pat Buchanan's book [*The Death of the West: How Dying Populations and Immigrant Invasions Imperil Our Country and Civilization*]? He makes sense.

"There is a red line if I get into the issue of Israel but the Jews, like everyone else, want to make money. Hollywood is not ethnic. There's English, Irish, Spanish, French, Roman."

"But movie and TV producers are 70 percent Jewish," I say.

"Yes. The studios are. That control is financial but not the creative aspect. You can't be more Jewish than Miramax [owned by Disney and operated by Bob and Harvey Weinstein, distributed last two Halloween films]. They financed me and I did it. But probably if I did something about Israel, they would not. So I get financing from overseas, such as when I did *The Message*."

Moustapha carries himself in a regal way and he speaks slowly and confidently. "I was born and raised in Aleppo, Syria. I wanted to be a film director in Hollywood. That was the joke of the town. We were an average family. My father worked as a government employee in customs. My father said, 'If you want to go, I can not really help you.' I had an American theater arts teacher Douglas Hill and he got me into UCLA. In 1954, when I was 18, I came to the airport to leave. My father said goodbye and put $200 in one pocket and a copy of the Koran in the second pocket. 'That's all I can give you.'

"I attended UCLA for four years and graduated in 1958. At the time, UCLA had the best film program. They had three productions per semester. USC at the time was not as rich as UCLA and the cinema department was smaller. If you wanted to do a film, you loaded up your station wagon and went to shoot. The New Wave [of filmmaking] developed at the time. The more realistic documentary approach to filmmaking. I wanted to expose myself to that and I went to USC for three years for my Masters.

"Then I started the starvation period. I applied to the seven giant studios for work and all TV studios and all advertising agencies for a job. Then [director] Sam Peckinpah wanted to do a movie about the Algerian revolution. So he approached UCLA to help him find a consultant, somebody from that area who speaks the language. They gave him my name and we got started. Then Algeria got its independence and the project was canceled.

"He took a liking to me. He was developing a movie for MGM called *Ride the High Country* (1962). He asked me to work with him. I was not paid. He always used to tell me to start from the top. 'You went to school for seven years. You can't go to work as a messenger boy. Sit down and write something.'

"I used to sit down and write every day and I'd bring it to him. He'd take it, read it and tear it up. I had applied everywhere for work and I always got the same question, 'What have you done?'

"I remember from my days at UCLA, I used to be invited into American homes. They always ask you, 'What do you think of the American food?' 'What do you think of the American woman?' 'What do you think about American education?' Everything you think about America, they like to know. I thought that would be a good subject to do a program on—how others see us.

"I made a small presentation to three TV stations to bring an African, European, Asian, and Latin American foreign student, with an American moderator and a different topic every week. The CBS and NBC both wanted it as a public affairs program on Sunday afternoons. NBC offered me $400 a week but no credit. CBS offered me $100 a week and the producer credit.

"So I went to Sam Peckinpah and I told him about my two offers. He asked which one I was going to take. I said, 'NBC.' He replied, and I've never forgotten, 'You sonofabitch. What do you want the money for? Take the credit.' I took the CBS offer.

"Now that I was a producer at CBS, I could call anybody and they'd return my call. I called United Artists and sold them a syndicated travel show, *Caesar's World*, hosted by Caesar Romero. Every week we traveled to a different country.

"I always advise anyone who aspires to be in this business Sam Peckinpah's advice. When you have something that somebody likes, play dumb on the money aspect. Tell them to talk to your lawyer or agent. But never compromise on the credit."

"How did you come to make your 1976 movie *The Message* [about the founder of Islam, the prophet Mohammed]?"

"I was making documentaries all over the world. I thought I needed to do something about Islam, which is not understood. At first I thought I'd make a documentary. Then I met Irish scriptwriter Harry Craig. He convinced me we should do it as a feature. I was able to raise the money from the Arab world."

"How was it received?"

"It was received fantastic but it was not American commercial for two reasons. You can not see the prophet. I get upset when I see Jesus or Moses portrayed by an actor. To me, you don't touch these things. The film is about Mohammed but he's not portrayed. Therefore, the camera takes subjective angles. It's good for those who know the religion. The movie was a big hit on video."

"How did you raise the money from Muammar al-Qaddafi for *Lion of the Desert* (1980)?"

"It was easy. I had the credentials now. The subject pertained to the Italian occupation of Libya. I had the freedom to work with the material. It was not religious, where you can't show this, you can't say this."

"Why do you think it didn't do better at the box office?"

"Publicity about Qaddafi hurt. They politicized it. The critiques [of the film] were good. I believe in the audience. If the audience do not come, I can not [boost the film]."

"Who distributed the film?"

"This is another thing. We had a hard time finding a distributor because of Khaddafy, prejudice, whatever. United Artists distributed it [around the time of the *Heavens Gate* debacle]."

"How did you connect with director John Carpenter in 1977 to make the first *Halloween* movie?"

"I was busy doing *Lion of the Desert*. He said he wanted to make a movie for $300,000. I laughed. You get worried when the budget is high or low. I asked him about the story. He told it to me in four words and I grabbed it. He said, 'Baby sitter to be killed by the boogie man.' The baby sitter part grabbed me

because every kid in America knows what a baby sitter is. I told him, 'Let's do it.'
I was spending $300,000 a day on *Lion of the Desert*. I gave John points [percentage of the gross receipts] so he made lots of money afterwards.

"The movie came in on budget. It was John Carpenter's movie. I saw the commercial aspect to it. We distributed it theater by theater, state by state. We made so much money we couldn't believe it."

"You must've funded it with pocket change from *Lion of the Desert*."

"Yes. Then two years later, 1980, Dino DeLaurentiis came to me wanting to do a sequel. I said, 'Sequel? This is not television. It's not going to make any money.' They said, 'We'll give you the profit in advance.' So they did and we made *Halloween II* (1981). It did good. I couldn't believe it.

"They came again. They said, 'Let's do *Halloween III* (1983).' I said, 'No way.' They said, 'This time we will change it a bit. We will do one without Michael Myers.' I wasn't for it, but I was out-voted. I said O.K. That was the big mistake. It was a big flop.

"Then I brought back Michael Myers and the basics, and *Halloween IV* (1988) was a big hit, perhaps the biggest hit [of the franchise]. We made the most money on *Halloween I*, the biggest box office on *Halloween H2O* [VII, 1998] but we had the most paying customers for *Halloween IV*.

"Drunk with our success, we did *Halloween V* a year later. That was a mistake. A few years later, Miramax came with an attractive offer to do *Halloween VI* (1996). Due to recent events, we're coming out with *Halloween VIII* in July.

"This *Halloween* [series] is a blessing. I feel like a father. Everybody wants to come chop the head of Michael Myers but I love this guy. I always try to keep to realistic stories. Somebody falling from the sky with ten ears and ten eyes isn't scary. But if you're locked inside a house and there's somebody there who wants to kill you, that could happen to anybody. You can relate.

"Why do people pay money to get scared? I asked my 17-year old son. He said, 'Dad, I take a girl with me to the cinema. After five minutes, I'm either grabbing her or she's grabbing me.'

"Donald Pleasance was asked by the press if we he was going to keep doing Halloween movies. He answered, 'No way. I'm going to stop at 22.' That's my answer too.

"With *H2O*, we chopped off his [Michael Myers] head. But was it really his head?

"This is something where you cater to the kids. Eighty percent of the audience now is kids. Home entertainment has become so sophisticated with the large screen, stereo, satellite, DVD, you can watch any movie a few months later. You can stretch your legs, smoke, drink. So why should adults bother to drive to see a movie? Kids have to go for dating and meeting. At my age [66 yo], you start losing touch.

"When my teenagers talk, I have a hard time understanding sometimes. We were casting *Halloween 8*. The director [Rick Rosenthal] suggested Busta. Do you know who Busta is?"

"No."

"I went home and asked my son about Busta. He lit up. 'Busta Rhymes?' He went crazy. I called the office and said, 'O.K., get Busta Rhymes.' He's one of those rap singers with the hair.

"Every time we shoot, kids gather around the studio. Another actor suggested was Tyra Banks. Do you know Tyra Banks?"

"I think I've heard the name."

"See? You're getting gray hair already. Again I went home and asked my kids. 'Tyra Banks? I'd marry her.' Tyra Banks is a black model who appears in underwear ads.

"When we test the movie, we bring kids. I've lost touch. All I do is preserve the storyline and the atmosphere of horror."

"How come you are the one person on all eight Halloween movies? Do you own the franchise?"

"Yeah. I paid for the first one. I guess it's a blessing. I didn't intend to sequels, but I had my lawyer read the contract and they put everything in. At the time, I didn't think of it.

"I spend 90 percent of my time on the *Halloween* franchise. If I am to direct, I only want to direct epic historic films. My favorite director when I was a child was Alfred Hitchcock. Then David Lean. I met him while I was student and he gave me advice. I'm now preparing an epic on Saladin and the Crusades, starring Sean Connery. We have a script. Financing is the issue.

"I love history. The best movies are comedies but I'm not good at that. I cannot direct a Western. You have to be able to live it to be able to direct it. Produce it, you can."

"The current atmosphere post September 11, is that good or bad for your Saladin film?"

"It is very good because Saladin exactly portrays Islam. Right now, Islam is portrayed as a terrorist religion. Because a few terrorists are Muslims, the whole religion has that image. If there ever was a religious war full of terror, it was the crusades. But you can't blame Christianity because a few adventurers did this. That's my message. Always there are fanatics but Saladin protected freedom of religion and different holy places. My sources on Saladin are all from the West. They all admit the chivalry of Saladin. The BBC did a beautiful four hours on the Crusades."

"Are there other Islamic filmmakers?"

"No. There are Arabic Christians like Mario Kassar."

"What is it like being a Muslim in Hollywood?"

"American citizenship is not an ethnic nationality. I practice my religion more freely here than I could anywhere in the Arab and Muslim world. Here it is not the rule of the majority but the rule of the constitution. Atheist lady Madelyn O'Hair sued the government and the next day, when she won, government schools were not allowed to mention the name of God. You get waves of hatred. You don't blame people after September 11 from having certain feelings against a certain group. That's normal. I was upset about it. Sometimes I am afraid to ride on a plane with someone [who looks like a young fundamentalist Muslim].

"We're living in a free society ruled by a constitution. The United States is like a corporation. The United States is the true United Nations. The whole world is represented here. We all have shares. How influential you are depends on how hard you work. But at the end, the media runs the world.

"My base is England. I have a studio there, Twickenham. It's not under my name. I did all of my work [on the two films he directed] there. My crew was mostly English. The best crews are English."

Akkad has produced such films as *Sky Bandits* (1986), *Free Ride* (1986) and *Appointment With Fear* (1987).

"How do you feel about being best known for the Halloween films?"

"Only with kids. The adults haven't seen it, but when I'm around kids, I feel good. How I feel depends where I am. When I am with kids, I feel like a king because of *Halloween*. With adults, they might know me for *Lion of the Desert*. Within the Arab-Muslim world, I am really big because they see me [as one of them] who's made it in Hollywood."

"Have you encountered much discrimination as a Muslim in Hollywood?"

"No. I make it very clear. I am proud of it. I don't try to hide it. Many suggested that I change my name. I would not. I respect other religions—Jewish, Christian, atheist. When I see somebody who, because he got married, changes his religion, I lose respect for him. One who's proud of his roots and his heritage, I respect.

"This is something that I practice in my home. When I lock the door in the morning and I leave the house, I am 100 percent American in my thinking, working. This is where I earned my education, my living, and my faith. Who's going to touch this country? Forget carrying the flags. Look at it from a practical point of view. I live here. My kids live here. My grandchildren live here. So I want security for this country America. It's a matter of practicality, not religion. I am open about it but I have never faced any [discrimination]. You might find something but I didn't feel it."

"Did you put a flag on your car after September 11th?"

"No. I hate this flag waving. People who fly a flag are trying to hide something. Why should I fly a flag? America is not a flag. It's a country with a constitution. Anything that affects this country, automatically affects me. I think these terrorists, the Taliban, are a bunch of animals. I thought of them as animals when they blew up those [ancient Buddhist] statutes. I wanted at the time to go hit them."

"Did you feel any moral qualms about taking funding from Muammar al-Qaddafi?"

"No. It all depends on what I do with it. If he put conditions. If I served his regime. At the end, he wanted to make a film about him and his revolution. I turned it down. I don't care where the financing comes from. It's what you make out of it. I can get it from anywhere."

"Even Osama Bin Laden?"

"I'd take the money from him, but what I do with it, that's what counts. I would correct his outlook and his animalistic approach to the whole religion."

35

Gerald Leider

Born May 28, 1931, Gerald Leider grew up in Camden, New Jersey. He attended public schools and Syracuse University. Awarded a Fullbright Scholarship, he studied drama at Bristol University in England, where he finished his masters. For several years, Leider worked as a producer/director on Broadway and in London.

"My mother had a flamboyant style but neither of my parents were in the entertainment industry. They were shopkeepers. My [three] sisters and I are first-generation Americans. My mother was born in Russia and my father was born in the Austria-Hungary [area]. They came to Philadelphia about the same year in the early 1900s and moved in across the street from each other. They got married and moved across the river to Camden.

"My parents were Jewish. I was raised religiously but I didn't take to it. We kept a kosher house though we had to keep our stores open on Saturdays. We lived on top of our store in a mixed neighborhood—Italian, Jewish, German, Dutch.

"The theater was my end-all and be-all. I headed the Drama Society at Syracuse. I married Helena [a non-Jew] in Britain. It last a couple of years.

"When I returned to the United States, I went to work at MCA [run by Lew Wasserman and Jules Stein]."

Jerry gets up and walks to the wall and points out a framed copy of his first paycheck stub ($108 for two weeks of work in 1955).

"Six years ago, Lew Wasserman had a couple of committee meetings at his house. I brought this over to show him. He said, 'Jerry, you're overpaid now and you were overpaid then.'

"It was in the middle of the winter, 1955-56. Peter Falk and I lived on a five story walkup on Ninth Street and Fifth Avenue. I was a secretary. My first bosses

222

were Freddy Fields and Dave Begelman. They both left New York two weeks after I got there, and came out to California.

"There was a terrible blizzard on Friday. MCA had a secretary on each floor on the Saturday from 9 a.m.–1 p.m. This was my Saturday. The subways and buses were closed. I walked for two hours to 58th and Madison through the snow. I got to the building at 9:05 a.m.. I walked in and got the snow off me and walked into the elevator. Just before the elevator closed, Lew came in. He was staying at St. Regents around the corner.

"I said, 'Good morning, Mr. Wasserman.' He looked at me and said, 'You're late.'

"On one of my last gigs as head of specials at CBS, I went out with Bernie Brillstein, a young agent at William Morris, to the Miss Teenage America pageant. Did we have a good weekend. Forget the teenage contestants, it was their hostesses."

"Did you read Bernie's book?"

"I read about half. James Aubrey, a gifted but strange guy, was my boss at CBS. He knew what he was doing for many years and then lost it. I bumped into him one day and asked him if he'd read the new book on Bill Paley. He said, 'No, I've given up reading fiction for a year.'

"After working for MCA for a year, I produced theater. In 1960, I began a three-year stretch at CBS. I was the Director of Special Programs.

"CBS chairman William Paley was remarkable. We had meetings every other week of department heads. I was the youngest one there. Bill had an uncanny ability, which I have not seen in anybody since then, to burrow in to the one thing you are most unsure of. Let's say you're giving a ten item report, and the one item that you were not quite sure of, he would spot and start probing in every area—news, operations, engineering.

"Jim Aubrey was tough, hard working guy. You'd come in on a Saturday afternoon and he'd be there. He was twisted. A lot of people thought Jim was a bad bad man. His peccadillos got the better of him. He made some good programming moves. He brought NFL football to CBS.

"Smiling Cobra is the name of a good book about Jim. That's what he was. I befriended him after his fall. Brandon Tartikoff nicely gave him a consultancy but he had a bad last ten years of his life. He lived in a small apartment on Santa Monica Blvd and Overland. He suffered from depression. He died in the emergency room and he lay unclaimed for three days. Like David Susskind dying in a hotel room. Why are we talking so morbid?"

"Did you guys think of yourselves as the Tiffany network?"

"Jim did. Mike Dann [key CBS executive] did. He's now a fulltime consultant for the BBC's Discovery Channel and for IBM. He's sharp as a tack and 81 years old. He had an 80th birthday party in New York September 11.

"There was an aura of invincibility.

"In 1963 there was a management change at CBS. Hubble Robinson came in and got rid of a bunch of us. Then I joined Ted Ashley at the Ashley Famous Agency. In 1965, the government broke up MCA [Lew Wasserman's dominant talent agency] and Ted hired many of the MCA agents and expanded rapidly.

"Steve Ross bought the agency in 1968 and then it was sold to Marvin Josephson in 1969. Steve Ross bought Warner Brothers and I moved to Los Angeles to run Warner Brothers Television.

"I married my present wife Susan Trustman in 1968. We have two boys, Matt and Ken. Susan was an actress on the TV soap *Another World*. She appeared in the 1965 Elvis Presley movie, *Stay Away, Joe*.

"In the summer of 1966, I met Susan in the middle of the West Hampton. Around noon, I pulled up my dinghy motorboat next to what I thought was the home of writer Peter Maas and his wife Audrey. It was a hot day. All the houses look alike. I had a date that weekend who never showed up. She told me later that she'd met a rich millionaire.

"I walked up the gangway and I saw this beautiful girl sunning herself. She was blonde and holy shit. I thought, 'Holy shit, I'm at the wrong house.' So I started slowly working my way back. Then I hear the slam of a kitchen door and Audrey comes out with a vodka and says, 'Jerry, what are you doing here?'

"She invited me back up for lunch. The girl was Susan Trustman. We never left each other's side. If Audrey had never left the house, I would never have met my wife 35 years ago.

"I got tired of the television packaging business so I took an opportunity to move to Rome to run Warner's foreign theatrical releases. I thought it was a good stepping stone to get into the feature side of Warner Brothers, so I packed up my wife and my little baby.

"After two years, I came back to Los Angeles with a two-year deal to produce movies for Warner Brothers."

Leider's first three productions were TV movies—*And I Alone Survived* (1978), *Willa* (1979) and *The Hostage Tower* (1980) followed by two features, *The Jazz Singer* (1980) and *Trenchcoat* (1983).

"Do you see yourself in *The Jazz Singer*?"

"A bit. Neil [a Jew] felt passionately about the story, and about the relationship between his father and his mom. As his mom and dad would say, 'We have two sons. We love them both. One is Neil Diamond and one sells swimming pools in the Valley.' Yeah. I bet you we know where they spend their first seder night."

"Everyone's telling me that the TV movie business is in decline."

"They're all stroking you. ESPN, A&E, SciFi, USA, Lifetime, TBS, Showtime, HBO, Hallmark, are all doing TV movies. Don't tell anyone. I'm busier than I've ever been. I'm calling on everybody. It's a myth. What has disappeared is the network TV movie that you can own."

"I've heard such pain and suffering."

"They're lazy. They're all my buddies. They're just too old. They're 40, 50 years old. They want to retire. They're full of it. Tell them to go into the shoe business."

"You've been making TV movies during a time of dramatic change in the business."

"Yeah. I remember when Barry Diller came to us at Warner Brothers [around 1969] and said, 'I'd like you to make these 90-minute picture [TV movies] for $575,000 each.' We said, 'That will never work.'

"But I don't like to talk about the past. I'm only interested in the future. I have a big career ahead of me. I'm sure you find that with all the guys my age who are still working."

"Find what?"

"That they're only interested in the future."

"You guys are like conductors."

Jerry stares. "The guys on the trains? For a writer, you're really reaching. Waiting for another one to come by?"

"No, like the classical music conductor, still going strong at 75 years of age."

"I was at Fred Silverman's home a couple of weeks ago, perhaps the biggest estate in Mandeville Canyon. He and his wife Cathy have two homes. He was the most brilliant TV programmer ever. He was my student at Syracuse.

"Fred told me that he'd just got this consultancy gig with Disney. Michael [Eisner] and Bob [Iger] needed some help. 'I like this idea better than producing. I never really liked producing.' I said, 'Freddy, you're sitting in this $20 million home. You were born in Brooklyn. And you're not sure that you like producing? You should be ashamed of yourself.' He laughed."

"Which of your movies has the most meaning to you?"

"*The Jazz Singer*. I had to get rid of the first director, Sidney Furie, and replace him with Richard Fleischer. I still meet people who love the movie. It was a big seminal event in their lives. I know every frame. I edited a lot of it. I wrote a few scenes."

"*Cadet Kelly* was the Disney Channel's highest rated show ever."

"We went in there to pitch a show. They didn't want it. They told us about the type of shows that they did. So I was sitting at home. I said to Susan, 'We should do a show at a junior high school setting that doesn't depend on that stupid opening shot of the kids coming down the hallways, with the lockers on both sides. How do you find a different junior high school scene?'

"I went to my computer and I found that there are seven military schools in the United States that are coeducational from seventh grade on. I came back to the dining room and said, 'Susan, *Private Benjamin* in military school.' I called my partner Robert Shapiro, former president of Warner Brothers features, and told him my idea. *Private Benjamin* was one of the movies he worked on."

"What happened to your movie *Fall From the Sky?*"

"That's a dreadful story. We were two weeks away from shooting when CBS pulled the plug. We were supposed to start shooting October 4th [2001]. They said the subject matter would not be acceptable for our audience. The story takes place in the future, in the era of big jumbo jets that can seat 700 people. During normal takeoff, one of the planes crashes. We find out later that it is pilot error. This is the story of a NTSB investigative team trying to find out why the plane went down. And they're pressured to say it was pilot error. They find out later it wasn't pilot error but a conspiracy between a couple of congressmen and the owner of the airline and the manufacturer to make it look like pilot error to hide a built-in flaw in the electrical system. It had nothing to do with terrorism."

"Post September 11, people don't want to make projects casting a negative light on government."

"Unfortunately for us, CBS decided that they had no liability for the bills we ran up. So we're going to have to sue them.

"I'm a consultant to the Miss America organization. We're working on a series of one-hour shows *Behind the Icon*. It looks like Hallmark wants to buy 13 hours. We're taking each of the Miss Americas, and doing a before, the year [of her reign], and afterwards. There are some fabulous stories. A lot of pain, a lot of heartache, warts and all."

"Wouldn't the Miss America organization want to put forward a certain sanitized image?"

"They're fine with this. It's promotion. It gets more people interested in the pageant.

"The Miss America organization is a non-profit agency founded in the 1930s primarily to keep tourists in Atlantic City for the week after Labor Day. Now it gives out millions of dollars worth of scholarships a year."

"What causes you to want to make something?"

"I pass on a lot of things that I don't think I can sell. That I sign on to a project does not mean that I am personally passionate about it. I have to be passionate about the opportunity. If I spot an opportunity, I get going.

"If I call an agent at CAA, he'll three or four days to return the call. If I call Michael [Eisner, Disney CEO] at 10 a.m., by noon, no matter where he is, I'll get a call back from him. The heads of companies are always like that."

"How do you feel about Warner Brothers, turning into this behemoth with AOL?"

"I have no feelings about it. It doesn't put a dime in my pocket. My job is still the same—to convince the guy sitting on the other side of the desk that my idea is a good idea. These big companies don't have exclusivity on ideas. If you sit down and say, 'Private Benjamin at a military school,' that's an idea. Ed Scherick said it best. 'The independent producer guy gets up in the morning, he shaves, he looks at himself in the mirror, and he says, 'I think I have a good idea today.' That's the power.'"

"What's your favorite part of the job?"

"Not being interviewed. Watching it happen. Seeing the pieces of the project come together. In the filmmaking process, my favorite part is post-production. I loathe casting sessions. They drive me up the wall. I can't stand seeing an actress come in, reading, and being dismissed. It's heart breaking. I like the script process. I like the beginning and end of a project."

"You have more control."

36

Frank Konigsberg

"I grew up in Queens and in Manhattan. My father was an engineer. My older brother William is a professor and scientist at Yale in bio-chemistry. We went to private schools. I've always liked the theater, movies, and books.

"I went to Yale where I majored in English. I graduated in 1953. Then I went to Yale Law School. I graduated in 1956. Six months later, I went to work at CBS, and then transferred to NBC after a couple of years where I negotiated deals for talent and programs. I met two guys who were selling shows to NBC. They wanted me to come to California to work for them in their business affairs division of their company—Artists Agency Corporation. It became the International Famous Agency (IFA) which later became ICM. I ran the West Coast office for about ten years. Then I became a producer.

"Bing Crosby was a client and I produced his Christmas specials. I knew all of the people running the networks from my days as an agent. My partner Sterling Silliphant and I sold a mini-series [*Pearl*, 1978] to ABC. We got the rights to use footage from *Tora! Tora! Tora!* (1970) and went to Hawaii and made it."

Frank speaks so softly that I have a hard time picking up his words. He seems bemused to be the subject of an interview.

"The golden era of TV movies seems over," I say.

"Probably because of the change in tax regulations [around 1986]. We used to have the investment tax credit where a portion of the money you spent on a film could be deducted directly from your income tax. For a long time, people turned out the same kind of movie over and over again. We got to be formula. We got to be uninteresting."

"Your first feature was *National Lampoon's The Joy of Sex* (1984)."

"Paramount was running out on their option on Alex Comfort's book. They had four months to start principle photography. They came to me and asked me to do it. They knew that in television you do things quickly. We threw together a

228

script. They wanted me to use director Martha Coolidge, who'd just made *Valley Girls*. It was a job. We just had to get it done. I didn't think it was a successful movie at all. It was awful. Martha hated it. I hated it."

"*Nine 1/2 Weeks* (1986)."

"I held the rights to the book for about eight years. I had a number of scripts written. I tried for years to get it set up with Zalman King directing. He tried to get the rights to the book out from under me. Finally, I washed my hands of it and sold it to Keith Barish. I didn't like the final movie. In the book, the guy's tight, controlled, and precise. They cast Mickey Rourke who's interesting but hardly a Wall Street commodities trader. The woman is repressed but Kim Bassinger is just sexy from the get go. It was awful. I hated the movie.

"It was supposed to be an interesting psychological study of carrying things to the limit. Like the Stockholm Syndrome, where the woman became increasingly attracted to this man who was abusive. It explored why people stay in abusive relationships."

"Is one of the joys of producing movies getting to vicariously explore things you would never touch in your ordinary life?"

"Yes. Like an actor, you get to play out different scenarios. Though you have to remain grounded in the reality of your own life or things can spiral out of control."

"Have you seen that happen to many of your peers?"

"No. In the television business, you can spiral downward but you don't spiral out of control. The feature business is much more excessive. In television, you're working with tiny budgets and tight schedules. It's more of a mass production factory. If you get a chance to do something really good, like some of my early films, it's because there's a lucky combination of a good executive who leaves you alone and subjects that are intriguing and fresh."

"Post production is a favorite of yours."

"I am a good editor. It's a complicated and intricate process and I like that best of all the aspects of making a film. You have the most control. It's more of a puzzle. You have all the pieces and you have to put them together. When you're on the set, it can rain or snow or a truck can go by. You're dealing with actors."

"Do you like pitching?"

"No. Does anybody?"

"Yes. Jerry Leider."

"Jerry's much more of a salesman than I am. He's probably much better at it than I am. I don't like it at all. I think the merits of my project are obvious and I shouldn't have to pitch it."

"Do you get frustrated dealing with idiots?"

"I don't think they buyer are idiots. We just come from different places. Most of them I like. They're bright people and their hearts are in the right places. There are just more corporate layers than when I was making films [in the 1970s]. Then, there was one guy at CBS who had a division called 'CBS Specials.' He had a mandate to make, say, six a year. He'd say, 'Go ahead. Develop it.' He didn't have to clear it with five other people. There was an appetite to do programs with some social value. I don't think they do that much anymore. The networks are much more into...getting an audience without being challenging. They still do the wife-beaters [stories]."

"Do you ever get frustrated with the medium? For instance, when you make a movie from a book, the book is always far more intellectually complex than the movie."

"It doesn't have to be. If you take *Guyana Tragedy: The Story of Jim Jones* (1980), the book just lays out all the facts. We picked the scenes that we thought were the most illuminating. If you read the book and you saw the movie, you'd probably like the movie better."

"How much artistic freedom to you feel to fictionalize movies like *Guyana Tragedy*?"

"Not much."

"Have you ever made a movie that you've looked back on as socially irresponsible?"

Frank laughs. "*The Joy of Sex*. I don't make violent movies or horror movies or things that will harm the youth of America. Those subjects don't appeal to me."

"Do you ever put messages in your films?"

"There are social messages in my films but I don't think they're inserted apart from the inherent nature of the subject."

"You don't feel that you are part of the anointed with a moral imperative to wake up the somnolent masses?"

"No. I have made some do-gooder films like *The Pride of Jesse Hallam* (1981) about illiteracy, but I think that the personal story of that man is what makes it compelling, not the statistics or the message at the end about calling the Illiteracy Council."

"Do you struggle between the conflicting aims of artistry and commerce?"

"No. I'm happy to do anything. I like to work."

"Tell me about Traci Lords."

"I worked with her on her life story. It was never made into a movie."

"Why?"

"A sudden degree of Puritanism was in the air when we delivered the script and nobody wanted to make the movie."

"Talent manager Bernie Brillstein says that the primary reason men get into the entertainment industry is to have sex with beautiful women."

"I don't think so. Do you?"

"I'm not sure."

"If you're successful or rich or powerful in any field, you can attract the opposite sex."

"You've never had an actress throw herself at you to get a part?"

"Never. You make me feel like I've missed out. I guess it says something about me."

"Which of your productions that we haven't mentioned have had the most meaning to you."

Frank laughs again. "I don't know."

"Tell me about your 1996 movie *Titanic*."

"As we were making it [for CBS], was looming behind us James Cameron, who's working with $120 million. And we have $12 million. We had tried to get Fox to give us a million dollars not to make it [as soon as Cameron's project started] but CBS wanted it and Fox didn't want to give us the money. I think our movie is good.

"We shot the movie in Vancouver in the middle of summer. We had a small tank at the University of British Columbia. Everyone's wearing fur coats. It's meant to be in the North Atlantic in the middle of winter. My partner says, 'Why isn't their breath showing? Why are they sweating? It's supposed to be cold.' You can't show people's frozen breath, and people shivering, when it is 110 degrees and you are shooting in a confined space with no air conditioning."

"Have you ever burned out?"

"No. I like this. Where else can you get well paid and meet interesting people and go places?"

"How could you a Jew make the 1999 movie *Jesus*?"

"I think it's a terrific story."

"Didn't you want to say, 'Hey, he was just a carpenter'?"

"He may have been a carpenter but he was a lot more than that as well."

"Do you believe Jesus was part of a triune godhead?"

"It is important for a lot of people to believe in that. It's certainly a story that's had sway over people for 2000 years."

"What would you parents have thought of you?"

"They weren't religious as Jews and they were tolerant of other religions.

"Have I exhausted you?"

"No."

April 18, 2002

"Mary Tyler Moore stars in [the 2001 TV movie] *Like Mother, Like Son: The Strange Story of Sante and Kenny Kimes.* She plays a mother who has an incestuous relationship with her son. They kill this New York socialite [Irene Silverman].

"We got the green light from CBS to do the project in November, 2000, and they wanted to air it in May. So we couldn't shoot it anywhere in the Northern Hemisphere. The story takes place over the July 4th weekend in New York City. The city was deserted and they had this big mansion to themselves. They lived in Las Vegas and Hawaii, which are warm weather, blue sky places.

"At one point we wanted to show the mother and son outside the home of a man (business associate of the late husband, Mr. Kimes) that they have been accused of murdering. They are now standing trial in Los Angeles for that crime, but at the time we were shooting, they had been accused but not indicted. CBS didn't want us to show them park outside the man's nondescript house.

"While we were shooting, the Kimes were indicted for the murder. Then CBS wanted us to change all the dialogue, identify the house, and put in everything that they had initially insisted we take out.

"We shot in Melbourne, Australia. We were able to find a couple of streets that we made resemble New York City. Hawaii was easy. Down the coast, we found a house with a Hawaiin name, built in Hawaiin style, overlooking the sea. When we surveyed it, it was a bright sunny day. When we shot there, after about two hours, the storm clouds came in. It started to rain and you couldn't see the sea. I was in Australia for six months. We left in mid-December, 2000, to find a crew, not realizing that everybody took a vacation in Australia from mid-December to mid-January.

"We met every possible crew member who wasn't in France or Italy. We got a crew together and started on the movie at the end of January. We did the post-production in Australia. It was difficult because CBS was back here. Every time we sent a cut back, it would take us two days to get a response. That slowed the process down."

"You weren't able to email it?"

"They didn't have the technology then. This was a year ago. Now I think you can get an optical line for $8000 a week, but they have to have the capacity to receive it."

"How was your Australian crew compared to an American one?"

"Our crew was a little slower. For all I know, there are probably great crews there."

"Are you married? Did you take your wife [Susanne]?"

"Yes I am, 40 years. No, I didn't take her. I think she was in Burma. She travels a lot on her own. Her trips didn't coincide with this and I didn't know when I'd be back.

"When I'm working, it's not much fun for her because I'm on the job 12-14 hours a day. I shot a miniseries (*The Tommyknockers*, 1993) in New Zealand. She spent a couple of days waiting around for me. Then she got a car and drove all around New Zealand by herself and then she left."

"What was your wife doing in Burma?"

"She just travels around. She likes to see exotic countries. She's an amateur archaeologist. She almost got her PhD in archaeology."

"About a third of the producers I've interviewed have been lawyers."

"It helps to have a business background as a producer because you're constantly up against legal, contractual and economic issues. At the same time, you can't have your mind constricted by those things. You have to be able to break out and have a creative vision. That's a hard combination."

"Do people team up to maximize their strengths?"

"Sometimes but it is rare to find a producer who doesn't have both skills. It's hard to find a producer who's solely business or solely creative. If they're solely creative, they go way over budget and don't get jobs again."

It hits me that I could never make it as a movie producer because you have to get along with so many people and make so many compromises.

"It would be nigh impossible for anyone to succeed as a producer who is antisocial because you have to deal with so many constraints and collaborate with so many people."

"It's important to maintain good relations with the network people, their legal department, standards and practices, the buying side and the creative side, the promotion and publicity department. It is sometimes difficult because they occasionally take positions that are wrongheaded."

"You have to suffer fools gladly."

"You have to hold yourself back. It's their money and you have to do what they say if you want to work again. You have to have your convictions though and fight for things you believe in with well-reasoned arguments."

"You lose a lot of those arguments."

"You do."

"The type of kid who wants to play with his toys by himself is not going to make a good producer."

"He'd be a better writer. Producers have to get people working together as a cohesive team and that's often difficult because there are disagreements amongst the crew. The costume designer wants to have everybody in red and the DP (director of photography) feels that red will spoil his color scheme. There are usually a lot of personality conflicts, often between the producer and the director and the production manager. The director will want to shoot longer hours and not stop for a meal break. The production manager has to point out the costs and the producer has to arbitrate."

"Often individuals, such as a director, will want to do things to impress their peers that don't add value to the final product for viewers."

"Directors, for instance, will often want to make a production as showy as possible."

"A narcissist wouldn't make a good producer."

"He'd be looking in the mirror all the time instead of at the monitor. You have to be more self-effacing. You don't get the credit as a producer. If the movie is good, the director gets the credit.

"When you start a project, you pick these people and they become your intimate family for months. Then you never see them again."

"This must be why so many producers I interview seem bland. They can't afford to flaunt their egos."

"Even when you read the biographies of moguls like Samuel Goldwyn, they gave a lot of leeway to the directors and the writers who were talented."

"Do you own your negatives?"

"Yes."

"I hear that is harder to do."

"It is probably impossible now. Ever since the [revoking of] financial interest rule [which limited the networks from owning their shows and movies], the broadcasters have insisted on owning more and more."

"Are you feeling increasingly squeezed as an independent producer?"

"Yes. I'm making fewer [TV] movies. I'm trying to make features. It's difficult. While television welcomes with open arms people with feature experience, it doesn't work the other way round. It's a different set of people and a different set of ideas about how they think about projects. In television, they want pre-sold stories—stories with a built-in audience and recognition value. They have a hard time getting attention.

"It's rare to find a big book these days that has enough name value. NBC bought the Tom Wolfe book *A Man in Full*, but it is not well known enough for them and so they're not doing it. USA is doing *Helen of Troy* and did *Attilla the Hun*. Everyone has heard of them though I would defy most people to tell the story of *Attilla the Hun*.

"Features are willing to do a subject that is more complex and less easily defined, aside from the action and the high concept films. Features are willing to tackle subjects, like *In the Bedroom*. A few years ago, that would've made a nice television movie. Now it wouldn't be made [as a TV movie] because it doesn't have a pre-sold audience. *Dead Man Walking* (1995) could've been a television movie from one of the cable companies.

"Features is much more concerned with who the director is. In television, it doesn't matter who the director is. You sell the project and then you hire the director. In features, you don't get financing until you have a director.

"A lot of it is a snobbery amongst the talent agents who don't like to expose their top writers and directors and agents to people who aren't currently hot in the feature field. In television, you get the project set up and then you go cast it. TV agents are eager. They want to get offers if not the actual job for their clients. But in features, the talent drives the project, be it the star cast or the star director. Their agents are much more protective. They don't like to send them out on things that may not get made."

"Why would they care if you already have the money?"

"If you already have the money, then they don't care. But if you are looking to set up a project, and to use their clients to move it forward, then they are much less eager to help."

"I sense that many film people despise television as an inferior medium."

"They think that. Though many feature people are crossing over because there's more money and the work is steadier. They're received like the Messiah. If a feature producer or director produces a TV show, even though they're not going to do anything on the project, just by attaching their name, they can get a lot of press for the project. Barbra Streisand's company did that TV movie on the lesbian army woman played by Glenn Close. Barbra Streisand didn't write it. She didn't direct it. She didn't star in it. But she put her name behind it and she got a lot of publicity for it. Networks are eager for that because it gives them that extra edge getting magazine covers, talk shows, etc. They don't have the budgets to pursue publicity so they have to get it through other means, such as attaching somebody."

"When you're trying to get a project set up, do you ever have to say who you are?"

"All the time. I used to know many of the people running the studios, but I can't call them to pitch an idea. So I am often meeting with people in their 20s and early 30s. I can't expect them to know me. It means selling myself again, which I really love.

"The ratios of movies that get made is much worse for feature producers than television. You stand about a one in three chance with a TV movie development deal. With features, your odds are about one in twenty.

"I'm not encountering age discrimination. If I were trying to do a TV series for Nicklelodeon, I suppose I'd have a hard time."

"Do you get pushed to aim for a young audience?"

"I don't get pushed to do it but that's what they want, so you try to develop something that will hit that narrow target. Often you will try to find a lead in that age range and a subject that will appeal to them. You tend to stay away from things like *The Golden Girls* [1985-92 series about old women] and the Walter Matthau movies *Grumpy Old Men* (1993, 1995).

"If you're pitching to Lifetime, you pick a movie that has a female lead and a subject that appeals to women. To USA, it's better to have a male lead and more testosterone action."

"Robert Kosberg says you have to be careful about pitching stories to studios that are too intelligent."

"Well, you can pitch them in a dumb way. If you were pitching Albert Einstein, or the Niels Bohr Story, you'd have a hard time. But they were able to dumb down *A Beautiful Mind*, so I guess you could dumb down the Albert Einstein Story."

"Are there topics that are too controversial?"

"Absolutely. I've been trying to sell a story about the recent priest-sex-scandal controversy. I have a particular way of doing it. It's not just watching priests diddle boys and girls. It was too controversial."

"Hollywood loves to make movies bashing Catholics."

"This was for television. They were afraid it would offend their more conservative viewers. But their decision baffled me. I don't think anyone believes that priests should be able to molest kids but anything that criticizes an established institution like the Catholic church will create controversy and controversy is bad."

"I thought controversy would create hype."

"There's a fine line between controversy and hype. They don't want to be criticized. Even the cable companies don't want to be criticized. They want to be talked about but not criticized. I think in that story you have to take a position. Obviously not all priests are bad and the entire church hierarchy isn't bad, but obviously there's something rotten there to allow this to go on for so many years. That's what needs to be dramatized."

"Other things you've found too hot for TV?"

"Female genital mutilation in Africa. In many tribes and country, it is a common practice. It was not well received. All the female executives were fascinated by it but they thought they couldn't get advertising for it.

"I had a good story on an adolescent girls physically abused, beaten by their boyfriends. That's common. According to a survey, about 30 percent of teenage girls in relationships are beaten by their boyfriends. The networks do wife abuse stories all the time and they rate well. But the advertisers hate it and they have a hard time selling the time. Even though they force one through every year or two, it is a big problem."

"Traci Lords."

"That wasn't about advertisers. It was more this whole southern conservative Jerry Falwell grassroots revolt against sex on television.

"I've tried to sell Mormon projects and they won't touch them. I had a wonderful script about Brigham Young's 27th wife. She was a young girl. He was in his 60s. She was engaged to someone else and he went ape over her. Because of his power and charisma, she married him under the condition that he would not have sex with anyone else. She had her own house and everything went great for a while. She got along with the other wives. Then after a few months, one of the other wives became pregnant. She objected. So he had her work in the fields. Then she led the wives on a revolt. They went shopping and refused to do what he wanted.

"She ended up speaking out against polygamy. She spoke before Congress, helping to pass the law against polygamy, which had him jailed. They felt that they'd get a lot of flack for it. That it was disrespectful to the Mormons."

37

Randall Emmett

April 10, 2002

Born March 25, 1971, Randall Emmett has 19 feature credits.

Brash and fast talking, he is in the mold of such producers as Avi Lerner, Joel Silver, and Don Simpson.

"I grew up in Miami, Florida," says Randy, a stocky kid. "I had no entertainment connections in my family aside from a distant cousin, Jerry Bruckheimer. I had always known about him. My mother grew up with him in Detroit.

"I started in the acting thing when I was young. I got a hold of a video camera and got into making my little video shorts.

"I spent my first college year at Delphi University in Long Island. I had a full scholarship for acting. I became mesmerized by the process of production. I loved being in that magical environment. In summer, I worked as a PA on the movie *The Hard Way* (1991) starring Michael J. Fox and LL CoolJ. I slept with my walkie talkie. It was the coolest thing in the world. As a PA, I got to lock up streets. I thought I'd arrived. I thought I was the big baller of PAs. At that point, I knew I had to be in movies.

"I wanted to go to film school and the only one I could get into was City College of City University of New York. I had no idea it was on 138th Street in Harlem. Here was this white Jewish kid from Miami, living on the Upper West Side. 'Oh, 138 St. It's just up 50 blocks, but once you pass Columbia University, it's a culture shock. I grew up in a sheltered environment. I had an 11:30 p.m. curfew. I was a little momma's boy. Now I'm on a subway in Harlem and I'm in gangland. That was my growing up year. I was one of the few Caucasians at the school.

"When I look back on it, I was crazy. I'd stay in the editing room until 10 p.m. and then walk a quarter of a mile to the subway, but that quarter-of-a-mile was gang infested. I guess I was blessed that nothing happened.

"Then I transferred to the School of Visual Arts on 23rd Street. I graduated in 1994. Everybody there wanted to be a director. I liked taking people's money and then budgeting it. These kids would have $15,000 and they would blow it. They'd never finish their projects. I became known as the production manager/producer. Every weekend for two years I was out shooting with these seniors. We did about 14 short films.

"We made a feature (*Eyes Beyond Seeing*, 1995) for $76,000. We went out to Long Island for four weeks. I put the crew up in a dorm. I had to have a star in the movie and the biggest one I could get was Henny Youngman. I called local TV stations to come out and cover us. We sold it for domestic release to UPN and we sold it foreign as well. I knew that I wanted to be a Hollywood producer.

"I was in my dorm room drinking a 40 [ounce beer] and eating a slice of pizza, with three dollars in my pocket, when Jerry Bruckheimer returned my call. He asked me what I wanted to do. I told him and then he replied, 'People will tell you what you do best. Instead of you deciding what you do best, people will tell you. You'll find your thing.' I found it in producing.

"I moved to Los Angeles. I worked as a development intern for Jerry Bruckheimer. I got a taste of Hollywood. I got to go to the editing room of *Bad Boys* (1995) and watch [director] Michael Bay. Unfortunately, I was jaded, because this was the highest level for a producer. I knew this was where I wanted to be but I didn't know there was a whole [spectrum] between Jerry Bruckheimer and nothing.

"One of my best friends was Mark Wahlberg. I met him the day I moved to LA. We hit it off. He loves film. I love film.

"Aaron Spelling wrote me a letter of recommendation and I took that to ICM with other letters of recommendation and I got my first assistant job, working for talent agent Nick Stein. Agencies are the nucleus of the business. If you want to learn how to be a producer, you need to go to an agency. That's where everything starts.

"I worked for Nick over a year. Then I left to work as a personal assistant to Mark Wahlberg for two years, leading up to his appearance in *Boogie Nights*. After 18 months, I left to work in foreign sales. I'd get on the phone and cold call people.

"A bunch of us producers started around the same time—Matt Rhodes, Tucker Tooley, Vincent Newman, David Glasser. We're all good friends. We all came up together. We'd all been burned by fake money guys. We'd met people who said they had $400 million to invest.

"Then I met my partner George Furla. He's a financier from a Wall Street background. I remember when he came into the room. He proves that you can't judge a book by its cover. I'm more of a stylish wear-it-on-the-sleeve kinda guy. My partner wears sweatpants and a T-shirt. If he's going to meet with the president, that's what he wears.

"He sat down in the room and I thought, 'Oh no. Another bullshitter. Another guy who knows a guy whose uncle in Kansas has $400 trillion.' I said, 'This movie's [*Speedway Junkie*, 1999] going. I need this amount of money to hold the actor. I need this amount of money to hold the script.' Maybe a total of $30,000.

"He reached into his pocket, no contract, nothing, and pulled out crumpled up checks. They were balled up. He starts writing checks. I thought it was a joke. He gave me three checks and then said, 'O.K, we've got to work out the deal.' I thought the checks would bounce like the NBA but they all went through. We opened up production offices and made the movie.

"During the production of that movie, we decided that we should partner up. We have a similar work ethic. I'm loud and obnoxious and in your face. George is reserved and calculating. If I go over the top, he's there to pull me back. If we need to step forward, I'm there to say, 'Let's go.'

"George took us public."

"Someone told me that you're a mini Joel Silver."

"I've heard that a lot. I don't know Joel personally. To me, that's the biggest compliment in the universe. People say that I'm a mini Don Simpson. If I could have one tenth of the success that either of these producers had, I could die happily. Yeah, I yell and scream a lot, but it is all for a movie. I don't go down the street and yell at the guy selling hot dogs. I'm yelling because I am a perfectionist and I want that movie to be the best. I have a partner who will sometimes say, 'Get back in your cage.'"

38

Joel Soisson

April 11, 2002

"My history seems to be that I hook up with a company, bankrupt them, and then move on. I never deliberately do this. I bankrupted Sandy Howard once or twice. I got hired by Bob Shaye at New Line and made one of the *Nightmare on Elm Streets* (1985). I thought they were about to go bankrupt, so I hopped over to DEG (De Laurentiis Entertainment Group, everybody in the '80 was an entertainment group) before I drove another company to extinction. And what do I do? I bankrupt DEG. Then I went to Cannon and bankrupted them. Then I worked with MCEG and bankrupted them. I did this horrible movie called *Boris and Natasha* (1992). That was MCEG's last gasp. I don't think they ever made another movie. I don't think DEG ever made another movie after *Bill and Ted's Excellent Adventure* (1989).

"Then I stopped bankrupting other people's companies and came close to bankrupting my own when I started Neo Arts & Logic in 1989. But we've held together for 12 years now. We've tottered a couple of times. People suggested that I call my company 7/11 Productions because I'm always considering which bankruptcy option to take.

"I'm holding on with Miramax now. I haven't bankrupted them yet. I gave them an off year or two, but I think I've turned the corner.

"For many low budget producers, the process of filmmaking becomes more important than the result. For them, a film is a sexy thing until you finish it. Then it's like yesterday's hooker. They don't even want to think about it. I can never be that way. I can't divorce myself from the agony of living and dying with a movie.

"Producer Lynda Obst says the only word that a producer should know is 'Next.' I find that something to aspire to.

"I'm locked into making low budget movies that are not meant to be permanent. They are not meant to be revisited at in ten years. They are not meant to be

241

paragons of art or social commentary. They are just meant to entertain somebody for 90-minutes.

"You grow old making these things and blow out your health. I want to evolve into that kind of producer who can just enjoy the process. The deal. I hate the deal. I despise the deal. I'm the reluctant producer. I came to the job through the backdoor."

"Tell me about your childhood."

"It's that typical Cleveland, Ohio story. I'm sure you've heard it from all the Cleveland filmmakers.

"I came late to the film bug. My father was a commercial and fine artist. I would have become a fine artist had I been convinced that I could be as good as him. I went to an art institute in New York where I was exposed to film as animation for the first time. I thought, 'Wow, this is cool. You can make drawings that move. I can smoke the old man. He's never done this shit.'

"I came out here in 1979 to make cartoons. I went to USC and then AFI (American Film Institute). Five colleges in all. I didn't graduate from any of them.

"We [Neo Art & Logic] have a little digital effects studio that's the last remnant of my artistic pretensions. I can go back and weigh in on 3-D animation, matte paintings, etc.

"I hopped around schools because I never found what I was looking for, aside from a sense of community and making contacts. The only way you learn is by picking up a camera and doing it. At school, I found everything was too theoretical."

"Your first credit was for writing and associate producing *Hambone and Hillie* (1984)."

"I worked for Sandy Howard, who was in the Roger Corman mold of: 'Screw the film, just get another one made. If it doesn't work, just make sure you have two more in the hopper.' By the time I left him, he was drafting his 12-14 Plan, which was to make 12-14 pictures, any pictures, a year. Just get them ground out. We had a slow year in my last year there. In 1986, we only made six films.

"With *Hambone and Hillie*, Sandy said, 'We need to do a family movie. Let's get a dog. Everybody loves dogs. We haven't done a dog movie.' I was a camera assistant at the time, on the verge of getting fired. So I knew that this was my chance to get another month of employment. I pitched him this dog idea. He said 'Write it up.' So I became a producer-writer. In those chaotic days, you did everything. As long as you were willing not to get paid for anything, you were like gold. It didn't matter if you had talent as long as you had initiative.

"This was about a dog who went from New York to LA. Because I was new, they only let me take the dog from New York to Philadelphia. Other writers took him the rest of the way, without any idea of what I had done. Sandy wanted to put his stamp on it. So he wrote the last leg where the dog got involved in a gang rape. I said, 'I thought we were setting out to do a family film.' He said, 'Yeah, but we still need drama.' I thought, 'Well, this man is pushing the envelope. I'm impressed.'

"I got to write the part where O.J. Simpson picks the dog off the turnpike and drives him a ways. They're sitting there motoring along. It was in the days where dogs didn't talk. O.J. was lamenting that he was a lonely trucker. His wife ran off with another guy. Thinking back, it's precious.

"I told an interviewer from the *LA Weekly* that the movie premiered on a TWA flight to China. I believe so because that's the only record I have of it being screened anywhere. A friend of mine flying to China saw it. Then I got this horrible letter back from Sandy saying that real producers don't denigrate their own work. He gave me that rule, which I have since broken at every chance. I've got a kiddie movie with a gang rape [rated PG] and I'm thinking, 'Thank God it premiered on a flight to China.'"

"Did anyone jump out of the plane?"

"I don't know but I'm sure it opened up a whole new world for the Chinese view of American culture.

"By the way, the dog didn't participate in the gang rape. He was a little dog so all he could do was nip at the heels of the assailants."

"What was Sandy's company called?"

"Many independent companies during the 1980s, including Sandy's, went bankrupt for a year and then came back under a new name. He had Sandy Howard International, Howard International, Sandy Howard Productions, Republic Pictures. If you stumble five times, you can go quiet for six months and then come back with big new fanfare. 'New astounding international company has a 12-picture slate for next month.' That's a salesmanship that I don't see as much anymore."

"It sounds like Menahem Golam and Yoram Globus of Cannon Pictures."

"Showmen. I worked with those guys for a while. I remember one time I went to Cannes and they had this big poster selling, 'Mitchum, Wayne, Taylor.' It was Chris Mitchum, David Wayne, John Taylor. Those guys would do anything. And they're all cheap.

"I got involved after Menahem and Yoram split up and had this holy war against each other. Yoram Globus was my guy. Yoram was more the producer/ financial side and Menahem was more of the creative guy.

"I got involved at the time of the Lambada dance craze. I had gone to Cannon Pictures from Dino De Laurentiis after making *Bill and Ted's Excellent Adventure*. Dino had phoned up his pal [Giancarlo] Paretti. We got a call, my partner Michael S. Murphey and I, to head up the new Cannon Pictures. We were totally jazzed to run a studio. We get there and meet with Chris Pearce, Yoram's back-room manipulating guy.

"We asked, 'So, what do we do?' Chris said, 'I'm not sure yet. There's another guy who wants to run the studio with you.' He sent us down to the script library to see if there was anything we wanted to make into a movie, something to kill time.

"We come back up after lunch. Chris said, 'We'll figure this all out later. Just go down and get your ID cards so you can get a parking pass.' I am so passive on these things. I say O.K. So I went down and the screening guy asked for my title. I said, 'Story Department.' That got me the Lambada job.

"They had this new dance wave coming. They didn't have a script. So they gave me this old script that had nothing to do with dancing about a math teacher in East LA. 'Just put some dancing in it. Make it the Lambada. I don't care if you know how to dance or not. Just say, whenever they dance, that it is the Lambada. Just put a sexy girl in there and let's go. We've got to beat Menahem. They're shooting now.' They wanted to totally destroy the other guy's company.

"So when's Menahem's thing coming out? 'He's only got a script. But we have the right to the title *Lambada* (1990). Menahem's called *The Forbidden Dance*.

"The two versions came out a week apart. One had something like a two week post. The other had a three week post. Both were awful movies. The box office on ours was $1100 per screen [not good]. But Yoram was triumphant because it was $200 more per screen than Menahem's made. It didn't matter that they were both abject failures. It was that we won. I just realized that so much of this business is all about ego.

"I'm the tightest. I'm cheap to a fault."

"Are you Jewish?"

"No, but I've learned enough that sooner or later, I am going to join the faith. I think it is only fair.

"It is physically impossible for me to squander money.

"I have made some turkeys in my career, but what has really done all these companies in is hubris. They have made far too many movies and sold too many rights away. The whole '80s was about overextension and greed. They'd make these giant monolithic companies with huge overheads, making movies that were completely antithetical to their original vision. Cannon was making an over the top $30 million Stallone turkey *Over the Top*. These companies suddenly want to be A list. It's an ego thing.

"Being successful making $3-5 million movies only gets you so far and then you need more gratification. In one year, Dino was making huge movies that were all $30 million out and one million in. The irony of my career is that the most successful movie I ever made bankrupted Dino. *Bill and Ted's Excellent Adventure* (1989). We made the movie for about $10 million and Dino sold it for a million because he thought it was a turkey. He didn't even test it. Orion picked it up and it tested through the roof. It was a huge box office success. I don't know that I can shoulder all the blame for these bankruptcies. I just find it peculiar that I am attached to so many of them.

"*Bill and Ted* can be accused of stupefying the world but it contributed to the American idiom. When the president spoke about his excellent adventure, it's an ego thing to make a movie that has actual cultural impact, even if it is negative. You go, 'That is so cool.' A friend of mine in distribution informed me that the movie tanked in your home country of Australia.

"I've had a good clean run for the past 12 years. I've forged a reputation for being commercially viable. My last unsuccessful movie was *Phantoms*, 1998. Miramax was on a roll that year, so it didn't affect the balance sheet too badly, but I was in the doghouse for a year.

"You never anticipate failure. You go into every movie thinking it will be a $100 million blockbuster. You have to think that way to work your ass off. You don't set off to make a bad movie.

"What's allowed me to survive some of my stumblings is that I've always behaved responsibly. During the 1980s, a lot of people were spending money wildly and blowing it up their nose, and the cars, and the lifestyle and all the trappings. That's what it was all about for them. They had no respect for what they were given to do.

"When tax shelters fell away, and video [sales] fell away in the early '90s, it made [independent films] risky. That's why for much of the '90s, I found myself making films for less than I did in the early '80s. It took me awhile to get back to making a $3 million movie. That's one of the glories of working with [Bob Weinstein's] Dimension Films. They are one of the few companies willing to gamble in that $3-10 million zone. That's the gray area between a typical direct-to-video movie and a theatrical level production. Being owned by Disney, they have Buena Vista underneath them. Buena Vista is one of the few video distribution companies that can put out video product and make money on it. You can buy Buena Vista videos."

"You make a lot of sequels."

"There's a chapter in William Goldman's last book entitled, 'Sequels equals whores,' because there's nothing original about them. It's about money over passion. You're working a concept until nobody will pay you anymore. I don't think any producer in history has done as many sequels as I have."

"Does that mean that you are the biggest…"

"Whore in history. I think I should say it before you did it. I have made a concerted effort to start focusing on original material."

"You sound like a whore who goes to church."

"And I do have a heart of gold. In my defense, because I'm not sure that you will come to my defense, it is so hard to make movies in this industry. It is even harder to make new or good movies. It is very hard to close the door when someone is pushing through a bag full of money to make a movie. So, yes, guilty as charged.

"It is not like I am running laughing to the bank. These movies are like ripples on water. Their budgets get smaller and smaller. They're pretty much invisible to the rest of the world but we still see them and that little chunk of change left to make them. We still even care. We have never set out to make a bad movie. Honest. How they come bad, I haven't figured that out yet.

"We've never set out, as many producers have, to go, 'They'll never know. It's just a box with shrinkwrap on it. If they open it up, that's not out responsibility. Our responsibility is getting it off the shelf.' Those are what they called in the '80s the poster movies. The box movies. Forget the script and the movie, get that art work. Get that picture on the cover of that cute chick with the gun. 'Nobody's going to care. They're buying the picture on the box. The roman numeral.'

"That's what we call sequels—roman numeral movies. It gives it more of a gothic feel."

"What are the Weinstein brothers like?"

"You must have heard many stories about them over the years but they are nothing if not unpredictable. They'll blow up at the slightest things but I've done scenes that came out hideous, or a movie that was a big disappointment, and when things are at their worst, when you want to jump off a high bridge, they are the most gracious guys on earth. They'll tear you down, but they'll never let you fall. Even when they are on one of their tirades, I know that it is just energy dissipation directed at the world.

"Harvey Weinstein fired me off a show [*Mother's Boys*, 1994] when I was supposed to be a supervised hitman for Miramax. I was supposed to shake down the production and get it back on track. I didn't do a good job and I got fired. After I got hired to make movies for Dimension, I used to avoid Harvey in the hallways in case he said, 'What's that guy I just fired doing back in my building?'

"Miramax has the art house mantel and Dimension the genre popcorn movies like *Spy Kids* (2001), *Scream* (1996), *Dracula* (1992). The adage in the industry is that Harvey scarfs up all the statutes and Bob makes the money. Ye Miramax is always considered the bigger."

"Do you get a lot of beautiful women throwing themselves at you to be in movies?"

"Daily. That's why I have a casting couch here. No, again, I am an anomaly. I've been happily married and living with the same woman since 1981. That whole thing has never been part of the game for me. I'd like to think that is because I have dignity and scruples. But a case could be made that nobody thinks that I have enough juice that I am worth sleeping with. I think I was flirted with in 1988 but it may have been a mistake in communications.

"You should interview this guy Don Phillips. He works with us. He's the most fascinating man I've ever known. He produced *Melvin & Howard* (1980). He cast *Fast Times at Ridgemont High* (1982), *Dazed and Confused* (1993). He's the antithesis of me. He is *Hollywood Babylon* on wheels. Or was. He's a good boy now."

39

John Hyde

April 11, 2002

John W. Hyde may run a big entertainment company, Film Roman, but he still wears blue jeans and cowboy boots into the office.

"I grew up in the small town of Bloomfield, outside Detroit, Michigan. It was a *Leave it to Beaver* (1957-63) childhood. I have a younger brother in Idaho and a younger sister in Santa Barbara. My father Neil was an executive at General Motors. I spent five years in high school because I got into so much trouble. This was a time, the late 1950s, when parents told you one thing but did another. I longed for a forum to express myself. This led me to New York.

"I studied Economics at NYU, graduating in 1963. I did graduate work in International Economics at the University of Lydon, near Amsterdam. The European Union had just formed. This was before Britain was a member. The Europeans said by the year 2000, there would be a common currency. I laughed at the time. Now we're there.

"In late 1963, I moved to Los Angeles and worked for ABC on a program of on-air promotional trailers. I've never gone back to Michigan more than a couple of times after I settled in California.

"I was immediately attracted to the casualness of the entertainment business. It was a sharp contrast to the formality I knew as a kid. I grew up in Bloomfield where it was suit and tie for everyone every day. You couldn't wear Levis to high school.

"I was raised an Episcopalian but I dropped out in my teens. It was High Episcopalian, just one degree off Anglican. Lots of pomp and circumstance. I discovered girls and other things on Sundays were more fun than going to church.

"When there was an opening at Universal Studios, I got a call and started in the mailroom with Mike Medavoy and John Badham. Mike's on the board of this company [Film Roman]. We've worked on several projects together.

"Ned Tanen took me out of the mailroom. He assigned me to this local television show, *The Lloyd Thaxton Show* (1961-68), an afternoon rock n' roll show, which MCA syndicated to 127 markets around the country. So at the tender young age of 25, making so little money I couldn't even qualify for credit cards, I'm suddenly flying around the country first class, with cars picking me up at the door, doing promotional tours.

"Ned convinced Lew Wasserman that the record labels MCA had weren't hip. So Mr. Wasserman gave us the approval to start a new music company—Uni Records. We signed Elton John, Neil Diamond. We shot the first two music videos in 1967, about a month before the Beatles did *Strawberry Fields*. Marcia Strossman (*Flower Children*) and Neil Diamond (*Brooklyn Roads*). Instead of sending the artists on tour, we could send these videos to all the local dance shows around the country. In those days, almost every city had a rock n' roll dance show on the air."

"Did you have much contact with Lew Wasserman?"

"This was when MCA had just taken over Universal. Lew Wasserman was aware of everyone who worked for him. You'd acknowledge him and he'd know you.

"Ned Tanen was one of my mentors. When I arrived at Universal, he was without portfolio. He got to be involved in any business he wanted to. He did the young filmmakers program. He started the record label. He oversaw some parts of television syndication. One of Ned's close associates was Jerry Perenchio, the entrepreneur behind Univision, Lowes theaters, Embassy Films. With Ned I got to network with a whole group of older, successful people.

"I left Universal in 1969 to work as an assistant to [Martin Ransohoff] the CEO of a company called Filmways, which was probably the hottest small production company in the world at that time. They had such TV shows as *The Beverly Hillbillies* (1962-71), *Green Acres* (1965-71), *Petticoat Junction* (1963-70), *The Adams Family* (1964-66), as well as feature films *Cincinnati Kid* (1965), *Catch 22* (1970), and *The Americanization of Emily* (1964).

"*Das Boot* had gone through several incarnations. At first it was supposed to be a tax shelter picture that starred Robert Redford and Paul Newman. That fell apart. To get it done, we shot it as a five-hour miniseries. Director Wolfgang Petersen brilliantly wove together the two-and-a-half hour script so we could cut it both as a five-hour miniseries and as a two-and-a-half hour film.

"We then did *Neverending Story* (1984). It was also shot in Bavaria and directed by Wolfgang Petersen. For two years, I flew back and forth to Munich one out of every three weeks. I clocked enough air miles to get two first-class tickets to Rio De Janeiro for a ten day New Years vacation.

"I was married in the 1960s to a dancer in West Side Story, actress Rita D'Amico. I have one son from that marriage who lives in Sydney, Australia. I've lived with my present wife [Kate Morris] since the late '70s. We got married in year 2000. People were always asking us, 'When are you going to get married?' Most of the people who asked us that, we saw marry, divorce, marry, divorce. We laughed and said we'd get married sometime when it was really special. Then we found out that the year 2000 was a special leap year that only happens once every 400 years. So we thought that makes it a perfect day. The last time there was a February 29th on a double zero even century was 1600. It won't come again until 2400. That's a great day, so we got married.

"My wife ran a number of companies that I oversaw or reorganized over the years. She also did all the subtitles and all the dubbing of Das Boot. We brought the original actors to London and she spent three or four months working with them getting the English-language version used for television, cable and video. She now runs our 1500-acre ranch, Fairlea Ranch, three hours north of here. The Ranch has 200-head of cattle, 110 horses, six Buffalo, five dogs and one pig. I spend every weekend there. Kate lives there full time."

"The 1970s were a great time for the movie industry."

"It was a time that was meant to come. Television had taken over motion pictures audience attention. The 1948 consent decree when the Justice Department required the studios to sell their ownership in theaters, burdening the motion picture studios. During the late 1950s and early 1960s, all the studios were having problems. Television production hadn't quite been accepted by the studios. In the 1970s television was part of every studio so studios could afford taking risks on films. There was a whole generation that just moved in together.

"When I worked at ABC in 1963, I met a guy who was working at a similar project. He was working at ABC until he could get in the William Morris mailroom. His name was David Geffen. Barry Diller was working with Leonard Goldberg then [at ABC] and they were doing the first of the [made-for-TV] movies. Television was just catching on to rock n' roll. People were realizing that music was as integral part of entertainment as were film and television. The generation of people who came out of the 1960s looked at music, TV, film as being part of a whole. We didn't separate them out. It was the beginning of the flexibility that allowed you to move between creative disciplines. That never happened before. If you were a television actor, you were only a television actor.

"Our view of television was so different from [traditional] motion picture people. The older studio executives looked at television as a threat. We looked at television as something that was part of our culture. This brought about an ability to work in all three disciplines and merge them together for the first time. Today when you see *Ally McBeal*, with music as an integral part of the program, or *Buffy the Vampire Slayer* (1997-2003), which opened the season with an incredible musical, this is the end product of what started in the late '60s."

"I remember your movie *Clan of the Cave Bear* (1986)."

"It was originally going to be an NBC miniseries. Peter Guber and Jon Peters said we should make this film using independent financing. Our partner at the time was Sydney Kimmel. He is probably the most successful clothing manufacturer in New York. He is the controlling shareholder and the founder of Jones of New York. He funded *Clan of the Cave Bear* and *Nine 1/2 Weeks*.

"*Clan* used a compromise form of signing and no real language. We used subtitling. It may have been a little too advanced. That was still the era when studios said you shouldn't use subtitles. Today people are used to seeing the bad guy being some other nationality and speak a foreign language and have subtitles underneath it.

"Peter Guber and Jon Peters had a vision for the picture and we convinced Warner Brothers to go with that vision. It was a noble experiment.

"We tested *Nine 1/2 Weeks* about 35 times before audiences. MGM had originally gone with our vision. There was a short period of time when MGM was purchased by an Australian. His first pronouncement was, 'I'm only going to do G and PG rated films.' He brought in new management. So, all of a sudden, the people who had bought *9 1/2 Weeks* and our vision of it, were gone. There was new management who said we should test it in front of an audience. We tested it in front of an audience. Women got up and walked out at a certain scene so we literally tested every single scene in the movie so that when we put it together, we had sequences that worked.

"[Director] Adrian Lyne did a brilliant job. He directed a film that is about testing the limits. It was simple. It was two people and a test of their limits. One had no limits and the other had limits. The film was about that clash.

"It was so controversial that while we were still shooting the film, people who had never even read the script were talking about how terrible it was.

"The ultimate proof is that it worked is the millions of videotapes and DVDs it sold. It was too bad that so many low cost sequels were done. When I look at it now, it is milder than most MTV videos. But at the time, it was groundshaking."

"What are your strengths?"

"I am able to get along with a diverse group of people. I'm good at pulling people and ideas together and moving them through the first few stages of a project or problem. Those stages are usually the toughest. Getting it from an idea to a story to the reality of production and then bringing together the elements needed. I've always been able to bridge the gap between creative talent and business talent."

40

Robert Marcarelli

April 16, 2002

"I graduated from Cal State Fullerton in 1972 with a degree in theater arts. I got married. I went up to the San Francisco Bay Area and worked in several theater companies. I had small roles in various TV shows such as *The Streets of San Francisco* (1972-77).

"We raised the money independently for my first two features—1992's *Original Intent* and *I Don't Buy Kisses Anymore*. The distribution on *Kisses* didn't work out because the movie became competition for the studio. When you make an independent movie, and you let a studio back it, and you're doing better business than their pictures, and they have $50 million tied up in a movie, and they have no money tied up in yours. Our per-screen averages were higher than the movies they left in the theaters because they were studio-made movies.

"It's the old consignment game. If you have a storefront and you've put thousands of dollars into a particular product developed in the back room, you'd be more inclined to want to push that as opposed to getting a commission on something you had nothing to do with it. On Monday morning, theater distributors are clamoring over theater space, and unless you're a break away hit, they're not going to keep you there because you're an obstacle to studio product.

"*Kisses* got good reviews but it was only out three weeks. My 1999 movie *The Omega Code* (produced by the Trinity Broadcasting Network) was in the theaters for 14 weeks and was the highest grossing film of 1999 among films that played in fewer than 600 theaters. Nobody expected it to hit but there was a big grassroots mechanism working for it and it platformed across the United States and did over $13 million at the box office.

"W could've done a tremendous amount of more business if we were prepared to open the picture wide after it hit. We opened in October. We didn't have enough prints. Then we were getting into the Christmas season, which meant competing in the Northeast corridor against all the big Christmas movies. We shipped a million videos."

"There was a groundswell of interest in the Bible Codes at that time. Are you an evangelical Christian?"

"I am. I like to do stories that are uplifting, or have a good character arc, some transformation of character. I would never do an exploitation movie where people are getting shot just for the heck of it or people are having sex just for the heck of it. Life affirming films are more enjoyable than exploitation films."

"Have you found your religion a creative straitjacket?"

"Not at all. I would say that 97 percent of scripts I get are things I would not want to do. I've turned down work of things that I felt were more part of the problem than part of the solution for mankind. That has nothing to do with religion. It's amoral. I just hate doing things where people do weird things and get away with it and we find ourselves sitting in the theater cheering for them.

"I have to point out that most of the top grossing films are PG or G rated movies. Half as many PG rated movies are made as R-rated movies, yet they do twice as much gross on average.

"I've seen some R-rated films that I would've been thrilled to direct like *Glory* (1989). There are a lot of hard edged movies that have a redemptive quality to them. I would not reject because it might get rated R. I look at the script to see what it is saying. If I find there's something offensive in there that doesn't have to be there to get the point across, then I'd usually lobby to soften it up."

"Do you believe in Bible Codes that foretell the future?"

"Neither *Left Behind* (2000) nor *The Omega Code* were my agenda. I look at Scripture as a template for my behavior and belief system. Scripture says that no one knows the future. I find it is fun to look at the future. There's tremendous latitude when you're dealing a story on End Times than when you're doing a historical movie on Joshua, David or Jesus, etc. Then you've got to do the research and try to honor the history that we have."

"What's the difference between a fundamentalist Christian and an evangelical Christian?"

"Evangelical means that you believe in your faith, that it is true, and that other people should hear about it. But a fundamentalist would tend to be more judgmental on specifics. They would be less tolerant. They would be more like the Pharisees or really fundamentalist Jews. When I was shooting in Israel, I remember the *Shabbat* elevators and other ways that people could get around using electricity. But they're still using it. But because they didn't touch the button. A lot of those things to me are low [in importance]. Yet they'll be very judgmental about people's lifestyles and behaviors, whether they have earrings or not. I think God's much bigger than that.

"We believe in the God of Abraham, Isaac and Jacob. We shout Him from the house tops. We tell people God is real, alive and sharper than a two-edged sword. That's an evangelical."

"What is it like to work in an atmosphere that is antithetical to what you stand for?"

"I would think that that would be the case in any job one takes. I don't see it as any different than if you're working for a university or a computer company. I think it makes a great mix. It gives one an opportunity to talk about spiritual things, especially if the project has some level of spirituality to it. It makes for great commissary conversation.

"I've just finished a western, *The Long Ride Home* (2003). Talk about an eclectic career, from Millenium thriller to romantic comedy to western."

"Do you prefer working on Christian themed films?"

"I prefer working on something that has a redemptive piece to it. I like to see a character come through the other side with hope. To enlighten and entertain. I'm not interested in preaching.

"You should want in a movie a sleek look, tense drama, exotic location, pulsating music and full-blooded characters."

"Do your religious leaders ever suggest that you should leave such a godless environment?"

"No. In fact, they encourage me to be involved. Television and film is where most people get their information. It's important to have some hope in there. That's where people gather on Sunday, more than they do in churches."

41

John Langley

As I walk down the hallway to John Langley's office, a blonde woman (his wife of 30 years, Maggie) warns me, "If you're not a smoker, throw your arms up in the air and say you can't do the interview here. He'll take you upstairs."

John's office is a largely empty stage. I look around and crane my head to the left where I find John, a tall strapping man about 60.

He asks me if I mind his cigar and I say I don't, but it would be nice to do the interview upstairs.

We pop into an editing bay and it looks like the guy is cutting homosexual porn, but it's just the TV show *Cops* (1989-???), Langley's most famous production. It debuted in 1989 on Fox, and is about to air its 500th episode.

John and I settle down on adjacent couches in an empty upstairs office. We put our feet up on the table and whine about lawyers.

"I was never in a lawsuit in my life until I got into this business, where it is almost inevitable."

"People will sue each other and then do business the next day."

"Absolutely. I wish we had the English [legal] system where loser pays. As long as you don't have that system, you are going to have a lot of litigious people suing just so they can get an insurance settlement."

"Where did you grow up?"

"West Los Angeles and Manhattan Beach. My father worked in the aircraft industry. My mother was a housewife. I have two older brothers and a younger sister. None of them are in entertainment.

"I was born June 1, 1944. At one time, I wanted to be an academic. I've always been a slow learner. At age 18, in 1961, I joined the Army. I didn't want to go to college right away. I figured this was a great way to see the world and get laid.

"I went into so-called Army Intelligence. I spent two years, nine months, 29 days, 13 hours, 22 minutes and 14 seconds."

"Did your being in Army Intelligence help you get laid?"

"Oh sure. I was in Panama for two years. Then I returned home, went back to school, piddled around, worked multiple jobs, and returned to school. I got my BA (English) and MA (Literature/Composition) from Cal State Dominguez and I did PhD work at UC Irvine in the philosophy of aesthetics. It was a movement at the time. I taught at those two schools and I thought I wanted to be a professor.

"In 1971, I finally said enough of this nonsense. I quit because I couldn't conceive of teaching the same courses year in and year out. I'm a Gemini. I need more stimulation. I loved academia and I loved literature but I burned out on Ivory Tower capitalism.

"I got married and worked for an airline for three years in public relations. It was a great gig but I made no money. I traveled the world. I've always been a writer. I published in Film News International. Someone (Steve Friedman) read a screenplay I'd written and asked me to help produce a movie (*The Crowley Testament*) for Warner Brothers.

"In 1980, we sold PCs and started a production company. We starved for a couple of years and then we did a documentary about drug addiction called *Cocaine Blues* (1983)."

"Was this based on personal experience?"

"Oh, there's a bit of that. Maybe it was my karmic debt. We had a film deal with somebody and they said, 'Do something small first just to show that you can do what you say you can do.' So we did *Cocaine Blues*, which had been developed for somebody else. In my naivete, I realized that making a film was one thing but selling it was another.

"We entered it in all the film festivals and won some awards. And that's how I got into television [and conceived the show *Cops*].

"I wrote a screenplay that sold years later. Then in 1987, I made the *Dolph Lundgren: Maximum Potential* exercise video. I hired Quentin Tarantino and Roger Avary as PAs. Quentin and Roger worked at Video Archives in Manhattan Beach, where I live. They were kids, 18-19 years old. We used to discuss film and BS. I loaned him my script for the film *Behind Enemy Lines* (1986). He showed me scripts he'd written.

"As a PA, Quentin was always bashing into nightstands and babbling to everybody. He's quite a talker and loves to get into debates about film. My partner would say, 'Fire that kid. He doesn't know what the hell he's doing.'

"Roger came to me once and asked, 'I want to be a director. I don't want to be a PA. How do I do that?' I said, 'Roger, if you want to be a director, direct. If you want to be a writer, write. If you want to be a producer, produce.' He thought about it and said O.K. The next day he came in and said, 'I quit.' I said, 'That's cool. What are you going to do?' He said, 'I'm going to be a writer and a director.'"

"Quentin finished out as PA on that project, picking up dog turds on Venice Beach and that kind of work. That was their intro to the film biz.

"For *Cops*, we always get permission from everybody. We have far more strictures than the news. They can show everything they want."

"Why do people sign releases to be on your show?"

"Fame."

"If you were arrested, would you sign a release?"

"Of course I would. I've told my children the same. *Cops* has become part of the pop culture. People who will yell, 'Get that news camera away from me.' But when they hear that it is *Cops*, they go, 'Oh, that's cool.' And they sign releases. You tell me why. I don't know why. Maybe it's because it is part of the landscape now. It's cool to be on *Cops*.

"A few years ago, I started a Web site Crime.com with the sole purpose of reverse convergence. It was everything you ever wanted to know about crime—information, news, entertainment. I wanted to turn it into a channel. I ended up selling it to USA Networks and being a cofounder of the cable channel, which has yet to launch."

"Have you had to tone down the violence on *Cops*?"

"No. The interesting thing about television is that you can show all the blood and guts you want. You just have to avoid sex and language. I've had some interesting discussions with Standards and Practices [internal network censorship units] over the years. For instance, you can't say 'Jesus Christ' or 'God damn it' on television. Yet I can show homicide. To me, a murder is far more obscene than language. I always try to push the envelope as far as possible. Not to exploit, but to be as real and as raw as possible because that's the programming mandate for the show. I wanted to show you reality as you have never seen it. You want to show what a homicide scene is and what a high speed chase is. My purpose is not to show blood and guts. I just want to show reality as unvarnished as possible. *Cops* is an existential variety show. It is unpredictable and immediate and as real as you can get without being there.

"Often there's a confusion between the message and the messenger. I am not a cop and I have never had ambitions to be a cop. I'm a child of the '60s. If you would've told me that I was going to do a show about cops, I would've said, 'What am I going to call it? Pigs?' I just happened to get in an arena that was dramatic and started doing documentary films about it that became so-called reality television. In doing it, I developed respect for people doing it, like cops, paramedics, firemen. Most of these people are in it for pro-social purposes. By and large, these guys are the good guys. When something like 9/11 happens, there's a great urge for order."

"Why have you chosen to specialize in crime?"

"Why do I do *Cops* and not *Accountants*? Certain professions lend themselves to drama. That's why there are so many medical, legal and crime dramas."

42

Don Phillips

A preacher's kid born December 21, 1940, Don "grew up in Ventner, New Jersey, a heavily Jewish town. All my fellow cub scouts were Jewish. I went to Hebrew School on Saturday so I could play basketball in the Jewish Community Center."

"How come you never converted to Judaism?"

"Because I believe in Jesus Christ. I am a Judeo-Christian. We both believe in the same God but I believe He has a son named Jesus Christ.

"When I was nine, we moved to another island next to Atlantic City, Ocean City. In high school, I decided that instead of writing a term paper, I'd write a play with my friend. We'd perform these plays. In my freshman year, we had a course in world history. At the time, there was a popular TV show called *Dragnet* (1951-59). We decided to call our show *Fishnet*. We were getting A grades for our plays.

"By my senior year, we were writing great stuff as well as playing all the sports. I said to my friend, Mike Fadden, who's since become chairman of the board of several of the biggest oil companies in the world, 'Why don't we become playwrights?' He said, 'Are you crazy? Only fags go to Hollywood.' I said, 'You're right.' He said, 'You either become a doctor or lawyer or insurance salesman or teacher. You don't go to Hollywood with all those fags.' That was 1957.

"I wrote and performed in plays in college. I first went to Kings College in New York and then I transferred to the University of Tennessee to play big time college basketball."

"Were you 6'6' then?"

"I was 6', which in 1960 was the tall guard. I was good sized for my position. The tallest guy on any given team might be 6'3. We used to call it playing below the rim. Now they call it playing above the rim. My life desire was to be a great college basketball player and then a great college basketball coach.

"When I was at the University of Tennessee, a couple of my buddies took bribes. It was a big scandal. We had no idea. So I left and went back to Shelton College in New York.

"They didn't like how I played basketball in the south. It was all slowed down. I was much more of a Bob Cousy-type player. I'd dribble between my legs and throw passes around my neck. That is more Eastern basketball so I didn't fit into the slow southern style.

"I graduated with a degree in Physical Education. I taught high school for three years. I was named teacher of the year. I left because I wasn't fulfilled and I wasn't earning enough money. All the teachers had to get a job at Christmas time and Easter time and during the summer to make ends meet. I knew I could never raise a family on that salary.

"One day in Manhattan, I ran into a guy I hadn't seen in ten years. He made industrial movies. He said, 'We're doing one on Tuesday for a paper company that sells school supplies. They want to appeal to the youth. We're going to film a rock n' roll group and have a disc jockey doing a voice-over. Don, how about you giving me one of your rock n' roll groups and I'll give them $500 for the day.'

"I showed up to the shoot on Tuesday. They've got 35mm cameras and lighting guys and grips and actors. I spend 12 hours that day watching them do it. My jaw drops open and I realize that this is what I want to do the rest of my life. I want to make films.

"The only guy I know remotely connected to show business is Tom Sullivan, who owns a PR firm on Madison Avenue. This is how God works. I tell him my story. 'But I don't know what to do? I'm not an actor.' He said, 'You could be an agent or manager.' I said, 'Tom, I've done that with the bands. I don't like flesh peddling.' He said, 'Well, there's always casting.'

"Casting? I go to Lincoln Center and I know some actors and I'm always watching a movie and thinking, wouldn't he be better in this movie?

"Tom's regular secretary is pregnant and is having her child. The temporary secretary is Marian Chinich. She'd just married Michael, who had experience in casting. He was starving. Tom set us up.

"We started out casting industrials, commercials and book covers. Our first movie was for Otto Preminger, *Such Good Friends* (1971). Otto Preminger was the tyrant of tyrants. If you ever got a chance to work for this man, you'd probably get fired.

"As Talent Services Inc, we cast *Thursday's Game* (1974), *The Effect of Gamma Rays on Man-in-the-moon Marigolds* (1972), *Summer Wishes Winter Dreams* (1973), *Miracle on 34th Street* (1973), *Cock Fighter* (1974), *Foxtrot* (1976).

"We got the job of casting day players and extras on *Serpico* [1973 film directed by Sydney Lumet]. *Serpico* was a humongous production because of its large number of actors. The extras who played policeman, and didn't have lines, weren't just up there for a day or so. They became characters because they were always shown in the precinct.

"There were creative differences between Al Pacino and John Avildsen, the original director. John left. Then producer Marty Bregman decided on Sydney Lumet, who was on the balls of his ass. He'd been making turkey after turkey. But they knew Sydney was a shooter with a love affair with New York.

"Casting director Shirley Rich had other commitments and had to leave the show. Sydney tapped me on the shoulder and said, 'Don, how would you like to cast the rest of the show?' What a break. Now we had the opportunity to cast the other speaking parts (130).

"I got my first taste of producing on [Polish] director Krzysztof Zanussi's film *The Catamount Killing* (1974). He was the darling of all the film festivals.

"He was a wonderful intelligent filmmaker who is good friends with the Pope. He was good friends with Roman Polanski. The Polish Wave with him, Polanski and Andrzei Wajda was coming on strong. Krzysztof got to make his first American movie, *The Catamount Killing.* I cast, was associate producer, accountant. I went on location. It won festival awards. It was a dime-store novel trying to turn into a psychological thriller.

"After we shot the picture, Chip Taylor, Jon Voight's baby brother, wanted to produce a film Zanussi had written. Chip wrote the song, *Wild Thing,* and *Just Call Me Angel of the Morning.* I put him in the movie as a sheriff. He was a little stiff. But Chip fell in love with Zanussi, with his mind and his philosophy.

"We flew to Berlin where Krzysztof was editing the picture. It is December, 1973, and Krzysztof wants to take us to Poland. We had to fly out of East Germany. Krzysztof told us to tell customs we are just tourists. Please don't mention my name.

"We had a great Polish cinematographer Witold Sobocinski. Witold was a rebel. He bought a Mercedes while in Germany. Witold's wife was a Jewish doctor who did research at Oxford and Cambridge. And they lived in a tiny cheap apartment.

"I've been known to have a big mouth. I was warned not to say anything. When Chip (who was quiet) and I got on the plane to go to Warsaw, I asked for some Polish newspapers. I figured they might have a picture of Zanussi. He was huge in Poland. In most Communist countries, the director is more lauded than any actor. They love the artist.

"The captain comes back. 'I understand you want the Warsaw papers. Do you speak Polish?' I said no. He said, 'Then why would you want to look at the Polish newspapers?' I said, 'I don't know, I just wanted to look at the pictures.' The captain went back and the stewardess gave me the papers.

"Chip said to me, 'Don, they think we're spies. You were told to keep your mouth shut.'

"We get to Warsaw. We're last off the plane. We're escorted off the plane by six soldiers with Uzis. Chip disappeared into customs. It felt clandestine and frightening. When you go into customs, they close a steel door and you're separated from the real world until they check your passport and open the steel door.

"I'd just separated from my wife and it was a crazy time for me mentally. I come to the customs. The guy takes my passport. He asks what I'm doing in Poland. I tell him I'm a tourist. The guy says, 'I don't believe you. Let's wait a minute. Would you like a cigarette?' I said no. He replied, 'No, you will smoke.' O.K., I will smoke.

"He said, 'Do you like women?' I said yes. He said, 'Do you want women?' I was in no mood to carry on this conversation. I said no.

"He opened up a drawer, pulled out a Luger and cocked it. He put it right in front of the window facing me. He said, 'Are you sure you don't want women?'

"I said, 'Listen pal. I don't want women. Why are detaining me? Give me my passport.' We've been chatting for 25 minutes. I take a cigarette. I'm getting crazy.

"I said, 'Listen, you motherfucker. I'm here to see my dear friend Krzysztof Zanussi and my dear friend Witold Sobocinski.' I said the right thing. He apologized, stamped my passport and hand it back, open the door and there are Krzysztof Zanussi and Witold Sobocinski waiting for me with open arms.

"Krzysztof Zanussi takes us around Warsaw. He speaks 13 languages. We were followed by guys in black raincoats. They were trying to entrap us to exchange money on the black-market.

"Krzysztof wanted to take a nine-hour train ride to Krakow. The city hasn't changed since the Ninth Century. We were going to visit Krzysztof's dear friend, Andrzej Wajda, who eventually made *Man of Marble* (1977). He ranks up there with Bergman and Fellini. Then we were to visit composer Wojceich Kilar, who eventually composed Francis Ford Coppola's *Dracula* (1992). Then we'd go see Kilar's parents.

"Between Zanusi's four years of studying physics, and four years studying philosophy, he took a vow of silence for one full year and lived in a Ninth Century monastery outside of Krakow.

"We were told Kilar's parents were in the country. On the way, we stopped at Zanusi's monastery. Zanusi rang the big bell and out walked the monk, with the old Catholic outfit on. Zanusi said he wanted to show his two friends from America (Chip and Don) where he slept, prayed, ate, etc. The monk looked around and said, looking at me, 'He can't come in because he can't keep his mouth shut.'

"I hadn't said a word, but he looked at me and saw that I couldn't keep my mouth shut. Zanusi says forget it, we'll go see Kilar's parents. We drive and it is Auschwitz. You walk in and there are bins in these buildings. One bin is just hair. One bin is just glasses. On the wall are pictures of everybody they gassed and killed. There are two shots of each person. One is full frontal and you can see they all weigh about 80 pounds. There's a side shot. Because they're so weak, there's a nail driven into the back of their skull so their head can be held up. These were Kilar's parents who were gassed and killed.

"The German were so proud of their medical experiments, that they filmed them. It was snowing that day and it was so brutal. It's now late in the afternoon. We drive back to Krakow to go to this Catholic church. Zanussi goes up the steps to the back of the rectory and this priest comes out. He has a key about two feet long to unlock the catacombs. The priest walks with us and talks with us. Franz Liszt's heart is buried in the church. The priest speaks good English. As we were saying goodbye, the priest says, 'If you had gotten here half an hour later, I wouldn't have been here, because I have to go to Warsaw tonight.'

"That priest was a Cardinal, the future Pope. He was Zanussi's best friend. He had written plays. He loved the theater and he loved the arts. Zanussi made a movie a few years ago that the Pope wrote the screenplay.

"When I got the phone call from producer Marty Bregman saying he wanted us to cast *Dog Day Afternoon* (1975), I knew this would be the highlight of my life. I'd read the script and I thought it was pure genius. All my early films had great scripts.

"Marty said he and Sydney Lumet approved me as casting director but I had to go through Al Pacino's approval. Al took artistic control of his movies like the *Godfather* took control. Rightfully so, because he knew exactly what he was doing. He'd waited a long time. Al was no kid when he got his first break.

"When they picked up Al in a limo from the airport, and called me from the limo to say that Al said I had the job, it was one of the biggest thrills of my life. I was intimidated by Al. I wanted to impress him.

"We were trying to cast the part of the transsexual. We decided that we would try every transsexual in the business to try to get the real thing. Sydney, Al and I looked at a zillion transsexuals. We also looked at ballet dancers. They were all too overt. They were over the top.

"I was feeling very competitive with Al. I wanted to show him that I knew more.

"I do not read actors. I pick the actors to read with the director. Rarely do they get to read with a superstar, but Al, and Jack Nicholson, happen to do that. Al had this trick. He would keep his head down during the scene and never look at the actor while saying his lines. If the actor was delivering a truthful performance, Al would lift his head up to look at the other actor. I got to know that if I asked to bring back the actor that Al liked, that was a point for me.

"During this process of looking at transvestites and transsexuals, this most beautiful woman I've ever seen. Her face was divine. The cutest breasts and the nicest legs. You could not tell it was a guy. I was about to tell this person that I'd like him to come back and read for Al Pacino and Sydney Lumet when he crossed · his legs. He didn't have any underpants. He had this 12' inch *schlong* that almost threw me off my chair.

"I decide that I am going to get Al. In the script, there's a confrontation and a big kiss. I told this man that he would read with Al and that I wanted him to get up, kiss Al on the lips, and then cross his legs. He said absolutely.

"A couple of days later, in walks this beautiful he-she. We sit down and do the lines. I see Al pick his head up and look at him. I can see in Al's eyes that he thinks this is the most beautiful creature he's ever laid eyes on. He gets up and plants one on Al. Then he sits down and crosses his legs with that *schlong* hanging down. Al got out of his chair and he almost choked me to death. He leaped at me. 'Get him out of here!'

"We were getting heavy into the movie. We'd meet Saturday mornings to talk about the script and the casting. We were rehearsing. I was trying hard to be a filmmaker. It was raining and I gave actor Al Lettieri a ride home. We were discussing this character Moretti eventually played by Charlie Durning. I actually got on bended knee and begged them to put him in the movie.

"Al said, 'Don, there's a problem. In the transition from the police detective to the FBI guy, there's no goodbye. It's too abrupt.'

"That next morning, Saturday morning, there's Marty Bregman and the other producer Marty Elfand, Al Pacino, Sydney Lumet and myself. We're discussing the script. I've been keeping my mouth shut, waiting to make my big entrance. I say, 'I know what the problem. Moretti disappears without a real ending.' Al looks at me. I think I've just said something brilliant. Al says, 'Don, you're a fucking liar.'

"Little did I know, later last night, Al Lettieri had met up with Al Pacino and discussed the script. Pacino knew that I'd taken his idea. I don't think I've ever told another lie in this business because that moment was earth shattering. To finish up the story, you're right. I meant to say that I agreed with Al Lettieri.

"Chris Sarandon eventually played the transsexual. He came into my office. He'd only been married six months to an actress named Susan Sarandon. He was telling me how macho he was. How he ran the track. He was up for the part of Sal, eventually played by John Cazale.

"I looked at my copy of *Life* magazine, which had a picture of the real transvestite. And I could not believe that Chris was a spitting image of the transvestite. And Chris had just got done telling me that he'd married the woman of the century. I'm about to ask him to come back to play a fag. He got all crazy and nervous when I asked him. I said to him, 'You can't think that way. You're an actor. Go home. Look at it. If you decide you want to come in and read with Al, fine. It's a chance of a lifetime.' He came back 14 times to read. He got the part and he got an Academy Award nomination for Best Supporting Actor on his first movie out of the box.

"I'll tell you the John Cazale story. We couldn't find anyone to play the part of Sal, a 19-year old boy. We couldn't find anybody on a one-to-one basis who could cut the mustard with Al Pacino. It was too threatening to them. After four months, I suggested another actor, who happened to be living with Al's ex-girl-friend. Al says, 'There's no way in hell, Don, that this guy who's sitting in my bedroom, watching my television, listening to my Hi-fi, with my girlfriend under the sheets, that I am going to be able to work with this guy. Come up with somebody better.' So I suggested John Cazale of *Godfather* fame.

"One of the producers of *Godfather* was Fred Roos, who was head of casting for Warner Brothers. Al said, 'I want you to call Fred Roos and I want you to tell him your suggestion.' I call Fred and he laughs at me. 'That's so funny, the Corleone brothers in drag. Good luck, bye.'

"Al wants to know what Fred said. I tell him. Al says, 'Let's get John in here.' John was genius. He died of cancer a few years later.

"After casting *Dog Day Afternoon*, we were considered the mavens of the East. I moved to Hollywood in 1975 and got a job right away at MGM.

"My mother and father were sitting on their porch in 1977 in Ventner, New Jersey. An elderly man came up the steps and introduced himself as Max, the [Jewish] furrier with a business on the boardwalk. He said he'd been observing my father for 30-something years. Max had decided to give my father and my mother an all-expenses paid trip to Israel for 17 days. He pulled out the tickets and gave them to my father. My father naturally said, 'Isn't that awfully expensive?' The guy said, 'I knew you were going to say that.' He reached into his other pocket and pulled out a ten-day trip.

"My dad, when he'd marry somebody, he'd give you the money back as a wedding present. If he buried you, he'd give you the money back. One time they gave him a bus, and he gave it back to the church. They gave him a house and he gave it back to the church. If you had a child in the hospital, my father would sit with your child. Dad was a giving man. When he was young, he used to preach like some dingdong, on a platform off the boardwalk. That's where most of the Jews who owned stores got to know my father. They got to know that he wasn't a fanatic but was a shy and humble man.

"My dad prayed about it. It was Israel. It was where Jesus walked. My dad could not pass this up. So he and my mother went to Israel. One day dad was going to fulfill his dream of baptizing a few people in the river Jordan, where Jesus was baptized. There he met another minister, Jess Moody, who was a minister to many presidents and had a humongous church in Van Nuys, CA. They met and they dug each other. They found out that both of their sons were in the movie business. Dr. Moody's son was working for Burt Reynolds and living in Georgia. I was in California doing every drug known to man and as far away from God as I could possibly be.

"A couple of years later, in early 1979, I was ready to shoot *Melvin and Howard*. My parents wanted to come out to LA. I said yes, they could stay in my five bedroom house but they could not mention God or try to get me to go to church. My father was excited about coming out so he could go see Jess Moody's church and hear him preach. They did that. At the end of the service, they got down at the altar, Jess and my father, and prayed for their sinful boys, their wayward sons.

"*Melvin and Howard* got made. It took another year before the studio allowed it to come out. There was nudity in *Melvin and Howard*, not to titillate, but just defiant nudity. Mary Steenburgen decides she's going to quit her job as a cocktail waitress at a strip joint. She pulls off her outfit, quits, and storms off naked. I'm sure that's one of the scenes that helps her get the Oscar [for Best Supporting Actress]."

"But my parents thought it was nudity. We weren't on speaking terms. Their boy had taken it to the limit. I had gotten married [to make-up artist Dottie Pearl]. We bought a beautiful home. We got ourselves a frenetic Cocker Spaniel. We called him Bo, after Bo Goldman who wrote *Melvin and Howard* and won an Oscar for Best Original Screenplay. It was 1982. Things were going well in our lives. I was not communicating with my mother and father. Dottie took a job doing make-up for Jessica Lange in *Tootsie*. When she got there, Dustin shut the show down because whoever was doing his makeup was doing a terrible job. So Dottie did Dustin's make-up.

"Dorothy decided to separate from me. She started dating someone else in New York. One day, after the phone call, little Bo decided to get the shits. He shit all over the walls, all over the floors, all over our beautiful furniture. Our house was architecturally gorgeous. So I cleaned it up off the walls. I got down on the rug and the smell was so bad, I was gagging so much, that I started to break down and cry. I guess things had come to a head in my life because I couldn't stop crying. Now I don't believe that God talks to you in this way but this is exactly what happened to me.

"I yelled out amidst my tears, 'OK God, what do you want from me?' And a voice in my head said, 'Call your father.' So I called my father and he said, 'Son, your mother and I have given you up to God. We can't help you anymore. We don't want to talk to you. We tried for so many years. Here's what I think you should do. You should go visit Jess Moody at his church.'

"I did. And hence my re-conversion and giving myself back to Church. Dottie and I remarried at the end of that summer in Paris."

"Tell me about *Melvin and Howard*."

"Art Linson, who was my partner on the project and the other producer, was someone I'd worked for on *Car Wash* (1976). I was the casting director and associate producer. Art told me to come to him with a story and we'd make a movie together. Art has since written a book called *A Pound of Flesh* about his stories of producing. He's got a whole chapter on *Melvin and Howard*.

"It took writer Bo Goldman about eight months to do a first draft. It was then called Sonny, the nickname of Howard Hughes. If you knew Howard Hughes, you didn't call him Howard or Hughes. You called him Sonny. Doing the research, Bo became more fascinated with Howard Hughes than Melvin Dumar. So my original idea for making *Melvin and Howard* was that we would bookend Howard Hughes and we would tell mainly about the ride. Bo wrote a different movie. But Ned Tannen, head of Universal motion pictures, said to Bo, 'This is a brilliant script but we need it to get back to its original focus. Universal is now making a television version of the life of Howard Hughes starring Tommy Lee Jones. I don't want another Howard Hughes movie.

"In those days, studios would have development deals with certain directors, giving them first-look capabilities. These directors were paid a handsome sum to say no to a lot of movies. Ned gave the script to Mike Nichols who was known for his ability to help a writer shape a movie. Mike loved the script and was hired to direct the movie. He worked for months at the luxurious Carlisle hotel on 79th Street in Manhattan. And three months later came a wonderful script called *Melvin and Howard*. Now it was time to cast the movie.

"At this point, 1978, Mike Nichols had directed six movies. Three were classics—*The Graduate* (1967), *Carnal Knowledge* (1971) and *Who's Afraid of Vrginia Wolff* (1966). After those three movies, he directed three turkeys—*Day of the Dolphin* (1973), *Catch 22* (1970) and *The Fortune* (1975). So Mike decided to return to directing Broadway. He'd been the premiere director of Neal Simon comedies.

"Jack Nicholson met with Mike Nichols at The Carlisle and Mike asked me if I'd be willing to wait a year for Jack Nicholson. I thought the Melvin character should be anonymous and that Jack would be a distraction, I said no. I pulled off my shoe and pounded the coffee table, which Mike Nichols sat behind, so hard that Mike's Valium went flying. And I said, 'There's no way in hell I'll wait a year.'

"Many major names were bandied about and they were just not right. They were green light names but they were not Melvin. Mike [Nichols] came up with the brilliant idea to cast Elvis Presley as Melvin. Elvis was on his last leg. He was fat and jowly and passed out. He wasn't the handsome leading man he once was. Mike knew the Colonel, Tom Parker, who ran Elvis's career. Mike met Elvis at a concert and asked him if he'd like to do Melvin. Elvis said he'd love to, after he finished his tour. That was in June, 1997. Elvis died six weeks later.

"We continued to cast. I saw this interesting movie *Citizens Band* (1977), directed by Johnathan Demme (although Paramount couldn't give tickets away to get people to see the movie). The star of the movie was Paul Le Mat, one of the premiere stars of *American Graffiti* (1973). He embodied Melvin to me but Mike did not want him. Then he started seeing more people and asking for rewrites. That's a delay tactic in making films. One of the rewrites was toning down the role of the wife/stripper played by Mary Steenburger, turning her into a waitress at a diner. It was a delay tactic that I thought was ridiculous. I also realized that Mike [Nichols], at this point in his life, did not want to do *Melvin and Howard*. He was afraid to make this movie. He did not have the protection of a superstar.

"So I went to Ned Tanen, the head of Universal. We went out on a limousine ride, ala *Godfather*, and I asked him to remove Mike Nichols. Ned said, 'Don, you do not fire Mike Nichols. You transfer him.' I gave him all the reasons why he should be transferred and eventually he was transferred to the movie, named appropriately, *The Jerk* (1979), which he did not direct either. Johnathan Demme eventually directed it.

"After the movie was made, the powers that be at Universal did not like the film. A president of distribution at the screening not only had an eye patch on because he had gotten drunk the night before and fallen down, he fell asleep six minutes into the movie. His report was that it will never play in the drive-ins and this is not a movie that should ever see the light of day. The movie hung around. They postponed it. They didn't send things directly to video in those years. We never gave up.

"Johnathan Demme had two friends in the business who were great directors, Bernardo Bertolucci and Frederico Fellini. Johnathan showed the movie to them separately. Fellini said, 'I'm influential at the Venice Film Festival. I'll get this movie in.' Bertolucci said, 'Johnny, I'm influential at the New York Film Festival. I'll get your movie in.' It's free. You don't have to spend any marketing money. It's a great way to open your movie.

"The two festivals said yes to it. The head of the Cannes Festival wanted it too. The movie was sent over to France to be subtitled. I got a call at 5 a.m. from the Cannes Festival, asking, 'Where is the print of *Melvin and Howard*?' I called the studio and they told me, 'We don't want your movie in Cannes, because then it will be known as a festival movie and we don't make any movies to be festival movies. So we've locked the print up in Paris. And you're not going on the trip.'

"I had the two other festivals up my sleeve. I waited for a couple of weeks and asked to put my movie in the New York and Venice film festivals. I was told no. I protested so much that they agreed to have a meeting. I brought Johnathan out from New York. We went up to the 14th floor. There's a long table and there were about a dozen executives there. I said it would be smart and wise to open in New York and Venice, because then we'd cover both bases, North America and Europe. And they said no.

"I couldn't take it any longer. I jumped up onto the table. I was dressed in my jeans and my jacket. I took my shoes off. I took my socks off. I took my shirt off. I took my jeans off. There I was in my underwear, yelling and screaming and walking around. And I told the boys that I was going to show them my ugly balls and my dick if they did not agree to put *Melvin and Howard* in the festival.

"A squeak came down from one end. 'We will allow you to be in the New York Film Festival if we are opening night.' Now, opening night is like the award that you don't know you get until two weeks before. You can not request opening night.

"But when I heard that I had a shot at it, I figured that I might as well put my clothes back on and take a shot. I said, 'Fellows, if they pick me for opening night, then I want to go to Venice. Do you agree?' They just wanted to shut me up. They just wanted me out of their hair. How much money could this cost them? A couple of plane fares and a print for Venice and New York? This is not the way you open a movie.

"We were picked opening night for the New York festival. It was a proud night. It was a standing ovation night. And now I can remember seeing some of those executives going around beating on their chests, saying, 'Yeah, we knew it.' They didn't know it. Eventually *Melvin and Howard* won 26 critical awards, including Best Picture of the Year from the National Society of Film Critics.

"I produced *The Indian Runner* (1991), written and directed by Sean Penn. I cast Sean in *Fast Times at Ridgemont High* (1982). I also cast Pam Springsteen as a cheerleader. She's Bruce Springsteen's sister. Sean fell in love with Pam and they got engaged.

"Pam got another part to do back in Virginia. In the meantime, Bruce sent a tape of his last album to his sister. Naturally she played it for her fiancee. Sean heard a song, *The Last Patrolman*, and not only did he weep, but he got Pam to call her brother up so he could tell Bruce that he loved the song and someday he hoped to do a movie based on it. Bruce gave him the rights.

"The song is a story of two brothers, one a cop and one a bad boy returning from Vietnam. Sean tried for many years to get the project off the ground. By 1988, Bruce was a superstar. Sean was long broken up with Pam. He'd been married to Madonna. He was making a movie in Canada with Bobbie DeNiro and Art Linson called *We're No Angels*. At the time, acting was make Sean sick. He'd get vicious headaches. He'd also get nauseous.

"He'd have some Scotch in his dressing room. He decided to make his time productive, he'd write this movie. He wrote *A Slow Dark Coming*. He showed the script to two producers with whom he'd made five films. They both said it was brilliant but there was no way in hell that you could make a movie about a guy who murders somebody and gets away with it at the end. It was too much of a downer. So Sean put the script away.

"In 1987, I decided that I wanted to make a great movie. I wanted to make the love story of Zhivago and the adventures of Lawrence Arabia combined into one movie. I'd been hearing a lot of sermons in church from Jess Moody who's a great storyteller about [19th Century British missionary to Africa] David Livingstone. I wrote down a treatment and I gave it to a great actor, a great producer, a great director and a great writer, just to find out if I was in the right track. The ·

actor was Sean Penn. He said, 'Count me in.' I wanted him to play Livingstone. The director, Hal Ashby, said, 'Count me in. This is some movie.' I gave it to Bo Goldman. Bo said it would make a wonderful movie. The producer was David Puttnam. David said, 'This is a wonderful movie. Go for it. I've got mononucleosis. I've just resigned from Columbia. I'm not going to do anything for a year. If you need any help, just call me.'

"So off I went to make David Livingstone. I ran into many problems along the way.

"In the summer of 1989, I have a meeting with Sean Penn. Sean informs me that he's never going to act again. He's going to do whatever it takes to direct a movie. I told him that I'd be honored to produce his first movie. He said, 'Really? Meet me at my house tomorrow morning at 9 a.m.'

"I met him at his beautiful home in Malibu, which burned to the ground around 1993. Sean said, 'Here's a script I'm fond of. It's called *A Slow Dark Coming*. It's written by Jay Vees McKnee, a prisoner on death row in San Quentin. I took it home and read it. Because of knowing many Bible stories, I had a tremendous affinity for this script, because it reminded me of Cain and Abel. And yes, at the end, one brother got away with murder and the other brother let him go because blood is thicker than water, and I understood.

"I met with Sean. I said, 'I don't care if this guy is on death row. I don't care if he mass murdered 60 people. This sonofabitch can write.' Sean said, 'I'm Jay Vees McKnee.' We shook hands and a year later we were shooting in Nebraska. This time we did get to go to Cannes and get a standing ovation.

"Producing is largely casting. You have to cast the right writer, the right director, the right actors and the right crew. Producing was natural for me. When I was a young man, I was always picking a team, finding someone to buy the uniforms, to get the equipment and plan our stupid football, basketball, and baseball leagues. That was preparing me for my life's work."

43

Karen Barber

<u>May 7, 2002</u>

"I grew up in Woodstock, New York. My parents were hippies. My father Ben Barber is now a famous journalist who covers foreign affairs for the *Washington Times*. My parents divorced when I was six years old.

"When my mom was 18, she did all the ink and paint for the Spiderman cartoons. She was the only person who drew with Stan Lee. She was going to move to L.A. to do Fritz the Cat with him. She took a month holiday and went to Israel where she met my dad, who's from London. He was on a holiday too. My mom gave up the art thing.

"I was born in Mendocino, California. We left when I was six months old and went to Hawaii and India. My dad had a big inheritance and was publishing his own books on foreign affairs and poetry and giving them out.

"If I'd have grown up with my dad, he would've pushed me to study more math and English. The big thing for my mom was art. I was the best artist in Catholic high school. Then I went to the Art Institute of Miami where everyone was the best artist from their high school and I realized that I was not very good. I was going to NYU but I had a boyfriend who wanted to kill me. So my mom insisted, three weeks before school was due to start, that I find another school.

"I thought graphic design was what I wanted to do. I was really into logos. But there were all these really talented artists around me and I did not think of myself as as talented as them. I have more of a head for business. I could never be a starving artist. I thought that art director for a magazine would be the right place for me.

"In my last year at college, we had to intern somewhere. I interned at a couple of magazines and I realized it was not what I wanted to do. I quit. I needed more intern credits. I was walking down the street and someone asked me if I wanted to audition for the Juliette Lewis part in the movie *Cape Fear* (1991), which was shooting in Miami at the time. I said no, I'm not an actress. But I need to intern.

I interned one day a week in the wardrobe department. I loved it. They wanted me to be there more and more. They ended up paying me.

"I loved going to thrift stores finding clothes. We had to find vintage stuff in double and triples because there was a lot of blood in [the movie]. When I went to the premiere of the movie, I was scared, even though I was on set all the time. That's when I knew I wanted to be in the movie business.

"I assisted the wardrobe woman for a year. I realized I didn't want to be a stylist. I didn't want to have clothes in my car all the time. I realized that all the wardrobe women were crazy.

"Then I went to work for a couple of low-budget exploitation movie producers. Those were the kind of movies they were making in Miami at the time. Skin flicks. We shot in Paradise Island in the Bahamas. We stayed in a resort. This wealthy man had $5 million and he wanted to direct his own movie. So he spent his own money and he wrote the script. Well, at least half of it. He thought he'd finish it while we were there. We shot half the movie and then he didn't want us to leave. We stayed in the Bahamas for a month doing nothing. I was the only young girl on the crew. I got freaked out because there these guys who were married who were knocking on my door at night.

"We would show up on the set and this guy [financier] would sit on a cooler and try to write what we were supposed to shoot that day. I thought that was how things were done. He didn't want us to leave.

"I then went to work at a New York talent agency for six months and hated it. I would come home every night and cry about it, it was so horrible. I thought I'd become a trainer. Then I got a call out of nowhere that producer Abel Ferrara needed an assistant. I said no but my mom and my boyfriend of the time talked me into it.

"Abel is out of his mind but he's extremely smart. He doesn't do anything by the book. He wakes up at 4 p.m. and wants me to work through the night.

"I'd been with him for a week when he had a meeting at October Films about the film *The Funeral* (1996) starring Christopher Walken. He showed up to this meeting with all these executives with a six pack in his hands. He said, 'Just tell everything to Karen,' and he walked out the door. I was 23 years old. The executives were all men. They don't say anything to me except to ask, 'Is he coming back?'

"I walk around the office looking for him. He's in the kitchen making a sandwich. He says, 'Make them tell you whatever they have to say.' I say, 'Abel, they don't want to talk to me.' He walks back in the room, 'I said you tell everything to Karen.' Then he leaves the building. That's how I got forced into everything. I ended up producing his life. He was a drug addict and he was paranoid of his agents and his lawyers. I did all the work. Everything came through me. I took care of him.

"We made a couple of movies during my two years with him. I helped him write and edit. He always wanted to cast Christopher Walken and Harvey Keitel. He doesn't watch many movies so I'd help him cast. If the script called for a 25-year old Mexican, he'd say, 'What about Chris Walken?'

"We made these *Subway Stories* for HBO. I read through hundreds of submitted scripts and chose some. I helped cast.

"I'd quit all the time and he'd beg me to come back. We had a codependent relationship. When I started, he was not as bad of a drug addict. It progressively got worse. I'd help him through rehab. Our movies went from O.K. to worse. The last two we did didn't even get distribution. Actors wanted to work with him but he was becoming incoherent because of the drugs.

"I helped write the script for *One Tough Cop*, which starred Mark Wahlberg. I've never answered phones and rolled calls. I didn't want to be an assistant. Marty Scorsese's office called me to see if I wanted to work as an assistant. I tried it for a week and went back to Abel. Then a couple of weeks later, I got a call from Robert DeNiro's office. It was one of the days when I was truly determined to quit Abel.

"I went down to DeNiro's office and there were all these people there interviewing. I had never interviewed for a job. All my jobs had been given to me. I didn't even have a resume. But an hour after I left, I got a call saying I had the job. The woman I replaced had been with DeNiro for 15 years. Robin Chambers.

"Working for Bob was the opposite of Abel. Bob does everything by the book. He uses his agents and his lawyers. I worked on the movie *Jackie Brown* (1997). I remember when Lawrence Bender would call. I felt so intimidated. DeNiro had so much going on. Abel gets up at 4 p.m.. Bob gets up at 5 a.m. and works out. I had a car service that took me everywhere. I ate lunch every day at Nobu. I made good money.

"I grew up in Woodstock with Todd 'Kip' Williams, who wrote and directed *The Adventures of Sebastien Cole* (1998). His wife Famke Jenssen and I told him that his first movie should be personal and done for no money. So in three weeks, he wrote *Sebastien Cole*. He had $250,000 in family money. He wanted me to quit my job to produce his movie. I kept refusing. He manipulated me. He said I was a loser. I'd been an assistant for so many years. I'd never amount to anything.

He convinced me to quit my job and produce his movie. My family contributed some money. I loved Todd's script. I'm a sucker for high school love stories.

"Through the contacts I made working for DeNiro and Abel, I got a great crew. Everyone worked for $500 a week. I got a camera package for nothing. We shot the movie in 24 days in Woodstock.

"I like getting things for free. I got every location for free. I got the Super 8 motel. I asked for the cheapest corporate rate and it was about $40 a night. I calculated how much we had to spend. It was about $15,000. They accepted it before they calculated how many rooms we'd need. It worked out to $16 per person per night.

"The only producer I knew, Ted Hope, advised us not to take the film to the Toronto Film Festival. We did anyway. Ted then advised us that if we got any interest in the film, if anyone was willing to distribute it, we should accept the offer, even if we weren't getting any money.

"Our film played on opening night. There was a line around the block for our screening. Six hundred people. Kip and I did a couple of shots of tequila before we had to speak in front of everybody. All the studio heads came by and said hello to us. David Dinerstein from Paramount Classics was moved by the movie.

"Our William Morris agent Cassian Elwes said five different people had made offers. We met with everyone that Saturday. We had breakfast, lunch, another lunch and dinner. The heads of studios would write down numbers on pieces of paper and pass them to us. We'd have another table at the other side of the restaurant. They'd make an offer and then Cassian and I would sit at our table and talk about it. We'd call my lawyer and the William Morris lawyers and come back with out counter offers. Then the heads of the studios would call their lawyers.

"One executive at a studio told us, 'This movie is brilliant. If we just reshoot the entire thing, it will be amazing.' Everybody said they loved it but everybody wanted to change it. Paramount Classics offered the most amount of money ($1 million for domestic distribution rights) and they best understood the movie. It was the first movie they'd bought after being open for a year. They'd asked us how much we'd made the movie for ($350,000) and I said I didn't know. When they found out, they were annoyed.

"I wanted to do my second movie with Kip. We optioned a John Irving book, *A Widow for a Year*. We pursued a book owned by the BBC. I was offered the *Pumpkin* (2002) project a few times and I passed. Finally my William Morris agent talked me into doing the movie."

Producer Deborah Del Prete tells me February 19, 2002: "I reject projects when I find the subject matter disturbing. A movie called *Pumpkin* was a success at Sundance. I haven't seen the movie. I saw the script two years ago. It's a black comedy about a sorority girl who has an affair with a retarded boy. It's a comedy that plays off him being retarded. It was incredibly distasteful. Despite having a commercial sheen to it, the script was making fun of people who were retarded. And I couldn't get on that bandwagon."

Karen responds: "The script is politically incorrect in every way. I met with the directors Anthony Abrams and Adam Larson Broder. They had a specific visual vision and I liked their ideas. It was a *Heathers*-type movie. It could go either way, depending on the director's vision. They brought me to meet the $2 million investor funding the movie. There were five other producers attached to the movie. They'd been trying to make the movie for years and anyone who promised them anything, they attached as a producer. I said that I didn't need to work with anybody. All the other producers were let go.

"I sent the script to some agents to try to attach talent. The first agent told me, 'Oh, I read the script a couple of years ago and it is not very good.' I was honest. 'I read it once and I was totally wrong about it. The script is so smart and there are so many different levels to it, that you'll only see it on a second reading.' She liked me and so she read it again. She called me and said, 'You're right. This is my new favorite script.' So this script which had gotten bad coverage at all these agencies, I would call the agents and tell them that they had read it wrong. So they'd reread it and it was their new favorite script."

"I've always been fascinated by sororities. I've never been a part of any group. I've never been in Girls Scouts or sororities. I've always had friends in lots of different groups. To me college is the most liberating experience, a time to try everything.

"My mother worked with mentally challenged kids. Some were high functioning to the point of normal and some were low functioning. If you have a 70 IQ, you're considered normal and you can be put in a Special Ed class in a regular school. If your IQ is 69, then you're retarded.

"The retarded kid in this film was put in with low functioning people and he never had anyone to inspire him. These people are locked up and they have no life.

"The director's vision was to take this sappy movie-of-the-week and do it as a satire. The point of the story is that these retarded kids are more intelligent than the girls in the sorority.

"I produced *Pumpkin* for Francis Ford Coppola's Zoetrope Studios. Because I'd only tried to do two movies, and got them both made, I was getting attention. People thought that with my specific tastes, I'd find the next *American Beauty*. I had a meeting at DreamWorks. I realized midway through the meeting that I didn't want to be locked up in a room trying to find the next *American Beauty*. I didn't want to stay in LA and drive to the studio every day. I wanted to find and make my own films. DreamWorks called my agent, 'We really liked her but she didn't seem interested in us.'"

"What happened to your John Irving book?"

"Kip is still trying to do it. The lead female character is about 45 and there's a lot of nudity. So a lot of the women don't want to do it. The movie would just be a sappy drama without the sexual tension."

"Annette Benning?"

"She won't get naked."

"She got pounded hard in *American Beauty*."

"But she didn't get naked."

44

Judd Bernard

Judd produced such acclaimed films as 1967's *Point Blank*, the first American film directed by John Boorman, and 1975's *Inside Out*, starring Telly Savalas.

Born June 20, 1927, he grew up in Chicago. "My father was a doctor. I studied pre-Med at the University of Wisconsin at Madison. I found out that I didn't want to be a doctor. So I studied English and history before I dropped out. I went to New York to seek my fame and fortune. I became a band manager instead. I wrote a magazine article and earned $200. A movie studio bought the article and they brought me on as a writer. It was a disaster. I got fired immediately. I got a job working for Stanley Kramer. We made such films as *The Men* (1950), *Cyrano de Bergerac* (1950), and *High Noon* (1952).

"I worked for Louis B. Meyer after he left MGM. He had an office on Canon and plotted how he was going to come back. We were going to make *Paint Your Wagon* but it never happened."

"How did you come to produce your first film, *Double Trouble* (1967), starring Elvis Presley?"

"I was trying to get another project off the ground starring Julie Christie. I was told that Irwin Winkler was her manager. Irwin and I had dinner at Cyranos on the Sunset strip, across from The Dome. We sat around until 3 a.m. talking, and we became fast friends. He said that if he delivered Julie Christie, he'd want to be a co-producer on the project.

"Julie Christie was in Madrid doing *Dr. Zhivago* (1965). MGM sent me to Madrid. I had lunch with director David Lean. I met Julie Christie at the Hilton. They were preparing to shoot the parade down the street in the snow. It was hotter than hell. Julie couldn't have been nicer except when I mentioned her manager Irwin Winkler. She said, 'He isn't my manager.'

"I formed a company [BCW Productions] with Irwin Winkler and his partner in New York Robert Chartoff [manager]. We had a deal with MGM.

"Once we got *Double Trouble* (1967) organized, I was in London. I saw this girl [Annette Day] on the street who looked like a girl in the script. I introduced myself to her and asked her for a photograph. She had this small black and white photograph. On the back it said 'Sam Shaw.' He was a big time magazine photographer. I had a close friend in London named David Steen who was also a prominent photographer. He took three color pictures of her and we blew them up.

"This girl had never acted a day in her life. She was 17-year old. She was good. She had no fear. She starred with Elvis Presley. Then she got married and never made another movie.

"I met my wife Patricia Casey on *Double Trouble*. I had two kids from my marriage to Australian model Pauline O'Dwyer—Adrianna (who died in 1995 in a car accident on Pico Blvd outside The Mint) and cinematographer Michael. I adopted Alicia, now Alicia Richards, who works as a commercials producer.

"I got divorced when I moved to London at the end of 1967. Patricia was working for me at Paramount and she moved to London when I did to do the Glenda Jackson movie *Negatives* (1968).

"Patricia later produced the first Monty Python movie, *And Now For Something Completely Different* (1971), a collection of skits from the first two years of the Monty Python TV show.

"*Point Blank* was John Boorman's first American movie. Patricia knew these two guys, David and Rafe Newhouse. David was a film editor. David and Rafe had optioned this book and wrote a screenplay.

"I was in the commissary at MGM eating lunch by myself. This guy came up to me and asked, 'Do you mind if I sit with you?' It was John Boorman who was taking a tour of the studio. I took him back to my house. He stayed and talked with me until 2 a.m. I gave him the script to *Point Blank* and the book.

"I was in London and Lee Marvin was doing *Dirty Dozen* (1967). I gave him the script.

"I saw this Canadian mini-thing about a coroner. There was a marvelous actor in it named John Vernon and a good actress named Sharon Acker. Boorman and I flew to Toronto to see them for *Point Blank*. We blew the jet engine out and we thought we were going to die. I remember saying goodbye to him. Somehow they landed the plane. We brought them back and they were in *Point Blank*.

"We wanted to shoot at Alcatraz. I called Jack Valenti [head of the MPAA], an advisor to President Lyndon Johnson. I got a call from my secretary at MGM with a number to call Jack. I dial. A man answers and says, 'Who's this?' I said my name and asked, 'Who's this?' And the man said, 'Lyndon Johnson.' It was a private phone at the White House. We were the first movie ever shot at Alcatraz.

"We were shooting at Alcatraz and at 3 a.m. this motorboat comes up with these two ladies in evening gowns—one a redhead and the other a blonde. They had a bottle of champagne. They said, 'We want to watch your movie.' QANTAS had had an inaugural flight from Sydney to San Francisco. This woman Hazel Phillips was a Sydney journalist. She so charmed Lee Marvin that he must've spent three days with her. And he never gave interviews.

"When I was in Sydney, I saw her on television.

"We had our first sneak [showing] of the picture at a Chicago theater. Everybody was stunned when it was over and nobody said a word. I don't know if it was ahead of its time or what. It was recently remade by Mel Gibson as *Payback* (1999).

"[Movie executive] Robert Evans had been a publicity client of mine. He became head of production at Paramount. He sent over his assistant Peter Bart, now editor of *Variety*, to have lunch with me. I [as Kettledrum Films] was the first producer they signed. I left my partnership with Winkler and Chartoff, the dumbest thing I've ever done. These guys became wildly successful making such movies as *Rocky*.

"Robert Redford was going to star in our film *Blue* (1968). Six weeks before shooting, he walked. We were desperate to find someone to replace him who had blonde hair and blue eyes. So we got Terence Stamp.

"When we got back from location, the hot thing was *A Man and a Woman* [1966 French film directed by Claude Lelouch]. I came up with an idea for a small movie. What if a guy working on a movie has an affair with a woman working on a movie. We made *Fade-In* (1968 TV movie). It starred Burt Reynolds and Eli Kazan's wife Barbara Loden.

"I think one of the reasons Paramount sent me to London was so that Peter Bart could take my house in Brentwood.

"Leslie Ann Down, at 15 years old, was an extra in my 1970 movie, *The Man Who Had Power Over Women*.

"*Inside Out*. We originally wanted to do the movie with Tony Curtis and Jimmy Coburn. John Calley, who ran Warners then, said, 'We'll get the biggest star in the world to play the lead. Telly Savalas.' It was Telly's first year as Kojak.

"When we shot at the flower market in Amsterdam, there were 25,000 people wanting to see Kojak. They had to call out troops. Then when we went to Berlin, Savalas walked into this police convention and they went crazy to see him.

"*Blood Red* [shot in 1986, released in 1988] was Julia Roberts' first movie. We cast her because her brother Eric was the lead and we needed somebody to play his sister. My son Michael worked on the movie. My daughter Adrianna, may she rest in peace, did her first job as a wardrobe assistant for [famous costume designer] Ruth Myers."

After our interview, Judd gives me a dozen tips, several producer referrals, a coat, lunch, and a subtitle for my book *The Producers—Profiles in Discouragement.*

45

Alexandra Rose

May 14, 2002

No woman has produced Hollywood movies for a longer time than Rose. She helped make *Big Wednesday* (1978), *Norma Rae* (1979), *Nothing in Common* (1986), and *Frankie and Johnny* (1991).

Born January 20, 1946, she grew up Green Bay, Wisconsin. "At the University of Wisconsin, I did a double major in Political Science and French. I then did a graduate degree in Political Science at the L'Institut D'Etudes Politiques in Paris. It was a program designed for foreign students. That school is where the future leaders of France go.

"I finished at the University of Wisconsin early. I decided to go to France with my friend Marian. In the late 1960s, we took a steamship across the Atlantic Ocean in the middle of winter. It was unbelievably stormy with waves the size of mountains. The north Atlantic in winter is a turbulent ocean. They gave us first class cabins but it was horrible because everybody was old. Everybody we liked was down in steerage.

"Paris was filled with rioting and strikes at the time. It was wild. The country went on a national strike for nothing. No buses, no trash. I loved it. To see all the cars come into Paris because there was no public transportation was amazing. People would walk across the roofs of cars to cross streets.

"We lived from pillar to post. We scrounged. We combined all our talents and put one ad in the International Herald Tribune. Whenever a call would come in, we would decide who would go apply for the job. Translating became my avocation. That's how I got into film. My then boyfriend-to-be, Patrick Kamenka, worked at the Cinemateque Francais. His grandfather founded it. I'd see six films a week there. In 1970, there was no foreign cinema in America. *I'm a Curious Yellow* (1966) was the first foreign film to become a hit in America.

"For me to see Cuban, Russian, Polish, and Chinese cinema was incredible. I became an historian of French film. My boyfriend's aunt and uncle had a French co-production company [that worked with an English company]. I would be called in to interpret for meetings and to translate screenplays.

"I came back to the States around 1971. I got off the plane in Los Angeles and went to an employment agency. There were two [entertainment] jobs available—one with a television company and one with a small film production company. Both companies were interested in me but the guy at the film company said, 'Stay. Start now.'

"I was a secretary. Medford Films had several small films in distribution. It was a wild outfit. The guys would wear their shirts unbuttoned to the navel, with gold chains. They couldn't write letters. They'd tell me to write, 'Dear so-and-so: That thing you sent me really sucks.' I'd translate it into proper protocol. I became the center piece of the office. I learned about film collections and theater bookings.

"Then, when Roger Corman was looking for someone to work in his new company, New World Pictures, I interviewed for the job and got it. I worked for Roger for about 30 months. The hours were exhausting but it was the best experience. Three weeks after I got there, his partners and head of distribution split up. Roger said he didn't want to bring in another distributor. 'So you can handle it. There will be no raise in pay but you will be head of distribution.'

"I had to oversee prints, trailers, ad campaigns. We'd buy these horrible films from Italy and we'd have to make them into American films. There wasn't anything I didn't do there, from reading scripts to casting sessions. We'd have casting sessions with lines down the block [of actors dying to get a job].

"I met Marty Scorsese there because Marty directed *Boxcar Bertha*. Marty was then living with Sandy Weintraub, the daughter of my husband of the time [Fred Weintraub].

"It was a wild and innocent time. A whole group of us ran around together—Paul Schrader, Marty Scorsese, Michael and Julia Phillips, Brian DePalma, John Millius. Julia Phillips was one of the strongest toughest most vulnerable people you'd ever meet.

"Tamara Asseyev [Brian DePalma's ex-girlfriend] and I formed a production company. She'd just produced a couple of films in Ireland on her credit card that I distributed through Roger Corman. She wanted a female partner for her production company.

"Tamara was the spearhead of the independent film movement. It was then considered outrageous to finance a film on credit cards.

"I had raised money using sub-distributors in a system pioneered by Roger Corman. At the time, there were 13 film distribution territories in the United

States. I went to these sub-distributors and raised money to make a karate film. Then the karate market fell out. After a few big karate pictures, all these others came out that had been sitting in vaults for years. The market was glutted. So I sent the money back.

"I had been doing research at the library at UCLA writing treatments for our own projects. They became our first films. We'd take the treatments to a famous writer, develop a script and then try to sell the project to a studio.

"Tamara was friends with director George Lucas and his producer Gary Kurtz. They wanted to do an African-American version of *American Graffiti*. Our version was called *Drive-In*. The project was similar to my life. I'd grown up as a teenager at the drive-in. I figured it was a great place to set a movie.

"We took it to Universal and we were all set to go, but 1975 was a politically sensitive time. There was a woman at Universal who was upset that they would have two white women producing this black film. So she created a lot of hue and cry. Universal got nervous. Their black expert was making trouble so they dropped the project.

"We raised the money independently and changed the race of the characters to white. Columbia bought the movie and we were in profit.

"Tamara and I got a deal at Warner Brothers. Two young USC graduates, Bob Zemeckis and Bob Gale, came to us with this idea of four young girls who want to see the Beatles. We pitched it to Warner Brothers and they decided to go for it. We were looking for a young hip director. We looked at all of them. We saw Bob Zemeckis's AFI thesis film and thought his 14-minute short was better than all these big films we'd been seeing, but Warner Brothers wouldn't go with a young inexperienced director.

"So we consulted our friend Steven Spielberg. He said that if we really wanted Bob to direct, he'd support us by executive producing the project. 'In case something happens, I'll be there.' Warners passed but Universal wanted it."

"*Big Wednesday*, directed by John Milius."

"Dennis Aaberg and I became friends. We decided to do a surfing film. John heard about it and said, 'Nobody can do a surfing film without me. I'm the big kahuna.'

"We took it to Warner Brothers and they didn't want to make it because John had all these other projects, but they agreed to develop the script.

"My job was to get John out of bed. I'd call him at 8:30 a.m. Then 8:45. Then 9. Because he had to do six pages a day. That was my job. To get six pages a day out of John. I'd go to the dentist with him. I'd go everywhere with him to get those six pages a day. He's a talented man but undisciplined."

"Were there other female producers at this time?"

"Julia Phillips worked with Michael but there were no just-female producers aside from Tamara and I.

"*Norma Rae* was a project I held for three years before I even showed it to my partner. Being in distribution, I knew the marketplace and I knew the marketplace was not yet ready for this project. I found the story in a *New York Times Sunday Magazine* piece. I didn't bring it out until *Rocky*, the first independently-financed "negative pickup" to be a huge hit.

"Negative pickup means the film is made with the bank's money but there's a promise made ahead of time that the studio will pay the cost of the film to the bank upon the delivery of the negative. The reason for this form of financing is to avoid union dues. It's a way of making a film outside the studio system.

"I figured that I could sell *Norma Rae* as a female version of *Rocky*. After we went to director Marty Ritt's office with *Norma Rae*, he asked his secretary who the two actresses were that were trying to sell him a project. She said, 'Mr. Ritt, they are not actresses. They are producers.'

"A film never gets green lit on its own. A film gets squeezed through a pastry tube until finally all it can do is come out the end. There are so many ways to say no.

"I had passion for this project. I'd held on to it for years. I knew this was a character I wanted to bring to the screen. I knew this was a character that was important for women. It was a character I identified with. I was a young woman. I wanted to see someone come up from nowhere with nothing, struggling and succeeding.

"Our agent Guy McElwayne helped us. He got us in to see Marty Ritt. Guy was one of the best agents I've ever met. He didn't care who you were or where your project came from. If it was a good idea, he went for it. And when he was president of Warner Brothers, he did the same thing. He didn't cover his tracks. He didn't protect himself. He'd get on board.

"Marty loved our project immediately. He said that if we'd get his friends the Ravetches to write it, he'd do it. The book on Norma Rae came out and sold about two copies. A book is a bad first draft of a script. It gives you a beginning, middle and end for a story. We optioned the book.

"We began giving the book to actors. We offered it to eight actresses (including Joanne Woodward, Louise Fletcher) before Sally Field. We couldn't get a studio to go for it. It was a tent-pole kind of film. Guy decided to get the project to Alan Ladd Jr at Fox. He was fresh from *Star Wars*. He sees projects in terms of a film, not in terms of protecting his corporate ass. He liked Norma Rae. We agreed to make the film for half our normal fees in return for a percentage of the profits. Ladd said, if the other filmmakers agree to do that, we can go ahead. We had to show our belief in the project.

"We shot the movie in Opelika, Alabama."

"Were there any indications on the set that you had a great movie on your hands?"

"Yes, I knew it from Sally. She would come to work every day so prepared, so eager, so knowing this character, so imbued with it. Everyone working on the film was outstanding. They were cohesive, prepared and so full of belief in this character. We all believed in the iconography of a character who hadn't yet become an icon.

"The film was budgeted at $5 million. We brought it in under budget and days ahead of schedule because Marty Ritts shot so economically and we were all so prepared. Any time a producer can get the financing entity to give one week at least in solid rehearsal time, on location, they should do it. That saves so much in time and money. We came in $500,000 under budget and nine days ahead of schedule."

"How did your life change after *Norma Rae*'s Oscar nominations?"

"The week we were nominated, I said to Tamara that we should call the president of the United States. Everybody took our call instantly. There wasn't one person who didn't pick up the phone. They were never busy."

"*Nothing in Common*, (1986), starring Tom Hanks, directed by Gary Marshall."

"We developed it as a TV movie. But the networks thought it was too multi-layered and didn't have a salient enough logline.

"I met my husband Rob on *Overboard* (1987). He'd sailed the boat from Australia."

Married to Fred Weintraub from 1974–84, Alex married Rob at the end of 1988.

"Tom Selleck was the driving force behind *Quigley Down Under* (1990). The script had been around for centuries. A number of fine actors wanted to do it, from Steve McQueen to Clint Eastwood.

"Quigley was a great character. That's probably the linking theme of my work. I glom on to projects with great characters, characters who stand up in the face of obvious oppression and resolves to make things right. It is usually a character who you wouldn't expect to have that role. That is my innate belief system in the human being that any person will do the right thing when the opportunity is forced upon them.

"We had script problems and Tom was excellent in fighting through the mish-mash of the studio's version of what it should be and the director's version.

"We got to Australia in 1989 during a national air strike. We were waiting in Sydney for Tom Selleck to come in. Tom's hairdresser Lonnie says, 'You better check some of this stuff out when you get to location. You need to take a look at these horses.'

"We took a private jet from Sydney to Alice Springs [central Australia]. We asked to look at the horses. We see this ridiculous horse for Tom. It's a short fat nag. Tom is a big man. He got on the horse and his feet dangled down near the ground. I said that the horse was not attractive. Can you see this horse on the poster? The horse crew said, 'Well, in those days horses weren't so big. It was 1870 and the horses were scrubby horses.' I said, 'Yeah, and you're going to tell that to the movie poster? Here's Tom Selleck on a scrubby horse because in 1870 Australia, that is what the horses looked like?' It was presented to me that it was out of the question to get another horse.

"We also brought with us from Montana this wonderful old cowboy. And there were two groups of workers on the movie—the horse guys and the stunt guys. The horse guys were the ones who got this scrubby horse. I created this split by refusing to accept the horse. I was told by a horse guy that I had created the split by calling their horse a short and fat horse. I said, 'It is a short and fat horse.' They were all upset.

"The stunt men were great. We chatted. They whispered that there was another horse in a trailer coming from Sydney. Tom refused to start shooting scenes until the horse was replaced. It caused a huge furor. It was a long drive from Sydney to Alice Springs but there was no other way to get the horse there. A couple of days later, the horse arrived and it was a big gorgeous horse."

"Every movie we've talked about so far you must've been pleased with how it turned out. Have there been any of your movies where you were disappointed?"

"*Exit to Eden* (1994). It's an interesting example of how genre and tone can get confused. *Exit to* Eden is a fun campy film but there's a tonal issue that never got resolved. We weren't sure of how much comedy and how much sex in the film. And the balance was never realized because none of us knew ahead of time how it was going to go.

"We were adapting Anne Rice's book. And you can't move away too much from an author's original intention. There's a disappointment when you move away from the source's intention. The book was a psycho-sexual fantasy. And we made a comedy-sexual fantasy. You not only alienate the fans of the book but you have to come up with Band-Aids for the script, as opposed to using the intrinsic material. For those reasons, the movie ended up different than what we expected. Because we didn't know what to expect, we didn't know what audiences should expect. If our intention as filmmakers is not clear-cut, then our intention can't be received."

"You tackled tough material, about developmentally disabled lovers, in 1999's *The Other Sister*. What were you thinking?"

"I thought the developmentally disabled couple represented that same theme of people who are unsung heroes. People who we don't think of as capable turn out to be enormously capable. We make a mistake in judging people a priori without giving them the benefit of flexing to the degree they can flex.

"The material is based on my family. I came up with the story. Garry Marshal knows my family well. He and I spent a weekend in Chicago where my sister Anne went to school. And we visited the school where she'd lived for many years.

"I'd shown Garry a picture of Anne and her new boyfriend. They were cute. Garry said, 'That's the movie I want to make. I want to make a love story between those two people.' So on my next trip to Green Bay, I interviewed on videotape my sister Anne and her boyfriend. Garry could then see the cadence of their speech and what they were about.

"Contrary to what Roger Ebert said, the movie is the most authentic film about mentally challenged people."

46

Chris Mankiewicz

May 20, 2002

"Louis B. Mayer's MGM was known to be a producer's studio," says Chris, one of three children of famed director Joe Mankiewicz (*All About Eve*, 1950). "In the old days, the producer was the assigned foreman of a movie, to see it from conception to completion. My experience was different. I worked at United Artists (UA) during the 1960s and 1970s. UA was the studio that wasn't a studio. It was meant to be a filmmaker's company. We didn't have a physical lot that had to be amortized. Filmmakers could shoot their movies any way they wanted to. We read and approved a script, financed it, and said to the director, go away and bring us back a movie. We didn't watch the dailies every night the way other studios do. We didn't micromanage the movie and try to see every draft of a script.

"Today studio interference is worse than ever. Everybody has an opinion. And the result is that nothing in Hollywood is at it appears to be. My father and I were seated at the home of well known director Jean Negulesco. And when there was nobody there, my father went over to one of the chairs, turned it upside down, and it said, 'Property of 20th Century Fox.' They used to loot the studios and bring a lot of the furniture home with them.

"There used to be one producer on a movie. Now there can be 10 producers on one movie. It's become a vanity credit. The role of the producer has been denigrated. Before, the studios put a producer in charge of a movie. Today studios are so filled with young would-be filmmakers [working as executives] that they find it irresistible not to produce the movie themselves though with all the films they're working on, they can't do it with the same dedication and time that an individual producer could. Yet they find it all so glamorous, and that's what they're in the business.

"We now have the rise of the line producer, formerly called the production manager. By definition, he's for hire and he doesn't have anything to do with the creative end. The creative producer in the studio system is a dying breed. The big producers in the studio system are salesmen and dealmakers.

"I remember when I worked for producer Marty Ransohoff. We did a film up in northern California and Marty came up once. I asked him why he didn't come up more often. Marty said, 'Chris, what am I going to do? Stand around and watch the director?' He could not think of anything more boring. For these guys, their big climax is making the deal. Once they have to pass over control to the director, they lose interest. It's boring and intolerable for most producers to stay with a project day by day.

"When I developed *A Perfect Murder* (1998), Arnold Kopelson was invited in on my project against my will by Warner Brothers. Arnold had a big deal with Warners and he didn't have many pictures, so Warners brought him on to my movie. Arnold told me he didn't like the script. I asked him what he did like about it. He said, 'I love the title [of Alfred Hitchcock's 1954 film *Dial M For Murder*].' I said, 'We can't use that original title. We're not making a remake.'

"I said to myself that this is insane. He looked around for something to find, and he looked for good titles. That's how deep it went. He never attended a single writers meeting during the entire development of the movie. As soon as the script was finished and we started looking for a director, it came time for him to strut his stuff. Suddenly he wanted to get involved. Suddenly his wife, Anne Kopelson, who I never even met, showed up in the credits as a producer. How bizarre! Gee, maybe I have a cousin that I could make a producer too."

"Has your wife ever shown up in the credits as a producer?"

"No. She has nothing to do with the film business, thank God."

"Tell me more about *A Perfect Murder*."

"It's not a happy subject. Arnold tried to package it with different combinations of mostly lowball talent.

"I've been a fan of Hitchcock material. I had a deal to develop projects at Warner Brothers. I thought that we should take one of his less successful movies, *Dial M for Murder*, which was shot as a 3-D stage play. It was made to get rid of a commitment to Warner Brothers. Hitchock was anxious to move on to Universal where he had a good deal.

"Warners had bought the play, *Dial M for Murder*. Hitchcock made no bones of the fact that it wasn't one of his terrific movies. It was stagy and not cinematic. It was a one-set play. And because it was shot 3-D, you couldn't pan without strobe problems with the 3-D cameras.

"I'm against remaking masterpieces but I thought this was a good opportunity. So we tried with one writer and it didn't work. Kopelson came in. We found another writer, Pat Kelly, who became the writer of the final script. He came up with an interesting gimmick: The person who's supposed to commit the murder, is not a down and out acquaintance as in the original movie, but is the wife's lover.

"Kopelson's original idea when he came on to the project was to do a big action piece like *The Fugitive* [a terrific 1993 action film directed by Andy Davis]. Pat Kelly tried a couple of versions of that and it was just terrible.

"Warner Brothers doesn't make movies unless it has a star. We couldn't find anybody for our film. Arnold tried to cut me out of the packaging. I was happy to let him package it. That was something he should be able to do well. In fact, he didn't do it well. In fact, he didn't do it at all.

"Andy Davis has a commitment to do a film at Warners that fell out. His agent CAA sent him a stack of scripts, including Pat Kelly's script of *A Perfect Murder*. Andy read it and loved it. He lives in Santa Barbara, near Michael Douglas. Andy took the script to Michael Douglas and said, 'Here's a wonderful script. Why don't we do this together?'

"We'd always had Michael Douglas in mind for the lead but we'd been told by a former employee of Kopelson's that Michael didn't want to play bad guys anymore and we shouldn't even consider him. But Michael read the script and wanted to do it. Thanks to the director, this movie happened."

"How did you get Gwyneth Paltrow?"

"My impression is that Michael Douglas suggested her. He wanted to make a movie with her, for whatever reason. You're not going to get me in front of a recording machine to say why he may have wanted to make a picture with her."

Douglas is a notorious womanizer who's been the driving force behind the selection of various beautiful young ladies to play opposite him in steamy movies.

"Paltrow was happy to finally have a payday and make some money. We paid her $3 million. She'd just made several independent movies.

"On this movie, I was aced out by Arnold. I was kept on the sidelines. I wasn't on the set. He said, 'Don't worry. You'll get your credit. You'll get your money. But let Arnold take care of this.' The picture was pretty good and did fairly well.

"The only thing that pissed me off was that Arnold Kopelson moved in on my project and never once in the history of this picture ever asked me to lunch or dinner or to have a drink with me, much less send me a gift Mercedes. 'Here, this is a present from me to you. Thank you for not minding that I barged in on your picture.' The guy has no class. I'm sure he's done this before. He has a famous saying around town. 'Movie projects are like subway cars. There's always another one coming down the track.' That says a lot about his attitude to individual movies. He's a salesman and he just wants the action. The condition of the subway car doesn't interest him much."

"Did you like how *A Perfect Murder* turned out?"

"I hoped for more. I think we could've done better with the casting of the artist. I think the directing could've been better. We had a much better ending, which is on the DVD. The original ending was the Gwyneth Paltrow character blows [the Michael Douglas character] away. Not in self defense, as in the Warners ending, where he hits her and she's knocked to the ground. It's more devious. She sets up the same trap for him that he set up for her.

"He's in the shower. He hears the phone. He goes into the kitchen and picks up the phone. There's nobody there. Then she steps out and shoots him in cold blood. Then she sets it up to look like they'd had a fight. So when the cop at the end of the movie says, 'I guess that's the way it was,' wink, wink. He realizes that she's gotten her own back.

"We had a preview of it and the other ending [Warners] scored better. Director Andy Davis didn't care one way or another, which is pathetic. A director doesn't care about the ending of his movie. The studios follow focus groups. We had one theater in a multiplex show one ending and another theater show the other ending. The studio totaled up the cards, and because the other ending did a little better, they decided to go with it.

"Today movies are a big business, and a big business immediately. A film can debut on 3000 screens. I understand they spent $50 million to open *Spiderman* (2002). The costs are so huge that testing and focus groups become essential. It's like saying to Picasso, oh, this angle tests better. These [studio] people are no longer artists. They no longer have a point of view. The studios take the point of view that it is their movie and they want it to be appealing to as large a population as possible. Directors responsive to that work more frequently that directors who don't.

"This picture *Unfaithful* (2002) was more than five weeks over schedule and over budget. Director Adrian Lyne's a taskmaster and a difficult man. Everyone got pissed off with him. Sometimes he did 40 or 50 takes, which typically drives a studio insane. Everything today is cost conscious, not quality conscious, because studios don't believe that the public cares about quality. But Adrian made a terrific movie.

"I could never see myself making a movie like *Spiderman* or *Star Wars*. Those are comic books.

"The budget on *A Perfect Murder* was about $55 million. It cost more than it should. If they had let me produce the movie, it would've cost significantly less.

But the moment you sign on a Michael Douglas, who gets about $22 million, and you take a producer like Arnold Kopelson who takes a couple of million for himself, and everything has to be grand, and money is no object, then the budget gets bigger and bigger. And it is a relatively small movie.

"The people who have the leverage are the people who run the show. The stars in particular and anyone attached to the stars. They set the tone for the kind of movie that is made.

"I'm trying to make this John Grisham movie with Will Smith. But Grisham, who has script approval and actor approval, will not approve Will Smith.

"Will Smith was going to get $20 million. He came with an entourage of eight people. The stories are well known today about the actors who have their own trainers and their own chefs. In the old days, the producer was empowered to hire and fire people. He was responsible for the cost of a movie. Stars were on contracts and could be punished and suspended. A producer today could get on a set and say no and everybody would laugh at him.

"It's a little different for a producer in the independent world. But if your financing hinges upon a certain star, and the star knows it, then you can't replace the star. Over 20 years ago, a friend of mine did a tiny movie in France. And the star actress, in the middle of the movie, decided that she wanted her boyfriend to get half the profits or else she would leave the movie.

"Today Tom Cruise is in the producing business.

"And let's say you have a director like Adrian Lyne who won't say print and keeps shooting. Who are you going to replace him with? Once the movie is over, the studio gets involved. The only place a producer has power is in the development process. In the old days, when I was an executive at United Artists and Columbia, the amount of meetings were nominal. You expected the filmmakers to come up with a movie that reflected your discussions. You didn't demand notes from everybody. Now everybody shows up with notes and comments and rewrites and drafts and it can go on for years. I'm developing something at Warner Brothers now and the writer has just finished over three-and-a-half years and 12 drafts of a picture. And every time we're about to start, the studio says, 'Oh, we just need him for a few more weeks to do another polish.' Today there are so many cooks that it is amazing that the broth ever gets served.

"I remember hanging out with Marty Scorsese in New York in the 1960s. He'd made one short film and he was teaching film. I said to him, 'You don't even know how to make a movie. How can you teach it?'

"There's a famous story from the British Academy of Film about director Karel Reisz, who made *Saturday Night, Sunday Morning* (1960). He wrote the

British Film Academy's book *Technique of Film Editing*. Marty gave me a copy of the book. Years later when I was going to direct a movie in England, an agent told me the back story. After WWII, the Academy didn't have any textbooks. So they sent people out to write texts on the [technique] of film editing, the [technique] of this and that. So Karel Reisz wrote this book long before he ever made a movie. Fade out. Fade in. Years later, he's making his first movie [*Momma Don't Allow*, 1955] and he can't get it to cut together. He's got all kinds of editing problems. So he calls the dean of English editors for help. The guy says to Karel, 'You want me? You, who wrote the definitive book on film editing, want little old me?'

"United Artists ended up doing a movie with Karel Reisz. I went to dinner with him and he told me that the story was accurate. He said that when he wrote the book he didn't mean to suggest that he was a great savant who knew everything about film editing. He was just compiling attitudes of other film editors but he was always stuck as the author of the book on film editing, which always amused the other film editors.

"The 1960s were a wonderful time in the sense that not knowing didn't stop anybody. Marty learned to make films pretty well. Everybody in the late 1960s wanted to make movies and it destroyed the old guard in Hollywood and turned the business into a director's world. To write a book about producers today is a sad story. Most companies would just as soon not have anything to do with a producer unless it is a line producer. On *A Perfect Murder*, they gave the line producer [Peter MacGregor-Scott] a producer credit. In the old days, he would've just been a production manager. He was a dreadful man.

"Today the director is king. Who knows who produces a Steven Spielberg movie."

"Walter Parks."

"Let me tell you a story about him. A friend of mine [David Scarpa] wrote a movie called *The Last Castle*. A terrific script [eventually directed in 2001 by Rod Lurie] bought by DreamWorks. The first thing they do is hire someone else to rewrite it several times. Then Walter Parks rewrites it. The director Rod Lurie, a closet writer, can't resist rewriting it. By the time they're finished, the movie is a piece of shit. It went into the toilet in about two weeks. It was a disaster.

"My father told me this story about Jack Benny, a consummate comedian who never really became a movie star. They (writers, director, studio executives) went out to Pasadena to preview a Jack Benny movie. The audience roared from beginning to end. They went back to the studio and sat around and they analyzed the reactions. They were convinced this was going to be a smash. And one person said, 'Yes, it was great. There was just this one little moment. If we cut it...' And another person said, 'Yeah, and there was this other moment.' And it snowballed. By the time they'd finished recutting the movie, it was a disaster.

"A friend of mine, Bob Downey, father of Robert Downey Jr, was an underground filmmaker. I got credit for playing a lunatic postman in Bob Downey's movie *Too Much Sun* (1991). We went to a screening of an early cut and it was too long. Things didn't work well but it was funny. They kept cutting it down and soon they cut out all the laughs in the movie. When I finally saw the final cut, it was terrible. I asked the editor what happened. He said, 'Instead of letting it breath, they kept trimming every scene. They compressed the movie down so much there was nothing left to laugh at.' The movie died, and Bob, even though he was a pioneer of underground cinema, has had a hard time as a filmmaker ever since.

"I see the same kind of thing happen in script notes and the development of movies today.

"My *bete noire* Arnold Kopelson did this movie *Outbreak* (1995). I know because I was developing another picture at Warner Brothers at that time with the same executive who was in charge of *Outbreak*. They had a two-guy writing team [Laurence Dworet and Robert Roy Pool] do the basic script. And they brought on board Dustin Hoffman who said that he'd like Elaine May to rewrite the movie for a million dollars. They refused but they said O.K. to Carrie Fisher for $750,000.

"She rewrote the script. The studio was not happy. They went off to Hawaii to make the movie. They brought back the original writers. Then the director, Wolfgang Petersen, thinks of himself as a writer. So he rewrote the script. In the mornings, before shooting, they'd all get together and have a paste-up. Each person had been rewriting the night before. They'd take a third of a page of this script and a line from that script and they'd put it together like a jigsaw puzzle. As a young man, I went through that on the *Cleopatra* (1963), which my father directed. There the scenes were written the night before. What was going on was an absolute template on how not to make a movie.

"This confusion is mirrored in the studio's willingness to give producers credits to anyone. Instead of giving someone a half a million dollars, they give a credit. Writers feel defensive because their work is changed. Star actors will sign on to a project and say, 'Oh, my character would never say these lines.' These practically illiterate actors will become the writers. The producers have spent years developing the dialogue, but that all gets chucked out the window. The lunatics have taken over the asylum.

"There were different sets of writers working on *The Fugitive* while it was shooting in Chicago. One person said to me that Andy Davis is the luckiest director in history that it all worked out. That picture should've been a total mess yet it came together. A producer today can only be a referee and try to stop people from killing each other.

"Today's big producers are mini studio heads mainly interested in the deal. When there were fights on *Outbreak*, Kopelson was nowhere to be found. The last thing a producer wants to do is to say to Dustin Hoffman, 'You're wrong,' because maybe next year he needs Dustin Hoffman for a movie. A producer doesn't want to be here when there's trouble. I just want to be here when the TV cameras are here and I can show them that I am in charge.

"I remember associate producing a movie that Brian Grazer produced—*Armed and Dangerous* (1986). It was a real piece of caca doodoo. Brian Grazer was never there except for when we had a really dirty sexy scene with a girl he was interested in taking a look at, and when they were doing a studio publicity thing about the making of the movie, suddenly he wanted to be there because he wanted to show everybody he was the producer.

"This line producer who just did *Don't Say a Word* (2001), which Arnold Kopelson produced, said to me, 'What kind of producer are you? Are you like Kopelson? Do you only show up when the star is there? Or are you going to be there everyday.' His point is that Kopelson ain't there except when he can show off to the big star. Such producers like to ingratiate themselves with the power, which is the movie stars. At all cost, they must stay in good with the movie stars, because those are the people who will get movies made.

"Sad to say, if I were that kind of producer, I'd probably be much happier with a much bigger track record of successful movies. I love to hang out with the crew. I love the process of making a movie. I grew up with my dad making movies. I hung out at the lot. It was summer camp for me. The actors have always intimidated me and made me nervous. With my mother being an actress and my father being a director, the battles that they waged with actors, I don't want to be involved with that. I want to be with the normal people who do real work. People who are less complicated. Actors can be cruel and mean and petty and self-centered. You can't relax with them.

"I remember when I was with Bernardo Bertolucci in England. The English censors wanted to edit *Last Tango in Paris* (1972). A group of us were sitting around smoking marijuana, but not Bernardo. He had to stay in control.

"My mother [Rose Stradner, a famous stage actress in Vienna before World War I] was an alcoholic. My father's brother Herman, who wrote *Citizen Kane*, was a big alcoholic. They could let themselves go and be drunk but [Joe] never could because he had to be on top of the situation. My father loved out of control actors because he could be the psychiatrist to them. The role that Bette Davis played in *All About Eve* was classic. He loved that kind of temperament. I find it too much a strain. I like to be with people with whom I can kick back and be myself and say whatever I want without worrying that you could walk away permanently scarred because I said something nasty.

"I find writers easiest. Writers are neurotic for different reasons, usually for good reasons, though I resent that they are the first ones to get good money on a project. Writers have to deal with people and their complexities. I'm developing something at Fox now with a young writer. We're starting the second draft. I spent hours talking with him about the characters. It's almost like psychoanalysis. For most producers, their attention span is too short. They want to build empires. They can't wait to show up at the big glamorous premieres. Being locked in rooms with grubby writers who have to work with their brains does not appeal to them.

"Most producers have to turn over so many projects to justify their existence. They have to be a big hoovering operation to suck up every script and book they can and schmooze with the actors and create an aura for themselves.

"Look at the pictures at the end of the year that get nominated for Academy awards. Most of them are not big studio pictures. Most of them are not even financed by the big studios. Most producers are not in business to make Oscar winning movies. They're in business to make as much money as possible.

"I supervised *Playing for Keeps* (1986), the only movie Bob and Harvey Weinstein wrote and directed (aside from a couple of animation efforts).

"You know how flamboyant and obnoxious the Weinsteins are. This was in extremis. The producers needed somebody to look out for their interests, so they hired me as their representative. They saw that the Weinsteins were wild guys who would not care at all about budgets. They asked me to be in effect the line producer. The Weinsteins looked at me as though I were the dreadful Nazi Herman Goerring. I was appalled by what they did. The Weinsteins were rock n' roll promoters then. They hired some guys from California on a nonunion basis to make this low-budget movie. The Weinsteins were paranoid and crazed and would scream and yell. They made this dreadful movie.

"I would call the financiers in London and say, 'Look out. It's getting worse. It's getting worse.' If you see the producer as a traffic cop or enforcer, those days are past. If you see a producer as someone who can work with the different elements and try to make everything fit together, that can happen. The third alternative is the producer as financier who is not really involved in the filmmaking process. He just raises money for other people to make movies.

"Now the Weinsteins are the Medicis of independent filmmaking. It seems inconceivable that these are the same people I worked with on that movie.

"In the 1970s, I worked in Italy as the head of film production company called Peah, an Italian film corporation headed by Italian producer Alberto Grimaldi. I fell in love with Europe. That run finished [circa 1977], and it became difficult for an American to work in the European film business. The Treaty of Roman, a circa 1960 agreement that governs how movies are made in Europe, requires that the producing elements be European. The only exceptions that are permitted are for cast. To qualify for the government subsidies, each producer had to be European. As is typical, the English refused to participate in this.

"There is a famous story about the head of the ACTT [leading British film industry union] shutting down a movie because it would've required going along with the fiction that Sydney Lumet was French.

"The Europeans would often make French-Spanish-Italian co-productions. Each government would kick in subsidies. Often you'd have a totally fictitious film that was dubbed in every character because each actor would be speaking a different language. The Spanish would say we have to have at least one Spanish star. The Germans would say, fine, we have to have at least one German star. The French would require a French star. You'd get these hybrid films put together as a result of the tax structure. There's a case of where being a producer means a lot. Even though you had all these auteur directors running around saying, I am Monsieur Cinema.

"I speak fluent Italian. I was married to an Italian woman [first marriage]. I worked with producer Alberto Grimaldi on the re-editing of the Serge Leone western *The Good, the Bad and the Ugly* (1966). Alberto is a shy lawyer but with courage and great instincts. He saw in me somebody who'd be a good liaison between him and United Artists and various filmmakers including director Bernardo Bertolucci.

"I joined forces with Grimaldi in 1971 while *Last Tango in Paris* was written in Paris. Director Bernardo Bertolucci didn't speak English. I worked with Bernardo and often translated for him. I went on the set of the film. We had an agreement with United Artists to make the film for U.S. $1 million. President Nixon then devalued the dollar and we needed another U.S. $200,000. United Artists refused to pay. I then offered the movie to every other studio in America and they all turned it down. Grimaldi put up the additional money. The picture made millions of dollars.

"When the movie was on the cover of *Time* and *Newsweek*, it was only playing in one theater in New York. Everybody in the country wanted to see it and there was no place but one theater in New York to see it, where it played on a reserve seat basis as if it was a play. They were afraid that people would think the movie was pornographic so the distributor [United Artists] wanted to do this classy thing of releasing it in a shy, timid way for the first six months.

"Frank Yablans at Paramount told Bertolucci he would've opened it in a thousand theaters around the country and would've made a gazillion dollars. David Picker [head of United Artists] got pissed off about the remark but it was an accurate remark."

"Which of your films are you most proud of?"

"None. My favorite film was one that was never made. It should've been [director Federico] Fellini's last movie. He saw *8 1/2* (1963) as the first part of a trilogy. The final movie, *The Voyage of Masturner*, was about himself and how he would end up. The final scene has God in the projection room. It was never made because Fellini and Dino DeLaurentiis had a big fight. Then Fellini begged us at United Artists to make the film and we didn't. Then later, Fellini became bugged about ever finishing the movie because it would be like the end of his life. He was superstitious.

"Being around such great Italian filmmakers as Fellini made up for my not staying in America, keeping my career moving so that I would become a multibillionaire.

"I lived in Italy from 1970-74, and then I moved to England for two years. I returned to America in 1976.

"I'm well known as an Anglo-phobe. If English was spoken in France or Italy, there would've been few Americans sitting in England freezing their asses off. There's a snob appeal about England. A lot of Americans loved the class of European life. England was the most pompous yet had a similar language. It was a natural headquarters for studios to run their European operations. Others simply wanted to live the high life. I found the English chilly. As Lord Byron said, 'The chilly isle with chilly women.'

"I went bankrupt in England. I lived off the dole and in people's basements.

"Even though I was born and raised in Los Angeles, I've spent most of my life in New York and Europe. My mother was Austrian. I'm reluctant to think of a particular place as home. I like to think of the world as my home. If you were to say that I was to live in Tahiti for the next year, I'd say, 'Great, let's leave tomorrow.' I can adapt to the lifestyle of different places. I have a facility with languages.

"I've spent much of my professional life as a film executive. I started at Columbia in 1963. I've also spent decades as an independent producer. So many pictures have not happened.

"I'm not a packager. I don't call packagers like Arnold Kopelson producers. They're almost in the agency business. I think of the producer as someone intimately involved in the creative process."

"You are not a philanderer like your dad."

"No. My brother [Tom, a director] is like that. I've never been a star fucker. [Director Joe Mankiewitz would sleep with his leading ladies, such as Joan Crawford and Gene Tierney.] I find actresses impossible to deal with. There's no one more psycho, insecure and self-centered than an actress. There's something about constantly offering yourself up for acceptance in auditions and it just frazzles them.

"In the old days, people loved being movie stars. They were at home in their own skin. Joe E. Brown is the guy who says, 'Well, nobody's perfect,' at the end of *Some Like it Hot* (1959). That guy used to have a yacht on wheels. He'd drive up and down Hollywood Boulevard at night looking for girls. They'd just bring the girls on board and fuck them. There was a sense of devil may care, let's have fun.

"There's this wonderful expression that Hitchcock is alleged to have said: 'Ingrid, it's only a movie.' We are not fashioning the Taj Mahal here. This is fun. We're like sports figures who get paid obscene amounts of money to play a game. We're not contributing anything to civilization.

"Today's stars live in Wyoming and Idaho and have enormous bodyguards and people who handle publicity. Getting to them is an impossible task. Mel Gibson is an example. People I know who've worked with him say what a huge process it is. You call somebody else and then that person calls somebody. The culture is different. People used to get together and have fun. They enjoyed being writers, directors, producers, actors. I remember as a kid the great parties when stars came together. That joy seems to have gone. I don't know if it is drugs or if people are shy today. It ain't the same world. It ain't the same business. The movie making business has become tougher. Everybody second guesses everybody. There's a culture afoot now where a man's word is not his bond.

"I remember Mike Frankovich, then head of Columbia Pictures, who said to me, 'If you ever get a submission from Swifty Lazar, be sure to go out and find out who really represents the talent.' Because Swifty stole everything from everyone else. While that is an amusing anecdote, today you almost don't have to say it. Actors. I don't want to say anything because we're casting right now, but it's amazing to me how many people who are available who are said not to be available. Then you find out that they signed to do something else when they said they were going to do it with you.

"Our director [Gary Fleder] on this John Grisham picture [*Runaway Jury*, 2003] has just met with two actors, one of them Jennifer Connelly, who supposedly wanted to play the female lead in our film. Our director met with her to find out that she'd never even read the script and couldn't even talk about it, but she took the meeting and nodded about it.

"I was fired from Columbia on my birthday, October 8, 1965. I went in to see about a raise and I was told to forget it. I was fired. People said, 'Don't worry about it. You'll be back here sooner or later.' And 15 years later, I was rehired at Columbia as the head of East Coast Production. I oversaw Jon Peters first movie, *Eyes of Laura Mars* (1978). It was 100 percent over budget and Peters walked around like he brought it in on budget. It was an absolute mess. At the time I left, we were developing *All That Jazz* (1979) with Bob Fosse, *Altered States* (1980) and *Kramer vs Kramer*.

"In 1978, I came to Los Angeles to work for Steven Bach and United Artists in the middle of the *Heavens Gate* fiasco. You'll read a lot about me in the Steven Bach book *Final Cut*. A lot of people have called me and said, 'I just want to speak to the person who was in this book.' He gives me a lot of juicy lines and he doesn't even tell the half of it.

"Then I got involved with Graham Chapman of Monty Python. I wanted to make a comic pirate movie [that became 1983's *Yellowbeard*]. We knocked out a treatment and I sold the project to Warner Brothers. Peter Cooke wrote a script. George Harrison's partner had a company called Handmade Films, which took over the picture. They wanted to make all the Monty Python films. We all went to England to do the picture. David Korda was hired as my line producer. Oh God, what a cold winter that was. Handmade chickened out.

"Terry Gilliam had just finished *Time Bandits* (1981) and it had gone way over budget. I got a call saying to fire everyone on the picture. Then one of the great betrayals happened. Graham was in financial trouble. He made a deal (netting him $600,000) behind my back with Orion Pictures and got rid of me as the producer of the movie. Orion dumped all of us and said, 'Sue us.' You can't sue on contingency [where the lawyer takes a percentage of the final judgment in lieu of a fee] like you can here and I would've had to put up a chunk of money. Orion went ahead and made the movie badly. It turned out to be a bomb. When it was over, Graham came back to Los Angeles to apologize to me about what had happened. A year later he was dead of cancer."

"He was an alcoholic and a homosexual, right?"

"Yes. He was flamboyantly on the wagon when I knew him. He used to order cases of soda pop. I remember going out with him and there was a tiny bit of alcohol in something and he refused it. He used to have these two different lovers. One would fly in when the other flew out. It was a mess.

"Of all the Monty Pythons that I knew, John Cleese was the funniest. John Cleese gave me his house in London. He loves American blondes and he was off pursuing one [psychologist Alice Faye Eichelberger] in California, a woman he eventually married. Graham was more complex. It's difficult to be generous when someone has stabbed you in the back and fucked you out of three years of your life. We spent thousands of hours together. The two people you can not go out to dinner with and not have a real laugh are John Cleese and Eric Idle. Graham was more professorial. He thought of himself as a doctor [he was an M.D.]. He used to smoke a pipe. One of the reasons that he was as funny as he was was that he was drunk. The stories that he regaled me with about being under the table at banquets because he was smashed. He had no caution because he had no inhibitions. When he stopped drinking, he was much more serious.

"I got a producing deal at Columbia when David Putnam took over. A project I developed at Warner Brothers called *Wounded Knee* was a heartbreak. I spent five years trying to get that made. It was the first Indian project but by the end it seemed like everyone else had made an Indian movie except us.

"My favorite movie is *Casablanca*. George Raft turned it down. Humphrey Bogart got lucky and happened to be in it. Ingrid Bergman was in it because she was waiting to do another film and she had nothing else to do. It was considered just a programmer. They were rewriting while the movie was going on. There's the famous story where Ingrid went to Hal Wallace, the producer, and asked how she was supposed to play the love scenes. 'Who am I going to be with at the end of the picture?' Hal said, 'We don't know yet. Just play it down the middle.'"

47

Ross Grayson Bell

May 23, 2002

"The job of a producer is to get the train to leave the station. While it is sitting at the platform, people can get on and off, and they will, but once it is gone, those who really want to be involved, jump on, and those who don't, get off. Or they're trapped."

"Where did you grow up?"

"In the lower North Shore, Sydney, Australia. I studied Political Economics for four years at Sydney University. I graduated in 1983 with first class honors. I backpacked around Europe for two years.

"Then I returned to Sydney and with a group of university friends, wrote and produced a cabaret in this little cafe, called Mick's Cafe on Oxford St. Those were the best six months of my life. We put our own money in and we performed the show and we made our money back.

"Australia is a great place to grow up but it is not a great place of ideas. Ideas come from struggle. When you go through Europe, which has destroyed and rebuilt itself in 50 years. Germans traveling to Paris for an exhibition of an Italian artist. It's mind blowing. I realized that I wanted to work in the dissemination of new ideas.

"The cabaret was about my experiences and the experiences of my friends, but at the end of the night, 40 people have seen those ideas. I realized that the only way to be effective was to film something, put it in a canister and ship it. Then anyone in the world has a chance to see it.

"I moved on from the cabaret group and started as an assistant, a runner as they call them in Australia, on films. I remember graduating to third assistant whose main job was to look after the extras, stop traffic, and make sure the dogs weren't barking.

"I did this from 1986-89. This American guy came out to cut a trailer and the Australian crew were rude to him. They felt it was us vs them, bad Hollywood vs good Australian independent films. I picked him up at the airport and showed him around. He said I should come to America.

"In 1989, four days after Tiananmen Square, I came on a vacation to Los Angeles. He said I could stay with him for two weeks. I had an around-the-world ticket. I was looking for a car. I wanted to drive across America and then fly from New York to London. In *The Recycler* [Los Angeles classified ads paper], they had a job for a production assistant on a film shooting in Colorado Springs. These kids had $100,000 to make a film (*Ice Pawn*, 1989). They had never been on a set before.

"I ended up line producing the film for free. It was a terrible movie.

"I returned to Los Angeles and interned for Roger Corman [B-grade film-maker]. Anyone willing to work for free can work for Corman. The ones that have commitment and dedication, he picks out. I didn't have anywhere to stay, so I used to sleep in the office. I'd get up before anyone came in and no one was the wiser. One morning he came in early and found me dead asleep in my sleeping bag on his couch. He said, 'Who the fuck are you?' I said, 'I'm Ross Bell. I work here and you don't pay me.' He said, 'That'd be right. Wash your face and come in and see me.'

"So I sheepishly wash my face and go back in. I think I'm busted. He said, 'Watch *Lethal Weapon* and do a scene by scene breakdown.' I did that and came back the next day. He said he wanted me to write a treatment that was a facsimile of *Lethal Weapon*. A buddy movie set in Peru.

"I realized that my breaking down a movie, and writing down what was happening in each scene, I learned structure. Chase, exposition, love scene.

"I went home that night, and following that structure, with a chase, explosion, love scene, I wrote up an idea. An American DEA officer goes to Peru to help on a drug bust. The American is the Mel Gibson character and the Danny Glover character is a Peruvian who doesn't want to be paired with the American. I came up with the title, *To Die Standing* (1990), from a Midnight Oil song. 'It is better to die on your feet than to live on your knees.'

"The idea was that the America DEA agent was ready to die standing. The guy in Lima, his wife had been killed by the drug cartel and so he was living on his knees. My first paragraph was the selling paragraph. Roger read it the next day. He read it over the phone to video distributor RCA Columbia who bought it. Corman said to me, 'I'll pay you $3000 to write me a screenplay. You've got two weeks.' So four weeks later, I hand it in a draft. He sponsors me for my greencard [permanent residency in the United States]. Six months later, I was a produced screenwriter.

"I think the wardrobe mistress had a go at rewriting me, but it was an amazing opportunity that could've happened nowhere else in the world and I never went back to Australia.

"It was never my intention to leave Australia to make it in Hollywood. I never liked Hollywood movies.

"In late 1989, I went to work for $300 a week for Brad Krevoy, Corman's sales guy. Brad had his own company which he sold for millions of dollars to Orion after making *Dumb & Dumber.*

"Brad had offices in this new building and it was $50 a month for parking. He wouldn't pay for my parking. I couldn't afford to pay. I didn't have a car. I did have an apartment. Brad gave me a car, something that he had stored at his grandma's condo. It was a TR7 Triumph convertible, low to the ground. The reason he wanted me to have it is that I could drive under the boom gates so I didn't have to pay the $50 a month. So I drove up to the boom gate. It would hit the windshield. I'd reach out, lift the boom up, and drive underneath.

"Those Triumphs are terrible cars. It was always breaking down. It cost me so much money. Then someone told me about a job for a VP of Creative Affairs (Tracy Barone, now married to Paul Michael Glaser) at Ray Stark's company. I realized working for Corman and Krevoy, dedicated B moviemakers, that you can stay in that world forever. But the A list is a different circle of people. This business is about contacts and relationships. You have to jump ship. At the time, you couldn't get more A list than Ray Stark. I worked there for three years.

"I also learned that the new filmmakers I was developing relationships with were never going to happen with Ray. He was with Larry Gelbard, Barbra Streisand and that crowd. But I learned a lot. During that time, he did *Lost in Yonkers* (1993) with Neil Simon, *Barbarians at the Gate* (1993) for HBO, *Mr. Jones* (1993). It was not a particularly successful time.

"What's the joke about producers? You can get rich as a producer but you can't make a living. You only make money when you make these things. I was talking to a writer the other day. He was bitching about all this work we were doing on a pitch. I said, 'Listen. If we sell this, you could make anywhere from $250,000 to $2 million. The producer only gets a development fee of $25,000, $12,500 upfront. If I set up four movies a year, I'm doing well as a producer. That's only $50,000.

"Since *Under Suspicion* (2000), it's been two years since I've made a movie. All the successful producers are brutal. I don't want to be that kind of person. I want to live a balanced life.

"The success of *Spiderman* makes it more difficult for films like *Fight Club* to get made. I've got an uplifting 1964 Olympic drama but it is hard to get it made.

"*The Economist* just did a piece on the economics of Hollywood. The theatrical release of a film is only 30 percent of its potential revenue. And this pie is shrinking. Theatrical release is now advertising for all the ancillary markets—video, DVD, pay cable, theme park rides, merchandise, sequels. If I'm running a studio, which is a small division in a huge corporate empire, am I going to invest in *Fight Club*? With no sequel potential and no upside in ancillary markets? So I go buy a spec script that Roland Emmerich just wrote about the end of the world. The concept will sell. I will get B-grade actors who won't participate in gross profits.

"Of course there are going to be more *Spidermans*. They are doing *Wonderwoman and Batgirl* and reinventing *Superman*. They're remaking *Miami Vice* as a film. We're recycling everything.

"If there isn't potential for a sequel, it can't get my same attention if I want to make a real business out of this. That's the dilemma. Do I stay true to my ideals and make great groundbreaking movies? Now every studio wants one or two of those a year for Oscar considerations, because Oscars enhance the brand of a studio.

"After September 11th, I was looking for stories about unity, but not in that cloying way with all the propaganda we were given after that event. In 1964, eight oar rowing was a sport dominated by college crews, particularly Harvard. The theory being that college kids have the resources and time to get together and train. This year, a group of older guys, with jobs and mortgages and kids, challenge them. They had this dilapidated old shell and they beat Harvard at the trials and eventually won the Gold medal.

"These older guys had trained in pairs and singles. And after their gold medal, it was realize that this was a better way of training a crew rather than the college way of having all eight guys train together in one boat.

"One of the great scenes is after they beat Harvard, the guys turn around and row back to the starting line, passed all the college boys collapsed in their boats.

"The sport doesn't interest me. What interests me is that there is no other sport like it where eight men have to be one. It's the *Dirty Dozen* (1967) of rowing and *The Magnificent Seven* (1954) of sports movies. Disney said, 'Why would anyone, after a long week at work, pay the nanny, get in the car, drive out to see this movie?' If it has to be an event movie every time, a feel good escapist, then movies are dead. You say that and then *The Rookie* (2002) comes out, which does well.

"When you look at the most profitable films at the end of the year, they are usually small films made for small budgets. *Crying Game* (1992), *Wedding Banquet* (1993), *Strictly Ballroom* (1992).

"It can be fun to work on movies that you don't care about so much. It frees you up."

"Like having sex without emotional involvement."

"I do that all the time. It's easy."

"How did you come to *Fight Club?*"

"I finished with Ray Stark in 1993. I built a company with Josh Donen (son of director Stanley Donner). Josh is now a CAA agent. For two years we put together movies. He produced *The Great White Hype* (1996) and *The Quick and the Dead* (1995). We were on the Fox lot when Kevin McCormick sent us the novel *Fight Club* by Chuck Palahniuk. Fox's book guy in New York, Raymond bon Giavani originally found it, flipped, and sent it over. The LA office [of Fox] was confused by it. Their coverage said, 'Don't make this movie. It is unconventional. It will make people squirm. No. No.'

"I read the book that night. Halfway through, it gets so dark, where they are burning each other with cigarettes. Then the reveal comes and it took my breath away. I felt my heart race and I couldn't wait to get to the end of each page to find out how it all wrapped up. I knew then that this was a movie I had to make.

"I called up Kevin and said that all the reasons given not to make the movie are reasons to make it. It is unconventional and it will make people squirm and you have to make it. I could hear him rolling his eyes over the phone. He didn't care about conventional. He cared about making money.

"I didn't know much then. I think that being naive allowed me to do things that I wouldn't do today, but then I was so gung ho. I got a group of actors together to do a read-through of the book. It took six hours. Over the next two months, I cut out stuff and started turning internal monologue into dialogue and making the structure more linear.

"Jim Uhls, an unproduced but fabulous screenwriter, wanted to do the script. Laura thought of *Fight Club* (1999) as *The Graduate* (1967), a film that will define a generation. She wanted to assign it to Buck Henry, who wrote *Graduate*. I said that was his generation. This is a new generation experience.

"Director David Fincher read the book and wanted to direct the movie. Then the studio rallied. The job of a producer is to give the financier the packaged movie before they have to pay for it. By packaging the director and the writer, I had made it more tangible.

"My actors' read-through was now down to 50-minutes. I taped it. I sent it to Laura Ziskin on a Friday. She listened to it in her car on the way to Santa Barbara on Saturday. She called up. 'I'm making the movie. You've got yourself a deal.'

"I'd been living off my credit cards for the past two years. I was deeply in debt.

"Jim handed in his first draft of the script. The ending was off. In the book, they blow up this building so it will fall on the Natural History museum. It symbolizes how you destroy culture and civilization. I suggested that they blow up the credit card companies. You have the scene with all the people coming out into the streets and their credit card statements are in shreds raining down. It would destroy and liberate civilization and the people would celebrate."

"And you had your own credit card debts."

"That's where it came from. And from my own background in political economy. I realized that if all the debtor nations in the world got together and formed a cartel and refused to pay their debts, they would destroy civilization. That would be the end of Western Civilization as we know it.

"David thought we would go through many drafts and several writers before we got it right. After we made this change, the script was ready. David committed to make it as his next film.

"From book to film was two-and-a-half years. That's fast.

"Film is a director's medium. We made *Fight Club* quickly because David got behind it. I'm not reducing the producer's role. *Fight Club* exists because I said so, but David made the movie and got the stars. The film is flawed because it is a David Fincher film, and it is genius because it is a David Fincher film."

"Many reviewers lambasted the film."

"Good. Hooray. It shows they're awake. There should've been lambasting. I think Kenneth Turan had a personal agenda against violence in movies. Columbine had happened and there was a lot of debate about how films were creating a more violent society. Anita Busch, editor of the *Hollywood Reporter*, wrote a commentary that we were morally irresponsible to make a film like this. I responded and she published my response.

"If you go to an AA meeting, you have someone stand up at the front of the room and talk about the horrors of drinking. It creates a catharsis. People see the horror and they recognize their lives. A burden shared is a burden halved. Imagine that this movie is David Fincher's confession to the world. Imagine the cinema as an AA meeting and the film is Fincher and me at the front. This is how we see the world.

"We're not encouraging anybody to go out and start fight clubs. We're sharing the burden. We live in a culture where we've been reduced to sound bites, where everything worth fighting for has been coopted and corporatized. We're expressing our beef with society.

"I say people go to that movie and it lets the pressure off. People have come up to me and said, 'Fuck. That was me up there. I understood that. I am now going to live my life the way I want to live it.'

"I also said to Anita in my column that the Soviet Union, in its first 70 years, also tried to create films that were socially responsible. Films that fit what the powers that be said was socially responsible to the glorious worker. And look where it got them? Complete breakdown and the emergence of freedom of speech. If Anita follows through on what she's saying, then we should all be making films that condone what Bush is doing in the war on terrorism, which is what is happening now. Bullshit! That's the death of freedom of speech.

"If movies are making a more violent society, show me the statistics. Come back to Columbine. They say they were wearing trenchcoats, like *The Matrix*. Those sad unfortunate guys who were so propelled to do that terrible thing, were shooting the jocks because they felt they were picked on. So I would argue that every film that has the jock as the heroic guy who gets the homecoming queen is also responsible. Look at how alienated [the Columbine killers] were feeling because they did not fit in with the buff jock image. And where is that promoted? In films and TV."

"Were you surprised by the ferocity of the reactions?"

"No. Chuck's work is all about run towards that which you are afraid of. If we stay knowing what we know, we are not going to evolve. But by embracing the unknown we evolve. The tribe in the village has to go across that mountain range and risk death to find out what's over there. That's evolution. Christ went into the wilderness for 40 days and broke himself apart. The ideas in *Fight Club* are fundamental to the evolution of humanity.

"There are only four real fight scenes in the movie. It is not as violent as people make out. But the ideas are confrontive and people think of that as violence.

"The marketing didn't work. Fox sold it as a fight movie. The stills that went out to reviewers showed bare-chested Brad with blood on his face, punching Ed Norton. It was one of those films that is hard to market. It was made for $70 million and the studio felt they had to market it as a big star-driven event movie and threw money into the campaign.

"Ideologically we were wrong because Tyler would've blown up Rupert Murdoch and Fox and the corporateness and inflated budget. It was untrue to what the film was saying."

"It's a low budget independent film."

"When it got green lit, David called up and said, 'They've just green lit a $70 million experimental movie.' The domestic box office was $38 million and it didn't do well internationally. Like every classic before it, it was misunderstood and misjudged at the time.

"*Fight Club* is a cultural reference point for many people while the latest Jennifer Lopez movie is not.

"After the disappointing box office, people involved with the film, agents and studio executives, all came back and said, 'We told you not to make that.' There was a rubbing of the hands and a smile on the face that said, 'You thought you were going to change the world. You didn't.' But in 15 years, they will be talking about my movie.

"I have a reputation for making challenging movies. It doesn't mean that anybody wants another one like it. Chuck Palahniuk, who wrote *Fight Club*, introduced me to his writing teacher, Tom Spandbaum. One of Tom's novels, *The Man Who Fell in Love With the Moon*, is a sister project to *Fight Club*. It is difficult, challenging groundbreaking. Director Pedro Almodovar optioned the book before me but never had a screenplay written. When he let the option lapse, I optioned it with the New York playwright Craig Lucas.

"I describe it as a buttfucking western. It's got every permutation of sexuality you can imagine. It's an interesting commentary on the destruction of native Americans, to destroy their mystery and take away their story, which is what the missionaries did. On one level it is a profound deeply moving story about the disintegration of humans by other humans. But again reviewers will go for the juicy sex and misread it. I will die to make this movie. No one will give me the money to make it but somehow I will do it."

"Did working on *Fight Club* change you?"

"No. Who I was enabled me to see *Fight Club*. Interestingly, Chuck had done The Forum [formerly EST] by Landmark Education. If you're nothing, if you're not your bad hair, the fact that your mother never loved you, that you're nothing, then you can create anything. I'd done The Forum too. We were somehow in sync. Art Linson passed on the book. It was sent to him before it was sent to Josh and me. And Art's son John championed the book.

"You are the sum of your experiences. I am the sum of my political economics degree, my study of Marx and Lenin. All of that led me to an opening to receive *Fight Club*, which has in turn opened me to further experiences."

48

Peter Samuelson

June 4, 2002

The fourth of five generations of Samuelsons employed in the film industry, Peter received his Masters Degree in English Literature from Cambridge. After serving as a production manager on *The Return of the Pink Panther* (1974), he emigrated to Los Angeles and produced *The Revenge of the Nerds* (1984), *Tom & Viv* (1994), *Wilde* (1997) and *Arlington Road* (1999).

"When you tell people that you are going to the film festival in Cannes, they think you'll spend your time walking up the red carpet wearing a tuxedo, surrounded by girls, hobnobbing with the rich and famous.

"This was my 20th year in Cannes. I arrived early Thursday with my brother and business partner Marc Samuelson. He's based in London. I'm based in Los Angeles.

"We've made this $20 million film *The Gathering* (2002) starring Christina Ricci. We didn't yet have an American distributor. We had a big screening planned for Friday night. The RSVPs went so high that we added a second screening at midnight.

"We were in Cannes eight days and we had 103 meetings. We had meetings every hour on the hour. Cannes is an amazing opportunity to do business. All the territorial buyers go in and it is like an enormous bazaar. Over 20 years, we've gotten many films off the ground because of Cannes.

"We have all our people there—lawyers, accountants, partners. The various soft money sources in Europe, sale-lease-back, the Isle of Man fund. Everyone is there and you can make projects happen. It is pure entrepreneurial producing.

"In between all our meetings, I'm phoning the cinema. 'Monsieur, we must come to rehearse the print for Friday night.' The cinema is saying, 'Monsieur, it is not necessary. We are professionals. You will not need to rehearse. Furthermore, you can't come rehearse your print because we have screenings all afternoon and evening.'

"I'm saying, 'This print is fresh from the lab. The film is still in post production. It is a double system print, meaning that the sound is separate from the picture. As you know, from our exchange of faxes, it is a flat 2.35 scope ratio print.' 'Yes, yes, it is not a problem. Don't worry about a thing.'

"Eventually I find out the last screening ends at 2 a.m. Friday. We arrive and test the sound. It's gorgeous. Then they throw the picture up. If the screen is 40 feet wide, our film is about 25 feet wide. If the screen is 15 feet tall, our film is 30 feet tall. It shows not only on the ceiling but on the floor. And what's showing on the ceiling has all the microphones in, and what's showing on the floor has the dolly track in, because, contrary to the exchange of faxes, they do not have the right lens nor the right projector aperture.

"So, after a lot of experimenting, it emerges that they do have a lens which is not really the right lens, but it makes the picture almost as wide as the screen. We're still missing about 5percent on the left and right, which is significant. When the credit of Brian Gilbert comes up, the screen says 'Directed by Ian Gilbert.' The 'Di' got cut off.

"We still have a tremendous problem with the spill of the picture top and bottom. This cinema has no curtains and no masking on the screen.

"Marc and I have a war council and decide to cancel the screening. It then emerges that names were not taken for the RSVPs. We don't know who's coming. We just know there are 600 of them.

"Marc and I fear that this will be a career killer. We will have to stand outside the cinema and send 600 people away at 10 p.m. tonight. I say we must try something else. Maybe we can mask it on the window of the projection booth. Maybe we can use tape or cardboard and cut off the top and the bottom.

"I say that we need black tape. They have none. I say we need cardboard. They say they have no cardboard. What about your calendar on the wall? The projectionist has a 2001 Cannes Festival calendar.

"At 4 a.m., we're kneeling on the floor of the projection booth with a razor blade, a metal ruler and the back of a 2001 calendar, cutting a rectangular hole. To avoid reflections, we tear up five yards of some 30-year old black tape from the carpet in the projection booth and it works perfectly.

"As a result of our screening, Mark Gill, the head of distribution for Miramax, comes out and gives me the Vulcan death grip, and says, 'Don't sell this film until I can get Harvey Weinstein in to see it.'

"Harvey Weinstein shows up the next night to our rehearsal screening for a different theatre, accompanied by eight people wearing little earplugs. He not only made us an offer for the United States and Canada, but he also buys Australia, New Zealand, South Africa, the United Kingdom and Italy. Their model for the release of *The Gathering* is *The Others* (2001). They plan a high P&A spend [prints and advertising].

"As we stood there drinking our champagne after closing the deal, I was thinking to myself, 'I'm going to get an enlargement of the photo being taken right now with the champagne, and I'm framing it in the piece of the cardboard that is the back of the calendar. I went back to the cinema, and the projectionist had written diagonally across the black carpet tape, 'Mr. Samuelson, thank you so much for having me in your team on *The Gathering*. Your projectionist, Albain. Cannes, 2002.'

"So I've now got my champagne pictured framed in the back of the calendar with the carpet tape. There you have the true arc of a producer, which goes from kneeling on the floor at 3 a.m. to drinking champagne after a huge sale to a studio.

"We developed *The Gathering* at Paramount in 1989. The executive, Ileen Maisel, left the studio and the picture was put into turnaround. We then set the picture up at Fine Line (sister company to New Line). Mark Ordesky was our executive. They fired our writer Anthony Horowitz and hired two lots of new writers before putting the project in turnaround. We then set the project up with Lauren Lloyd at Hollywood Pictures in the mid '90s. They brought in a new writer. Then Lauren Lloyd left Hollywood Pictures and went to Touchstone. Our project went with her. Then she left and Touchstone put the project in turnaround. We briefly set it up with Savoy Pictures. That company imploded. We then got all the rights back and threw away all the versions of the script except the original.

"A couple of years ago, we partnered with Granada, a big British TV and film company, to make the film. It has the great central premise that when Christ was crucified, people gawked. Those gawkers were fated to be reincarnated in every generation. They roam the earth and feed on human catastrophe and misery. They choreograph and orchestrate it.

"We may be the only people to benefit from last year's threatened strike by the Screen Actors Guild. We were able to finance the film out of foreign sales. Under ordinary circumstances, the foreign buyers might've said, 'Where is the American deal?' We were able to say, 'We can't do an American deal now because if we do, and there's a strike, [American actress] Christina Ricci wouldn't be able to work.'

"We'd sold *Tom & Viv* to Miramax. We had a morning screening in Milan for foreigner buyers but all the American buyers showed up anyway. Marc and I were disappointed all afternoon because nobody had made an offer. When we got back to the hotel, we had dozens of envelopes stuffed in the boxes behind the concierge with offers for *Tom & Viv*. The best one was from Harvey Weinstein. Everyone else's letter was three pages long and had terms and conditions. Harvey's letter said, 'Dear Marc and Peter, Miramax Pictures will pay you $500,000 more than anyone else. Best regards, Harvey Weinstein.' And indeed they did."

"How did you come to make *Tom & Viv?*"

"Marc saw it as a stage play in London. We thought it was the great untold story of T.S. Eliot's first wife, who, like a quarter of a million other English women between the Wars, was too uppity to satisfy her man. They were committed to asylums forever, diagnosed with a hysterical mental illness. That is what T.S. Eliot had done to his wife. She lived for years in an institution. He never visited her. She's been largely written out of the story of his life and she had been his muse for years. She'd given him the title for *The Waste Land*, edited *The Waste Land*, and made as big a contribution to it as Ezra Pound. So the film set out to put that to rights.

"That led to making the film *Wilde* three years later about Oscar Wilde. It was our first film where we put up a website (www.oscarwilde.com). On the site, you can send emails to the producer. They come out on my laptop and I can see that the film played on latenight cable in Finland because I will get 21 Finnish emails. I can see when school goes back and people get assigned reading in Oscar Wilde. It was the first time that Marc and I had direct interaction with thousands of audience members.

"The United States release of *Arlington Road* was harmed by the tragedy at Columbine High School. That happened a couple of weeks before we were supposed to be released and it just wasn't the responsible thing to do, to release a film about domestic terrorism and people building bombs in their suburban garage. So Sony pulled the film and it eventually went out in the teeth of the summer, which was a mistake."

"How did you come to *Arlington Road* in the first place?"

"I am a final stage judge of the Nicholl Fellowship of the Academy of Motion Picture Arts and Sciences. I read this amazing script by Ehren Kruger. I couldn't put it down. I read it twice in one night. Because of the ethics of being a judge, I had to wait until the results of the competition were published in *Variety*. Then it was open season. With the permission of the Academy, I then bought the rights.

"Then Marc and I went on a search for a director. We wanted someone who could sell the paranoia of Jeff Bridges' character. And our thoughts went to an MTV kind of a director. But the trouble with those guys is that they often can't span a 100-minute narrative. They are used to telling a story in four minutes.

"We saw director Mark Pellington's show reel. It was brilliant. We saw his one feature film, *Going all the Way* (1997). While the script was flawed, the execution was good. What really did it for us was a documentary he made, *Father's Daze*, about how the terrible scourge of Alzheimer's Disease took over the life of his father. He made it over many months. His father was a vibrant football player who was devastated by the disease.

"We met Mark. He's about nine feet tall, a gentle giant. We hired him. My phone rings and it is John Matoian, who was then running HBO. John says he's read the script and he will immediately green light it. I go in to see him and he says 'I am green lighting this film.' I say, 'That is kind of you. What are the contingencies?' He says, 'None. But you have to say yes now.'

"He lays out an appropriate high-end HBO deal. I say, 'I have to talk to my partner.' I call Marc on my cell phone and we agree that it is mad for us to say yes now. We haven't even tried to sell it as a feature. We will give ourselves the ten days of Cannes to set it up as a feature. And if not, we will take the HBO deal.

"We went to Cannes. We met with Tom Rosenberg, the head of Lakeshore Entertainment. He committed to making it as a feature using his Paramount output deal. Lakeshore would sell the foreign rights. 'But if you leave the room, the deal is off.' We said we had to talk to our lawyer. He asked us to come back at 3 p.m.

"We couldn't find a lawyer in Cannes. Our lawyer, Libby Savill, was leaving for London that day. Her partner, David Bouchier, was due to land at 2 p.m. at Nice airport. We drove to the airport, found David's limo driver and sent him away. When Bouchier came out of customs, we said, 'Hi, we're your limousine. By the way, you're negotiating a deal for us with Lakeshore in 50 minutes.'

"We then drove at 100 mph to Rosenberg's hotel with Marc driving and me briefing Bouchier, who threw himself into it with gusto. We were on time for our appointment and made our deal. And four months later, we were in pre-production."

"I found *Arlington Road* terribly disturbing."

"It was intended to be. We had terrible fights over the ending with the studios. You can only name a couple of American films where the hero dies in the end. We thought it was an article of faith that the Jeff Bridges character Michael Faraday [an anti-terrorism expert] had to die. The film is a horror story with domestic terrorism as the monster and it would be completely specious and morally bankrupt to do a classic American studio film where you paper it all over at the end and everything is sweetness and light.

"We've learned in the three years since the film was made that it was prescient. We've learned that terrorism is infinitely powerful and infinitely difficult to stop. It empowers extremists who have always been marginalized and treated as the crackpots they are. It gives them a bully pulpit. And the forces of civilized society are ill-equipped to stop it.

"It wouldn't have been worth making the film if Jeff Bridges had saved the day, put it all in a neat box, and sent the Tim Robbins character to jail. We were forced by the studio to shoot two endings. In one, Jeff Bridges did not die. The DVD shows this alternate ending. We had the FBI guys dragging him away from the explosion site to a cell.

"When we tested the film, the scene that was most liked by the audience was the cathartic, grim but realistic ending of the movie. And that was the last we heard from anybody telling us that we had to be the millionth American film where the hero saves the day.

"I don't know why it is in the American studio system that catharsis is unacceptable in a motion picture other than in horror films. Drama began in ancient Greece where they had comedy, drama and tragedy. And catharsis, making the audience experience something that frightens them, was always an integral part of Aristotle's Poetics. And that has remained true throughout the generations. Where's the happy ending in *King Lear* or *Hamlet*?

"There is only one exception in modern culture—the last 60 years of American studio filmmaking. I think it has more to do with the can-do frontiers optimism of the early immigrant studio heads than the tastes of the audience. I don't think American audiences are any less open to all Aristotle's different forms of drama and I believe they can be touched and made to cry and made to feel a cathartic release. People in studios don't seem to agree with that."

"The producers of *Sum of all Fear* (2002) came under pressure from Arab-Islamic groups not to cast the bad guys as Arabs or Muslims."

"We were specifically focused on right-wing domestic terrorism.

"I have a European Community passport and an American passport. I grew up in the UK. I lived in France for a year and now I live in Los Angeles. I really do see both sides of the Atlantic Ocean clearly. There is a perverse cultural hegemony and even an imperialistic arrogance to the way that America portrays its worldview through film. I don't justify the fomenting of anger against America in the Third world and the Islamic world, and major parts of Europe, but I think I partly understand it. It partly feeds on jealousy because so much of the world's wealth is here. But it is also that America is perceived as a cultural fortress that pays little attention to the cultures of the rest of the world, let alone to their religions. While tolerance within the United States is part of the Constitution, understanding and outreach to other foreign beliefs and ways of living are not historically core values of the American way. There are exceptions like the Peace Corps and the famous American tradition of a junior [college] year abroad, backpacking through Europe.

"That only one American citizen in ten even owns a passport is not a statistic that goes without notice in the rest of the world. I believe there is an opportunity and a responsibility for the American entertainment industry to build some cultural bridges into the rest of the world. Or at least to stop building mine fields.

"It's an amazing thing that a recent Gallup poll in Saudi Arabia had about 75percent of young educated Saudis agreeing with the anti-Americanism of Al Qaeda if not with its methods. On the other hand, American video cassettes and DVDs are the staples of entertainment across the Middle East and the world. I don't think there's been any period of history since the Roman Empire where there's been such cultural hegemony. I do believe that the frustration in certain parts of the Middle East is partly fueled by realizing that in virtually every piece of American entertainment where they need bad guys, they historically have been Arabs. That we almost never see positive Arab images is not unrelated to the anger and frustration in certain parts of the world of Islam.

"We are working with producer Debra Hill on a project called *Blood and Sand* about a young American and a young Saudi who meet at an American postgraduate college and then run into each later in the Middle East as enemies and what then brings some minor but crucial understanding between them. I think we need to do a lot of that. We need to stop the stereotyping of who the enemy are—three guys with rags on their head who look like they haven't had a bath in a year building a bomb in the back of a cafe. This is not how to make friends and influence people."

49

Al Burton

I interview Al Burton at his light and airy French/English style Beverly Hills mansion.

A spry man in his seventies, he stands about 5'3" tall.

"I worked for Norman Lear for ten years. I started as director of development and I became a close friend of Norman and an executive vice-president. During this time, he would call on me to go to events he couldn't make. In 1974, he asked me to make a speech for him at a conference in Aspen, Colorado. I was not welcomed warmly by some of the people.

"I did not know then that Ben Stein [a *Wall Street Journal* TV critic] had written a bad review of *The Jeffersons* (1975-85). Norman wanted to know what this guy was like.

"The first day that Ben and I started talking to each other, it was clear that we were going to be close friends. I'd brought my wife with me to Aspen, Colorado. I invited Ben to lunch. He walks in and my wife had half-a-dozen anti-Nixon books. She was reading *All The President's Men, The Final Days*, etc. Ben says, 'I'm sorry. I think you should know that I wrote speeches for Richard Nixon.'

"We were knocked out by Ben. He was funny. He was diametrically opposed to everything my wife stood for. I'm not much of an ideologue, but the severest word you could give against George W. Bush, my wife would probably subscribe to.

"I had a tape of the *Mary Hartman, Mary Hartman* (1976-78) pilot with me. I asked Ben if he'd like to see a show that had not sold. It'd been turned down by ABC and CBS. He said yes and we played it for him. Then he asked if Norman would mind him reviewing it.

"My guess was that Norman would welcome a review. I called Norman and he said of course he can review. So Ben wrote a five-column wide review atop the

Wall Street Journal under the headline, 'A Dandy Show You Might Never See.' We blew that up as a poster and that's how we sold the show.

"We invited 25 TV executives from around the country to dinner at Norman's home in Brentwood. That's how we started syndicating the show. And it was a smash hit from the beginning.

"It turned out that Ben had only criticized *The Jeffersons* for one thing, and I agreed with him. That the show was the *Amos & Andy* (1951-53) of its time.

"I got a chance to put him on as a consultant to a show called *All's Fair* (1976). Richard Crenna plays a right-wing conservative and Bernadette Peters plays a left-wing liberal. And Ben contributed the far-right thought. He claims that he was hated by everybody [at Norman Lear's production company]. It's not true. They thought he was funny, but they hated his politics. They were 1935-style communists.

"Ben's book *Dreemz* is about his move to California. I greeted him at the airport with a limo and five adorable cheerleaders [in short shorts] with T-shirts that read, 'I'm Benjy's.' He had come from a cubicle at the *Wall Street Journal*. It was a terrific beginning for his stay in Hollywood.

"Ben was not an actor. He did appear in *Ferris Bueller's Day Off* (1986). He delivered an ad-lib drone in the background. When he finished doing it, everybody laughed so hard that they aimed the camera at him. He was not supposed to be in the shot. I then put him as an actor in *Charles in Charge* (1984-90). I made Ben the villain. He was Mr. Willard. He never had a steady job. He was the nemesis of Charles. He was the loan officer and the psychologist. Then he got *The Wonder Years* (1988-93). *Win Ben Stein's Money* (1997-2002) catapulted him to the top.

"It was complicated to get him to do the show. At the time, it sounded like I wanted him to be a gameshow host. I knew that it would make him. I knew he would get press. He's a journalist's star. I knew that he's so smart that he can answer those questions. I devised a game that nobody else could play. He's now a sought-after speaker on college campuses. He's probably given more commencement addresses in the past three weeks than anybody but the president. In an airport, he's mobbed.

"On the *The Late, Late Show With Craig Kilbourn* (1999-???), he did 'The Steins' as a takeoff on the Osbournes. We taped his wife, son and dog. Ben did the father. Ben would even speak like Ozzy Osbourn. The plot was that his show didn't sell. He said, 'MTV loused me up. They f——me, they f——me.' Each one got bleeped like Ozzy on MTV.

"I claim that I have just celebrated my 56th birthday. I've celebrated it for a number of years already. I was born in Chicago but grew up in 14 different states because my father managed a dime store (Neisner Brothers out of Rochester, NY) like Woolworths. He had three kids and he moved every six months to open a new store.

"I went to Northwestern University in Illinois. I met Edgar Bergen, father of Candice Bergen. He's a ventriloquist. I knew Candice Bergen when she was three years old. Edgar got me a scholarship. He liked that I was commercially minded while most kids at Northwestern were in their ivory towers.

"At age 19, I graduated with a degree in Speech. I came to Hollywood. I sold a teenage television show (*Tele-teen Report*) on which I appeared. I was the editor of a mythical newspaper that covered 72 schools in the LA area. That led to other shows. At one point, I was doing five teenage television shows a week.

"That background gave me the impetus to invent the Miss Teenage America pageant in the early 1950s. I did not continue with it. I went to pick it up again in 1962 when MCA called me to say they're doing their own Miss Teenage America pageant. They offered to help me promote my pageant if I changed the name. So I did to Miss Teen USA. It became Miss Teen International. I ran these pageants until 1973.

"The first Miss Teen International was Ewa Aulin who baby-sat my daughter. Ewa starred in the movie *Candy* (1968), based on the Terry Southern novel. It was a dirty movie. It embarrassed the hell out of me because I was going on with my clean wholesome teenage image. But she was adorable. Norman Lear put her in *Start the Revolution Without Me* (1970), playing a Marie Antionette duplicate.

"After *Candy*, she moved to Italy and married Roberto Rosselini Jr, the love child of Ingrid Bergman conceived on the island of Scromboli. Ingrid had an affair with Roberto Rosselini, who she later married and divorced. Ewa Aulin was a superstar in Italy. She divorced Roberto and married John Sperrow. She starred in some big Italian movies.

"The girls in the pageant were aged 15-19. That age is adorable. A reviewer once wrote, 'The problem is that at this age they are all Juliets. And they become Lady MacBeths.' A telling line. If you stop to think, it is more true than it should be. All I dealt with ever were Juliets. I loved these young ladies.

"I met my wife in the middle of this career. When we went out socially and people asked her what her husband did for a living, she said, 'He exploits teenagers.' She put up with me somehow. She had to walk in all the time to see me with bikini-clad beauties."

"Did you ever date any of them?"

"Oh sure, that's why I got into the business I'm in. Why does anyone become a producer?

"When I was at Northwestern, I was a little short guy. But I put on a show on [TV station] WEAW in Evanston, Illinois. I dated beautiful blond girls and they liked me. They were all high school girls.

"When I came to Los Angeles, I was going to housewarming parties that lasted 20 days. I had a nice life. I've always claimed that I was a wholesome person. I didn't do drugs. I barely drank liquor."

"Did you date any contestants from the Miss Teen USA?"

"No. By that time, I was grown up. I married when I was 27 years old. My wife is also short. My daughter is tiny.

"One time we were driving in the car and listening to the radio. A report said that dwarfs are 4'10 or less. And my daughter said, 'Oh my God, I'm a dwarf.' But at that time she was 12. We did take her to a doctor to check on her height. He took one look at Sally and me and said, 'What do you expect?'

"But I used the plot for the Gary Coleman character in *Diff'rent Strokes*. I think I was helpful to Gary because I was a short guy who had obviously achieved something.

"My daughter (Jennifer Burton Worthy) is adorable. She stands about 5' high. She's successful. She's married with two kids and lives in Hillsborough in the San Francisco Bay Area. She's been a designer of upscale hotels. If you've been to Disneyworld in Orlando, Florida, she designed the beach resort. She designed Paris Disney. She designed the biggest hotel in San Francisco, the Hilton. Now she's the head of the architecture review board of Hillsborough.

"In 1962, I created the world's first exposition for teenagers, the Teenage World Fair. Tom Wolfe from Esquire magazine came to that fair and wrote about a car at the fair. His essay was called 'The Kandy-Colored Tangerine-Flaked Streamlined Baby.'

"We did the Teen Fair at the Hollywood Palladium. It went on to play at 50 cities around the US as well as Toronto and Tokyo.

"I met Norman [Lear]. I was doing a TV show called *Hollywood A-Go-Go*, which was syndicated worldwide. I had the Rolling Stones on, and Jan & Dean, the Beach Boys, Sonny & Cher, and the Beatles. The Beatles were in love with Ewa Aulin so they came down to the fair when it was in Detroit. Dominick Dunne worked on the show.

"We did five television shows out of the ten-day Teen Fair. We produced the Miss Teen USA and Miss Teen International pageants. We did television fashion shows. It was the pinnacle of the babyboom and they were just the hottest thing in the world."

"Did the messes of the 1960s spill over to your Teen Fair, with the drugs and riots and crime?"

"Yes it did. It may have been why I was ready to go join Norman Lear in 1972. In 1968, Martin Luther King was assassinated. Until that moment, the Teen Fair was totally out of knowing anything about Vietnam and drugs. Of, if it were, it never crossed my threshold of knowledge. Then King was killed and LA turned bad and negative.

"The Teen Fair was like Orange County. It was just out of the mainstream of anything that was really hip. We never had gangs. The joke about me was that I was chickenhip. It meant that I did a namby pamby bland event. In Detroit, we had a riot. Then in 1971, there was a murder and I stopped letting my kid go to the event.

"Norman came to me in 1966. He asked to have lunch with me. His opening question was: 'Where do you get the girls for *Hollywood A-Go-Go?*' I said that I got them from Gazzarris [hip nightclub on the Sunset strip]. Gazzarris had the greatest looking girls. By then I was a total expert on great looking girls. When they are out on the floor dancing, I, or one of my associates, would pick them and ask if they want to come on the show.

"I would send one of them, whose taste I could trust, to a place called Hole-in-the-Wall. I'd tell her to pick out outfits she liked that the girls could dance in. Norman thought they were just great. He said, 'I'm doing a special called *Where It's At* (1969) for ABC and I'd like you to be the casting director.' That was Dick Cavett's first hosting job.

"I took Bud Yorkin [Norman Lear's assistant] to meet a group in my office—the Mommas and the Poppas. They had never been on any show before. He turned them down.

"I came in to see Norman in 1972. He said he wanted to do a soap opera that played on two levels. I want people who like soap operas to get addicted to it, but I want people to call their friends after they see it and say there's something here you've got to see. Out of that conversation came *Mary Hartman, Mary Hartman.*

"I brought back a *Life* magazine about a couple bored to death on the job. It was about blue collar assembly-line workers. I said we should do this story but with good looking people. Gail Perrin wrote 27-pages but I rewrote her 27-pages and that was the beginning of the series. I was a smash. That got me out of the teenage business. I developed *Diff'rent Strokes, Facts of Life* (1979-88), *Square Pegs* (1982-83), *Silver Spoons* (1982-87)."

"To what do you attribute your success?"

"My serious answer is that I am an inveterate optimist. I can't get pessimistic or cynical. I can write cynical humor but I am not a cynic. I think the world is great.

"My others answers are that you should eat at Pinks a lot [hot dog stand on La Brea Blvd] and always stand to the right when they take your picture so your name will show up first in the caption. And write your own theme song for the shows you do.

"Alan Thicke introduced me to that. He and I wrote the themes to *Diff'rent Strokes, Facts of Life*. Then I did *Charles in Charge* and *Hollywood A-Go-Go*. My original ambition was to be a songwriter but then the world left me. In 1954, rock came in. Rock just killed the kind of songs that I wanted to write.

"I've developed a show called *White People*. Do you know the group called The Waitresses? They do the theme. They talk-sing. The theme goes, 'White people, white people. Pasty faced and pasty brained, should've had their gene pools drained. Scared your kid might date a Jew? Say hello to Abdul Abu.'

"The show is about three families in a cul-de-sac-Middle Eastern Arab, WASP and Jewish. Their kids intermix.

"The show *Facts of Life* was based on my girl's private school—the Westlake School for Girls. It was a spinoff. Do you want all this?"

"Yes."

"I still can't figure out what the point of your book will be."

"I figure it out as I go along."

"I apologize for interfering with your journalism.

"We did *Diff'rent Strokes*. It was a shocking instant hit. Within the cast we had the wonderful character actress Charlotte Ray. I went to school with her. Charlotte was so well received by the audience that NBC, in desperate need of programming, said get us a show with Charlotte quick.

"I got to Charlotte and handed to Norman and two writers the idea for a show about a private girls school with uniformed girls, well to do, or charity cases. I changed the name of the school to Westland. Then Standards and Practices changed it to Eastland.

"We scouted the school. I take Charlotte to lunch with the girls. In the hall of Westlake, they're all beauties like my teenage beauty pageant. They're all gorgeous. Charlotte spots this stout little girl Mindy Cohn off to the side who was getting laughs at the table. We pull her over to our table. Charlotte pitches her to be on the show.

"I met with her mother and of course she wanted her to do it, but I didn't want to louse the kid up and make her a Hollywood kid. I didn't want her to get a Hollywood education. I wanted her to get a Westlake education. So we got permission from the school board to make one exception for Mindy. We cut her hours down so she could continue to go to Westlake and get a decent education.

"Hollywood kids don't get a decent education. There aren't enough strictures."

Born May 20, 1966, Mindy got her degree in sociology from Loyola Marymount in 1995.

"How did the Harvard school react to the show?"

"They loved it. There was never a complaint."

"Tell me about Dana Plato and *Diff'rent Strokes*."

"I discovered Dana Plato at a dance group. We were looking for a girl for the show *Hello Larry.*

"E!'s *True Hollywood Story* on Dana used tape from the show *Diff'rent Strokes* when we were all sitting together. Dana at the time is under the influence of something and is fuzzy when she recounts her story of how I found her.

"I called Dana in and she was just fabulous. She was 13 years old. I didn't check her lineage well enough. Her mother was mentally ill.

"She was not that necessary to the show but she was adorable. When she was 16, it was clear that she was under the influence of something. We couldn't tell whether it was mother, manager or agent. We dropped her from the show in its last year because she got pregnant. She didn't know that it was wrong to get pregnant. That gives you an idea about the problems that that kid had.

"I bumped into her a few years later after she'd done a layout for *Playboy*. She said, 'Can you imagine? Todd Bridges is in jail. Gary is suing his parents and I just posed for Playboy. Mr. Drummond is a terrible father.' It's a great line. It's a gag writer's line that came out of her mouth.

"I was not paying attention to her when she died. I helped Todd Bridges at one point when he was in jail. I tried to help her and she would have none of it. I said, 'Dana, come in. I'll find you something.' I got Todd a job on *Lassie* but she turned me down.

"Todd today is fine. He's financed by a church group. I've done some jokes with Gary Coleman. Gary gets sporadic work. He's self-destructive. Todd is not. He's just got a tough road to hoe.

"In my early days of *Tele-Teen Reporter*, I had a cute girl on the show who was an acrobat. She danced. She's cartwheeling on live television and a falsie falls out.

The camera goes to the falsie and just hangs there. I am so upset. I'm Mr. Clean and I don't want to upset anybody.

"The girl's name is Joy Vogelsang. I believe that she grew up to be a choreographer and a dancer. I've never talked to her since. She's the mother of Nicholas Cage."

"What do you think about beauty pageants for kids five years old?"

"I'm against them. My consciousness was also raised in the 1970s when I went to work for Norman Lear. Norman Lear's consciousness was raised beyond consciousness. I didn't do anything after 1973 that would've been exploitation.

"I did an episode of *Charles in Charge* where I extolled the virtues of being in a beauty pageant. I thought somebody should. The truth is that young women who get into beauty pageants, their self esteem is raised, even if they don't win. I have enough personal experience to tell you that if a girl in a high school in Oklahoma gets into the Miss Teen USA pageant, and then gets sent home because she only came in 40th, she's referred to as Miss Teen USA in her home town. Time and time again they call girls who get into the pageant as Miss Teen USA in their home town.

"There were two daughters in *Charles in Charge*. The younger one enters the pageant. The older one, by far the greatest beauty on the show, was so against her little sister entering the pageant because it was exploitative, a meat market, etc. Somehow we got the message across that it did the younger one a world of good to be in the pageant. She got attention. She got recognized over her older sister.

"I don't think I'd operate a pageant in the same way. I'd score Olympic style and it would have to be on not just beauty but comeliness, presentation. In the days I did it, I blatantly went for beauty. We didn't give a scholarship. We gave money and a car. I didn't know there was anything wrong with that."

"Would you have allowed your own daughter to participate in a beauty pageant?"

"Yes. Not when she was nine, but when she was 14. Yeah, because I saw it was a great confidence builder. The excellence of beauty pageants is that they have experts in extolling the virtues of being in good health, fit and looking great.

"I did a show two years ago with Norman [Lear]. It was called *The Big Pitch*. We sold it to 20th Century Fox. It was never aired."

"It sounds like Bob Kosberg."

"I know him from so long ago. He's an operator. He's really an operator. I'm in awe of him. He was too high powered for me."

"Too intense."

"Yeah. I like a calm life. I like to enjoy my life. I can't imagine his marriage situation."

"He's married."

"For a long time?"

"Yes."

"God love him. I may be wrong. But he was one of those who I thought was too peripatetic to have a family. I'm family oriented. I would not let television or a deal interfere with my family. So sometimes I don't do something. I don't shoot in Vancouver, British Columbia. I'm very impressed with him but I want to keep my belt fastened."

"How did working for Norman Lear change you?"

"I have a picture from a company picnic we went to with Norman. My assistant, who was then called 'secretary,' came wearing my credit on a T-shirt on her chest. It said, 'Developed by Al Burton.' When I show that picture today, I realize that I would not do that today.

"He made me understand that there was such a thing as sexual harassment, though we were all guilty, including Norman. In 1975, you didn't know it was wrong to pat a girl. You didn't know it was wrong to hold on to a girl in your office. You certainly didn't know that there are some girls you don't hug and some girls you don't kiss. Because we were huggers, kissers, touchers all the time.

"Norman employed certain people who started telling us, 'I'm not comfortable with this.' In the old days, none of this touching was considered bad. Now it would be considered offensive sexual harassment."

"In many ways, you had more freedom 30 years ago."

"Are you kidding? A man had more freedom. I wouldn't say a woman had more freedom."

"Why wouldn't a woman have more freedom too? She could object back then."

"That's the nub of the argument. There are women who say, 'You think we could've spoken up, but if we said anything, we would've been regarded as troublemakers.' Political correctness has some basis in fact. And if you were black or Chinese...I am Jewish. Somehow Jews grow up knowing they are going to be harassed.

"Norman was an extremely civicly conscious man. I wasn't. I'm not an ideologue. I understand that you're supposed to be supportive of certain causes. The one that I focus on because of Sally is animals. We're major animal-rights people. Norman was the most ethical businessman that I've ever worked with."

"Your overall experience with the television industry sounds like a positive one."

"Totally positive. I'm sure I've been ripped off through the years many times. But I've lost an idea. I can get another idea. So that's why I am not cynical. Producer Arnold Shapiro has a cartoon on his wall. One guy says, 'I see the glass half empty.' Another guy says, 'I see the glass half full.' I'm saying, 'I see the glass overflowing all the time.'

"I've been married over 40 years. We have one kid. At the time we had our first baby, we didn't want to stop traveling. We figured that the second baby would force Sally to stay home."

50

Harry Ufland

June 11, 2002

"I was born (around 1936) and raised in New York City. I attended PS (Public School) 187. I went to Columbia for two years.

"My brother was a publicist. My aunt worked for Shuberts theatre. She used to come to dinner Friday night with tons of movie star pictures. My father was in the textile business. I went into the army for two years, 1956-58. I then started in the William Morris mailroom at $35 a week. There were half a dozen Phi Betta Kappas [elite students] in the mailroom. That kind of training doesn't happen anymore.

"I remember bringing something over to an actress at her home and she offered me a dollar. I turned it down. She said, 'I know how much money you make. Take it.' So I did.

"Ever since I knew I couldn't play professional baseball, I've wanted to be a producer. I thought that would be the way to do it. Little did I know that I'd be an agent for 23 years first.

"I started an industrial films department, which no other agents had. I signed director Marty Scorsese and actor Robert De Niro in New York. William Morris asked me to move to Los Angeles in 1972. It was much more corporate. They tried to get us to wear ties. Marty Scorsese's film *Mean Streets* (1973) was playing at Lincoln Center and William Morris wouldn't pay for me to go see it.

"I got a call from Freddie Fields and Guy McElwaine, asking me to join their agency CMA (which became ICM). They made me an offer that was considerably more than I was making. That was great until they sold the company to Marvin Josephson in 1974. I never liked Marvin. In 1976, I left and set up my own agency, The Ufland Agency. I represented Marty Scorsese, Bob De Niro, Adriane Lyne, Ridley and Tony Scott, Peter Bogdanovich, Harvey Keitel, Roger Donaldson [and Jodie Foster]. I burned out. I had a dozen employees. It was a large small agency."

Ufland is tightly coiled. I can sense the volcanic temper just below his surface. He's known around town for screaming at people over the most petty matters.

Many producers, including Dino De Laurentiis, tried to go around him to the stars he represented.

"I helped a friend of mine, Joe Roth, get started in Los Angeles. I'd met him in New York. We had lunch at Le Dome one day on Sunset Blvd. I said I couldn't stand what I was doing. His suggestion was that we partner up on a production company. We couldn't get out of our own way at the beginning. They weren't wonderful movies [that Harry produced and Joe directed, such as *Moving Violations* (1985), *Off Beat* (1986), *Where the River Runs Black* (1986), and *Streets of Gold* (1986).] We folded the agency into a management company and then phased out all the clients except Marty and Bob. I found myself reading their stuff before mine. I thought that if I ever really wanted to do it [as a producer], I had to really do it. So I set Marty and Bob up at CAA.

"Mary Jane joined our company as vice-president. The minute she walked in, I thought we'd get married. And we did in 1985.

"What did you think of Peter Biskind's book about 1970s Hollywood, *Easy Riders, Raging Bulls?*"

"I didn't read it. I heard about it from friends. He was silly not to call me. He would've gotten great stuff about Marty if he'd phoned me. I thought he was foolish not to. A lot of these things are not well researched. People write them with their opinions, which they had beforehand and they don't want to be deterred."

"How did you get hooked up with *The Last Temptation of Christ* (1988)."

"It'd been Marty's obsession since *Boxcar Bertha* days (1972) when Barbara Hershey told him about the [novel by Nikos Kazantzakis]."

"You loved the novel?"

"Yes. We knew it was controversial. We didn't dream that this stuff would happen."

"I don't understand why you didn't understand that there would be that much fury."

"Now it is easy to look back and see how organized they were. They were so unbelievably organized. They were selling anti-*Last Temptation* kits. All the letters were the same. They were form letters. These people, not only had they not seen the movie but they hadn't read the book.

"When you think about it, Marty is so deeply religious."

"He is?"

"Yes."

"Didn't you realize this was a sensitive topic? You're dealing with a guy who is regarded as God by two billion people."

"We realized it was a sensitive topic. People didn't really know right-wing fundamentalism at that point. You'd be silly not to know that something like that could happen now. The orchestration of the campaign was just amazing. I remember driving out to Universal one day and they had Southern California kids in shorts who they paid to hand out leaflets and to demonstrate. Who dreamed that would happen?

"I had sold it to Tom Pollock [at Universal]. He had been our lawyer. They had the guts to buy and to make it and then at the end they chose to let it go. Wasserman's house was threatened. These people really went to town.

"Universal opened the movie without any fanfare. Unfortunately, the people who wanted to see it, went to see it in the first week or so. The rest got afraid. They didn't want to go to the movies and risk getting blown up.

"During the time that Barry Diller [at Paramount] put it in turnaround, and we went around town trying to set it up, we felt that whatever move we made, something was ahead of us. We found out that Salah M. Hassanein, the head of UA Theaters who worked for [movie magnate] Marshal Naify, a Muslim, told studios that if they did anything to get this movie made, their movies wouldn't play at his theaters.

"Salah hadn't read the book. He assumed this would be an anti-religious picture. The book is a deeply religious book. It is certainly not an anti-Christ book.

"Joe Roth is married to Sam Arkoff's daughter. We knew that Sam knew Salah Hassanein. We couldn't get to him so Sam got to him for us.

"We were in New York. Salah Hassanein sent a van to pick us up. So Marty, Joe and I went out in this unmarked white van. He was charming. He admitted he hadn't read the book. He said something that I will never forget. 'You don't understand. You make the movies. They don't come to your theater and destroy the theater.'

"He was basing that on a movie called *Messenger of God* [about the Islam prophet Mohammed]. And they destroyed the theater.

"I said to Salah, 'I don't care if you hate the movie but let us get it made. Please don't follow us around and tell people not to do it. Then do what you want when the movie is made.' And he promised to back off."

"What was the key to getting the movie made?"

"Tom Pollock stood up for it. They [Universal] wanted to be in business with Marty. Whenever you get a controversial movie made at a studio, you have to have someone who will stand up and say, 'I want this movie.' The same thing happened when we did *Not Without My Daughter* (1991). There was a lot of nonsense about that too.

"Marty never went over budget. I thought it was a good picture."

"How did Universal react to the firestorm of criticism?"

"Badly. That's easy for me to say. I didn't run the company."

"So what did they do? They just didn't put much into advertising? They just let it die?"

"Pretty much. They could make a case for saying that the business wasn't there. And I don't think the business was there. But I think it could've been.

"People thought they could get hurt by going to see it. And there were enough bomb threats to justify that fear. It's a lesser version of the aftermath of 9/11 when people didn't want to fly."

"What did you love about the film?"

"I'm prejudiced because I know how much it meant to Marty. For me, the idea of presenting Jesus as an ordinary person was an extraordinary thing to be able to do."

"Do you have a Christian background? Are you Jewish."

"I am Jewish. I was not raised religious."

"What was your role on the film?"

"We seem to be going far afield from producing. There are things about that that I just don't want to go into."

"Tell me about *Not Without My Daughter*."

"We were sent the manuscript of the book (by a book agent at William Morris) as it was being written. The book and the movie came out at the same time, the same time as the Persian Gulf war and we were accused of trying to exploit the war. Like we knew that the war was going to happen at that time.

"It's so tough to get a movie made. It wasn't nearly what I thought it might be. It's a flawed movie."

"What happened?"

"We had a bad director [Brian Gilbert]. Even though it was a flawed movie, we still run into people at parties who love that movie. Particularly women."

"How did you get the movie green lit?"

"When Sally Fields signed on. Although I think [MGM studio executive] Alan Ladd would've made it without her. It was Ladd's suggestion that we go with Brian Gilbert as director. Brian rewrote the script and it was his version that got it made.

"We shot in Israel using the production services of Globus [owned then by Menahem Goland and Yoram Dohan]. That was something. We worked with a guy named Itzik Kol, who was a charming rogue. He was sharp and funny and fat. He wore jeans with suspenders. We lived in Israel for almost a year. There are people we met on that shoot who've remained lifelong friends.

"Living in Israel is different from going on one of those five-day junkets. When you go on a five-day trip, everything you see is wonderful. When you live there, you see what's wrong with it."

"Tell me about 1993's *Freaked*."

"Alex Winter and Tom Stern came to us with it. Mary Jane, Joe Roth and I thought it was their thing, their vision, it's not going to cost much, so let's back it. It is a flawed movie. Some of it is very funny. That was probably the nicest time we ever had on a movie. Everybody rolled up their sleeves. We funded it partially through Fox and partially through private funds. We had to make a speech before the crew that we didn't have the money now but we will work it out. And everybody stayed and worked for nothing.

"Movie crews are extraordinary. They want to help. I have never seen a crew that doesn't want to help. The only thing that turns them are foolish producers and directors who just won't acknowledge them. I've said to directors, 'Do you know the names of anybody? Why don't you just acknowledge them?' It's extraordinary that some directors get so into their own head, that they don't acknowledge anybody."

"Tell me about *One True Thing* (1998)."

"I was given the book [by Anna Quindlen] and I just loved it. My wife and I love true stories [this novel was based on Quindlen's life]. The movie disappointed me. You are happy to have gotten it made. But the process can you take you to a place you don't want to be. Everybody sees things differently. The movie that Karen [Croner, screenwriter] and I wanted to make is not the movie got made."

"You worked with Kathleen Kennedy and Frank Marshall on 1999's *Snow Falling on Cedars*. They are regarded as the top producing team in the business."

Harry rolls his eyes. "Good for them. And good for the people who regard them as such."

"Tell me about your 2001 movie *Crazy/Beautiful*."

"Oh God. Mary Jane and I went in to see [studio executive] Todd Garner. He said he didn't want to do another comedy. He wanted to do a melodrama about high school kids. So we met with a bunch of writers and started thinking about what we wanted to do and we came up with the thought that it would be terrific to have a good Latino kid and a bad white girl. We went with two young writers we liked a lot [Phil Hay and Matt Manfredi]. Then we went through the process of getting a director. [President of Disney's movie division] Nina Jacobson insisted on John Stockwell."

Harry's voice has turned grim.

"Were you pleased with the final result?"

"No. I thought it was very flawed. It was not the movie we set out to make. The movie I wanted to make was about his dreams and it no longer is. The whole experience was a disappointing experience."

"That's common theme through our conversation. These movies are breaking your heart."

Harry laughs. "My little boy asked when I'm going to make a movie I like. I said, 'If you ever like them, they start getting worse.' People see things differently. Because of availabilities and everybody having different opinions, you get to make movies with people you'd probably prefer not to make them with."

"When did you sense the project getting away from you."

"When Nina insisted on John Stockwell."

"Have you agreed with the direction of any of your directors, aside from Scorsese?"

"That's part of the problem. When you grow up in this business with perhaps the best director in the world, it makes it hard to work with people who are significantly less. The reasons that these movies happen is so strange. Disney decided they wanted something and were willing to go with somebody they shouldn't have gone with. Nina liked him. She's entitled to like him but everybody does have different taste. I would always want to shoot higher. When you're working with Marty or people I used to represent like Ridley Scott, you are working with guys who are really talented."

"Are you pleased with the final result of any of your films?"

"No, I think they all could've been much better. There are so many people involved in the process that it has hurt the final result."

"I hear that in features the director is the king."

"I'll never forget the first day of shooting *Not Without My Daughter*. When director Brian Gilbert said 'Action,' behind me Alan Ladd and Jay Kanter [MGM/Pathe studio executives] said, 'The ship has sailed.' It turned out to be true. The studio today does back the director unless he goes wildly over budget. It becomes hard once you start shooting to do anything."

"Do you sense that the producer today has less power than when you were an agent?"

"Much less power unless you are a Jerry Bruckheimer."

"How do you and your wife divide up your roles?"

"Mary Jane is extraordinary with writers. She has enormous focus and patience. She's the fastest reader I know. I'm a bird dog in getting the material and getting the deals made. I also have a good ability at picking new directors, . which is what I did as an agent. We both have to like it to pursue a project and we work on it together.

"I can get along well with writers. I don't like an hour meeting taking six hours. I don't have the patience."

"Is it good for a marriage to work so closely together?"

"I think it is great. Dick Zanuck and Lili Zanuck are close friends of ours. They've done it and it's been great. Lauren Shuler and Dick Donner."

"Has being a father changed you as a movie producer?"

"Yes. I had five kids in my first marriage but it was a different time because I was on my way up. Mary Jane and I have a wonderful ten-year old boy who is one of the main reasons we work from home, so we can be around him. We're always talking about making movies that he can see. Not that I would ever want to come away from the tougher pieces we have done."

"Have you ever worked on a film that has changed you?"

Harry pauses. "That's a good question."

He turns to his wife. "Mary Jane, Luke has just asked me if we've ever worked on a film that has changed us, has changed me."

Mary Jane makes an inaudible comment and Harry gives a cynical laugh.

"Mary Jane says that each one leaves an imprint. My answer to that would have to be *Last Temptation* because it showed me that you never give up. That took 18 years. If you believe in it, you have to stay with it. The speed mentality of weekend grosses and then go on is not who we are. If there's a fault, it's probably that we work on them too long."

"Was it worth the trouble?"

"Oh yeah. It was worth it because it was something Marty had to do. And my devotion was to him and I would do anything to help him realize his desire to make that movie.

"We're doing a complicated script now based on the Jerry Spence book *Going For Justice*. It's a case that Jerry had 25 years ago. A friend of his was blown up by a bomb set by a psychopathic maniac. Jerry took the case as a prosecutor. And he's vehemently against the death penalty. And this case became a death penalty case. It's the case in his life. I hope we get to make it. It gets tougher to talk these people [financiers a.k.a. studios] into something of value. And every time there's a *Spiderman* [smash hit], then it makes it worse. People don't realize it. They think it is good for the movie business. I think it is terrible for the movie business."

"You seem to be primarily a story-driven producer."

"Characters drive us. Even though we say, 'Gosh, we've got to get out of this true-story thing because it is so hard to do them,' we do like them."

"I find Martin Scorsese's films disturbing."

"That is the reason the numbers haven't been greater. But a lot of life is. Marty's movies are very real and you get an experience from those that you don't get from anybody else."

"Your least favorite parts of your job?"

"Shooting is not exciting. Going to studios. Driving to studios bothers me, and then having to sit with all those people. The process of selling a movie is extremely frustrating. It's out of both sides of the mouth all the time. 'We think this should open the third weekend in July.' Then, two minutes later, 'We think the best time would be the second weekend in February.' There's no rhyme or reason for any of it. I find the process of using testing insanity.

"I'll never forget the time I was representing Bob [Robert DeNiro] and we were out testing *Deerhunter*. In Detroit, the projection broke and the thing was a disaster. All the Universal people weren't talking to us. And the next night in Chicago, everybody loved the movie so we were all best friends again."

51

Brian Reilly

June 20, 2002

"I grew up in Manhasset, Long Island, a suburb of Manhattan. I have two brothers and a sister. We went to a private Catholic school for 12 years. I hated it. It was the birthplace of my rebellion against authority.

"Wanting to do something meaningful, I got a job at NBC News at 30 Rockefeller Dr in New York. I was a film editing assistant. I was there for two years. I then worked freelance production in Manhattan for a few years. Then I met the Madison brothers. These two filmmakers had made a marvelous documentary about the effects of architecture on children's self worth. I thought this was great. This is what I wanted to do. I want to make these kinds of stories. I went into business with these two talented filmmakers and seven years later, I'd produced a ton of television commercials and no documentaries.

"I made some money at real estate ventures. I wrote a few screenplays but they were bad. I was such an inveterate New Yorker that I never considered going to California. I had a summer place in Amaganset where I met the wonderful woman [Barra Grant, daughter of 1945 Miss America Bess Myerson] who became my wife. We got married in 1982 and moved to Los Angeles in 1983.

"I didn't know what I was going to do. Having television commercial credits doesn't mean much to the people in the motion picture business. In my New York career, I had sold a lot of soap. Now it was time to learn how to make a movie.

"I took a number of film and screenplay courses at UCLA and began to read as many screenplays as I could. I met as many people in the industry as I could. A friend from New York introduced me to Bobbie Newmyer, who was leaving Columbia Pictures to produce independently. I had some money, which is a good thing for someone who wants to be a producer. It's hard to make money right away.

337

"Before long I found a script called *The Real World*, [which became 1991's *Don't Tell Mom the Babysitter's Dead*] which was in turnaround at Fox. We redeveloped the script and took it to Susan Cartsonis at Fox. Roger Birnbaum, who ran Fox at the time, told us we had to get certain elements, such as actress Christina Applegate to play the lead.

"It so happens that during my time in New York, I'd run a restaurant. I hired someone who became a good friend and successful actor [Ed O'Neill]. I went to Ed's TV show (*Married...With Children*, 1987-97) and he introduced me to Christina. The next Monday, Christina said she was interested. Big day! Then Fox gave us a short list of directors. Stephen Herek was on the list. He said yes. Another big day! On a Friday, Fox said they were going to make the movie. On Monday, they changed their minds. They had another family comedy (*Home Alone*, 1990) and they didn't want to compete with themselves when it came time to market the two films. This was a bad day. We ended up making it for about $10 million for Cinema Plus, part of HBO Films in New York. Subsequently, the Time/Warner deal came about and our little comedy became a Warner Brothers release and a box office success."

"Tell me about *The Santa Clause*, the third highest grossing film of 1994."

"Martin Spencer, an agent at CAA, sent it to me. I had never read anything like it. The premise was wildly original and very funny. I remember sitting at my desk and laughing out loud.

"The screenwriters had known Tim [Allen] from the comedy club circuit. Tim was a big star as a stand-up comedian. It so happened that the writer's manager and Tim Allen's managers were in business together at the time. Tim became aware of the script as we were about to submit the screenplay to the studios. To be honest, I would've never thought of Tim to star in the movie. We were thinking of people who were established movie actors. Meanwhile, we learned that Disney's Jeffrey Katzenberg was looking for a movie for Tim to star in. I asked to see some of his *Home Improvement* (1991-99) shows on tape. I remember sitting watching those shows and thinking, 'This guy could really do this.' He had the comedy chops in spades, and he was able to play emotional scenes. It was an exciting day."

"It was a challenge getting to know him because he's a guarded person. He had had so much success and he was brilliant as well as funny. But over time, we've developed a lasting friendship. He asked me to produce for him.

"We'd struggled over the script for *The Santa Claus 2* for two years and it still wasn't ready. When we postponed it, that created an opening in Tim's schedule. Fox's Tom Rothman wanted to put something together for Tim. They sent over a couple of projects. *Joe Somebody* (2001) offered Tim the opportunity to do something that he had never done before in the movies—to play a straight part. It was Fox's pursuit that made it happen."

"How did you feel about the material?"

"Conflicted. The original script needed to be a smaller movie. I was surprised by the level of money that was put into the movie. Fox had a vision of the movie that wasn't on the page. We had a reading and it wasn't that funny. It wasn't intended to be funny. The investors wanted the movie to be more of a comedy. We rushed to make the movie before the [proposed] strike. The studios wanted product in the pipeline. It was not the best environment for Tim to chart a new direction in his career."

"You worked with some powerful producers such as Arnon Milchan and Arnold Kopelson on that movie."

"That's part of the challenge. The original movie script presented to Tim was mostly a dark drama. Once the studio did the arithmetic on how much money was being spent to make this movie, they wanted to make a different movie. And to get their money back, they wanted to transform the script and make it into something it wasn't. Many writers were brought in. We all felt the need to be responsible to the studio's need to make a film that would appeal to a large, Tim Allen audience. Tim had signed on for one thing and the studio pressured him and everyone involved to make another movie. In the words of one of the studio execs, 'It was a classic bait and switch.'"

"The most harmful decision that robbed a lot of people of the opportunity to see the film was the release date, which was during the 2001 Christmas glut, on the same day as *The Lord of the Rings*. None of us who worked on the film ever thought it was a big family comedy for Christmas release, but that's what the studio wanted it to be. The release date doomed the prospects of the film making money."

"What was the message of the film?"

"This guy Joe chose badly with his first wife. She dusted him off when she found a younger man. She was immune to the fact that her daughter was witness to this. Joe lives a loveless life. The fight with the bully, in front of his daughter, wakes him up to the need to find something that will put passion in his life. Julie Bowen, the human resources manager, challenges him to take responsibility for his life. And ultimately what he wants in life is to be with her."

"What does the movie want you to think about Allen's desire to fight the bully?"

"Joe was fearful. The Jim Belushi character allows him to deal with that on a physical level. Joe comes prepared to fight. And with his working out and his training with Belushi, he would've beaten the bully. But that would've been a different way to go. Maybe it would have been a better way for the story to unfold. There was always a dilemma about what to do in the film because either way you can't win. By not fighting the bully, you are going to disappoint and anger much of the audience, particularly young guys. But there was another tack, to show that Joe had to earn the capacity to not fight the guy, and to make a statement that has an impact on the bully and on all the co-workers who cheered Joe on. It was always thought of as a high school drama with the adults behaving like teenagers and the pre-teen daughter behaving as the parent."

"If you were Joe Somebody, would you have fought the bully?"

"Probably. I think I would've fought him as soon as he hit me. I would've wanted to run him over."

"And would you have advised your son to fight back?"

"No. I'm not a fan of violence. It's a tough call. In the moment, I would want to get in the car and run the bastard over."

"I think the moral response is to fight back."

"I don't know if that is the moral response. Should human beings be hurting and killing other human beings? Stephen Hawking's greatest fear for the future of the planet is man's aggressive tendencies. I agree. What is the root of all the horrible things that happen on this planet? That men can't contain themselves. 'He hit me. I'm going to hit him harder.'"

"If you had a boy, and he was punched at school, would you teach him to punch back or to turn the other cheek?"

"I would certainly have him prepared to fight, certainly if it is in self defense and to avoid getting hurt. If a guy hits you and taunts you and it becomes a psychological game, then I hope a sense of self would prevail rather than the need to prove oneself. I think people show who they are in moments like that. That's where character is revealed. I could never give a hard and fast answer. There are too many gray areas. There are some people you have to hit. You shoot them if you need to."

"Were you bullied as a kid?"

"Everybody's bullied. As a teenager, I had a big guy come after me once because of a girl. He was drunk and I wasn't. It was a huge mistake on his part. I just got out of the way in plenty of time and he did the rest himself. He just kept flailing away and I would just take a little shot until he was exhausted."

"How did you get this niche of family producer?"

"It just happened. If you're lucky in life, you get to do what you want."

"Were you pleased with *Don Juan DeMarco* (1995)?"

"No. That's the single best script that was ill treated. There was so much complexity and wisdom in the writing. Johnny Depp was brilliant. The potential of that story was great. That's the one that's most troubling to me because it had the potential to be a great movie."

"Have you ever seen a movie that's changed you?"

"The first movie that made a significant impact on me was *Who's Afraid of Virginia Wolf?* starring Elizabeth Taylor and Richard Burton. They're drunk and always fighting. Movies before that were from the Mary Poppins world. I went, 'Oh boy, that's powerful. That's not just passive entertainment.' I'd seen *On the Waterfront* (1954) on television and I knew that movies could be that. It was an amazing experience to sit in a dark room and witness these raw emotions."

A few days later, Brian calls. "When's your deadline?"

"I don't have one. I'm still researching the book."

"How do make money?"

"I sold some writing a year ago and I'm living off that for the next two years."

"Are you one of those English eccentrics who can get by on a piece of string?"

"Exactly."

"When was the last time you picked up a meal for more than three people?"

"I can't remember."

"I'm the biggest producer you've got on your list."

"I've got Stephen J. Cannell, who's produced a billion dollars worth of TV programming."

"That's television shit."

"I interviewed Barnet Bain. He produced the $60 million Robin Williams film *What Dreams May Come*."

"Where's Sydney Pollock?"

"I haven't secured that interview yet."

"I want better names on the list before this book goes to press. You've got Edgar Scherick. That's a good name to list. People can't call him up and check with him about you because he's sick. You need some serious names. Now that you've got me, you can do better. Use me as your low point."

"You will be the rock upon which I build my book."

"Don't embarrass me now. Wear some clothes [unlike the Chabad 'I did a mitzvah for Israel' T-shirt I wore to his interview]. Look like you know what you're doing and that you got a check recently. Good luck."

52

Susan Cartsonis

June 20, 2002

"I grew up mostly in Arizona in a small town west of Phoenix, Litchfield Park. I spent two years of high school in Eastern Canada. My mother was a social worker and my father is an architect and urban planner. He helped plan the town I grew up in. I have four younger brothers and sisters. Organizing and taking care of them was my best training for being an executive in the movie business.

"I graduated high school at age 16. I got my bachelors in Theater from UCLA. I did a year of graduate work at UCLA in writing. Then I transferred to NYU (New York University) where I received a masters in Dramatic Writing.

"I got a job in New York reading scripts for Fox. At the end of nine months, Scott Rudin, then a young president of production at Fox [in Los Angeles], called me up. 'I really like this coverage you did. Why don't you come out to work for me?' I said, 'I don't know. I have a good life here. What would I be if I came out to LA?' I didn't want to be an assistant. He said, 'You could do research for me.' I blew him off. I think that made me more appealing.

"I was doing good work for him. I enjoyed my job of reading and being paid for my opinion. I didn't know the parameters for a readers job. I was coming up with ideas for movies and handing them over. If I found a book, I'd write a treatment for it. Scott took notice of that and he kept calling me. I said, 'I'm not coming to be an amorphous thing.' He said, 'What would it take to get you out here?' I said, 'You will have to make me an executive.' He said, 'OK, you're an executive.' I said, 'K, I'll be out in two weeks.'

"I came out. He still didn't know exactly what my job was. Nor did I know what my job was. I had a little dial phone, answer machine and an office. I had no assistant. I felt my way. I was on the bottom rung of the ladder but I was at least on the ladder. I started the day after Labor Day, 1986 and I stayed at Fox until the day after Labor Day, 1995 [when Susan was Senior Vice President of Production]."

"So, it was a good experience?"

"'Good' is not a word I would use, though there were good times. 'Interesting. Educational. Fascinating. Insane. Hilarious. A life-lesson.'"

"What do you love and hate about Hollywood?"

"I love the idea that groups of people come together to tell stories that are sometimes profound, or sometimes just unite us by making us laugh together. I love the fun of it. I love to be part of a business that can transport people. Sometimes I love the process. Sometimes I hate the process. Sometimes I like the result and sometimes I don't like the result. I love movies. I'm a great audience. I can watch a movie like somebody who's never had anything to do with making a movie and just enjoy it. I can enjoy most genres though extremely violent movies can take me out of it because I am so repulsed.

"I hate and love that the intense competitiveness of the business brings out the best and worst in people. You get to see what people are really made of. You learn who you want to spend your time with. I love dealing with smart people and there are a lot of smart people in this business. I hate the devaluation of writers and producers. They are taken for granted. Writers want to do their jobs well to make actors and directors look brilliant. People forget so quickly there was ever a writer. Producers, if they do their job well, make it appear that there was never a producer on the movie.

"What I hate most in Hollywood is the blatant self promotion. It was ingrained in me since I was a small child that that is evil and abhorrent. I work for three Midwestern guys and I find that they are soft spoken and lead with their talent, rather than drawing attention to themselves. The sad thing is that talent doesn't always immediately draw attention and publicity can be an effective tool. I don't know what so disturbs me about self promotion. It's probably deeply psychological."

"What's the polite way of saying, 'Let's see who swings the biggest male organ.'"

"I'm a woman. I don't have to do that. I see a lot of it. It makes me laugh. I'd like to think that as more women infiltrate the business, there will be less dick swinging and more collaboration."

"When did you last say, 'Love you babe.'"

"I don't say that. I come from a family where we didn't do that among each other so I would hardly say it to a stranger. If someone says it to me, I do feel the need to say it back. I can get the words out. My family tells me there's a certain amount of hyperbole in my speech. By Hollywood standards, I'm low on the scale."

"Do you find yourself telling people, 'I loved your last movie,' when you hated it?"

"Do I lie? I try hard not to. I try to lie only when it is about preserving somebody's feelings and to tell the truth when it is about business or something that will affect them in the long run. I don't like to be lied to. I love it when people tell me the truth, even when it is painful."

"What do you say after a screening when you hate the film?"

"If you publish this, I'm sunk and I will have to come up with something new. But I like to say, 'What an accomplishment! Congratulations.'

"You meet so many people in this business, especially as a studio executive, because you're essentially a banker and people come to you for money to finance their films. It's hard to remember who you've met and who you haven't met, so there's become this Hollywood ritual of saying, 'It's nice to see you,' instead of, 'It's nice to meet you.' Because, God forbid, somebody makes a mistake of saying, 'It's nice to meet you,' to someone they've already met.

"The people who've been around a while are really good at faking it. Faking it is something one has to both hate and admire. When I was a young executive, I once heard a famous Hollywood producer give notes [to a writer] on a script he hadn't read it. I knew he hadn't read it. He started out by saying, 'I love the idea. The first act is spectacular. I love the way the characters are developed. Then in the second act, it loses its way. Around page...' Then the writer chimed in, 'Around page 50?' The producer said, 'Exactly. From page 50 to 75, I lost sight of the focus of the story. The main character, what's his name?' 'Bob.' 'Bob! He just wasn't funny enough. He wasn't emotional enough. And there wasn't enough action. The ending was good but there was something missing.'

'At which point, the writer chimed in, 'Well, maybe this or this.' And the producer, 'Yes, yes.' The producer did a brilliant job of faking it because what he said could be applied to almost any script in the dead center of development and not quite ready for production. Every script needs help with the second act. Every script can have a better ending. Most scripts are good in the first act. It was the most wonderful, incredibly inspiring, episode of bullshitting that I've ever seen in my life.

"Then, I had another meeting with the same producer with a writer who was experienced and had won an Academy Award. I wondered, how is he going to get out of this one? How will he pull the wool over the writer's eyes? This time the producer had read it. Whenever the producer would give a note, the writer would have ten questions, narrowing and honing in on what exactly the problem was. The writer was like an experienced shrink trying to get to the core of a problem, or somebody running a focus group after the marketing screening of a movie. This writer was incredibly astute. I thought, 'If I ever become a writer, I will want to do exactly what this writer did.'"

"Have the movies you've produced and developed turned out as you envisioned?"

"No, they've all turned out differently. In some cases it was most painful. My time at the studio inured me to it. I learned that yes, it is a collaborative process and it is led by a director's vision. Once you sign on with a director, you've made your bed. Then you just go with it and see what it is going to become. It's like having a baby [Susan has no children]. You don't know how a baby is going to turn out."

"Were you happy with *What Women Want* (2000)?"

"I'd be an ingrate to say that I was anything less than happy with the way that the movie turned out. Every producer dreams of a movie as successful as *What Women Want*. It was a short development process to the release of the film—three years. The writers came up with such an original idea that they executed wonderfully. Director Nancy Myers shaped it and made it more sophisticated. Who could ask for a greater gift than Mel Gibson in a movie? He's a gift to the audience because he's a pleasure to watch, and charming and willing to try anything on screen and afraid to throw himself into the fray. He's a gift to producers because he sets a tone on the set. He's incredibly professional and has no snobbery. Everyone is to be dealt with with respect. *What Women Want* is the highest grossing romantic comedy ever."

"You said in a 1997 interview with *Variety*, 'We are defined by our choices, so we've opted to handle material that means something to all of us. It doesn't matter if the project is a cable movie or a full-length feature. All that matters is the message.' What did you mean by that?"

"I don't know. It sounds like meaningless hype. If there were ever a message that I'd want to convey, it would be about humanity, whether it's a broad stupid comedy or a dark sensitive drama. What does it mean to be a human?"

"Do you guys talk about message?"

"Never."

"What words do you use instead of message?"

"Nothing like that. I don't know what I was thinking. That was five years ago."

"We do ask ourselves what's the movie about. What's the story we're trying to tell. What's the lead character trying to do."

"Are there messages you don't want to send?"

"If it is saying something disgusting or drag people down and make them want to commit suicide, yes, we'd ask questions about it."

"Has that come up?"

"We've been offered projects that are too dark. We ask ourselves, 'Why would anyone want come to see this? Why would we want to spend years of our lives making this?'"

"Do you need to relate to the movies you make?"

"Yes, in a visceral way. I don't think I could get financing for a film unless I was excited about it."

"So you loved all 20 projects you developed at Fox?"

"I loved every one of them. There was something about each of them that spoke to me."

"Have you worked on a film that's changed you?"

"Yes. The first film I was thrown into at Fox—*How I Got Into College* (1989). It was another executive's movie. He got sick. I was asked to take it over. It was tremendously troubled. The director was replaced [credited director is Savage Steve Holland]. There wasn't enough money to finish it. There were production problems. I learned how to be a producer and how to create comedy from nothing.

"*For The Boys* (1991). I worked on it with Bette Midler, [producer] Bonnie Bruckheimer and [producer] Margaret South. There were a couple of creative choices made on the film just to be expedient in getting it out there that were not the right ones. The movie came out the same week as the Gulf War and nobody had a stomach for a war movie. The movie tanked. And the lesson for me was that it would've been better to wait for the casting to come together in a better way.

"*Buffy the Vampire Slayer* (1992) changed my life. I thought we were just making a cute mixed-genre movie. A short time after it came out, I realized that it was a cultural phenomenon. It sent a message to young women that you could be both cute and powerful. I speak at NYU from time to time and girls in their early 20s say, 'That movie changed my life.'

"*The Truth About Cats and Dogs* (1996). We had a tough production. I spent a lot of time on the set. I rolled up my sleeves and worked side-by-side with the producer and the director to help out. It was the kind of detailed work that executives don't normally do. Somebody on set said to me, 'Susan, I've never seen an executive do what you did.' That sent a message to me that I shouldn't be doing what I was doing. That I should be a producer. That wasn't a compliment. That was somebody telling me that I was doing the wrong thing. It was a huge moment of change for me.

"I'm much happier working as a producer. I went through six regime changes at Fox. They were fascinating but grueling.

"The most profound experience was working on *Where the Heart Is* (2000). It was a book that I read while working at Fox. I fell in love with it and saw the movie in my head. There's something about the story that taps into my own experience."

"Stan [Seidel, Susan's late husband] and I joked that *Where the Heart is* and *One Night at McCools* (2001) made at the same time, were the same movie. They were the story of a young girl who wants more than anything else to have a home of her own, and goes to any lengths to achieve it. *Firelight* (1997) is about the same thing. A woman unanchored looks for a home. She finds a family in this unusual way.

"*Where the Heart is* changed my life. It was the first time that I was a full-time on-set producer. It was stressful because we made the movie independently. We only had four weeks of preparation. We had a first-time director [Matt Williams]. It was grueling. The heat in Austin, Texas, was intense. The personalities on the set were intense. Matt had a vision of the movie fueled by his personal experience that helped rally the troups and got us through the process. Everyone shared a passion for telling the story. The script by Lowell Ganz and Babloo Mandel was great, and though the shoot was hard, everyone felt a part of something special."

"How have you kept your moral compass on due north?"

"I made a decision in the first year that I came to LA as an executive. I looked around at the people in senior positions and asked, 'Who do I want to be? How do I want to succeed? On what terms do I want to succeed? On what terms will success be meaningful to me?' I made decisions about how I would and how I wouldn't behave. I had a good sounding board in Stan.

"I decided that I wasn't going to suffer over losing a project or fight with a colleague. If I did my work that which was meant for me would come to me.

"If you don't make a conscious choice to keep your compass on due north, you will slip into telling yourself lies. If you are able to lie to yourself too well, you won't be able to tell the truth about character and stories."

"I've heard that females are particularly suited for producing because it is a nurturing position."

"True. Some men have those qualities too. Women are trained from an early age to collaborate and there's a natural nurturing quality that women have that lends itself to producing."

"Why do you think Hollywood is so afraid of stories involving organized religion?"

"I don't know. I've never been a member of an organized religion. I've often wondered why Jewish executives are so afraid of Jewish material. That was a very strong feeling in me when I was starting out but with movies like *Schindler's List* that's lifted. Maybe organized religion feels exclusive. Movies about a specific faith may shut out large parts of the audience that are not in that faith. Maybe it's a marketing decision."

"When PG-rated films make more money than R-rated ones, why does Hollywood produce so many R-rated films?"

"Maybe because human experience is R-rated. Oedipus acted out on the screen in a contemporary way. Do you think it would be PG-13? I don't think so."

53

Hillard Elkins

June 25, 2003

A short elegant American with a small carefully shaved beard, tuffs of white hair, and an occasional British accent, Hilly strikes me as smart, energetic and tenacious.

He works in a home office covered with posters, photos and memorabilia from his career.

Born October 18, 1929 on Eastern Parkway in Brooklyn, Hilly ran with a gang as a kid. He was knifed a couple of times. He spent time in a reformatory school after forging a check for $500.

"While attending law school, I went to work at William Morris as an office boy. Within five months, I was working as an agent, and then as head of the theatrical department. Then I was drafted. I did my time in the Korean War by making various training films in Manhattan. I returned to the agency business. I didn't like it.

"I started my management company in the 1950s when most managers wore black pinky rings and fixed the lights in Las Vegas. At this time, actors, directors and writers didn't have managers. I started something unique. That was then and this is now when you can't walk out the door without tripping over managers, most of whom I wouldn't let do my laundry, let alone my career.

"I represented such actors as James Coburn and Robert Culp (who are still clients), Steve McQueen, Mel Brooks, Herb Ross, as well as Charles Strouse and Lee Adams, who ultimately wrote score to the musical '*Bye Bye Birdie*. I subsequently hired him to write the score for *Golden Boy*."

"How did you meet Claire Bloom?"

"I knew Claire and [her husband of the time] Rod [Steiger] for years. If you were in film or theater in New York, you hung out. I was on my third marriage at the time, which was breaking up. Rod invited me to have dinner with Claire and him. Rod was preparing to go to Europe to do a film. He said to me, 'Look after her.' I don't think that what resulted was what he had in mind. Claire and I became involved and fell in love and got married. The marriage lasted five years [1969-74]."

"Does she mention you in her book?"

"Oh boy, does she!"

Hilly opens a drawer. "I will show you something. I won't give it to you but you won't find it anyplace else. I find it amusing. The London papers have a tendency to go over the top."

Hilly pulls out a photocopy of a newspaper article with this large headline: "Hilly stole me for a willing partner in his dark sexual games."

"That was totally untrue, but the size of the headline would make you think it was World War III.

"[Director] Arthur Penn was a close friend of Elaine May [actress, director]. I adored Elaine. She asked me to read a screenplay she had written [*A New Leaf*, 1971]. I read her script and liked it. She hadn't been able to get it on. I offered to produce it. With her help, I got Walter Matthau interested in starring.

"It was Elaine's first film. Her first cut was long. With the help of Bob Evans, who was running Paramount, we reedited the film. It was released and got good reviews and good box office. Elaine wanted to sue for damages. I said, 'What damages? You got good reviews and we're going to make a good deal of money.'"

"Edgar Scherick told me Elaine May was a handful."

"He's right. She's brilliant and a handful."

"*Oh! Calcutta!*"

"Ken Tynan [conceivor of *Oh! Calcutta!*] was a friend of mine. He'd wanted to put on the show in London but Lord Chamberlain, the censor, would not allow it to go on.

"I represented director Jacques Levy, who Ken wanted to direct the show.

"Ken wasn't feeling well. I suggested he could stay at my house [in New York] until he was feeling better. I went to California to close a film deal on *The Rothschilds*.

"The trip was a short one. We didn't close the deal. When I returned to New York, I stayed at a hotel so I wouldn't disturb Tynan in my house.

"Tynan went to David Merrick to produce *Oh! Calcutta!* in New York. David wanted total control so the deal didn't happen. I said I'd be delighted to produce the play. It opened in May of 1969.

"I raised $200,000 to stage the play. I used some of my own money.

"While we were in rehearsal, I was able to get a list of the people who were going to be on the Johnny Carson Show, which then came out of New York. I invited them to see the show. Some of them said it was marvelous. Some of them said it was a terrible piece of sexual crap. Whatever they said sold tickets.

"Once we opened the show, we got the worst set of reviews in the history of show business. I had a party at Sardis. I called Claire in London with the reviews. She started crying. I said, 'Don't cry. It will be fine.' I decided that if I were going to go out, I'd go out with a bang rather than a whimper. In those days, theater tickets were $10. I raised the price to $25 a seat. I expected we'd run three nights and then we'd go home.

"Then the limos started rolling in. The people started coming. It became the talk of the town. We were on the cover of *Esquire* and *Time* and *Newsweek*. Fortunately, the mayor [John Lindsey] was an ally because there were an awful lot of people who wanted to close it. The show ran 20 years."

"Did it always have so much nudity?"

"Oh yes, we didn't change anything. The nudity was primarily in the dance. Nudity was an issue with Actors Equity. What [director] Jacques Levy did when we auditioned people, was first audition them as singers and dancers. If they qualified, he'd give them an improvisation which required them to take their clothes off. The better the actor, the less inhibited they were.

"When it came time for rehearsals, it was Jacques' idea to give them lockers for their clothes and blue robes, with *'Oh! Calcutta!'* on the back and their names on the front. They were terry robes that untie as you move about. On the first day or two, a lot of tying went on. By the fourth day, they didn't bother tying their robes. By the fifth day, they took their robes off. They took great pride in being able to work without clothes and not be self conscious. The opening number of the play was called, 'Taking off the robe.'

"This was a show about sex. It was not a show about politics or a comedy."

"How did you feel about the film version (1972)?"

"There was no film version. Some folks offered a good deal of money to show the piece in a limited number of theaters. So we videotaped the show. I warned them about the censorship they faced. They ignored the warning and were closed down in a fair number of theaters.

"I found a lab that could convert that to 35mm. I made a deal with the company and it went out theatrically. It made a fair amount of money. Of course they screwed me. If you do a show about screwing, you expect to be screwed."

"Let's talk about *The Rothschilds*."

"Everybody thought I was nuts to do a play about Jewish bankers. Hal Linden played Meyer Rothschild. Michael Kidd did the choreography and ultimately directed it. Jill Clayburgh had a small part. The show was a tremendous hit in LA and out of it Hal got [a role on the TV show] *Barney Miller* (1975-82).

"I wanted to do some plays with Claire. We were both fond of Ibsen. We thought a double-bill of *A Doll's House* and *Hedda Gabbler* would be an adventure. We did that off-Broadway.

"It was a success and did well on the road. We did a film version with Claire, Anthony Hopkins, Sir Ralph Richardson, Denholm Elliot, and Dame Edith Evans."

Hilly points to a photo on the wall of four men.

"I think you will recognize the players. It's Harry Belafonte, Sammy Davis Jr, Martin Luther King and me."

Above the picture is a framed letter from Dr. Martin Luther King to Hillard Elkins, thanking him for *Golden Boy* and for coming to Selma, Alabama to march.

"I closed the show and we all went to Selma and marched. When we came back, I wanted to do something for Dr. King. I put on a show *Broadway Answers Selma*, raising money for Dr. King. We had Walter Matthau, Sammy Davis Jr, Dennis O'Keefe, Carol Burnett, Ethel Merman, Lou Gossett Jr, Tom Bosley, Victor Borge, Alan Arkin, Alan Alda, Carol Channing, Martin Sheen, Sir John Gielgud, Martin Sheen, Buddy Hackett, Barbra Streisand, Maurice Chevelier. I even got the Nazis to work."

"You got who?"

"I'm kidding. I even got a lot of right-wing people to support Dr. King's cause."

We look at a flier for a show called *The Meeting*.

"In 1989, I produced a show for PBS about an apocryphal meeting between Dr. Martin Luther King and Malcom X.

"I did the first Athol Fugard play, the anti-apartheid *Sizwe Barnzi is Dead*. I also produced Athol's *The Island*. That refers to the island that imprisoned Nelson Mandela and most of his followers. I saw Athol's two plays in London and I fell in love with them and I was determined to bring them over [to New York]. I did in partnership with several producers. The plays got brilliant reviews. Nobody at the time could pronounce 'apartheid', let alone know what it was. Nobody came. We kept the play open. We then won the first-ever double Tony [award] for the two South African performers, Winston Ntshona and John Kani. Then everybody came, for all the wrong reasons, and saw the play.

"I also did a play by my friend Gore Vidal, who's one of Claire's best friends. *An Evening With Richard Nixon and his Friends*. We told the truth about Nixon and nobody believed us. It was three months before Watergate. We called him a thief and a liar. We closed in two weeks. It was Susan Sarandon's first play on Broadway."

Hilly points at another poster.

"I produced the first concert film—*Richard Pryor: Live in Concert* [1978]."

"Are you married at the moment?"

"No. I am living with the young lady I've been with for 18 years, Sandi Love, a former costume designer, who is much too smart to marry a five-time loser."

"I found this quote by author Kurt Vonnegut. 'I sold the rights to *Cats Cradle* for all eternity to Hilly Elkins. He's never done anything with it, never will, and won't sell it back.'"

"Interesting you say that because I just closed a deal last week on *Cat's Cradle*.

"It was in the sixties and Kurt was broke. Strangely enough, I had some money, so I bought the rights for a good deal of money. He's quite right to be pissed off. It's one of my favorite pieces and I am going to get the bloody thing made."

"How long did you live in England?"

"About four years."

"I don't hear many Americans using the word 'bloody.'"

"I have this terrible habit, when I'm on the phone with someone from London, I get more and more British as the conversation goes on. Some of my best directors and wives have been British."

"Who did you marry after Claire Bloom?"

"A young lady named Juliette, who I'd known for years. We married a year after Claire and I parted."

"Was she another's producer's wife at the time?"

"She was married to Andrzej Gutowski, who produced Roman Polanski's first film. My marriage to Juliette resulted in a son named Daniel, who's a chef living in France. My older boy is a song writer and a book writer. We are trying to produce his animated musical Romeo and Juliet."

Hilly refers to another poster on the wall. "I did a concert in Israel for the Huberman Centenial. Huberman was a German violinist who started the Israeli Philharmonic. I learned about him while having a drink at the Hilton with Zuben Mehta, who was doing an extraordinary evening at the Mann Auditorium, with some of the world's best violinists—Yitzhok Pearlman, Pincus Zuckerman, Isaac Stern. The Jewish mafia. The concert lost a lot of money but I'm proud I did it."

54

Phyllis Carlyle

June 26, 2002

Phyllis produced such films as *The Accidental Tourist* (1988) and *Se7en* (1995), and guided the careers of Willem Dafoe, John Malkovich, Pierce Brosnan, David Caruso, Geena Davis, Salma Hayek, Joseph Fiennes, Andy Garcia, Melanie Griffith, Jude Law, Ewan MacGregor, Jon Stewart, and Lou Diamond Phillips.

Phyllis lives alone with half a dozen cocker spaniels. Married twice, she has no children.

"I was born in Cleveland, Ohio. I grew up traveling. My father Russ Carlyle had a big band orchestra.

"I got married to a radio disc jockey and I went back to Cleveland for a year. Then we moved to Chicago. I divorced after a year. I stayed in Chicago. I worked at a talent agency and then I started my own.

"My goal has always been to make movies. I moved to Los Angeles [around 1973]. My cousin [Jeanira Ratcliffe] had written a book, *Will There Really be a Morning?* It was the autobiography of Frances Farmer. She'd had a dramatic life and had lived with my cousin for 15 years before her death. The story that was eventually made into the film *Frances* (1982) starring Jessica Lange was not the truth."

"My first word, as a two-year old, was 'movie.'

"I came to Los Angeles believing that I could use some of my financial relationships I had in Chicago to make movies. It's funny because I am still doing the same thing. I was way ahead of everything. I look back and I am surprised I saw the future.

"I met Barbara Boyle [who now runs Gail Ann Hurd's operation]. She's an attorney. She liked me. She agreed to be my lawyer. Shortly after that, she went to work for Roger Corman. We thought that an investment group I knew might match up to a slate of Corman films. The investment of $750,000 would've been spread over four films but the group decided not to invest. Two of the Corman movies, *Big Bad Momma* (1974) and *Death Race 2000* (1975), turned out to be the top moneymakers he ever had.

"My friend Kathy Bishop, a commercials producer from Chicago who moved to Los Angeles before me, got me work as a commercial casting director. I probably became the top commercials casting director.

"Naivete can be a great quality because you think everything is possible. While if I had listened to the advice I was receiving, I would've done nothing. Everybody cautions you against everything. I didn't know any better. I decided to start a management business. From my work as a casting director, I saw a lot of young talent. And I started picking people out of that pool to discuss management. I figured that I would build their careers. They would become stars. I would learn the film business.

"I took this master plan to a producer. He looked at me and said, 'Why don't you just produce?'

"One of the people I managed was John Malkovich. There was a tremendous amount of interest in him [around 1986]. Mark Rosenberg, who ran Warner Brothers at the time, offered John a production deal. This was my master-plan come true. I went to John. He said, 'Oh honey, I don't want to do that. Why, do you want to do it?' I said, 'Oh yes.' John said, 'O.K. As long as you don't bug me with it, go ahead and do it.'

"So we put together a two-year deal at Warner Brothers. I think John showed up twice in two years. That was the beginning of my relationship to a studio.

"Mark Rosenberg was fired about four months later. Mark was a truly wonderful man—intelligent, creative, kind. That's of course why they fired him. He wasn't fitting the mold. He was succeeded by Mark Canton who was in bed with Jon Peters. I was among the first women with a production deal.

"A William Morris assistant in New York tipped me off to the book, *The Accidental Tourist* by Ann Tyler, while it was still in galleys. I bought the rights. The exec I worked with at Warners was Bonnie Lee. We got Frank Galati, a professor at Northwestern, to do the screenplay. Nobody knew who the hell he was. Mark Rosenberg thought Frank was a great creative choice. The new regime didn't agree.

"I got a call from Bonnie. She said, 'I've got good news for you. A wonderful director wants to do the project.' I said, 'Well, we haven't even talked about directors. Just do me a favor. Promise me it isn't George Roy Hill.' There was dead silence on the other end of the phone. Finally she said, 'How do you know?'

"I said, 'Bonnie, he's wrong for the project.' She said, 'Phyllis, he's a world class director. He's making a few notes now on the script and then he wants to meet with you. At least give him a chance.' The notes dragged on for two months and it turned out that he was writing his own script. I read it and it was truly horrible. Even the studio had to agree. He took this sad and wonderful story and turned it into something that Walt Disney would do with dogs.

"It turned out that Warners had a huge deal with George. They paid him an enormous amount of money every year and he didn't make anything. This was the first thing he liked and this was how they were going to pay themselves back. Warners was sure he was right for the project.

"I caused enough trouble that Mark [Canton] wanted to see me. He told me, 'This is my studio. If you don't like it, get the fuck out. If you want to do everything your own way, go get your own money and your own studio and do your own movies. But if you're going to stay here and make this movie with my money, you're going to do it my way. George Roy Hill is going to direct this movie and Bill Murray is going to star in it.'

"My head of development was with me. We were walking back to my office. He said, 'I've never heard you that quiet.' I said, 'I've never been that close to killing anyone.'

"I racked my brain trying to think how to save my project. I got a call an agent at UTA (United Talent Agency) who said that Larry [Kasdan] would love to talk to me about directing the project. We sent him the script on a Thursday and by Monday morning I got a call back saying Larry would love to do the movie. I called Bonnie. 'I have such wonderful news for you. A world-class director wants to make this movie. Larry Kasdan.' There's dead silence. Larry Kasdan was very hot at this time.

"Warners had this Chevy Chase movie *Funny Farm*. They called George and asked him to direct it. 'Chevy loves you. *Accidental Tourist* isn't ready yet. This movie is ready to go. Do this movie while we're getting *Tourist* ready and we promise you we will then bring you on to *Tourist*.' Once they had George signed, sealed and delivered, they dumped him from the *Tourist* project."

Funny Farm (1988) was George Roy Hill's last film.

"After we saw the first cut of *Tourist*, it was strong. Larry wanted to test it. He didn't get the test scores he wanted. They were only in the seventies and he thought they should be in the eighties. Larry had the right to final cut. He was that strong then as a director. So he rewrote and re-shot half of Kathleen Turner's scenes, because in the test results, people didn't like her. She was reduced to this character on the phone. One of the strongest scenes I've ever seen was cut out of the movie because it tied too strongly into the essence of her original character.

"In the original version, she was a deeply conflicted woman over the death of the child. Warners exec Lucy Fisher oversaw the project. She sums up completely what I felt about the movie. After Larry re-cut, re-shot and re-edited the movie, I wrote a five-page letter to him pleading for a return to the original version. Lucy tried to talk to him as well. Larry told us, 'History will show that I was right.' I said to Lucy, 'Isn't there anything we can do?' She said to me, 'Phyllis, we had brilliance. Now we will have to settle for very good.'"

"How did you feel about the casting?"

"It beats Bill Murray, doesn't it? Bill is talented but he would've been the funny version of the character. He wouldn't have been the true version. I'd developed *Accidental Tourist* for my clients Melanie Griffith and John Malkovich. Melanie turned it down to do *Working Girl* (1988)."

"Did you know at the time that in the studio process, once a director signs on, he becomes the king of the project?"

"I learned that. I learned some hard lessons, particularly if you are somebody who has an independent spirit. I was slapped around right and left by everybody. And nobody cared. I was really hurt. I'd just gotten married to my second husband. And I'd just be sitting there at 4 a.m. staring at the wall. I'd loved movies since two years old. I'd come to Hollywood to make wonderful movies and I'd run into the boys club, the politics, and things you don't have a reference for. It was horrible. It was done in such a brutal way. I was robbed of much of the credit I should've had for that film.

"I had brought Larry to the picture. Then Larry was finalizing his contract with Warner Brothers. I got a call from Peter, Larry's agent at UTA. He said, 'We're almost done with Larry's contract. We just have a couple of deal points left but they pertain to you. I want to run them by you. The first one is, we want to remove you as the producer. The second one is that we want to be attached to your turnaround in case we don't make the movie at Warners. I said, 'Peter, you want to remove me as the producer, but in case anything happens, you want to be attached to the project so that you can fuck me at another studio? Is that what you're saying?' He said, 'Yeah, pretty much.'

"Larry wanted me off the project because I'd never produced a movie. He had his own producing team. I didn't know enough at the time to preserve my producing credit. But I had this powerful attorney (Jake Bloom) who'd worked hard to convince me that he was going to take care of me. I told him the situation. He calls me back in 20 minutes and says, 'Phyllis, I don't want you to get emotional about this. This is your first movie. You're going to get it made. You're going to get a credit. I think we should take the executive producing credit and give them their turnaround clause.'

"I said, 'Jake, why would I want to do that?' He said, 'Ach, I knew you were going to get emotional.' There was just nowhere to turn. That ended my relationship with my attorney. So I agreed to everything because they were going to throw me off the picture completely if I hadn't. When the picture was nominated, I had to fight to get a ticket to the Golden Globes.

"I got to *Se7en* because Jim, a partner at UTA, sent me the script for a client. I read the script and I liked it. The studios were turning it down.

"[Director] David Fincher had not done a film since *Alien 3*, which he got a great deal of slack for. I was initially against hiring him. I thought he was a music video guy who'd had his shot. I heard all these stories about how difficult he'd been. I was very wrong. He was brilliant."

"Were you on set?"

"Not much. There wasn't any need."

David Fincher says: "Michael De Luca [former President and Chief Operating Officer of New Line Productions] went to the mat for *Se7en*. When we needed 18 more days to reshoot on *Se7en* and Phyllis Carlyle was saying, 'We need to fire this guy. He's a music video guy. He doesn't know what he's doing. We need to redo the ending. The head can't be in the box.' When all that shit was going on, Mike De Luca was watching my back."

Phyllis: "I did not try to fire David Fincher. I think almost all of us thought that the head in the box was too much. Arnold Kopelson wanted to change the ending. He walked around saying, 'I'm not making a fucking picture with a woman's head in a box.'

"Brad [Pitt] did change the ending. The shooting draft had Morgan [Freeman] pulling the trigger. Brad argued strenuously with David that his character should do it.

"When a movie does what *Se7en* did, you keep quiet. Everyone was right and we did it perfectly.

"I had so many arguments over the years with people on how to do *Se7en*. Paramount had this list of changes. I said, 'Why don't you do those things with the ten movies you've already got?' I went outside of the system completely to revive this project. New Line eventually financed the film. They called Arnold Kopelson in to help produce. Arnold is a complex guy. One part of him is a big teddy bear that will take care of the world. Then there's this other side of that is ego and has a hard time sharing any credit."

55

Jeff Wald

July 2, 2002

Jeff Wald's office is covered by pictures of Jeff with Presidents Clinton, Ford, Carter and Bush Sr. He's friendly with such celebrities as Barbra Streisand and Sylvester Stallone. During our interview, he takes a call from Jimmy Connors, the ex-tennis champ.

Jeff's third wife, Deborah (an English actress), took the *People* magazine cover photo of Barbra Streisand and hubby James Brolin, one of eight Wald clients.

As we talk, Jeff has a woman in the room screening his calls and a man working on a laptop computer.

Wald is a short squat balding man with a pot belly. On his desk is a plaque that reads, "Jeff Wald—Prophet, Genius."

"I grew up in New York. I was born Jeff Sommers. My father, a doctor, died when I was eight. My mother, a school teacher, remarried and changed my name. I didn't like and I shortened it to Wald. My son Jordan now uses the name Sommers.

"A couple of things made me want to go into this business. When I was eleven years old, Mike Todd was married to Elizabeth Taylor. He was 5'5" with the same bad accent that I have. He was from the Bronx. He threw a birthday party for Elizabeth Taylor at Madison Square Garden. He brought her in on an elephant painted pink. I saw this guy on television talking. I thought if he could do it, I could.

"I went to the same all-boys high school (De Witt Clinton in the Bronx) as Neil Simon, Garry Marshal, Paddy Chayefsky, Ralph Lauren, Calvin Klein, Stokely Carmichael, Milton Berle, Burt Lancaster. Ralph Lauren was in my class. He was then Ralph Lipshitz.

"I was a rough kid. I was always in trouble. I fought a lot. I had a big mouth and a short fuse, so I hit first. I was somebody's bad news. I didn't like to be fucked with. I had taken a test to get into a special school. I was admitted. Then they wrote my mother a letter saying they didn't want discipline problems. In high school, I was a truant. I spent a lot of time in Harlem going to the Apollo Theater. I was arrested for fighting but I was never convicted."

"What's your ethnic background?"

"Jewish."

"Were you raised religious?"

"Not a fucking chance. All those religions are full of shit. With your pedophiles in the Church. It's all about controlling people and sexual repression.

"I grew up in the du-op era of music. I started in the music industry after getting kicked out of NYU for gambling along with 63 other guys. I didn't fix games but I knew guys who did. One was a relative of Vito Genovese, a big Mafia guy.

"I moved to Buffalo in 1963. This [black] singer-songwriter Oscar Brown Jr came through town. I hung with him. He asked me if I wanted to be in show business. I said yes. I hopped in my car and I followed him to Chicago. I lived in his house. I was his gopher.

"A few months in, he fired his manager. I became his manager. I didn't know shit. But I did know that in the business there were a lot of drugs, money and women. I got to meet Martin Luther King through him and Malcom X and Elijah Mohammed.

"I stayed with him for six months. Then I left Chicago."

"Were you run out of town?"

"Basically, by the police. It was a political time. We had the Alley Theater Company and it used what we called title funds from the government to go into inner-city schools and teach kids different things. The kids we worked with were a street gang called The Mighty Blackstone Rangers. They are the biggest street gang in the US to this day, bigger than the Crips and the Bloods. The guy who ran it is now in jail for the rest of his life for murder—Jeff Fort.

"The police in those days would shoot a Blackstone Ranger and leave a Disciples jacket near the body to foment gang violence.

"The police didn't like anybody trying to help those kids. I was told that if I didn't leave, I'd have an accident.

"I was brought to Bobby Kennedy who was interested in how those government programs were working.

"I moved back to New York. I realized that I didn't shit about the business. I got a job at William Morris talent agency in the mailroom."

Jeff points at a framed couple of pages from the April, 1998 issue of *Vanity Fair* about all the people who started in the W.M. mailroom.

"Did you have to fake a college degree?"

"Yeah. I lied. I met David Geffen in the mailroom. We became friends. I married [Australian singer] Helen [Reddy] in 1964. I met her on a Friday and I married her on a Tuesday. I proposed to my current wife on our first date and married her five weeks later.

"I actually dated my second wife. That was my big mistake. I'd just gotten out of Betty Ford [drug addiction clinic], so what did I know? I stayed six weeks for the four-week program. Betty Ford kept me two extra weeks because she said I was suffering from terminal uniqueness. She and her husband are good friends of mine.

"The marriage [in 1987] last eight months."

Assistant: "I have to pass gas. Do you mind turning that off?"

Jeff: "Get out of the fucking room, you asshole.

"I was at William Morris for a year and then left and went to Ashley Famous Agency. I lasted three weeks and I got fired.

"You know Ann Miller? She was an actress who did a lot of movies in the forties and fifties. Then she had a revival of her career doing a play on Broadway with Mickey Rooney called Sugarbabies. They used to call her 'Big Hash.' She had big hair. She was a big tall dancer. Not a rocket scientist.

"I was a junior agent in the nightclub division. A friend of mine, Tom Milius, was a senior agent. Our boss was an Irish guy named Joe Higgins. He was usually drunk in the afternoons and he'd never use an intercom. He'd just yell, 'Tom Milius, get in my office.'

"One day, Tom came out of Higgins' office with a long face. 'We've just signed Ann Miller and I have to take her out to dinner at the Copacabana.'

"The next day, Joe Higgins yells, 'Tom Milius, get in my office.' So I yelled out, 'Yeah, tonight they want you to fuck Lassie.' Ann Miller was standing there with Ted Ashley. I got fired on the spot.

"I was out of work for four months. I got two job offers on the same day in 1967. One [thanks to a recommendation by David Geffen] was with a management company called Chartoff-Winkler. They were a shitty management company that had Buffy Sainte-Marie, a little Indian girl who was a singer-songwriter, a fat comic named Jackie Vernon who's now dead, and a rock n' roll group called The Happenings. They offered me $125 a week.

"The same day I got an offer from a company in Chicago that owned a string of nightclubs. That job paid $325 a week. I had a lot of parking tickets in my glove box. So I moved to Chicago with Helen and my daughter. I booked talent for the club—people like Flip Wilson, Dione Warwick, Joan Rivers, Tony Fields, Shecky Green, Ramsey Lewis, Miles Davis, Richard Pryor. I was with Richard the night that Martin Luther King got shot. We had to close the club because the troops were in the streets controlling the riot. We drove around and smoked a joint and watched all the shit happen.

"Miriam McCaver worked at the club. The night that she opened, she announced her engagement to Stokely Carmichael, who was head of SNVCC (Student Non-Violent Coordinating Committee). It was actually violent. He wore combat boots. Those were the black militants of the time.

"I lasted ten months, until the Chicago Democratic convention and the riots. I wanted out.

"Bill Cosby had come to town. I told him I had to get out. I couldn't spend another winter here. He told me to call his manager Roy Silver. They'd formed a [management] company Campbell-Silver-Cosby. Roy said that if I was ever in California, I should give him a call. I flew out that night. I showed up at his office the next morning. I got hired. I rented an apartment in West Hollywood.

"I flew back to Chicago. I quit my job. I put Helen and my daughter in the car and we drove to LA. We got here with $8 cash. I bought a $5 bag of grass on Sunset Strip and spent the remaining $3 for food.

"I was at the management company four minutes and we signed Tiny Tim. In a minute, I got one of the biggest acts in the world. We had an unbelievable 18-month ride. The money's pouring in.

"I produced a show on Broadway starring Mohammed Ali, Bigtime Buck White. It ran six days.

"Norman Brokaw, the chairman of William Morris, told me that Roy Silver was not handling Cosby's funds in the appropriate way. That if I wanted to have a career in the business, I should quit. I was making $600 a week. I was driving a new car. I wasn't saving anything. I was doing drugs—mainly grass but some coke.

"William Morris loaned me $30,000 to go into business and set up my own office.

"In 1970, I convinced a guy at Capitol Records to give my wife Helen Reddy a deal to make one single. She did a song from Jesus Christ Superstar, 'I don't know how to love him.' It went top ten. I dropped all my other clients and concentrated on her between 1971-75. I produced a TV series for NBC in 1973 called, *Flip Wilson Presents the Helen Reddy Hour*. It was an eclectic show. It was the biggest thing I'd ever produced. I had acts like The Eagles, Cheech and Chong, Jim Crow, B.B. King, The Temptations, Gloria Steinem. I got into this huge fight with the president of NBC who wanted Ken Berry and Florence

Henderson on the show. I said they were never walking on my fucking stage. So the guy hated me and canceled the show after eight episodes.

"Then I made a specials deal. On the last one I did, I remember telling one of the executives that I'd gotten Jane Fonda to do her first variety show. She was going to do a 160-song medley with Helen. I flew to Hawaii to talk to the guys running NBC. They said, 'I wish you would've gotten me Cindy Williams instead of Jane Fonda.'

"It turned out that NBC didn't want Jane Fonda on because NBC was owned by RCA, a huge defense contractor. They didn't want Hanoi Jane.

"I got into another huge fight with the president of NBC, Michael Weinman. This time I threatened to kill him. The show I'd done was supposed to air on Mother's Day. And NBC was going to fuck me and put it on in August, when nobody's watching. I went berserk. I offered to buy it back for what they paid, $580,000. I wrote a check for $580,000 and I owned the most expensive home video in America.

"I convinced ABC to put it on Mother's Day. I made a $50,000 profit. I'm the only producer of television in history who's bought back his show because he didn't like its time slot, and then put it on another network. The show won its time slot and came in in the top 20 for the quarter.

"It was the only good press I ever got. Weinman got fired. *The New York Times* wrote this great article about David and Goliath. I was David for a change beating Goliath, a man who took, on principle, his special back from the network. It wasn't principle. I was coked up. I had a lot of money and an attitude."

"Where did you make your money?"

"With Tiny Tim, Deep Purple and those acts. Then in 1975, I developed a huge management company. I signed Donna Summer. She was making $400,000 a week in Las Vegas. Helen was making huge money. I signed Sylvester Stallone right out of Rocky. I still speak to him most every day. I had Chicago and Flip Wilson, Crosby, Stills and Nash, Marvin Gay, Miles Davis. I produced one of Stallone's movies, *Paradise Alley*. It's the only movie I've ever acted in. I did TV specials with Donna and Helen. I've got a huge coke habit."

"How come you're not dead?"

"I came close. I overdosed a couple of times.

"I was six years on the LA Olympic organizing committee. I was four years on the national board of USO (United Servicemen's Organization), appointed by President Carter. I was four years on the Economic Council of California. I was big in politics. You saw all those pictures of me with Carter, and Humphrey and Teddy Kennedy and John Tierney. I was riding a nice wave.

"Then Donna Summer found God. She started trashing gay people. I didn't want anything to do with that politically. She wanted me to sue Neil Bogart (founder of Casablanca Records). I wouldn't do that. He was my friend. Donna and I split.

"In 1983, the divorce with Helen Reddy was ugly and expensive."

Jeff pulls out an issue of *People* magazine with Helen and Jeff's divorce as the cover story.

"Then Marvin Gay's dad killed him. That didn't help my business. Chicago fired me. Stallone and I split at my request, which was stupid. One day I got coked up and I basically told him to fuck off. We wound up staying friends. I went to his wedding. I went to his honeymoon. I will probably wind up producing some films with him this year.

"I made a movie in 1985 called *Opposing Force*. It was one of the biggest pieces of shit ever made. I did it in the Philippines for Mike Medavoy's Orion. Mike wanted me to make another war picture while I was down there. I passed. I wouldn't even read the script. It turned out to be *Platoon*.

"I made the wrong war movie. But I'd spent three months down there and it was enough. They were at war. I was bribing the Marcoses and the guerillas. People were shooting at us. It was three months of insanity. I came back and went to Sly's wedding and honeymoon. I came back and overdosed. I was at Cedars Sinai for 18 days and then I went to Betty Ford for six weeks. I've been clean since January 25, 1986.

"Ali McGraw saved my life. She found me unconscious. My kid called her up and said, 'I can't wake him this time.'

"That was the end of my tenure with Crosby, Stills & Nash because David went to jail (in Texas for gun possession and drugs) the same day I went to rehab.

"I married [*American Graffiti* (1973) star] Candy Clark, January 1, 1987. That lasted eight months.

"I was friendly with producer Burt Sugarman, producer of the TV show *The Midnight Special* (1973). He'd just produced the movie *Children of a Lesser God* (1986). He'd just bought the company Chuck Barris Industries, which produced *The Newlywed Game, The Gong Show, The Dating Game*. I met with him and we formed a partnership company called Barris-Wald. That lasted four days. I said to him, 'The company is a piece of shit.' He said, 'If you don't like it, change it. You're the president.'

"So I fired 127 people in one day out of 129 employees. I hired 127 new people. I went over to the shows and fired everyone on the shows—all the producers, everybody. They'd been doing the show for 24 years.

"I produced 3000 hours of TV. I did a miniseries called *Switched at Birth* (1991)."

"What's your view on Michael Ovitz?"

"I've never liked him. I always thought he was bad for business. He was always the antithesis of everything that this business is about for me. I like being involved in music, television, movies and records. I think it is a privilege to be able to make a living doing this stuff. The people that I started in this business with, the Geffens of the world, had a passion for this business. This guy was about killing people. He was about leveraging. He was not collegial. He took a lot of the fun out of the business. It was always competitive but there were always gentlemen running the business. You didn't always judge your success by other people's failure. But to him, it was all about that.

"I started attacking him in 1990 when they were calling him the most powerful man in the business. I called him a jerk. For him to be so disingenuous to blame a gay mafia, please. Blame yourself and your fucking hubris."

"Are you afraid of the gay mafia?"

"No. They're my friends. I love David Geffen. I think he's an incredibly talented guy. And the rest of these guys [Ovitz] names are friends of mine. I grew up with them. They're sexual orientation has nothing to do with me."

"Is there a secret gay mafia running Hollywood?"

"There's a generation running Hollywood, all of whom come from the same backgrounds, from the William Morris mailroom and places like that. [Ovitz] is a fucking asshole. He's not talented at the end of the day. He was all about the wrong things and he's getting it in the ass like he deserves. He's done nothing right since he left CAA. He fucked his partners at CAA. He fucked them all. He lied to them. He did everything wrong for them and his clients. Then he did a shitty job at Disney. Then he invested in an Internet business that tanked. Then he fucked around with the NFL and cost LA from having a team. He started this AMG (Artists Management Group) which was a fucking joke. It's all about his incompetence, stupidity and venality.

"James Brolin has been my client for 24 years and my friend. I executive produced his TV series *Pensacola: Wings of Gold* (1997-2000). I executive produced *The Roseanne Show* (1998). It was the worst experience of my life. She's probably the single worst human being I've ever dealt with on any level. I signed Mike Tyson at the same time. I'd take ten Mike Tysons on a bad day rather than her on a good day any day.

"I thought I could handle her. I thought I could change her. I thought I could control her. I thought I could deal with her. I turned out to be 100 percent wrong but the money was so good that I stayed. I was with her for almost five years."

"I made a movie a few years ago called *Two Days in the Valley* (1996). I'm proud of that. I'm hands on. I read every script of *Pensacola*. I was on the set every day of *Two Days*. I helped the design the favored nations deal for the movie where everyone got paid $20,000 a week. Instead of paying people scale, I had the best caterer and the best trailers. I had a band on Fridays so people could dance. People looked forward to coming to work. So I ended up with no meal penalties [for being more than five hours between meals], no overtime…

"It was Charlize Theron's first film. I gave her the job at the audition. We were in this tiny room. The director, me, and the casting director. Normally the secretary knocks on the door and hands you a resume. The actor comes in. There's two minutes of small talk and they read with the casting director. We'd been doing that all day. It was hotter than shit. There's no knock at the door. Someone comes crashing through the fucking door. She throws herself on the floor and does the death scene from the end of the movie. That was Charlize's audition."

"What's the most meaningful part of your work?"

"The money."

September 5, 2002

Jeff calls. "You have a fucking death wish?"

"No."

"Let me tell you something. First of all, you had no right to reprint my son's poem, which is copyrighted. [Jeff showed it to me at his office and I published it on my website.] That's the first fucking lawsuit you're going to get. Between me, [Mike] Medavoy and Anita Busch, you are going to have a lot fucking problems because I am going to finance everybody's lawsuit against you. Let's see how much money you have to go fucking do depositions and the rest of the shit. So you better get my kid's poem right the fuck off of there, that's for openers.

"Secondly, you are so fucking inaccurate, you can't even get names right. Your spelling and your fucking listing of names is just fucking unbelievable. So let me tell you something. I'm now making it a career to go after you and break you. So you better get my shit off your fucking website.

"Anita Busch is not too happy with you and neither is Mike Medavoy. So if you think you can come into this town you little snot-nosed fuck and just put shit like that up there, let's see how much you can afford fucking lawyers. I'll own your fucking shirt when I'm finished because I can just afford to keep your fucking ass in fucking depositions for the rest of your fucking life. Do you understand that?"

"Yeah. What would you like me to do?"

"Get my fucking shit off the website especially my kid's fucking poem, which as far as I'm concerned, I haven't decided whether to call the police and say you stole it off my desk."

"I'll take it off right now."

"That's the fucking position that I am going to take with everybody in my office, that you stole it. You came in my office and stole it. You're a little mother-fucker. You came in here. You were going to write a book. You put up all that shit on the website and you think you can come into this fucking town and trash everybody. You're not Julia Phillips pal. She had a long fucking history with me and a long history in this town. She's an Oscar winner. You're a fucking pimple on my goddam ass.

"I'll break you the fuck down like you've never seen in your fucking life. You want to see some shit? Let's see how much fucking money you have. You'll never have a fucking dime as long as you live. Because that's how long I'll fucking keep you in court. And I don't give a fuck if I lose. I'll just keep going after you in fucking court. Do you understand that? I'll make sure that every fucking penny you earn for the rest of your life will go in fucking lawyers. I can finance that with my residuals."

"I've taken it off. Is there anything else you'd like me to do?"

"Lose my fucking name. If I see one more word with your name attached to me, and you're fucking dead. Do you understand that? You can tape-record that. You can put that as a threat and anything else. You're financially fucking dead. O.K., and if I were you, I'd leave Anita Busch alone. She's got a lot of fucking friends in this town. And right now they're not real happy with you."

"Is there anything else you'd like me to do?"

"That's all I want you to do. Get it the fuck down right now. Don't let me go on a website and find anything with your name and my name."

I have a signed release from Jeff Wald, dated July 2, 2002: "I give Luke Ford permission to quote from my interview with him in his forthcoming book on Hollywood and articles on the entertainment industry. I understand that I will not be compensated for this."

A Hollywood source writes me: "It was always noted by the business managers who handled the Walds that Jeff was disgusting before he ever got on coke. The end of 1982 and beginning of 1983 Jeff had bankrupted everything his wife earned and was coked out of his mind. When Helen left Jeff his intent was to take their son to punish her for leaving him. He paid Marvin Gross his attorney, out of the proceeds of the sale of the community property home, an unknown 'bonus' to accomplish this. An evaluator, on a list in the Santa Monica courthouse, said Jeff was suitable, under the Father's Rights law for 50/50 time. I believe, but never checked the file, that it was Dr. Rocco Motto, psychiatrist, whose license was "retired," in 1987 who did the job. Dr. Motto was also asked to resign as head of Rice-Davis rather than be fired. Jeff was running around town screaming "I aced my MMPI," The Minnesota Multiphasic test, designed for the likes of Detroit auto workers to try and weed out potential crazy's. Several hundred yes or no boxes to check, any sociopath could ace it. Jeff then co-parented his son, who was a straight A student, who's weekend job, when he was with his father, was to watch Jeff binge until he passed out. When a lump of coke worked its way to Jeff's brain and Jeff was dying, Jordan found him and got help. Jeff rented a house on Malibu Road. The paramedics knew the address by heart. If Jeff hadn't purchased the use of his son for his own purposes, he would probably be dead."

September 6, 2002

Jeff calls. "You think it's funny with Medavoy's letter and Anita Busch? You're playing with the wrong people. I want my whole thing down. I want nothing to do with you. I'm fat with a pot belly? Who the fuck do you think you are? I can make you not fucking breathe. Everyone else will be polite and send you a letter like Medavoy did. I'll stop you from breathing. Do you understand me? You can put that up there and quote it. I'm just telling you something right now. We will crush you with fucking lawyers. And that will just be the fun part. That will be the part of your day that you fucking enjoy when you run out of fucking money. Now take it the fuck done. You came in here under false pretenses. Take the whole fucking thing down. And you've got that shitty thing on Anita Busch up there. What the fuck is the matter with you? Do you want to win friends here and get any kind of cooperation? I'll put your name all over this fucking place. I'll send out emails to everyone in this fucking town and nobody will take your fucking calls when I'm finished. I'm just telling you something. You're fucking with the wrong guy here. You put up all the times I've been arrested. They were for assault pal."

"I sent you most everything I wrote about you."

"I got it. I don't like it. You twisted things. You got things wrong. I'm just telling you I want it down. I want nothing to do with you. Don't write about me. I will sue the shit out of you. I don't give a fuck if I lose. I'll just re-sue you. You can't afford the lawsuits. I'll fucking hire a lawyer fulltime right out of fucking law school whose job will be nothing but to file depositions and shit on you and make you defend yourself. I'll break you."

From Jose Lambiet's Star Confidential column in the December 17, 2002 issue of *The Star* tabloid (www.starmagazine.com):

Headline: "You're Dead! James Brolin's Rep Lets Dirt Digger Have It"

Wald recently left several death-threat-laden messages on Internet scoop Luke Ford's voice mail after Ford ran on his website, lukeford.net, a warts-and-all profile of the former drug addict Wald.

Some choice passages from Wald's messages: "If I see one more word with your name attached to me on your website, you're (swear word here) dead. Do you understand that? You can tape-record that."

A day later, Wald obviously hadn't let off all his steam. He didn't like Ford's description of his potbelly and other physical unpleasantries. (Remember, this is Hollywood, where you are what you look like!)

"So, I'm fat with a potbelly?" he bellowed. "I can make you not (really bad word here) breathe. Everyone else would be polite and send you a letter. I'll stop you from breathing."

An unapologetic Wald tells Confidential: "Let him go to the (another bad word here) police then!"

December 9, 2002

Jeff phones. "You slimy piece of shit. So you had to go to *The Star* with it? It's against the law in the state of California to tape phone calls. So I'm going to the District Attorney along with a whole bunch of other people to put a stop to you. This is not about you breathing or anything else. This is about you tape-recording phone conversations without permission. I never left a message on your voicemail ever. You know who this is, I take it?"

"Yes, it's Jeff Wald."

"So you're going to keep doing to everybody and think you're going to get away with it, you little shit? Harry Ufland and everybody else you're doing numbers on now? You're out of your fucking mind, do you know that? Now I'm going to get lawyers and you are going to spend the rest of your life in depositions and court. If I lose it, I'll file something else. I'm going to the District Attorney's office because it is against the law in the state of California to tape conversations."

"You said I could tape it."

"No, I didn't. No I did not. No I did not. I never told you you could tape me. You're a lying piece of shit. And I've got witnesses here who were sitting here when I called you. I never told you you could tape anything. It's against the law to tape the conversation. That's a felony by the way. I just want you to know that. Now you're going to the Star with everything? Good luck to you pal because now you're really in fucking trouble. Your shitty little website nobody gave a fuck about, now you've got to print it in Star magazine? Now you're going to see what happens. So have fun."

Jeff hangs up.

A friend writes me: "Too bad that Jeff hung up before you could mention that what California law actually prohibits is recording 'confidential communications,' and that by admitting that he had 'witnesses here who were sitting here when I called you,' he's made it impossible for him to prove that the conversation was being 'carried on in circumstances as may reasonably indicate that any party to the communication desires it to be confined to the parties thereto.' [Citation to statute omitted so as to aid Wald's attorneys in billing as much time as possible in looking into this matter.]"

56

David Friendly

July 9, 2002

David is the son of Fred Friendly, the former president of CBS News.

"Normally when I talk to a reporter, I have a single agenda. I stick to my script, no matter what question I'm asked. This is different because it's for a book. But you have to be careful in what you say for publication. I've said a throwaway line and it has come back to haunt me."

Off the record, Friendly gives me a sizzling example.

"Good quote."

"It was a good quote but it was upsetting to them. I busted them. In the end I thought, 'Not very smart.' I wouldn't do it again because I need to work with these people. I'm getting a minute of pleasure for a pithy quote that ultimately could've endangered my long-term relationship.

"I inherited my father's tendency to sometimes say what is on my mind."

"Like Ovitz and the Gay Mafia quote. Many people in the industry talk about the Gay Mafia, they just don't do it on the record."

"Exactly. And for good reason."

"Because you get your head handed to you."

David laughs. "Your job is to get those people to say those things that they wouldn't normally say."

We discuss my first book about sex in film.

"I know people who are adverse to doing a movie with any action. They're not into violence on the screen. They feel it contributes to violence in the culture. So you say, well, you can do comedy and drama. But look at what movies are working today. *Bourne Identity. The Minority Report.* Action is a big part of the American movie-going experience. And so is sex. Imagine if you had to eliminate that. You'd be fighting with one hand behind your back against people using two hands.

"So what's your thesis in this book?"

"I don't have one. Just that it is about the different kinds of producers."

"There is no specific definition of a modern day producer. Many producers do it in different ways and many of them are successful are doing it differently. I was trained under Brian Grazer. He was my mentor and boss and the person who recruited me from the halls of journalism into the plusher halls of show business. Brian is a different producer from a Scott Rudin who is different from Jerry Bruckheimer. Yet they are all wildly successful.

"I have been intimately involved in all my movies and I want to change this so I can make more movies. I'm not trusting enough to turn that over to other people, but the guys that get five movies a year done have whole systems so they can delegate. I'm trying to get to that place because I have aspirations to be a bigger producer. But I've found that it is highly important to be around all phases of producing a movie.

"For instance, on *Big Momma's House* (2000), I sat next to director Raja Gosnell every day, from first shot to last shot. It was good to have a second opinion there. Directors get so caught up in the technical and what they need to accomplish to have the scenes cut together that it is good to have somebody like a producer sitting there to say that this didn't play quite as funny as we thought. Or did you notice that he's wearing the hat differently in this take. It's good to have someone to manage the outsized personalities.

"Some producers don't go to the set. You can't criticize it. It's just a different way of doing it.

"For me, the creative satisfaction is having input in the process. If I'm not there, it's hard to have input, either in the present or later, because you don't have the credibility of having been around. For example, Betty Thomas, who directed *Dr. Dolittle* (1998), is a character. She's eccentric, prickly and funny with strong opinions. We would dailies every day on this eight-wheeler truck. If you weren't at dailies, how would you possibly have a strong point of view about how you wanted to shoot the movie? Unless your philosophy is: I develop the project. I put the elements together. I let them go make the movie."

"Like Bob Kosberg, the pitch man."

"He sells ideas. That's different from producing."

"He still gets the credit."

"That's the thing that still makes producers a little crazy because you have this broad spectrum of people who call themselves producers. It's like anybody can have a business card printed and describe their occupation as producer. The people that I look up to—the Brian Grazers, the Doug Wicks, the Scott

Rudins—these people are not here to go to premieres and cocktail parties. They're creating movies."

"But a Brian Grazer is not on the set."

"He has built an infrastructure. When he and Ron Howard were starting out, creating movies for Paramount together like *Night Shift* (1982), he was on the set. But as his system grew, and he got more financial wherewithal, he was able to recruit a team of people he trusts and he lets them do their job. Who can quibble with his success?

"Dick Zanuck is about 75 years old and he goes to the sets. He lives on the movies he produces."

"What did you think of the movie *The Player*?"

"It was exaggerated. People have gone to great lengths to sell ideas in this town but the goofier approaches usually don't work. There was a point where David Permut sent out a pitch on videotape and he sold it.

"You can bracket the different types of producers. There are the salesmen [like David Permut, Bob Kosberg], the creative producers, the line producers. I pride myself on being a creative producer. On the first day of production, that becomes the director's movie. I get to come back in in post-production but when we're making the movie, there can be only one boss on that set, and that boss has to be the director.

"There's an old expression that in pre-production, the producer holds the gun. On the first day of production, he hands the gun to the director. I live by that rule. My job is to keep that director calm and focused.

"When we were doing *Courage Under Fire* (1996), I was in Texas with [director] Ed Zwick. We were shooting a scene next to a private airport. It was an intense scene between Denzel Washington and Matt Damon. Denzel was interviewing this kid and finding out that he was hiding things about his drug use. Every take was getting blown by these little airplanes. After one particularly rough take that had been going well and then was blown because of sound, Ed Zwick took his headphones off, threw them to the ground and stamped on them. It was like watching a kid have a temper tantrum. Then he said, 'You're the fucking producer. Do something about this.'

"To that point, he and I had this brother to brother relationship. I decided to send one of our PAs to the terminal, a 1000 yards away, with a walky talkie, and ask the air traffic controller to wait to send the planes between the takes. It ended up working out.

"I left my home a week after my son was born and I spent six months in Texas on *Courage Under Fire*. My family joined me for one month."

"How did you meet your wife [Priscilla Nedd-Friendly]?"

"She's a film editor. I was an executive at Imagine Entertainment. I was over-seeing *The Dream Team* (1989) starring Michael Keaton. We had a music super-visor named Becky Mancuso, who was a good friend of my wife. I was having dinner one night with Becky. She said, 'Oh, I want to bring this friend of mine.' It wasn't a setup or anything. We quickly struck up a relationship. We've been married eleven years."

"How do you feel about her having a hyphenated name?"

"It's fine with me. That's her choice. I love seeing her name on the credits with 'Friendly' at the end. I've learned about movies from being married to an editor. Studio executives want to have input but because they don't get to pro-duce the movie or experience the editing process, their opportunities to have input are based on a couple of screenings. That's not to say their opinion isn't valid but it's not from within the eye of the storm.

"A producer like Jerry Bruckheimer is close to being a director. He's proactive, both in the process of making a movie and especially in post-production. In many of his movies, he'll work with directors who are controllable."

"When you were a kid, what were your career ambitions?"

"I grew up in the shadow of a famous journalist. My father was a larger-than-life human being devoted to his journalistic mission. I thought that was my path. I edited my high school newspaper. I went to Northwestern [outside of Chicago], which has an excellent journalism school. While at Northwestern, as a sopho-more, I got the producing bug by becoming the concert chairman. I had an office and I was on the phones to the coast every day and I got Billboard magazine and I loved putting on a show. I produced concerts with the Beach Boys and Jethro Tull and The Grateful Dead. My ego came out. I made it part of the deal that any band played Northwestern, I had to introduce them or we wouldn't do the deal.

"At the same time, I produced a radio show that was hosted by the dean of the journalism school. When I graduated, I had a couple of offers to work for big Chicago concert promoters. But because of the influence of my father, and my major, it didn't seem serious enough. So at age 22, I got a summer internship at *Newsweek* and I stayed there for six years (1978-84). I was one of the youngest staff writers in the history of the magazine. It was a crazy job because they had reporters out in the field sending in files and then you as a staff writer compile everything and boil it down to six paragraphs. So from Monday to Thursday, you're sending out queries and monitoring the reporting, and then Friday morning, the pressure was on. It was not what I wanted to be doing. It froze me. It was too much too soon.

"I wanted to be a reporter, out in the field interviewing people. I didn't want to be sitting in a little office in New York writing up files. So I transferred to *The LA Times* covering Hollywood.

"What got frustrating for me as a journalist was that I got tired of observing life and I wanted to participate in life. I was 30 years old and I out interviewing people in my same age group who were driving BMWs and had big beautiful offices. Then I'd drive back to this windowless cubicle at the *Times*. It wasn't exciting enough for me. I had bigger dreams. And, I don't think I was as good at journalism as I wanted to be."

"You had a once-a-week column like Patrick Goldstein."

"Mine was called First Look. His is The Big Picture. I look at his column all the time and I can always tell when he was out of ideas and he does some story, like a couple of weeks ago, about a father-son producing team. You do that when you're stuck. That's just the run of the mill profile. I don't begrudge him. It's hard, even if it is just once a week, to come up with a good column."

"Did you break any stories?"

"I did a Sunday Calendar story about the leaders at Disney. I called them 'Team Disney' and the label wound up sticking. It was all about the new regime at Disney. The lead was about this black convertible mustang rolling into the lot at 6 a.m.. It was all about Katzenberg and his crew. I was proud of the fact that they started calling themselves Team Disney.

"I also did a piece on why there hasn't been a *Godfather III* (1990). Later there was one. I did some controversial stuff. My column got a lot of attention. I concentrated on the business. I wasn't interested in doing profiles of stars. I tried to give the reader a window into the day to day process of movie making.

"I did a piece about writer Dale Launer—*Ruthless People* (1986), *Blind Date* (1987). He didn't have an agent. He did his own deals. David Permut was producing *Blind Date* with him. I published Launer's fee, which at the time was about $150,000. The head of the studio, Jeff Sagansky, didn't want that published. That was the angriest any source got at me. I remember holding the phone two feet from my ear, with Jeff screaming away: 'You've made it impossible for Tri-Star to do business in this town.' It was like something out of a movie. It was great. And all I'd done was print the number that David Permut had shown me."

"Were you ever conscious of writing beat sweeteners?"

"I've never heard that term. It's great. A story that would help your relationship with an important source. I don't think I ever consciously set out to do a puff piece on a guy, but there were people I was definitely seduced by. My favorite source was veteran producer Larry Gordon. He always spoke the truth from his standpoint and he is an incredible raconteur. He represented what appealed to me about the movie business—large than life characters who were fearless. This guy gave the best quotes. Everything was wrapped in a wonderful anecdote. There was a Southern accent on the end of the phone. He remains a good friend and a mentor. He was the kind of guy I'd give a lot of breaks to because he was so entertaining.

"The best ones understand that they have a job to do when they talk to the press, and that's to entertain.

"Some of these guys were just so tough. I remember going to a lunch at Paramount. Barry Diller was running the studio. There were a couple of dozen people at the lunch. I was introduced to Barry Diller. I said to the head of publicity, Deborah Rosen, for five minutes with Mr. Diller for a piece. She told me to be at his office at 2:30 p.m. Now it was 1:15.

"So I went to his office. I walked in. He was sitting at this desk that devoid of any paper. He was looking at a legal pad. When I walked in, he said, 'And you are?' It was a naked power move. It was jarring to me. Why is he saying this to me? I had just met this guy an hour ago. I'm the press, who everybody courts in this town. It rattled me. I don't remember what the story was about but I remember that moment because it was somebody demonstrating power and freezing you."

"Did you ever withhold writing something you believed to be true and accurate and you just didn't want to burn a source?"

"If something I thought was germane to the story, I'd figure out a way to tell it. If I had to shade it, by not identifying the source, I would say, 'one industry observer.' I wasn't out to embarrass people or cost anybody their job but I wrote some tough pieces."

"Did anyone you write about come back to haunt you as a producer?"

"No. In fact, the opposite. When I started working for Imagine, I had a two year deal. Shortly after I started in 1987, there was a writer's strike. You could not meet with writers. And when you're a young development executive, that is what you do. Your day is meeting writers. I was sitting in my office when I got this call from Brian Grazer. He said, 'What's going on?' I said, 'Not that much. I can't meet with any writers because of the strike.' He said, 'Don't think we're going to keep you around just because there's a writers strike. You better go out and find a movie for us.' I was petrified. When I hung up the phone, I was shaking. I'd just given up a nine-year career in journalism and now I was being told that if I didn't find a movie, I was going to be out on my ass. I couldn't go back to journalism.

"I called a young agent at CAA. I said I need to get to other sources of movies. He said he'd slip me a list of every producer in Hollywood and I could go see if they had any projects they'd want to bring to Imagine. I got to Rafaella De Laurentiis, who I had profiled in my column. It had a famous picture of her with her feet up on her desk, barefoot. I called her. 'Rafaella, I've got to come see you. I'm coming over. I need a script.'

"I came to her office. She was running DEG at the time, DeLaurentiis Entertainment Group, for her father Dino. She said, 'Look, I don't really have anything that you would do. I've got this one movie about firemen but you guys wouldn't do it.' I said, 'Sounds great. Let me read it.' I read it and I gave it to Brian and Ron [Howard]. Over the weekend, everyone at the company read it. On Monday morning, they went around the table at the staff meeting. Everyone was dumping on it. It gets around to me. I said, 'I would make it. It's a strong concept. People are interested in what firemen do.' Brian said, 'Yeah, I like it too and so does Ron.' Ron then took it on to direct [*Backdraft*, 1991].

"After the meeting, Brian came to my office and high fived me. So in a five day period, I went from the verge of being fired to being the hero. And a lot of that came from having a relationship with Rafaella."

"How did you come to Imagine?"

"About every Monday, I would call about 25 different people in the business. Brian was one of them. He courted the press. After about two years at *The LA Times*, I was interested in crossing over. Somebody said to Brian, 'You could hire this guy.' We ended up having a drink at the Sportsmen's Lodge. We had another meeting and he offered me a job at his new company.

"It was a fantastic place to learn. Brian and Ron are two of the most successful people in the history of the business. I was there for seven years, eventually becoming president of production. But ultimately it is the Ron and Brian show, as it should be, and I hit the glass ceiling. I left there and partnered with John Davis, who was a producer at Fox. I wanted to produce movies. I didn't want to be just a guy running a company. There was no chance to have your own byline.

"John came after me to run his company and to produce the movies with him. In three years, we produced four movies together: *Daylight* (1996), *Out to Sea* (1997), *Courage Under Fire* and *Dr. Dolittle*.

"By going to live on the movie set of *Courage Under Fire*, my first call and last call of every day was to Laura Ziskin [who ran Fox 2000]. That was a difficult movie. Through that experience, Laura said I'd done a good job and she would give me a producing deal. I said, I definitely want that. That's how I got the opportunity to open up Friendly Productions."

"Do producers share techniques with each other?"

"Producers talk to each other about challenges and frustrations and out of that you get a sense of how the other people do it. But like a good poker player, they're not going to give away all their moves. Different producers have different attitudes about it. I loved about Brian that he would go to movie theaters to watch movies with the public. He would not go to premieres. It made him uncomfortable to sit there with his competitors.

"You have these relationships with other producers but you're in friendly competition with them. Michael Caton-Jones is going to direct this movie I'm doing with Pierce Brosnan [*Laws of Attraction*, 2004]. Michael is off the market now. He's not available to other producers."

"Were you excited about all the movies you made or were some just a job?"

"I had a movie that didn't work, *Here on Earth* (2000), but I was really passionate about it because it was my idea. Those are the ones that I get most excited about—when I generate the concept and turn it into an actual movie. *Laws of Attraction* is an idea of mine to do a modern day's *Adam's Rib* (1949) about two divorce attorneys who can't stand each other and fall in love on opposite sides of the case.

"Once you decide to make a movie, you have to be passionate about it or it doesn't get made. Producing is pushing a boulder up a hill every day. And the boulder weighs two tons and I weigh 170 pounds. If I don't have the passion, I can't push that boulder up the hill. The studio or financier that green lights the movie, if they don't sense that in the producer, they are not going to make the movie."

"Is it possible to make an intelligent movie at a studio?"

"It all depends. I look back on *Courage Under Fire* as a smart movie. Laura Ziskin championed the movie. It was a problematic story to tell because it had this rashamon quality. I come from the studio world. I'm now doing my first independent film, *Little Miss Sunshine*. I don't like vast generalizations of any kind. *American Beauty* was a studio movie. Good work comes from many different places."

"Yet you told *Variety* when you started this company that you now sought 'independent fare that has the potential to break through as mainstream entertainment.'"

"At the time, I wanted to attract a different kind of script than I had normally been associated with. Sometimes you say things that are salesmanship. We have a mix of movies here. There are the mainstream high concept comedies that are my bailiwick but we're also drawn to independent fare. My partner would rather make independent movies but the mainstream movies pay the bills.

"I'm like every other producer. You're looking for a great script. You're looking for a script that wows you and seduces you. You don't categorize studio or independent. You're just trying to find good stories like a journalist is trying to find good stories. I don't think you set out to say, 'Well, this is where the story is going to come from.' You do 100 interviews and maybe the guy you did as a favor for somebody turns out to be the best interview. It's hard to go in and pre-fab the movie.

"What's great about independent features is that there are fewer rules. Studios today are into event movies. Look at what's out there—*Men in Black II* (2002), *Stuart Little II* (2002). Sequels, high concept saleable entities that can become a theme park attraction. The independent world is more about interesting characters and dynamic situations but it doesn't have to be high concept.

"It's hard to get a movie like *American Beauty* made by a studio. But when it is made, it is great because they put the same marketing muscle behind it as they would behind a regular feature. *Road to Perdition* (2002) looks like an independent movie that's being sold by a studio. That's the best of both worlds."

"Is your pecking order among your peers totally calibrated according to box office results?"

"I don't think so. Mark Johnson, for instance, is the epitome of the class producer. He's done a range of material. But he's not Jerry Bruckheimer. He doesn't have Jerry's economic success but I respect him equally. I'd like to achieve the economic success of a Brian Grazer or a Jerry Bruckheimer but I'm more drawn to the kinds of movies that Brian does than the movies that Jerry does.

"There are a handful of producers out there who can make what they want to make—Scott Rudin, Brian Grazer, Jerry Bruckheimer. When they call a studio head and say, 'I want to make this movie,' the studio head will generally trust their taste. That's true power because most of us have to sell all the time. Then the response comes back, 'The idea sounds good. Write the script. Get us a star.' You get the star and then you have to get a director."

"The movies you've made reflect you and your taste?"

"Somewhat. There are movies I would have liked to have made but haven't that I feel best reflect my taste. I wanted to produce *Dr. Dolittle* because at the time my kids were small and I wanted to make a movie that would make them smile and that they would watch over and over again.

"I love comedy. I find it to be a tonic for the world. But I like comedies with heart. I don't like doing big broad dumb comedy. Bob Simons has the market cornered on those. Growing up, I was drawn to much darker fare. I think the best movies our business has ever made were in the early '70s—*The Deer Hunter, Serpico, Dog Day Afternoon, The French Connection, The Godfather*. With all the technology and everything available to us today, I don't think the movies are as good. Yet I don't want to make those dark movies. I have a family now and I'm sheepish about violence. I'm not quite to the point where I think that violence in movies contributes to violence in society but I'm not drawn to: 'In this scene, do we want the guy strangled with a wire or we should just have him shove a knife into the back of his hand.'

"We change as people. You bring a family into the world and your tastes change and what you want out of a movie changes. I want to make movies that my kids can see. I'm proud of what I've done but I don't think I've done what I'm capable of doing."

"In many ways, we have less freedom to create today than we did 30 years ago."

"Good point. You have to be conscious about what is politically correct about smoking, language, women, dialogue, race. So how do you create interesting characters within those rules?"

"Have you found yourself running into things that are forbidden?"

"Not really. Our tastes are mainstream. *Little Miss Sunshine* is a movie about a family going through a beauty pageant in south Florida with a little girl. We have to be very careful how we deal with that because of the Jon Benet Ramsey incident. It's not a movie about beauty pageants. It's a movie about a family coming together, but there's a scene at the end of the movie where she dances at a pageant and we have to be careful how we treat that. We've had a lot of discussion about that."

"Why are studios so afraid of themes of organized religion? In a country as religious as the United States, you'd think that if you wanted to make family entertainment, you'd do some religious themes."

"A lot of the conflict in the world today is based on religious differences. A lot of the terrorism that we're facing now has its origins in religion. Studios want to avoid risk. To them, the world of religion is fraught with risk. *The Last Temptation of Christ*."

"That was a blasphemous movie. Most producers don't get it because they're not active in an organized religion."

"There was picketing and controversy but they had Marty Scorsese saying he wanted to make a movie and he's everybody's favorite director in this town. We don't turn him down.

"I've never been a particularly religious person. I grew up Jewish in New York. I went to Hebrew school. I was *bar mitzvah*ed in a Reform temple. I take Rosh Hashanah and Yom Kippur off and go to services. My wife who is not Jewish comes with me and really enjoys it. So I'm now drawn to those projects. I don't find them entertaining. I associate religion with history. I wouldn't make a movie about history either unless it has great conflict at the center."

"Yet 40 percent of Americans go to religious services weekly."

"Bowling is the most popular sport in America, yet nobody is making bowling movies."

57

Lewis Chesler

July 9, 2002

"I was a Cultural History major at Amherst College in Massachusetts. I was interested in literature. I found fiction to have a more vivid truth than nonfiction.

"After college, I joined the Peace Corp and went to Venezuela for two years. I was a child of the sixties. It was a romantic time and I was there supposedly to promote universal fraternity and brotherhood. Really I was stoned out of my mind for two years (1968-70).

"After school, I thought I might go into broadcasting but I found after working in the medium that it was reductive, dogmatic and propagandistic. I was then drawn to producing works of dramatic fiction.

"Now, even speculative fiction, has become didactic. Stories have become tendentious and moralistic. They are not filled with contradiction and they are not allowed to be messy complicated or interior. They are forced by market demands to be simplistic, formulaic and one dimensional.

"After Venezuela, I came back to New York and I started working in the performing arts as a producer and administrator. I had a girlfriend who was a dancer. I fell in love with her. I eventually lost her but I kept the love of the dance. I ran several modern dance and ballet companies. At the time, it was a fast growing entertainment form (it's since lost its appeal). I still love dance. I think it's the purest art form there is. It's simply the body as idea.

"I recognized that you couldn't make a living working in the performing arts because there is no support for the arts in America.

"I then went to work in the mass media. Entertainment is a serendipitous business. Through a series of random events, I came to the West Coast and became a theatrical producer of spectacle entertainment like theater, rodeo and rockn'roll shows. I became the artistic director of the Long Beach Convention and Entertainment Center.

"In 1979, I lost that job because of funding cutbacks (Proposition 13). I was stranded here in LA. I looked around for work.

"At the Center, I'd created a theatrical event televised on HBO. I'd met television producer Riff Markowitz who I'd introduced to an executive at Home Box Office, Michael Fuchs, who subsequently became the chairman of HBO.

"Through our joint relationship with Michael, Riff and I became one of the leading independent producers for pay television. We made a lot of event programming for HBO like concerts (Crystal Gale), one-man shows starring great performance artists and comedians like George Burns and Red Skelton (who taught me that great clowns are not about making us laugh but about breaking our hearts).

"Network television was strictly hierarchical then. It was hard to gain entry unless you'd started at an agency or studio or network and worked your way up. Because cable was an emerging industry, it allowed you lateral entry. I went to Michael Fuchs and said that I wanted to do drama. I created an anthological concept (*The Hitchhiker*, 1983-91) inspired by *The Twilight Zone* (1959-65) and the *court metrage* (European notion of small films).

"HBO was then chiefly a purveyor of film, not conventional television programming. We discovered that the creative license of pay television allowed us to produce these shows like features with creative licenses not available in standard network television. We used a European flavor with a more graphic visual presentation. We had more license with language and provocative ideas.

"This made the programming distinct and a value to HBO, which was trying to sell itself as a premium service. HBO wanted the audience to understand that they were getting something of value for their subscription."

"I remember in high school people were talking about it because it had a lot of nudity."

"I wanted to deal with emotion, sexuality and psycho-erotic ideas in a way that no other American mass medium allowed you to do. Sexuality is a fundamental part of the dramatic conflict. In the 1960s and early '70s, it was a part of American filmmaking but since then American film has become chaste. Even suspense has been removed from storytelling. American films are star driven. Because you have to protect the longevity and the heroic value of the star, you know that Julia or Tom is going to be all right. So what's the point of seeing the movie? Once you have invested so much in personage, there's no investment in story.

"*The Hitchhiker* was also distinct because it was done as a Canadian-French co-production. It was a progenitor of the possibility of globalization. I've long been a fan of European cinema. I used directors like Paul Verhoven, Philip Noyce, Roger Vadim and Wayne Wang who'd rarely worked in North America and never in television. HBO was not a signatory to the Directors Guild of America at the time. I became the definitive expert on Eastern European and South Pacific directors. They in turn brought in feature talent like Klaus Kinski, Gary Busey, Willem DeFoe, Karen Black and Peter Coyote.

"European television at the time was state-run television. It was rudimentary.

"The last 25 30-minute episodes of *The Hitchhiker* were made in Paris.

"There's a tradition in Europe of the small movie. That's what we were making."

"You've made a ton of stuff over the past three years, most prolific."

Lewis laughs. "Until today we were. It is getting more difficult because of the fragmentation of the market, the collapse of the world economy, the collapse of the broadcast market in places like Germany, Italy, Spain and the UK."

"There was a glowing article about you in *Variety* a week ago."

"Yeah. I hope it is not my obituary."

"How do the sinking stock prices of companies like Vivendi, AOL, etc affect you?"

"Those are the distribution streams we sell to. Now they are taking their cash and not spending it on content but on keeping their own companies afloat. It's all changing and at such exponential rates. Fifteen independent distributors have gone out of business in the last 12 months."

"How much time do you spend in LA a year?"

"As little as possible, because the more time I spend in LA, the more time that I am not working. I like to supervise production. I've just returned from six months in Paris where we shot *Tempo* for Canal Plus. I usually spend about three months a year in LA."

"Are you married?"

"I was in a long term relationship."

"That must be hell on your relationships."

"It's hard. Is this a personal interview or a professional interview? I've been a gypsy for 20 years. I love the excitement of it. I love to experience new things. I love the interchange with creative people. We're crazy. This is a community of misfits. We live on the marginal edges of reality or too directly in the center."

"What is the filmmaker's moral responsibility to society?"

"To subvert. Artists are not supposed to be good citizens. It's not their work. They must challenge the system, not reinforce it. American studio films reinforce preconceived notions of behavior."

"Have you ever read a script and thought, 'This is too immoral for me to make.'"

"No. Immoral is not a word I use as a judgment.

"There's no point to humor unless it wounds."

"What are some of the taboos you've run into?"

"You couldn't do a movie now about pedophilia. It's part of the human condition and you should be able to do a film about it so that people can make their own judgment on it."

"What did you think of *American Beauty?*"

"I thought *American Pie* was better."

"It doesn't seem that the projects you work on live up to the ethos you espouse?"

"It's hard because the market compromises everything you do."

"Which producers do you admire?"

"I think the Weinstein brothers are the most interesting American producers and entrepreneurs."

"Why is your industry so afraid of themes dealing with organized religion?"

"Many things are taboo—politics, religion. Many things can not sustain legitimate discourse in American life. We're not an introspective culture."

"What's the most desperate thing you've ever had to do to get a film made?"

Lewis thinks. "In comparison to the truly desperate things that some people have to do to survive, I haven't had to do anything desperate. Mostly what you have to do to get films made is lie."

"How do you handle bad reviews?"

"Nothing bothers me. I have no character. I don't get that invested. As my former partner used to say, 'At the end, it's just a TV show, not a religious crusade.' I've always separated myself from the produce of my labors."

Chesler is a founder of The Los Angeles Museum of Contemporary Art and is on the board of numerous ballet and modern dance companies.

July 19, 2002

Lewis still wears a white singlet.

"I fear that I may have made my last movie. So if this interview is going to be my epitaph, I have some things to say about the industry."

"Why so dour?"

"The independent movie business has collapsed. With the concentrations of the big media companies, with the nature of the changing viewing patterns of the public, it may never come back. I hate to be dire. There have just been many sea changes in viewer interest, demand, taste, satisfaction levels and cultural changes in notions of originality and authenticity versus the lack of need for them. Those things are no longer valued.

"This is prevalent not just in popular culture, but was first introduced in high art, where authenticity was no longer valued. The aping of means of mass reproduction, with people like Warhol, became valued. Warhol did it in an ironic fashion. His was a critique that had value and originality but in the 40 years since Warhol, it has overwhelmed us. This has impacted on story telling and people's response to story and the values they look for in story. Stories are no longer sequential, linear, interior, contradictory or original. The audience wants some level of reassurance that formula and engineered response provides them.

"There was a review today of *K-19* by Kenneth Turan that said the film was fundamentally undermined by the fact that it was so predictable in its key moments, in comparison to the definitive submarine piece of *Das Boot*.

"There are a number of factors that mitigate quality work. We're an ahistoric culture. There's a despotism of the present. We're a reductive culture. Everything is reduced to compressed, simple, intense ideas. I think that's the influence of advertising and the exponential growth of information. The only way to take in all this information is to compress it. Unfortunately, we've lost essential information in the process.

"We've lost the deliberation of information and knowledge. The kind of knowledge we receive does not permit us reflection. There is no contemplation any longer. There's certainly no contemplation in popular art, film or television. There's not only an intellectual change in the way we perceive things, but thanks to the introduction of the computer, there's a sensory change in the way we receive information. We're no longer a linear, sequential, chronological culture. We're now a random binary culture. Thanks to video games and music videos, our narrative structure has been altered significantly.

"Why we can't deal with other kinds of information is of interest to me. American culture defends itself against pain and suffering and history, loss, death and ultimately life. We're a death-denying culture. We're a life-denying culture. We're a sex-denying culture. This is a residue of the fact that we're fundamentally a Protestant culture and therefore we're a culture that is sexually guilty and bodily shameful.

"There is no willingness in America to deal with dark intent. We had artists who did—Edgar Alan Poe, Nathaniel Hawthorne, Norman Mailer—but they don't speak any longer to the culture. American life has been homogenized and sanitized. We're the residue of an English culture. Remember the E.M. Forster comment about the English not being disposed to accep human nature.

"I think that most of it has to do with sexual guilt. I have always felt there's a relationship between sexual repression and the violence that is so endemic to American culture. One part of American's fascination with horror and violence is that horror and violence is basically sexual projection and sexual repression. If there was a greater genuine sexual permissiveness, we would be less violent. The moralistic self-righteous critics of American culture say there is too much permissiveness. I find it to be a coy permissiveness. It's manufactured. It doesn't allow the genuineness, the pain, the raggedness of real emotion and therefore sexuality.

"Our notions of beauty have become artificial. The constructed, the manufactured, the augmented breast, is now what is perceived as the ideal. The human, the regular, the slightly misformed is repressed and denied. This is a residue of the Protestantism of the American culture. One of the premises of that paradigm was grace through good works and purification and that we be an insistently self-improving culture. This process of self amelioration denies and attempts to cleanse human nature, which I think is impossible.

"It's not unlike when Marquis De Sade wrote."

"Is he a good guy in your eyes?"

"Oh no."

"He seems to be the opposite of everything you've decried."

"The point of Sade was to critique the utopian hope of the Enlightenment. He wanted to subvert or challenge the investment in reason and science as salvation by saying that not withstanding the progress in those areas, man was still ruled by fundamentally bestial, aggressive, and libidinal impulses."

"What did you think of the movie *Quills* (2000)?"

"I didn't like it. It was too flamboyant and theatrical. I like the French version of Sade. I'm not an expert on Sade. I only read him because he turned me on as an adolescent.

"The other principle, by the way, that we deny in our culture is the principle of pleasure. Even our popular culture doesn't give us pleasure. It gives us engineered sensation but not genuine pleasure the way a great work of art should. It should be erotic, tactile."

"I don't get why you didn't love *American Beauty* because it glorifies the homosexual couple, portrays everyone else as screwed up."

"I thought the targets were easy."

"But they're all the targets you just named."

"But I thought it was too easy. It wasn't wounding enough. It wasn't scabrous enough. It didn't truly pierce to the heart of anything. It presented it all with a sitcom irony. These are things that have been addressed by other ironists and satirists in American culture in a deeper way."

"Who has pierced through and been scabrous enough?"

"I like the black artists."

"Spike Lee. *Clockers* (1995)."

"Yes. Chris Rock. Richard Pryor."

"Quentin Tarantino?"

"Yes and no. He's more about form. He's more of an aesthete than a social critic. His art is about art. His filmmaking is about filmmaking, which is ok. Art is self referential and a lot of art has become about the process of art.

"The reason I think I am citing some of the black artists is because the outsider has nothing to lose. They can have the courage to be most damaging. When Roseanne did her best work, because she was fundamentally an unattractive woman in the conventional sense, she was so audacious and honest in her pain, that I thought, even in the context of a sitcom, there was real humor in what she did.

"It's been almost impossible for [true artists] to work [within the system] in the last 10-15 years because the economic forces of the market are so overwhelming."

"Are there some pornographers that you find piercing and scabrous enough?"

"Not that I know of. I've watched it randomly but I wouldn't know anybody specifically.

"I also like the lyrical and the tender. I don't think that's present in a lot of American work either. That's a result of a desensitization of feeling. We've become feeling less. We are not permitted to be vulnerable. That is some kind of a warding off or a defense against some of the notions I've talked about.

"You asked me about morality. I think that's a religious or social term. The point of art is to engage taboo not to recede from it."

"What did you think of photographer Robert Maplethorpe?"

"He was an aesthete. He forces us to deal with issues of gender, sexuality and politics, which is where art went. Everything in recent art has been seen through the prism of identity. This sometimes ignores our common humanity. We are all searching for the same thing—love, affirmation, and intimacy. I don't care what social or political group you come from. I say that so much of American work has become didactic and propagandistic because it focuses more on social-political association and connection then it does on human need. There should be no censoring the human heart."

"So who are the guys in town who are fighting this good fight?"

"I don't think anybody is. I can't cite a commercial film that was moving or valuable. I think there are films made by North Americans that have tremendous energy of form, style and skill. But I don't care about the sophistication of film. When special effects come on, I close my eyes. I was never interested in cinema as a kinetic art. I've always treated film as pictorial literature, and maybe that's not fair to film. Maybe film is its own thing and I should look for the qualities that I want in film in literature.

"I remember films of greater depth, complexity and beauty or even greater commercial energy. I just watched *Training Day* and I don't know how to comment on it when I compare it to a film like *French Connection*.

"*Training Day* was completely manipulative. It was so posed that every frame was a tableau. There didn't seem to be any arc to the cinema let alone to the character or the story. There didn't seem to be any truth. I didn't believe a single moment.

"Maybe everything has been said. Maybe there are no more stories to be told."

"Could you get any darker and more pessimistic?"

Lewis laughs. "You're young. There are guys who preceded me who said this.

"I once read a quote by Jean Luc Godard. It said that anytime that anything good is successful, it must be the result of a misunderstanding. I said, how wry, how clever, how sardonic. Then I was reading an exchange of letters between Heinrich Mann and his brother Thomas in which he says that anytime that if anything good is successful, it must be the result of a misunderstanding. I said, wait, Jean Luc Godard plagiarized. And he was one of my cultural idols.

"But after I thought for a second, I said, 'But of course. That's exactly what he was about. Appropriation. Godard's work was always about deconstruction and appropriation."

"So what great loss did you suffer that made you so cynical?"

"I've always had a forlorn view of life."

"It doesn't go any deeper?"

"What else is there? For *Citizen Kane*, it was his sled Rosebud. For Proust, it was his tea cookies. Ultimately, it's all irony and pathos."

"It doesn't have to be. Why do you want to choose that?"

"Because I don't know how else to treat the world."

"That's it. Secular life is so reductive that if you are intelligent, there's no alternative but the dark view."

"Faith. I can't partake in it. I might find some transcendence through art."

"You have no hope."

"I can always hope for an increase in my MasterCard line."

"Why do you get up every morning and keep doing this?"

"Because of pleasure. I have pleasure in experience and learning. You should learn something new every day. Life is a matter of wasting time."

"When was the last time you were starstruck?"

"I was never starstruck. I've never had a hero."

58

Cary Solomon, Chuck Konzelman

July 16, 2002

Cary: "[Don] Simpson and [Jerry] Bruckheimer said that if you write a great script, you'll own the town. We believed them. We wanted to run a studio. Our goal was and still is to be like Louis B. Mayer and Irving Thalberg. So we've concentrated on writing scripts, and eventually it started working for us.

"There are two types of producers: There's a producer who's a schmoozer. He gets material and takes it with him to star actors and directors and studio contacts and puts the package together. And then there's the creative producer."

Chuck: "I don't know how the producers on the lowest rung of the food chain, who are strictly producers, are able to function these days. The studio system as it exists today presents those guys with an unfair set of hurdles. Projects are no longer bought simply because the script is based on a good idea. A script has to be in shooting form before anybody is going to put up a nickel. This means the producer is forced to acquire the material with his own money and somehow bring it up to snuff. I don't know how they make a living."

Cary: "You have a two-tier system. You have the low-end producer who lives off foreign pre-sales and manipulating this and that. They make $150,000 off one movie and the next thing you know they're working in the circus that just left town. Then you have the major in-house studio producers like Joel Silver and Arnold Kopelson.

"We want to produce and direct. We want to be as writer friendly as possible and become a Statute of Liberty for writers. We leveraged our way in with the writing and now we're starting to direct. And because of our heat as writers—we're doing *The Inferno* with Joel Silver and Warner Brothers and we're working with Stan Lee and Bruce Willis on a project called *Femizons*. We've

391

become A list. And now we get approached by independent money sources. It's a town of legal extortion."

Chuck: "The more acceptable term is 'leverage.' That's how the business works. You negotiate the best deal you can based on what you bring to the table. Most industry people call it clout. Dealmakers back East used to call it 'drag.'

"Because the international market has monopolized that 'under $10 million' feature range, we've become landed immigrants for Canadian purposes (the Canadian equivalent of resident alien status in the United States). Now we don't get shut out on the producing end from the Canadian and Canadian-Euro subsidies. We qualify for 'soft-dollar' subsidies and tax credits everywhere in the world.

"We lost our series *The Immortal* (2000). It was a good idea that became an awful 22-hour series because we weren't 'landed' at the time."

Cary: "We had a brilliant idea for a TV show. At the time there were four stars in syndicated TV who were considered worth $100,000 an episode. The only one whose series had just been cancelled was Lorenzo Lamas. We took it to his manager on a Friday. By Monday we had a deal. He had another series deal in the final stages of negotiation, but he walked away from it to do ours. Our ex-managers—who were the XP's on the show—came to us at the last moment and said, 'You're not Canadian. We're shooting the show in Canada. You're screwed.' We balked at their offer, and after some acrimonious negotiations they ended up paying us $16,000 a week to walk away and do nothing. Since it was already financed for a guaranteed run of 22 episodes, we agreed but the downside is they castrated the show. They turned it into a piece of shit because they had no idea what the hell they were doing.

"One of the problems of going to a B producer is that it's all about the money. They take what they can. If it were the same situation now, we'd be able to make a hit show and get the credits and residuals for the rest of our lives. We decided we weren't going to let this happen to us again and now we're eligible for every tax credit in the world.

"The rest of the world is joining up to beat up on Hollywood."

Luke: "Who did you have to sleep with to get this special landed status?"

Chuck: "Like everything else in this industry, it comes down to money. There's an attorney in Toronto who specializes in doing this. There's nothing illicit about it, but the Canadians are pretty specific about who they want to qualify, mainly producers and directors, people who are held to be 'work creators' as opposed to those who fill a slot which could be serviced by a Canadian citizen."

Cary: "We were in Artisan Entertainment the other day. They're talking about doing business with us. We brought up the fact that we were landed, and they went crazy (in a good way). They said we could work forever because in some cases we'd be eligible to get 30 percent of the budget subsidized."

Luke: "How did you guys meet?"

Cary: "My mom and dad divorced when I was a junior in high school. We moved out to New Jersey. Chuck was the guy next door. I felt sorry for him."

Chuck: "I let him follow me around and it was the mistake of my life. I went to college at Notre Dame and studied accounting finance. I audited mutual funds for a few years. Cary and I opened a brokerage for a few years. We made a lot of money but we decided we hated our lives and our business. We'd rather make movies. So we figured if we were successful in one business, we could be successful in Hollywood."

Cary: "Our decision did not make our girlfriends too happy."

Chuck: "We had no idea how difficult it would be to get into this business. We now refer to it as the paradox of Hollywood: Anyone who is raised in Los Angeles typically doesn't understand the types of movies that excite the rest of the country. And the rest of the country doesn't understand anything how movies are made. And it's incredible difficult to find someone who understands both sets of realities."

Cary: "We started in the mutual funds business having no contacts and ended up making incredible amounts of money. We were doing a convention speech in Philadelphia. We had offices in 20 states. After my speech, I said to Chuck, who was about to go on stage, 'Do you want to go to Hollywood and make movies?' He said, 'Yeah.' That was it. We were off.

"If you come to town to make movies, the hardest part is making an entry into the business, because you are going t o suffer and be humiliated, no matter what. It's a ten year ordeal. The industry is a terrible mistress, but if you can somehow endure, after ten years, you know everyone. Mathematically, you can't help bumping into people at a diner."

Chuck: "As Dick Wolf [creator of *Law & Order*, 1990-???] points out, success is largely about outlasting everyone else."

Luke: "People tell me that the best asset for a producer is some money in the bank, because there are such long dry spells."

Chuck: "Yup. Especially if you're not a creator, you're going to need money to option or purchase scripts. Paying for rewrites, running an office. It all adds up. Sooner or later, someone without basis for it is going to try to block your access to a property you legitimately own the rights to. So you need at least $50,000 on hand to hire a good attorney to squash that suit."

Cary: "It's not like you can't do it without money. We did it."

Luke: "Wait, you just told me you made a ton of money before you came here?"

Cary: "When we came out, we couldn't take a lot of that money with us. We were living high at the time, which was a mistake. We were arrogant and said, 'We've conquered Wall Street, we can conquer Hollywood.' Because we were 3000 miles away, they gobbled the business up and stopped sending checks. We went from wealthy to having to buy 69c burritos to survive.

"In our heyday, we were spending hundreds of dollars for dinner. We'd take eight friends out and end up footing a bill for hundreds of dollars."

Luke: "Did your girlfriends come with you to Hollywood and share in your pain?"

Chuck: "Mine came with me for six months."

Cary: "Mine promised she'd love me forever. That ended the day I quit my business."

Chuck: "She could tell we were headed for the 69c burritos."

Luke: "Women have good antennae."

Cary: "I don't blame them for leaving. What we went through for the next five years, I wouldn't put anyone through. The tragedy of Hollywood is that there are so many creative people who will never get a chance because of Hollywood's caste system."

Chuck: "It's as bad as being a serf in the Middle Ages."

Cary: "You have this great piece of material and you can't get a meeting or an agent."

Chuck: "No one will look at it and no manager or entertainment attorney wants you for a client because you don't make any money."

Cary: "If you've got the stink of no one wanting to talk to you, how do you break in? You have to scrape your way in from the bottom like a gladiator rising out of the pits. Our first writing job was for $250 to take a script from Polish to English. We did our first producing jobs for free for the experience. Then you meet five, ten, fifteen people and over time, people see you and hire you."

Luke: "Tell me about your film school experience at USC. I hear that's the best place to make Hollywood contacts after Harvard."

Cary: "We bought into their accelerated six month program for $50,000 each. We didn't know anything about film. We heard it was the most prestigious film school in the world. The guy told us on the phone, 'This is going to be four awesome years crammed into six months. You're not going to have time to eat or sleep.'

"We went in and they were teaching us all this useless crap. They spent six weeks teaching us about film from 1908. They know all about pre-WWII Russian documentaries, but the professors hadn't bothered to see the blockbuster films of that year."

Chuck: "Then we broke into little groups to do a 16mm color sync sound-short. The director of the program asked us to stop scaring students because we were too intense. We wanted to learn everything we could in the shortest amount of time. We had only one good professor, Herb Pearl. He was a director of photography. He would only teach on Saturday or Sunday because he was working the rest of the week. He would teach more in those two days than everybody else did in the other five."

Cary: "We finished the program in two months and got in our car, drove back to New Jersey, moved all of our stuff out here and went to work. It was a worthless program. You learn by doing. If you want to be a producer, roll your sleeves up and go to work. Do everything. Assist someone. We have interns by the bundle. We believe in helping people. You need to find a mentor, because that's better than film school.

"In the nine years we've been out here, we've seen the whole industry change. It used to be you could go to a meeting at a studio, pitch an idea and they'd rip out a check for $750,000. That doesn't happen anymore. You have to go through 50 ranks before and then they ask you, 'What's your quote?'

"A quote is the fee you get for your services. If you are a writer-producer, and your quote for your first movie was $125,000, then that's your quote. If you don't have a quote, they are going to start you at $75,000."

Chuck: "Studios have become good at 'sidestepping.' Studios don't honor production company quotes, even if they are from big production companies and they've actually paid you. Studios will try to depress your price on your first studio gig. Here's how you gauge whether they really want you: Our manager responded to a quote squabble six months ago by saying, 'Let the quote write the script.' In other words, if you want the project from these guys, you are going to have to pay more. And they did."

Cary: "We worked with a guy whose quote to produce is $750,000. We came to him with a smaller project, which he loved. But he couldn't do it because his cut would only be $300,000. And if he did that, then everyone would think he was on the slide.

"This is a hard time to be a producer but the magic of seeing your film on screen keeps everybody going.

"I suggest to prospective producers, if you can, write and direct. It gives you additional bullets for your gun. If you can't, you can still schmooze your way through it. It's just harder.

"You have to decide early on what you want—art or commerce. If you want to make money, you have to work within the studio system. If you want to make art films, you have to make them independently.

"We're working on a small independent called *Bad Karma*, which we wrote and are going to direct. We want to take it to Cannes and the other film festivals. We want to make both independent films and studio films. We can do both so long as everyone knows that it's a conscious decision on our part to go independent, not because we're failures.

"One of the great things in this town is the publicity machine. You need to learn how to spin things because people get destroyed over perception. In Hollywood, it is not about who you really are but about how you are perceived. If you don't get a hold of your image quick, you're dead.

"You say to your agency—our agency is ICM—we're doing this because, damn it, we're artists. And you tell them 90 times because you want them to get it through their heads. They are so deluged with so many clients and material."

Chuck: "Unless you're born wealthy or well-connected, you have to find the most powerful advocates you possibly can to champion your material. Credibility comes from being vouched for by other people who are perceived as being credible. That's why it's so tough for an unknown outsider to break in. He or she may have written a brilliant piece of material but people out there probably won't recognize it as brilliant. Or, if they do suspect that it is something special, they will be afraid of their own convictions. And if they hear any negative reaction from anyone, they will tend to say, 'Oh well, I guess that wasn't as special as I thought it was.'"

Cary: "We were lucky that we mapped out a plan whereby if we could get our hands on great material, sniff it out like a Thalberg, then we could show it to stars and get it made. Most of the talent can't predict great material. We've been fortunate to have a manager who goes around town every day telling people, 'This is great. This is hot.'

"We started off with an entertainment lawyer who had no idea what he was doing. Now we have the best lawyer in town, Mike Adler. He reps Tarantino, Soderberg and Streisand as well.

"You need a 'battle plan' to conquer Hollywood. You need to plan everything.

"If you were to come to town and suddenly make a big deal and become an overnight success, it would probably wipe you out. You wouldn't be able to handle it. You don't know anything yet, and likely couldn't duplicate the success. Don't believe it? Look back at the writers of all the big spec script sales of six to eight years ago. Most haven't been seen or heard from since."

Chuck: "You need to get one person to like you and your work. Then you get other people to like you. We have a spec script going out in the next week. It was a sneak to one star who wanted to be attached to it. If the star didn't want to be attached, everyone's perception would be damaged."

Cary: "I have chancy material that I won't move right now. It goes in the treasure chest. When you've got the heat, you can let it out.

"If we end up selling this spec script for a million and end up producing for another $250,000, and the result is good, we get heat. Then that piece I put on the shelf is ready for daylight. All of the sudden, we're geniuses and we're daring. Five months earlier, it would've been written off as 'over the top'.

"You've got to turn your heat into meetings with the right people. You've got to build associations with the right people to move forward."

Chuck: "Most chronic gamblers begin with a lucky first day at the track and it's all downhill from there."

Luke: "Many producers tell me that their best experience was making their first film and everything has been downhill from there."

Chuck: "Because they rounded up independent money for that project and they had nearly complete creative control."

Cary: "Later on everybody gets involved."

Chuck: "The moment you take that studio check, you have to realize that you are beholden to them. They are in charge."

Cary points to a poster from one of his projects gone bad, *Race Against Time* (2000).

"If I were to teach a film course, I'd make people read the original script and then watch the movie. And see how 30 extra people in the process destroyed something brilliant.

"It was a piece called *Gabriel's Run*. It won several screenwriting awards. It built our careers."

Chuck: "It was watered down for cable TV. We only let it go because it was supposed to be a backdoor two-hour pilot for a series."

Cary: "The agent sold it for fast money. We thought it was going to be a feature and it ended up on TNT. But we still send out *Gabriel's Run* as a writing sample of our work and a lot of our career was built on it. MGM saw it a few months ago and a Senior VP was very excited about whether or not it was still available."

Chuck: "It's what got us the Stan Lee—MGM—Bruce Willis project."

"Many film producers are bringing in 60-70 percent of the financing from funds under their control. They expect complete creative control but they still end up having to meet numerous studio criteria."

Luke: "How do you guys divide up?"

Cary: "He's great analytically. He's great with numbers and finances and planning."

Chuck: "I always want to bring things back to structure. He's the great intuitive thinker. He thinks outside the box."

Cary: "We have the same goal. We want to run a studio. Everything else is subservient to that goal. We know that we're better together. McCartney and Lennon were better together. Simon and Garfunkel were better together.

"People laugh at us when we say this. They think we have audacity. It's simple. We want to do it the way Simpson and Bruckheimer could've done it. They had the opportunity but chose to stay producers because it was more lucrative. At their height with Paramount, they were getting nine percent of the gross from first dollar."

Chuck: "We're willing to take a cut in pay for the opportunity to determine which movies get made and how."

Cary: "We want to reinvent a workable form of the old studio system. I believe you can pick the winners. We know what good material is. We write it all the time. We're starting to direct. We have no doubt that our profile as directors will flare up. If you do good work, and put your heart and soul in, you will be noticed.

"People fail in this town because of sex, drugs or parties or greed or ego. Too often one of the nasty traits becomes dominant and destroys everything.

"If you ask these veteran producers about their goal, you might find out that some of them got lost along the way.

"Money follows success. When I was in my last business, and I was making $100,000 a month, people were calling me and offering $10 million. It's the same thing in Hollywood. Once you get a profile going, it builds on itself."

Luke: "Tell me about your manager Jeff Wald?"

Chuck: "If Jeff believes in you, he will strap on a sword and shield and go out and do battle against any dragon."

Cary: "He made our career. Let me tell you a story. Our manager at the time, Mark Skelly, took us in to meet Jeff in November of last year. He sits behind his desk. 'Who the fuck are you? I've read your shit. I know that you guys want to write and direct and produce and run a studio. It ain't gonna happen.'

"For the first hour, he just hits you with cannon shells. Then he said, 'But you guys have something special. I know. I can do this for you.' He gets on the phone. 'I can make you guys. I'm going to get you a $500,000 deal right now.'

"Jeff makes a call. We're at Stallone's house an hour later. Stallone says, 'You guys are good.' Six hours later, we have a $500,000 deal because Stallone wanted us to rewrite a project that's been bouncing around town for years."

Chuck: "It was a fantasy project (based on the novel *The Green*) that nobody could get a take on. We didn't even have to pitch our take on it. We just got the assignment and ICM became our new agents.

"*The Green* is the story of a golf hustler (Stallone) who gets sucked into the world of Ryder Cup play. We have a quirky black comedy sense. Stallone read *Bad Karma* and was tickled by it, and essentially said, 'I want these guys for the rewrite.'"

Luke: "What should I be asking producers?"

Chuck: "If you're looking to find out what these guys really know, you won't find the answers from asking direct questions. Because you'll frame those questions based on things you think up in your head. The real secrets of producing are hidden a lot deeper and you have to hope they're willing to unfold those things before you. If you're not experienced enough, you won't know what questions to ask."

Cary: "It's like anything else. Ten years on the police force, and a cop knows exactly how to talk to somebody. He can tell when somebody is lying."

Chuck: "The power producers are defined clearly. Are they gross percentage players? Do they get a set percentage of gross box office revenues? There aren't half a dozen guys in town who can legitimately make that claim."

Cary: "They came from a different time. They came when things were flexible. Everyone was shooting from the hip. Everybody was go-go-go. James Cameron started as a model maker, then worked as a writer, then director, now producer. He forces projects through because of his clout. He can direct one movie and produce five based on his muscle. The new producer is the creative producer who can write, direct and produce."

Chuck: "And in many ways, this tough market works to our advantage. We can go out and find material that's just inside the 20-yard line and polish it up to where it gets across the goal line."

Cary: "Stuff that nobody else is paying attention to."

Chuck: "Big agencies now complain, behind closed doors, that they've been too successful. They've managed to get fees so high for their A-list stars that very few movies can be made. There isn't enough work to go around.

"Americans have traditionally spent about seven percent of their disposable income on entertainment every decade of the past century. That held true even during the Great Depression. So ultimately a bottleneck in studio production creates a demand for more hours of entertainment product."

Cary: "When I came out here, I did not understand why studios didn't accept unsolicited scripts. I now understand. We just had to shut down our development arm. There was potential for too many lawsuits. We had a production company. We'd take in 3000 scripts a year, and our people would read them panning for gold. Maybe we bought five.

"There just wasn't enough 'gold in them thar hills' to justify the expense. Ironically, it's not the good scripts that create a potential liability. The good ones you buy, and that's it. Or if the writer has unreasonable expectations about what it's worth, you just say 'oh well,' forget about it and move on. It's the unreadable piece of junk where one of your readers read the first ten pages and passed without even doing coverage on the screenplay. We've never been big on wasted labor. Why spend two hours of writing to say a script is no good? But the writer of that screenplay is out there somewhere, liable to file suit if they have the least suspicion that you might have knocked off their script because you do something in a similar genre. I now understand that the studios only accept material from the agencies, because the agencies filter out most of the nonprofessional junk."

Chuck: "There's a saying around town: Feature people invite people to their premieres. TV people invite people to their homes."

59

Mark Frost

I meet Mark Frost (born in 1953) at a deli in Bel Air.

Billionaire Steve Bing jogs up. He moves like an 18-year old jock. He wears shorts and a Taj Mahal T-shirt. He yells at a friend like a high school student and they slide into the deli.

Brian Wilson of the Beach Boys sits with his back to us.

"Tell me about your transition to writing novels."

"Everything is on a smaller scale. The money is less.

"I grew up in New York. We moved to Los Angeles when I was a kid. My father [Warren Frost] was a stage manager of Philco Playhouse of *Playhouse 90* (1956-61) when they were doing live shows weekly. That dried up. My father wanted to be an actor and he thought LA was the place for that. With three young kids, I was the oldest, he wasn't able to make a go of it.

"After seven years, he decided to get his doctorate in Theater. He joined the faculty of the University of Minnesota in Minneapolis, where I went to the university high school. It was a radical shift in reality after being brought up on both coasts. I worked as an intern at the Guthrie Theater. I wrote plays. Guthrie produced one of my plays (*Between Looks*) as a high school tour show.

"I went to Carnegie Mellon University in Pittsburgh as a playwright. For about 30 years, it was the preeminent theatrical conservatory along with Julliard. A vast network of alumni came into this business. When I was ready to leave after my junior year, I met Steve Bochco, who'd graduated ten years before. It was 1974 and Steve was the story editor of *McMillan and Wife*.

"Steve introduced me around Universal and I had a job within three weeks. I wrote for *The Six Million Dollar Man*. My college gave me credit for working in Hollywood and I graduated while making a living. When that year was over, I wasn't ready to commit to working in television. So I went back to the Guthrie and worked there for three years as a literary associate and a playwright. While taking a vow of poverty for several years, I had plays done all over the mid West.

"I began making documentaries for the local PBS station. One got national exposure—a portrait of my friend Jim Beattie, a former heavyweight boxer. A big white guy, 6'8" and 240 pounds, he'd been recruited by a consortium out of New York. Sonny Liston was the champ then and he was a poster boy for bad behavior.

"To make a long sad story short, he realized that the guys paying the freight were Frank Costello and the mob. He tried to get out of his contract. They tried to kill him. They drugged his water bottle in a fight at Madison Square Garden. It ruined him. He was almost killed in the ring. His life fell apart. He moved back to Minnesota. He was cast as the Great White Hope in the movie *The Great White Hope* (1970). He's the guy who beats up James Earl Jones.

"Jim pulled himself back together. He started a halfway house for young felons. He started boxing again. He eventually won the heavyweight championship of Minnesota.

"It was 1983. I came out to Los Angeles to write for the third season of Bochco's *Hill Street Blues*. I worked on the show for three years. That put me on the map. I was the youngest guy on the staff.

"Then I wrote and associate produced a movie with John Schlesinger, *The Believers* (1987). I took the job because I wanted a master course in filmmaking. Schlesinger, a generous guy, took me on. I was involved from the first story meeting to the last preview. I did some second-unit directing. I sat in the editing room with him for four months. Then I met David Lynch. One of our mutual agents at CAA thought it would be interesting to put us together and see what happened.

"I wrote a script for a movie that David was going to produce, an adaptation of a book by Anthony Summers about Marilyn Monroe, *Goddess*, for United Artists (1988). The movie was never made but David and I hit it off.

"We both had an outsiders mentality. I had never embraced the industry as a way of life. I saw it as a way to make a living. I had many interests beyond film and television. David was the same way. We both had some wild ideas about how to shake things up.

"We had this opportunity to create a show for ABC, then the third place network. We demanded and received complete creative control. *Twin Peaks* (1990-91) came out of that. *Twin Peaks* was the not the product of a network clusterfuck. It was two guys going off, creating their own studio, owning their own show."

Mark eats a chicken tostada. He drinks a coke. It's *Tishu Be'Av*, a Jewish fast, so I can't eat or drink.

"David and I worked together for about five years. In 1992, I wrote and published my first novel, *The List of Seven*, which had great success. That was a turn in the road for me though I've sporadically gone back to television. *Buddy Faro* (1998) was a fun show that had a disappointing experience with the network [canceled before it had a chance to establish an audience]. The landscape had changed drastically with the elimination of rules forbidding networks from owning their own shows to the detriment of the creativity of the product involved."

"What went wrong with *Twin Peaks* in the second season?" I ask. "The conventional wisdom is that it got too weird."

"David and I were getting pulled in different directions. Because of the success of the first season, we had numerous opportunities. It was a rocket ride. The network was not helpful. They changed its schedule to Saturday nights, a blow to the solar plexus of the audience. In the middle of the season, the Gulf War started and we were preempted nine out of ten weeks. The show depended on your ability to see it on a regular basis and stay up with its story lines.

"We honestly began the show with no thoughts of it turning into *Falcon Crest* [another nighttime soap opera]. We were trying to do the anti-*Falcon Crest*.

"By the end of the second season, we were gearing up. We wanted to put back on the body armor and ramp the thing up one more time. And if there had been a third season, it might've been good. Our interest had been rekindled."

"That must be a heady feeling to have the most talked-about TV show?"

"It was bizarre. For this industry, that's as good as it gets. And then the wheel turns and you have to move on."

"Did you make any deals while your stock was hot?"

"Perversely, I didn't. I went out and made a small independent movie [*Storyville*, 1992], and wrote a novel. I didn't want to capitalize on *Twin Peaks* fame because I'd already done everything I wanted to do in television. A weekly TV show has a crushing pace.

"I was most disappointed about the adaptation of my novel *List of Seven*. I was eager to make it as a film. It came within a hair breadth on two different occasions with Jim Cameron producing."

"How did you come to work for Aaron Spelling on *Buddy Faro*?"

"He was eager to broaden the profile of the kind of shows he was known for. At this time, the networks began to own their own shows because of the FCC ruling. That's the line of demarcation between the industry that was and the industry that is now. It's been a disaster creatively. It's created a monopolistic situation where there is no creative tension between producer and network anymore. The network calls all the shots and as a result the shows are increasingly watered down, copycat and timid. The appeal is to the lowest common denominator.

"Network television as we have known it for the last 40 years is over. The competition for the average viewers free time that is now offered by cable, DVD, Internet, a 100 channels on satellite, is overwhelming. The networks are still behaving as if they the cultural hegemony they had in the 1960s. I can't think of a single show now that I would go out of my way to watch."

"I don't watch any television."

"It is now blatantly what it has always been surreptitiously—an advertising medium. The programming is a viral cover for the real message—advertising."

"Who watches commercials now there's TIVO?"

"I don't. I taped the British Open this morning and I watched six hours in 90 minutes. Commercials go by like one of those sequences in *Shop of Horrors*."

"Did you understand what David Lynch's *Mulholland Drive*?"

"It started as a conversation David and I were having about a sequel to *Twin Peaks*. We wanted to take the Audrey Horn character, played by Cheryl, to Hollywood. I proposed *Mulholland Drive*, which I lived on, as a title. He sold it as a pilot to ABC and then convinced the French that if he shot 45 more minutes, he could make something out of it. I haven't seen it. I heard it was a mess. I knew that the pilot was a mess.

"David's strength and weakness is that he is often able to transcend story because he's such a master creating mood. His failing is that he's not a strong storyteller. He doesn't have a lot of interest in telling a story. He's not as interested in character as fragments of personality. He's a surrealist."

"He's got a great eye for hot looking women."

Mark smiles. "That was always one of his strengths. The mistake that people make about David is that they assume he's an ironist. He's not. He's a sincere simple guy. He doesn't work things out. He's not that good in logic. When people spend a lot of energy trying to figure out exactly what he meant by *Mulholland Drive*, I can assure you that he didn't know.

"I exchanged emails with Roger Ebert at one point. He was conducting an online seminar about the meaning of *Mulholland Drive*. David works like a painter. He throws a canvas up there and you interpret it any way you want. He doesn't have a strong point of view. It's about sensation and feeling and arousing emotions."

"Are you married?"

"For eight years. My second marriage. The first was from 1984-90. My wife has a doctorate in Psychology and she's working on a book. It's important to find somebody who understands the creative process. She supports my switch to novels. For ten years, I hardly drew a breath that wasn't related to making a television show. I've learned to dial that back and I've become happier and healthier for it.

"I write every morning first thing. I'm usually at work from 8 a.m. to noon. I take a break for lunch and then come back for an hour afterwards.

"I usually spend three months a year at my summer home in New York. It's where I grew up. It's where my family's from. It's seven acres on a lake in the middle of country. It's people I've known all my life. It's two hours from New York if you want the stimulation of the big city. It's completely different from the feeling you get from being in LA in a one-industry town.

"I write on a computer. I bought the first MacIntosh in 1984. I started working on screenplay programming before there was even one out.

"Books last longer than a television show. You feel like you're creating more of a legacy than writing episodic TV,"

"You're not an angry bitter man."

"Right. I've largely lived my life apart from the business. I don't read the trades. My fortunes don't rise and fall with today's phone calls or how someone is feeling about me. I've made enough money to give me a cushion."

"Where do you think your creative impulse comes from?"

"Curiosity. It comes from a desire to understand reality and people. It began with an unsatisfied to know more deeply what was going on, not only out there but within me."

"My family has supported my journey. My father, having been in the industry, understood the pressures and pain of it. I cast him in Twin Peaks and he then went on to have a wonderful late-life career. My brother Scott is a screenwriter. My sister Lindsay Frost [June 4, 1962] is a successful actress."

"Why does Hollywood not take religion seriously? For instance, in the movie *Castaway*, Tom Hanks is marooned on a desert island for four years. He develops a relationship, not with God, but with a volleyball."

"If he doesn't have God in his background, it doesn't make sense. America is becoming a secular country. It was founded as a secular country with a specific division between church and state.

"There's been a growing dissatisfaction with religion as the place to get answers to the questions that trouble people. Faith has become less of a given. People are more questioning. In the 1960s, *Time* magazine declared that God was dead. In America, people think of religion as a private issue. It's a country suspicious of any attempt to proselytize.

"I'm supportive of religion in people's lives. I have big questions about how the Catholic Church has operated for a 1000 years, but the tenets of Judaism and pure Christianity, almost impossible to find now, are obviously great moral compasses for conducting a life. They don't make for great drama unless there's some kind of tension, like *A Man For All Seasons* (1966), where you pit somebody's religious principles against the complicated world they're living in. It's hard to find stories where religion can play a central role.

"The people in this business are well educated if not over educated, affluent if not with too much money, and completely disconnected from the concerns of people who live in small towns. The shows reflect the people who make them. The lack of moral accountability in so many movies and TV shows is appalling.

"A lot of the people in this business are godless and corrupt. That's without dispute. And it's been that way for 80 years, going back to Fatty Arbuckle and William Desmond. Creativity often creates unbalanced people. When you take an unstable personality and add fame and wealth and freedom of movement, you're going to get amorality. It's certainly not going to create moral rectitude. It's what Martin Amis called, 'the moronic inferno side of show business.' It's unavoidable. It's part of human nature that weak personalities, given those temptations, will succumb to them."

"I'm sitting here watching [billionaire] Steve Bing in the parking lot. I'm thinking about the perpetual teenagehood of many men in this industry."

"The industry encourages childishness. It doesn't reward adult behavior. It responds to success."

"Steve Bing moves like an 18-year old. He's a 37-year old jock wearing T-shirts and shorts."

"The California culture is casual. Many of those guys from the surfer generation never grew up. They're still smoking dope and watching sunsets. The process of moving through life and recognizing the stages of life, and what each stage demands of you, does not prepare you for a long career in Hollywood. They prefer to keep you in adolescence because that's the consciousness they feed on. They want to get 16-year old kids seeing the movie three times. The industry tends to freeze and suspend maturity at a certain age."

"I've found in my 100 interviews with producers, that the event in their life that has changed them the most is parenthood. They want to make product that they can show to their kids. They become more socially responsible."

"One of the documentaries I worked on years ago was about the poet Robert Bly. He said about people stuck in that adolescent rut that they were in 'the moon palace.' They were still seeing the world by moonlight, which is dominated by magical thinking and adolescent desire. He said that the only sure cure for getting somebody out of the moon palace was changing diapers because that grounds you in the reality of every day life."

"What are your favorite parts of your producing role?"

"One was the excitement of gathering a troup of people together to work on something. It's like Tom Sawyer getting his friends to paint his fence. But it wasn't so that you could sit back and watch. It was so you all could pitch in and feel like you had a common hand in something worth doing. Two was the satisfaction of seeing something you've written come to life. Three was seeing how people reacted to what you've made."

"I've found out that some people became producers through the route of procuring bodies to satisfy the sexual urges of stars or directors or producers."

"It's a time-honored path to the top throughout history. Hollywood is like a medieval courtiers system. There are fiefdoms of power that are like principalities where money and power get concentrated. Those people behave like the Medicis, usually with the same lack of moral acuity. They are city-states. That's human nature."

"See the corruption inherent in the system. The people who go to synagogue to pray three times a day are not going to make movies."

"They are the pillars secretly holding up the world that the Satanists in the business are trying to tear down."

"I know from my own religious community, that if you were ever to do anything truly creative, your community would throw you out."

"That's the tradeoff. I think of myself first as a writer. It's a writer's job to illuminate the human condition, not to judge the human condition. You have to straddle many different communities and worlds. A producer's job is to make money for everybody around him, primarily himself. So writers and producers are often at odds with each other. I became a producer purely as a defensive gesture, to protect my property. The writer in Hollywood might as well have a sign in his back that says, 'Kick me.' The industry, in its heart of hearts, doesn't trust or respect writers. It sees them as a necessary evil."

"Did you have women throwing themselves at you during the height of *Twin Peaks?*"

"Yes, but they're the kind of women who don't value themselves, so what value can they bring to you?"

"How have you kept your moral compass on due north?"

"I have a strong family that is grounded in reality and morality. My mother is religious. She was raised Presbiterian and she still goes to Unitarian church. I did go to Sunday School as a kid. I grew up in a house where right and wrong were clearly delineated. My father grew up hating organized religion."

"I thought it was required to have at least one Jewish parent to enter this industry?"

"No. I'm the last of the goyim. That will be the title for my autobiography."

"Judd Bernard gave me a title for my book on producers. *Profiles in Discouragement.*"

"It's a good title."

"But you're not a good candidate."

"Because I've endeavored to build a life outside of this business. I saw my father's disappointment early on. I realized this was a terrible way to make a wonderful living. If you became wholly invested in it as a lifestyle as well as a career, then discouragement and disappointment were bound to be daily companions."

"I've found as a writer that my best characters are bad guys. And you?"

"I've got a book coming out about a good guy [amateur golfer Francis Quimet], *The Greatest Game Ever Played.*

"This guy led such an exemplary life. He promised his father he'd try to become a businessman. Francis had an exemplary career and raised a wonderful family, and started a college fund for caddies that's now the largest endowment of its kind in the world. They give a million dollars a year. They've helped over 5000 kids go to college.

"He's a wonderful subject for a book because he's so good. Dickens was a genius at creating good characters and throwing them into an evil universe and seeing them get crushed and then rise back to the top. That was his own experience. That was the book he wrote over and over. Name the last movie written for the screen like that?"

"I can't."

"Part of the problem is that often good people don't have the kind of conflicts that make for interesting drama."

"Do you have any reaction to Mike Ovitz's burnout?"

"He used to represent me. He was a great agent. The tragedy, not many people would call it a tragedy, was that he didn't learn ever how to create the win-win situation. Mike had to win and the other guy had to lose. Whatever demons were driving him to make that kind of deal with himself in life, he's now paying the price. It's a classic morality tale. It's the kind of story that makes Hollywood feel good about itself. 'Oh, we've weeded out the bad guy.' It's not so simple. Everything he did in this business, he did with the complicity of many other people. What he did wasn't anymore rotten than what you find in other cut throat businesses at the highest levels.

"Mike had the hubris to believe that his success as a representative would transfer to other arenas, without having the education, grounding and experience to be successful in them. So naturally he failed. He only knew how to do one thing. He was a kind of idiot savant. The degree of self pity in that [*Vanity Fair*] article was startling and indicative of the huge disconnect inside of him between who he thought he was and the effect he was having on other people around him. He hurt a lot of people and he pissed a lot of people off and he refused to take responsibility for it. Eventually, the chickens came home to roost."

60

Herb Nanas

July 18, 2002

Herb Nanas returns my call. "[Jeff Wald is] a piece of shit. He's the worst human being whoever lived. He wouldn't know how to produce his foot. Only because I was partners with him was his name on the movie [*Two Days in the Valley*]. A fraud. I was in business with him twice in one lifetime so I've got angel wings. He's a wretched fucking human being."

Jeff Wald calls. "Herb had nothing to do with that fucking movie. You can call the director and ask him.

"I went back to him years later because I felt badly for the way I fired him [in 1976]. I fired him at 5 a.m. I sent two bodyguards to his house. I got him out of bed and had him go to the office and clean his shit out.

"Years later I went back into business with him [1995-97] for a minute [in Wald Management] and realized that wasn't going to work either. He's just a sleazeball and he didn't work. He sat around all day and waiting for shit to happen. I don't work like that. I'm proactive, not reactive. I walked out of the partnership. I took Roseanne with me, who couldn't give a fuck about him."

July 22, 2002

I interview Nanas at his office in Sherman Oaks. He wears a Hawaiin shirt. Herb doesn't own a tie, except for a black tie, which he wears with his Armani suits and closed shirts.

"I grew up in the Bronx. I grew up with an interesting group of people, 95 percent Jewish. Ralph Lipshitz a.k.a. Ralph Lauren (fashion designer), Calvin Klein (fashion designer), Penny Marshal (actress-director), Robert Klein (comic), Gloria Leonard (pornographer). For 35 years, my license plate has read "PS80BX" [Public School 80 in New York City's Bronx borough].

"I used to explain to my kids: For the first six years of your life, your home with your mother and grandmother. Then the first day of school, you step into the street and immediately you see 400 kids your age that you never saw before. From that moment on, it's all about who's the fastest, who's the toughest, who gets the most dames, who's got the biggest dick. You don't get that [intense competitiveness] in California.

"I made *The Scout* in 1994 starring Albert Brooks and Brendan Fraser. We were in Yankee Stadium. I used to take a train there as a kid, ten minutes from my house. Here I was in Yankee Stadium, taking a leak in the bathroom of the dugout and I'm calling everybody I grew up with. I'm pissing where Ruth pissed. I'm pissing where Mantle pissed. That felt more important than anything else I've ever accomplished.

"When I was raised in the Bronx, it was mostly Jews and Italians. On Jewish and Christian holidays, school closed.

"The Grand Concourse in the West Bronx was like the Champs Elisee [in Paris]. It ran to Yankee Stadium. There was all that beautiful architecture built at the turn of the century. In our lobbies, there were marble floors and velvet drapes and fountains in the courtyards.

"When I went back in 1994, there were cops all around. There was a police precinct at Yankee Stadium. There was graffiti all over the buildings.

"When I grew up, you never locked your apartment door. You walked everywhere at night. There was no terror, violence, guns."

"Were you raised religious?"

"The family was Orthodox but about the time my last grandparent died, Orthodoxy disappeared quickly. My last surviving grandparent was my grandmother. My father would leave the house on a Jewish holiday and go to the racetrack. But he was raised Orthodox.

"I graduated high school in 1958. I wanted to be an actor. I went to the University of Bridgeport to study theater arts. After four months in school, I dropped out and joined the Air Force for four years. I had four friends on one drunken night who were leaving the next week for the Air Force and I decided to go along.

"I was in the Air Force about a day when I said, this is a serious mistake. On the second day of guys screaming and yelling, I decided that I would rather be the yeller rather than the yellee. I passed the OCS (Officer Candidate School) test. I had to wait several months for an opening for Officer Candidate School, and the week I was supposed to go, a directive came down that said no college education, no OCS.

"So I spent three years in the Philippines in Air Force intelligence. I married Felisa, a Filipina, in 1960. She already had a two-year old daughter. We had two boys by 1962. We all came to Hollywood. I took acting classes. I started a theater company in Hollywood. I did that for almost two years when I realized that I wasn't making enough money.

"There were a couple of agents at William Morris who knew me, George Shapiro and Howard West. They subsequently became Jerry Seinfeld's managers. George had seen me in Summerstock and off-Broadway theater. Here I was just a short New York guy and everyone was blond and blue-eyed out here.

"George got me a job at the William Morris Agency. I had a meeting with agent Phil Weltman. Phil said to George, 'I really like this kid but how is he going to live off $50 a week?' George said, 'His father will give him $25 a week.'

"It usually takes years to become an agent. I moved up quickly. I became Phil's secretary after a few months. I worked the building because I wasn't out looking for dates. I put out everybody's mail at 6 a.m.. William Morris paid overtime. I hung out at the building until closing time, introducing myself to everybody.

"After a year, I became an agent. George Shapiro wanted me to meet 'Albert Einstein.' George's cousin is Rob Reiner. Rob and Albert Brookes grew up together in Beverly Hills. One day in 1968, Albert Brooks walked into my office and made me laugh for ten hours.

"Within nine months, I had Albert on every television show—*Steve Allen, Tonight Show, Dean Martin*. A few months later, I decided I just wanted to spend my life with special people like Albert. So I became a manager in 1969. I've never had an employer since.

"Albert didn't want to be a comedian. He wanted to be a film actor and filmmaker. Around 1973, he stopped doing standup.

"I met Sylvester Stallone on the street in Los Angeles in 1974. I'd seen him in *The Lords of Flatbush* (1974). Everyone was talking about Henry Winkler and Perry King. I said the big kid is the movie star.

"I said to him, 'I'm your biggest fan in the world. You are going to be a major movie star.' I didn't know his name.

"He said, 'I'm represented by William Morris. I live in New York. I'm auditioning for the movie *Stay Hungry* (1976).'

"I saw him in the Roger Corman movie, *Death Race 2000*.

"I ran into him several times. I didn't hear from him for months. Then he called me up one day. I said I wanted to get into his life. This is a few years before *Rocky*.

"He had a woman manager who died of cancer. So I became his manager. He said to me one day, 'I'm a writer.' He gave me three amazing scripts. One was on Edgar Alan Poe. One was on Charlie Becker, who was the only tenderloin detective in New York City at the turn of the 20th Century. He was executed for a murder he didn't commit. And a thing called *Hell's Kitchen*. He'd optioned it to somebody for 22c.

"We got it to Irwin Winkler and Bob Chartoff. They wanted to make it. It's about two brothers in boxing smokers and the exploitation of the third brother. We ultimately got to make it as a wrestling movie called *Paradise Alley* (1978). It was the first movie I produced, though I wasn't credited as the producer.

"The two guy (John F. Roach and Ronald A. Suppa) who had the option on the script sued Stallone for plagiarism and won $250,000. As part of the settlement, they would get credited as producers on *Paradise Alley*.

"I said to these guys, 'Why don't you let Irwin Winkler produce this movie? He's got a deal at United Artists.' These guys were cocky. 'We don't need you.'

"I jumped over the desk and grabbed one of them, the lawyer, by the tie. I looked him in the face and said, 'You'll never produce this movie. You don't know how to produce a movie.' It was like a war.

"The day that Stallone and I moved on to the Universal lot to make the film, I said to Ned Tanen, 'I will only make this deal if we kick those two guys off the lot.'

"I went to the guys' office. I told them, 'Pack your bags. Security will be here in an hour. Get off the lot.' That was it. Those guys never had a career.

"I started liking the process of putting people together and watching a movie take form.

"I managed Stallone until the middle of *First Blood* (1982). We did *Nighthawks* (1981), *Escape to Victory* (1981), *Rocky II* (1979) and *III* (1982). I loved Stallone but he was tough on people. Recently his brother asked me, 'You guys were best friends. What happened?'

"I've represented people since 1969 and I've never had a signed contract with anybody. This is about passion. If you don't like me anymore, or if I don't like you, I'm ineffective.

"What I like best about my long career is that there is no bad story about me. I don't mind breaking a guy's balls to make a huge deal for talent but then, go do your job. Don't make everybody's life miserable.

"He [Sly Stallone] really didn't want to do *First Blood*. Everybody, including his CAA agent Ron Meyer, said the picture was too violent. When I read that script, I saw that guy in the milieu of Rocky. He was an underdog. There were no machine guns and no fighting with the enemy that the rest of the movies became. It was simply a guy going to visit his friend after Vietnam.

"The script reminded me of a Kirk Douglas picture that Stanley Kramer directed years ago. *Home of the Brave* (1949). The last guy in America still riding a horse stops in a bar in contemporary Texas and winds up in a fight. He's brutalized in jail.

"I told [Stallone], the public knows you. They touch you when you walk down the street. They don't touch Robert DeNiro or Paul Newman or Gregory Peck. But you're accessible to them. You're an underdog. I was proud of *Nighthawks* and *Fist*. I think director Norman Jewison should've ended *F.I.S.T.* (1978) at Sly's victory. Sly never wanted to do *First Blood*. He was out of control on set. He was late every day. He was tough on everybody. I left three-quarters through the movie and we didn't reconnect for seven years. I needed to go home and breathe. It wasn't worth the money."

"How far do you go back with Jeff Wald?"

"When I was an agent at William Morris, pre Albert, Jeff came into my office one day and said, 'I married this chick who's a singer. I hear you're terrific. Your from the Bronx. I'm from the Bronx.'

"I'm a few years older than Jeff. I was the only guy in town who helped Helen Reddy [Jeff's wife] when they didn't have ten cents. They lived with me for a while when they moved out here. I put her on some television shows. When I first left William Morris, we shared offices together. Then Jeff and I started a management company together that Sly was part of [after *Rocky*, about 1977]. Our clients included Sly, Albert, Ray Sharkey, Donna Summer. Jeff had Helen Reddy making a zillion dollars. That wasn't in the mix.

"Jeff may be the worst human being I ever experienced in the 61 years of my life. On every level. I went into business with him twice [1977 and 1993-97]. He's the worst human being God ever put on the earth.

"Jeff likes to take credit for producing *Two Days in the Valley*. All he did was to get an entire crew to duck when he showed up. He told the Teamsters, 'Park my car.'"

"You must've been pleased with the success of *First Blood*?"

"When Sly first saw that picture, he offered to pay the producers the cost of the negative and burn it. I was the only person who believed in that movie. I even screamed at him one day driving in a tunnel in Canada, 'John Rambo will make you a bigger star than Rocky Balboa.'

"Years later at a screening, David Geffen said to me, 'Herb, what a brilliant concept to marry him to that project.' I said, 'I don't manage him anymore.' David said, 'I fucking hate all the talent.' And he turned around and walked away.

"At one point, I hear that Sly said to Jake Bloom, his attorney: 'I guarantee you that Herbie's standing on top of a mountain saying, 'I'm right.' Jake said, 'He stood alone.' I did stand alone.

"Sly and I had a tough 1982. He really thought I had railroaded him into the movie. His wife Sasha read the script and told him he should do the movie. It didn't make a difference."

"Did he eventually call you and tell you that you were right?"

"No, never. We didn't talk for seven years. Then one of his guys called me one day and said that Sly would love to have dinner with me. So we had dinner. I'll always be fond of him. We had about six years that were fantastic. I now have a good relationship with him as a friend.

"We were in a golf cart the other day. He asked about my son Ricky. 'How old is he going to be?' I said he will be 40. Sly was at Ricky's *bar mitzvah*, before *Rocky*.

"Sly always acknowledged me being part of *Rocky*. My wife remembers me standing in his living room and saying to him, 'You must play this role [Rocky]. You cannot sell this script.'

"He would've sold the script. The offer was up to $135,000. He didn't have ten cents. I'd put him in *Kojak* (1973-78) and *Police Story* (1973-77). I needed the money too. But I said, 'You can't sell this script. You created this for you.'

"He had a pay or play contract [is paid his full fee even if he's fired from the picture]. We always believed that he'd shoot two days and United Artists would fire him. So we made them change the contract before he started shooting to pay and play so they couldn't fire him."

"Tell me about working with Albert Brooks."

"Someone will always make an Albert Brooks film and nobody bothers you when you do it.

"One of my favorite Albert Brooks movies is the one I didn't make with him, *Modern Romance* (1981). I thought it was the ultimate courage of a single guy defining the difference between the strength of men and the strength of women after a breakup.

"I get a different thing out of Albert Brooks's films than other people do because I have been with him his whole adult life. I get some catharsis out of his movies out of private moments between him and I. They are in all of them—some of his fears and joys. In *Defending Your Life* (1991), there's a scene where he has to speak in front of people [and he can't]. There's a guy downstairs saying, 'They're waiting for you, man. They're out there.'

"That was a big moment between him and I at the end of his personal appearance business. We had sold out theaters in Boston and he said, 'I don't want to do this anymore.' I walked him to the stage. 'You can do it. They're waiting. If you don't, they'll burn this house down. Just do one show.' That was the last standup he ever did [in 1974]. I was the guy downstairs in that scene."

"What was it like working with Bob Rafelson (about 70 years old) in your latest film, *The House on Turk Street* (2002). How did he choose this project?"

"I don't think people are offering Bob Rafelson movies. His choices are narrowed. He works hard. But everything you've ever read about him he still is at age 70. I got along great with him. I was with him from the beginning when he was doing rewrites to the end of the movie. Bob doesn't seem to care if nobody likes him on the face of the earth. There's no part of his brain that thinks, 'Is there a nice way to say this?' It's jarring. It was the most damage control I've ever done in my life.

"After saying something to somebody, Bob would say to me, 'You don't really like it when I do that, do you?' No, I don't. Because that is going to be a big job to pull us back together again.

"Bob just speaks without giving one shit about whether it will hurt your feelings or not. I never met anybody like that. He's not even mean spirited. He's bright. He's interesting to be around. I enjoy his company. But whoa, is there no censor mechanism? He still likes to be a bad boy."

"What's your strong point as a producer?"

"Dealing with personalities. Bringing the elements together. I'm not in the schlock movie business. My films are all interesting intelligent films. I have the ability to embrace everybody on a movie set every morning to make sure everyone's happy. When a movie's going, I know every human being on a set.

"I love talent. Whether it is Charlize Theron remembering me as the producer who gave her first big role or Sam Jackson saying to me afterwards, 'Any movie you want to do. I love you. You're the greatest.' Sam is not the kind of guy to say things like that easily."

"Are there things that you do just for appearances?"

"I think that's a truism for life. I stopped doing that illusionary thing years ago. I no longer felt I had to drive a fancy car. David Geffen drives a Mustang. You get to like yourself.

"I've ridden motorcycles for 40 years. I became a pilot in my fifties. I dove every ocean in the world. I sailed boats. I saw my kids grow up. That's why I didn't build AMG [Michael Ovitz's company sold in 2002 to Jeff Kwatinez]. That's why I'm not Brad Grey or Bernie Brillstein.

"There are a lot of guys driving Mercedes who don't have a dime. A lot of guys in Hollywood are living in houses that they can't afford. People who are secure with themselves need less flash than people who are not secure with themselves.

"In the drug days, I had the ability to go home at 1 a.m. rather than get the next bundle of drugs. I had to feed my kids. Everybody else I know has been in an AA program.

"I don't seek fame. I seek accomplishment.

"I get up every day and say, 'Today is going to be a great day.' I've always had these kids I was nuts about. I have four granddaughters. My wife is a great chick. I start out every day surrounded by affection and people I like. My greatest victory in the world is when people tell me I have the greatest kids. That's far more important to me than all the one-sheets [movie posters] on the wall."

"How much time do you spend producing as opposed to managing?"

"I'm looking to spend 99 percent of my [working] life producing. I'm 61 years old. I'd like to do this for another 18 years. I'm young and healthy for a guy 61 years old."

"How do you lead a typical day, like today?"

"I got up around 7 a.m. I played golf. I sat around the pool in the sun for a couple of hours and took a bunch of phone calls. I went to lunch with a friend who sells foreign films. Then I came in here and met with you. My day can be anything. I don't ever have to come to the office.

"I'm leaving this office next week and I am going back to working out of my house."

"How much time do you spend on the road?"

"I was three months in Montreal on the Samuel Jackson movie. I'll be doing a WWII movie in Europe for a few months. My wife comes a bit but she has grandkids. She doesn't like to leave. My kids grew up with movie stars in the house and none of them are in show business. They saw behavior that was just different from the way the rest of the world operates and it never appealed to them."

"What do you think of the Michael Ovitz meltdown?"

"Mike Ovitz, Ron Meyer, the whole CAA team and I were at William Morris together. We've been acquaintances. I was closer friends with Ron Meyer. I gave him Sly Stallone at his peak.

"Lew Wasserman told me in the early seventies when I sat down at his office. It was great to see a desk with nothing on it. He said to me, 'The only power in Hollywood is talent and money.'

"Ovitz had all the talent. He gave up the king spot. He was the most powerful guy in Hollywood. He won't be on any list ever again. He ain't even number 500. He's done. People won't return his calls.

"It used to be in Hollywood that the big guys understood that there was enough in the community for everybody. Don't pick on little guys. Let them have their coin. Ovitz changed that game. Let's go out and get everybody and swallow them all up. That he was brutal and callous and dogmatic in his approach, and Ron Meyer isn't. It's easy when you start to slip, in any business, for people to piss on you.

"I started to read the *Vanity Fair* thing but I don't care. Who cares if he was a victim?

"Because of the way I lead my life, I have a hard time wondering why a guy who has $250 million goes to work when there's an entire universe to scour.

"Somebody asked me when I was in the William Morris mailroom, what I wanted to do with my life. I said that I wanted to represent the biggest actor in the world. One day I did [Sylvester Stallone]. I was satisfied.

"It was something to be in a position where everyone picks up your call. They don't return your call. They pick up your call. People would say, 'Thank you so much for calling me back.'

"I was with Roseanne Barr from 1987-92. She'd been in town three days when I met her on *The Tonight Show*.

"A friend of mine, Jim McCauley who died of cancer, for 25 years booked the comedians for *The Tonight Show*. He always wanted me because I had Albert, and at one point, I represented a lot of comics. I had Bill Hicks, who was brilliant. He wound up with cancer and killed himself.

"Jim called me. He wanted to put Gary Busey on *The Tonight Show*. I'm sitting talking to Judy Busey. Gary is on with Johnny Carson. Johnny says, 'Tonight, first time on *The Tonight Show*, is a housewife from Salt Lake City, Roseanne Barr.'

"I just glance up at the screen. Roseanne says, 'I'm not a housewife. I'm a domestic goddess.' In 30 seconds, I said to Judy Busey, 'Hold that thought. I can make her the biggest star in America.'

"I walk backstage to talk to Jim. I ask him if she's really from Salt Lake City. He asked if I liked her. I said, 'She's a star. She's Erma Bombeck. The camera loves her. She could be American's favorite mom.'

"Jimmy says, 'That's the only reason I put Gary Busey on. I knew I could never get you down here to see her. I knew I couldn't get you to the Comedy Store to see her.' I met her in the hall that night. I was her manager the next day.

"In my final days with her, she wanted to be Lenny Bruce. I told her she was Erma Bombeck. That's what America wants. The second you say 'Fuck,' the audience leaves. That's the only reason our relationship came apart. I wouldn't let her curse.

"Rodney Dangerfield was in the audience one night. He asked her to tell a story. She said, 'I can't. My manager's here. He won't let me curse.'

"In my first 30 seconds of seeing her, I saw *Roseanne* (1988-97). I said that she will never have to learn how to act. She will have a fat husband. She will have three fat kids. I broke her when I put her on the Julio Iglesias tour.

"Judy Busey used to say to me, 'What made you see it?'

"Roseanne said to me, 'You said to me everything I dreamed anyone would ever say to me.'

"I did a second shot with Jeff Wald from 1995-97. Then Roseanne went off with Jeff.

"Roseanne made everyone so crazy on her pilot that I never thought the network would pick it up.

"One night at a Mike Tyson fight in Las Vegas a few years ago [1997], Roseanne said to me, 'I want you to come back into my life. I've been through so much shit in my life. Everybody has fucked over me. Everybody's pissed on me. You're the only person who's been straight with me in my whole life. You are the only honest person I've ever met since the day I got into show business.

"She came back to me for management at that point. It was the last year for the Roseanne show. It wasn't too much fun.

"I kept pushing her off to Jeff. I produced the movie *Mother*, and I had a series with Lorenzo Lamas. Jeff, in the interim, was talking to Michael King about doing a talkshow with Roseanne. Jeff did not tell me. He was just wretched to people. So we split. Then I had about 20 people tell me, 'Herbie, I'd do business with you, but not a fucking chance with Jeff around.' He did some serious damage. He may be the most disliked human being in this community. He's a tarantula in that old story about the tarantula and the alligator. He can't help it.

"I didn't care that he fucked me out of the Roseanne series. He said to me, 'Herbie, we may get a talkshow. If we do, I'll pay you X amount of dollars.' I said O.K. He never paid me.

"Doing her talkshow put him in the hospital. She did him in. She says he ripped her off. They deserve each other."

61

Marian Rees

July 26, 2002

I drive 40 minutes to Studio City for breakfast at Al's Deli on Ventura Blvd.

My appointment with Marian Rees is for 8:30 a.m.. At 8:38, I see Marian chatting with two female waitresses. I introduce myself. Marian says she'll be with me in a minute.

She's wearing peach-colored pantsuit. She has short hair and glasses. She takes her time talking to the waitresses. When she finally sits down at my table, she acts like she's a cop and I'm a convict. "What's your motive for writing this book? What is the personal profit to you? What's point? Your last book was obviously exploitive. I didn't read it. Just from the title [*A History of X: 100 Years of Sex in Film*]. I don't understand why you are writing this one."

When I try to explain, she interrupts me. She's hostile. I haven't encountered this before from a producer. All the ones I've spoken to are friendly. Many producers have asked me why I am writing the book and what my longterm goals are but there's a hateful edge to Marian.

Whenever I try to reply to her questions, she cuts me off, telling me why my answers are inadequate, inaccurate, untruthful, unnecessary and ill formed.

She repeatedly apologizes for her hostility.

"I suppose my journey to this book began eight years ago," I say, "when I came to Los Angeles and pursued acting. I eventually abandoned that because I found it too collaborative."

"Stop right there. What do you mean 'too collaborative?' Working with other people is the essence of this business. I can tell we are not going to get along. I'm not going to give you an interview."

"I guess I prefer to work alone on projects I can control."

Marian eats a bowl of oatmeal with fruit. I eat two hardboiled eggs with fruit. The check comes. I take it.

"You better give me that."

I hand it over to her.

"I'm not going to give you an interview so I might as well pay for breakfast."

Marian wants to know what I think of producers. She's on the board of the Producers Guild.

"I found fewer cowboys than I expected. I thought I'd encounter more sleazy types. People who'd trash their peers and would just be in the business to chase girls. Instead, every producer I've interviewed has been intelligent, well mannered, professional and willing to submerge his ego for the sake of the production."

Marian says she's shy and rarely talks to reporters. She thoroughly checks them before she does. She's wary of being misquoted even though she's never yet been burned.

She discusses a nine-hour interview she did with a black male journalist for *Emmy Magazine*. She admitted she wasn't happy with her work. She found it shallow. She wanted to be a sociologist. The journalist told her that her work had great meaning and because she tackled serious issues like racism, she was a sociologist. That made her feel good.

62

Andre Morgan

"I was born in French Morocco. My father served in the American Navy. My mother is English. An only child, I traveled back and forth. We moved, on average, every six months. I went to twelve different grade schools, mainly in England and the States. I learned French and German.

"When it came time to go to university, I needed a scholarship, so I decided to enroll in whatever department gave me the greatest opportunity to gain a scholarship. That was the Department of Oriental Languages and Literature at the University of Kansas. So I majored in Chinese and got a draft deferment.

"I've always loved the film industry but I had no particular penchant for the Chinese language."

"Were you a good student in high school?"

"I was average. I guess I was usually in the top ten percent of my class."

"And you were a film buff from what age?"

"As soon as I began sneaking into theaters, around age ten. In England they had this rating system where you, as a child, could only get in to see certain kinds of movies. We figured out how to get somebody in the theater, run around the back and open the emergency exits and we'd all slip in the back door."

"What did your parents think of your obsession?"

"They didn't discourage it. From any parent's point of view in the 1960s, they just hoped their kid would go to school, get a job, be a lawyer or engineer or something respectable, and don't end up getting arrested for doing drugs.

"I left the University of Kansas in my senior year in 1972. I dropped out, with one semester left, to go to Hong Kong to polish my Chinese. I was supposed to be in Hong Kong for one year. Then I planned to return to Kansas to finish my degree.

"Then, when I got the job with [Raymond Chow's film production company Golden Harvest] and got to Hong Kong, it became obvious to me after a few months that I wasn't going back to academia. I was already in the industry I loved."

"How did you get the job?"

"The head of the Chinese department at Kansas had been a close friend of Raymond Chow's in the late 1940s. They'd set up Voice of America in Hong Kong together. When I told my professor I wanted to go to Asia, he said he'd make a few phone calls and see if there were any jobs available. Serendipitously, Raymond Chow had formed Golden Harvest five months previous. They made a compact that if I were to come out and spend a year in Hong Kong, working for a local Chinese salary, he'd give me a job as an office boy.

"I met Bruce Lee on my second day in Hong Kong. We were the only two Americans in the company. Bruce Lee was born in San Francisco. He was becoming a superstar in southeast Asia.

"Before I got to Hong Kong, I didn't know Bruce Lee from any other actor. I had vague recollections of having seen him in a couple episodes of *The Green Hornet* (1966) and in one episode of *The Streets of San Francisco* (1972-77). But when I arrived, they sat me down and, before I met him, I screened Bruce's first two movies (1971), *Fists of Fury* and *Big Boss*."

"Were you star struck?"

"No. You can't really be in this business and be starstruck. The magic of the industry is watching the impact that the talent has on the public. I remember the first time I met Steve McQueen, I was starstruck. It's like anything else. Once you get to know the people, they tend to lose their aura.

"I stayed in Hong Kong until 1985 [when British prime minister Margaret Thatcher decided to give it back to the Chinese]. I started as an office boy and by the time I left, I was running the largest division in the largest film company in Asia. We had offices in London and Los Angeles. We had a huge theater system to distribute our English-language and Chinese pictures.

"In 1972, we were at a point in Hong Kong cinema where there were no rules. We were making up the rules as we went along. Nobody in America at this time really knew what kung fu was. There had been one *Billy Jack* movie and a bad TV series called *Kung Fu*. Once we introduced the Bruce Lee films, and got over the initial market resistance, it was a trip to watch the number of kung fu fans grow. Over time, it's been fun for me to watch it spawn new generations and new genres."

"Do you have a personal attachment to kung fu?"

"No. I've never studied kung fu. I've never had any interest in studying kung fu. But I recognize and appreciate it as an important skill set for young action stars. I've worked with some of the top action stars in the world like Bruce Lee and Jackie Chan, you realize the tremendous amount of skill, coordination and study required.

"Hong Kong has gone through many changes over the past 30 years. In 1972, it was a sleepy colonial backwater port that was primarily a low cost manufacturing center for wigs and computer chips and a transshipment center for raw produce going in and out of China in the days when embargoes were still in effect because of the Vietnam War. That's what you see in *Enter the Dragon* (1973). The big oceangoing fishing junks in Aberdine Harbor. Hong Kong has a skyline but it is not a dynamic skyline. It's a picturesque skyline. In the mid seventies, Hong Kong's became a finance center for the region. In the eighties was the real estate boom and the transition from being a manufacturing center to a service center."

"Did you feel happy or sad when the sovereignty of Hong Kong changed from Britain to China?"

"Both. It was sad because it was the end of an era in which I'd grown up. I got to Hong Kong when I was 20 years old. On the other hand, for China and the people of Hong Kong, it was a good thing the British were gone and it had returned to Chinese sovereignty. If they do a good job of reabsorbing Hong Kong into the bosom of the mainland, it will only facilitate a more peaceful and rapid solution to the China-Taiwan issue."

"How did you come to set up this huge studio in China?"

"We've been going in and out of China since 1978. We've been waiting for the right opportunity, meaning, the infrastructure to support the day to day grind of filmmaking. The bureaucracy had arrived at a level of workable understanding with the film and television industry. We also had to gauge the American market to see if there was a renewed interest in things Chinese. You realize after 30 years in the industry that everything has an ebb and flow. Every eight years or so, there's a new cycle and everything Chinese and Asian is hot for a year. Then America loses interest for a while.

"We concluded the timing was right for several reasons. One, China was close to achieving entry into the WTO (World Trade Organization) and they were making a significant bid for the 2008 Olympics. We met local entrepreneurs in China who represented what is the first generation of private sector enterprise in China. We had the opportunity to put the studio together without having to joint-venture it with the old rustbelt state-run organizations."

"Do you feel comfortable with comparisons to Armand Hammer?"

"No. I'm not selling pencils and I'm certainly not selling secrets. We have little in common except that he went behind the Iron Curtain in his day and I've been going in and out China for 24 years."

"Are there rumors that you are a Communist spy?"

"No, that I am CIA. I just heard that from somebody who's been working for me for nine months in Shanghai. That was the rumor amongst the Australians there.

"Under the Freedom of Information Act, I should probably pull my file. But then again, who cares? You can get obsessed with this stuff or just get on with living your life."

"Are you married?"

"For six years. My second marriage. It's my Chinese phase.

"My home was Hong Kong until 1985. Then I re-domiciled to LA. I met my first wife, a Philipino-American, in 1987. We were married for 18 months and . then divorced.

"I took John McTiernan to Malaysia to do a location survey for *Medicine Man* (1992), starring Sean Connery. They needed a rain forest. We were in Kuala Lumpur, where the rain forest is second growth. It's been harvested once. John wanted to go to where we shot Farewell to the King. We charted a flight and flew back down to Borneo where I bumped into my now second wife (Maria) in the coffee shop of the hotel in Kuching. She's pure Chinese."

"Is she in the entertainment industry?"

"No. She has a masters in Psychology. She was a director for PR and marketing for a hotel chain in Asia called Pan Pacific Hotels."

"How much are you on the road these days?"

"Last year I was gone ten months but that was an incredible bizarre year because of 9/11.

"We were on location [in Shanghai, China] shooting [on 9/11] while watching this whole nightmare unfold on CNN, MSNBC and BBC.

"We decided to shoot the TV series [*Flatland* (2002) starring Dennis Hopper] in high definition digital video. We created the first entirely digital post production facility in China. Then we set up our own CGI department in China to do the graphics, because the show's look is *The Matrix* meets *Crouching Tiger* (2000)."

"Is there a network for this show?"

"Not yet. We're in negotiation for it right now."

"That's bold going out there and shooting a show before you sell it."

"It's certainly out of the box. We've spent close to $40 million in the past year on the studio and the series.

"We decided that the fastest way to train people was to do TV. It was reminiscent of things we'd done in Hong Kong in the early seventies when we made kung fu movies for $100,000 a piece. We set up the studio. We set up the training program. We bought 500 hectares built three soundstages in the first four months of 2001."

"Did you use slave labor?"

"No, but we worked three shifts, 24/7, banging them out."

Andre shows me pictures of the work.

"That stage is 18 meters high, that's five stories. We started shooting on the 15th of July. We'd just finished our first section with Dennis Hopper. We'd shipped him back to the States. I was getting ready to come back to the States.

"Shanghai is twelve hours ahead of New York. This came down at dinner time, at 8:45 p.m. our time. First you're getting the news reports on Chinese television. We had many Americans in Shanghai working on the show who were cut off from their loved ones in the United States. They could leave China but they couldn't land on the West Coast of the United States.

"We decided to keep shooting, that it was better for the Americans to keep them busy working the normal 12-hour days. That way they're only watching CNN in their off hours.

"We were flying, on average, three actors a week to China to be guest stars in the TV series. We couldn't get anybody out of the United States for two weeks. We couldn't get any equipment out of the US. We had people stuck in Seoul, Beijing and Hong Kong.

"It disrupted our production for three weeks. In selling the series, it set us back a good six months. After 9/11, the fall TV season was delayed. We'd originally planned to sell the series in December. We're out there selling the series now."

"Have you lost any projects because of 9/11?"

"It's a good excuse but if it is a good product, you'll find another way to reconstitute it and get it going. I consider some things delayed but I don't consider any project killed by 9/11."

"What's *Flatlander* about?"

"It takes place in Shanghai in the year 2010. It's the story of Saint Michael versus the Devil. Dennis Hopper plays Saint Michael who's out to catch the Devil. Dennis Hopper is the meanest baddest angel they got. His job is to catch the Devil and round up the Devil's colleagues on earth. We have various villains who are white and black and Asian. The idea is to make it non-race specific, the same we did [the TV series] *Martial Law* (1998) for CBS."

"Weren't you concerned about hiring Dennis Hopper, whose got a reputation for being psychotic?"

Andre laughs. "Dennis is a sweetheart. If you want to believe everything that is ever put out about any actor or director or producer, you can always find stories that will convince you that they are crazy. My experience in dealing with these guys over the years is that if you come on to them straight, and you don't play games, they'll deal with you honestly. It's only if you start messing around that you'll have trouble. What drives people nuts is people who shine them on.

"Nobody's perfect. We all have temper tantrums from time to time and we all scream and yell and we all melt down. So, if they're having a bad hair day, you ask, 'What triggered their bad hair day?' You cut through and figure out the real problem. If you've been straight with people, they'll usually be straight with you. You will rarely get a truly psychotic actor unless they're having a serious drug or alcohol problem. And that's a different issue, and something you have to watch like a hawk.

"We did two movies with Burt Reynolds and two movies with Tom Selleck. I've heard all the stories about these guys and they were pussycats. But you have to deal with them straight. It doesn't mean you have to go in and suck up to them and kiss their ass.

"The relationship between a producer and an actor has to be a two-way street. You need them to do things for you that go way beyond just giving a good performance—to promote the film, to do interviews. They are going to want things from you that aren't in their contract. Their agent can't anticipate everything that can come up. If you're reasonable, you're going to find a way to work things out. That's part of being a producer. You've got to keep the family going. Don't sit there and think you're the headmaster and you're going to cane everyone. At the end of the day, you want everyone working together because they are getting your vision on the screen.

"In any large gathering, there are bound to be personality problems and conflicts of interest. So if you can set yourself up as the person who is fair, you can have a successful production."

Andre takes a long drink of coffee. "My first cup of the day."

"How many cups do you normally drink?"

"It depends. I used to own a coffee plantation. I've had periods where I've drank ten cups of coffee a day. And then I go to China and I don't drink any."

"What are your other guilty pleasures?"

"Smoking. You've got me on the first day of me quitting smoking for the fourth time this year. I quit for seven years twice."

"Which actor drove you to resume?"

"This is probably a terrible insight into a producer's psyche. I started smoking when I was 14 because it was cool. I went off to Hong Kong when I was 20. Everybody smokes there. Then I quit smoking for four years. I came back to the United States in 1985, and out of boredom, picked up a cigarette. My partner, Al Ruddy, smoked like a chimney. In 1991, we decided we were going to quit smoking. In 1992, I signed us up for a quit-smoking clinic. We'd tried everything—hypnosis, this and that. This quit-smoking class worked even though my wife is a chain-smoker and smokes two packs a day. Al lasted a year-and-a-half. I didn't have another cigarette from June of 1992 until December of 2000.

"I'm sitting in Malaysia, two days before New Year's Eve, having a Margarita. 'Gee, that smells good. Why don't you give me a puff?' I'm thinking, what's the big deal? It tasted so good that I decided I was going to smoke through the New Year and then I'd quit when we left Malaysia for Hong Kong. And I've been smoking ever since.

"I smoke about two packs a day."

"What are your other guilty pleasures?"

"Everything. You indulge all your sensory perceptions all the time. It's all part of living. Filmmaking is an extension of life. How can you draw on life if you haven't lived it and experienced it?

"I've been watching this program on the History Channel about the History of Sex in WWII. They had something about Jack Kennedy. He talked about war being hours of boredom interrupted by minutes of abject fear. That's exactly what producing is all about. You sit around for weeks and months while the script is whipped into shape. You wait for the actors and studio execs to read it. You get someone to agree to make the movie. The making of it is the fun part. Then you go into the editing period, probably the single most important period.

"Each ones of those periods requires a different part of your personality to come into play, whether I'm indulging my passion for smoking or good wine or spicy food. When you've got the stress from managing multiple projects, why are you going to put restraints on yourself? I thank God that I never had a serious drug problem."

"Many producers tell me that their least favorite part is the shoot?"

"That's because they are not in control. But if you've done your job right, and you have the right director and the right actors, it's fun to watch. Most producers, by definition, are control freaks. You are so used to micro-managing different things it's hard to let go and let the director run with it. My perspective is different from most producers because at Golden Harvest, I was overseeing the production of ten movies a year. You learn to be dispassionate.

"Many producers are frustrated directors. I do not want to direct. Do you know how boring it is to wait on a set all day long to get the one take you think is right while the lighting crew fiddles around? That is a death of a thousand cuts."

"How did you come to partner up with Al Ruddy?"

"We've known each other a long time. We teamed up at Golden Harvest to do the *Cannonball Run* (1981, 1984) movies.

"When I decided to return to the States in 1984, Al suggested we set up a company together and see what trouble we could get into. We looked at Ruddy-Morgan as a loose fraternal organization of non-dedicated tennis players that evolved into today's company.

"Al is like a big overstuffed teddy bear and one of the kindest people you'll ever meet. He loves this industry. We both came out of a different time and place when it was possible to put things together on your own. We're probably the only guys in town who, if we want to make a movie, and the studios say no, that doesn't mean anything. Studios aren't always right.

"*Cannonball Run*. That script sat around for two-and-a-half years and everybody said, there's no point in making this movie. By the time we had put Hal Needham and the script together, every studio had passed on it twice. By the time we had put Hal Needham, Roger Moore and Farrah Fawcett together, the studios had passed on it three times. When we added Burt Reynolds to the mix, every studio said they had made a mistake and they wanted to reconsider that they had passed on the project. Our job is to make a sexy package that people want to buy."

63

Scott Kroopf

July 29, 2002

"I was born in Palo Alto, California. My father was a doctor. Two of his children went into show business. My older brother Sandy wrote *Birdy* (1984). He's going to produce a movie in Italy, *Under the Tuscan Sun* (2003).

"I went to the University of California at Irvine. I had no idea for the first quarter what I wanted to do. I took a nature of drama survey course from Professor Robert Cohen. He was such a brilliant lecturer that it got me into drama. I wrote an autobiographical play, *Alice Through the Needle*, which I produced and directed. It's the story of a young boy, disappointing all of his friends, by going out with a wrong druggie hippie girl and how all of them, three years later, were coming to him to score pot, having gone through their own ridiculous transformation.

"I wrote the story in detail and then I had the actors improv the whole thing. It came out great. I was off to the races. I studied directing and acting. I went to the American Conservatory Theater's summer acting program in San Francisco. I worked the Utah Shakespeare festival. I graduated in 1973 and made my first strategic career mistake. I chose to stay in Los Angeles instead of moving to New York. If I had moved to New York, I would've most likely stayed in theater.

"My brother got me a job as a reader for a friend of mine who worked in the TV business. I worked on commercial and documentary crews. I got a job in 1982 reading for Embassy Pictures, owned by Norman Lear and Jerry Perencio. I became a story editor and then production executive over the course of three administrations. Norman and Jerry didn't see eye to eye so it was hard to get movies through. I worked on *The Sure Thing* (1985), *A Chorus Line* (1985), *The Emerald Forest* (1985), and *Stand by Me* (1986).

"I worked with Lindsay Durand, the only person from Embassy they kept. She went on to work for Paramount and then ran Sydney Pollack's company. She then became the head of UA (United Artists) and she now has a deal with us. She was my mentor.

"Not knowing what was going on at my company (it was being sold to Coke Cola) in 1984, I phoned up Lindsay to talk about Interscope, run by Robert Cort and Ted Field. She got me in to see Robert and he hired me. My first movie was *Outrageous Fortune* (1987). It was a baptism of fire because we had the classic problems. The studio hated Bette Midler's wardrobe and hair and made a meltdown over it. Bette Midler and Shelley Long didn't get along resulting in a large fracas to which Jeffrey Katzenberg said to Robert and I when we phoned up about it, 'That's why you guys are producers and I am a studio executive. I don't have to deal with it. You take care of it.'

"Then I produced *Bill & Ted's Excellent Adventure*. Warners put it in turnaround. DEG (Dino De Laurentiis Entertainment Group) picked it up. Dino had no idea what it was about. He didn't understand what dudes were until someone explained to him that 'dudes' meant guys who had big dicks. Then he said, 'Oh, great, now I get it.'

"We finish the movie. We never test it. Rafaella and Alan Rich are out. Howard Koch comes in. The company is circling down the toilet to bankruptcy. Everyone's bailing out. I'm facing my baby being released on HBO. I went in to see Rick Finkelstein, who used to work at DEG. He moved over to Nelson Entertainment owned by Barry Spikings. Rick had always liked the movie. I said, 'Rick, you can buy this movie for ten cents on the dollar. For a million bucks and you get all rights.' So they did. They tested it. They immediately realized that it tested great.

"It was amazing to me that none of the DEG guys bothered to test the movie. They just all looked at it in a screening room and decided it was no good. It was too silly.

"Between *Excellent Adventure* and *Outrageous Fortune*, I got a strong producing start. When we screened *Fortune* for Disney executives, several of them thought it was awful. Then it tested well and they loved the movie.

"In the last five years, producers have become the low man on the Hollywood totem pole. Writers have surpassed us. 'Producer' has become such a watered down credit that people think that producers do nothing other than be lucky. There are a ton of do-nothing producers. I don't want to name any. They fall into categories. They are the tagalong producers. Either they're managers or someone who knew someone. The obscurity of the connection and the desperation that people cling to these credits. I understand about putting your foot in the door, but if you don't do anything, then what's the point of the foot in the ·

door? There are packaging producers. They find good material, let the studio develop it, and never walk on a set. Then there are line producers who creatively do nothing.

"The difference between a good producer and a bad producer is how much courage they have to confront people over problems. Now, you don't want to take on a director in front of an entire crew. I've seen it done. It's folly. But you've got to confront over problems. More often than not, producers don't confront. They let things slide.

"Some directors will not pay any attention to actors because they are more interested in the technical things. Sometimes a producer must work with the actors and let them express themselves, but without undercutting the director's authority. If a director won't give people what they need, be they actors, technicians, makeup artists, someone's got to go in and do that. But you don't then want that person turning to you after a take before they look at the director.

"One guy told me that the job of the producer is to keep the atmosphere on a set like a freshly opened bottle of champagne. Keep everyone's spirits up. Parties are good. Little signs of appreciation. Bring a masseuse on to the set. Anything from icecream to hats. It's like camp. There's the army metaphor and the camp metaphor. You want to keep the atmosphere light because people can get hunkered down.

"We're doing *Texas Chainsaw Massacre* (2003). I was in Texas last week. The actors were working in a van while the temperatures outside were over 100 degrees. They were acting their guts out. So we gave them each a one-hour massage this weekend as a show of thanks."

"What are your guilty pleasures?"

"I have smoked. I don't anymore. Occasionally, if I need to really think about something, I'll get a cigarette. I've drunk countless double espressos and iced cappuccinos. I'm always trying to not eat all the time. You can sit, if you're working with any level of anxiety, at a crafts service table and just eat yourself to death. Then you end up feeling like hell. I think a drink at the end of the day is a good thing. I drink martinis. I've found you can't drink at dailies because it results in too much exhaustion.

"I like a good party. I'm the last guy out of the office type. I'll go to all the dailies. I've had a couple of movies with outstanding party schedules. One of the best was *The Gun in Betty Lou's Handbag* (1992) because the director, Allan Moyle, was a brilliant party thrower. We shot in Oxford, Mississippi for ten weeks. We had parties at every different duke joint in 100 miles.

"Whenever there's that level of partying, it's never good for the movie. People just burn out. Actors can party because they get a lot of down time. It's really hard on department heads, directors, to party.

"We had a great wrap party on an 80-acre cotton farm. I can't call it a plantation. We had four blues bands and a Mardi Gras-style parade where the grip, electric and camera department dressed up as women and threw junk at people."

"It's good to find sporting events and concerts for people to go to. It's always good to hang out with your actors because the producer is usually the one who has to ask them favors."

Married 18 years, Scott has a 14-year old son and 8-year old twins.

"How has being a father affected you as a producer?"

"It helped me focus. I'd always thought about directing. Then, when I had kids, I made the judgment that if I put my mind to producing, it would be better for my family. If I wanted to direct, I'd have to go backwards and fight my way up. My first kid was great. For about five years, you can pack them up with you. My wife, Kristine Johnson, is a screenwriter (*I am Sam*, *Imaginary Crimes*, 1994). I met her at Embassy Pictures. She was the head of acquisitions.

"We'd bring our son on location. But once they are in school, it's no good. Once the twins came, it let me know I was really a father. I had to go off and do a movie (*Terminal Velocity*, 1994) shortly after they were born. The first day of the movie was the big 1994 earthquake. I'd hoped it would go smoothly and I could bail out. It turned out to be a battle to finish it. It was a big action movie that wasn't budgeted as big as our director's appetite. It built the appropriate resentment from my wife.

"Everyone goes through the on location resentment. Now I'm running a company and I'm doing more executive producing, though I find it the most fun to be on the set all the time.

"I love development, because it is pure. You are just dealing with a writer. You don't have a big committee yet. I find packaging interminable and agonizing. Then I enjoy production. Editing is tough. It means previews and the attendant anxiety. You get to figure things out and if necessary, re-shoot. We made many movies initially with Disney and I don't think there was a movie where they didn't do a re-shoot."

"Tell me about Ted Field."

"I've worked with him 18 years. He's a friend. Ted gets a bad rap. Anyone who comes from a wealthy family, there's an immediate stamp on them that they are a dilettante. Ted works hard. He has multiple businesses. He has so much money there's no reason he couldn't take six vacations a year and roll into the office at 11 a.m. He shows up at 9:30 a.m. like everyone else. He works late. He goes out 365 nights a year. He has his finger on the pulse of American culture. He sees every movie including weird little independent movies. He sees music. He has a great sense of the marketplace. We see eye to eye on commercial material. We disagree on artistic movies. He loves dark indie movies.

"The key part of our business is making commercial movies. While we'd like to make movies like *Very Bad Things* (1998) and *Gridlock* (1996), it's an indulgence. You are making movies to break even because they are artistic."

"Which of your movies have broken your heart?"

"*What Dreams May Come* was disappointing. It was such a great script and bold idea. The movie looked the way we wanted to, yet it didn't catch on. When we finally tested our best cut, we realized that this movie, which we thought all women in the world were going to love because it was a story about love that never dies, the people who really dug it were boys under 25. It was dark and visually cool and twisted, all the things that young guys dig.

"We made a couple of miscalculations. As a parent, I always had this bad feeling and everyone told me not to worry about it. I had this bad feeling that when you kill two kids in the beginning that an adult audience would have a difficult time recovering and they would just tune you out because it was just too painful to go there. That got us. There's nothing worse for a woman than the idea of her own child dying.

"Gene Siskel was a gigantic fan of the movie. Of course, he was in the process of dying."

64

Jay Stern

September 19, 2002

As director Brett Ratner's producer, Jay runs Rat Entertainment.

"I was a studio exec for 12 years, at Disney and then New Line. I don't think I've really proved myself as a producer yet."

"That's O.K. There are no definitions of the term producer."

"That's part of the problem. Anyone who passes the book store and says, 'Oh, that looks like an interesting title. I should producer that.' That person becomes a producer.

"Another problem is that there is no training ground for producers. They come out of being agents and studio executives. There's no system for creating good producers."

"It's the most undefined role in Hollywood."

"That's why producers get as little respect as they do. Many producers don't deserve respect."

"Tell me about your upbringing."

"I grew up in New York City. My father's a dentist. My twin brother is a psychiatrist. My sister has a doctorate in Scandinavian Folklore and works in computers. I graduated from Yale with a degree in psychology. I was on the nine-year plan. I was one of the only guys to graduate Yale in two terms—Nixon's and Carter's. I dropped out a couple of times. Then I was in a doctoral program in Clinical Psychology for about a year and a half. After leaving the program, I moved to Los Angeles for the film business."

"How did your family feel about your getting into the film industry?"

"Initially they were dubious. My mother would've preferred me to become a lawyer. It's scarey. I have a six year old boy. It's scarey to think, 'Is he going to make his way in the world? How rough is it going to be for him?' You want your children to avoid pain and have satisfying lives. My parents are happy now about my choice."

"What essential values did you inherit that allowed you to make your way in Hollywood?"

"I've been fortunate enough to last in the movie business. One thing that's helped, I basically like people. I'm asked all the time, how could you go out to lunch with all those agents and managers? Because I enjoy most of those lunches. I actually like a lot of those people. Or let's say that I find something to like and enjoy about most of them. Aside from that, I try my best to be fair and respectful in every situation, to deal with real integrity. Over time, that's helped me build relationships, where people know they can trust me. Being completely selfish or singlemindedly opportunistic may help other people do what they do, but it's not how I'm constructed. I don't walk into meetings with complicated strategies. I don't walk into meetings expecting a fight. If you do expect a fight, you'll be more likely to get one. I try to keep an open mind about what's best for the movie, which always takes precedence over what's necessarily best for me Jay. Hopefully they coincide more often than not—in my experience they usually do.

"What's fun about working with Brett [Ratner] is that he is so collaborative. He'll ask anybody, 'What do you think?' If someone has a good idea, Brett will use it. He creates his vision partly out of all the smart things said around him. He hunts and sniffs out smart stuff around him like a rabid truffle hog."

"Is this a polite industry?"

"No. People are animals. Most people say that if you turn your back and give someone else the advantage, you're dead. I'm usually looking for agreement and resolution right off the bat. Maybe I'm not as successful as I could be because I'd rather resolve things than have a sustained confrontation, but everybody has to work as best as they can with their natures and constitutions.

"I started my career working for producer Michael Peyser. I read hundreds of scripts a year and did more notes than anybody should have to do. Over that time, I honed my tastes and my instincts. I learned how to give notes to a writer. It's different in every situation. You can have the most brilliant notes in the world, but if you are not able to get the writer or director to embrace those notes, you might as well not give them. You can't force a creative person to come up with inspired work if you can't get them to agree with you. Half of the battle is getting them to embrace your direction. Part of what you're fighting all the time is that you don't want to alienate the creative person. It's like being a good coach.

"We [New Line] bought the *Rush Hour* (1998) script for Brett. His film *Money Talks* (1997) had been a sort of dress rehearsal for *Rush Hour*, although we obviously didn't know it at the time. We had a director walk off *Money Talks* three weeks before we were to start shooting. Brett came in for 20 minutes and talked about why he had to do the movie, and what it meant for him. We [DeLuca and I] hired Brett.

"After *Money Talks* came out, Brett said, 'You should come run my company.' I thought he had to be kidding. He was a child. I was a relatively established studio executive. He'd only directed one movie. After *Rush Hour* came out, I had to take him seriously."

"How has being a father affected you as a producer?"

"It's much tougher to get through the pile of scripts on a weekend because you want to spend time with your wife and son [Eli]. It makes you a more compassionate person. I've got to figure out what's the best thing to do. It's not just about you. But what's the best thing for this young developing wonder? Figuring out ways to empower and nurture him isn't all that different from what I try to do with writers and directors. He's also a brutal negotiator, so my negotiating skills have definitely been honed by being a Dad.

"We were on vacation in Bermuda. My wife Vicki had seen the promos for a new show called *Samurai Jack* (2001-???). She said we should watch it. We thought it was great. I got back to Los Angeles. Brett's assistant David Steiman had seen it on his vacation to the Caribbean. We thought the show was unbelievable and that we should do it as a live action movie. I tried to get the rights to it. I got Toby Emmerich involved. He got it immediately. We showed the premiere episode to Brett. He called me at 8 a.m. to say he loved it, and he never does that.

"Eli has fantastic taste. David, Brett and I happened to share it."

"How did you come to make so many black pictures?"

"I'm only white on the outside. Skin deep, baby. I went into New Line right after Helena Echegoyen had left. She'd developed a number of black movies. New Line has a tradition of doing urban movies. *Love Jones* (1997) was the first one I did. I do, by the way, have a natural affinity for urban culture. There were a couple of movies lying around that I could jump on and develop. Then Mike started giving me those projects and the community started sending me those scripts. What I want to do is *A Room With A View* (1985), only with black people."

"Did white people go to see movies like *Love & Basketball* (2000) [about middle class blacks]?"

"I think it did some crossover. There are [urban a.k.a black] movies that do $35 million box office and almost no crossover [into a white or Asian audience]. I'm guessing that *Barbershop* (2002) had an 80-90 percent urban audience.

"I think we could've gotten more blacks into *Love & Basketball* too. I think black males shied away from it because of the love side of it and black females shied away from it because of the basketball side. In the trailer and the commercials, there was a scene where he said, 'What are we playing for?' And she said, 'Your heart.' I think that young black males stayed away from the movie because of it. I tried to get involved in the marketing. I wasn't able to convince the filmmakers that that was going to have a cooling effect. It was still a good movie, New Line still made money on the movie, but I was a little frustrated it didn't find a bigger audience. *Money Talks* did about $40 million box office to an audience that was probably 75 percent urban. Chris Tucker was not that known a quantity yet in the white world. People weren't rushing to see Charlie Sheen at the time.

"When there's a big urban turnout to a movie, it scares whites away. Ten years ago, when there were some fatalities in theaters, there were black people who hesitated to go to a theater house packed with an urban audience. They think there's going to be trouble. For the same reason they're not going to a street fair with an overwhelmingly urban crowd. They fear there's going to be trouble. And plenty of white people are terrified to go to a movie theater where the audience will be largely black.

"Theater owners love Eddie Murphy and Will Smith but if they don't know the black person in the movie, they're hesitant to pick up the movie. Booking the theater can be the biggest problem for black movies, particularly in white suburbs."

"Producer Rob Long just told me that he didn't know what any studio executive had to contribute by going on set."

"Television tends to be driven by the show-runners (executive producers)."

Jay's mom calls. Jay tells his assistant: "Tell her I will have to call her back. I'm in a meeting."

"If he was like most producers in Hollywood trying to get features made, I don't think he'd be saying that. There are some smart people out there trying to make the movie better. I think that's another [example of the] 'Creatives vs. the suits' attitude. I guess there are brilliant directors who are auteurs. I've heard that [director] Michael Mann is tough and doesn't like to listen to the studio. Most people in this business have to be collaborative to survive.

"To work your way up in the studio system, you have to be willing to eat some shit and smile while you're doing it. Nobody likes someone who is eating shit and actually grimacing.

"It helped my career that I was on the slow track. I got to observe and learn. People often overplay their hand. They get themselves in positions of power where it feels like they can do anything and they can't. You overplay your hand a bit and the people above you tend not to appreciate it."

"Does the low status of producers in the business bother you?"

"Yes. I had a tough time moving over from studio exec to producer. Respect is built into the job of studio exec because you're a buyer. The tendency on most studio executives' part is to be dismissive of the producer. It's habitual. I don't know if Jerry Bruckheimer or Scott Rudin run into it but I certainly run into it. I run into it at every level—notes, creative and deal.

"When they give me notes, I have to come up with good arguments. I enjoy the autonomy of being an independent producer as opposed to an exec."

"Have you had any conversations about switching the race of a protagonist?"

"Many. Brett was interested in doing a movie called *Paycheck* (2003). Denzel Washington and Nick Cage were interested in playing the same character. Denzel and Will [Smith] are the names that come up as [blacks] who could come in and replace a white lead. You then ask the question if his love interest can be white or do you have to go black all the way. To be safe, you may want to go black all the way, or at least a person of color. It's easier to go black and Latino than black and white because there is a bias in the black community against black men and white women. I don't think you're going to have a black man and a white wife that works [in a sitcom or movie] any time in the next few years."

"How do black leads play overseas?"

"That's a huge consideration. That's the biggest reason why there aren't more black leads. The traditional conventional wisdom is that they don't sell overseas. The economics dictate this. These days, 60 percent of a studio movie is paid for by overseas. The exceptions are Will Smith, Denzel Washington, Eddie Murphy and Chris Tucker.

"You can make a movie for up to $20 million and turn a profit from just your domestic market but you're not going to make a $40 million movie starring black people unless one of them is Will or Denzel."

"Is there a type of movie you make best?"

"Certainly multi-racial action comedy is what I've done best till now but I swear there's *A Room With A View* in me with South American pygmies. People do tend to send me action comedies."

"Have you been recognized by the black community for your contributions to black cinema?"

"I don't know that I have been but I should be. A friend of mine used to joke that I'm the hottest black executive in town.

"It's all about Brett [Ratner] and Chris [Tucker] and Jackie [Chan]. They don't know I exist.

"As a producer, you have to put your ego aside. The actors and director will always command more attention."

"How much would it mean to you to win an Oscar?"

"It would be really nice."

"Do you ever dream of receiving a Best Picture Oscar?"

"I'd be lying if I hadn't told you that I'd fantasized at least a few times about it. It's not like I thought I would ever get up there for *Rush Hour 2* (2001) and say, 'Ladies and gentlemen of the Academy.' I didn't think it was in the realm of possibility. If all I ever do is movies like *Rush Hour*, that would be O.K. One *Room With A View*, one statuette, that would be O.K too."

65

Mark Damon

September 19, 2002

Born Mark Harris in Chicago, Illinois, on April 22, 1933, Mark was the romantic lead in Roger Corman's *The House of Usher* (1960).

He created the Producers' Sales Organization (PSO) in 1977 and helped father the independent film movement. Damon oversaw distribution of such international blockbusters as *Das Boot, Once Upon a Time in America* (1984) and *Prizzi's Honor* (1985).

I'm surprised at how young he looks.

Mark speaks in measured tones. "When I was an actor, I resolved that I would always take care of myself."

"Somebody told me that six years ago you were ready to quit the industry."

"Never. I have no hobbies. My two grown children have left the house. I couldn't sit around my home all day. My wife wouldn't know what to do with me."

"How did you find the process of working on your book?"

"Exhilarating at first, frustrating later. Exhilarating because I kept a lot of correspondence from certain periods in my life and I was able to go back into it and capture some of the emotions I felt. Frustrating because the mind plays tricks. You think something happened in 1967 and it happened in 1965. It's difficult to corroborate things. You have holes in certain periods of time. I had a photographic memory as a kid. But when so many things go on in your life, a lot of things get blurred. Since I've never kept a journal, it was frustrating not to be able to put everything together.

"What was interesting with my book was that after going through my entire life, I began to see a thru-line. Sometimes I picked it up. Sometimes my biographer picked it up. Where the drive started. What fed it. What were the things that never changed—my desire to be number one at everything. My determination to leave no stone unturned to accomplish anything I wanted to accomplish.

"Through looking back over all the years, it became obvious where some of the inciting moments were. You can't control what happens but you can control how you deal with things. No matter how adverse the situation, I will be able to cope with it. No matter how chaotic the situation, this gives me the opportunity to define an order that wasn't there before."

Five minutes into our conversation I leave so Mark can take a private call from Kevin Spacey, who's headed to South Africa with ex-President Bill Clinton to raise money for a charity.

Thirty minutes later, I return to Mark's office.

"What killed PSO?"

"[In 1986] We formed a union with Lou Corman, who was running the film fund Delphi. We called our company PSO-Delphi. Lou Corman took us to Allen & Company to raise funds. They raised $25 million for us in private placement. Part of our business plan called for us to invest money not just in film production but with producers, giving them overhead deals so that we would have a flow of product. The plan was to produce a certain number of pictures per year.

"Meantime, we finally closed a credit line for $140 million with the First National Bank of Boston and the Chemical Bank of New York. The $25 million raised through private placement and put into escrow was contingent on the $140 million line of credit closing.

"Mike Spiegler, who negotiated the deal with us, was let go from the First National Bank. We were operating on a handshake basis. Then we found out there was an internal fight going on between Chemical and First National. First National was concerned that our line of credit would be too highly leveraged. When Spiegler tried to fund us, they let him go and brought in people who were not entertainment industry bankers. They looked at the credit line and concluded it was to highly leveraged. So instead of giving us a $140 million line of credit, they would give us an $80 line of credit.

"At that time, we'd made deals with producers and we were shooting five pictures (*Short Circuit, 9 1/2 Weeks, Flight of the Navigator* (1986), *Eight Million Ways to Die* (1986), *Clan of the Cave Bear*) and executing our business plan based on a $140 million line of credit.

"We made money on all the pictures except *Eight Million Ways*, which was Hal Ashby's last picture. Ashby at that time, his mind was blown. He'd had too much coke, whatever. It's a flawed picture with moments of brilliance. It was from a script by Oliver Stone and rewritten by Robert Towne, two of the best writers we had. Ashby threw the script out and had the writers improvise every day. It was mind boggling.

"Once our credit line was changed, our $25 million was blown because it was contingent on a $140 million line of credit. We were out of business at that point. We'd spent $11 million of the $25 million. We'd depended on a handshake while the documents were drawn up. That's what really happened.

"Since then, John Miller of Chase and Franz Zoffman of Credit Lyonaisse said that the stupidest thing the bank could've done was pull the plug on PSO because PSO had been so highly successful.

"If I had wanted to be in the courts for the next five years, we would've won against the banks.

"It was not production that finished PSO."

"That's the general perception. PSO moved from sales to production and they went belly up."

"That's a total misperception."

"Where did you go after PSO?"

"I went into a state of paralysis. Having had such a successful company, I didn't get that involved in the banking end of it. That's what my partner John Hyde was doing. We'd agreed that he'd handle most of the banking and financing and I would handle the sales and marketing and production. I was as shocked as anybody.

"I'm proud that we protected the other producers. They got all their money. Nobody got hurt except John and I, and we had no personal liability.

"I was flying so high. PSO was the platinum diamond in the business. There was almost no picture we made a mistake on.

"I would get up in the mornings [after the bankruptcy] and hear the soundtrack for *Short Circuit*, which was about to come out, and I was paralyzed. All these pictures that I put my heart and soul into are now going out without my overseeing the marketing. The pictures were just thrown to the winds. *Eight Million Ways* got short shrift. *Flight of the Navigator* was neglected. It was the first picture to use CGI [computer generated images].

"About nine months later, I revived myself and began a company with Peter Guber and Jon Peters called Vision. I sold the company to Credit Lyonaisse in 1993 and started MDP Worldwide [a production, sales and distribution company] on about $10,000. By 1998, we'd made about $12 million on lower budget pictures. We became a public company. We're now worth about $50 million. Because we are one of the few independents with cash, all these projects are coming to us. We have every important project available thrown at us now because most of the other independent companies are just out of money. We crawled back up."

"How do you deal with rip-off producers?"

"You'll have to be more specific."

"I heard Moshe Diamant turned your hair white with his shenanigans."

Mark laughs. "Moshe is a smart guy. He's also an Israeli. He's an egomaniac. He's a control freak. He knows how to produce pictures. People say he has no taste. The last two pictures of his we handled got about the worst reviews I've ever seen—*The Musketeer* and *FearDotcom* (2002)."

"Will Moshe make more pictures for you?"

"No. I think that business relationship is over. We've had enough of each other in business, hopefully not socially."

"How much are you going to reveal in your book?"

"Pretty much everything. I think the only way to do a book that's interesting to the public is if they see your vulnerabilities. I read the book *The Kid Stays in the Picture*. I thought it was good. I thought the documentary was brilliant.

"Here was a crazy egomaniac who ruined his life on drugs. I went all through the *Cotton Club* (1984). What you don't have there..."

Mark points to my notes. "You have the list of movies I took producer credits on. Imdb doesn't list the 300 pictures I helped finance and distribute. *The Cotton Club* would not have been made without our involvement."

"Do you look at the book *The Kid Stays in the Picture* as a model?"

"There's a certain similarity that we were both actors and we both became successful producers. Bob was crazier than I was. Bob rose to greater heights of prominence than I did. My claim to fame will be the fact that I basically, coming from an acting background, became what they call the godfather of independent films. The one who invented the foreign sales business. The one who invented ways to get films financed.

"How did somebody do what I did? Because I didn't know better. I came in with such fresh viewpoint because I'd been an actor and I didn't know anything. Then I got into distribution in Europe. I began to meet European distributors and I understood that these guys were better than the major studios. They were more careful with their money. They got every nickel's worth of publicity. They knew the provinces better than the majors. But they couldn't get big pictures. It became my goal to get them big pictures.

"I went on a crusade for years to show that you could make much more money if you distributed your pictures independently through PSO (Producers Sales Organization) than if you went through the studios."

66

Rob Long

Rob Long walks into his Paramount office and asks about the overnight ratings. A golf cart clatters by.

"Are people too lazy to walk?" I ask.

"Yes. Most of the executives have carts so they can get some place quickly."

"It makes that much of a difference?"

"It makes no difference at all. I don't think an executive ever has to be anywhere on the lot quickly. They shouldn't be on the lot at all. They should be in their office. There's almost nothing that happens on movie lots that an executive can contribute to.

"People don't like to walk. You might encounter somebody."

"I only saw positive reviews on your book, *Conversations With My Agent.*"

"Depends how you read the reviews. If the review says it's a great book, but this part didn't work so well, and you wrote the book, you think, 'What the hell?' If you're just reading the review, you think it's a great review. I got a bad review from *Entertainment Weekly*. They gave me a B+."

"That's a great review."

"I thought it was a snide snarkey review."

Vanessa I. Friedman writes in the January 24, 1997, issue of EW: "The only jarring moment occurs at the end, when the writer and his partner perhaps succeed in selling a new comedy to a nascent network. Suddenly all irony is abandoned in favor of mature assessment and a weird kind of personal-growth statement. One of Long's pet peeves is the tendency of everyone in his business to give him notes on his shows, but the temptation is suddenly irresistible, so here goes: Skip the last page."

"That's almost the worst kind of review. It means the person enjoyed the book and wrote a thoughtful response to it that you have to take it seriously.

"Nobody bought the book so I'm always gratified to hear that certain people enjoy it. If everyone who ever enjoyed it, bought it."

"I checked it out of the library."

"Most people picked it up at the bookstore, it's so short, they read it while standing in line. By the time they finally got to the cash register, they'd read it. Put it this way, the book caused me no tax trouble.

"People always say, I want to write a novel. My old agent used to say, 'Look, if you want $800, I'll give you $800.' That's about how much money you'll make off your first novel."

"Was there any negative fallout from the book?"

"No. Only the young people take themselves and the industry seriously. If you're a vice-president of something, you tend to be naive and stupid. I don't think I've ever met anyone with that title who didn't take themselves and their jobs seriously. By the time you've been around six or seven years, you realize it's ludicrous.

"Everyone tends to believe that they are the island of sanity. So, when they read about how crazy everybody is, they go, 'Oh boy, are you ever right? I'm surrounded by them.' When, in fact, part of the book is about that person. People tend not to recognize themselves or they tend to be flattered. Most of the people in my book are composite characters who come off O.K."

"No one who matters is afraid of you?"

"Unfortunately not. Unfortunately, I inspire zero fear or respect in anyone. I think fear and respect are the same thing. People make little jokes about it. 'Oh, this is going to show up in your next book.' I think they're secretly hoping it does. To work in this industry you have to be unembarrassable. Big producers like it when people talk about how dumb they are. They think it's funny."

"Have you had any huge feuds?"

"No."

"Do you have any huge enemies?"

"No."

"I saw this interchange in Harpers between two sitcom writers who hated each other."

"Wasn't that awful? I don't even know what they were arguing about but one guy came off to be a lunatic. There are almost always crazy people but if you just do the job, there should be no trouble. It's [television] a collegial place. There are only a few people who work so everybody's got to get along. You prepare yourself for these awful meetings. You tell yourself, 'I'm really going to blow up.' Then you don't because you figure, what's the point?

"There's a whole cottage industry here on the apology. What gift to send to apologize. Where the meeting will be where you apologize. I'm so conflict averse. Today at 4 p.m. we were going to have a meeting in which I was absolutely, in my shower, just eloquently devastating about the idiotic notes we had to listen to."

"Have you ever had any notes sessions in your shower?"

"No. That's what keeps me back. That I am embarrassable."

"Has the Gay Mafia ever done anything to you?"

"No. That was a weird thing of him [Michael Ovitz] to say. In order for that to work, all of those people would have to get along. That particular community is often riven by feuds. They're certainly emotional people. So I don't think they can even agree on their enemies.

"I shouldn't say this as a heterosexual Episcopalian. But as an observer, the most complicated person is the gay Jewish guy. He's got all kinds of things going on. I heard that when they liberated Kabul in Afghanistan, they found two Jews. And they hated each other. They preferred the Taliban to each other."

"What's it like being an Episcopalian in this business?"

"It's good. You learn a new language. The industry is so open. They don't care. This is the most open major industry in the world. I hear people say, 'Oh, it's closed.' There's nothing closed about it. You've just got to write the script. Someone's got to read it. It's going to be hard but it's hard for everybody equally.

"And you have to do something that most people don't do—you have to actively manage your own career. Most people get a job and they go where the company directs.

"There are categories of people and you have to hire the right people to put you in the right category. There are funny writers who write vaguely disgusting comedy over here. Girl writers who write romantic comedies, Nora Ephronish but younger, over here. You want to make sure you are in the columns you want to be in. You don't want anyone else defining you. I got a call once from an agent pitching a writer. 'The thing about her is she's great administratively.' What the hell is that? She's not too great with story or jokes, but administratively she's great?"

"Do people ever try to make you feel inferior because you work in television rather than film?"

"I find that people who are sitting at Starbucks working on their screenplay, who've never sold anything, tend to look down on people who write for television. But people I know who write features don't at all. They all want to get into television. It becomes so exhausting going to meeting after meeting, and the project never goes anywhere, and the money's not so good, and you see your friends who write for television, and they cast it and they hire and fire the director, and put it on TV.

"For TV writers like me, who do it for a while, and you do meeting after meeting and you're just trying to get your show on the air. You get it on the air and you get a 12 share and they don't promote it. You think you'd rather sit at home and write your features. Each side wants to do the other thing.

"I only encounter the snobbery from people who aren't working."

"Do you yearn to go into features?"

"It'd be a great job if you were in semi-retirement. To work for a living writing features is a tough job. You need to be able to walk away. You need to have the power of the alternative. The great semi-retirement job is that you come in for two weeks, punch it up, and you leave. If I was going to go into features, I'd want to go in as the boss. It's hard to go from here, where you're the boss, to features where you are not the boss."

Rob is single and has no kids.

"Let's talk about race. I was raised in America to believe that race doesn't matter but in casting characters in TV and movies, race matters."

"When people declare things like that, that race doesn't matter, what they're really saying is that race is the only thing that matters. It's the biggest giantest hugest thing. It's a giant sub-current in every political or financial conversation. It's like the sub woofer. It goes through everything. You may not be able to see where it is coming from, but it's there. And you are not allowed to talk about it. It's rude."

"I can just picture you going to a network and pitching a new show and then saying, everyone's black."

"They wouldn't mind that because then it would be a black show. It's a solid performer. There's a financial category for that. You need them. They're evergreens.

"Everyone is so polite and careful that you are never going to be able to get anyone to have an honest conversation at any point anywhere in America unless the door is locked and they're there with their family and they've got, 'I've got shit I could tell people that you said too.' You have to have some kind of mutually assured destruction to have that kind of conversation honestly.

"If you are trying to construct a series, you're just looking for fertile ground. You're looking for fields that are funny. I don't think that I would ever arbitrarily select race unless I knew that it would be funny.

"We wrote a black character for a Bob Newhart show because it was funny having him play against Bob Newhart. But that's why we picked it. We weren't making a statement. We thought it could be fruitful to see a conservative Catholic uptight white guy with a young black guy."

"How often does race come up?"

"It has a financial ramification and a scheduling ramification. People think they can have a psuedo-frank conversation about—is it a black show, a white show or a multiracial show? If it's a black show, we can have two areas on our schedule where we can schedule black shows. If it is a black show that cuts young, that's good because it syndicates well. Make it, put it on the WB, syndicate it in the afternoons and make a lot of money. People talk about that—the nuts and bolts—because it makes sense to them and no one can complain about that. But if you're talking about anything else, it's just uncomfortable."

"Could you write a cutting-edge black show?"

"No. It isn't me."

"What are the financial ramifications of a multiracial show?"

"It depends on how old the people are, whether it is male driven. A black show has a certain niche for the financial backers. The problem is that multiracial shows don't work. maybe because they are all so pious. We did a show about young guys last season for the WB with a black lead, and a Cuban-American, but it was mainly a guy show about guys chasing women. It didn't have a racial attitude."

"On the day President Kennedy was shot, journalist Tom Wolfe visited various ethnic neighborhoods in New York and discovered that each ethnic group was blaming another group for the assassination. He wrote the story and turned it in but it was never published because the American newspaper is too much of a 19th Century Victorian gentleman."

"You can't write the truth because it doesn't fit your audience. That's trouble. It hurts the very groups you're trying to protect. When the homeless were in, under President Reagen, every homeless person was revealed to be a family of four that has fallen on hard times. He's a skilled carpenter and she's a nurses' assistant and they don't have any money and this is terrible. We live in this terrible Reaganite world. The problem is that the people walking up and down the street, their eyes said the homeless tend to be drug or alcohol abusers or mentally ill.

"The media kept hitting this story of no room at the inn, and Joseph and Mary and their baby, and the truth is it was really something else. It delayed a legitimate conversation about the homeless because it was hyper-politicized by the media who wanted to blame it on Reagen. We didn't really want to deal with the topic. We didn't really want to say that part of the problem is that state mental hospitals were closed because they were terrible places. And we had all these people saying in the early seventies that even if all these people live on the street, they're better off on the street than in a state mental hospital.

"I think the same thing happened with AIDS. It wasn't the choreographer or the photographer's assistant but the guy who just got it from the thing and the girl who was a guy one time and all these people who were statistically insignificant. It socialized the risk. The two things that people heard about AIDS when it broke was one, everyone can get it, and two, don't worry, it's not an epidemic. And people just turned off.

"The tragedy is, the very people you're trying to psuedo-protect by lying about it, end up not helping. So the incidence of HIV infection among young gay men is going up. So how have we helped?

"When *Friends* (1994-2004) came out, it was a cultural phenomenon. It was a show about single young people in New York. People forget that there had been a hit show on Fox for a year before called *Living Single* (1993-98)—about single young people in New York City. But they were black. When NBC moved *Friends* to 8 p.m. Thursdays, you had a white and a black version of the same show on at the same time. Nobody mentioned it because it was rude."

"Do you ever fear that you are in an industry that is fundamentally degrading the country?"

"I don't believe there is an industry. It's too fragmented. It's a matter of the amount. People watch too much TV. They're always doing studies that show Americans are busier than ever. So busy they don't even eat at home anymore. They pick up food and eat it while they drive. But they still watch three hours of TV a day. I hope people will develop appointment viewing."

"Do you go to church regularly?"

"No. I haven't been to church in years. I don't think there's a church around. There's a Lutheran Church around the corner but I'm scared. If I were to pick a church, it would be a church that doesn't require a great deal of faith. Being Episcopalian, faith isn't what it's about."

"How much do you think the lack of religiosity of people who make TV affects the final product?"

"They've done studies that show that people who don't go to church have a hard time believing that anyone else goes to church or that there's anything to be found there. Some of the biggest, longest running, hits on TV have been church related—*Touched By An Angel* (1994-2003), *7th Heaven* (1996-???). I think the theory is that religion is a private thing and you don't want to turn anybody off. You've got to be nice and generic and broad. You can God up there on a big cloud but you can't get too specific about it because you have too many people out there and you don't want to turn anybody off."

"Would you be willing to risk your life to do a TV show called *The Last Temptation of Mohammed*?"

"If I could do it funny. You don't want to do it just for controversy. I saw *The Last Temptation of* Christ and it was a bad movie. I couldn't tell if it was irreverent or blasphemous or what. I was just so bored by it. A movie about Mohammed wouldn't have any appeal to them because it is only fun to offend your neighbor."

"Do you do things for appearances?"

"No. A traditional film producer needs to do that. You need to be out and to look like you're busy. When you have a skill, you don't need to do any of that stuff. I live at the beach [in Venice] and I find it really hard to turn around and go back [to Los Angeles proper]. I will do anything after I leave work to avoid going east of Lincoln Blvd."

"Do you go to many parties that you don't want to go to?"

"I don't get invited to parties. Every now and then you get invitations to charity benefits. Then you look at it and try to figure out who put you on the list and you try to figure out if you have sent that guy invitations to your charity events. People who have given money to your cause, you give to their cause. That's as political as I get.

"I'm political in that I listen to notes. I'm polite and respectful even if the person is a moron. Making sure that everyone feels they have a stake in the project. Be easy to work with. That always pays off and the opposite always penalizes you."

"How do morons get to be executives?"

"That's how they hire them. They're a separate class of person. It's not like the old days when they'd say to someone like me, 'Are you exhausted? Come be vice-president of development.' Instead, they have people whose job is to watch me do my job. It doesn't seem economical.

"It used to be that you had a big boss who expressed his taste. That's how you programmed a network or built a slate of films. This picture needs a pretty girl in it and that picture needs a monster. Now there's nobody like that. I don't know one writer or director who wouldn't want to work for one of those old fashioned moguls, because at least you know where they are coming from. There's one guy left who's kinda like that—Les Moonves [who runs CBS]. He's infuriating and difficult and aggressive and scary but you know where he's coming from. He's expressing his taste as opposed to a guy looking at the numbers and the testing.

"There's no scientific formula. When NBC gets *Friends*, the first thing they do is to try to put on five other shows like Friends, as if they somehow came up with *Friends*. What gave them Friends was that they hired three people to write a good script and make a good show. NBC fought them every step of the way. In the process of those three people not listening to the network and not doing what the network told them to do, they got a hit show. The lesson from that the network received was—we know how to create hits. The lesson they should've learned was—we have no idea how to create hits, which would be so liberating. All you'd have to do is find people whose work you liked and then hire them do their work. See if it works. If it doesn't, put on something else."

"What's the most meaningful part of your work?"

Long pause.

"I don't know. I like doing my work with the camera and the people performing...I like being on the set and making the show funny. But the minute it's over, the studio and the network have ideas. You have to cut the thing."

"Are most comedy writers misanthropes?"

"The good ones are. It's not an attractive trait to have a job where you joke around. When you sit in a room with a bunch of writers and everybody is making jokes and you're trying to top each other. Because it is quasi-social, you can convince yourself that is your group of friends. This is your social life. It's not. It's a collegial job. It's not friendship. It's not the job of your real friends to make you laugh.

"You should try to be the guy who comes up with the line or the fix that is so great that everybody gets to go home early, that's the person you should aspire to be if you want a career. My career goal is to go home. That story editor is a huge star to me."

"Do you think about comedy as various degrees of cruelty?"

"That's probably true. There's something hilarious about cruel humor. People who write great comedy can also write great drama while people who write great drama can't always write great comedy."

"What are your favorite parts of Hollywood culture?"

"The awards shows are my favorite if I'm nominated. And if I'm not nominated, they are my least favorite."

Nominated twice, Long has never won an Emmy.

"The show [*Cheers*, 1982-93] got an Emmy for a show I wrote with my partner. I didn't get a statute.

"The best thing is the first two months after your product is a certifiable hit. You have a grace period for a couple of months where you can do whatever you want. No one will deign to give you notes.

"Television is a matter of fact place. You don't have to be or do anything so long as you have a skill. If you're a writer, you always want to let other people think they are discovering you because then they will have more of a stake in promoting you. We tend to spec [submit] our ideas rather than pitch them. They come to the desk fully formed and already written and there's an element of surprise to whoever is reading it. It may take an extra month to write the thing, rather than just pitch an idea, but it is much easier in the long run.

"The worst Hollywood ritual is pitching. I hate it. It's stupid. When you go in a room and pitch someone a story, then go write it. For two months, your idea of what you're writing and their idea of what you're writing grow miles apart. You turn in something they don't recognize.

"In January, all the scripts come in. The networks go nuts. They make frantic calls. 'What else do you have?' If you are a writer who wants to get a show on the air, write a spec pilot, put it in your drawer, and send out January 6. Because they will be so disappointed in the stuff that they ordered.

"It's even worse in features. They take 30 pitches a day in tight bits of ideas that eventually have to become long stories. It never works out."

"Any pop culture profs see great profundity in your work that you never realize existed?"

"They used to do that with *Cheers*. *Cheers* was an officially approved intellectual piece of work, which always made us laugh. One of the guys who used to run the show remarked that the characters on the show are awful to each other. But because the theme song is so friendly, people get the sense that the people love each other.

"Some guy did an interesting piece about what an ancient form *Cheers* was. These are natural archetypes. You are naturally going to have these characters in your play. They go back to ancient Greece. The sassy barmaid. The bragging know-it-all guy in uniform. The poor schlub who has a wife he can't stand and he has to drink all day. I'm sure it never occurred to the Charles brothers who created the show. They are smart guys but they weren't trying to resurrect some of the famous archetypes of comedy."

"Do you tell strangers what you do for a living?"

"No. I say I'm a financial journalist or a merchant banker. Neither one has any follow-up. Before I did that, people would always respond, 'Do I know anything you've done?' Probably not. I've had a couple of shows canceled. And there was that concern that you'd get. Don't worry. Failure is rewarded around here."

"Do you encounter people who start lecturing you about the immorality of television?"

"Yeah, when I go to right-wing events. You just say, 'What do you want me to do? I write things that I think are funny.' I don't think TV is instructional. I think TV is the worst place to learn anything. It's pure entertainment."

"Is there a common thread through your work?"

"I hope not."

"Have you ever been in therapy?"

"No, I don't think I would do well. I'd think, 'How would that guy know? He doesn't know me.' This girl was telling me about behavioral therapists. You go to them with a problem. 'I can't start anything on time. Instead, I have to do it at the last minute.' These guys are really good. They give you tricks and cues and ways to discipline yourself to accomplish a task. Big sports team use them. That might be cool."

"But you are not interested in why you do what you do?"

"I couldn't be less interested. I don't believe I could learn that from somebody else."

"You don't read on psychology?"

"No. I don't believe in it. It has fun buzz words you can use.

"You pay the guy to ask you questions. I don't know. What are you going to tell me that I don't already know? It would be hard for me to go and tell somebody what actually happened that day without being bored by it. I think I'd make shit up or make it more entertaining. I often do that in life. I think that would be bad for therapy.

"I'm surprised when I see Larry David's show, *Curb Your Enthusiasm* (2000-???). If I were his therapist, you'd know the guy is lying. You'd know from watching the show."

"Have you ever had a chick tell you to go to a therapist?"

"No. I'm dating a girl who's studying to be one. It's interesting when she talks about personality disorders.

"If I ever met a therapist who I thought was funny, I might be interested, but most of them seem earnest."

"You don't see yourself replaying relationships you had as a child?"

"God no. I see myself taking language from people and using it [in scripts]. It's a pastiche. It's more like dreams where the content is not as important as the emotional story. It's all about how you feel.

"I'm currently having a weird dispute with a friend. He says it happened to him and I'm certain it happened to me. I was driving on Wilshire Blvd and some guy pulled up next to me and said in an English accent, 'Hey, use your fucking indicator!' I'm convinced it happened to me and my friend Tim is convinced it happened to him. He says his wife was in the car but I've already had run-ins with his wife's memory, which is really bad."

67

Erica Huggins

"I decided that the only way I could make documentaries was to get into editing. [In 1987] I had a high school friend who worked at Cannon Films. I got off the plane from [Hampshire] college and my friend said Cannon was looking for apprentice editors. They hired me for $300 a week non-union. My first movie was *Firewalker* (1986) with Chuck Norris. I worked for an editor who was a drunk. Instead of giving us apprentice work, he'd just give us scenes to cut.

"I worked on Michael Cimino's *The Sicilian* (1987). He fired me and hired me and fired me."

"He's a bizarre character."

"He was turning into a bizarre character on *The Sicilian*. I always respected him because he was so smart about filmmaking. I didn't work on any good movies with him but he was so smart. He was challenging. He'd go through assistants like chewing gum. We connected. The editor I worked with, Françoise Bonnot, was a well-known French editor. She just needed somebody who would take care of Michael. He always wanted to come in to work with her. She wanted to be left alone to cut the movie. 'You play around in there.'

"I was then hired as an assistant editor on John Waters' *Hairspray* (1988). My husband, my then boyfriend, was a huge fan of John Waters from the Polyester days. He knew all the characters in John's movies. I was more naive. I read *Hairspray*. I went off to Baltimore for six months [in 1988]. I met Janice Hampton, the film's editor. We worked together exclusively for the next six years. I went from being her assistant to being an editor. She took me under her wing and she became my mentor. She needed somebody and I was looking for somebody.

"We worked on *The Gun In Betty Lou's Handbag*. It was produced by the guys from Interscope—Scott Kroopf, Robert Cort and Ted Field. Janice had done some fixes for New Line on Allan Moyle's *Pump Up The Volume* (1990), which was a big success. So Allan hired Janice and she hired me to be the second editor.

"Allan was not cut out for *The Gun In Betty Lou's Handbag*. He hated the script. He didn't get along with the leading lady. It was a bad situation. Allan lost his mind on the movie. He would never come into the editing room. He was down the hall playing X-rated video games. Janice went off to cut another movie and I finished the movie with the producers. I formed a relationship with Scott and Robert. Interscope had just had a big hit with *The Hand Rocks the Cradle* (1992). Interscope was closing a deal with Polygram and Robert needed to hire some people. He called me up one night [in 1992] and asked if I wanted to be a producer. I said 'Yeah!'

"We struck a deal. After three months, if it wasn't working, no harm, no foul. For the first three months, he'd give me half my salary, and an office and he would introduce me to everybody that he knew. He would let me be in every meeting he was and go to every lunch he went to and be at every breakfast and be at every phone call, and he kept his word."

In 1997, Robert Cort left to form a company at Paramount. "I think it was time for us to move apart. At a certain point with a mentor, it's hard when you want to movie on. With Janice it wasn't easy, we didn't talk for ten years. We talked but it wasn't friendly. For the last five years, it was very unfriendly. She's working for me on a movie I just made this summer [*How To Deal*, 2003]. It's funny how it comes back around.

"Robert handed me a script called *Boys* [in 1994]. I worked with him to Winona Ryder and all of a suddenly we had a movie. He let me go off and produce it. I'd been on so many movies that he trusted that I knew how to tell a story. He believed that I was a storyteller from the back part of the movie, and that if I could tell it from that side, that I would be good at doing it from the beginning. It was horrible.

"The first few years were just miserable because I didn't have any contacts. I'd call agents and they had no idea who I was. I was so naive about how things worked. But I had Robert and he backed me up. Cut to I've been here ten years.

"*Gridlock'd* (1997) was the second movie I produced. It was Tupac Shakur's last movie. He and Tim Roth had a fantastic relationship. It was one of those movies where everyone had a great time making the movie, which is rare. Tupac was a total pro. Then you wake up the next morning and read about what he did the night before, after you wrapped, and he was out gangbanging with his friends and you think, who is this guy? How can he be such different people? He couldn't get out of the other life, even if he wanted to. [Tupac was murdered soon after.]

"*What Dreams May Come* was the biggest movie I've ever made. Director Vincent Ward had made *Map of the Human Heart* (1993), a $17 million movie. We won an Academy Award for *Dreams*, the first that Interscope had ever won but it was just such a hard movie to make.

"Vincent was so insecure about the largesse of this movie and the actors that he had, like Robin Williams, it intimidated him. He shut down. Instead of dealing with all the people on the movie, he'd ask people questions in areas that weren't their specialty. He ended up getting half the information and it hurt the movie.

"I made that movie before I had kids. The movie's about two kids dying in the first ten minutes. I now wonder, what was I thinking? The movie should've been made for women in their 30s who had children but I don't think it was an easy movie for women to see. I wasn't experienced enough to know. I hadn't had the life lesson of knowing what it was like to have children.

"Then, the wife in the movie committed suicide. Then the hero of the movie went to heaven, and instead of looking for his children, he looked for his wife. It just doesn't make any sense.

"I can never forgive [fellow producer] Stephen Simon for the way he treated everybody. He's very metaphysical. Robert used to call him the Mooney. They'd [Stephen Simon and his producing partner at the time, Barnet Bain] always had a cosmic explanation for why something wasn't working the way it should. Stephen had this horrible temper and he was just so nasty to people. He didn't live the life he espoused. It was an awkward relationship. He despised me. He just didn't think he needed me. Why can't we just go off and make our own movie? They were making an $80 million movie and I was there to produce the movie creatively for our company [Interscope] and watch the money for [distributor] Polygram."

"Rob Long says, I don't know why executives ever come on a set. There's nothing they can contribute."

"You can't. When you're put in that position, it's complicated. No matter what choice you make, it's going to hurt. If you make the financially sound choice, creatively you're in trouble. If you make the creative choice, it always ends up costing you. You can't be true to the movie. That was the one movie where I played both roles and it was not fun. It did not work. I was an executive at a studio, because Polygram was financing the movie, while I was creatively producing the movie for our company Interscope. Those two roles don't work together. They never have. Since then, we've just been producers on movies."

"Did you realize all along that you were in trouble with this movie?"

"From the first day of the scout, I knew there was a problem. We were in Montana in East Glacier National Park, the most beautiful location in the world. We were creating heaven. We had these amazing locations. We needed helicopters to get out. We had to build trees on cliffs. We painted flowers on hillsides.

"Vincent couldn't find a location for the first day of shooting—Robin wakes up in heaven and finds the dog. We're in the middle of this fabulous location and Vincent decides we're going to use the hill behind the hotel. You had to keep the camera down so you didn't see the hotel. He shot and shot and he didn't shoot any dialogue the first day. I remember Robin called me into his trailer and said, 'This is a debacle. What are we doing here?'

"I remember having a meeting with Vincent and he said, 'I am the director.' When you get a person who is so terrified that they have to shut everybody out. He didn't really have a producer. I was Interscope. Stephen and Barnett were keepers of the script, the book and the metaphysical angle. He didn't have anybody he could call at 2 a.m., when he was freaking out, that he could trust. I think that's the most important relationship you can have with your director. They can call you and be completely panicked and you are not going to panic. He didn't have anybody to confide in. Maybe he's not capable of trusting people. I didn't even know what he was thinking so I couldn't help him get what he wanted.

"Vincent stopped talking to Robin about his performance once we got to San Francisco. So Robin had nobody to talk to about his performance. After dailies, Robin would call me at 1 a.m. to find out how it was. He needed some feedback.

"About a month ago, Robin had a good interview on NPR about *One Hour Photo*. He said being a [stand-up] performer and being an actor are two different things. Being a performer, you put yourself in front of the audience and it flows. Being an actor, you have to come up with a personality you're willing to become. It's harder to be an actor than a performer. When you're an actor, there's so much more you don't know.

"We hoped this movie would have the two things Robin was good at—humor and compassion. You couldn't get through the movie to even see if that was there.

"My colleague Scott Kroopf was close with Marsha, Robin's wife. The bonding against Vincent was unfortunate but we didn't want to lose our actor too. We couldn't get to Vincent. He wouldn't let us in.

"I haven't seen the movie since it came out. I have no idea about how I feel about it now. I just couldn't watch it anymore. It was such a disappointment. It deserved to win the Academy Award for digital effects. At the end of the day, I think that's what Vincent is most interested in—the artistic effects. It was an $80-million art movie."

Vincent Ward hasn't shot a movie since.

"That first night in Robin's trailer, there was an unspoken understanding that he would be O.K. with making a change. He felt insecure about the way Vincent was directing, but Michael Coon, who was head of Polygram at the time, wouldn't make a change. Nobody wanted to mutiny against Vincent. He just wouldn't let anybody in. It took me years to get over it.

"Then Polygram fell apart. We had just made *Pitch Black* (2000), a big success, but not for Polygram because the company couldn't last. We didn't have a good run with Polygram. They expected us to do international movies and we were a company that historically done female-driven comedies. Robert [Cort] had a way of doing things that Michael Coon didn't understand.

"Now it's fun. Ted [Field] is our sugar daddy. We have a big library of material. We have a good track record. We are a family of people who have worked together for more than ten years. We made seven movies this year."

68

Edgar J. Scherick

February 14, 2002

Confined to bed by a stroke, Edgar J. Scherick, creator of ABC's *Wide World of Sports*, lies dying.

A big man, he looks beaten down by life. Oxygen tubes go up his nose. A color television plays silently in front of him. I sit beside his bed and ask him about his childhood. He speaks in a growl.

"My parents (Jacob Jay and Jenny) were born in the United States. They were of German and English stock. My father was a manufacturer of boys' sailor suits. My mother was a beautiful woman from the lower East Side. They were married in 1910. In 1919, my sister Shirley was born. I was born in Manhattan on October 16, 1924.

"When I was two weeks old, the whole family moved to Long Beach, New York, on the south shore of Long Island.

"My earliest memories are selling blotters and little things around my neighborhood. My father was a fisherman, and at five years old, I started fishing in the bay. I fished until I had a stroke in 1998.

"I remember going to silent movies like *The Ten Commandments* (1923). I can still see the pages of the Bible as they were burning. I remember being scared out of my wits by horror pictures and having terrible nightmares. I loved Abe Lincoln in Illinois. I loved any picture where Indians were getting shot. I liked Errol Flynn in *Captain Blood* (1935). I liked swashbuckling films. My parents liked movies too. Everybody went to the movies in those days.

"The local theater had circulars, which told what the program was for the week. I gave these circulars out house-to-house and my pay was a free pass to the movies anytime I wanted to go. On Mondays and Tuesdays, they ran a double feature. Then they changed to a new double feature. I saw all four movies every week. I found out the day the news reel changed.

461

"They say that a pool player is a sign of a wasted childhood. I can tell you the name of practically every character actor in Hollywood from those days. I like these stations that show black and white movies from my youth.

"I was a precocious kid. I went to a private kindergarten. I could read and write when I was four years old.

"My family was wiped out by the Great Depression. My father had earned a good living. His business was wiped out. He was worth a good hunk of money. He was out of business for a month, commuting into New York, without telling my mother that he had closed his business. We lost our house to the bank. My mother began to sell off stuff we'd accumulated to put food on the table—cut glass, wine. She held the family together. I never went hungry.

"My father was very unhappy. He lost everything in the depression. He was cranky as hell. My mild-mannered mother gave us the best food. It was a dysfunctional family. There was a lot of tension in the house over my father's position in the household. He started a screaming session every morning but he never hit us.

"My mother's sister Edna Roth used to spend summers with us. She was vivacious and funny and beloved by her friends. She was in all these philanthropic organizations like Hadassah.

"I was raised by three women—my mother, my aunt and my West Indian nanny Rose Dunbar."

"What did your dad do after he lost his business?"

"He hung around and got sick. He sent me out every morning to go to the candy store to get two cigars and a newspaper. He ran up a considerable bill at these mom-and-pop stores. He never worked again. He had a couple of shots at things but they never worked out. He got a political job at City Hall as an assistant tax commissioner but he never amounted to anything. He was a big Democrat.

"My mother earned the money. Everything foreclosed in Long Beach during the depression. She would go to the bank and rent a house. She'd fix up apartments in the house and people would come down to spend the summer in Long Beach. She accumulated enough money to live through the following winter. She amassed $15,000 in the bank before she died.

"My father Jacob died of a heart attack in 1949 at age 74 and my mother Jenny died in 1962 at age 82.

"I had a remarkably happy childhood. I lived on an island that had a bay on one side and the ocean on the other side. I grew up with nature.

"Rose used to wheel me on the boardwalk in a stroller. Another black woman did the same thing with another kid. These two women became friendly and the boy in the stroller became my lifelong friend, Martin Warshaw. He now lives in Ann Harbor, Michigan. He was a professor of business at the University of Michigan.

"I had a whole coterie of friends."

"Any of them become famous?"

"I'm far and away the most famous."

Most of Edgar's friends were Jewish. Though he's always believed in God, he rarely went to temple and he never had a *bar mitzvah*.

"Did your family keep kosher?"

"Are you kidding? We were lucky we could eat. As my sister used to say, 'I follow the Ten Commandments, that's my religion.' I think she fasted on Yom Kippur."

"Did you grow up believing Jews were smarter than other people?"

"No. There was no sort of superiority taught in my house. Everybody was equal."

Scherick attended the public (and largely Jewish) Long Beach High School.

"What were the most influential books you read as a kid?"

"*Microbe Hunters* by Paul DeKruif. It was about great scientists like Louis Pasteur. I read a lot. *The Count of Monte Christo. Treasure Island. Kidnapped.*"

I meet with Edgar a dozen times during 2002. It's rare that he gives me more than 30 minutes at a time.

"I was a good student at school. Teachers liked me. My friends and I created the newspaper and took on projects. I served on the yearbook and played intermural sports. I was 5'10 and I was never a great athlete though I played everything in its season. I graduated high school in 1940 at age 16. I went in to New York to work as an office boy at an advertising agency and a runner at the export area. I didn't make much money but whatever I earned, I brought home. I went to New York City College at night.

"I realized that I was attractive to women but I didn't worry about it. We used to play spin the bottle at age 14.

"I entered the Army in March of 1943 and served for three years. I was a meteorologist running a little weather station in Iceland for two years. It was terrible. I learned discipline in the military but it was unpleasant. I was lucky that I didn't get shot. I didn't want to see combat. I'm a card-carrying coward.

"They said to me in basic training, 'Your size is perfect for tail gunner.' I said I was claustrophobic. Heaven forbid you stick me in there and have people shooting at me.

"I was happy to go in. In those days, the worst thing that could happen to you was to not go into the war. The war was so important, what was at stake, the thought of staying at home and not participating was frightening.

"I first saw a television after the war in Long Beach, New York. There was a radio store that sold tubes and small AM radios. There were no FM radios then. This particular store in Long Beach had a television set with a glass top. They televised a game from Ebbets Field between the Cincinnati Reds and the Brooklyn Dodgers. That was the first baseball game ever televised. They had a television at the Worlds Fair in New York.

"I got into Hobark College in upstate New York. It was populated by professors from Harvard. I became interested in Harvard and I transferred there.

"Beginning at Harvard was difficult. I went to the Veteran's Advisor and said, 'I could die in my room and nobody would know I was dead until the body began to smell.' It was impersonal."

"Did you date a lot at Harvard?"

"No. Those Radcliffe girls were not my idea of heaven. I had some lovely experiences.

"I majored in Economics and English. I graduated in 1949 Magna Cum Laude and was elected to Phi Beta Kappa. My classmates included Henry Kissinger, Arthur Schlessinger, and Bobby Kennedy."

After graduation, Scherick served as Assistant Campaign Manager for Boston mayoral candidate John B. Hynes who defeated the incumbent James Michael Curley. The contest inspired the novel *The Last Hurrah*. After the election, Scherick co-founded the New Boston Committee, an organization dedicated to reforming city government and the public schools.

"I liked Boston and wanted to stay. I got a job working for a man who ran a chain of clothing stores. He advertised on WHGH-TV and I would go over to the studio to work on the commercials. These were talkshows with live commercials. I decided that was what I wanted to do. I wrote documentaries for WHGH.

"Television was just beginning. I came to New York to work in television. I tried to get an interview with Doris Ann, who ran NBC's religious programming. She wouldn't see me. At an employment agency, I saw an ad for a time buyer for $60 a week at Dancer, Fitzgerald & Sample. It said you must know Nielsen. I wanted to know where you had to go to meet this guy Nielsen.

[Most of Edgar's stories sound like he's told them a hundred times. He gives me no scoops. He takes his secrets to the grave.]

"I was interviewed by several people. One of them [Lyndon Brown, head of marketing] said, 'Do not let this man out without giving him a job.' I was an impressive young man.

"I got the job as an assistant in the media department. The clients included General Mills and Proctor & Gamble. It was the number two broadcasting agency. I stayed there six years. It was my graduate school. I had a terrific mentor who taught me the broadcast business. I met the presidents of all the networks.

"Dancer, Fitzgerald & Sample manufactured programming that they placed on ABC, like The Lone Ranger. CBS would not take other people's programming if they could avoid it.

"I started as a time buyer and then became media supervisor on the Falstaff beer account. Then I became director of Sports and Special Events."

In early 1953, Falstaff wanted to sponsor baseball on network TV. They were already broadcasting locally the games of the St. Louis Cardinals and Browns. Scherick's plan was to black out the major league cities and broadcast to the half of the country that supported minor league ball. Edgar worked out a compensation package to reimburse the minor leagues for the potential loss of fans. The Broadcast Committee of the National Association of Baseball turned him down.

So Scherick lined up broadcasts of the Indians, the White Sox, the Philadelphia A's, and the New York Giants with commentator Dizzy Dean. Falstaff sponsored and ABC broadcast the "Game of the Week."

When baseball's "Game of the Week" moved to CBS in 1955, Scherick was approached to become head of sports. National sales manager for the network, Tom Dawson, asked Edgar what he thought of CBS's operation. Edgar replied, "It could be improved." CBS hired Bill MacPhail, head of publicity for the Kansas City A's.

"In those days, TV stations would send out circulars advertising their local shows. One day, across my desk comes a flyer from a station KMTV, Omaha. And it offered me in Omaha the home games of the Chicago Bears and Chicago Cardinals football teams. Falstaff Beer had a brewery in Omaha. I investigated and found out that ABC was feeding a patchwork network of stations on Sunday mornings when the Bears and the Cardinals were home. I went to my boss and said, 'We've got to talk to the president of ABC.' I arranged for us to buy half of those games [for Falstaff Beer].

"I felt there was a TV sports revolution coming. I took a job at CBS in 1956 as a sports specialist. I shaped the regional networks that provided the basis for

CBS's entrance into pro football broadcasting. I negotiated those rights with Bill McPhail, head of CBS Sports. They had those rights for 40 years and then lost them."

At CBS for only eight months, Edgar ran into a familiar problem with sports programming—the lack of events during the first quarter of the year. Big Ten Basketball was the only sports programming CBS had on during that time and it received low ratings. So Scherick phoned Bill Reed, the lieutenant of Big Ten Commissioner Tug Wilson. 'Bill, you're getting cancelled by CBS. You'll never make it as a national vehicle but you can as a regional one and I can clear the regional network and sell it so that Big Ten basketball can have a very fruitful and long life.' Reed gave his go ahead for Scherick to set up that regional network.

Ed left CBS in 1957 and through his company Sports Programs Inc formed the Big Ten Basketball Network. He signed on Standard Oil of Indiana as a major sponsor.

In his 1978 book, *The Thrill of Victory: The Inside Story of ABC Sports*, Bert Randolph Sugar names Scherick as a key figure in the rise of ABC Sports. "Described by many of his former colleagues as a high-strung Mad Hatter, Scherick was a combination midwife, clairvoyant, and public-address system for the coming sports revolution in the late 1950s."

"There was a guy who controlled the Sterling drug account," remembers Edgar. "He said he had a nephew who's supporting his mother and needs work. I said that I'd see him. In walks a kid with green Dartmouth socks on. Jim Spence [future Vice President of ABC Sports]. I hired him."

Edgar's other hires included [future head of NBC Sports] Chet Simmons, and producer Chuck Howard. In 1960, Scherick hired Roone Arledge to produce ABC's NCAA football.

Chet Simmons remembers Scherick tangling with his director Jack Lubell. "Lubell literally lifted Scherick off the floor with his hands around Ed's neck. I thought Jack was going to kill him, because all the while Scherick was making these gurgling noises with his tongue hanging out. Finally, Jack let him go and said, 'Don't worry about it. But we will take care of this later.' I don't even recall what they were battling about because they were always scrapping, but it wouldn't have shocked me if murder had been committed." (Spence, pg. 55)

"The first instant replays came in with NCAA football," says Scherick. "In those days, the Ampax [videotape recorder] machine was huge. [The year 1958 marked the first use of videotape.] We had it on a trailer and we dragged it to the football game in a truck. And I'd see a play and say, 'That's one.' We'd mark it.

And when halftime came up, we'd replay the highlights of the first half. There was no instant replay.

"I went back to Dancer, Fitzgerald & Sample. They had General Mills for a client and Wheaties was one of their products. Wheaties had great days as the breakfast of champions. But they could no longer afford to buy the rights to games. I said I would create and buy pre-game shows. I did some research and found out that these pre-game shows got 40 percent of the ratings of the games.

"I knew that sports was the best vehicle for delivering mature men to TV advertisers. Affiliates loved having sports. When the guy went to the country club, he could say, 'We've got the Dallas—Washington game this weekend.' That made him a big man at the country club."

Scherick gave ABC's head of programming Tom Moore the idea to televise the November 1958 Bluegrass Bowl. It was a postseason college football game (between Florida State and Oklahoma State) played for the first, and only, time in Louisville, Kentucky. It was the last broadcast of Harry Wismer, a one-time giant of sports broadcasting, and the first national telecast of newcomer Howard Cosell.

"I flew down with Howard on the plane, and I had to listen to him tell me for three hours that he is the greatest announcer in the history of the world.

"Here is the first football game I produced for ABC. We televised a game in six above zero between two nondescript college teams. The players wore sneakers, and they slipped and slid all over the field, facing empty stands of 2,100 people. On either side of me, two of the greatest sports characters in the history of sports broadcasting. It's got to be the low point of my life." (Sugar, pg. 41)

"The Gillette razor company, the biggest razor company, had a programming on NBC called Friday Night Fights. [In 1959] NBC decided the program wasn't up to their standard of quality, so they threw Gilette off. And this was Gillette's most efficient advertising vehicle. Gillette got upset and came to ABC and asked if we would put on their Friday Night Fights. ABC said yes, if you will back us on NCAA Football and baseball's Game of the Week, we will give you Wednesday Night Fights. We made a huge deal."

The $8.5 million Gillette paid ABC enabled the network to buy the right to NCAA football in 1960-61, and financed ABC's Wide World of Sports, which helped ABC secure the rights to the Olympic Games. "Of the major milestones in the history of ABC Sports, only "Monday Night Football" (begun in 1970) owed nothing directly to Gillette money." (Rader, Benjamin G. *In Its Own Image: How Television Has Transformed Sports*, pg. 103)

ABC told Scherick not to hire Howard Cosell because he was Jewish. "They said, 'Don't let him on the microphone. Don't give him a job.'

"I liked Howard. He was smart and a seething mass of insecurities. He had total recall.

"The first time I saw Jim McKay, he was doing five minutes of sports on the CBS news. I used to say to him, 'Jim, sit tight. I'm going to get a literate sports show for you.' Then Wide World of Sports came on and I brought him on. It was my show until I merged with ABC Sports in 1961. It was a tax-free transfer. We exchanged stock for stock. I then turned over sports to ABC's sports department, which was essentially under Roone Arledge."

Jim Spence remembers:

> The first [NCAA] game we [ABC] did—in 1960—was between Alabama and Georgia with Fran Tarkenton, who later would work fro ABC Sports, quarterbacking for Georgia. The madcap Scherick just about drove Gowdy, Christman, Arledge and everyone else crazy with his antics. Never quiet, he'd race back and forth between the mobile unit where Roone, who was producing the telecast, and the others were trying to call the shots, and the booth were Gowdy and Christman were trying to call the game. It was so bad that, before our third telecast, Gowdy and Christman met with Roone and threatened to quit if Scherick didn't stay out of their hair. Roone didn't want Ed in the mobile unit, either, and told him how critical it was for him not to interfere. Still, Scherick showed up at Lawrence, Kansas, for the next game. Unwelcome in the booth, an intrusion in the truck, he became frantic as he tried to find a place where he could watch the telecast. Finally, he wandered into a nearby building on campus, saw an open office with a television set, and promptly made himself at home. He turned on the set, propped his feet on the desk, and was fretting about the coverage of the game when another man appeared at the door and said, "Excuse me, sir?"
>
> Ed said, "Be quiet."
>
> "Excuse me, sir?"
>
> "Be quiet," Sherick sharply told him. "Can't you see I'm trying to watch this telecast?"
>
> "The other guy stood his ground. "Excuse me!' he replied, "but I'm Dutch Lonborg, and I'm the athletic director here at Kansas, and you, sir, are sitting in my office." (Spence, pg. 59)

In February of 1961, Scherick merged his company with ABC and Edgar became ABC's Vice-President of Sales.

The debut of *Wide World of Sports* (4/19/61) made TV history. ABC televised live the Penn and the Drake Relays, cutting back and forth. The initial ratings were terrible.

Arledge and McKay discussed that the most important thing with sports was not the technical achievements but the people involved: "Who they were, where they were from, how they got to this moment, how they might handle it, why it was so important to them—all the personal dreams and insecurities with which the viewer could identify. This human approach expanded from Wide World to our coverage of ten Olympics, and, in time, to all networks' coverage of sports." (McKay, Jim. *The Real McKay: My Wide World of Sports*, pg. 90)

"Roone Arledge gets all the credit," complains Edgar. "I hired him out of total obscurity. Nobody would've ever heard of him were it not for me. Though he was talented. I made Roone Arledge the president of NCAA football, when his experience did not warrant it at all."

"Do you have any good stories about Roone Arledge?"

"None that I want to talk about. He's not my favorite person in the whole world. He couldn't share credit where credit was due. He had to get all the glory for himself."

In his 1988 autobiography, *Up Close & Personal*, former Vice President of ABC Sports, Jim Spence, writes, "ABC Sports stands today as a monument to Roone Arledge. I have only one quarrel with that: Some other names should be on the monument, and the name at the top of it should be that of Ed Scherick."

"Tell me how you got the rights for ABC [for the 1960 and '61 seasons] to NCAA football?"

"In those days, only a certain number of college games were televised. And that was controlled by the NCAA. They sold the package of those exclusive rights. I decided we wanted those rights back. The main contender was NBC. Their sports department was run by Tom Gallery, former cowboy actor and husband of Zasu Pitts. I knew he was the guy to beat. So I head to figure out how to do it.

"We came up with a good figure to bid [on March 14, 1960]. I found the most innocuous guy in the company, and I said to him (Stan Frankel). 'You're going over to the hotel where the bidding takes place. You're going to watch what Tom Gallery does. He'll sit with the back of the chair in front of him with his legs over it. When the bidding comes around, he'll look around to see if there's anybody he recognizes. He'll have a low bid and a high bid. After he puts his envelope down on the table, you get up and say, 'I represent the American Broadcasting Company.' And put down your envelope.

"I sent another guy right behind him. I told him, 'If the first guy falls down and breaks his leg, you've got the same envelope with the same bid.' I told them, 'If anybody asks who you are, don't lie. Tell them you work for the American Broadcasting Company.'

"Asa Bushnell represented the NCAA. He said, 'It's time for the bids.' Gallery got up and put an envelope on the table. Then Stan Frankel did exactly what I told him to do. They adjourned to the back. When they came back, they were stunned. They announced that the rights were awarded to ABC. Quite a coup for me.

"I got announcers Curt Gowdy and color man Paul Christman, who'd been a great star with the Chicago Cardinals. I called him up and offered him the job. He says, 'Mr. Scherick, thank you but I'm doing color for the Chicago Cardinals. I live in Chicago. I have a paper box company. Doing this show is good for my box business.' I said, 'How much do you make?' He said, '$375 a game.' I said, 'I'll double it.' He said, 'I'll take it'."

"I produced numerous closed-circuit boxing matches for Irving Kahn. They played in theaters with a big projection screen."

In 1963, ABC's head of programming Dan Melnick quit. Scherick, ABC's sales manager of the time, went in to the head of ABC, Leonard Goldenson, and said, 'That's my job.' Scherick got it. His official title was Vice President of programming. He developed such shows as *Batman*, *The FBI*, *The Hollywood Palace*, *Bewitched*, and *Peyton Place*. His employees included such future producers as Scott Rudin, Robert Lawrence, David Nicksay, Brian Grazer and Michael Barnathan.

"November 22, 1963. President Kennedy is shot."

"I was the only executive in the building. Everybody else was out to lunch. I got a call from the newsroom. I sent word to the guards. 'Don't let anybody out of the building.' I didn't know what was going to happen. And then traffic started again and people went in and out.

"It was a different time. We did not feel that we could put commercial programming on the air with the president lying on a bier. We took all commercial programs off the air. I had to program the time with new programming."

"Tell me about your series *The FBI* (1965)."

"Benny Kalmenson was president of Warner Brothers after Jack's retirement. Tom, who ran ABC, loved the idea of doing the FBI. Benny was well respected in those circles. He was an American patriot. He contacted the FBI to see if they were willing to do it. I remember every script was vetted by the FBI. Nothing was done that they did not totally approve of."

"*Peyton Place* (1964-69)."

"That was already in development when I took my job as head of programming. We made the pilot. And the network was so nervous about it because they thought it was pornography. Finally, *The New York Times* magazine wrote an article about the social significance of *Peyton Place* and that took the curtains off. It was a huge success. It changed habits in America. People didn't go out on certain nights when *Peyton Place* was on. It was the first primetime soap opera."

"Did you have moral qualms about the show?"

"Not at all. It was the biggest hit I was ever associated with. I remember *Newsweek* referred to me as 'the house intellectual' at ABC. I thought more than most people. I wasn't just wedded to television. I had a sense of society as a whole and what made it tick. And what television's place was. Somebody said to me, 'How can you, a Jew from New York, pick programs for the entire country?' I said, 'I'm no different from the guy in Rockford, Illinois. We like the same things, so I don't worry about it. Things that I like, he invariably likes too.'"

"You had many disputes with *Peyton Place* producer Paul Monash."

"They couldn't get a story I liked. I raised hell and brought a woman in, Erna Phillips, the queen of the soap opera. Monash opened the files of our exchange of memos to *TV Guide*. And *TV Guide* wrote an article that made me look foolish. And I resented that. I thought those memos were private. I would never do that to him. But that's a long time ago. And if I see him, it's all forgotten."

"Do you remember turning down the TV show *Get Smart* (1965-70)?"

"I didn't turn the show down. I turned down the people who brought it to me. Danny Melnick brought it to me. The funniest experience Danny Melnick ever had in his life was when he walked by a manure pile. I just didn't believe that he could make something funny. Then they went out and got Leonard Stern and he made *Get Smart* into a hit with the help of Mel Brooks."

"Do you regret turning it down?"

"Sure. You don't want to lose any hits. Nobody's infallible."

"What other shows did you turn down that you later regretted?"

"None that I can remember."

In his autobiography, *Beating the Odds*, former ABC CEO Leonard H. Goldenson wrote about Scherick's departure: "[T]he head of network programming has to have his hands in so many pies simultaneously that it's difficult to concentrate on any one program. So it's hard to leave a personal mark on any show in particular. This became a source of frustration to Ed. Soon after *Batman* debuted, he resigned to start his own company." (pg. 250)

Ed told an interviewer from the TV Academy:, "To see a company like ABC turn and become successful was exciting. I felt like that I was handling so much, I wasn't concentrating on anything. I wanted to take a project and get deep into it. When you're an executive, you never get deep into anything. At that time, the studios were shaky. Leonard [Goldenson] owned 400 movie theaters at the time. I said, 'Leonard, you've got to get into the manufacturing of film.' So he made a deal with me to form a subsidiary company called Palomar Pictures and I made pictures for ABC."

Would ABC take anything you did for them?

"No. Sam Clark, who headed the record operation, was in charge of motion pictures. I had to go through him. He was my immediate superior. But I had no problem. He liked what I wanted to do. At that time, I was the only producer who successfully made the switch from television into feature films."

After Scherick formed his own production company in 1967, he first made feature films, then TV movies and miniseries (more than anyone) such as *The Kennedys of Massachusetts* (1990), *On Wings of Eagles* (1986), and *The Phantom of the Opera* (1990).

Edgar married for the first time (Carol) in 1960. It lasted 20 years. Then he remarried. His Japanese-American wife Marge Iwasaki, a doctorate in Bio-Chemistry, divorced him in 1998 after he suffered a stroke. Scherick has four kids from his first marriage—Greg (Beverly Hills), Jay (a screenwriter living in Brentwood), Brad (Beverly Hills) and Christine.

"I met my wife on blind date," Scherick told a 1991 video. "We went to Baskin & Robbins. Marge rubbed my back. I was as tight as a drum. She thought I was insane, because I was. She came from one background and I from another. I think I was the first show business person she'd ever met, and a show business person in torment, which is even worse."

Edgar tells me, "After I got a stroke, my second wife, who I didn't deny anything to, didn't want to be married to a man with a stroke."

A source friendly to Edgar says that Marge thought of herself as a movie star after she married Edgar. She loved going out with him and meeting important people. When Edgar had his stroke, she kicked him out of the house and wanted nothing to do with him.

Edgar watches TV as he talks to me. "There's Lesley Ann Warren, a friend of mine. She worked in some of my films. What a pistol she is.

"I didn't fool around on my marriages. Not once.

"Nobody ever gave me a boost. I earned everything."

"Why did you leave ABC and start up your own production company?"

"Because I wanted to. All my life, since I was a boy, my mother had said to me, 'You will learn the business and then you will go into business for yourself.'"

"What do you remember about making your first movies like *For Love Of Ivy* (1968)."

"How unpleasant and hard it was. We were shooting at night at a department store in Long Island and it was costing a lot of money. I didn't like how the production managers were running things."

"*The Killing of Sister George* (1968)."

"It was a controversial picture because it was about two lesbians and a young girl. It had one shocking scene. It was an X-rated picture."

"*The Birthday Party* [1968]."

"I thought it was a good picture but nobody would pay any money to go see it."

"*Take the Money and Run* (1969)."

"We got a script from Woody Allen who had never done a movie. In those days, a picture would open on a Wednesday. We'd get reviews Thursday and Friday you'd run a big review ad for the weekend. On Thursday, I got Woody to come to the advertising agency while we culled the reviews. And the reviews were good. I sat with him. Woody never says anything. Then he says, 'If they like this picture, just wait.' That was the only thing he said to me the whole time. I thought Woody talented and funny. He's very smart. He's done some stupid things in his life like marrying his [step] daughter. His movie *Crimes and Misdemeanors* was brilliant."

"*Ring of Bright Water* (1969) was one of the big movies of my childhood."

"We showed it at a screening in Hollywood. After the otter was killed, a scream went up and a woman leaped up and started for the lobby. I ran out to the lobby and she said, 'You killed that beautiful otter.' I said, 'Go back and watch the rest of the picture.' It was Gypsy Rose Lee. She came up to me afterwards, 'That was a beautiful picture.' She loved animals."

"*Jenny* (1969)."

"I had put Marlo Thomas on the air with *That Girl* (1966-71). This script came in and she liked it. I decided, 'What the hell, I'll make it.' It wasn't much of a script and it wasn't much of a movie."

"*The Man Who Wanted To Live Forever* (1970)."

"That was a television movie. I don't want to comment on television movies."

"*Sleuth* (1972)."

"The only picture in history where the entire cast was nominated for an Academy Award."

"I heard you had a lot of fights with director Joe Mankiewicz?"

"In the play, there was an intermission and I wanted to put in an intermission into the movie. He didn't. I thought he could've been more efficient spending money.

"One day I'm reading a book of the memos of [studio exec] David Selznick. I come across something that makes a precise statement about something that is going on with *Sleuth*. I copied it out. At night, I'm having a drink with Joe at his quarters and I whipped this paper out."

"*The Heartbreak Kid*."

"It was a short one-page story by Jay Friedman that we'd acquired. One day Neil Simon read it. I got a call. 'Neil Simon wants to write a screenplay based on this.' I said fine. We made a deal for heavy bread, which almost committed you to make the picture. It was directed by Elaine May, who was talented but crazy in a wonderful way. I was the only producer who constrained her at all."

"*Gordon's War* (1973)."

"That was a black picture we shot in New York. I said to the producer Robert Schaffel on the first dailies, 'The audio is no good.' So he said, 'It's freezing cold. And the sound man is freezing cold and going up to his apartment and sitting up there.' I said, 'You get him on the street.' He went and got the guy to come down on the street. They had an argument. Finally, the producer fired him. The guy replied, 'I'll never work for a Jew again.' The soundman said to him, 'I'll never work for a Jew again.' The producer said, 'What business are you going into next?'"

Edgar has a big scene in his 1974 movie *Law and Disorder*.

"*The Stepford Wives* (1975)."

"This was a book by Ira Levin that titillated me. That men would order their women to get bigger tits. The picture became a cult movie. The term 'Stepford Wives' is part of our language. Scott Rudin and I are doing a sequel for Paramount."

TV Academy interviewer says, "*Born to the Wind* [1982] had an all-Indian cast."

Edgar: "I had a writer-friend who was fascinated by American Indian culture and lore. I sold [to a network] the idea to do a series of one-hour shows with a strictly Indian cast. It never got a chance to succeed. Fred Silverman killed it twice at NBC. It played in England and got good notices."

Luke: "*Shoot the Moon* (1982)."

"I bought the script for $25,000. That's a pretty auspicious list of movies you're running down there. Not bad for a guy lying in bed."

"*I'm Dancing as Fast as I Can* (1982)."

"Michael Eisner said, 'Let's make the first Valium movie.' I think it is the only Valium movie. I hated the guts of our lead actress Jill Clayburgh. She was cruel to everybody. I hate cruel people.

"It wasn't a bad book. Jill Clayburgh was Michael Eisner's cousin or something like that. He wanted to make a picture with Jill Clayburg. I never thought much of the picture."

"*White Dog* (1982)."

"Paramount owed me a movie. Michael Eisner said, 'Get me a picture and I'll make it.' I'd worked hard on a feature that didn't make it. They had a script called *White Dog*. It was a controversial film about black relationships. I can hardly own up to it to this day because I had little to do with it."

I pause to pat the dog.

"Your time is going to run out here so you better keep going."

We've talked for 15 minutes.

"*He Makes Me Feel Like Dancin'* (1983)."

"The only picture to win an Emmy and an Academy Award the same year. It was a documentary on a ballet studio in New York."

"*Evergreen*, 1985 miniseries."

"Based on a best seller. NBC's Brandon Tartikoff was stunned that it was successful. I said, 'Brandon, you don't understand this picture. It's about family. A family is a marvelous theme.'

"Brandon was so smart. He was a great man. He treated me with great respect. Rightly so. Brandon had an instinct about the history of the business. He knew my place in it. Fred Silverman, a bit of a historian, says there have been three great periods of network programming, and Edgar Scherick's was the greatest. He looked at what came out of that period and the people who worked with me. He respected what I did. Having been in that position, he understood the difficulty.

"I should charge you for this interview."

"What do you remember about your 1985 miniseries *Evergeen*?"

"It was about something that interested me—immigration into the United States. Lesley Ann Warren was the leading lady and she was a pain in the ass. When we'd be ready to shoot, there'd be no Lesley Ann Warren. She'd be in the make-up trailer, and I'd have to go get her. She'd be sitting in her chair, taking three strands of hair, curling them to the right and then curling them to the left. Finally, I'd get her out of the make-up trailer onto the set so we could shoot. She then did a good job.

"About a month after the picture was finished, Lesley Ann Warren walked by. I yelled, 'Lesley Ann, you came out of the trailer.' We laughed. I had a good relationship with her. She was a little crazy, highly neurotic. She got the director, Fielder Cook, ill. Something got clogged up in his intestines. We had to take him to the hospital. They were wheeling him into a room when one of those heavy intravenous things fell off the stand and hit him on the head. He recovered and was back to work the next day."

"Why does the topic of immigration interest you so much?"

"I'm an American. And I'm of Jewish heritage. So that should answer your question. It's the story of America."

"How did you get involved with the Wednesday Morning Club [a group of Hollywood non-liberals founded by ex-radical David Horowitz]?"

"They came to me and asked me if I would be one of the founding members. I said I would be happy to. They knew I was conservative."

"Looking at your peers, would you say they were 80/20 Democrat?"

"Much more than that. They're heavily biased towards Democrats and liberals."

"95/5?"

"Yes."

"How did you deal with that throughout your Hollywood career?"

"It never bothered me. I never worried about someone's politics. It had no material effect on the project. I've always said what I wanted to say. I shocked some people."

"*On Wings of Eagles.*"

"We needed someone to play Lieutenant Colonel Arthur E. 'Bull' Simons who led the raid into Iran. Burt Lancaster was the logical guy. His CMA agent, the late Ben Benjamin, named a figure [of about $1 million], which for television was a lot of money. We paid the price. Burt had just had a bipass operation. I had to pay a big premium for insurance for him. We finished the picture on a mountain near Mexico City and I was concerned about the thinness of the air. I brought an ambulance and doctor in on a 24-hour basis. And he was fine."

"Your 1987 TV movie *The Stepford Children.*"

"It was based on a good idea—the children of Stepford were being Stepford-ized. The script [by William Bleich] turned out middling. Somebody who worked for me called me on the phone. 'The director [Alan J. Levi] is walking off the picture. What do I do?' I said, 'You go in and direct for the rest of the night. We'll worry about it tomorrow.' I don't think the director walked off. As soon as they find out someone else is going to direct, they don't walk so fast."

"Tell me about NBC Entertainment head Brandon Tartikoff."

"I was fond of him. He was an exceptional man. Smart, funny, knowledgeable. I'd done the same job he was doing at another network years before. He was the best I'd ever seen at that job. We got along famously."

"*Hands of a Stranger* (1987)."

"Larry Elikann directed and he was one of my favorite television directors. I enjoyed this because it went smoothly. The cast were friends of mine—Armand Assante and Beverly D'Angelo. I was in love with Beverly D'Angelo. From a narrative point of view, it may be the best mini-series I've ever made."

"*Uncle Tom's Cabin* (1987)."

"When news got around that I wanted to make this picture, there was roiling among the black community, who did not want this picture made. To them an Uncle Tom [was bad]. I wanted to find someone of authority to say, 'That is a good idea. Go make this picture.' The head of the NAACP, Sydney, said, 'This is one of the great classics of American literature. It had a great effect on the Civil War. Absolutely this picture should be made.' So we made it for little money in Mississippi in terrible heat. Edward Woodward was playing Simon Lagree. His wardrobe was a jacket and a weskit [vest]. And I said to him, 'Edward, what are you doing out here in this heat?' He said to me, 'Edgar, when again will somebody ask me to play Simon Lagree?'

"We had a plantation house. And they called me to the set. 'There's a crucial moment here where we need a line.' Uncle Tom had great faith. He believed that all things would be solved by faith. I came up with this terrific line that solved the problem perfectly.

"We had a screening at Jackson State University. I wanted to see how the picture played at a black college. Avery Brooks [who played Uncle Tom] went with me. When he walked in, the women went crazy. They loved him. He was like a matinee idol among the blacks.

"We screened the picture. Afterwards a young kid got up and said, 'How come all my life I've been taught that Uncle Tom was a flunky?' Then an English teacher stood up and said, 'There's a book in the library called Uncle Tom's Cabin. It hasn't been taken out of the library since 1932.'"

"*The Kennedys of Massachusetts*."

"I was in England when I got a call from a colleague in New York. 'Doris Goodwin is writing a book about the Kennedy clan, and I have an outline of it.' She got it to me in England. I said I was interested. My friend said, 'Instead of flying back to California, why don't you go see Doris Goodwin?' So I went to Concord, Massachusetts, where she lived with her husband Dick Goodwin. I stayed with them that night and we got to know each other. She liked me, and I got the rights. There were a lot of people after it. She won the Pulitzer Prize for that book."

"Have you heard that she did a lot of plagiarism on that book and others?"

"I've heard that. I don't believe it. Who could she plagiarize?"

"*The Secret Life of Ian Fleming* (1990)."

"That's a fake. I thought that up. I just wanted to get into business with [executive] Scott Sassa who was over at Turner Broadcasting. It was the first movie they made. I knew that Ian Fleming had a house in the West Indies. So I thought we should make up a story about his life. We made the movie with Sean Connery's son [Jason], a very nice looking young man. I don't know what happened to him. I thought he was going to be a prominent actor."

"*Phantom of the Opera* (1990)."

"We went back to the original book. I shot it in France. Tony Richardson directed it. A real miserable man. He was terrible. I didn't know he was sick with AIDS at the time. I had countless run-ins with Tony Richardson. He caused me untold trouble. He rewrote the script without anybody authorizing him to. I had to spend a week restoring the script to its original form, the script the network approved. The two women who worked with him said, 'To get along with him, just let him do whatever he wants to do.' I said, 'That's not my style.'"

"In the TV movie, the producer is in charge."

"I don't know what that means. That means a lot of discussion."

"Doesn't that mean it is your vision that should prevail?"

"I just finished a picture for HBO called *Path to War* (2002). It is the picture of director John Frankenheimer from start to finish. He consulted no one.

"*Fever* (1991) was a picture I made for HBO about the thrill of criminal behavior. Larry Elikann directed. Those films I really liked, I remember. Marcia Gay Harden was the actress. I found her and I liked her a lot and nobody knew much about her. The guy at HBO didn't want her and I really leaned on him. I said to him, 'By the bowels of Christ, bethink ye that ye might be mistaken. You are wrong, wrong, wrong.' He cast her finally. After I got done with 'the bowels of Christ,' he was speechless."

"*Rambling Rose* (1991)."

"I read the book by Calder Willingham and I thought it was a beautiful book. I employed Calder Willingham to write a screenplay and he wrote a lovely screenplay. I couldn't get it shot. Finally, I gave it to Martha Coolridge to read. At that time, she was a director of no note. She gave it to her friend Laura Dern. Laura loved it. Laura was living with Finnish action director Riny Hall, and she told him that she wanted to make that picture more than anything in the world. He had some pull with Miramax and they wanted to do what he wanted to do. That's how the movie got made."

"Was that the last feature you made?"

"No, *The Wall* (1998). You make it sound so final. I'm not done by a long shot. Since you've been here, I've sold a picture to Showtime on the telephone. It's called *[Time of Crisis*, 2003]. It's about what happened in the Whitehouse on September 11. Lionel Chetwynd is writing it. He's at the Whitehouse doing interviews. He's on a president's council and so they opened up to him. Lionel is speaking to everyone who was with the president that day.

"What else do you want to know? Come on, I'm getting tired of you already."

"*Betrayed by Love* (1994)."

"Aren't we all?"

"*The Good Old Boys* (1995)."

"That was based on a Texas novel that I read and liked. I sent it to Tommy Lee Jones. I knew he'd read it. Years ago, Tommy Lee Jones was a football player at Harvard. And I saw in the monthly Harvard magazine that Tommy Lee Jones wanted to be an actor. I had enjoyed him as a football player. So I called him. 'Look, I'm in the movie business. I don't have any jobs for you but the next time you come to New York, call me up.' So he came and called me up. He said, 'They're making a picture at Harvard called *Love Story* (1970). There's a scene in there with several Ivy League jocks. I'm an Ivy League jock.'

"So I called the producer of the picture and Tommy got a job. There's a scene in *Love Story* where the guys are playing poker in one of the dormitory rooms. One of them was Tommy Lee Jones. That was his first appearance on film. He never forgot that. So if I sent him something to read, he'd read it.

"He said he liked the book. Two weeks later, 20 pages of the script arrived. Without me asking, he started writing a script. So the person I worked with on the movie said, 'Look at this? What's going to happen? He's writing a script. What are we going to do?' I said, 'Look, it's pretty good. Let him write.' He wrote the script for the picture. Tommy Lee Jones is smart. He's almost a legend at Harvard."

Jones made his directorial debut with *The Good Old Boys*.

"*Tyson.* [I was an extra in the 1995 movie, playing a reporter.]"

"It's a story of Cus D'Amato and Mike Tyson. I was close to boxing. I did a lot of championship fights. And I knew Tyson's foster father Cus D'Amato. I produced the telecast of the fight where Ingemar Johanson knocked out Floyd

Patterson. Then the night that Floyd Patterson won the title back, Cus D'Amato and I stayed up all night talking. It was such a great moment.

"I saw Tyson's sixth fight and I knew his story well. There was a book on Tyson by Jose Torres, a former light heavyweight champion. I acquired the book and used it as the basis for a screenplay, which I sold to HBO."

"*Ruby Ridge* (1998)."

"My then-wife took off the Internet the summary of some senate hearing. And I read that and said, 'Oh, that's a movie.' I sold it as a four-hour miniseries to CBS.

"It was a controversial project because Randy Weaver was a hero to many Americans. Many people felt strongly that he had been terribly wronged by the US government and that they should protect him."

"The TV movie business has changed."

"It's getting smaller and smaller."

"Did you see it coming?"

"No. It doesn't affect me. I can sell ice to eskimos."

"Why does it not affect you?"

"Because I am able to sell things. I never made the traditional movie. I always asked a question of a piece of material—is it touched by singularity? If you try to sell the same old rot, it's not going to work. I looked for subjects that would touch inside me."

"Which of your projects have had the most meaning to you?"

"*Raid on Entebbe. The Path to War.* It was something I lived through [Vietnam]. I was thinking lying in this bed that I've probably lived through more history than any other man alive. My whole life is part of the panorama of American history, beginning with the Great Depression, which affected me deeply. Then WWII, the Vietnam War. I've had a little to do with each of those epochs."

"What did you have to do with the Vietnam War?"

"I made a movie called *The Wall.* Did I have anything to do directly with the war? No."

"Were you opposed to the war?"

"I didn't spend a lot of time thinking about it, yeah or nay."

"Who are your favorite people in the industry?"

"Adolf Hitler, Benito Mussolini. That's a silly question."

"Which of your peers do you respect the most?"

"Larry Gordon. It's hard to say. I don't spend much time thinking about them."

"Did you socialize much with the industry?"

"No, I was a family man essentially, though I moved among all circles with ease. Everybody knew me. Everybody's door was open to me. I went where I wanted. I am one of the few men in Hollywood today who can get anybody on the telephone. From Lew Wasserman on down."

"Which of the titans stand out most clearly in your mind?"

"Lew Wasserman. David Selznick. A giant. But I didn't know when I was with him. I didn't realize what a giant he was."

"Did you have many dealings with Barry Diller?"

"I hired Barry Diller out of William Morris into ABC. I remember how smart he was and how nice he was and is to me."

"Michael Eisner."

"I like him a lot. Michael Eisner once said on a public forum that Edgar is the first man to ever pitch him a project in this business. It was a TV show for ABC, *Tales of the Nunandaga*. It was about a fictional American Indian tribe.

"Come on, let's get down to cases here."

"What do you think of the increasing consolidation of the entertainment industry?"

"I've never thought of consolidation as a good idea. It eliminates competition of ideas.

"I don't think your book is going to be too interesting based on these questions you're asking."

"What part of your work did you enjoy the most?"

"The creative part. Coming up with an idea and seeing it through to fulfillment."

"And which part of your work did you dislike the most?"

"The wrangling and the arguing. The duplicity. Next."

"Do you have a pet project you've been nursing for years?"

"I just pitched a project based on a book called *The Shadow of Blooming Grove*. It's a biography of Warren Gamiel Harding, America's worst president. That's what I want to call the project—*America's Worst President*. What a schlemiel this guy was.

"What else? This is trivia we're talking about now. Not to me, but to readers. What do they care what I think I want to do now?"

"What do you want to be most remembered for?"

"Honesty. And good taste. And courage."

"What have been some of the most courageous things you've done?"

"Told the truth in all conditions. I didn't give in to the stroke. Here I am. It's pretty debilitating. I can't have anyone around me who doesn't tell the truth."

"Who do you hate the most in the industry?"

"I don't hate anybody. I hate no man on earth. It's debilitating to hate. It saps your energy. I'm very angry with my ex-wife."

"Did you find you had to change the way you did business in Hollywood?"

"No, I've always done business on a forthright basis."

"How do you think you've changed over the years?"

"I'm less loud. More subdued."

"Why were you so loud?"

"I was frustrated by inefficiency and stupidity and the only way I could get through was to raise my voice, which is the least effective way to get through."

"Why did you develop that trait?"

"When I was an infant, my mother hired a West Indian woman to take care of me. She was hard of hearing. As I grew up, I had to talk loud so I could get through to her. It affected me for the rest of my life."

"What part of your meaning in life has come from your work?"

"The meaning I've found in life comes from the accomplishments of other people. So many people have done so many wonderful things."

"Were you a workaholic?"

"No. I always went home to my family in the evenings."

"What kind of a father were you?"

"Dutiful. I have good children. There was never anything they did, any athletic event, that I was not there. I was in total attendance to their lives."

"Who are your heroes?"

"Franklin Roosevelt. I can't think of anybody off hand. I can think of hundreds of people. La Guardia. Herbert H. Lawman, Governor of New York for many years."

"Any books which have most influenced you?"

"I can't think of any now. Somebody came to me today and said, 'I have a friend who has the rights to *Profiles in Courage*. Would you be interested?' I said, 'That's old hat by now.' It was an interesting book. There were stories in there that were exciting. Any time a man stands alone for something he believes in, that's exciting. Where he lays it all on the line, it can't get any bigger than that."

"Were there any people in your life who did that when you were a kid?"

"No."

"Perhaps heroes on a movie screen?"

"Ask me what movie popped in my mind now—John Ford's *Young Abe Lincoln.*

"I've been fortunate to spend my life in the company of some exciting people—writers, actors, directors."

"Have people stuck by you in the past few years?"

"Sure. I have plenty of good friends. Have they turned around and called me up to say, 'Hey, here's something we want you to do'? No. The business is not that way. But I have no complaints."

"Why do you think there are so many Jews in television?"

"Jews gravitate towards entertainment. There's something especially gratifying about it as a career."

"How do you feel about television?"

"I think it is a miracle. Tonight I am going to watch the Olympics in Salt Lake City. I never cease to be in awe of television."

"How do you relate to the view that TV is the tool of the devil?"

"That's bullshit. But it can be dangerous for children. It has to be regulated."

"What do you remember about producer Scott Rudin?"

"He worked for me for five years. He's brilliant. Driven. The smartest man whoever worked for me. I secretly renamed him, 'Scott Rude.'"

"What do you remember about Brian Grazer?"

"He was a little pipsqueak. He was always working to better himself. He was a hustler, always calling up people. He never impressed me with having much intelligence."

I return to Edgar's bedside a few days later. I'm largely out of questions but I want to keep him company in his final days.

"I hear you keep the Sabbath?" he asks.

"Yes, I'm an observant Jew."

"Good for you. I respect that."

"What should I be asking you that I haven't?"

"I think it is quite amazing, that in view of the fact that I've had a stroke and am more or less bedridden, that I can operate with my mind and my telephone. I've through it well. I'm pleased and proud of myself. There are a lot of things that I should be doing that I'm not doing. Reading is impossible for me because I can't hold a book in my hand. I've only got one hand that works (right) and one hand doesn't work at all."

"Tell me about your stroke in 1998."

"I was eating at a restaurant. I go to the restroom and I leave my credit cards on the table. I told someone that I was picking up the check. I come back. I'm having a strenuous conversation and all of a sudden, I fell over. The next thing I remember is being on a gurney and being put on to an ambulance and taken to the hospital. I was in the hospital for weeks."

"At what point did your wife Marge leave you?"

"Not until I got home. As long as I was in the hospital, I wasn't cramping her style."

"What kind of relationship did you have with Marsha before your stroke?"

"Very good, I thought. I took care of her. I gave her everything she wanted. She was a church mouse when I found her and she turned into a fully flourishing woman, culturally and intellectually."

"How did she break it to you?"

"She said, 'I'm selling this house [across the street from the Harvard-Westlake prep school].' They moved me into here. I'm dependent. Blanche DuBois' last words in *The Streetcar Named Desire*. 'I've always depended on the kindness of others.' I'm totally dependent on Linnette [Edgar's devoted Filipino nurse]."

"You've always been in charge. What's it like to be dependent?"

"Very unpleasant. I've learned a discouraging amount about the fallibility of human nature."

"Has it been an opportunity for spiritual growth?"

"Yes. Because of Linnette, I was exposed to Catholicism. I never really got much spiritual input from Judaism. About a year ago, I converted to [Roman] Catholicism."

I'm shocked.

"Has that been good for you?"

"Oh, I like it. Yes. It helps me. I went to Church Sunday. During the Eucharist, I cry. It touches me deeply."

"What about Catholicism appeals to you?"

"The everpresence, the ever healing protecting presence of Jesus. See Jesus up there by the television set?"

I notice it for the first time.

"And you never found that in Judaism."

"I'm very proud of my blood. The blood of heroes in my veins. They can never take it away from me. I'm proud of being a Jew. I consider myself a Jew. In formal religion, I consider myself a Catholic. I was converted in this room by a Jesuit priest who was a friend of mine. I've known him a couple of years, but only from this bed. I've been in this bed for about five years."

"Are you able to get out every day?"

"Most of the time, if there's somebody there to help me. To get me into the chair. I can't walk."

"Do your friends from the industry call you?"

"Not socially. But from the point of view of business, yeah."

"Have you been surprised by the people who have not stayed in touch?"

"No. I've been pleased with the fact that nobody has been deterred from doing business with me because I had a stroke."

"When was the last time you heard from your wife?"

"I had a meeting with her in the lawyers office six months ago. If I had a gun, I'd shoot her. She's now suing me for half of what I have in this world. That's the law in California. A terrible, terrible law."

"What went wrong with your first marriage?"

"Carol had a nervous breakdown and then she turned to health food and became overwhelming and dominated the whole house. I don't mind that the kids were raised vegetarian but she was telling me what I could eat and what I couldn't eat. It was terrible. Oppressive. That was her religion. I used to sneak out and have a hamburger. I used to get some migraine headaches. I'd have to turn out the light and lie down. And my son walks in and says, 'The reason that you have this headache is that you ate sushi last night.' I said, 'That's enough. I'm out of here.'

"She administered to her mother in her mother's last days and tortured her. What she did to her mother—no oxygen. She's basically a good woman. I don't have strong negative feelings. I'm telling you about what happened more than 20 years ago. She lives in New York. When she's out here, she comes to see me. And it's always pleasant."

"What were some of the most common scams you've seen?"

"In the early days, they talked about kickbacks to production manager. I was a time buyer at an advertising agency. I spent thousands of dollars. Only once was I offered a couple hundred dollars to do something dishonest. I refused. My only motivation as a producer was to protect the picture and the money of the financiers."

"Hollywood has always been known for its creative accounting."

"Nobody creative accounting'ed me. I never went into a picture expecting huge returns on net points."

"Tell me about the Wednesday Morning Club, created by Michael Horowitz."

"We've had some great speakers like George Will, who says, 'Ever year is divided into two parts. Baseball and the void.' I agree. Baseball is a big part of my life. It's filled with strategies. You have to be courageous. Hitting a round ball with a round bat is an athletic feat. I live and die with the New York Mets. Mostly die."

"Did you put your values into your movies?"

"I put no messages in anything. I remember once I was looking at a rough cut of one of our movies. This man hits a woman. And then he hits her again. I got upset. 'How can you do that? That kind of unmitigated violence is out.' One hit was enough. I hate violence."

"On TV and in movies, liberals are always pushing liberal messages."

"I don't know what you're talking about."

"Have there been topics and materials that you wanted to work with but couldn't due to Hollywood's liberal mindset?"

"No. My politics, to my knowledge, have never interfered with anything I wanted to do."

"Why do you think Hollywood has never made a movie celebrating the Persian Gulf War where we kicked the Iraqis out of Kuwait?"

"It's yesterday's newspaper."

"We've made an endless number of movies about Vietnam."

"That was a national trauma. The other one wasn't. It was clean and delineated."

"Could it be that most of Hollywood isn't patriotic?"

"Not so. It just wouldn't make an entertaining movie. It was inconclusive. Sadam Hussein is still there. You seem to be consumed with this idea of messages. I think you're way off base."

"Well, liberals are always pushing liberal messages in the *LA Times, NY Times, Washington Post*, the movie studios, and the networks."

"I don't think it's hurt the country. We're in good shape except for this war. I spoke to Gore Vidal today. He thinks of Bush as an unmitigated disaster. I want to do a movie about America's worst president—Warren G. Harding. Gore says Bush."

"Gore Vidal is nuts."

"He may be nuts but he's Gore Vidal. He's very smart. He's Al Gore's cousin. I have to read a book of Vidal's on Hollywood. I like him. He's so smart."

"Is that the trait you value most in people?"

"No. Honesty. Forthrightness. Honor. Keep your oaths. I admire character. I hate duplicity. I hate lying."

"Well, Hollywood is rife with lying, duplicity and bad character."

"Somehow I've escaped it."

"What do you think about the large number of homosexuals in the business?"

"I've always thought that homosexuals probably have a sensitivity and creativity that other people might not. That's why they gravitate towards the entertainment business. There's no homophobia in me."

"You worked on many movies with Dan Blatt."

"He's capable, intelligent, hard working, well trained in the business. He's a good friend of mine. When I'm dead, I want to be cremated. If they have a memorial service for me, which I don't want, Dan Blatt would be the man to conduct it. He knows me well. Dan is special. I don't know if you got that out of him."

"He doesn't say much."

"He's not used to being interviewed. I've been interviewed all my life. I want to hire a publicity man for [the two-and-a-half hour HBO movie] *Path to War* and for him to publicize my role in it. It took ten years of development."

"Why did it take so long to get made?"

"Because it was a complex script. It had to be vetted on every point to make sure it was totally accurate."

"Do you own most of your films?"

"No, just a couple. The picture is owned by the financier."

"Do you regret not starting your own financing entity?"

"I've done good work and I'm satisfied. There's only one guy in this business I refuse to talk to, and that's the manager of English director Tony Scott, brother of director Ridley Scott. The manager did something to me that's just inexcusable. If I see him, I just walk right by him.

"I brought Tony Scott over from England. We traveled to Chile together. We got close. He was at my house all the time. I wanted to see how he was. I called him up one day. And I got a call back from his little mouse manager who says, 'Edgar, if you want to talk to Tony, you should go through me.' I never spoke to him again. It was an insult of monumental proportions."

"Did you speak to Tony Scott again?"

"No, I didn't. After that, I don't want to talk to him."

"Who were your favorite people to deal with?"

"Anybody who was straight forward, I liked."

"Hurry up, you're hanging by a thread here. I'm giving you my valuable time. Where do you get all these questions? You sit in your house and think them up?"

"I research and write down questions. I've tracked down every reference to your name on the Internet."

"Do you go to *shul* every Friday night?"

"Yes. And Saturday morning. And most every day, I'm in *shul.*"

"Good for you. Can you read Hebrew?"

"A bit."

"I was a crackerjack. The rabbi at the Talmud Torah [afterschool Orthodox Jewish education] loved me."

"When was the last time you talked to a rabbi?"

"Years. I find most of them pompous. The guy who used to interest me was the head of Chabad, Rabbi Menaham Schneerson. He used to hand out dollar bills. He's dead now."

"He had a stroke."

"He ate too much *schmaltz* [chicken fat]."

"Did you have any other favorite rabbis?"

"Rabbi David deSola Pool was a big Sephardic rabbi on Lexington Avenue in New York."

"Do you have any favorite priests?"

"I like the Pope. I think he's an interesting man. One of the important men in the world today. He speaks many languages. He writes plays. A courageous man."

"So you've found some solace in Roman Catholicism?"

"Yes. I feel Jesus' presence. When you turn the lights out here at night, it's black and you're all alone. I have nobody except Linnette in the other room. I feel that Jesus watches over me."

"How often do your kids come to visit?"

"Every weekend."

"What was the last book you read?"

"Bernie Brillstein's. It was wonderful.

"Director Irvin Kirshner made a lot of money directing *The Empire Strikes Back* (1980) so he doesn't have to work. He goes around and lectures under the title 'Hollywood and Pickled Herring.' Why? 'Everybody thinks that the people in Hollywood want to make film. If they could make the same amount of money making pickled herring, they'd make pickled herring'."

"Is that true?"

"Not true at all."

"If you had not gotten into TV and film, what would you have done?"

"I probably would've been a sportswriter. I was the sports editor of my high school newspaper and my college yearbook. Or I would've been a teacher. It's the most noble profession.

"Let's keep going. This is not interesting to me."

"Who have been your closest friendships in this industry?"

"William Morris agent Larry Auerbach, now a USC professor.

"I want you to see this videotape, 'The First 1600 Years of Edgar Scherick.' There was a place that helps people who are partially sighted. And they wanted to honor me with a dinner. That's how they raised money. I agreed. I worked at it and I raised more money than they ever had before. I figured that nobody at the dinner would know who I was, so we better get something that shows a bit about me. So they followed me around [in 1991]."

On the tape, Edgar hams it up: "The state of morality in this country and in this town leaves a lot to be desired. Every single thing we touch involves some element of twisting, turning, maneuvering to find some worthless irrelevant advantage. Everybody is out to position themselves a little bit better regardless of what is said about themselves. Today there are no more mentors and initiators. I was fortunate enough to have a mentor at the advertising agency Dancer, Fitzgerald & Sample. He was a pioneer in broadcasting. And in the six years I was at the agency, he taught me the business and it served me in good stead all my life. I've tried to be a mentor like he was to me.

"If you look at the Hollywood Hills, there must be a wealth of people of age and maturation, be it writers or directors, who could be of such value to this business. We must build a bridge between them and the younger people. Today the young people have nowhere to turn. One 26-year old with a question turns to another 26-year old, who doesn't know what to do and gives him back the same amorality. They feed off each other. And people wonder why principles disappear. Because there's no handing down of the torch.

"If a guy gives you something to read, either buy it or don't buy it. You don't give him a critique. He didn't send it to you for a critique."

March 18, 2002

Stephen Abronson, Scherick's assistant, phones: "Edgar says it's now or never. He's in a good mood. I'd go now."

I drive two miles west to Edgar's pad.

"I've just been through six books on you. Leonard Goldenson's book on the history of ABC television."

"Bad book. The author [Marvin J. Wolf] wasn't a good writer. He's a friend of mine. I shouldn't say that. It was a strange book, broken up into sections."

"Bert Randolph Sugar wrote about how crazy you were, like a Mad Hatter."

Edgar laughs. "I guess I was in those days. You need to read the book *Cowboy at the Mike* by Curt Gowdy. He tells a wonderful story about me running back and forth at this NCAA game. They lost the cues at the end to get us off the air."

"I read this story about how you were thrown out of the trucks because you were too kinetic."

"Apocryphal. Nobody throws me out of anywhere I belong. I am that truck. That's my domain."

"I read Jim McKay's book."

"That prick. He didn't write anything about me. I'm responsible for his career."

"He wrote a couple of pages about you."

"He was afraid of Roone Arledge."

"I looked up every book that might have a section on you. I was going to bring them to you."

"I don't want them. I don't get any kick out of reading about myself. I have little interest. Jim Spence wrote a good book. It was all true. I hired him because he had Dartmouth green socks."

"He said that if a monument was ever built to ABC Sports, your name should be at the top."

"He's right. He spent his whole career there. He was the only person in his book to clearly acknowledge me for starting *The Wide World of Sports*. And he was there. He knows."

"Jim couldn't stand Roone Arledge."

"A lot of people couldn't."

"I just read Marc Gunther's book on Roone Arledge and ABC News."

"I called up Fred Pierce, president of ABC, when the job [head of ABC News] opened up. I said, 'If you don't put Roone Arledge in that job, two men in white suits will come and take you away. You'd be crazy not to avail yourself of that piece of manpower that you've got sitting there.' I never got credit for that.

"Roone Arledge was a real prick to me. He ignored me completely. He told lies about things. When I said to Roone, 'How could you say something like that?', he'd say, 'I never said it. I don't read all that stuff. People write it and then they put it in a book.'

"ABC published a book about *Wide World of Sports*. The introduction to that book angered me. He denied that he ever read it. He's full of shit. Everything that had his name in it, he read. There was an article in *The New York Times* not long ago on the anniversary of *Wide World of Sports* and its derivation. I really nailed Roone Arledge on it and said how it all really happened. Roone wrote a nasty letter to the editor, saying that the article was all wrong."

Edgar's voice rises dramatically. "That article was exactly right. I'm going to die sooner or later. What's a better place to have it written than *The New York Times*? 'All the news that's fit to print.'

[After Scherick's death, *The Times* devoted 458 words to his obituary. When Arledge died three days later, *The Times* devoted 3908 words.]

"An article in the *Duke Alumni News* credits me for starting *The Wide World of Sports*."

Edgar removes the oxygen nozzles from his nose. "The doctor wants me to stay on oxygen because of the lung thing I had in the hospital. A medicine I'm taking caused a toxicity in one of my lungs. Now let's go back to business because your time is limited."

"What have you been doing?"

"I told you how I sold a movie about the White House on September 11th. We're working out a deal with the writer Lionel Chetwynd. His greed may exceed his enthusiasm for the project and if that continues, I'm going to throw his ass out of there."

"I was at a party for director David Lynch Saturday night."

"He is wonderful. He always wears his shirt buttoned up to the neck with no tie. I loved his picture *Blue Velvet* (1986). He's not working enough.

"I see that Liza Minnelli got married to some guy named David Guest. I don't have a clue who he is. That says something about the guy."

"What?"

"Who the fuck is he?"

We look at the TV show *Extra* and see a shot of the new building that will host the Oscars.

"I haven't been in this building yet. I cancelled my tickets. It's too much pushing and shoving for me. They're having a big argument about seats. Tickets are $350 each. I've been many times. It's all the same. I was there when the little Indian girl Little Feather, got up to accept the award for Marlon Brando. I'm on the executive committee of the producer's branch of the Academy. I vote yeah or nay on new entrances. They call me 'Black Ball Edgar.'"

Scherick smiles. He's kidding again. "To get admitted, you have to produce two pictures and fill out this huge application and have some sponsors."

"What does an Oscar mean to you?"

"It means a lot."

"What about the Emmys?"

"No. I'm going to win an Emmy for *Path to War* [it doesn't happen]. They're going to wheel me out on the stage and I'll say, 'When I make an entrance like this, I feel like Larry Flynt.' Everyone will laugh. I'd rather have an Emmy than not have one. But there's nothing more forgettable. Once you're an Academy Award winning director or producer, that's part of your name forever. That's not true of Emmys. Everybody's Emmy award winning this, Emmy award winning that. I don't participate in anything with the Television Academy."

"Why?"

"Because I don't think it's worth the powder to blow it down."

Edgar stares at the TV. "Look at Liz Taylor. She looks terrible. She's a remarkable woman for what she's gone through. There's Mickey Rooney, the most talented man in his prime that Hollywood ever produced."

"What are your favorite TV shows?"

"*NYPD Blue* and baseball."

"Who have you been talking to of late who's interesting?"

"Depends who you consider interesting. [*Variety* columnist] Army Archerd? He's a friend of mine. He's been writing that column for 50 years and he's never said a bad thing about anybody. It's pretty hard to write a gossip column for 50 years and not write something bad.

"Come on, you're wasting your own time."

"I'm sorry, I don't…"

"You're not prepared. Put the tape on and maybe we'll see something that will get me started."

"The Edgar Scherick acting tape? These are your acting roles?"

"Just put it in and shut up.

"I never turned down a part [until the stroke]."

"What have been your favorite roles?"

"I liked working for Marty Scorsese in *King of Comedy*. His dressing room was next to mine. We'd broken for lunch. I knew he wasn't satisfied with the first scene after lunch. He has asthma. He was making such terrible noises in his dressing room. So I sat down with a piece of paper and rewrote the scene and slipped it under his door. That was the scene he essentially ended up shooting.

"He's a marvelous, intense Italian gentleman. He's smart about movies. Almost encyclopedic. I was with Frederick De Cordova, who produced the Johnny Carson Show for years. And they were talking about Crimson Pirates. And Scorsese told them what the Crimson Pirate wore in his hatband. Scorsese supposedly had four TV sets in his room and four tapes going at the same time.

"He wanted me to go to Africa to produce *The Last Temptation of Christ*. And I wasn't about to go to Africa. And I wasn't interested in the project.

"I remember auditioning Kevin Costner for a role in *Mrs Soffel*. Diane Keaton made me promise to destroy the tape because she wasn't made up. I destroyed the tape because I promised her I would."

May 6, 2002

I sit through *Path to War* at USC. Larry Auerbach introduces Scherick. Tomorrow Edgar flies to New York and Washington D.C. for more screenings, his first plane rides in six years.

Larry: "Edgar, why did you make this film?"

"Because two gentlemen (Howard Dratch and Daniel Giat) who I had never met before, and who had no real experience, came into my office one day and said they wanted to make a movie about Clark Clifford and the Vietnam War. I said that Clark Clifford was an attendant meant to fill a scene or two. The real story is about Lyndon Baines Johnson. If you are interested in doing a film about Lyndon Johnson, I'd be interested in pursuing it with you. Lyndon Johnson was the greatest pure politician we've ever had.

"I'm proud of how this movie turned out. In twenty years, when students want to know what it was like inside the Johnson White House during the Vietnam War, this picture will be brought out and viewed.

"Michael Gambon is an Irish actor who was afraid of playing such a purely American Texas character. Jack Valenti's son John plays Jack in the LBJ administration.

"Barry Levinson initially agreed to direct the picture. He jerked us around for two years. I think it is the luckiest thing that ever happened that Barry Levinson didn't agree to do this picture. This is John Frankenheimer's meat."

Larry: "I remember in 1963, I was a William Morris agent who'd sold a lot of stuff to ABC.

"We had done a special with Sammy Davis Junior. In those days, when one of the networks put a black man on coast-to-coast in a special, that was news.

"One of my associates sold a Sammy Davis Jr. show to NBC and never told me. I thought, what am I going to tell Edgar? I knew he would find out.

"Edgar called. I want to see you and your boss Wally Jordan in my office at 9 a.m. tomorrow.

"They were the two leading television agents in New York.

"I never went to a buyer without something under my arm that I could sell. So I had an envelope under my arm. Edgar had this long office. We walked in and he says, 'Sit down gentlemen.' And he starts in. 'How dare you!' And he starts screaming and yelling and kicking. 'How could you do that?'

"I say to Wally Jordan, 'We better get out of here.' As we get up to leave, all he wants to know is what is under my arm. I knew that I didn't want to try to sell him something now because he's upset. And rightfully so. He follows us out to the envelope. He said, 'You and you and everyone else from William Morris are barred from the second floor of ABC.'"

Edgar: "I was his best customer."

Larry: "We had a lot of shows on ABC because nothing could stay too long. Four o'clock that afternoon, I'm at J. Walter Thompson advertising agency, the leading advertising agency. I'm sitting in a conference room with half a dozen guys trying to pitch something. And the phone rings. And it is for me. And Edgar reads off a list of our shows that he's canceling. He cancelled every deal we made. The man was rightfully upset with me but we are together today."

June 9, 2002

I walk into Edgar's bedroom.

"I'm on the edge," says Edgar.

"Edge of what?"

"The edge of shuffling off this mortal coil."

Edgar's substitute nurse Craig brings ice tea and sits down with us. I'm grateful for his company because I'm running out questions. Scherick intends to take his secrets to the grave.

"You got on the plane for the first time to fly to New York and Washington D.C. for premieres of your new film."

"When we got there, there was a wheelchair for me. I got into a van. The putz driver didn't know where the Plaza Hotel was [it's in Manhattan].

"I'd bought a beautiful black jacket with me but it was nowhere to be seen. I thought it had been stolen while we were out of the room. I reported it stolen and the detectives came up, blah, blah. When we got back, it was in the closet. I love that jacket.

"The Washington screening was at the French embassy. I went over to Ben Bradlee [former *Washington Post* editor]. He said, 'That's the most beautiful picture I've ever seen. I cried from the beginning to the end.' That made the trip to Washington worthwhile. I have a lot of respect for him.

"The retiring senator from Tennessee was there, Fred Thompson. Jack Valenti [runs the Motion Picture of America Association]. There were many Representatives. A friend in New York told me it was the best thing I've ever done. I received universal approbation."

"It was very interesting."

"John Frankenheimer went to the hospital for an operation. He had two discs removed from his back."

[John dies a month later.]

"Why did you make so many sequels to the *Stepford Wives*."

"For television, to earn some money."

"What do you remember about casting Matt Damon in your 1995 film *Good Ol' Boys?*'

"I liked him. Very handsome. He had a beautiful girlfriend. Ben Affleck's father [Tim, a former social worker] lives in this building. He was in *The Taking of Pelham 1-2-3* (1974)."

"You had Sydney Poitier in your movie *For the Love of Ivy* and *Guess Who's Coming to Dinner* (1967)."

"He was the number one box office star in the United States. Wherever we went, the women went crazy about him because he was so handsome."

"What do you remember about Robert Aldrich who directed *The Killing of Sister George?*"

"He was a tough bird. I read the script. And one of the stage directions seemed impossible to me. So I called him up. He said, 'That's a stage direction. I never read stage directions.' A good director doesn't read stage directions. He does his own directions.

"He used to cause me problems. I finally figured it out. He was always fighting the system. I had a three picture deal with him. He'd pick up the phone in the morning and say to himself, 'How can I screw this guy today?' And he'd do something ridiculous. Then I caught on and I didn't get upset about. And we stayed good friends until he died."

"What do you remember about working with Billy Friedkin?"

"He was a pain in the ass. We were in England and we had a difference of opinion. He goaded me and I got upset. Someone asked him, 'Why do you treat Edgar like that?' He said, 'Because it makes me happy to see him so upset.' He was a real prick. He's talented. It looks he's run out of steam. I'm mellower now. I have good thoughts about him."

"You used to get upset more easily?"

"I was in a perpetual state of upset. I cared about every detail. I couldn't stand stupidity. I couldn't stand anybody who was duplicitous. If you tried to bullshit me, it was a problem."

"What do you remember about Cybil Shepherd in *The Heartbreak Kid*."

"She was having an affair with Peter Bogdanovich. Peter was in Europe. We were shooting in a Miami Beach hotel. The telephone rings. It was for Cybil

Shepherd. The last thing I was going to do was pull her off the set to Peter Bogdanovich. So I said something to him and that was that.

"I remember how breathtakingly beautiful she was in a bathing suit. She was very polite. At that time, I don't think she could act a lick. Elaine May really worked with her to get a performance."

"What do you remember about working with director Gillian Armstrong in 1984's *Mrs. Soffel?*"

"She said that she didn't work with anybody over 40 years of age. I put that aside quickly. I got to be like a member of her family. I was like Uncle Edgar. I think about her a lot lying here. I think about that picture and Mel Gibson. I like the Australians. She had a lot of Australians on the crew. She wasn't going to have any strangers around her if she could avoid it."

"Tell me about Jaclyn Smith [on her fourth marriage] who appeared in two of your movies, *Nightmare in Daylight* and *Rape of Dr. Willis.*"

"Her ex-husband [Anthony B. Richmond] was a cinematographer. She was professional and beautiful. She had lovely children. She was a good mother. When you looked at her, you couldn't believe she was so beautiful. A classic kind of beauty. A Titian [Italian painter] kind of beauty. You don't know who Titia was? Wow, you're supposed to be an educated man. He was an Italian painter who painted voluptuous women during the Renaissance."

"What about that scene in *Rambling Rose* with Rose and that 14-year old boy in bed."

"It's right out of the book. It takes 80 pages. The book is autobiographical. The guy who wrote it was pure animal."

"What do you remember about working with Bette Davis in *Little Gloria: Happy at Last?*"

"We were shooting in the Flagler mansion in Palm Beach, Florida. And unbeknownst to us, there was a city ordinance forbidding shooting movies in that area. So Bette Davis stormed to the front of the mansion and said, 'Arrest me. It will be all over the country.' So they let us finish the shoot.

"She wrote me a letter once about what a beautiful picture she thought it was, but she only signed 'Bette,' not 'Bette Davis,' so I couldn't sell her autograph. She was a tough wizened old bird.

"We had a deal that she could not be called to the set except one minute before they were ready to shoot. They didn't want her waiting around. But she didn't want to miss anything. She'd stand there while the next scene was lit.

"We used a classic Canadian actor in that mini-series. He's simultaneously playing Iago on Broadway. It's becoming time for the Tony awards. The critics are coming. He didn't want to miss the evening performance. So, to keep him happy, I'd hire a helicopter to come out to Rhode Island and fly him out of there at 4 p.m. That pissed Bette Davis off no end. She'd say, 'Is that sonofabitch in this picture or isn't he?'"

Craig: "Tell him the Robert DeNiro story."

"When he started off, he was broke. I'd buy him lunch at the Players Club. He was nobody. A few years ago, I called him up in New York. His assistant said he'd call me the next day. So, the next day, the housekeeper comes in. 'Robert DeNiro is on the telephone.' She was awestruck."

Craig: "Edgar's more impressed with sports figures than actors."

Edgar: "I've got thousands of anecdotes. Joe Mankiewitz won the Academy Award as a writer and a director in two consecutive years, a feat unequaled. He directed *Sleuth*.

"Now the play *Sleuth* had an intermission where the police inspector comes back as a detective. I thought we should have an intermission with the movie. Joe was unalterably opposed. We locked horns.

"We went to New Haven for a screening. I still thought it needed an intermission. So I'm sitting in one limo and he's sitting in another limo. Somebody said, 'Why don't you go over and talk to Joe?' I said, 'If he wants to talk, he can come over here and talk to me.' I wouldn't get out of the car. Finally we talked but we never had an intermission. He said, 'That's the worst idea I've ever heard. I'll go to the press and I'll blacken your name all over the country.'"

"I interviewed his son Chris the other day."

"He used to work for me. Lazy, lazy, lazy. I haven't seen him in 25 years and I am not anxious to see him."

"Your former assistant Brian Grazer."

"He was assiduous in pursuit of his own interests. There's nothing wrong with that. He wasn't a tower of moral strength. He did certain things that I thought were reprehensible. There was a football coach at USC named John [Robinson]. Brian married his daughter. They had a son and Brian paid no attention to him.

"I purchased a screenplay by Bo Goldman called *Twitching*. It later became *Shoot the Moon*. I wanted to get Al Pacino to play in it. I talked to Pacino's agent Stan Kamen at William Morris. They sent the script to Pacino. The word came back that he wanted to hear the script read. So I called up Juliette Taylor, who'd done a lot of casting for me in New York. She said she was too busy to set up a reading. 'But I'm going to give you a young man who will do a good job for you. His name is Scott Rudin.' He set up the reading and it was set to perfection.

"After the reading was over, Pacino went into his shell to communicate with himself. Then Stan Kamen called. 'Al wants it read again.' We went through the whole routine again. He'd just made a movie called Bobbie Deerfield, about a racing driver. It was a failure. He was nervous about doing another introspective picture so he ended up not doing it.

"Scott Rudin worked for me for five years. He had an encyclopedic knowledge of show business.

"Alan Parker directed *Shoot the Moon* [starring Albert Finney and Diane Keaton]. Alan was an arrogant pain-in-the-ass.

"Luke, you're almost out of here."

"In your battles with directors, any of them get the best of you?"

"Not really. I'm not interested in getting the best of anybody. I had some real scenes with Elaine May."

"So what do you think about most of the time?"

"I lie in bed and I watch television. I have the newspaper read to me. I think about what's going on in the world. I think about my life."

"And what do you think about your life?"

"It's tinged with sadness. Fishing was a great hobby of mine. You should get a copy of an essay I wrote called 'Redfish.' Every once in a while I see men standing in water up to their knees with a fishing rod. That was my favorite activity and I can't do that anymore."

"What else do you think about?"

"Women."

"Which ones?"

"All my ex-girlfriends. I was basically monogamous. Once I was married, I was completely monogamous. I never cheated on one of my wives once."

"How many women were you with in your life?"

"God knows."

"Any actresses?"

"I stayed away from actresses. Don't shit where you live.

"I went with one girl for five years [before Edgar's first marriage]. Her name was Hatfield Orly. At the end of five years, I asked her to marry me. She said no. I was stunned. She did me the biggest favor. We were not meant for each other. She was the biggest party girl. Always with a glass of Jim Bean."

Craig: "How did you meet your first wife [Carol]?"

"I was working in the advertising business. We had a Falstaff Beer account. Falstaff would sponsor the radio broadcast of the St. Louis Hawks baseball team, which moved from Minneapolis. Ben Kerner owned the team. One day he said to me, 'My office assistant Jeanie Bilgray is coming to New York with a friend. Look out for them.' I had scheduled a fishing trip to Bermuda. I had a guy who worked for me, Jack Lubell. He was a television director. A real character. An alcoholic. He was the neatest drunk I ever saw. Immaculate. I told him to watch out for these people and I went fishing.

"I caught a 210 pound Marlin. When I came back to New York, my arm was in a sling. Those two girls came to my office to give a box of chocolates to Jack Lubell for taking care of them. That was the first time I'd ever seen my first wife, Cal Roman. I took her out that night and began a romance that culminated in my first marriage and the birth of my daughter.

"She'd come up from St. Louis to New York for a week. I didn't want anyone to find out that she was staying at my apartment. There was a hotel across the street. I lived at number two Fifth Avenue. There was a hotel at number one Fifth Avenue. I got her a room where she could get messages but she really stayed with me. There was something about her that I liked. She was classy.

"One day she calls me up from St. Louis in tears. 'I'm pregnant.' In the blink of an eye, I said, 'Come on up. We'll get married.' There were all these churches around but they wouldn't marry you unless you'd posted ahead of time announcements that you were getting married. She wanted to get married in a church. I finally found a place on the island I was raised, Point Lookout, Long Island. It was a little community church. The minister called up some people from town as witnesses and he married us in that church. The minister ended up christening some of my children."

"Have you worked on any films that have changed you?"

"*Raid on Entebbe*. The emotional ties to that story have never left me."

"You were on Larry King a few weeks ago. I remember Larry King asked you that."

"I was on with Jack Valenti, John Frankenheimer and Donald Sutherland."

"Do you ever feel like you are living out one of your movies?"

"I had gone to weather school in the army at Grand Rapids, Michigan. Now I was stationed at Winsla, Connecticut. They are getting ready to ship me north to Prestile, Main, from whence I would go overseas. There was a guy named Ben. His father was a commanding general. We went into town to the USO on an overnight pass. We met two girls and we home to their apartment. Barbara Rappenport was the girl I met. There was no real sex, just holding on to each other. We went to sleep. Wherever our bodies had touched each other was wet with perspiration.

"I lied to her about myself [about age and education]. We had a passionate correspondence for six months. It kept me sane in Iceland for the first six months. Then I stopped writing to her because I didn't think it was fair of me to perpetuate this myth that I had created. I come back from overseas [two years later]. I get her number and call her. I say, 'Barbara, this is Edgar Scherick.' She says, 'I'm being married in two weeks.' And she hangs up. That's quite a story. It would make a marvelous film. All men have bullshitted a woman."

"Were there any innovations you introduced?"

"I was closer to editing than most producers. I made this television movie *Good Ol' Boys*, directed by Tommy Lee Jones. I wanted to make some cuts in it. I thought it was slow in moments. I spent a full day making edits and then I called him. 'Tommy Lee, I've made some cuts. I'm going to send you a tape. Anything you don't like, I will restore it the way you had it.' He bought all the cuts and that is the way the picture went.

"A guy sent me a book called *Jaws*. I read the book. In those days, I would fly home from Los Angeles to New York to be with my family for the weekend. I get on the airplane and [Producer] David Brown says, 'Edgar, how are you?' I said I'm pretty good. He said, 'Have you seen anything good lately?' I said, 'I've seen a book that I think is interesting and I am in negotiations with the agent.' He said, 'What's that book?' I said, 'It is called *Jaws*.'

"On Monday I called the agent and he said he was in negotiation with David Brown [who secured the rights].

"I had 70 pages of a book [manuscript] called *The Godfather*. I gave it to Stanley Jaffe at Columbia Pictures. His father was a big mogul. Nothing happened. Later, Stanley said to me, 'I didn't know you had access to Bristol Myers money. I would've done something with you.'

"I wanted to do a picture with Francis Ford Coppola called *The Conversation*. I went up to San Francisco with agent Jeff Berg, now president of ICM, to see Francis about financing his picture. He was cutting *The Godfather*. He was cutting the scene where Marlon Brando got shot.

"I went to a screening in New York of Coppola's first feature, *You're a Big Boy Now*. When I'm coming out, I run into Steve Canther, a movie critic for *Time* magazine. He asked me what I thought. I said, 'A new American filmmaker has made his debut. This guy is talented.'

"Coppola was like an Eastern potentate. He walked around in these velvet robes in his hotel room.

"One day Albert Brooks came to me. He said he wanted to do a movie for $750,000. I asked him to let me read the script. He said, 'There is no script.'"

"Which producers are you jealous of?"

"I'm jealous of no one except David Geffen, because he's a billionaire. If I were a billionaire, I could have my specially constructed fishing boat with a hoist. And I could go fishing.

"I was never money oriented. I never did anything purely for money in my life. I thought that if you did good work, money would follow. And that's the way things worked out."

"What are you most ashamed of?"

"I'm not ashamed of anything. Well, I once had a difference of opinion on *Rambling Rose* and I did this guy (Michael Houseman, personal producer of director Milos Foreman) out of a credit. I'm ashamed of it.

"I was never egomaniacal. I was only concerned with one thing—the work. The world is divided into two groups. Group one is those people who are more interested in themselves than in the work. Group two is the people who are more interested in the work than in themselves. I've always belonged to group two.

"I believed in live and let live. You get the best out of a person if he is free to use his creative powers."

July 15, 2002

Scherick, 77, was rushed by ambulance to Cedar Sinai hospital a week ago, suffering heart-attack-like symptoms. After numerous tests, the doctors concluded there had been no heart attack and he was released.

I pay him a visit. He seems sicker than usual. He's covered with black and blue splotches from all the blood tests he's endured.

I don't have any prepared questions for him but I want to say hello. I remember how much I appreciated that when I was sick.

After a minute spent on his physical condition, Edgar cuts me off. "Do you want to talk about my health or do you want to talk about your book? How's it coming along?"

"Slowly."

"That's because you're not working hard enough. I think that you're in trouble with it. You have no focus."

I sit beside the bed.

"I need to find a narrative. What have you been doing?"

"We have an idea for a movie, which I think I am going to sell. We've set up a series of appointments this week to sell it."

"You're going out to these appointments?"

"Yes, all around town until I find a buyer."

"Which people in the industry know you best?"

"Most people will give you superficial comments. Producer Dan Blatt knows me well. Bob Phillips. I'd say Michael Eisner and Jeffrey Katzenberg but they won't talk to you. Elaine May would be good."

"If you were writing a book on producers, what questions would you ask them?"

"What causes you to respond to a piece of material."

"What else would you want to know if you were going around talking to your peers?"

"Are they getting laid."

"When producers turned to you for advice, what were their questions?"

"What do you think I should do in this situation. I remember Marty Bregman was making *Dog Day Afternoon*. He was telling me stories about the [original] director. I said, 'Fire the sonofabitch!'

"We had a saying in our shop. 'Writers write, directors direct, actors act and producers produce.'"

"What were the most common problems producers turned to you for?"

"Pictures were getting out of hand. There's nothing worse than a runaway picture."

"Did that ever happen to you?"

"No. I went over budget but it was always controlled. Most people in Hollywood don't like to share their problems. They like to keep them quiet.

"Irwin Winkler and I didn't get along well. We were doing a picture once, *They Shoot Horses, Don't They?* I brought in Irwin and his partner Robert Chartoff. I have to give Irwin credit. He went to Europe and got Jane Fonda. There was a lot of internal warfare, firing of people."

"You never had the desire to direct a movie?"

"I directed in the middle of things. When they were making *Heartbreak Kid*, I went down to the set on a yacht club in Florida. Elaine May is fucking around. I said, 'Elaine, let's get going.' She said, 'You direct it,' and walked off the set. So I directed the scene."

"So why do you think Hollywood is so afraid to tackle themes of organized religion in movies?"

"I'm not sure people want to pay money to see pictures about organized religion.

"I wasn't crazy about that *American Beauty* picture. It was morbid, almost anti-American. It had no relief in it. It went one from one bad situation to another."

"What do you think your body of work says about you?"

"That I'm interested in the human psyche, soul, morality. That I'm a man of taste."

"Have your attitudes to any of your movies changed over the years?"

"Yes, *For the Love of Ivy*. I like that movie now more than when we finished it. It was racially forward.

"You better hurry up. I'm running out of gas."

"What were your weak points as a producer?"

"Technical stuff. I didn't know about the different types of cameras."

"What do you think of the Gay Mafia?"

"Why are these people a mafia? Ridiculous."

"Has the gay mafia ever threatened you?"

"No."

"Threatened to break in and redecorate your apartment?"

"No."

Edgar's assistant Stephen Abronson says, "They did, can't you see?"

"I've had good relations with homosexuals."

"Because they find you attractive?"

"No, because I respect their proclivities. I never tell a man who to do or how to live."

"If you had to wear a dress for an acting role, would you be willing to do it?"

"Of course."

"What if you had to kiss another man in an acting role?"

"It would depend on the script. There are men that I am attracted to but I don't kiss them.

"I worked on *And the Band Played On* [eventually produced by Aaron Spelling]. I was never comfortable with the material. The story just petered out at the end.

"I learned a lot about homosexual practices, fisting and things like that."

"Don't you think that's disgusting?"

"No, it doesn't disgust me. It's not the most attractive thing I can think of."

"Do you think AIDS is God's punishment on homosexuals?"

"No. How's world Judaism?"

"Things have been better in Israel lately. We have *Tishu'Bav* Wednesday night, when we mourn the destruction of the two temples."

"I may vacillate in my religion, but I've always been proud of my heritage. I have the blood of heroes in my veins."

"I've met this genius rabbi at *shul* who studies ten pages of Talmud a day. That's unheard of."

"That's tricky stuff. It never says exactly what it means."

"It's the most difficult material I've ever studied."

Edgar and I do not speak again. He dies of leukemia December 2, 2002.

I walk up to his funeral Sabbath afternoon, December 7th, and see a friend from my Orthodox synagogue, Hugh Taylor.

"What are you doing here?" he asks.

"I'm writing a book about producers. I interviewed Edgar a dozen times this year. And you?"

"I was his head of production."

About 200 people attend the memorial service at the All Saints Episcopal Church, I see the Harry Ufland and his blonde wife Mary Jane, and tall aristocratic blonde grandmother Dorothea Petrie and her much shorter husband Dan.

I see a young curly-haired handsome priest (Rev. Jimmy Bartz) in his vestments.

Edgar's first wife Carol stands with big black jazz musician Illinois Jaquette, her close friend since the late seventies when he taught her the piano and other things.

I do not see Edgar's second wife Marge.

I can't sign the guestbook because it is the Sabbath, a holy day when a Jew is not permitted to write or do any form of "work."

I suspect most of the crowd is Jewish. Jewish Law forbids a Jew from entering a church but Jews in Hollywood are rarely observant of their tradition.

I've read comedic scenes about Hollywood types at funerals doing deals. If that's going on here today, it's so low key I can't see it.

I walk inside the church and sit near the back. About 40 of Edgar's former assistants have shown up to pay their respects along with about 40 producers. Most of the crowd seems to come from entertainment.

The service begins on time with the priest walking down the aisle reciting a prayer in English about the Resurrection. Then he leads the congregation in the 23rd Psalm, which traditional Jews sing in Hebrew about now as part of the Sabbath's third meal.

Edgar's family say they plan to scatter his ashes off the coast of Long Island.

The speakers remember the deceased as brilliant, temperamental, tempestuous and funny. The priest describes how much Edgar loved the Pope.

At 5:30 p.m., the crowd repairs to the Museum of Television and Radio on Beverly Drive for drinks, hors d'oeuvres, a video presentation and more speeches.

A woman named Zane talks about her favorite memories of Edgar. She recalls their first meeting. Edgar was hungry. He asked his assistant, on his first day on the job, fresh from Harvard, to get him a Turkey sandwich, with lettuce and tomato on the side and coleslaw in the sandwich.

Forty minutes later the kid returns and puts the styrofoam container on Edgar's desk. He opens it and his face goes purple. "You're fired," he screams at the kid, who hasn't been seen in Hollywood since.

The lettuce and tomato were in the sandwich and there was potato salad on the side. Edgar said if the kid couldn't get his order right, he couldn't get movies right.

December 26, 2002

I speak by phone with Michael Dains, a former assistant to Scherick, who I met at the funeral.

"Much of my job was being his driver and accompanying Edgar to meetings. I was with him from the early morning until late at night. He always did business on his car phone.

[Edgar was a bad driver with a poor sense of direction. In 1989, he caused a bad accident on Sunset Boulevard and was lucky he wasn't killed.]

"It was impossible to get Edgar to stop what he was doing to go to meetings. We would start giving him warnings well in advance. He also could not stand to be 30 seconds late. He had to be places on time. That's a real challenge in LA.

"If I was ever going to take Edgar somewhere, I'd drive the route first. You never wanted to be lost with Edgar.

"Edgar believed he always knew the best way to go, which was not always true. I went my way. He said, 'If we're late, you're fired.' I laughed. He said, 'No, I'm serious.' We arrived on time.

"Being his assistant meant being part of his brain. He was so busy, and had so much on his mind. When you're talking on the phone, you usually have an assistant listening in and taking notes. If you're in the car, you're only hearing half the conversation and you're driving. You can't take notes.

"Edgar was uncomfortable with me being his assistant. He said to me once, 'You driving me around is like a thoroughbred pulling a garbage scow.' I just wanted to learn as much as I could from him. Some of his assistants didn't pay attention.

"Michael Barnathan told the story at his memorial service that when he was hired by Edgar, Edgar told him to just sit there. Michael thought he was supposed to do something but all he was supposed to do was listen and learn.

"I recall sitting with Edgar in an editing session for *Passion for Justice* with the director and editors. Edgar had a photographic memory. We were looking at a scene when Edgar said, 'Wasn't there another shot of this?' There was. There was one reaction shot. Edgar suggested using it. It changed the whole scene and made it better.

"Edgar was willing to fight for things and it was fun to watch him fight and to see when he would back down. Edgar told me about throwing furniture around the room.

"Edgar yelled. One assistant just before me quit because she couldn't take being yelled at.

"I felt like my relationship with Edgar was a father-son relationship. I saw assistants who'd come and go because they'd get pissed off with him and wouldn't deal with it. There was one time I was ready to quit on the spot but he came back and apologized. It was a moving moment. He realized that he had gone too far."

Michael Dains gave me a tape of Edgar J. Scherick speaking at a "Producers on Producing" forum at AFI May 9, 1985. Here are highlights:

"What's important is to take your work seriously and not yourself. We are transient. We don't matter. This town has been going on for 80-years and the titanic clashes are all forgotten and what lives on are the pictures.

"I have four children. All are in the industry in one form or another. I have not got one of them a job. I've never told any of them what to do.

"If you have a reasonable idea of yourself, you shouldn't have difficult evaluating other people. You look at a person and you can pretty well tell if that person is going to be any good or not.

"*The Taking Of Pelham 1-2-3* is a terrific picture. United Artists distributed it. It was the first time I had done a picture for a studio. Freddy Goldberg was in charge of advertising. They prepared an oil painting (at a $5000) for the campaign of a scene inside a New York subway station. One man was standing with a sub-machine and another man had a woman around his throat. It was beautifully done.

"We snuck the picture in New York and it went like gangbusters. The audience was screaming. But the movie didn't open well. I was working with a company that was an exceptional merchandiser of packaged goods. They had nothing to do with the movie business. I knew a guy in the marketing research department. I told him I wanted to find out why this picture was not clocking them.

"He set up some research. The motion picture had never done this before. No business ever marched on so blindly ignorant of their own market as the motion picture business. He set up research in which he checked what the expectations were from seeing the advertisement and what the reaction was after seeing the movie. Out of that came a lesson—an advertisement sets up expectations for a movie. If the audience's expectations are not fulfilled by the movie, they come out and give you lousy word-of-mouth, the key factor in selling a movie.

"This advertisement created a violent milieu and all the violence freaks zapped into that movie and it wasn't really a violent movie. And the violence freaks came out and told all their friends, 'Screw it. It's no good.' But the people who went into it who weren't violence freaks, and who didn't see the ad, liked the picture and came out speaking positively about it. We had spent millions of dollars convincing the real audience for this picture not to come.

"The man who did that research quit his $17,000-a-year job and came to Hollywood and became one of the most important figures in market research and telling the movie companies what to do. His demise began when he advised Warner Brothers not to do *Star Wars*.

"I don't think I've ever made a movie I wouldn't have my children watch."

January 7, 2003

I call Dan Blatt. "When did you first meet up with Edgar?"

"In 1969. I represented ABC in a termination agreement [with Scherick]. Edgar and I didn't become friendly right away. There was a mutual respect. In July of 1970, Selig Seligman died and everybody from ABC East came to [Los Angeles for] the funeral—Leonard Goldenson (who created the ABC network as David Sarnoff created NBC and Bill Paley created CBS), Si Segal (Leonard's number one man). Edgar asked me to pick him up at the plane. We spent the day and that's when it started.

"Edgar made a deal with Bristol Myers [to finance his movies]. He called me up and asked me to work for him. I left ABC and moved back to New York to work for him as head of business and legal affairs. My condition was that I would only report directly to him. We made junky pictures in the beginning.

"We had a tiny company, with five employees. I was doing many different things. On *The Heartbreak Kid*, [director] Elaine May and [writer] Neil Simon had a falling out. And the contract between Simon and Palomar was that we couldn't change a word without his approval. He agreed to write the script under the Dramatists Guild contract [playwrights have far more power than screenwriters, you can't change a word of their plays without their permission]. It's the only script he ever wrote that wasn't based on an original idea of his. It's based on a short story by Bruce Jay Friedman called 'Change of Plan.'

"Elaine wanted to make changes but she and Neil wouldn't talk to each other. So they had to find a conduit to go back and forth and negotiate the changes. I was chosen for the job. I'd sit with Elaine and she'd tell me what the wanted and I'd go to Neil and I had to find a way to effect creative compromise.

"We had some problems on *Sleuth*. I was chosen to go to London to meet with [director] Joe Mankiewicz and the art director Ken Adam. I felt the picture was too long. So now I was getting involved with the script. I learned from the seat of my pants. Those two pictures got nominated for six Academy awards."

Blatt's first producer credit came in 1977 on *Circle of Children*, followed by *Raid on Entebbe*.

"We didn't get renewed at Bristol Meyers. I was the first one to say that we had to move to California."

"Did Edgar scream at you?"

"No. In the beginning, a few times. When I decided to leave, it became rupturous."

"You screamed at him?"

"I'm not a screamer but it was emotional. We were together a long time. It started out that he was my employer, then he was a partner, then he was the closest of friends, and then there was a break-up, like a marriage. He was clearly older than me. We'd been through a lot of good things and a lot of bad things together.

"When I first met him, I thought he was fantastic. I still do. But when you're with somebody 16-hours a day for a long time, everybody gets to know everybody's strengths and weaknesses. We were really close. The breakup [in 1979] was an emotional, difficult situation. There was money involved."

"You wanted to go out to work on your own because?"

"That's what I wanted to do."

"He felt like he couldn't continue to be friends if you did that?"

"It's like when you breakup with your wife or girlfriend, do you stay friends right away? It doesn't work that way. There were a lot of things going on at the same time. His marriage was in trouble. Moving to California."

It took until 1984 for Dan and Edgar to re-establish their friendship.

"I've heard Edgar was one of the legendary screamers?"

"He was volatile. I didn't think it was appropriate."

"Was it pleasant working for him?"

"It wasn't boring. He was smart with great ideas. He had bursts of energy. The guy that you interviewed at that bed, that's the guy. He wasn't the same person anymore but you captured who he was. When I read the interview, I said, 'This is vintage Scherick.' When he said, 'If I could pick a gun and shoot Marge [his sec-. ond ex-wife].' That kind of stuff.

"Like 99 percent of people, he didn't fulfill his potential. He did great things but he didn't come close. With a different emotional makeup, he could've been a bigger producer. I don't want to get into it."

"He didn't seem terribly interested in money."

"That's not true."

"He wasn't terribly successful with money then."

"Right. He wanted money. Everybody wants money. But that wasn't the driving force. He was interested in making good projects and receiving credit for doing wonderful things."

"He wanted glory."

"You're putting words in my mouth. Listen, everybody wants to be recognized. Everybody wants to score the winning touchdown. Everybody wants the cameras going off as they go into the end zone. No one wants to miss the four-footer on the last hole.

"It's a generational thing too. Ed was an Eastener. He went to Harvard. He was a product of the Depression. His father lost all his money. Read about Irving Berlin and you'll see a guy who came out of the ghetto. I guarantee you that when Irving Berlin caught a cab and the fare was $1:40, he didn't just flip $2 at that cab driver. He grew up understanding the value of money. You can't escape that. At the same time, Irving Berlin took some of his royalties and sent them to charity. New York and Hollywood are two different towns requiring two different kinds of people. Some guys made the transition easily and other guy haven't.

"Ed was educated. He had an intellect."

"And he liked to let you know."

"That was his insecurity. Most people who have done things suffer from a combination of megalomania and insecurity. That's a tough combination to live with—for the person and for those around him. It forces you do things that you hate yourself for doing. Then you're in a business in which no one knows what will really work. There's all that insecurity selling, making and just holding your breath.

"Edgar did quality work, which doesn't necessarily translate into financial reward. The movie he did with [director] John Frankenheimer, *Path To War*, that was an attempt to do a quality piece of work about something. That's not *Caddyshack* (1980)."

"How well do you think he pulled it off?"

"By that time, Ed was a sick person. You can't say he made that film. He started that picture. It's a subjective thing. Did you think that guy was Lyndon Johnson who everyone said was so great?"

"No. The movie didn't work for me."

"No, he wasn't Lyndon Johnson. When you saw *The Gathering Storm* (2002), was Albert Finney Churchill? It was remarkable. Was Marlon Brando the Godfather? As soon as that picture opened, you said, 'Ohmigod, what is happening here?' Peter Finch was Yitzhak Rabin."

"Edgar told me he wanted you to speak at his funeral and you did."

"As I said at the funeral, Edgar had a great eye for talent. He was a charismatic character. He had a command of the room. He was literate. He appreciated good work. Edgar was one of a kind, plus and minus. When they [Brian Grazer, Scott Rudin, Michael Barnathan, et al] worked for him, he was the boss. You may have walked away mumbling but it didn't matter."

"Was he a happy man?"

"What do you think?"

"No. His last years were particularly bitter. The man I met was bitter."

"The golden years to him weren't golden. This is not a business for older people."

"When you had dinner with Edgar, what sorts of things came up most often in conversation?"

"Movies, politics and sports."

"Did you ever turn for help to Edgar once you'd gone out on your own?"

"No."

"Did he ever turn to you?"

"Yes, periodically, he'd call me and ask what I thought. That's more to his credit than mine."

"Could you give me an anecdote about Edgar?"

"I was working with a director [Alan Parker?] who was brilliant but not interested in the project. Ed was frustrated with the guy and said, 'You're so arrogant, you don't even know you're arrogant.' I think that's the best line I ever heard."

"Edgar always wanted good people to work for him. He had the ability to spot them. [Edgar] fucking hired Roone Arledge. Anybody who tells you differently is a liar."

"What were his relationships like with guys like Michael Eisner and other studio chiefs?"

"A lot of these guys worked for Edgar. Leonard Goldberg. Scott Rudin. Brian Grazer. Larry Gordon. Robert Lawrence. Michael Barnathan. Chris Schenkel.

Frank Barton. Edgar was there before they were. Eisner respected him. ABC was a distant third when he took over and the shows he put on the air, like Batman, Batgirl, helped propel ABC into competition with NBC."

"Edgar championed women."

"When he started out, there weren't many women in the business. Joan Scott was one of the first. Edgar had nothing to do with her but if you want to do a good story about someone in the business, Joan Scott. She created Writers and Artists Agency. She saw that there was no way that a woman could become a partner in an agency and she said, 'I will create my own agency.' Harrison Ford, Armand Assante, Jimmy Woods, she found all of them. She's a manager now in New York. She's in her seventies. She's vibrant and beautiful and smart and funny. Joan Scott will demonstrate what a woman could do and couldn't do."

Edgar told a TV Academy interviewer, "Women in Film gave me an award for husbanding the careers of more women than most. It's called the Martini Award and I was the first man so honored. I was raised by three women (mother, sister and aunt). I feel terribly close to women. In many cases, I preferred working with women."

"Did Edgar have a lot of friends?"

"What's your definition of friends? He had a lot of people who liked him. They had a nice turnout at the funeral. Bob Daly [former co-head of Warner Brothers]. Edgar was the last of an era. An era when a person could walk into a room and with the sheer enthusiasm of their passion for a project could sell it. It doesn't work like that anymore because everything is so layered and corporate."

"I'd see people in my research for my book on producers and they'd mention they knew Edgar. I'd mention that I saw him regularly and they'd say, 'Give him my best.' I thought, 'Why don't you call him and give him your best?' Part of the reason I went to see him so many times was that I thought he wanted the company. Then you'd get there and he'd throw you out after 20-minutes."

"He was tough on visitors. 'You can leave now.' Fuck you, Ed. I don't want to be told I can leave now. I didn't drive over here to be told I can leave now. Right?"

"Yes."

"Did you feel that way?"

"Yes."

"Don't tell me to leave. I'm not rude to you. He was in bad shape. He was heavy. He was lying flat on his bed. He had leukemia. It was sad for me to see him like this.

"He liked baseball, fishing, literature. He appreciated a good sentence. He liked a good meal. He loved the business. He was a great salesman."

January 26, 2003

I sit down with Hugh Taylor, who worked for Scherick for four years (1988-90, 92-94).

"Tell me about your book—*The Hollywood Job-Hunter's Survival Guide*."

"It's basically a how-to-be-an-assistant to Edgar Scherick thing. It started over at Saban, when we were hiring a lot of people and this was going to be a guide on how to do coverage, etc. It eventually became a book.

"He was a larger-than-life character. He was about 62-years old. According to a lot of people, he'd already calmed down a lot but he was still a powerful personality in the full swing of his career. He yelled and screamed. He could be rough on people. I remember once he asked me to move his car and I didn't give him back his car keys and he yelled at me for five minutes that I had caused him to worry that he wouldn't know where his car keys were. He was like that all day long—breathing fire.

"He would mellow out towards the end of the day and tire himself out. As he got older, that would happen earlier in the day.

"He had many people in that assistant job over the years. If he feels like he likes working with you, he brings you more into the process. He barely spoke to me for the first month or two I worked there. He would tell me to type things up and read scripts. There was almost no dialogue. Then somehow that began to change. As we were driving around, he'd say, 'What did you think of that script?' I would tell him. Over time, we would talk more. He'd give me little assignments, say, 'I want to make a movie about the boyhood of Mozart. Go research that.' I would go to a library and write up a treatment.

"Then he began taking me into meetings and I could sit in a meeting.

"It was better for Edgar to have fewer people. The more people he had, the more harried he would become. He would feel that everybody would come at him from a million directions and he'd go crazy. He'd be on the phone and someone would poke their head through the door and he would say, 'I am not a hydra-head. I can't talk to two people at the same time.'

"He'd use a lot of classical and medieval terms. If he were busy, and he wanted someone else to take over a project, he'd say, 'You need to take up the cudgels and start fighting on this one,' like it was some kind of medieval contest. He'd talk about having the sword of Damocles hanging over his head. How Portcullis would come down and cut him off from somebody.

"I was so not-Jewish at that time. I went to a meeting at NBC and they ordered sandwiches. They asked what I wanted. I said, 'Ham on white with mayonnaise.' [Jewish Law forbids eating meat and milk together.] Susan Baerwold, executive at NBC, said to Edgar, 'That's a real goyisha menu.' Now I'm Orthodox and Edgar is Catholic.

"Edgar didn't realize that I was Jewish for the first two months that I worked for him. He was talking to his wife and he said I was a Gentile. I said, 'No, I'm Jewish.' That was right around the time the relationship improved, when he realized I was Jewish."

"You went around with your *tzitzit* (fringes) tucked in."

"I didn't even know what *tzitzit* were at that time. If I had seen an Orthodox Jew eating a ham sandwich in a car on Saturday, it wouldn't have struck me as odd."

"What was Edgar's relationship with his Jewish identity?"

"He was ethnically Jewish. He used a lot of Yiddish expressions. He was sensitive to anti-Semitism when he perceived it. He wasn't observant at all [of Jewish Law]. He had no affiliation with Judaism."

"Did he have many encounters with anti-Semitism?"

"Very little. I think ABC in the fifties and sixties had some. That was a time when Jews were still on the outside of advertising and TV. It wasn't as Jewish as it is now. Obviously the CEO Leonard Goldenson was Jewish but there were people at ABC who didn't have a high opinion of Jews."

"He liked to show how literate he was."

"He was smart and well-read. He used to do the crossword puzzle and he'd ask me for clues. He'd say, 'Who's a ninth century monk whose name started with the letter A.' If you didn't know, he'd say, 'You're not paid not to know. You went to Harvard. You should know these things.'

"He was fond of quoting Oliver Cromwell. If a network passed on a project, he'd write them a letter, 'By the bowels of Christ, methinks you may be mistaken.'"

"Why did you leave him in 1994?"

"It was a decision mostly to get out of the business. Working for him was stressful. It did take a toll on me. In the ABC deal [1993-94], I was the only executive there. I administratively ran the place and I was in charge of development. It wore me out. I didn't like the business after a while. We were doing a lot of true-story rights acquisition—calling up people who'd been victims of crime and trying to buy their rights. Not that I am so pure, but I became uneasy with twisting true stories around to make a dramatic point. Taking advantage of ambiguity in a story.

"There are incidents where someone innocent is convicted of a crime and their trial testimony will make it look like they did something, and because of the way the rules work, you can dramatize that trial testimony as real and people will view it as real and that's the way the story will be known. I became uncomfortable with that.

"One of the moments when it clicked that I had to get out, I went down to Florida to pursue the case. There was a woman who had been wrongly imprisoned for murdering her husband. It was a great TV movie story. You could imagine Jaclyn Smith wrongly accused of killing her husband. The woman had not gotten a proper trial. I met with her lawyer, one of these $500 an hour Miami lawyers, and he said, 'I think my client probably did shoot her husband to death but the fact is she didn't get a fair trial, so she deserves to be let out of jail.' I say, 'Well, that's O.K. I can make her look innocent in the movie.' As soon as I said that, I thought, 'Wow, is that what I went to college for? Is this what I want to do with my life? I've got to get out of here.'

"That's what the business had become at that point. That trend [of women in peril] came to an end. I could just picture the movie. Jaclyn Smith walking into jail and the door clanging behind her.

"I miss the creativity of it. Once for fun, Edgar and I made up a fake true story. Edgar needed to make a living so he would make these movies, but he really didn't like them. He didn't like crime and exploitation. Once for fun we made up a story of a nursery school teacher who was a prostitute and serial killer and we called it *She Kills By Night*. We typed it up as a newspaper article and we faxed it to the network and one of the network executives phoned, 'This is great.' 'Well, sorry, it is fake.' Edgar could get away with that. If it had been me, I would've never worked in this town again."

We chat about the January 1994 earthquake centered in Northridge.

"Edgar went crazy. He basically blamed me for the earthquake and that his life was inconvenienced. I just thought, 'This is crazy.' The day after the earthquake, the city was chaos. The police said, 'Don't leave your house. Don't use your phone.' He wanted me to come over to his house. He was trying to make phone calls. Nobody was in. He said, 'You failed me.'

"After I left, I would check in with him periodically. There were a group of us who had a strong attachment to him and we would visit him in the hospital.

"He had his stroke in 1996. I was engaged to be married."

"What was his relationship like with his second wife Marge?"

"Until the stroke, it was a good relationship. They had a lot of respect for each other. She was an interesting woman. Her daughter was Laurie Iwasaki. Then she married [after Edgar] someone named Scott, so she was Marge Scott Scherick.

"She was supportive of him [until the stroke]. She put up with a lot. He loved her. He was devoted to her in a lot of ways. They traveled together to productions in New York, London or Toronto. I used to book them on fishing trips to Costa Rica. The best fishing places are in the middle of nowhere. These trips were uncomfortable. You'd get on little planes, boats, cars. She would have to go down there and sweat it out down there in the fishing camp with him. Someone once said to Edgar, 'I didn't realize your wife was into fishing.' He said, 'She wasn't but now she is.'

"Fishing was his escape. That's why they bought a little place down in Texas."

"Were there any movies you made with Edgar that embarrass you?"

"I was never embarrassed. We made a few movies that weren't that great. We never made a porno movie or anything really stupid and horrible. We made a couple of high concept low-end television movies. One was about a neurosurgeon who got raped and the rapist ended up on her operating table.

"Edgar involved himself diligently in all those things. I never heard him say, 'This isn't an important movie so I'm not going to get involved.' He'd be on the set and he'd supervise the editing and he'd go page-by-page with the director. He took to heart the maxim that you're reputation is what you make. Even if it is only a dumb movie for Sunday night, it better be as good as it can be. That's why he was able to work for so many years. Most people's careers [in Hollywood] don't last 20 years and he was in television for 50 years and in features for almost 40."

"How come Edgar had so many producing deals?"

"I wouldn't say he burned bridges, but he could become a handful for whatever company that had him. Companies wanted him because they knew if they took him in, they'd get at least a couple of movies out of it. His TV movies were valuable at that time for creating bigger distribution portfolios internationally. If a studio like Fox could produce three or four TV movies a year, they could add that to the package they'd syndicate along with *Die Hard* and other hits.

"Edgar would clash with people. He said something revealing to me once. We were having a big fight over casting with the network. He wanted to cast Marcia Gay Harden, who's now a big actress but was then unknown. Big fight, arguing on the phone for an hour a day for a week, and he said, 'You don't really win regardless. Even if you win, you lose, because you've stained the relationship.'

"People wanted to work with him. If you have a [difficult] director or actor, someone like Edgar can handle them. Not everyone can, but it always has its own blowback.

"The business changed. Ten years ago, they were making a lot of TV movies. Now almost none. Deficit-financing television movies to distribute internationally [go into debt making TV movies for American networks in hopes of selling right overseas for a profit], that business barely exists anymore."

"Was there anyone who wouldn't return his calls?"

"Not that I know of. There were people who didn't like him and sometimes it was mutual. I don't think he had any kind of relationship with [agent] Mike Ovitz. What happened at the end, which was sad and revealing of how the town works, was that there were people who didn't know who he was anymore. When he was 70 in 1994, and we'd call New York to find out rights on a book and talk to a 27-year old book agent at ICM, the agent would say, 'Who's Edgar Scherick?'

"I didn't tell Edgar, 'This guy doesn't know who you are.' It would've hurt his feelings and he would've gotten so angry that he would've called the head of the agency. So I faxed over the bio and said, 'This is Edgar Scherick. He is someone who can make this book into a movie.'

"With features, I could understand how that would work, because by 1994, Edgar hadn't had a feature film, aside from *Rambling Rose*, in about ten years."

"Did you see him lose touch?"

"His stroke definitely affected him. He still got a few things made but he was dealt a big setback. There are certainly people who are disabled who make movies, but the perception that you are getting old and sick is bad. I don't know what happened to him and features. I don't know why he didn't continue to make features. I think he missed a generation of executives and once that happens, it's difficult to recover. He could call the people at the top, Jeffrey Katzenberg, Barry Diller, but he missed the middle layer.

"The people who ran networks (Bob Iger, Sandy Grushow, Ted Harbert, Jeff Sagansky) had respect for Edgar. They knew he had been head of a network and that there was this connection. They liked to talk to him about what was going on. He helped a lot of those guys along the way."

"Which of his protégés was he most proud of?"

"He was very proud of Scott Rudin. He felt a lot of gratification that he had seen the potential in Scott Rudin early. I think Rudin was 19-years old when he brought him out here [from working in New York as a casting director]. I think he always felt proud that people like Brian Grazer, Larry Gordon, Dan Blatt, Michael Barnathan, went on to great success."

"Was Edgar a happy man?"

Hugh pauses for almost ten seconds. "Good question. I think the short answer is no. I think he was happy to the extent that he enjoyed making movies and being involved with interesting people. He spent much of his time grousing at people and intense conflict. That would make me unhappy. I don't know if it made him unhappy. To some extent, he thrived on it. He got to live a life and do things that a lot of people want to do and don't get to. Especially in later years, he had a nice relationship with his children. He was happy in a lot of ways. His day-in, day-out existence was unpleasant at times. He couldn't let go of things that bothered him."

"What were his strengths and weaknesses?"

"One of his strengths was his ability to recognize quality material—find books, see the movie in a book or play, conceptualize it, sell it. He was strong at managing the volatile producing process. There are many things that can pull a production apart from the star who won't come out of his trailer to the director who has visions beyond the budget. He could keep all that under control.

"His weaknesses revolved around his temper. He would reach a point where he would lose his temper beyond any reasonable need. He was aware of it after the fact, after damaging a situation, potentially costing him the ability to do things. Organizationally he would suffer. One of the reasons he would have people like me around would be to pick up all the pieces and make sure that this paper got filed in the right place."

"How come he was never able to keep any of his employees for long?"

"He was hard on them. Sandy Carrio worked for him for 14 years as his secretary. Her secret was that she was mellow and she didn't let it get to her. She had also worked for Don Simpson. She'd seen it all. His formula was to bring in people awfully young, pay them under the going rate, give them a lot of experience, and then they would move on. He expected that. He wanted people to go on to succeed on their own. He used to say, 'I don't want another replaceable part. I want a guy who's fired up who will go on to produce on his own.' He got that. Sometimes he got people who wanted that but couldn't pull it off and just burned out. Edgar had high standards. He worked with line producer Lynn Raynor for about 25 years. He worked over and over again with director Larry Ellikan."

"What parts of his job did Edgar enjoy and which parts did he hate?"

"He hated managing and administrative stuff. He hated managing politics between people who worked for him. It's a pain for anybody. If he had two employees arguing over a project, he'd just get this look on his face, like 'Get out of here! I don't want to deal with this.' Edgar liked to make pictures. He used to say, 'You're not making money unless you're making a movie.' He didn't like developing. It was a necessary part of the process.

"He enjoyed holding court. He liked to have people listen to him talk. He used to have a party every year at the holidays and everyone would sit around and listen to him tell stories."

"How many people did he fire while you worked for him?"

"At least 20. Everybody who was there when I started was gone within a couple of years. A lot of people were induced to quit. Some people couldn't handle it. I had my own psychological litmus test for someone handling Edgar. If someone had difficulty with their own father they could not handle Edgar at all. They would crumble because he was the ultimate big bad father figure. He'd humiliate people. He'd ridicule people.

"He was going to bring in a new assistant. We brought this guy in for a trial day. Edgar sent him out to get lunch and the sandwich didn't have mayonnaise on it and Edgar fired him. Edgar said, 'I only want people who can be producers and this guy can't produce lunch.' In some ways that's harsh, but that was his thing. But in some ways it was like families where there's an alcoholic and everyone is tiptoeing around making sure that person doesn't get upset."

"Was there anyone who replied to Edgar with equal rage?"

"His wife [Marge] could give it pretty good when she wanted to. She didn't always take the bait. She would sometimes settle him down. Sue Pollock in New York could handle him. She didn't get angry back. There were people at his level in the business, not in the office, who said, 'Edgar, maybe you should calm down.'

"I remember writer-director Larry Cohen used to have screaming arguments with Edgar.

"Director Tony Richardson used to scream back at him. They would just go at it. It was like the Fourth of July. The network has strict rules about the length of a movie. It has to be exactly 93.5 minutes. Tony turned in a first version of *Phantom of the Opera* that was about 62-minutes long. Edgar went ape on him and Tony replied (in his upper-class British accent), 'So they will make it a three-hour miniseries. Who the fuck cares?' 'You can't do that to me. How dare you?' It was a battle of the titans."

"Edgar was volcanic."

"That's a good word. That's probably why he had a stroke, that surge of aggression."

"How would Edgar have liked his funeral and memorial service?"

"I think he would've been into it. He would get reflective. He was at that age where a lot of his friends were dying. Part of my job was to keep his rolodex up to date and typed up. One day he said, 'I'm going to erase all the people in my book who are dead.' So he spent an afternoon, 'He's dead. He's dead. He's dead.' He'd get all reflective.

"We think of Edgar as being old but Edgar was actually young for that first generation of television. All those big classic guys were dying off."

"Did Edgar get accused of unethical behavior?"

"There was a studio person who accused Edgar of being on the take. It wasn't true and Edgar hated him for it. I don't think Edgar carried a lot of grudges."

"Did Edgar see himself accurately?"

"There were certain areas where he did not appreciate his stature outside the world of entertainment. For example, he was interested in writing an article for *The New York Times Sunday Magazine* about television. They had a column called 'About Men.' He said, 'I don't want that. I want to write a feature article for *The Times* about my job.' We had to explain to him that nobody was interested in that.

"Once we were flying to London for a movie and he made a big stink with the airline about something. His wife was saying, 'Edgar, this isn't the Polo Lounge [at the Beverly Hills Hotel]. You're just another guy on this plane.' Edgar's not only the person to have this type of difficulty. He's a big person in the entertainment industry but elsewhere...

"He knew that his temper could get out of control. I worked for him. I wasn't his confidant. I was younger than his youngest son."

"He had good relations with homosexuals?"

"Yes, he was very accepting. I never heard him make an anti-gay remark. We were the original producers of *And The Band Played On* movie [about the origins of AIDS]. He pushed hard for that to get made. It shows how networks change because in 1989 NBC didn't want to make it because it was too gay.

"He was a big proponent of women. Being of an older generation, he could get away with things that if a younger person had done would've been called sexist. He launched a lot of women in the business and as far as I know, he never did anything inappropriate.

"Once we were in an elevator with an actress who had just auditioned and was good looking, and I (only 22 years old) made some crack that she was smiling at him. He replied, 'Don't be a wiseguy. I've never had a dalliance with an actress.'

"He had a funny story about a man who worked at ABC in the 1960s, named Ed Sherick. And this man had a mistress who called the network and got Edgar's office and was talking to Edgar's secretary. 'I'm supposed to meet Mr. Sherick at the Carlisle Hotel.' His secretary was so embarrassed. It was a mistake. Wrong guy.

"Edgar was old fashioned in that way. He was strict. He wasn't a liar. He could bend things around if he wanted to make a deal but he didn't really need to lie. He made all these movies.

"One reason he succeeded so long as a producer was that he never laid a lot of bullshit on a network or studio. If something was going wrong on a shoot, he wouldn't hide it from the network or studio. He taught me something important. 'Do not mention a problem without having a solution that you can discuss at the same time.'"

"Was he a workaholic?"

"No. He took his job home with him. He had been a workaholic. He'd cancel vacations with the family at the last minute because something had happened. That's not great if you are the family and packed to go to the Bahamas. He had a consuming job. You're working all day, then you have to read stuff at night and socialize…

"He enjoyed acting. *The King of Comedy* was his best part. He played Louis B. Mayer in *The Kennedys of Massachusetts* but I think that scene got cut. He always liked to go to the hairdressing trailer and get his hair cut."

"I think that 1991 ten-minute video was revealing."

"He was hamming it up. What they didn't show on that video was when he lost it. Then he'd get really ugly if someone made a mistake. Let's say a writer turns in a script, an executive with Edgar's company looks at it and turns it into the network. And Edgar decides the script wasn't ready and shouldn't have gone out. The script is already gone. So Edgar rides him. 'Why did you do that?' 'I thought it was finished.' 'Well, you shouldn't think that much. I'm not paying you to think. Why did you do that?'

"That could go on for half-an-hour.

"Edgar had a driver after his accident in 1989. I was responsible [in 1988] for getting Edgar's first car phone. He was talking on the phone when that [1989] accident happened. His wife then forbade him from driving and talking on the phone."

"Was he in good health when you knew him?"

"He was vigorous and robust but he had heart problems for years before the stroke. He had high blood pressure. Invisible ailments.

"When I first started working for him and he was screaming and yelling and carrying on, Michael Barnathan said to me, 'His doctor has told him to calm down and he's much calmer than he used to be.' Wow, what was he like before?'

"I asked people at studios if they'd make a feature movie with Edgar or is he just finished? They said they would make one if the right thing came along. He was eligible. He just didn't have the right project.

"Also, movies changed. The kind of movies he liked to make were getting made on cable. Movies have become so stupid. Intelligent feature films from studios are rare."

"Where did Edgar's demons come from?"

"I think a lot of his demons were innate—rage control, excessive brain power. Not suffering fools gladly. That his father became virtually inert during the depression after having suffered a business failure was probably a strong motivator. Edgar had to 'be the man' when he was just a kid. According to his sister (who was about 10 years older), his mother was afraid of him he was so smart. He could talk circles around her. The Depression forced a lot of kids to skip childhood and become adults too early."

July 11, 2003

I speak by phone with Scherick's cousin Eric J. Feldman. "Edgar was a very private guy. I'm the only one in the family, outside of his immediate family, to see him in ten years. I don't know why Edgar never kept in touch with anyone. At Edgar's Century City apartment, I met his son Brad, an extended cousin of mine, who didn't know that I existed, or that his father had an extended family. I explained to him how I was related and he said, 'That's just like my father.'

"Edgar's mother and my grandmother were sisters. He's my mother's first cousin.

"I believe he moved to California when I was a teenager. I'm not sure if he cut off all contact with his family, or if he kept to himself while in New York. I don't remember him ever coming by my house while I was growing up. My mother always characterized him as an 'intellectual snob,' in other words, someone who was very bright who would not be afraid to remind you of that fact. He always liked my mother. He and my uncle did not get along. I don't think he got along with many people in the family.

"There was a mystique about Edgar. I was too young when he was with ABC to be aware of his accomplishments there. I do remember when I was a kid, he had put out his first film—*For the Love of Ivy*. There was this big buzz about it. Everyone in the family was talking about him.

"Everyone in the family referred to him as Eddie. No one called him Edgar except me, and that was after I got to know him. Our cousin Stanley (who also lived in Long Beach) used to come to my house all the time. He was the one who kept in touch with Edgar during those years (1970's). He always relayed the news that Edgar had a movie coming out in the theaters or on television. Edgar was quite prolific during those years. That is what built this mystique in the family about him. He was certainly the most famous in the extended family. While the majority of the family became successful in their fields, no one in our family had anything remotely related to his kind of success.

"In the late '60s, early '70s, Edgar had a house on Point Lookout a small beach front community near Long Beach. I remember my grandfather taking me over there. Edgar had four kids, all within a few years of my age. I think I saw them once while growing up. He was married to Carol, his first wife. He drove a Volkswagen bus to carry his clan around. There was nothing flashy or ostentatious about him. His family would never mingle. I didn't know any of his kids. He kept to himself. He stayed in touch with those in the family he wanted to—his cousin Stanley, his sister Shirley, and occasionally my mother. His sister Shirley and my mother were best of friends until Shirley passed away.

"I remember Edgar and his sister Shirley at my *bar mitzvah*. I remember that he gave me a generous gift. Shirley is responsible for my first drink. I remember her exclaiming 'There's the *bar mitzvah* boy,' and dragging me off to the bar. Edgar gave me a generous gift, more than anybody else gave.

"The last time I think anyone in the family saw Edgar was 1991 when my oldest brother got married and Edgar went to the wedding. He sat [with his second wife Marge] a couple of tables over from me with the older people. I remember him and Marge getting up to go outside to get some air. He sees me and he gestures for me to come with him. I walk out with him. And you should've seen the looks of all the relatives as I went for a walk with Edgar. I think shock best describes it as no one knew I had a relationship with him. I don't think many people spoke with Edgar that night. Maybe it was because they were afraid or intimidated, or just did not know what to say to him. He could be an intimidating guy.

"I called him in 1999 to tell him my grandmother (Edgar's Aunt) had passed away. He'd already had the stroke and he was already bedridden. I'd heard he was ill but I didn't know the extent of it. I made a major faux pas. I didn't know [Marge had divorced him].

"When Edgar called me back, I could tell his voice was different. It was husky and his speech was slurred. I told him that his aunt (his mother's sister) had passed away. I asked him how Marge was. I had no idea what happened between them. He replied, 'She's fine.' We were only on the phone a few minutes when he said, 'I can't talk now. I'm tired.'

"I didn't talk to him much for a few years. I figure he's ill. I'm busy.

"Last September, I went to LA to work at a trade show. I go to see Edgar at his Century City apartment. He looks happy to see me. I say, 'Edgar, how are you?' And he says, 'I'm an invalid.' He looked vastly different. He'd gained a lot of weight. He had an eye patch.

"We talked for a while. He had a massage therapist out. It was just like the old days. Edgar was firing questions at me. His first question was, 'So, how many relatives do I have alive?' He asked many questions about the family. He asked me if I was married. I said no. He said, 'Why not?' I try to say something funny like, 'No girl asked me yet.' He ignores me and goes to the next question.

"I told him that I'm real proud of him. With a puzzling look on his face, he asks why? I told him about watching the movie *Path To War* on HBO in April. As the movie unfolds, I say to myself, this looks like something Edgar would do (I was not aware that the film was his). The movie ends and there are the credits, and it is his film. I told him, I knew you were ill. Millions of people never make a movie in their life and you made it from here [the sick bed]. His eyes lit up. He was so happy. And he started telling me about the film. He told me more about his work in that little time together than my whole life with him.

"When I was on my way out the door, and we were saying good-bye, he says, 'If there's anything I can do for you, let me know.' I made him a happy man when I said, 'Edgar, I've got everything I want.' He had the biggest grin on his face because he knew that I came to see him to see him. Not to ask for a favor. I think in retrospect that reason was why I was one of the few in the family he ever bothered with."

Index

0-595-32016-3

Printed in the United States
33457LVS00004B/52